Contents

Introduction

Phyllis L. Newcomer

This book of readings may serve as a companion piece to my book *Understanding and Teaching Emotionally Disturbed Children and Adolescents*, or it may be used independently. The works included were selected not from current literature but from the volumes of publications pertaining to emotional disturbance that have been produced over the years. Each piece conveys the flavor of the time in which it was written.

The first section consists of excerpts from two books that convey aspects of the history of emotional disturbance, Reginald Scot's *Discoverie of Witchcraft* and *Remarks on Prisons and Prison Discipline* by Dorthea Dix.

The second section contains articles and segments from books written by many of the most significant theorists associated with various approaches to understanding emotional disturbance, including biological, psychodynamic, behavioral, cognitive, phenomenological, existential, and ecological perspectives. Each reading is a seminal work. This section also includes papers that illustrate the humanness of these innovative individuals by revealing their attitudes toward one another and toward alternative frames of reference.

Section III presents important papers discussing childhood disorders. Included are two highly influential papers pertaining to infantile autism and childhood schizophrenia, written in the 1940s by Leo Kanner and Lauretta Bender, respectively. Bruno Bettelheim's fascinating case study of a schizophrenic child rounds out the section.

Section IV presents the work of leading therapists depicting therapeutic applications of each theoretical perspective. The case studies and interventions are classic examples of each unique approach to helping individuals with emotional disorders.

Section V presents the work of innovators in the use of group therapy and activity and non-verbal types of therapy, such as play, drama, music, art, and dance.

The individuals whose works are included in this volume have made monumental contributions to the study and treatment of emotional disorders. Their names are familiar to many, but their original work is often less familiar, probably a result not only of the passage of time but also of shifts in attitudes. I think the modern reader will be surprised and pleased at the quality of these works and as interested in their content as the reading audience for whom they were originally written.

Section I

HISTORICAL BACKGROUND

Reginald Scot's book *The Discoverie of Witchcraft* is an extremely rational attempt to persuade his sixteenth-century audience that the prevailing belief in witches and the wholesale persecution of persons accused of practicing witchcraft by "witchmongers" was little more than nonsense—an attribution of God's exclusive supernatural power to mortals. He sought to protect those he described as poor, aged, and simple, a group that undoubtedly included persons whose serious emotional disorders caused behavior sufficiently deviant to arouse their neighbors' fear and hostility. This excerpt clearly conveys the author's logic and the spirit of the time in which he lived.

Several centuries later, Dorthea Dix's compassion for the insane in prisons is conveyed in her book *Remarks on Prisons and Prison Discipline*. Like the investigative reporters of today, she sought to document whether prisoners were driven insane in prison as well as to explore the humaneness of their treatment. She also discusses the early nineteenth-century custom of paying fees to visit prisons and view the inmates, much like watching animals at a zoo.

Excerpts from
The Discoverie of Witchcraft

Reginald Scot
1584

THE EPISTLE.

To the right worshipfull Sir
Thomas Scot Knight, Etc.

Sir, I see among other malefactors manie poore old
women convented before you for working of miracles,
other wise called witchcraft, and therefore I thought you
also a meet person to whom I might comend my booke.
And here I have occasion to speake of your sincere administration of justice, and of your desteritie, discretion,
charge, and travell emploied in that behalfe, whereof I am
oculatus testis. Howbeit I had rather refer the reader to
common fame, and their owne eies and eares to be satisfied, than to send them to a Stationers shop, where manie
times lies are vendible, and truth contemptible. For I
being of your house, of your name, & of your bloud; my
foot being under your table, my hand in your dish, or
rather in your pursse, might bee thought to flatter you in
that, wherein (I knowe) I should rather offend you than
please you. And what need I currie favour with my most
assured friend? And if I should onelie publish those ver-
tues (though they be manie) which give me speciall occasion to exhibit this my travell unto you, I should doo as a
painter, that describeth the foot of a notable personage,
and leaveth all the best features in his bodie untouched.

Note. From *The discoverie of witchcraft* by R. Scot, 1584, Menston, York-
shire, England: Scolar Press Limited.

I therefore (at this time) doo onelie desire you to consider of my report, concerning the evidence that is commonlie brought before you against them. See first
whether the evidence be not frivolous, & whether the
proofs brought against them be not incredible, consisting
of ghesses, presumptions, & impossibilities contrarie to
reason, scripture, and nature. See also what persons com-
plaine unto them, whether they be not of the basest, the
unwisest, & most faithles kind of people. Also may it
please you to waie what accusations and crimes they laie
to their charge, namelie: She was at my house of late, she
would have had a pot of milke, she departed in a chafe
bicause she had it not, she railed, she curssed, she
mumbled and whispered, and finallie she said she would
be even with me: and soone after my child, my cow, my
sow, or my pullet died, or was strangelie taken. Naie (if it
please your Worship) I have further proofe: I was with a
wise woman, and she told me I had an ill neighbour, &
that she would come to my house yer it were long, and so
did she; and that she had a marke above hir waste, & so
had she: and God forgive me, my stomach hath gone
against hir a great while. Hir mother before hir was
counted a witch, she hath beene beaten and scratched by
the face till bloud was drawne upon hir, bicause she hath
beene suspected, & afterwards some of those persons
were said to amend. These are the certeinties that I heare
in their evidences.

Note also how easilie they may be brought to confesse
that which they never did, nor lieth in the power of man to
doo: and then see whether I have cause to write as I doo.
Further, if you shall see that infidelitie, poperie, and
manie other manifest heresies be backed and shouldered,

and their professors animated and hartened, by yeelding to creatures such infinit power as is wrested out of Gods hand, and attributed to witches: finallie, if you shall perceive that I have faithfullie and trulie delivered and set downe the condition and state of the witch, and also of the witchmonger, and have confuted by reason and lawe, and by the word of God it selfe, all mine adversaries objections and arguments: then let me have your cuntenance against them that maliciouslie oppose themselves against me.

My greatest adversaries are yoong ignorance and old custome. For what follie soever tract of time hath fostered, it is so superstitiouslie pursued of some, as though no error could be acquainted with custome. But if the lawe of nations would joine with such custome, to the maintenance of ignorance, and to the suppressing of knowledge; the civilest countrie in the world would soone become barbarous, &c. For as knowledge and time discovereth errors, so dooth superstition and ignorance in time breed them. And concerning the opinions of such, as wish that ignorance should rather be mainteined, than knowledge busilie searched for, bicause thereby offense may grow: I answer, that we are commanded by Christ himselfe to search for knowledge: for it is the kings honour (as Salomon saith) to search out a thing.

Aristotle said to Alexander, that a mind well furnished was more beautifull than a bodie richlie araied. What can be more odious to man, or offensive to God, than ignorance: for through ignorance the Jewes did put Christ to death. Which ignorance whosoever forsaketh, is promised life everlasting: and therefore among Christians it should be abhorred above all other things. For even as when we wrestle in the darke, we tumble in the mire, &c: so when we see not the truth, we wallow in errors. A blind man may seeke long in the rishes yer he find a needle; and as soone is a doubt discussed by ignorance. Finallie, truth is no sooner found out in ignorance, than a sweet savor in a dunghill. And if they will allow men knowledge, and give them no leave to use it, men were much better be without it than have it. For it is, as to have a tallent, and to hide it under the earth; or to put a candle under a bushell: or as to have a ship, & to let hir lie alwaies in the docke: which thing how profitable it is, I can saie somewhat by experience.

But hereof I need saie no more, for everie man seeth that none can be happie who knoweth not what felicitie meaneth. For what availeth it to have riches, and not to have the use thereof? Truelie the heathen herein deserved more commendation than manie christians, for they spared no paine, no cost, nor travell to atteine to knowledge. Pythagoras travelled from Thamus to Aegypt, and afterwards into Crete and Lacedaemonia: and Plato out of Athens into Italie and Aegypt, and all to find out hidden secrets and knowlege: which when a man hath, he seemeth to be separated from mortalitie. For pretious stones, and all other creatures of what value soever, are but counterfeits to this jewell: they are mortall, corruptible, and inconstant; this is immortall, pure and certeine. Wherfor if I have searched and found out any good thing, that ignorance and time hath smothered, the same I commend unto you: to whom though I owe all that I have, yet am I bold to make other partakers with you in this poore gift.

Your loving cousen,
Reg. Scot.

TO THE READERS

To you that are wise & discreete few words may suffice: for such a one judgeth not at the first sight, nor reprooveth by heresaie; but patientlie hereth, and thereby increaseth in understanding: which patience bringeth foorth experience, whereby true judgement is directed. I shall not need therefore to make anie further sute to you, but that it would please you to read my booke, without the prejudice of time, or former conceipt: and having obteined this at your hands, I submit my selfe unto your censure. But to make a solemne sute to you that are parciall readers, desiring you to set aside parcialitie, to take in good part my writing, and with indifferent eies to looke upon my booke, were labour lost, and time ill imploied. For I should no more prevaile herein, than if a hundred yeares since I should have intreated your predecessors to beleeve, that Robin goodfellowe, that great and ancient bulbegger, had beene but a cousening merchant, and no divell indeed.

If I should go to a papist, and saie; I praie you beleeve my writings, wherein I will proove all popish charmes, conjurations, exorcismes, benedictions and cursses, not onelie to be ridiculous, and of none effect, but also to be impious and contrarie to Gods word: I should as hardlie therein win favour at their hands, as herein obteine credit at yours. Neverthelesse, I doubt not, but to use the matter so, that as well the massemoonger for his part, as the witchmoonger for his, shall both be ashamed of their professinos.

But Robin goodfellowe ceaseth now to be much feared, and poperie is sufficientlie discovered. Nevertheles, witches charms, and conjurors cousenages are yet thought effectuall. Yea the Gentiles have espied the fraud of their cousening oracles, and our cold prophets and inchanters make us fooles still, to the shame of us all, but speciallie of papists, who conjure everie thing, and thereby bring to passe nothing. They saie to their candles;

I conjure you to endure for ever: and yet they last not a pater noster while the longer. They conjure water to be wholesome both for bodie and soule: but the bodie (we see) is never the better for it, nor the soule anie whit refrmed by it. And therefore I mervell, that when they see their owne conjurations confuted and brought to naught, or at the least void of effect, that they (of all other) will yet give such credit, countenance, and authoritie to the vaine counsenages of witches and conjurors; as though their charmes and conjurations could produce more apparent, certeine, and better effects than their owne.

But my request unto all you that read my booke shall be no more, but that it would please you to conferre my words with your owne sense and experience, and also with the word of God. If you find your selves resolved and satisfied, or rather reformed and qualified in anie one point or opinion, that heretofore you held contrarie to truth, in a matter hitherto undecided, and never yet looked into; I praie you take that for advantage: and suspending your judgement, staie the sentence of condemnation against me, and consider of the rest, at your further leasure. If this may not suffice to persuade you, it cannot prevaile to annoy you: and then, that which is written without offense, may be overpassed without anie greefe.

And although mine assertion, be somewhat differing from the old inveterat opinion, which I confesse hath manie graie heares, whereby mine adversaries have gained more authoritie than reason, towards the maintenance of their presumptions and old wives fables: yet shall it fullie agree with Gods glorie, and with his holie word. And albeit there be hold taken by mine adversaries of certeine few words or sentences in the scripture that maketh a shew for them: yet when the whole course thereof maketh against them, and impugneth the same, yea and also their owne places rightlie understood doo nothing at all releeve them: I trust their glorius title and argument of antiquitie will appeare as stale and corrupt as the apothecaries drugs, or grocers spice, which the longer they be preserved, the woorsse they are. And till you have perused my booke, ponder this in your mind, to wit, that *Sagae, Thessalae, Striges, Lamiae* (which words and none other being in use do properlie signifie our witches) are not once found written in the old or new testament; and that Christ himselfe in his gospell never mentioned the name of a witch. And that neither he, nor Moses ever spake anie one word of the witches bargaine with the divell, their hagging, their riding in the aire, their transferring of corne or grasse from one feeld to another, their hurting of children or cattell with words or charmes, their bewitching of butter, cheese, ale, &c: nor yet their transubstantiation; insomuch as the writers hereupon are not ashamed to say, that it is not absurd to affirme that there were no witches in Jobs time. The reason is, that if there had beene such witches then in being, Job would have said he had beene bewitched. But indeed men tooke no heed in those daies to this doctrine of divels; to wit, to these fables of witchcraft, which Peter saith shall be much regarded and hearkened unto in the latter daies.

Howbeit, how ancient so ever this barbarous conceipt of witches omnipotencie is, truth must not be measured by time: for everie old opinion is not sound. Veritie is not impaired, how long so ever it be suppressed; but is to be searched out, in how darke a corner so ever it lie hidden: for it is not like a cup of ale, that may be broched too rathe. Finallie, time bewraieth old errors, & discovereth new matters of truth. Danæus himselfe saith, that this question hitherto hath never beene handled; nor the scriptures concerning this matter have never beene expounded. To prove the antiquitie of the cause, to confirme the opinion of the ignorant, to inforce mine adversaries arguments, to aggravate the punishments, & to accomplish the confusiō of these old women, is added the vanitie and wickednes of them, which are called witches, the arrogancie of those which take upon them to worke wonders, the desire that people have to hearken to such miraculous matters, unto whome most commonlie an impossibilitie is more credible than a veritie; the ignorance of naturall causes, the ancient and universall hate conceived against the name of a witch; their ilfavoured faces, their spitefull words, their cursses and imprecations, their charmes made in ryme, and their beggerie; the feare of manie foolish folke, the opinion of some that are wise, the want of Robin goodfellowe and the fairies, which were woont to mainteine chat, and the common peoples talke in this behalfe; the authoritie of the inquisitors, the learning, cunning, consent, and estimation of writers herein, the false translations and fond interpretations used, speciallie by papists; and manie other like causes. All which toies take such hold upon mens fansies, as whereby they are lead and entised awaie from the consideration of true respects, to the condemnation of that which they know not.

Howbeit, I will (by Gods grace) in this my booke, so apparentlie decipher and confute these cavils, and all other their objections; as everie witchmoonger shall be abashed, and all good men thereby satisfied. In the meane time, I would wish them to know that if neither the estimation of Gods omnipotencie, nor the tenor of his word, nor the doubtfulnes or rather the impossibilitie of the case, nor the small proofes brought against them, nor the rigor executed upon them, nor the pitie that should be in a christian heart, nor yet their simplicitie, impotencie, or age may suffice to suppresse the rage of rigor wherewith they are oppressed; yet the consideration of their sex or kind ought to moove some mitigatiō of their punishment. For if nature (as Plinie reporteth) have taught a lion not to deale so roughlie with a woman as with a man, bicause she is in bodie the weaker vessell, and in hart more inclined to pitie (which Jeremie in his lamentations seemeth to confirme) what should a man doo in this case, for whome a woman was created as an helpe and comfort unto him? In so much as, even in the lawe of nature, it is a greater offense to slea a woman than a man: not bicause a man is not the more excellent creature, but bicause a woman is the weaker vessell. And therefore among all modest and honest persons it is thought a shame to offer violence or injurie to a woman: in which respect Virgil saith, *Nullum memorabile nomen faminea in pœna est.*

God that knoweth my heart is witnes, and you that read my booke shall see, that my drift and purpose in this enterprise tendeth onelie to these respects. First, that the glorie and power of God be not so abridged and abased, as to be thrust into the hand or lip of a lewd old woman: whereby the worke of the Creator should be attributed to the power of a creature. Secondlie, that the religion of the gospell may be seene to stand without such peevish trumperie. Thirdlie, that lawfull favour and christian compassion be rather used towards these poore soules, than rigor and extremitie. Bicause they, which are commonlie accused of witchcraft, are the least sufficient of all other persons to speake for themselves; as having the most base and simple education of all others; the extremitie of their age giving them leave to dote, their povertie to beg, their wrongs to chide and threaten (as being void of anie other waie of revenge) their humor melancholicall to be full of imaginations, from whence cheefelie proceedeth the vanitie of their confessions; as that they can transforme themselves and others into apes, owles, asses, dogs, cats, &c: that they can flie in the aire, kill children with charmes, hinder the comming of butter, &c.

And for so much as the mightie helpe themselves together, and the poore widows crie, though it reach to heaven, is scarse heard here upon earth: I thought good (according to my poore abilitie) to make intercession, that some part of common rigor, and some points of hastie judgement may be advised upon. For the world is now at that stay (as Brentius in a most godlie sermon in these words affirmeth) that even as when the heathen persecuted the christians, if anie were accused to beleeve in Christ, the common people cried *Ad leonem:* so now, if anie woman, be she never so honest, be accused of witchcraft, they crie *Ad ignem.* What difference is betweene the rash dealing of unskilfull people, and the grave counsell of more discreet and learned persons, may appeare by a tale of Danæus his owne telling; wherein he opposeth the rashnes of a few townesmen, to the counsell of a whole senate, preferring the follie of the one, before the wisdome of the other. . . .

THE DISCOVERIE OF WITCHCRAFT

The first Booke.

The first chapter.

An impeachment of Witches power in meteors and elementarie bodies tending to the rebuke of such as attribute too much unto them.

The fables of Witchcraft have taken so fast hold and deepe root in the heart of man, that fewe or none can (nowadaies) with patience indure the hand and correction of God. For if any adversitie, greefe, sicknesse, losse of children, corne, cattell, or libertie happen unto them; by & by they exclaime uppon witches. As though there were no God in Israel that ordereth all things according to his will; punishing both just and unjust with greefs, plagues, and afflictions in maner and forme as he thinketh good: but that certeine old women heere on earth, called witches, must needs be the contrivers of all mens calamities, and as though they themselves were innocents, and had deserved no such punishments. Insomuch as they sticke not to ride and go to such, as either are injuriouslie tearmed witches, or else are willing so to be accounted, seeking at their hands comfort and remedie in time of their tribulation, contrarie to Gods will and commandement in that behalfe, who bids us resort to him in all our necessities.

Such faithlesse people (I saie) are also persuaded, that neither haile nor snowe, thunder nor lightening, raine nor tempestuous winds come from the heavens at the commandement of God: but are raised by the cunning and power of witches and conjurers; insomuch as a clap of thunder, or a gale of wind is no sooner heard, but either they run to ring bels, or crie out to burne witches; or else burne consecrated things, hoping by the smoke thereof, to drive the divell out of the aire, as though spirits could be fraied awaie with such externall toies: howebeit, these are right inchantments, as *Brentius* affirmeth.

But certeinlie, it is neither a witch, nor divell, but a glorious[a] God that maketh the thunder. I have read in the scriptures, that God[b] maketh the blustering tempests and whirlewinds: and I find that it is[c] the Lord that altogither dealeth with them, and that they[d] blowe according to his will. But let me see anie of them all[e] rebuke and still the

[a] Psal. 25.
[b] Psal. 83.
[c] Eccles. 43.
[d] Luke. 8. Matth. 8.
[e] Mark. 4, 41. Luke, 8, 14.

sea in time of tempest, as Christ did; or raise the stormie wind, as[f] God did with his word; and I will beleeve in them. Hath anie witch or conjurer, or anie creature entred into the [g]treasures of the snowe; or seene the secret places of the haile, which GOD hath prepared against the daie of trouble, battell, and warre? I for my part also thinke with Jesus Sirach, that at Gods onelie commandement the snowe falleth; and that the wind bloweth according to his will, who onelie maketh all stormes to cease; and[h] who (if we keepe his ordinances) will send us raine in due season, and make the land to bring forth hir increase, and the trees of the field to give their fruit.

But little thinke our witchmongers, that the [i]Lord commandeth the clouds above, or openeth the doores of heaven, as *David* affirmeth; or that the Lord goeth forth in the tempests and stormes, as the Prophet [j]*Nahum* reporteth: but rather that witches and conjurers are then about their businesse.

The *Martionists* acknowledged one God the authour of good things, and another the ordeiner of evill: but these make the divell a whole god, to create things of nothing, to knowe mens cogitations, and to doo that which God never did; as, to transubstantiate men into beasts, &c. Which thing if divels could doo, yet followeth it not, that witches have such power. But if all the divels in hell were dead, and all the witches in *England* burnt or hanged; I warrant you we should not faile to have raine, haile and tempests, as now we have: according to the appointment and will of God, and according to the constitution of the elements, and the course of the planets, wherein God hath set a perfect and perpetuall order.

I am also well assured, that if all the old women in the world were witches; and all the priests, conjurers: we should not have a drop of raine, nor a blast of wind the more or the lesse for them. For [k]the Lord hath bound the waters in the clouds, and hath set bounds about the waters, untill the daie and night come to an end: yea it is God that raiseth the winds and stilleth them: and he saith to the raine and snowe; Be upon the earth, and it falleth. The [l]wind of the Lord, and not the wind of witches, shall destroie the treasures of their plesant vessels, and drie up the fountaines; saith *Oseas*. Let us also learne and confesse with the Prophet *David,* that we[m] our selves are the

causes of our afflictions; and not exclaime upon witches, when we should call upon God for mercie.

The Imperiall lawe (saith *Brentius*) condemneth them to death that trouble and infect the aire: but I affirme (saith he) that it is neither in the power of witch not divell so to doo, but in God onelie. Though (besides *Bodin,* and all the popish writers in generall) it please *Danaeus, Hyperius, Hemingius, Erastus, &c.* to conclude otherwise. The clouds[n] are called the pillers of Gods tents, Gods charios, and his pavillions. And if it be so, what witch or divell can make maisteries thereof. *S. Augustine* saith, *Non est putandum istis transgressoribus angelis servire hancrerum visibilium materiem, sed soli Deo:* We must not thinke that these visible things are at the commandement of the angels that fell, but are obedient to the onelie God.

Finallie, if witches could accomplish these things; what needed it seeme so strange to the people, when Christ by miracle[o] commanded both seas and winds, &c. For it is written; Who is this? for both wind and sea obeie him.

The second chapter.

The inconvenience growing by mens credulitie herein, with a reproofe of some churchmen, which are inclined to the common conceived opinion of witches and omnipotencie, and a familiar example thereof.

But the world is now so bewitched and over-run with this fond error, that even where a man shuld seeke comfort and counsell, there shall hee be sent (in case of necessitie) from God to the divell; and from the Physician, to the coosening witch, who will not sticke to take upon hir, by wordes to heale the lame (which was proper onelie to Christ; and to them whom he assisted with his divine power) yea, with hir familiar & charmes she will take upon hir to cure the blind: though in the [a]tenth of *S. Johns* Gospell it be written, that the divell cannot open the eies of the blind. And they attaine such credit as I have heard (to my greefe) some of the ministerie affirme, that they have had in their parish at one instant, xvii. or xviii. witches: meaning such as could worke miracles supernaturallie. Whereby they manifested as well their infidelitie and ignorance, in conceiving Gods word; as their negligence and error in instructing their flocks. For they themselves might understand, and also teach their parishoners, that [b]God onelie worketh great woonders; and

[f] Psal. 170.

[g] Job. 38, 22.

[h] Leviti, 26. verse. 3, 4.

[i] Psal. 78, 23.

[j] Nahum. 1.

[k] Job. 26, 8. Job. 37. Psalme. 135. Jer. 10 & 15.

[l] Ose. 13.

[m] Psa. 39, &c.

[n] Exod. 13. Isai. 66. Ps. 18, 11, 19.

[o] Mar. 4, 41.

[a] Joh. 10, 21.

[b] Psal. 72, & 136. Jeremie, 5.

that it is he which sendeth such punishments to the wicked, and such trials to the elect: according to the saieng of the Prophet *Haggai*,[c] I smote you with blasting and mildeaw, and with haile, in all the labours of your hands; and yet you turned not unto me, saith the Lord. And therefore saith the same Prophet in another place;[d] You have sowen much, and bring in little. And both in [e]*Joel* and [f]*Leviticus,* the like phrases and proofes are used and made. But more shalbe said of this hereafter.

S. *Paule* fore-sawe the blindnesse and obstinacie, both of these blind shepheards, and also of their scabbed sheepe, when he said; [g]They will not suffer wholsome doctrine, but having their eares itching, shall get them a heape of teachers after their own lusts; and shall turne their eares from the truth, and shall be given to fables. And [h]in the latter time some shall depart from the faith, and shall give heed to spirits of errors, and doctrines of divels, which speake lies (as witches and conjurers doo) but cast thou awaie such prophane and old wives fables. In which sense Basil saith; Who so giveth heed to inchanters, hearkeneth to a fabulous and frivolous thing. But I will rehearse an example whereof I my selfe am not onelie *Oculatus testis,* but have examined the cause, and am to justifie the truth of my report: not bicause I would disgrace the ministers that are godlie, but to confirme my former assertion, that this absurd error is growne into the place, which should be able to expell all such ridiculous follie and impietie.

At the assises holden at *Rochester,* Anno 1581, one *Margaret Simons,* the wife of *John Simons,* of *Brenchlie* in *Kent,* was araigned for witchcraft, at the instigation and complaint of divers fond and malicious persons; and specieallie by the meanes of one *John Ferrall* vicar of that parish: with whom I talked about that matter, and found him both fondlie assotted in the cause, and enviouslie bent towards hir: and (which is worse) as unable to make a good account of his faith, as shee whom he accused. That which he, for his part, laid to the poore womans charge, was this.

His sonne (being an ungratious boie, and prentise to one *Robert Scotchford* clothier, dwelling in that parish of *Brenchlie*) passed on a daie by hir house; at whome by chance hir little dog barked. Which thing the boie taking in evil part, drewe his knife, & pursued him therewith

even to hir doore: whom she rebuked with some such words as the boie disdained, & yet neverthelesse would not be persuaded to depart in a long time. At the last he returned to his maisters house, and within five or sixe daies fell sicke. Then was called to mind the fraie betwixt the dog and the boie: insomuch as the vicar (who thought himselfe so privileged, as he little mistrusted that God would visit his children with sicknes) did so calculate; as he found, partlie through his owne judgement, and partlie (as he himselfe told me) by the relation of other witches, that his said sonne was by hir bewitched. Yea, he also told me, that this his sonne (being as it were past all cure) received perfect health at the hands of another witch.

He proceeded yet further against hir, affirming, that alwaies in his parish church, when he desired to read most plainelie, his voice so failed him, as he could scant be heard at all. Which hee could impute, he said, to nothing else, but to hir inchantment. When I advertised the poore woman hereof, as being desirous to heare what she could said for hir selfe; she told me, that in verie deed his voice did much faile him, specialle when he strained himselfe to speake lowdest. How beit, she said that all times his voice was hoarse and lowe: which thing I perceived to be true. But sir, said she, you shall understand, that this our vicar is diseased with such a kind of hoarsenesse, as divers of our neighbors in this parish, not long since, doubted that he had the French pox; & in that respect utterly refused to communicate with him: until such time as (being therunto injoined by M. D. *Lewen* the Ordinarie) he had brought fro *London* a certificat, under the hands of two physicians, that his hoarsenes proceeded from a disease in the lungs. Which certificat he published in the church, in the presence of the whole congregation: and by this meanes hee was cured, or rather excused of the shame of his disease. And this I knowe to be true by the relation of divers honest men of that parish. And truelie, if one of the Jurie had not beene wiser than the other, she had beene condemned thereupon, and upon other as ridiculous matters as this. For the name of a witch is so odious, and hir power so feared among the common people, that if the honestest bodie living chance to be arraigned therupon, she shall hardlie escape condemnation.

---

[c] Hag. 2, 28.
[d] Idem. cap. 1, 6.
[e] Joel, 1.
[f] Leviti. 26.
[g] 2 Tim. 4, 34.
[h] 1 Tim. 4, 1.

Excerpts from *Remarks on Prisons and Prison Discipline*

Dorthea L. Dix
1845

The officer designated to report the case of insanity to the Warden of the other prison, *forgot it;* the insane man refused to work, was accused of obstinacy, and repeatedly flogged till his shrieks and tortures compelled his ignorant and hard-judging officers to suspend the horrid punishment. He was removed to a hospital for the insane. An officer in another of the most approved prisons on the Auburn plan, testifies that a prisoner was committed, who declared himself unable to work. The officer believing him to be *obstinate,* flogged him repeatedly, (as the rules of the prison required,) but fearing he might be wrong, the Warden was summoned, who considered it a case of mere deception. The flogging was repeated very severely in the afternoon; the following morning the man was found dead in his bed. The post-mortem examination discovered extensive disease! Had there been a resident physician present, or had the responsible physician been called, what misery might have been spared. While I would speak respectfully of the ability of Physicians who attend at most of the prisons, I must express the opinion that often too little time is spent in examining the physical and mental condition of the convicts.

THE INSANE IN PRISONS.—From the Massachusetts State prison '7 insane convicts are reported to have been transferred to the State Hospital, during the year ending September, 1844.' In the Connecticut state prison, July 1844, '2 only are represented as wholly insane, and 4 partially; all being so at the time of commitment.' 'No provision,' writes the physician, 'is made for sending an insane convict to the Hospital at Hartford.'

Inquiring at the prison at Auburn, concerning the *insane,* I found, that having no authority to send their patients to the State Hospital, they have conveyed them to the Bloomingdale Asylum, when so violent as to require much active care. The quiet patients are employed in the shops. One poor fellow, who had served out his time, and was but a degree above idiocy, was discharged the day I was last at the prison; the officers appeared to commiserate his friendlessness and incapacity to take care of himself, and took much pains, after clothing him comfortably, and giving him some money, to make him understand its value and use. He was no subject for convict discipline, and the Warden assured me never had been.

Of the insane in the prison at Sing Sing, one of the Inspectors writes to me as follows:—

"Aug. 28, 1844. As to the insane, it is difficult to give you any satisfactory answer. The line of demarkation between the sane and the insane is not easily defined. We are making a thorough investigation on this subject. We are not authorized to send any of our prisoners to the State Hospital for the Insane at Utica. We are therefore now

Note. From *Remarks on prisons and prison discipline* by D. L. Dix, 1845, Philadelphia: Kite & Co.

erecting an out-ward for the treatment of the insane upon the plan pursued in our best regulated asylums. At present the provision for them is exceedingly imperfect."

A deplorable necessity that, which urges the construction of a hospital within the boundaries of a prison.

In November 1844, the committee reported, that beside four insane sent to Bloomingdale, 31 of the 868 convicts were insane. Most of these were insane when committed. Insanity is sometimes developed in this, as in all other prisons, but so also is it in communities; and I consider neither the 'silent' nor 'separate' systems as specially disposing convicts to insanity; but the want of pure air in the lodging-cells is, I doubt not, one of the many exciting causes of this malady in all prisons, and in all institutions in which ventilation is defective.

In the Eastern Penitentiary, during 1844, twelve convicts were admitted in a state of insanity. Within two years, *twenty-seven* have been received in that condition, charged with various crimes. These were entered as insane by the sheriffs who delivered them to the custody of the warden, and known to be so at such times, and long previous.

In February last, I saw six insane convicts in the prison at Trenton, all of whom I ascertained to have been committed in that condition. From this prison, as from the Eastern Penitentiary, I traced the history of these convicts to the several counties, whence they were committed, in order to assure myself of the absolute fact of insanity *previus* to their committal.

In the Western Penitentiary, August, 1844, I found but *one* absolutely insane convict; three were simple, or of very weak understanding. A letter from the chaplain of this prison contains the following reference to this subject.

"I have given the subject particular and close attention, only for a short time; but, in the period of my labors here, I am ready to testify, that the 'separate' system has no more tendency to produce insanity than any other form of imprisonment. The *mild influence* which soothes the convict in his separate cell; the frequent presence of the officers, who carry his food, instruct him in his employments, receive his work; together with the aids of the moral instructor, the visits of the physician, the warden, and inspectors, and the use of books, unite to maintain an equable state of mind."

In the prison at Columbis, I saw two decidedly insane; in the prison at Baltimore, the same month, *three,* but not excited. In the prison at Richmond, *two;* the persons of these, and the cells, all indicated care on the part of the several officers in charge. Great, very great inconvenience is experienced from this unhappy class of prisoners in all prisons; they cannot receive from the prison-officers that appropriate and peculiar care their condition demands.

VISITORS.—Visitors' fees at Auburn, in 1842, were $1692.75, and, in 1845, $1942.75,—making $3635.50; at 25 cents each, we have for two years, at one prison, of paying visitors alone, 14542 persons. At Sing Sing, of paying visitors, was received, in 1843, $311.75, and in 1844, $236.62, making $548.37; (children half price) 2194 visitors, counting only one at 12½ cents. Income from visitors for two years at Charlestown, $1487.75; allowing 25 cents for each paying visitor, there were admitted 5951 persons. At Wethersfield, the visitors' fees amounted in the last two years to $548.12½, allowing 25 cents each, there were admitted 2192, allowing but one at half price; but, if the fees are less than 25 cents, as is sometimes the custom, the number is greatly larger. At the prison in Windsor there were in one year 796 visitors, and during the same period in New Hampshire about 500 paying visitors, allowing 25 cents, more if a smaller sum. In Columbus, Ohio, in one year, 1844, was received $1038.78 for paying visitors, admitting, if we allow all to have been adults at full price, at 25 cents each, above 4150 persons. It might be supposed that the exposure of the convicts to such larger numbers of spectators, would not aid the moral and reforming influences of the prisons. This source of revenue would be better dispensed with.

Section II

THEORETICAL APPROACHES TO EMOTIONAL DISTURBANCE

This section begins with a paper by Ivan Pavlov that adheres to a biological perspective of emotional disorders and reflects some of the most avant-garde scientific thinking of the 1930s—the experiments in classical conditioning. Note Pavlov's meticulous investigation of the excitatory and inhibitory processes of the nerve cells and his application of theory evolved from studying dogs to the human disorders paranoia and obsessional neurosis.

The next selection illustrates the psychodynamic perspective: excerpts from the early studies of hysteria that Sigmund Freud and Josef Breuer published between 1893 and 1895. This work shows the change in Freud's attitude toward hypnosis. Although he initially was excited to discover that patients' hysterical symptoms disappeared when hypnosis was used to help them recall events that caused the symptoms, Freud eventually abandoned hypnosis as a form of treatment. The reading also conveys the development of Freud's belief that sexual factors were the etiology of neurosis and that hysteria occurred, not as a separate clinical entity, but in combination with other anxiety neuroses.

In the early twentieth century, when the work of Freud had gained international repute, the American behaviorist John B. Watson reported his reaction to the tenets of the psychoanalytic movement. Like many persons interested in the study of human behavior, he was impressed with the accuracy of Freud's observations, though not with Freud's interpretations of behavior. Read how Watson rephrases psychoanalytic tenets in the language of systems of habits.

In the much more recent work of Albert Bandura, the behavioral position itself changes. Bandura was a leader in directing behavioral psychology away from a primary focus on external events as determiners of behavior, deemphasizing the link between stimuli and responses and the reinforcement of adaptive behavior. He emphasized instead the importance of cognitive processes in acquiring and retaining behavior. Known as a social-learning theorist, Bandura made extraordinary contributions to the study of human behavior by describing the processes whereby imitation or modeling of observed behavior and self-evaluation strategies determine behavior. The paper on self-efficacy theory included in this section is a brilliant example of Bandura's scholarly and systematic approach to theory development and validation. Don't be put off by the length; there was nothing in the article that any conscientious editor could delete.

The next article in this section is by Albert Ellis, the father of Rational-Emotive Therapy. Like Bandura, Ellis was convinced that cognitive processes were the primary cause of emotional distress. Unlike Bandura's perspective, however, which was based on his training as an academician and learning theorist, Ellis's conclusions emanated from his knowledge of clinical psychology and his experiences as a psychotherapist. His insights regarding the importance of an individual's negative or self-defeating self-talk as a constant reflection of an irrational belief system address the key issue of how an emotionally disturbed person maintains "illogical" behaviors in spite of the less than desirable consequences they evoke. Although this article was written in 1957, the ideas presented are not dated. Indeed, cognitive therapy has become the most influential approach to treating emotional disorders in the 1990s.

From cognitive theory we move to the phenomenological perspective as represented in excerpts from Abraham Maslow's seminal work on the theory of human motivation. Maslow evolved a sequence of basic human needs that served as goals for behavior. The highest of these needs, self-actualization, is the ultimate in human fulfillment—being all you can be. As a leading figure in the humanistic movement in psychology, Maslow took a very positive view of human beings. His writing illustrates his respect for others and his optimism about society, all the more remarkable given that he was a German who came to the United States to escape Hitler.

The next work in this section is by Rollo May, the esteemed existential therapist. Like Maslow, May reveals concern and respect for the unique qualities of each human being. Reacting against psychoanalytic theory, he cites the inadequacy of focusing attention on innate drives and instincts believed to govern behavior, noting that the individual's essence is overlooked. This treatise on existential psychology reflects the same obvious belief in the potential of human beings that underpins all of May's extensive writings on such fascinating issues as will, love, hate, and creativity.

The discussion of theoretical approaches continues with an interesting symposium on the control of human behavior by two great representatives of radically different perspectives about the topic: the phenomenological theorist Carl Rogers and the behavioral theorist B. F. Skinner. Skinner writes first, putting his faith in the ability of science (that is, the experimental method as practiced in operant conditioning) to bring about a better society. In response, Rogers voices his aversion to any systematic method for shaping behavior to conform to static values such as obedience or happiness. Like Maslow, Rogers emphasizes the constructive, inner-directed evolution of humankind toward self-actualization made possible by the acceptance of individuality and the avoidance of a controlled or closed society. In his reply, Skinner questions Rogers's assumptions about an individual's ability to be self-directing and to progress toward self-actualization without external structure. He calls for evidence to prove these premises and reiterates the necessity of applying science to achieve constructive social goals. These two great psychologists had many fascinating exchanges during their lives. This particular exchange captures the essence of their beliefs.

The last paper in this section, by Joseph Wolpe, is a relatively recent (1981) expression of the author's frustration over the persistent use of psychoanalytical procedures to treat neuroses, in spite of behavior therapy's proven efficacy. Wolpe attacks the psychoanalytical approach for not proving clinical effectiveness, defends behavior therapy against charges that its treatment is inhuman, and discusses the social implications inherent in the continued use of unverified procedures. He notes that the specific values that determine scientific effect are subjective and lie outside the scope of that effect.

An Attempt at a Physiological Interpretation of Obsessional Neurosis and Paranoia

Ivan Pavlov
1934

The starting-point for a physiological understanding of the above-mentioned diseases consisted in some new laboratory facts obtained in the course of the study of conditioned reflexes in dogs.

When conditioned stimuli are elaborated out of various external agents (we may take for an example conditioned food reflexes), the first reaction elicited by the established conditioned stimulus usually consists in a movement towards the stimulus, i.e., the animal turns to the place where the stimulus is to be found. If the stimulus is within reach, the animal even tries to come in touch with it, namely, by means of its mouth. Thus, if the conditioned stimulus is the switching on of a lamp, the dog licks the lamp; if the conditioned stimulus is a sound the dog will even snap at the air (in case of very heightened food excitability). In this way the conditioned stimulus actually stands for the animal in place of food. In the case of several conditioned stimuli arising from different directions the animal naturally turns towards each of them.

In one of our dogs, besides other conditioned reflexes, there was formed a conditioned reflex to an extremely feeble noise issuing from under the right side of the table on which the animal was standing (experiments of I. I.

Filaretov). Trying to catch this noise, the dog went to the very edge of the stand, sometimes even stretching out one or other paw over the edge and bending its head to the utmost in the direction whence the sound proceeded. Other conditioned stimuli were to be found at various other places, but when they were put into action the dog still preferred to turn towards the place where the noise had been produced.

This fact appeared particularly strange when, in the course of experiments with other stimuli, the application of the noise was discontinued, but the motor reaction towards the place whence it had originated invariably remained, and still exists up to the present time—that is, a year and a half after this stimulus was dropped. On the application of any other stimulus originating in quite a different place the movement of the dog was always directed to the place where the noise had formerly been heard; this continued until food was served, and then only would the animal turn to the food-box.

Towards the end of the usual interval between conditioned stimuli, i.e., before the setting-in of the next stimulus, dogs often get into a state of "feeding excitement" (time reflex), either turning towards the food-box, or to the place of one or other conditioned stimulus. The above-described animal turns only towards the place from which, long before, the noise had been heard.

Evidently this reaction ought to be considered a pathological one, since it is senseless and crude, distinctly con-

Note. From "An attempt at a physiological interpretation of obsessional neurosis and paranoia" by I. Pavlov, 1934, *Journal of Mental Science, 80,* 187–197.

tradicting the existing relationships. Such being our opinion, we decided to put the animal under treatment. A positive result would, of course, have been a further proof of the indisputable pathological character of the reaction. To this end we selected bromides in adequate doses, since we already knew of a great many cases where they had been of decisive help in our experimental neuroses, and even in cases of constitutional failings of the nervous system.

Under this treatment the reaction weakened considerably. On the application of other stimuli it disappeared altogether, being superseded by an adequate and legitimate motor reaction directed towards the place where these diverse stimuli were situated. Later on the same phenomenon was observed in some other dogs; in one of them similar abnormal reactions were completely obliterated by means of bromides.

It is clear that in the above-described facts we have a pathological disturbance of the activity of the nerve cells, an alteration of the normal balance between two sides of their activity (the excitatory and the inhibitory processes) with an abnormal predominance of the excitatory process. This found confirmation in positive results obtained with bromides—agents which are known to increase the inhibitory function of the cells.

As the extreme weakness of the external agent provoked an unusual tension not only of the general motor orientating apparatus, but also of the special adjusting apparatus of the receptor in question, the overstraining of the excitatory process must be looked to as the proximate cause of the pathological phenomenon in the experiment described.

Soon we were able to add to this another similar fact. On a dog of a weak type (but of a stronger variation), and on several castrated dogs of different types, we undertook an investigation on the solving of a difficult problem. The problem consisted in the transformation of the conditioned action of a pair of metronomes with different frequency of beats and opposite conditioned significances into the reversed action. The stimulus provoking excitatory process in the cerebral cortex was transformed into a negative one, and the stimulus provoking the inhibitory process into a positive one (experiments of M. K. Petrova). For this purpose the metronome with well-elaborated positive effect was applied without reinforcement, and the inhibitory stimulus, on the contrary, was invariably accompanied by feeding. In one of the castrates of an exceptionally strong type the procedure met with a complete success. In the other animals which were submitted to the same test, transformation seemed to be in the act of taking place, when a peculiar state of affairs set in. In some animals it seemed even as if the object had been obtained; several times in succession the metronome gave results corresponding to the new conditions of the experi-

ment. However, later on, either gradually or at once, everything returned to the original relations, in spite of the fact that the procedure of transformation had been repeated some scores of times and was still being continued.

What was the meaning of this? Was it possible that at this stage of experimentation, in spite of the external likeness in the action of metronomes to their former action, everything relating to the nature of the excitatory and inhibitory processes in the cell had remained without alteration?

This had to be solved by means of a special investigation. The experiments that were undertaken revealed serious disturbances of the normal relationships in the nerve cell. The excitatory process now is not what it had been. It has become more stable and less inclined to yield to the inhibitory process. Or it might be understood as if the inhibitory process had weakened considerably, and thus led to the predominance of the excitatory one. The experiments were as follows: When the metronome evoking this changed excitatory process was applied repeatedly in the course of the same experiment without reinforcement by food, that is, was made to undergo extinction, it decreased considerably less and much more slowly than other positive stimuli in similar conditions. And still another peculiarity. Very often after the extinction of the transformed stimulus we failed to observe diminution in the usual effect of the succeeding conditioned stimuli (secondary extinction). This suggested insufficient participation of the inhibitory process in the procedure of extinction of our stimulus. On the other hand, immediately after the extinction of other conditioned stimuli (until zero reaction) the aforesaid stimulus hardly underwent any change except, perhaps, a very slight weakening. At the same time, other positive stimuli decreased considerably, and even on the following day showed lowered effects. We had here a case of an evident stability of the excitatory process of the cell, alongside a weakening of the inhibitory one. Simultaneously we became aware of a great difference among other auditory conditioned stimuli as to the stability of their excitatory process. Stimuli differing most from the metronome in the character of their sound, namely, tone stimuli, remained normal. Stimuli with elements of striking sound approached, in respect of stability, the pathological action of the metronome.

Thus in these experiments, on the transformation of the action of metronomes, we obtained the same abnormality as in the case first described: there in the cells of the motor analyser, here in those of the acoustic; in the first case as a result of overstrain of excitation, in the latter as a result of a clash between excitation and inhibition. In both cases normal relationships were restored after the administration of bromides. This gave one more reason for regarding the weakening of the inhibitory process as one of the mechanisms of the new pathological state, and also enabled us to understand why this fact was observed on castrated animals of the strong type. We have long known that one of the main results of castration consists in the lowering of the inhibitory function of the cell.

Many descriptive names may be applied to the above-mentioned pathological phenomenon—blockage, unusual inertia, increased concentration, exceptional tonicity. Henceforward we shall preferably use the term "pathological inertness."

These new data serve as confirmation and expansion of our older more general finding, that by functional means (without mechanical interference) one might experimentally obtain in the cortex a very limited pathological point. In our former experiments such a point was represented by paradoxical and ultra-paradoxical phases, i.e., corresponding stimuli gave greater effect while diminished in strength, contrary to what takes place in normal conditions, or even produced a negative effect instead of a positive. The given point either remained in this condition without affecting other points of the hemispheres, or passed on into the next pathological stage, when its stimulation by the corresponding agent led to a disturbance of the activity of the whole cortex in the form of a general inhibition of this activity. In our last case also we have isolated pathological points, but their pathological state represents a peculiar phase, which is expressed in the abnormal inertness of their excitatory process.

The foregoing is sufficient evidence for assuming that under the influence of various morbific factors of a functional character in the cerebral cortex, distinctly isolated pathologic points or areas may originate. Consequently we may expect that this experimental fact will also take its place in the pathology of the higher nervous activity in man.

I feel justified in thinking that in stereotypy, iteration, perseveration as symptoms, as well as in the substance of obsessive neurosis and paranoia, the fundamental pathophysiological phenomenon is one and the same, namely, that which was observed in our experiments, and which we decided to designate by the term of "pathological inertness." Stereotypy, iteration, perseveration are pathological inertness in the motor area of the cortex (of the general skeleton movements as well as of the special verbal ones); in obsessive neurosis and paranoia we have similar inertness in other cortical cells relative to our other sensations, feelings and conceptions. The latter statements, of course, do not exclude the possibility of the appearance of the same pathological state in the lower sections of the central nervous system.

Now let us turn our attention so to say to the clinical setting, in the various neuroses and psychoses, of this pathological phenomenon as an expression of one of the phases of the pathological condition of nerve cells. For instance, stereotypy and perseveration are no uncommon symptoms in hysteria. A hysterical woman complained that when she began to comb her hair she was unable to stop—to put an end to this occupation in due time. Another patient, after a provoked catatonic attack of short duration, could not pronounce a word without numerous reiterations, or pass over to the next words of the sentence. Still more often these phenomena occur in cases of schizophrenia, where they form the characteristic feature of the disease, especially in its catatonic form. Pathological inertness in the motor area either affects separate points or spreads over the whole skeletal-muscle system, as is to be seen in some catatonics in whom any group of muscles once made to move passively continues to do so an enormous number of times.

Further, we shall concentrate our attention specially on the obsessional neurosis and paranoia as separate, independent diseases, where the phenomenon we are interested in constitutes either the essential characteristic symptom or the whole of the disturbance.

If pathological inertness is evident and must be accepted as a fact in motor phenomena, it is indeed hardly possible to object to the possibility of the same facts being lawful and admissible in relation to all sensations, feelings and conceptions. Now these phenomena, taken within the limits of the normal, are undoubtedly manifestations of the activity of the nerve-cells. Consequently obsessional neurosis and paranoia would be pathological states of the corresponding cells of the cerebral cortex—in this case a state of pathological inertness. In these forms of morbid disturbances we have stable conceptions, feelings, and, later on, actions which correspond neither to man's relations to nature at large nor to his normal, strictly specialized, social relations. Therefore they bring him into difficult, trying, detrimental conflicts with nature, with other people, and, most important of all, with himself. All this, however, applies only to morbid conceptions and sensations; outside their sphere these patients think and act as perfectly healthy people, and may even possess capacities above the average.

Obsessional neurosis and paranoia, from the clinical point of view, are sharply differentiated as two morbid forms. Not all neurologists and psychiatrists, however, recognize this distinction in the same measure. Some admit transitions from one form to the other, ascribing differences between them to different intensities and phases of the pathological state, and other additional factors.

Here are some quotations from the latter authors. Pierre Janet says: "Persecutory delusions and obsessions are very close to each other, and I wonder why they ever came to be so completely separated." E. Kretschmer: "In connection with the old disputable problem of the existence of any essential difference between delusional and obsessive ideas, we can come to a precise conclusion in the negative sense." R. Mallet: "In this way the delusion would come into line with the obsession . . . the organic injury would be of the same kind."

These two morbid forms differ in two fundamental characteristics. In the case of obsessive neurosis the patient is conscious of the morbid nature of his pathological state, and struggles against it as far as he is able, though on the whole in vain. In paranoia the patient does not possess this criticism of his state; he is in the power of the disease, in the possession of the persisting sensation, feeling, and conception. The second difference consists in the chronic course and incurability of paranoia.

But these distinctions of the two forms do not essentially exclude the identity of the chief symptom. The more so as many clinicians have doubtless observed cases of acute as well as of chronic transition of obsessions with retention of critical faculty into obsessions without it. The difference between these forms which has served as a foundation for their clinical separation may have depended on the kind of ground on which their general essential symptom has originated, and on the kind of means by which this symptom has been provoked in each separate case.

First of all let us direct our attention to the predisposing factor and causes of the disturbance investigated in our laboratory material. We have long known in our animals that different experimental neuroses can be produced by one and the same morbid agent, depending on the inborn type of nervous system. Only representatives of the weak type and those of the strong, but unbalanced, type become easily diseased. Of course, it is also possible by intensifying morbid agents to overpower and break even a strong, well-balanced type, particularly if previously the subject was made to undergo some organic disturbance—for instance, castration.

More especially in the case of the transformation of opposite conditioned reflexes (a method of provocation of the above-described pathological inertness) we had a great variety of results within the normal limits, as well as among pathological deviations, depending on the individuality of the animals. In strong and perfectly normal types this transformation runs regularly towards that required, though differing greatly in speed and in details. In a giant of nervous strength (even after castration), the like of which I have not met during thirty years' work with conditioned reflexes, this transformation started from the very first, and without fluctuations was completed in the fifth experiment. In other dogs the procedure failed to attain complete success in spite of numerous repetitions; either the new positive stimulus did not reach the effect of the previous one, or the new inhibitory stimulus, contrary to the former, did not attain zero secretion. In some animals it was the positive stimulus which underwent trans-formation earlier, in others the negative. All this takes place in cases of successful transformation.

Likewise a great variety of results in relation to the solving of this problem are observed in cases of pathological deviations. As has already been mentioned at the beginning of this paper, either one or other of these deviations takes place. And pathological inertness, as one of the results of transformation, also either speedily changes into some other form of the disturbance or remains more of less stationary. In the weak type, pathological inertness usually soon gives place to some other pathological state. Chronic pathological inertness is particularly often observed in castrated animals of the strong type.

I am now intentionally dwelling on our laboratory material in order to show how various must be the methods of solving the same life problem by people of different types of nervous system, and how diverse must be the pathological results in abnormal types with an incapacity to overcome this difficulty.

So much on the importance of the fundamental factor. As to the proximate causes of the disturbance investigated, we saw in our present experiments (not yet very numerous) two factors provoking its appearance. At one time it is a strong and continuous excitation, i.e., an overstraining of the excitatory process, at another time a clashing of the opposite processes.

When we turn to human beings, we must naturally bear in mind here also the different causes as well as different predisposing factors which will determine various degrees and various courses, even of one and the same fundamental morbid disturbance.

Already the first cause which has been studied in our animals opens a wide range of possible causes for the disturbance investigated in humans. Irregular development, occasional accentuation of one or other of our emotions (instincts), disease of some internal organ or of a whole system, may cause the corresponding cortical cells to be temporarily or permanently, excessively and unlimitedly excited. This finally brings about their pathological inertness—an irresistible conception and sensation which continues to exist long after its real cause has been withdrawn. The same might result from strong and overwhelming life experiences. No fewer, if not more, cases of pathological inertness should be due to our second cause, since the whole of our life is an incessant struggle, a conflict of our innermost aspirations, wishes and tastes with general natural and special social conditions.

The above-mentioned causes would localize the pathological inertness of the excitatory process in different levels of the cerebral cortex. It may take place either in cells receiving immediate stimulation from external as well as internal agents (first signalizing system of reality), or in different cells (kinaesthetic, auditory, visual) of the verbal system (second signalizing system). In both cases pathological inertness may reach different degrees of intensity, at one time remaining on the level of conceptions, at another increasing in strength up to real sensations (hallucinations).

In our dogs we saw that sometimes, owing to pathological inertness, the effect of the corresponding stimulus distinctly rose above the normal effects of other stimuli.

As to the predisposing factor, it will be a common one in obsessional neurosis and in paranoia, i.e., a nervous system inclined to disease, as in our laboratory data. It may be, however, the weak type of the nervous system as well as the strong but unbalanced one. Our laboratory experience has taught us already how essential this difference may be in relation to the character of the disease. It is hardly possible to raise objections in this respect against the lawfulness of the transfer of conclusions from animal to man. Naturally, besides inherent predisposition one inevitably meets with cases of unstable or fragile nervous systems incapacitated by unfortunate occurrences, such as trauma, infections, intoxications and violent emotions.

Consequently, the difference between our two forms of disease in relation to chronicity and incurability is reduced to a difference in the immediate causes of the disease and in the types of nervous systems. The immediate causes of the disease may be either temporary or permanent. In its turn the excitatory process may either be relatively weak, unstable in its nature, easily giving place to the inhibitory one (in the weak type), or strong from the start, altogether dominating the inhibitory process. It is clear that in the latter case pathological inertness has little or no chance of being completely removed or reduced to a lesser degree, relatively normal for the given animal. This may be confirmed by the following fact from our laboratory data; in one dog of a more or less strong type, with an obsessive movement, bromides distinctly diminished the obsession, while in another dog of an indisputably weak type the same treatment removed the obsession completely. Besides, it has already been mentioned that a more chronic pathological inertness occurs mostly in castrates of a strong type. In this connection it is interesting to note E. Bleuler's remark in the latest edition of his text-book—that in cases which he had studied thoroughly he would not like to regard the coincidence of paranoia and sexual insufficiency as accidental.

As to the other feature of distinction between the two forms (the absence of criticism in relation to the morbid symptom in paranoia and its presence in obsessional neurosis), it must naturally be reduced to the difference in the intensity of pathological inertness. It follows from what has been said before that pathological inertness of the excitatory process in a strong type must be considerable. And this will account for its greater independence and even its inaccessibility to the influence of other undam-

aged areas of the cortex, and thus will physiologically determine the absence of criticism. Besides, it is probable that the inert excitatory process of considerable force on its periphery will, in accordance with the law of negative induction, initiate strong and irradiated inhibition. This, again, must lead to the same result, i.e., the exclusion of the influence of the rest of the cortex on the above-mentioned process.

Let us illustrate general considerations by concrete examples. Imagine an individual of an excitatory type—that is, one whose excitatory process predominates over the inhibitory. Let us suppose that in his emotional fund (instincts) prevails a rather common tendency to superiority. From his childhood he ardently desires to distinguish himself, to be in the first row, to be leader, to raise admiration. But nature at the same time either did not endow him with eminent talents, or unfortunately for him they were not discovered at the proper time, or his conditions in life did not permit of their being applied to practice. In consequence the individual concentrated his energy on an activity foreign to his nature. Inexorable reality denied him everything he aspired to: there was no influence, no laurels; on the contrary, there were rebuffs and blows. Nothing remained but to submit and to reconcile himself to the part of a humble drudge—that is, to inhibit his aspirations. But the necessary inhibition is lacking, and the emotion continuously and imperiously insists upon its own.

Hence at first excessive and vain efforts in one's unfortunate choice of a profession, or a change to some other with similar results. Later on, in accordance with the type (strong), a retirement into self-indulgence by means of constant and vivid representation of one's real or imaginary endowments, rights and privileges, with associated and supporting notions of intentional hindrances and persecutions on the part of the surrounding people. Thus sets in, naturally, a sufficiently conditioned phase of pathological inertness in corresponding points of the cortex, and obliterates there the last remains of inhibition. And now manifests itself the absolute strength of the idea. Not by means of active inhibition based on other associations, signals, witnesses of reality, but with the help of passive inhibition or negative induction it switches off everything inconsistent with it, and changes into a phantastic conception of imaginary greatness and success. The emotion lasts to the end of the subject's life, while alongside of it the morbid ideal lives on, but remains isolated, disturbing nothing that does not come in touch with it. We have genuine paranoia in the sense of Kraepelin.

Now I shall analyse two cases from Kretschmer's book, *Der sensitive Beziehungswahn.* They deal with two girls of a more or less weak type, but businesslike, modest, with claims only as to their honesty in religious, moral and social relations, without pretensions to rights and privileges in life. Pretensions of the last kind very often, nearly always, combine with a strong excitatory type.

Having attained maturity, the girl experiences a natural sexual attraction towards a man. Individual, ethical and social requirements have not allowed, have detained and are detaining the realization of this attachment. A clashing between nervous processes takes place. A disturbed state of the nerve activity ensues, and finds expression in pathological inertness in those parts of the cortex which are connected with struggling feelings and conceptions. The girl receives the insurmountable, obsessive conception that her sexual attachment is reflected in her face in the form of crude sensuality. In the ward she hides her face in the pillow even before the doctor. Before that stage she avoided going out into the street, as it seemed to her that people looked at her, spoke of the expression of her face and laughed. Although these conceptions are imaginary, so far everything remains within the limits of the really possible. Further comes a jump, incomprehensible even as the work of pathologically connected thought. Under the influence of a conversation with a friend, who affirmed that Eve in Paradise conversed with the serpent, not as an intellectual, but as a sexual seducer, the patient attains at once the unexpected and irresistible conception and sensation that a serpent dwells in her inside. It moves continually, and sometimes its head seems to mount as far as the pharynx. We have here a new inert idea. But how, by what process, has it originated? Kretschmer calls the phenomenon "inversion," and believes it to be a reversion of reflex nature (*reflektorischer Umschlag*).

In connection with an identical phenomenon in another clinical case Kretschmer says: "It has arisen in the manner of a reflex without logical mediation, even in direct opposition to it." What sort of reflex is it, then? Where does it originate and how does it stop? We have met and known this process in the laboratory and can understand its physiological mechanism. At this stage I find it essential to mention, to emphasize, that in this case the physiological and the psychological overlap most evidently; in fact they closely coincide, and, one may say, become identical.

Let us remember the pair of oppositely-acting metronomes, one excitatory, the other inhibitory. If in the cortex there arises a general inhibition, in the form of hypnosis for instance, or locally within the area of metronome action, the positive metronome becomes negative and the negative positive. This is what we call an ultraparadoxical phase.

In the above-described unexpected conclusion of our patient we come across this very physiological fact. The girl possessed a constant and deeply-rooted conception of her sexual purity and inviolability. She held it a moral and social stain to experience sexual attachment, even if sub-

dued and not in the least realized. This conception, owing to the generalized inhibitory condition in which the patient resides and which, in weak nervous types, is usually accompanying a state of difficulty, irresistibly, physiologically, changes into a reversed one (slightly veiled). The latter, reaching the intensity of a sensation, causes the patient to feel the presence of the sexual seducer in her very body. Exactly the same takes place in the persecutory delusion. The patient wants to be esteemed, and is smarting under contrary and imaginary conceptions of continuously inflicted insults; he wants to possess secrets, and is haunted by an obsessive idea, an opposite conception, that all his secrets are penetrated by others. Such a physiological interpretation I have already given in an open letter on the subject of obsessive feelings (*les sentiments d'emprise*) addressed to Prof. Pierre Janet.

Consequently, in the present case, at the basis of the delusional state are to be found two physiological phenomena—pathological inertness and ultraparadoxical phase, existing either separately or side by side, or relieving each other.

Approximately the same took place in the case of the other girl described by Kretschmer; the same conflict of a natural sexual attachment with a worldly-wise and pertinacious idea of an incongruous difference in years, the object of love being much younger; the same consequences, including the inversion, when the patient becomes tormented by the absurd idea of being pregnant, in spite of the fact that the object of love had never even noticed her inclination to him because of the reticence in the expression of her feelings.

This last case, studied by Kretschmer in the course of many years, shows clearly how obsessive ideas and sensations sometimes reach the intensity of real ideas and sensations and cease to be accepted by the patient as morbid, how they remain at this stage for some time, and then again are recognized by the patient objectively as symptoms of disease. The changes in this case took place in connection with repeated complications in the surrounding circumstances, and consequent changes in the stages of the nervous system, either recovering or again oppressed and weakened. Finally, with advancing years everything naturally settled to the normal.

While perusing some books on neurology and psychiatry I was glad to come across a mention of a theory formulated by the French psychiatrist de Clérambault. According to this theory the primary phenomenon in paranoia consists in the appearance of "intellectual automatism," "parasitic words and ideas," as de Clérambault calls them, round which later the delusion develops. What can be understood under the term of "intellectual automatism" if not a point of a definite pathologically inert excitatory process round which concentrates (according to the law of generalization) everything intimately connected with it, related, similar to it, and from which is repulsed, inhibited (according to the law of negative induction), everything that is foreign to it.

I am no clinician (I have been and remain a physiologist), and, of course, at present (so late in life) would have neither the time nor the possibility to become one. Owing to this, in my present conclusions as well as in my former excursions into neuropathology and psychiatry, while discussing corresponding material, I dare not aspire to sufficient competency from a clinical point of view. But I certainly shall not be erring now if I say that clinicians, neurologists and psychiatrists, in their respective domains, will inevitably have to reckon with the following fundamental patho-physiological facts: the complete isolation of functionally pathological (at the aetiological moment) points of the cortex, as well as the pathological inertness of the excitatory process and the ultraparadoxical phase in them.

Excerpts from
Studies on Hysteria

Sigmund Freud
1893

IV

The Psychotherapy of Hysteria

(1)

For my own part, I too may say that I can still hold by what is contained in the "Preliminary Communication." None the less I must confess that during the years which have since passed—in which I have been unceasingly concerned with the problems touched upon in it—fresh points of view have forced themselves on my mind. These have led to what is in part at least a differing grouping and interpretation of the factual material known to me at that time. It would be unfair if I were to try to lay too much of the responsibility for this development upon my honoured friend Dr. Josef Breuer. For this reason the considerations which follow stand principally under my own name.

When I attempted to apply to a comparatively large number of patients Breuer's method of treating hysterical symptoms by an investigation and abreaction of them under hypnosis, I came up against two difficulties, in the course of dealing with which I was led to an alteration both in my technique and in my view of the facts. (1) I found that not everyone could be hypnotized who exhib-

ited undoubted hysterical symptoms and who, it was highly probable, was governed by the same psychical mechanism. (2) I was forced to take up a position on the question of what, after all, essentially characterizes hysteria and what distinguishes it from other neuroses.

I will put off until later my account of how I got over the first of these two difficulties and what I have learnt from it, and I will begin by describing the attitude I adopted in my daily practice towards the second problem. It is very hard to obtain a clear view of a case of neurosis before one has submitted it to a thorough analysis—an analysis which can, in fact, only be brought about by the use of Breuer's method; but a decision on the diagnosis and the form of therapy to be adopted has to be made before any such thorough knowledge of the case has been arrived at. The only course open to me, therefore, was to select for cathartic treatment such cases as could be provisionally diagnosed as hysteria, which exhibited one or more of the stigmata or characteristic symptoms of hysteria. It then sometimes happened that in spite of the diagnosis of hysteria the therapeutic results turned out to be very scanty and that even analysis brought nothing significant to light. On other occasions again, I tried applying Breuer's method of treatment to neuroses which no one could have mistaken for hysteria, and I found that in that manner they could be influenced and indeed cleared up. I had this experience, for instance, with obsessional ideas, genuine obsessional ideas of the Westphal type, in cases without a single trait which recalled hysteria. Consequently, the psychical mechanism revealed by the "Preliminary Communication" could not be pathognomonic for hysteria.

Note. From *The standard edition of the complete psychological works of Sigmund Freud* (Vol. II, pp. 255–267) by J. Strachey (Ed. and Trans.), 1955, London: Hogarth Press. Copyright 1955 by Hogarth Press. Reprinted by permission.

Nor could I resolve, merely for the sake of preserving that mechanism as a criterion of it, to lump all these other neuroses in with hysteria. I eventually found a way out of all these emerging doubts by the plan of treating all the other neuroses in question in the same way as hysteria. I determined to investigate their aetiology and the nature of their psychical mechanism in every case and to let the decision as to whether the diagnosis of hysteria was justified depend upon the outcome of that investigation.

Thus, starting out from Breuer's method, I found myself engaged in a consideration of the aetiology and mechanism of the neuroses in general. I was fortunate enough to arrive at some serviceable findings in a relatively short time. In the first place I was obliged to recognize that, in so far as one can speak of determining causes which lead to the *acquisition* of neuroses, their aetiology is to be looked for in *sexual* factors. There followed the discovery that different sexual factors, in the most general sense, produce different pictures of neurotic disorders. And it then became possible, in the degree to which this relation was confirmed, to venture on using aetiology for the purpose of characterizing the neuroses and of making a sharp distinction between the clinical pictures of the various neuroses. Where the aetiological characteristics coincided regularly with the clinical ones, this was of course justified.

In this manner I found that neurasthenia presented a monotonous clinical picture in which, as my analyses showed, a "psychical mechanism" played no part. There was a sharp distinction between neurasthenia and "obsessional neurosis," the neurosis of obsessional ideas proper. In this latter one I was able to recognize a complicated psychical mechanism, an aetiology similar to that of hysteria and an extensive possibility of reducing it by psychotherapy. On the other hand, it seemed to me absolutely necessary to detach from neurasthenia a complex of neurotic symptoms which depend on a quite different and indeed at bottom a *contrary* aetiology. The component symptoms of this complex are united by a characteristic which has already been recognized by Hecker (1893). For they are either symptoms or equivalents and rudiments of *manifestations of anxiety;* and for this reason I have given to this complex which is to be detached from neurasthenia the name of "anxiety neurosis." I have maintained [Freud 1895b] that it arises from an accumulation of physical tension, which is itself once more of sexual origin. This neurosis, too, has no psychical mechanism, but it invariably influences mental life, so that "anxious expectation," phobias, hyperaesthesia to pains, etc., are among its regular manifestations. This anxiety neurosis, in my sense of the term, no doubt coincides in part with the neurosis which, under the name of "hypochondria," finds a place in not a few descriptions alongside hysteria and neurasthenia. But I cannot regard the delimitation of

hypochondria in any of the works in question as being the correct one, and the applicability of its name seems to me to be prejudiced by the fixed connection of that term with the symptom of "fear of illness."

After I had in this way fixed the simple pictures of neurasthenia, anxiety neurosis and obsessional ideas, I went on to consider the cases of neurosis which are commonly included under the diagnosis of hysteria. I reflected that it was not right to stamp a neurosis as a whole as hysterical because a few hysterical signs were prominent in its complex of symptoms. I could well understand this practice, since after all hysteria is the oldest, best-known and most striking of the neuroses under consideration; but it was an abuse, for it put down to the account of hysteria so many traits of perversion and degeneracy. Whenever a hysterical sign, such as an anaesthesia or a characteristic attack, was found in a complicated case of psychical degeneracy, the whole condition was described as one of "hysteria," so that it is not surprising that the worst and the most contradictory things were found together under this label. But just as it was certain that *this* diagnosis was incorrect, it was equally certain that we ought also to separate out the various neuroses; and since we were acquainted with neurasthenia, anxiety neurosis, etc., in a pure form, there was no longer any need to overlook them in the combined picture.

The following view, therefore, seemed to be the more probable one. The neuroses which commonly occur are mostly to be described as "mixed." Neurasthenia and anxiety neuroses are easily found in pure forms as well, especially in young people. Pure forms of hysteria and obsessional neurosis are rare; as a rule these two neuroses are combined with anxiety neurosis. The reason why mixed neuroses occur so frequently is that their aetiological factors are so often intermixed, sometimes only by chance, sometimes as a result of causal relations between the processes from which the aetiological factors of the neuroses are derived. There is no difficulty in tracing this out and demonstrating it in detail. As regards hysteria, however, it follows that that disorder can scarcely be segregated from the nexus of the sexual neuroses for the purposes of study, that as a rule it represents only a single side, only one aspect, of a complicated case of neurosis, and that it is only in marginal cases that it can be found and treated in isolation. We may perhaps say in a number of instances: *a potiori fit denominatio* [i.e. it has been given its name from its more important feature.]

I will now examine the case histories that have been reported here, with a view to seeing whether they speak in favour of my opinion that hysteria is not an independent clinical entity.

Breuer's patient, Anna O., seems to contradict my opinion and to be an example of a pure hysterical disorder. This case, however, which has been so fruitful for our knowledge of hysteria, was not considered at all by its observer from the point of view of a sexual neurosis, and is now quite useless for this purpose. When I began to analyse the second patient, Frau Emmy von N., the expectation of a sexual neurosis being the basis of hysteria was fairly remote from my mind. I had come fresh from the school of Charcot, and I regarded the linking of hysteria with the topic of sexuality as a sort of insult—just as the women patients themselves do. When I go through my notes on this case to-day there seems to me no doubt at all that it must be looked on as a case of severe anxiety neurosis accompanied by anxious expectation and phobias—an anxiety neurosis which originated from sexual abstinence and had become combined with hysteria. Case 3, that of Miss Lucy R., can perhaps best be described as a marginal case of pure hysteria. It was a short hysteria which ran an episodic course and had an unmistakable sexual aetiology, such as would correspond to an anxiety neurosis. The patient was an over-mature girl with a need to be loved, whose affections had been too hastily aroused through a misunderstanding. The anxiety neurosis, however, did not become visible, or it escaped me. Case 4, Katharina, was nothing less than a model of what I have described as "virginal anxiety." It was a combination of anxiety neurosis and hysteria. The former created the symptoms, while the latter repeated them and operated with them. Incidentally, it was a case typical of a large number of neuroses in young people that are described as "hysteria." Case 5, that of Fräulein Elisabeth von R., was once again not investigated as a sexual neurosis. I was only able to express, without confirming it, a suspicion that a spinal neurasthenia may have been its basis.

I must add, though, that in the meantime pure hysterias have become even rarer in my experience. If it was possible for me to bring together these four cases as hysterias and if in reporting them I was able to overlook the points of view that were of importance as regards sexual neuroses, the reason is that these histories date some distance back, and that I did not at that time as yet submit such cases to a deliberate and searching investigation of their neurotic sexual foundation. And if, instead of these four, I did not report *twelve* cases whose analysis provides a confirmation of the psychical mechanism of hysterical phenomena put forward by us, this reticence was necessitated by the very circumstance that the analysis revealed these cases as being simultaneously sexual neuroses, although certainly no diagnostician would have refused them the name of hysteria. But an elucidation of these sexual neuroses would overstep the bounds of the present joint publication.

I should not like it to be wrongly thought that I do not wish to allow that hysteria is an independent neu-

rotic affection, that I regard it merely as a psychical manifestation of anxiety neurosis and that I attribute to it "ideogenic" symptoms only and am transferring the somatic symptoms (such as hysterogenic points and anaesthesias) to anxiety neurosis. Nothing of the sort. In my opinion it is possible to deal with hysteria, freed from any admixture, as something independent; and to do so in every respect except in that of therapeutics. For in therapeutics we are concerned with a practical aim, with getting rid of the pathological state as a whole. And if hysteria generally appears as a component of a mixed neurosis, the situation resembles that in which there is a mixed infection, where preserving life sets a problem which does not coincide with that of combating the operation of one particular pathogenic agent.

It is very important for me to distinguish the part played by hysteria in the picture of the mixed neuroses from that played by neurasthenia, anxiety neurosis and so on, because, once I have made this distinction, I shall be able to express concisely the therapeutic value of the cathartic method. For I am inclined to venture the assertion that that method is—as a matter of theory—very well able to get rid of any hysterical symptom, whereas, as will be easily understood, it is completely powerless against the phenomena of neurasthenia and is only able rarely and in roundabout ways to influence the psychical effects of anxiety neurosis. Its therapeutic effectiveness in any particular case will accordingly depend on whether the hysterical components of the clinical picture do or do not assume a position of practical importance in comparison with the other neurotic components.

There is another obstacle in the way of the effectiveness of the cathartic method, which we have already indicated in the "Preliminary Communication." . . . It cannot affect the underlying causes of hysteria: thus it cannot prevent fresh symptoms from taking the place of the ones which had been got rid of. On the whole, then, I must claim a prominent place for our therapeutic method as employed within the framework of a therapy of the neuroses; but I should like to advise against assessing its value or applying it outside this framework. Since, however, I cannot in these pages offer a "therapy of the neuroses" of the sort needed by practitioners, what I have just said is equivalent to postponing my account of the subject to a possible later publication. But I am able, I think to add the following remarks by way of expansion and elucidation.

(1) I do not maintain that I have actually got rid of all the hysterical symptoms that I have undertaken to influence by the cathartic method. But it is my opinion that the obstacles have lain in the personal circumstances of the patients and have not been due to any question of theory. I am justified in leaving these unsuccessful cases out of account in arriving at a judgement, just as a surgeon disre-

gards cases of death which occur under anaesthesia, owing to post-operational haemorrhage, accidental sepsis, etc., in making a decision about a new technique. When I come to deal with the difficulties and drawbacks of the procedure later on, I shall return to a consideration of failures from this source. . . .

(2) The cathartic method is not to be regarded as worthless because it is a symptomatic and not a causal one. For a causal therapy is in fact as a rule only a prophylactic one; it brings to a halt any further effects of the noxious agency, but does not therefore necessarily get rid of the results which that agency has already brought about. As a rule a second phase of treatment is required to perform this latter task, and in cases of hysteria the cathartic method is quite invaluable for this purpose.

(3) Where a period of hysterical production, an acute hysterical paroxysm, has been overcome and all that is left over are hysterical symptoms in the shape of residual phenomena, the cathartic method suffices for every indication and brings about complete and permanent successes. A favourable therapeutic constellation of this kind is not seldom to be found precisely in the region of sexual life, owing to the wide oscillations in the intensity of sexual needs and the complications of the conditions necessary in order to bring about a sexual trauma. Here the cathartic method does all that can be asked of it, for the physician cannot set himself the task of altering a constitution such as the hysterical one. He must content himself with getting rid of the troubles to which such a constitution is inclined and which may arise from it with the conjunction of external circumstances. He will feel satisfied if the patient regains her working capacity. Moreover, he is not without consolation for the future when he considers the possibility of a relapse. He is aware of the principal feature in the aetiology of the neuroses—that their genesis is as a rule overdetermined, that several factors must come together to produce this result; and he may hope that this convergence will not be repeated at once, even though a few individual aetiological factors remain operative.

It might be objected that, in cases of hysteria like this, in which the illness has run its course, the residual symptoms in any case pass away spontaneously. It may be said in reply, however, that a spontaneous cure of this kind is very often neither rapid nor complete enough and that it can be assisted to an extraordinary degree by our therapeutic intervention. We may readily leave it for the moment as an unresolved question whether by means of the cathartic therapy we cure only what is capable of spontaneous cure or sometimes also what would not have been cleared up spontaneously.

(4) Where we meet with an acute hysteria, a case which is passing through the period of the most active production of hysterical symptoms and in which the ego is being constantly overwhelmed by the products of the illness (i.e. during a hysterical psychosis), even the cathartic method will make little change in the appearance and course of the disorder. In such circumstances we find ourselves in the same position as regards the neurosis as a physician faced by an acute infectious disease. The aetiological factors have performed their work sufficiently at a time which has now passed and is beyond the reach of any influence; and now, after the period of incubation has elapsed, they have become manifest. The illness cannot be broken off short. We must wait for it to run its course and in the meantime make the patient's circumstances as favourable as possible. If, during an acute period like this, we get rid of the products of the illness, the freshly generated hysterical symptoms, we must also be prepared to find that those that have been got rid of will promptly be replaced by others. The physician will not be spared the depressing feeling of being faced by a Sisyphean task. The immense expenditure of labour, and the dissatisfaction of the patient's family, to whom the inevitable length of an acute neurosis is not likely to be as familiar as the analogous case of an acute infectious disease—these and other difficulties will probably make a systematic application of the cathartic method as a rule impossible in any given case. Nevertheless, it remains a matter for serious consideration whether it may not be true that even in an acute hysteria the regular clearing up of the products of the illness exercises a curative influence, by supporting the patient's normal ego which is engaged in the work of defence, and by preserving it from being overwhelmed and falling into a psychosis and even perhaps into a permanent state of confusion.

What the cathartic method is able to accomplish even in acute hysteria, and how it even restricts the fresh production of pathological symptoms in a manner that is of practical importance, is quite clearly revealed by the case history of Anna O., in which Breuer first learnt to employ this psychotherapeutic procedure.

(5) Where it is a question of hysterias which run a chronic course, accompanied by a moderate but constant production of hysterical symptoms, we find the strongest reason for regretting our lack of a therapy which is effective causally, but we also have most ground for the appreciation of the value of the cathartic procedure as a *symptomatic* therapy. In such cases we have to do with the mischief produced by an aetiology that persists chronically. Everything depends on reinforcing the patient's nervous system in its capacity to resist; and we must reflect that the existence of a hysterical symptom means a weakening of the resistance of that nervous system and represents a factor predisposing to hysteria. As can be seen from the mechanism of monosymptomatic hysteria, a new hysterical symptom is most easily formed in connection with, and on the analogy of, one that is already

present. The point at which a symptom has already broken through once . . . forms a weak spot at which it will break through again the next time. A psychical group that has once been split off plays the part of a "provoking" crystal from which a crystallization which would otherwise not have occurred will start with the greatest facility. . . . To get rid of the symptoms which are already present, to undo the psychical changes which underlie them, is to give back to patients the whole amount of their capacity for resistance, so that they can successfully withstand the effects of the noxious agency. A very great deal can be done for such patients by means of prolonged supervision and occasional "chimney-sweeping." . . .

(6) It remains for me to mention the apparent contradiction between the admission that not all hysterical symptoms are psychogenic and the assertion that they can all be got rid of by a psychotherapeutic procedure. The solution lies in the fact that some of these non-psychogenic symptoms (stigmata, for instance) are, it is true, indications of illness, but cannot be described as ailments; and consequently it is not of practical importance if they persist after the successful treatment of the illness. As regards other such symptoms, it seems to be the case that in some roundabout way they are carried off along with the psychogenic symptoms, just as, perhaps, in some roundabout way they are after all dependent on a psychical causation.

I must now consider the difficulties and disadvantages of our therapeutic procedure, so far as they do not become obvious to everyone from the case histories reported above or from the remarks on the technique of the method which follow later. I will enumerate and indicate these difficulties rather than elaborate them.

The procedure is laborious and time-consuming for the physician. It presupposes great interest in psychological happenings, but personal concern for the patients as well. I cannot imagine bringing myself to delve into the psychical mechanism of a hysteria in anyone who struck me as low-minded and repellant, and who, on closer acquaintance, would not be capable of arousing human sympathy; whereas I can keep the treatment of a tabetic or rheumatic patient apart from personal approval of this kind. The demands made on the patient are not less. The procedure is not applicable at all below a certain level of intelligence, and it is made very much more difficult by any trace of feebleness of mind. The complete consent and complete attention of the patients are needed, but above all their confidence, since the analysis invariably leads to the disclosure of the most intimate and secret psychical events. A good number of the patients who would be suitable for this form of treatment abandon the doctor as soon as the suspicion begins to dawn on them of the direction in which the investigation is leading. For patients such as these the doctor has remained a stranger.

With others, who have decided to put themselves in his hands and place their confidence in him—a step which in other such situations is only taken voluntarily and never at the doctor's request—with these other patients, I say, it is almost inevitable that their personal relation to him will force itself, for a time at least, unduly into the foreground. It seems, indeed, as though an influence of this kind on the part of the doctor is a *sine qua non* to a solution of the problem. I do not think any essential difference is made in this respect whether hypnosis can be used or whether it has to be by-passed and replaced by something else. But reason demands that we should emphasize the fact that these drawbacks, though they are inseparable from our procedure, cannot be laid at its door. On the contrary, it is quite clear that they are based on the predetermining conditions of the neuroses that are to be cured and that they must attach to any medical activity which involves intense preoccupation with the patient and leads to a psychical change in him. I have not been able to attribute any deleterious effects or danger to the employment of hypnosis, though I made copious use of it in some of my cases. Where I caused damage the reasons lay elsewhere and deeper. If I survey my therapeutic efforts during the last few years since the communications made by my honoured teacher and friend Josef Breuer showed me the use of the cathartic method, I believe that in spite of everything, I have done much more, and more frequent, good than harm and have accomplished some things which no other therapeutic procedure could have achieved. It has on the whole, as the "Preliminary Communication" put it, brought "considerable therapeutic advantages." . . .

There is one other advantage in the use of this procedure which I must emphasize. I know of no better way of getting to understand a severe case of complicated neurosis with a greater or lesser admixture of hysteria than by submitting it to an analysis by Breuer's method. The first thing that happens is the disappearance of whatever exhibits a hysterical mechanism. In the meantime I have learnt in the course of the analysis to interpret the residual phenomena and to trace their aetiology; and in this way I have secured a firm basis for deciding which of the weapons in the therapeutic armoury against the neuroses is indicated in the case concerned. When I reflect on the difference that I usually find between my judgement on a case of neurosis *before* and *after* an analysis of this kind, I am almost inclined to regard an analysis as essential for the understanding of a neurotic illness. Moreover, I have adopted the habit of combining cathartic psychotherapy with a rest-cure which can, if need be, be extended into a complete treatment of feeding-up on Weir Mitchell lines. This gives me the advantage of being able on the one hand to avoid the very disturbing introduction of new psychical impressions during a psychotherapy, and on the other hand to remove the boredom of a rest-cure, in which the patients not infrequently fall into the habit of harmful day-dreaming. It might be expected that the often very considerable psychical work imposed on the patients during a cathartic treatment, and the excitations resulting from the reproduction of traumatic experiences, would run counter to the intentions of the Weir Mitchell rest-cure and would hinder the successes which we are accustomed to see it bring about. But the opposite is in fact the case. A combination such as this between the Breuer and Weir Mitchell procedures produces all the physical improvement that we expect from the latter, as well as having a far-reaching psychical influence such as never results from a rest-cure without psychotherapy.

Behavior and the Concept of Mental Disease

John B. Watson
1916

For some years I have been attempting to understand the physician's concept of mental diseases. Not long ago I had the pleasure of attending a medical meeting and of listening to a physician who has been very successful in his treatment of neurasthenia. Several cases of neurasthenia were described. Since none of the patients showed general organic disturbances of a serious kind and since all of the neurological tests showed normal functioning of the reflexes of the central nervous system, the physician concluded that the disease was "purely mental." He then began to describe the condition of such a patient's ego—the general content of consciousness, the inward reference of attention, and the peculiarities of the field of attention. At the end of his discourse two or three eminent physicians stated their satisfaction that the speaker had been willing to come out clearly and say that the disease was "*mental.*" In other words, they expressed their approval of the fact that the speaker did not, in functional nervous cases, deem it necessary to find lesions in the central nervous system or even a toxic condition of the nervous system before admitting that the patient had a disease.

Being the only psychologist present, I did not like to admit that I did not understand the physician's use of the term "mental." (I do not wish by this assertion to stir up strife or bitter argument, but rather to confess ignorance on my own part and to seek for some common ground of

discussion.) As a sequel to this meeting I began to attempt to formulate my own ideas as to the terminology I should use in describing a mental disease. I think that at the outset I should admit that I know a good deal more about terminology than I know about diseases of any kind. I am strengthened in this attempt to give my concept of mental diseases by the difficulty I have had in understanding the terminology (involving throughout and often transcending the current concept of consciousness) of the psychoanalytic movement.

I have been for some years an earnest student of Freud (and other psychoanalysts), but the further I go into their terminology the more sure I am that there is a simpler and more common-sense way (and at the same time a more scientific way) of describing the essential factors in their theory. I am convinced of the truth of Freud's work, but as I teach the Freudian movement to my classes I drop out the crude vitalistic and psychological terminology, and stick to what I believe to be the biological factors involved in his theories (Freud himself admits the possibility of this). The central truth that I think Freud has given us is that *youthful, outgrown, and partially discarded habit and instinctive systems of reaction can and possibly always do influence the functioning of our adult systems of reactions, and influence to a certain extent even the possibility of our forming the new habit systems which we must reasonably be expected to form.*

To my students in psychology I usually introduce the habit terminology somewhat as follows:

Long before Freud's doctrine saw the light of day William James gave the key to what I believe to be the true explanation of the wish. Thirty years ago he wrote: ". . . I

Note. From "Behavior and the concept of mental disease" by J. B. Watson, 1916, *The Journal of Philosophy, Psychology, and Scientific Methods*, 13(22), 589–597. Reprinted by permission.

am often confronted by the necessity of standing by one of my selves and relinquishing the rest. Not that I would not, if I could, be both handsome and fat and well dressed, and a great athlete, and make a million a year, be a wit, a *bon-vivant,* and a lady-killer, as well as a philosopher, a philanthropist, a statesman, a warrior, and African explorer, as well as a 'tone-poet,' and a saint. But the thing is simply impossible. The millionaire's work would run counter to the saint's; the *bon-vivant* and the philanthropist would trip each other up; the philosopher and the lady-killer could not well keep house in the same tenement of clay. Such different characteristics may conceivably at the outset of life be alike *possible* to a man. But to make any one of them actual, the rest must more or less be suppressed."

What James is particularly emphasizing here is that the human organism is instinctively capable of developing along many different lines, but that due to the stress of civilization some of these instinctive capabilities must be thwarted. In addition to these impulses which are instinctive and therefore hereditary, there are many habit impulses which are equally strong and which for similar reasons must be given up. The systems of habits we form, *i.e.,* the acts we *learn* to perform, at four years of age will not serve us when we are twelve, and those formed at the age of twelve will not serve us when we become adults. As we pass from childhood to man's estate we are constantly giving up thousands of activities which our nervous and muscular systems have learned to perform and which they still have a tendency to perform. Some of the instinctive tendencies born with us are poor heritages; some of the habits we early develop are equally poor possessions. But whether they are "good" or "bad" they must give way as we put on the habits required of adults. Some of them yield with difficulty and we often get badly twisted in attempting to put them away, as every psychiatric clinic can testify.[1]

I then try to show that such habit systems need never have been "conscious" (and here all I mean by being "conscious"—and all I believe the psychopathologists mean by it—is that *the patient can not phrase in terms of words the habit twists which have become a part of his biological equipment*). The implication is clear that in the psychoneuroses I should look for *habit disturbances*—maladjustments—and should attempt to describe my findings in terms of the inadequacy of responses, of wrong responses, and of the complete lack of responses to the objects and situations in the daily life of the patient. I should likewise attempt to trace out the original conditions leading to maladjustment and the causes leading to its continuation. To these statements most psychopathologists will subscribe, but most of them will insist

that maladjustments can not be stated wholly in behavior terms. It is just here that I think my difficulty in understanding the psychiatrist's position begins. I believe that the description of "mental" cases can be completed as well as begun in behavior terms.

I think the chief difficulty in completing the description in terms of the every-day language of habit formation lies in our failure to look upon *language* (the patient's here) as being only a system of motor habits. As a short cut—a system of economy—the human animal has formed a system of language habits (spoken words, inner speech, etc.). These language habits are built up from and always correspond more or less closely to the general system of bodily habits (I contrast here for convenience of expression *language habits* and *bodily habits*) such as the eye-hand, ear-hand, etc., systems of coordination and their complex integrations. This general correspondence between language and bodily habits is shown clearly in the football field, where we see the player making a complex series of movements and later hear him stating in words what systems of plays he employed; and in the case where we hear a man tell us what acts he is going to perform on a horizontal bar and later see him executing these acts. Words have grown up around motor acts and have no functional significance apart from their connection with motor acts. I have come recently to the view that speech should be looked upon as a vast system of *conditioned reflexes.* In a previous paper[2] I sketched the method of establishing motor and secretory conditioned reflexes. As Pawlow [*sic*] and Bechterew have shown, the central feature of the method consists in the fact that almost any stimulus can, under suitable conditions, *be substituted for another stimulus* which has a very definite act of its own as a consequence. An electric contact applied to the sole of the foot will produce a defensive reflex—a jerking up of the foot. A monochromatic light produces no such effect. If, however, the light is allowed to fall upon the retina of the eye at the moment the foot is stimulated electrically, we will (after repetition) bring about a condition such that the light alone will produce the defensive reaction of the foot. Words as words are learned largely by imitation, but words receive their standing as functional units in integrated habit systems by virtue of the fact that they become *substitutable for the stimulus which originally initiated an act.* A simple illustration will possibly serve to make clear my point. The cold air from an open window leads a child who has gone to bed to draw up the covers. The words of the nurse "cover up, dear" will lead to the same act. Of course in habit systems as complex as those in speech, words get

---

[1] From a written but unpublished lecture.

[2] "The Place of the Conditioned Reflex in Psychology," *Psychological Review,* March, 1916.

further and further divorced from the original stimuli for which they were substituted (*i.e.,* from the original integrations in which they first played a part). The final test of all words, however, is the question whether they can stand adequately (be substituted) for acts. We often see an instructor despair of telling a student in words how to conduct an experiment. He then resorts to acts and goes through the experiment for the student. Our words thus stand as a kind of shorthand sketch of our repertoire of acts and motor attitudes.

I have developed these points at length because a great many of the symptoms of so-called mental cases consist in disturbances of speech-functions—in maladjustments of that nice balance which should exist between speech acts and bodily acts (and, perhaps even more, disturbances among the "speech functions" themselves). For fear that I may be misunderstood in my use of the term "disturbance" of speech I wish to say that I have no reference here to aphasia. I mean, among other things, by speech disturbance what the Freudian means: For example, in the manifest content of dreams one finds new words, misplacement of words, condensation of words, etc.; and in the association test the failure of words and an increased reaction time between stimulus word and response. These are speech disturbances and hence *habit disturbances,* exactly on a par with the paralysis of arm or leg in hysteria, defensive reactions, compensatory reactions, and the like. All such disturbances of habit— superfluous and useless conditioned reflexes—may be found to date back to some primary stimulus (possibly to sex trauma, exposure,[3] masturbation, etc., in childhood) which is the conditioning cause operating just as the electric shock given jointly with a visual stimulus operates in forcing the visual stimulus finally to release a group of responses which, until the current was applied, brought none of them.

Motor tics, the seeming paralysis in hysteria, etc., are to be envisaged in the same way; as types of conditioned reflexes, which are no more wonderful and no less wonderful than the cases in the laboratory where the sound of a bell does not at first cause a subject to jerk back his arm, but which later comes to do it after we have jointly stimulated the hand with an electric current and the ear with the bell. Nor will the objection hold that conditioned reflexes arise only in the laboratory. Dr. Lashley has shown that numerous such conditioned reflexes exist in the functioning of the parotid gland in man, and that these reflexes arise in the regular course of daily activity. So pronounced are they that a subject can not very well

experiment upon himself. If he reaches forward to get a pipette full of acid to test its effect in increasing the activity of the gland, the gland begins to function as he reaches for the acid. Now if conditioned reflexes can arise in the salivary gland, they can and possibly do arise in all glandular and muscular portions of the body. The possibility that tics and hysterical manifestations generally arise in this way is very great. It seems to me to be the only biological formulation possible in the present state of our knowledge.

Is it not simpler, then, to look upon all such manifestations as special forms of conditioned reflexes? As long as they do not disturb the subject's ordinary reactions to the objects around him, we do not class the patient as being "mentally" disturbed (as in the psychopathological disturbances we see in daily life); the moment, however, that an arm is incapacitated or the glandular and muscular elements of the sex organs become involved we must take notice of such grave disturbances and try to see what can be done. If now we can take what appears to me to be a sensible point of view about language habits ("thought") and come to look upon them as obeying the laws of all other habits, and describe our patient's symptoms wholly in terms of habit disturbance, and trace the conditions which have led to the disturbance, we shall have come a long way. We could throw over bodily the enormous and burdensome terminology of a description in terms of consciousness—disturbances of the affections, misplacement or withdrawal of the libido (a concept which, in Jung's latest book on the "Subconscious," has become the equivalent of Driesch's entelechy), repressions into the subconscious, and the like.

I think I can illustrate what I mean by describing a hypothetical "neurasthenic dog." Suppose I take a dog to a canine psychiatric clinic and tell the physician nothing about the dog's previous history. The physician puts the dog through a searching neurological examination, makes a thorough test of heart action, examines the urine, etc. Absolutely no pathological disturbances are found. He finds, however, on testing the dog's reactions to his normal canine environment that there are serious functional disturbances. When the normal dog sees a piece of red meat, he snaps at it. The "neurasthenic" dog, however, lies down and becomes absolutely motionless. When brought near a female of his own kind, far from exhibiting the usual reactions, he begins to shed tears. When spoken to in gentle tones, he hangs his head, puts his tail between his legs, but when spoken to gruffly he brightens up and lifts his head and licks the speaker's hand. When preparing to sleep, instead of turning round and round and lying down with anterior and posterior ends in close relations, the dog jumps up and down and finally lies down on his back with his paws pointing to the stars. The physician surely finds here serious conflict with reality

---

[3] I believe it takes more than a single shock or disturbance to bring such conditional reflexes in its train. Usually I believe it is a long-continued struggle with environment which brings them.

and a woeful lack of normal compensations. But since there are no organic pathological disturbances, the physician diagnoses the case as neurasthenia with compulsion neurosis—the disease is mental.

When I come to the clinic and see the physician and talk with him I explain that there is no need to introduce any concept of the "mental," I tell him that I have *trained the dog* during the past five years to do just these things. The trouble with the dog is that his habits are twisted. Now if I had started with a dog whose instinctive reaction systems were (possibly) perverted in the beginning (heredity) and I had superposed in addition the above bizarre group of habit reactions, he would seem a pitiful object indeed when trying to cope with his environment.

Now as to the cure of the dog. I should begin step by step to *retrain* the dog along lines which would make him better fitted to cope with his environment. If there were sufficient plasticity left I should undertake it with a good deal of hope. The length of time required for the cure and the rapidity of the cure would depend upon several factors—such as my luck in fixing upon just the right method for breaking up the old non-serviceable habits, the length of time the old habits had been in force, upon the tractability of the dog, etc.

If I understand their teachings, this cure which I suggest is the keynote of the work of the psychopathologists. It is certainly that of Adolf Meyer. I doubt if Dr. Meyer will go as far as I do in holding that the time has already come for describing "mental diseases" wholly in terms of twisted habits, and yet it was a conversation which I had with him three or four years ago that first led me to think over functional nervous cases in this way. Nor can I see where the straight Freudian adherents can have any cause for complaint. Every psychopathologist begins with a conversation with his patient. In the conversation certain words begin to give indications of the "complex" (maladjustment). The habit twist is made still clearer by the results of tests with the word-association method, by the analysis of the patient's dreams, by inference, and by common-sense observations. In course of time the maladjustment is completely located, and its origin, development, and consequences are fully traced. Now during the process of study, the patient's reeducation (usually, but not necessarily, along sex lines) has already begun. In fact it began the moment the physician secured sufficient acquaintance with the patient to begin analysis. (Brill states that he will not attempt analysis until he has known the patient for at least a week.)

Several psychopathologists have thought that the objective methods and terminology which we have sought to introduce would necessarily do away with conversation with the patient. This is not true. Speech is just as objective as tennis-playing or any other muscular act and should be looked upon in just as objective a way. The difficulty has been that instead of looking at speech as at other muscular acts, we have looked upon it as a revealer of "thought"—the sacred inner secret of the "mind." Now in testing out a neurasthenic patient one of the first things we do is to find out what disturbances there are in the movements of hands, arms, and body as a whole. We watch and describe them in wholly objective ways. Is it not possible to look upon speech disturbances in just such an objective way and see in them merely signals which will lead us to the disturbed systems of bodily integrations? In a particular case we may find (without admitting that we must find it so) that the speech defects point to the "incest complex" in one form or another. The faulty and unwise behavior of a mother has led the boy to react to her in many particulars as does her husband. Such a group of integrations on the boy's part seriously disturbs the forming of suitable boyish habits and may bring in its train a vast series of conditioned reflexes which may show themselves in general bodily disturbances, such as tics, paralysis, etc., or in speech defects, such as failures in word responses, lengthened reaction time, etc.

My thesis so far has concerned itself with *motor habits*. The muscles form only a part of the total reaction system. Every motor reaction calls for a simultaneous response in the glandular system (corresponding in part at least to the *affective values* of the psychologists and psychopathologists). Now the chief symptom in many cases of mental disease is the disturbance of "affective values" (withdrawal of the libido, etc.). It is to take account of this puzzling transfer that has led the Freudian school to speak as though the "affective process" could be disembodied from any particular response and hang suspended as it were in mid-air[4] (the "subconscious" is introduced here by Freud). From time to time, to be sure, it attaches itself to certain responses, but these responses may bear no relation to the original stimulus which called it forth.

The modern notion of emotional[5] reactions calls first

---

[4] I quote from Ernest Jones who is interpreting Freud's theory of affective processes: "Most significant, however, is the assumption that it has a certain autonomy, so that it can become released from the idea to which it was primarily attached, thus entering into new psychical systems and producing widespread effects. This displacement of affect from one idea to another Freud denotes as transference (*Uebertragung*), and says that the second idea may in a sense be termed a representative of the first. A simple illustration of the process is when a girl transfers the affective process properly belonging to a baby to that of a doll, and even takes it to bed with her and makes attempts to feed it, thus treating it in all possible respects as she would a baby." Papers on Psycho-Analysis.

[5] I prefer to keep the term "emotion" in objective psychology. I, however, throw away all of the conscious implications. To me an emotion is a bodily state which can be observed in man and animal equally well, such as the bristling of hair, shedding of tears, increase or decrease in respiration, sighing, heightened muscular activity, and the

for the presence of an emotionally exciting stimulus, which will, through hereditary mechanisms, excite neural arcs leading through the central and the autonomic systems, finally arousing activity in the glands—especially in the ductless glands. The latter then set free certain substances, *e.g.*, adrenin, among other things, which, on getting into the blood, continue the emotional activity just as though the original stimulus were present. As I view the matter we have here just the situation for arousing *conditioned emotional reflexes*. Any stimulus (non-emotional) which immediately (or shortly) follows an emotionally exciting stimulus produces its motor reaction before the emotional effects of the original stimulus have died down. A transfer (conditioned reflex) takes place (after many such occurrences) so that in the end the second stimulus produces in its train now not only its proper group of motor integrations, but an emotional set which *belonged originally to another stimulus*. To apply this in detail in functional cases oversteps my ability as well as my present interests. At any rate the suggestion seems to me to give a reasonable clue as to the way in which such shifts in the emotional constituents of a total integration can occur. Surely it is better to use even this crude formulation than

to describe the phenomenon as is done in the current psychoanalytic treatises. What is simpler than to speak of a transferred or conditioned emotional response, giving both the object (or situation) which originally called out the emotional response and the object (or situation) to which it was transferred?

In conclusion I wish to say that I am not attempting to launch criticisms at the head of the psychopathologist. If his terminology is involved it is the fault really of psychology, since he perforce had to use the concepts which psychology had developed. I have tried in this paper merely to raise the question whether the psychopathologist can not reshape to some extent his formulation of problems (without doing injustice to the patient) so as to avail himself of biological and behavioristic concepts.

Psychological terminology is, I believe, being fast outgrown. Dunlap's recent inquiry[6] into the definitions of psychological terms shows, I believe, more clearly than I can state, just how little agreement there is among psychologists in the use of common psychological terms. It seems to me to be a mistake for as useful and fascinating a growth as psychopathology to allow itself to become encrusted with the barnacles of an outgrown terminology.

---

like. Some day we shall be able to mark off these objective states and classify them with respect to the types of stimuli which call them out (sex, food, shelter, noxious odors, etc.).

[6] Knight Dunlap, "The Results of a Questionary on Psychological Terminology," *John Hopkins Circular*, 1916, No. 5.

Self-Efficacy: Toward a Unifying Theory of Behavioral Change

Albert Bandura
1977

The present article presents an integrative theoretical framework to explain and to predict psychological changes achieved by different modes of treatment. This theory states that psychological procedures, whatever their form, alter the level and strength of *self-efficacy*. It is hypothesized that expectations of personal efficacy determine whether coping behavior will be initiated, how much effort will be expended, and how long it will be sustained in the face of obstacles and aversive experiences. Persistence in activities that are subjectively threatening but in fact relatively safe produces, through experiences of mastery, further enhancement of self-efficacy and corresponding reductions in defensive behavior. In the proposed model, expectations of personal efficacy are derived from four principal sources of information: performance accomplishments, vicarious experience, verbal persuasion, and physiological states. The more dependable the experiential sources, the greater are the changes in perceived self-efficacy. A number of factors are identified as influencing the cognitive processing of efficacy information arising from enactive, vicarious, exhortative, and emotive sources. The differential power of diverse therapeutic procedures is analyzed in terms of the postulated cognitive mechanism of operation. Findings are reported from microanalyses of enactive, vicarious, and emotive modes of treatment that support the hypothesized relationship between perceived self-efficacy and behavioral changes. Possible directions for further research are discussed.

Current developments in the field of behavioral change reflect two major divergent trends. The difference is especially evident in the treatment of dysfunctional inhibitions and defensive behavior. On the one hand, the mechanisms by which human behavior is acquired and regulated are increasingly formulated in terms of cognitive processes. On the other hand, it is performance-based procedures that are proving to be most powerful for effecting psychological changes. As a consequence, successful performance is replacing symbolically based experiences as the principle vehicle of change.

The present article presents the view that changes achieved by different methods derive from a common cognitive mechanism. The apparent divergence of theory and practice can be reconciled by postulating that cognitive processes mediate change but that cognitive events are induced and altered most readily by experience of mastery arising from effective performance. The distinction between process and means is underscored, because it is often assumed that a cognitive model of operation requires a symbolic means of induction. Psychological changes can be produced through other means than performance accomplishments. Therefore, the explanatory mechanism developed in this article is designed to account for changes in behavior resulting from diverse modes of treatment.

COGNITIVE LOCUS OF OPERATION

Psychological treatments based on learning principles were originally conceptualized to operate through peripheral mechanisms. New behavior was presumably shaped automatically by its effects. Contingency learning through paired stimulation was construed in connectionist terms as a process in which responses were linked directly to stimuli. Altering the rate of preexisting behavior by reinforcement was portrayed as a process wherein responses were regulated by their immediate consequences without requiring any conscious involvement of the responders.

Growing evidence from several lines of research altered theoretical perspectives on how behavior is acquired and regulated. Theoretical formulations emphasizing peripheral mechanisms began to give way to cognitively oriented theories that explained behavior in terms of central processing of direct, vicarious, and symbolic sources of information. Detailed analysis of the empirical and conceptual issues (see Bandura, 1977) falls beyond the scope of the present article. To summarize briefly, however, it has now been amply documented that cognitive processes play a prominent role in the acquisition and retention of new behavior patterns. Transitory experiences leave lasting effects by being coded and retained in symbols for memory representation. Because acquisition of response information is a major aspect of learning, much human behavior is developed through modeling. From observing others, one forms a conception of how new behavior patterns are performed, and on later occasions the symbolic construction serves as a guide for action (Bandura, 1971). The initial approximations of response patterns learned observationally are further refined through self-corrective adjustments based on informative feedback from performance.

Learning from response consequences is also conceived of largely as a cognitive process. Consequences serve as an unarticulated way of informing performers what they must do to gain beneficial outcomes and to avoid punishing ones. By observing the differential effects of their own actions, individuals discern which responses are appropriate in which settings and behave accordingly (Dulany, 1968). Viewed from the cognitive framework, learning from differential outcomes becomes a special case of observational learning. In this mode of conveying response information, the conception of the appropriate behavior is gradually constructed from observing the effects of one's actions rather than from the examples provided by others.

Changes in behavior produced by stimuli that either signify events to come or indicate probable response consequences also have been shown to rely heavily on cognitive representations of contingencies. People are not much affected by paired stimulation unless they recognize that the events are correlated (Dawson & Furedy, 1976; Grings, 1973). Stimuli influence the likelihood of a behavior's being performed by virtue of their predictive function, not because the stimuli are automatically connected to responses by their having occurred together. Reinterpretation of antecedent determinants as predictive cues, rather than as controlling stimuli, has shifted the locus of the regulation of behavior from the stimulus to the individual.

The issue of the locus at which behavioral determinants operate applies to reinforcement influences as well as to antecedent environmental stimuli. Contrary to the common view that behavior is controlled by its immediate consequences, behavior is related to its outcomes at the level of aggregate consequences rather than momentary effects (Baum, 1973). People process and synthesize feedback information from sequences of events over long intervals about the situational circumstances and the patterns and rates of actions that are necessary to produce given outcomes. Since consequences affect behavior through the influence of thought, beliefs about schedules of reinforcement can exert greater influence on behavior than the reinforcement itself (Baron, Kaufman, & Stauber, 1969; Kaufman, Baron, & Kopp, 1966). Incidence of behavior that has been positively reinforced does not increase if individuals believe, based on other information, that the same actions will not be rewarded on future occasions (Estes, 1972); and the same consequences can increase, reduce, or have no effect on incidence of behavior depending on whether individuals are led to believe that the consequences signify correct responses, incorrect responses, or occur noncontingently (Dulany, 1968).

The discussion thus far has examined the role of cognition in the acquisition and regulation of behavior. Motivation, which is primarily concerned with activation and persistance of behavior, is also partly rooted in cognitive activities. The capacity to represent future consequences in thought provides one cognitively based source of motivation. Through cognitive representation of future outcomes individuals can generate current motivators of behavior. Seen from this perspective, reinforcement operations affect behavior largely by creating expectations that behaving in a certain way will produce anticipated benefits or avert future difficulties (Bolles, 1972b). In the enhancement of previously learned behavior, reinforcement is conceived of mainly as a motivational device rather than as an automatic response strengthener.

A second cognitively based source of motivation operates through the intervening influences of goal setting and self-evaluative reactions (Bandura, 1976b, 1977). Self-motivation involves standards against which to evaluate performance. By making self-rewarding reactions conditional on attaining a certain level of behavior, individuals create self-inducements to persist in their efforts until their performances match self-prescribed standards. Perceived negative discrepancies between performance and standards create dissatisfactions that motivate corrective changes in behavior. Both the anticipated satisfactions of desired accomplishments and the negative appraisals of insufficient performance thus provide incentives for action. Having accomplished a given level of performance, individuals often are no longer satisfied with it and make further self-reward contingent on higher attainments.

The reconceptualization of human learning and motivation in terms of cognitive processes has major implications for the mechanisms through which therapeutic procedures alter behavioral functioning. Although the advances in cognitive psychology are a subject of increasing interest in speculations about behavioral change processes, few new theories of psychotherapy have been proposed that might prove useful in stimulating research on explanatory mechanisms and in integrating the results accompanying diverse modes of treatment. The present article outlines a theoretical framework, in which the concept of *self-efficacy* is assigned a central role, for analyzing changes achieved in fearful and avoidant behavior. The explanatory value of this conceptual system is then evaluated by its ability to predict behavioral changes produced through different methods of treatment.

EFFICACY EXPECTATIONS AS A MECHANISM OF OPERATION

The present theory is based on the principal assumption that psychological procedures, whatever their form, serve as means of creating and strengthening expectations of personal efficacy. Within this analysis, efficacy expectations are distinguished from response-outcome expectancies. The difference is presented schematically in Figure 1.

An outcome expectancy is defined as a person's estimate that a given behavior will lead to certain outcomes. An efficacy expectation is the conviction that one can successfully execute the behavior required to produce the outcomes. Outcome and efficacy expectations are differentiated, because individuals can believe that a particular course of action will produce certain outcomes, but if they entertain serious doubts about whether they can perform the necessary activities such information does not influence their behavior.

In this conceptual system, expectations of personal mastery affect both initiation and persistence of coping behavior. The strength of people's convictions in their own effectiveness is likely to affect whether they will even try to cope with given situations. At this initial level, perceived self-efficacy influences choice of behavioral settings. People fear and tend to avoid threatening situations they believe exceed their coping skills, whereas they get involved in activities and behave assuredly when they judge themselves capable of handling situations that would otherwise be intimidating.

Not only can perceived self-efficacy have directive influence on choice of activities and settings, but, through expectations of eventual success, it can affect coping efforts once they are initiated. Efficacy expectations determine how much effort people will expend and how long they will persist in the face of obstacles and aversive experiences. The stronger the perceived self-efficacy, the more active the efforts. Those who persist in subjectively threatening activities that are in fact relatively safe will gain corrective experiences that reinforce their sense of efficacy, thereby eventually eliminating their defensive behavior. Those who cease their coping efforts prematurely will retain their self-debilitating expectations and fears for a long time.

The preceding analysis of how perceived self-efficacy influences performance is not meant to imply that expectation is the sole determinant of behavior. Expectation alone will not produce desired performance if the component capabilities are lacking. Moreover, there are many things that people can do with certainty of success that they do not perform because they have no incentives to do so. Given appropriate skills and adequate incentives, however, efficacy expectations are a major determinant of people's choice of activities, how much effort they will expend, and of how long they will sustain effort in dealing with stressful situations.

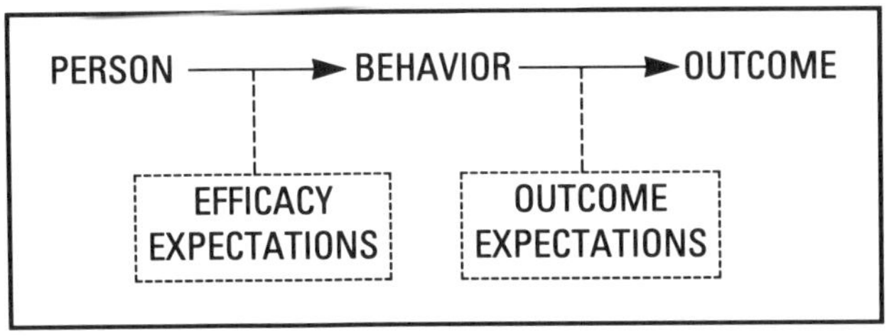

Figure 1. Diagrammatic representation of the difference between efficacy expectations and outcome expectations.

DIMENSIONS OF EFFICACY EXPECTATIONS

Empirical tests of the relationship between expectancy and performance of threatening activities have been hampered by inadequacy of the expectancy analysis. In most studies the measures of expectations are mainly concerned with people's hopes for favorable outcomes rather than with their sense of personal mastery. Moreover, expectations are usually assessed globally only at a single point in a change process as though they represent a static, unidimensional factor. Participants in experiments of this type are simply asked to judge how much they expect to benefit from a given procedure. When asked to make such estimates, participants assume, more often than not, that the benefits will be produced by the external ministrations rather than gained through the development of self-efficacy. Such global measures reflect a mixture of, among other things, hope, wishful thinking, belief in the potency of the procedures, and faith in the therapist. It therefore comes as no surprise that outcome expectations of this type have little relation to magnitude of behavioral change (Davison & Wilson, 1973; Lick & Bootzin, 1975).

Efficacy expectations vary on several dimensions that have important performance implications. They differ in *magnitude*. Thus when tasks are ordered in level of difficulty, the efficacy expectations of different individuals may be limited to the simpler tasks, extend to moderately difficult ones, or include even the most taxing performances. Efficacy expectations also differ in *generality*. Some experiences create circumscribed mastery expectations. Others instill a more generalized sense of efficacy that extends well beyond the specific treatment situation.

In addition, expectancies vary in *strength*. Weak expectations are easily extinguishable by disconfirming experiences, whereas individuals who possess strong expectations of mastery will persevere in their coping efforts despite disconfirming experiences.

An adequate expectancy analysis, therefore, requires detailed assessment of the magnitude, generality, and strength of efficacy expectations commensurate with the precision with which behavioral processes are measured. Both efficacy expectations and performance should be assessed at significant junctures in the change process to clarify their reciprocal effects on each other. Mastery expectations influence performance and are, in turn, altered by the cumulative effects of one's efforts.

SOURCES OF EFFICACY EXPECTATIONS

In this social learning analysis, expectations of personal efficacy are based on four major sources of information: performance accomplishments, vicarious experience, verbal persuasion, and physiological states. Figure 2 presents the diverse influence procedures commonly used to reduce defensive behavior and presents the principal

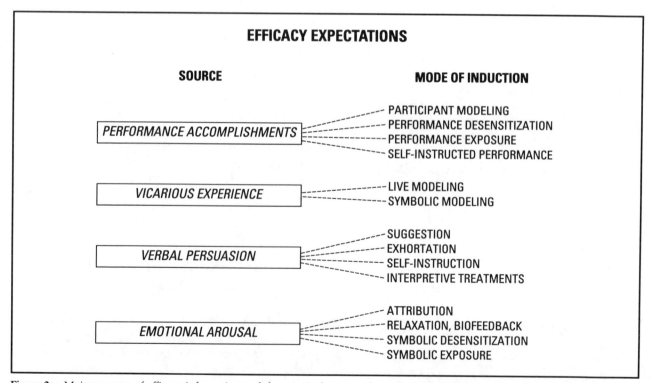

Figure 2. Major sources of efficacy information and the principal sources through which different modes of treatment operate.

source through which each treatment operates to create expectations of mastery. Any given method, depending on how it is applied, may of course draw to a lesser extent on one or more other source of efficacy information. For example, as we shall see shortly, performance-based treatments not only promote behavioral accomplishments but also extinguish fear arousal, thus authenticating self-efficacy through enactive and arousal sources of information. Other methods, however, provide fewer ways of acquiring information about one's capability for coping with threatening situations. By postulating a common mechanism of operation, this analysis provides a conceptual framework within which to study behavioral changes achieved by different modes of treatment.

Performance Accomplishments

This source of efficacy information is especially influential because it is based on personal mastery experiences. Successes raise mastery expectations; repeated failures lower them, particularly if the mishaps occur early in the course of events. After strong efficacy expectations are developed through repeated success, the negative impact of occasional failures is likely to be reduced. Indeed, occasional failures that are later overcome by determined effort can strengthen self-motivated persistence if one finds through experience that even the most difficult obstacles can be mastered by sustained effort. The effects of failure on personal efficacy therefore partly depend on the timing and the total pattern of experiences in which the failures occur.

Once established, enhanced self-efficacy tends to generalize to other situations in which performance was self-debilitated by preoccupation with personal inadequacies (Bandura, Adams, & Beyer, in press; Bandura, Jeffery, & Gajdos, 1975). As a result, improvements in behavioral functioning transfer not only to similar situations but to activities that are substantially different from those on which the treatment was focused. Thus, for example, increased self-efficacy gained through rapid mastery of a specific animal phobia can increase coping efforts in social situations as well as reduce fears of other animals. However, the generalization effects occur most predictably to the activities that are most similar to those in which self-efficacy was restored by treatment (Bandura, Blanchard, & Ritter, 1969).

Methods of change that operate on the basis of performance accomplishments convey efficacy information in more ways than simply through the evidence of performance improvements. In the course of treatments employing modeling with guided performance, participants acquire a generalizable skill for dealing successfully with stressful situations, a skill that they use to overcome a variety of dysfunctional fears and inhibitions in their everyday life (Bandura et al., in press; Bandura et al., 1975). Having a serviceable coping skill at one's disposal undoubtedly contributes to one's sense of personal efficacy. Behavioral capabilities can also be enhanced through modeling alone (Bandura, 1971; Flanders, 1968). However, participant modeling provides additional opportunities for translating behavioral conceptions to appropriate actions and for making corrective refinements toward the perfection of skills.

Most of the treatment procedures developed in recent years to eliminate fearful and defensive behavior have been implemented either through performance or by symbolic procedures. Regardless of the methods involved, results of comparative studies attest to the superiority of performance-based treatments. In the desensitization approach devised by Wolpe (1974), clients received graduated exposure to aversive events in conjunction with anxiety reducing activities, usually in the form of muscular relaxation. A number of experiments have been reported in which relaxation is paired with scenes in which phobics visualize themselves engaging in progressively more threatening activities or with enactment of the same hierarchy of activities with the actual threats. Findings based on different types of phobias consistently reveal that performance desensitization produces substantially greater behavioral change than does symbolic desensitization (LoPicollo, 1970; Sherman, 1972; Strahley, 1966). Physiological measures yield similar results. Symbolic desensitization reduces autonomic responses to imagined but not to actual threats, whereas performance desensitization eliminates autonomic responses to both imagined and actual threats (Barlow, Leitenberg, Agras, & Wincze, 1969). The substantial benefits of successful performance are typically achieved in less time than is required to extinguish arousal to symbolic representations of threats.

More recently, avoidance behavior has been treated by procedures involving massive exposure to aversive events. In this approach, intense anxiety is elicited by prolonged exposure to the most threatening situations and sustained at high levels, without relief, until emotional reactions are extinguished. Several investigators have compared the relative success of prolonged exposure to aversive situations in imagery and actual encounters with them in ameliorating chronic agoraphobias. Real encounters with threats produce results decidedly superior to imagined exposure, which has weak, variable effects (Emmelkamp & Wessels, 1975; Stern & Marks, 1973; Watson, Mullett, & Pillay, 1973). Prolonged encounters that ensure behavioral improvements are more effective than distributed brief encounters that are likely to end before successful performance of the activity is achieved (Rabavilas, Boulougouris, & Stefanis, 1976).

The participant modeling approach to the elimination

of defensive behavior utilizes successful performance as the primary vehicle of psychological change. People displaying intractable fears and inhibitions are not about to do what they dread. In implementing participant modeling, therapists therefore structure the environment so that clients can perform successfully despite their incapacities. This is achieved by enlisting a variety of response induction aids, including preliminary modeling of threatening activities, graduated tasks, enactment over graduated temporal intervals, joint performance with the therapist, protective aids to reduce the likelihood of feared consequences, and variation in the severity of the threat itself (Bandura, Jeffery, & Wright, 1974). As treatment progresses, the supplementary aids are withdrawn so that clients cope effectively unassisted. Self-directed mastery experiences are then arranged to reinforce a sense of personal efficacy. Through this form of treatment incapacitated people rapidly lose their fears, they are able to engage in activities they formerly inhibited, and they display generalized reductions of fears toward threats beyond the specifically treated conditions (Bandura, 1976a).

Participant modeling has been compared with various symbolically based treatments. These studies corroborate the superiority of successful performance facilitated by modeling as compared to vicarious experience alone (Bandura et al., 1969; Blanchard, 1970b; Lewis, 1974; Ritter, 1969, Röper, Rachman, & Marks, 1975), to symbolic desensitization (Bandura et al., 1969; Litvak, 1969), and to imaginal modeling in which clients visualize themselves or others coping successfully with threats (Thase & Moss, 1976). When participant modeling is subsequently administered to those who benefit only partially from the symbolic procedures, avoidance behavior is thoroughly eliminated within a brief period.

The findings summarized above are consistent with self-efficacy theory, but they do not shed much light on the mechanism by which specific mastery experiences produce generalized and enduring changes in behavior. Verification of the operative mechanism requires experimental evidence that experienced mastery does in fact alter the level and strength of self-efficacy and that self-efficacy is, in turn, linked to behavior. We shall return later to research that addresses itself specifically to the linkages between treatment procedures, perceived self-efficacy, and behavior.

Vicarious Experience

People do not rely on experienced mastery as the sole source of information concerning their level of self-efficacy. Many expectations are derived from vicarious experience. Seeing others perform threatening activities without adverse consequences can generate expectations

in observers that they too will improve if they intensify and persist in their efforts. They persuade themselves that if others can do it, they should be able to achieve at least some improvement in performance (Bandura & Barab, 1973). Vicarious experience, relying as it does on inferences from social comparison, is a less dependable source of information about one's capabilities than is direct evidence of personal accomplishments. Consequently, the efficacy expectations induced by modeling alone are likely to be weaker and more vulnerable to change.

A number of modeling variables that are apt to affect expectations of personal efficacy have been shown to enhance the disinhibiting influence of modeling procedures. Phobics benefit more from seeing models overcome their difficulties by determined effort than from observing facile performances by adept models (Kazdin, 1973; Meichenbaum, 1971). Showing the gains achieved by effortful coping behavior not only minimizes for observers the negative impact of temporary distress but demonstrates that even the most anxious can eventually succeed through perseverance. Similarity to the model in other characteristics, which increases the personal relevance of vicariously derived information, can likewise enhance the effectiveness of symbolic modeling (Kazdin, 1974b).

Modeled behavior with clear outcomes conveys more efficacy information than if the effects of the modeled actions remain ambiguous. In investigations of vicarious processes, observing one perform activities that meet with success does, indeed, produce greater behavioral improvements than witnessing the same performances modeled without any evident consequences (Kazdin, 1974c, 1975). Diversified modeling, in which the activities observers regard as hazardous are repeatedly shown to be safe by a variety of models, is superior to exposure to the same performances by a single model (Bandura & Menlove, 1968; Kazdin, 1974a, 1975, 1976). If people of widely differing characteristics can succeed, then observers have a reasonable basis for increasing their own sense of self-efficacy.

The pattern of results reported above offers at least suggestive support for the view that exemplifications of success through sustained effort with substantiating comparative information can enhance observers' perceptions of their own performance capabilities. Research will be presented below that bears more directly on the proposition that modeling procedures alter avoidance behavior through the intervening influence of efficacy expectations.

Verbal Persuasion

In attempts to influence human behavior, verbal persuasion is widely used because of its ease and ready availability. People are led, through suggestion, into believing they can cope successfully with what has overwhelmed them in the past. Efficacy expectations induced in this manner are also likely to be weaker than those arising from one's own accomplishments because they do not provide an authentic experiential base for them. In the face of distressing threats and a long history of failure in coping with them, whatever mastery expectations are induced by suggestion can be readily extinguished by disconfirming experiences.

Results of several lines of research attest to the limitations of procedures that attempt to instill outcome expectations in people simply by telling them what to expect. In laboratory studies, "placebo" conditions designed suggestively to raise expectations of improvement produce little change in refractory behavior (Lick & Bootzin, 1975; Moore, 1965; Paul, 1966). Whether this is due to the low credibility of the suggestions or to the weakness of the induced expectations cannot be determined from these studies, because the expectations were not measured.

Numerous experiments have been conducted in which phobics receive desensitization treatment without any expectancy information or with suggestions that it is either highly efficacious or ineffective. The differential outcome expectations are verbally induced prior to, during, or immediately after treatment in the various studies. The findings generally show that desensitization reduces phobic behavior, but the outcome expectancy manipulations have either no effect or weak, inconsistent ones (Howlett & Nawas, 1971; McGlynn & Mapp, 1970; McGlynn, Mealiea, & Nawas, 1969; McGlynn, Reynolds, & Linder, 1971). As in the "placebo" studies, it is difficult to make conclusive interpretations because the outcome expectations induced suggestively are not measured prior to the assessment of behavior changes, if at all. Simply informing participants that they will or will not benefit from treatment does not mean that they necessarily believe what they are told, especially when it contradicts their other personal experiences. Moreover, in the studies just cited the verbal influence is aimed mainly at raising outcome expectations rather than at enhancing self-efficacy. It is changes on the latter dimension that are most relevant to the theory under discussion.

Although social persuasion alone may have definite limitations as a means of creating an enduring sense of personal efficacy, it can contribute to the successes achieved through corrective performance. That is, people who are socially persuaded that they possess the capabilities to master difficult situations and are provided with provisional aids for effective action are likely to mobilize greater effort than those who receive only the performance aids. However, to raise by persuasion expectations of personal competence without arranging conditions to facilitate effective performance will most likely lead to failures that discredit the persuaders and further

undermine the recipients' perceived self-efficacy. It is therefore the interactive, as well as the independent, effects of social persuasion on self-efficacy that merit experimental consideration.

Emotional Arousal

Stressful and taxing situations generally elicit emotional arousal that, depending on the circumstances, might have informative value concerning personal competency. Therefore, emotional arousal is another constituent source of information that can affect perceived self-efficacy in coping with threatening situations. People rely partly on their state of physiological arousal in judging their anxiety and vulnerability to stress. Because high arousal usually debilitates performance, individuals are more likely to expect success when they are not beset by aversive arousal than if they are tense and viscerally agitated. Fear reactions generate further fear of impending stressful situations through anticipatory self-arousal. By conjuring up fear-provoking thoughts about their ineptitude, individuals can rouse themselves to elevated levels of anxiety that far exceed the fear experienced during the actual threatening situation.

As will be recalled from the earlier discussion, desensitization and massive exposure treatments aimed at extinguishing anxiety arousal produce some reductions in avoidance behavior. Anxiety arousal to threats is likewise diminished by modeling, and is even more thoroughly eliminated by experienced mastery achieved through participant modeling (Bandura & Barab, 1973; Bandura et al., 1969; Blanchard, 1970a). Modeling approaches have other advantages for enhancing self-efficacy and thereby removing dysfunctional fears. In addition to diminishing proneness to aversive arousal, such approaches also teach effective coping skills by demonstrating proficient ways of handling threatening situations. The latter contribution is especially important when fear arousal partly results from behavioral deficits. It is often the case that fears and deficits are interdependent. Avoidance of stressful activities impedes development of coping skills, and the resulting lack of competency provides a realistic basis for fear. Acquiring behavioral means for controlling potential threats attenuates or eliminates fear arousal (Averill, 1973; Notterman, Schoenfeld, & Bersh, 1952; Szpiler & Epstein, 1976). Behavioral control not only allows one to manage the aversive aspects of an environment. It also affects how the environment is likely to be perceived. Potentially stressful situations that can be controlled are construed as less threatening, and such cognitive appraisals further reduce anticipatory emotional arousal (Averill, 1973).

Diminishing emotional arousal can reduce avoidance

behavior, but different theories posit different explanatory mechanisms for the observed effects. In the theory from which the emotive treatments are derived, emotional arousal is conceived of as a drive that activates avoidance behavior. This view stresses the energizing function of arousal and the reinforcing function of arousal reduction. Social learning theory, on the other hand, emphasizes the informative function of physiological arousal. Simply acknowledging that arousal is both informative and motivating by no means resolves the issue in dispute, because these are not necessarily two separate effects that somehow jointly produce behavior. Rather, the cognitive appraisal of arousal to a large extent determines the level and direction of motivational inducements to action. Certain cognitive appraisals of one's physiological state might be energizing, whereas other appraisals of the same state might not (Weiner, 1972). Moreover, many forms of physiological arousal are generated cognitively by arousing trains of thought. When motivation is conceptualized in terms of cognitive processes (Bandura, 1977; Weiner, 1972), the informational and motivational effects of arousal are treated as interdependent rather than as separate events. We shall return to this issue later when we consider the differential predictions made from social learning theory and from the dual-process theory of avoidance behavior concerning the behavioral effects of extinguishing anxiety arousal.

Researchers working within the attributional framework have attempted to modify avoidance behavior by directly manipulating the cognitive labeling of emotional arousal (Valins & Nisbett, 1971). The presumption is that if phobics are led to *believe* that the things they have previously feared no longer affect them internally, the cognitive reevaluation alone will reduce avoidance behavior. In treatment analogues of this approach, phobics receive false physiological feedback suggesting that they are no longer emotionally upset by threatening events. Results of this procedure are essentially negative. Early claims that erroneous arousal feedback reduces avoidance behavior (Valins & Ray, 1967) are disputed by methodologically superior studies showing that false feedback of physiological tranquility in the presence of threats has either no appreciable effect on subsequent fearful behavior (Gaupp, Stern, & Galbraith, 1972; Howlett & Nawas, 1971; Kent, Wilson, & Nelson, 1972; Rosen, Rosen, & Reid, 1972; Sushinsky & Bootzin, 1970) or produces minor changes under such limited conditions as to be of little practical consequence (Borkovec, 1973).

Misattribution of emotional arousal is another variant of the attributional approach to modification of fearful behavior. The strategy here is to lead fearful people into believing that their emotional arousal is caused by a nonemotional source. To the extent that they no longer label their agitated state as anxiety, they will behave more

boldly. It may be possible to reduce mild fears by this means (Ross, Rodin, & Zimbardo, 1969), but the highly anxious are not easily led into misattributing their anxiety to irrelevant sources (Nisbett & Schachter, 1966). When evaluated systematically, misattribution treatments do not produce significant changes in chronic anxiety conditions (Singerman, Borkovec, & Baron, 1976), and some of the benefits reported with other dysfunctions cannot be replicated (Bootzin, Herman, & Nicassio, 1976; Kellogg & Baron, 1975). There is also some suggestive evidence that in laboratory studies the attenuation of fear may be due more to the veridicality of arousal information than to misattribution of fear arousal to an innocuous source (Calvert-Boyanowsky & Leventhal, 1975).

Any reduction in fear resulting from deceptive feedback is apt to be short-lived because illusory assurances are not an especially reliable way of creating durable self-expectations. However, more veritable experiences that reduce the level of emotional arousal can set in motion a reciprocal process of change. In the social learning view, potential threats activate fear largely through cognitive self-arousal (Bandura, 1969, 1977). Perceived self-competence can therefore affect susceptibility to self-arousal. Individuals who come to believe that they are less vulnerable than they previously assumed are less prone to generate frightening thoughts in threatening situations. Those whose fears are relatively weak may reduce their self-doubts and debilitating self-arousal to the point where they perform successfully. Performance successes, in turn, strengthen self-efficacy. Such changes can, of course, be reliably achieved without resort to ruses. Moreover, mislabeling arousal or attributing it to erroneous sources is unlikely to be of much help to the highly anxious. Severe acrophobics, for example, may be temporarily misled into believing that they no longer fear high elevations, but they will reexperience unnerving internal feedback when confronted with dreaded heights. It should also be noted that in attributional explanations of the success of behavioral treatments the heavy emphasis on physiological arousal derives more from speculations about the nature of emotion (Schachter, 1964) than from evidence that arousal is a major determinant of defensive behavior.

COGNITIVE PROCESSING OF EFFICACY INFORMATION

The discussion thus far has centered primarily on the many sources of information—enactive, vicarious, exhortative, and emotive—that people use to judge their level of self-efficacy. At this point a distinction must be drawn between information contained in environmental events and information as processed and transformed by the individual. The impact of information on efficacy expectations will depend on how it is cognitively appraised. A number of contextual factors, including the social, situational, and temporal circumstances under which events occur, enter into such appraisals. For this reason, even success experiences do not necessarily create strong generalized expectations of personal efficacy. Expectations that have served self-protective functions for years are not quickly discarded. When experience contradicts firmly established expectations of self-efficacy, they may undergo little change if the conditions of performance are such as to lead one to discount the import of the experience.

The corrective value of information derived from successful performance can be attenuated in several ways. The first involves discrimination processes. The consequences individuals anticipate were they to perform feared activities differ in circumstances which vary in safeguards. As a result, they may behave boldly in situations signifying safety, but retain unchanged their self-doubts under less secure conditions. Such mitigative discriminations can extend to the treatments themselves, as well as to the situational circumstances in which behavioral attainments occur. This is especially true of treatments relying solely on symbolic and vicarious experience. Achieving reductions in fear to threats presented symbolically is unlikely to enhance perceived self-efficacy to any great extent in people who believe that success in imagery does not portend accomplishments in reality. Information conveyed by facilely modeled performances might likewise be minimized by anxious observers on the grounds that the models possess special expertise enabling them to prevent injurious consequences that might otherwise befall the unskilled. Because such discriminations, even though objectively mistaken, impede change in self-efficacy, observers will be reluctant to attempt feared activities and will be easily dissuaded by negative experience.

Cognitive appraisals of the causes of one's behavior, which have been examined extensively in investigations of self-attributional processes (Bem, 1972), can similarly delimit gains in self efficacy from behavioral attainments. It was previously shown that attributions of affect and actions to illusory competence have little, if any, effect on refractory behavior. This does not, of course, mean that causal appraisals are of limited importance in the process of behavior change. Quite the contrary, performance attainment is a prominent source of efficacy information, but it is by no means unambiguous. As already mentioned briefly, people can gain competence through authentic means but, because of faulty appraisals of the circumstances under which they improve, will credit their achievements to external factors rather than to their own capabilities. Here the problem is one of inaccurate ascription of personal competency to situational factors. Successes are more likely to enhance self-efficacy if performances are perceived as resulting from skill [rather] than from fortuitous or special external aids. Conversely, failures would be expected to produce greater reductions in self-efficacy when attributed to ability rather than to unusual situational circumstances. The more extensive the situational aids for performance, the greater are the chances that behavior will be ascribed to external factors (Bem, 1972; Weiner, 1972).

Even under conditions of perceived self-determination of outcomes, the impact of performance attainments on self-efficacy will vary depending on whether one's accomplishments are ascribed mainly to ability or to effort. Success with minimal effort fosters ability ascriptions that reinforce a strong sense of self-efficacy. By contrast, analogous successes achieved through high expenditure of effort connote a lesser ability and are thus likely to have a weaker effect on perceived self-efficacy. Cognitive appraisals of the difficulty level of the tasks will further affect the impact of performance accomplishments on perceived self-efficacy. To succeed at easy tasks provides no new information for altering one's sense of self-efficacy, whereas mastery of challenging tasks conveys salient evidence of enhanced competence. The rate and pattern of attainments furnish additional information for judging personal efficacy. Thus, people who experience setbacks but detect relative progress will raise their perceived efficacy more than those who succeed but see their performances leveling off compared to their prior rate of improvement.

Extrapolations from theories about attribution and self-perception to the field of behavioral change often imply that people must labor unaided or under inconspicuously arranged influences if they are to convince themselves of their personal competence (Kopel & Arkowitz, 1975). Such prescriptions are open to question on both conceptual and empirical grounds. Cognitive misappraisals that attenuate the impact of disconfirming experiences can be minimized without sacrificing the substantial benefits of powerful induction procedures. This is achieved by providing opportunities for self-directed accomplishments after the desired behavior has been established. Any lingering doubts people might have, either about their capabilities or about probable response consequences under unprotected conditions, are dispelled easily in this manner (Bandura et al., 1975). The more varied the circumstances in which threats are mastered independently, the more likely are success experiences to authenticate personal efficacy and to impede formation of discriminations that insulate self-perceptions from disconfirming evidence.

Results of recent studies support the thesis that generalized, lasting changes in self-efficacy and behavior can best be achieved by participant methods using powerful induction procedures initially to develop capabilities, then removing external aids to verify personal efficacy, then finally using self-directed mastery to strengthen and generalize expectations of personal efficacy (Bandura et al., 1975). Independent performance can enhance efficacy expectations in several ways: (a) It creates additional exposure to former threats, which provides participants with further evidence that they are no longer aversively aroused by what they previously feared. Reduced emotional arousal confirms increased coping capabilities. (b) Self-directed mastery provides opportunities to perfect coping skills, which lessen personal vulnerability to stress. (c) Independent performance, if well executed, produces success experiences, which further reinforce expectations of self-competency.

Extensive self-directed performance of formerly threatening activities under progressively challenging conditions at a time when treatments are usually terminated could also serve to reduce susceptibility to relearning of defensive patterns of behavior. A few negative encounters among many successful experiences that have instilled a strong sense of self-efficacy will, at most, establish discriminative avoidance of realistic threats, an effect that has adaptive value. In contrast, if people have limited contact with previously feared objects after treatment, whatever expectations of self-efficacy were instated would be weaker and more vulnerable to change. Consequently, a few unfavorable experiences are likely to reestablish defensive behavior that generalizes inappropriately.

We have already examined how cognitive processing of information conveyed by modeling might influence the extent to which vicarious experience effects changes in self-efficacy. Among the especially informative elements are the models' characteristics (e.g., adeptness, perseverance, age, expertness), the similarity between models and observers, the difficulty of the performance tasks, the situational arrangements under which the modeled achievements occur, and the diversity of modeled attainments.

Just as the value of efficacy information generated enactively and vicariously depends on cognitive appraisal, so does the information arising from exhortative and emotive sources. The impact of verbal persuasion on self-efficacy may vary substantially depending on the perceived credibility of the persuaders, their prestige, trustworthiness, expertise, and assuredness. The more believable the source of the information, the more likely are efficacy expectations to change. The influence of credibility on attitudinal change has, of course, received intensive study. But its effects on perceived self-efficacy remain to be investigated.

People judge their physiological arousal largely on the basis of their appraisal of the instigating conditions. Thus, visceral arousal occurring in situations perceived to be threatening is interpreted as fear, arousal in thwarting situations is experienced as anger, and that resulting from irretrievable loss of valued objects as sorrow (Hunt, Cole, & Reis, 1958). Even the same source of physiological arousal may be interpreted differently in ambiguous situations depending on the emotional reactions of others in the same setting (Mandler, 1975; Schachter & Singer, 1962).

When tasks are performed in ambiguous or complex situations in which there is a variety of evocative stimuli, the informational value of the resultant arousal will depend on the meaning imposed upon it. People who perceive their arousal as stemming from personal inadequacies are more likely to lower their efficacy expectations than those who attribute their arousal to certain situational factors. Given a proneness to ascribe arousal to personal deficiencies, the heightened attention to internal events can result in reciprocally escalating arousal. Indeed, as Sarason (1976) has amply documented, individuals who are especially susceptible to anxiety arousal readily become self-preoccupied with their perceived inadequacies in the face of difficulties rather than with the task at hand.

DIFFERING PERSPECTIVES ON SELF-EFFICACY

The phenomena encompassed by the construct of self-efficacy have been the subject of interest in other theories of human behavior. The theoretical perspectives differ, however, in how they view the nature and origins of personal efficacy and the intervening processes by which perceived self-efficacy affects behavior. In seeking a motivational explanation of exploratory and manipulative behavior, White (1959) postulated an "effectance motive," which is conceptualized as an intrinsic drive for transactions with the environment. Unlike instigators arising from tissue deficits, effectance motivation is believed to be aroused by novel stimulation and is sustained when the resultant inquisitive and exploratory actions produce further elements of novelty in the stimulus field. The effectance motive presumably develops through cumulative acquisition of knowledge and skills in dealing with the environment. However, the process by which an effectance motive emerges from effective transactions with the environment is not spelled out in White's theory. Nor is the existence of the motive easy to verify, because effectance motivation is inferred from the exploratory behavior it supposedly causes. Without an independent measure of motive strength one cannot tell whether people explore and manipulate things because of a competence motive to do so, or for any number of other reasons. Although the theory of effectance motivation has not been formulated in sufficient detail to permit extensive theoretical comparisons, there are several issues on which the social learning and effectance theories clearly differ.

In the social learning analysis, choice behavior and effort expenditure are governed in part by percepts of self-efficacy rather than by a drive condition. Because efficacy expectations are defined and measured independently of performance, they provide an explicit basis for predicting the occurrence, generality, and persistence of coping behavior, whereas an omnibus motive does not. People will approach, explore, and try to deal with situations within their self-perceived capabilities, but they will avoid transactions with stressful aspects of their environment they perceive as exceeding their ability.

The alternative views also differ on the origins of efficacy. Within the framework of effective theory, the effectance drive develops gradually through prolonged transactions with one's surroundings. This theory thus focuses almost exclusively on the effects produced by one's own actions. In the social learning theory, self-efficacy is conceptualized as arising from diverse sources of information conveyed by direct and mediated experience. These differences in theoretical approach have significant implications for how one goes about studying the role of perceived self-efficacy in motivational and behavioral processes. Expectations of personal efficacy do not operate as dispositional determinants independently of contextual factors. Some situations require greater skill and more arduous performances and carry higher risk of negative consequences than do others. Expectations will vary accordingly. Thus, for example, the level and strength of perceived self-efficacy in public speaking will differ depending on the subject matter, the format of the presentation, and the types of audiences that will be addressed. The social learning approach is therefore based on a microanalysis of perceived coping capabilities rather than on global personality traits or motives of effectance. From this perspective, it is no more informative to speak of self-efficacy in general terms than to speak of nonspecific approach behavior. To elucidate how perceived self-efficacy affects behavior requires a microanalysis of both factors.

Discrepancies between efficacy expectations and performance are most likely to arise under conditions in which situational and task factors are ambiguous. When performance requirements are ill-defined, people who underestimate the situational demands will display positive discrepancies between self-efficacy and performance attainments; those who overestimate the demands will exhibit negative discrepancies. Therefore, in testing predictions from the conceptual scheme presented here it is important that subjects understand what kind of behavior will be required and the circumstances in which they will be asked to perform them. Moreover, performances and the corresponding efficacy expectations should be analyzed into separate activities, and preferably ordered by level of difficulty. In this type of microanalysis both the efficacy expectations and the corresponding behaviors are measured in terms of explicit types of performances rather than on the basis of global indices.

The social learning determinants of self-efficacy can be varied systematically and their effects measured. Hence, propositions concerning the origins of self-efficacy are verifiable with some precision. A slowly developing motive, however, does not easily lend itself to being tested experimentally. Another dimension on which the alternative theories might be judged is their power to produce the phenomena they purport to explain. As we shall see later, there are more diverse, expeditious, and powerful ways of creating self-efficacy than by relying solely on novel stimulation arising from exploratory actions.

With the ascendancy of cognitive views of behavior, the concept of expectancy is assuming an increasingly prominent place in contemporary psychological thought (Bolles, 1972b; Heneman & Schwab, 1972; Irwin, 1971). However, virtually all of the theorizing and experimentation has focused on action-outcome expectations. The ideas advanced in some of the theories nevertheless bear some likeness to the notion of self-efficacy. According to the theory of personality proposed by Rotter (1966), behavior varies as a function of generalized expectancies that outcomes are determined by one's actions or by external forces beyond one's control. Such expectations about the instrumentality of behavior are considered to be largely a product of one's history of reinforcement. Much of the research within this tradition is concerned with the behavioral correlates of individual differences in the tendency to perceive events as being either personally or externally determined.

The notion of locus of control is often treated in the literature as analogous to self-efficacy. However, Rotter's (1966) conceptual scheme is primarily concerned with causal beliefs about action-outcome contingencies rather than with personal efficacy. Perceived self-efficacy and beliefs about the locus of causality must be distinguished, because convictions that outcomes are determined by one's own actions can have any number of effects on self-efficacy and behavior. People who regard outcomes as personally determined but who lack the requisite skills would experience low self-efficacy and view activities with a sense of futility. Thus, for example, a child who fails to grasp arithmetic concepts and expects course grades to be dependent entirely on skill in the subject matter has every reason to be demoralized. While causal beliefs and self-efficacy refer to different phenomena, as we have already noted, causal ascriptions of behavior to skill or to chance can mediate the effects of performance attainments on self-efficacy.

The theoretical framework presented in the present article is generalizable beyond the psychotherapy domain to other psychological phenomena involving behavioral choices and regulation of effort in activities that can have adverse effects. For example, the theory of learned helplessness advanced by Maier and Seligman (1976) assumes that as a result of being subjected to uncontrollable aversive events, organisms acquire expectancies that actions do not affect outcomes. Because they come to expect future responding to be futile, they no longer initiate behavior in situations where outcomes are in fact controllable by responses. Although this theory posits an expectancy mechanism of operation, it focuses exclusively on response-outcome expectancies.

Theorizing and experimentation on learned helplessness might well consider the conceptual distinction between efficacy and outcome expectations. People can give up trying because they lack a sense of efficacy in achieving the required behavior, or they may be assured of their capabilities but give up trying because they expect their behavior to have no effect on an unresponsive environment or to be consistently punished. These two separable expectancy sources of futility have quite different antecedents and remedial implications. To alter efficacy-based futility requires development of competencies and expectations of personal effectiveness. By contrast, to change outcome-based futility necessitates changes in prevailing environmental contingencies that restore the instrumental value of the competencies that people already possess.

MICROANALYSIS OF SELF-EFFICACY AND BEHAVIORAL CHANGE

To test derivations from the social learning analysis of the process of change, an experiment was conducted wherein severe phobics received treatments designed to create differential levels of efficacy expectations, and then the relationship between self-efficacy and behavioral change was analyzed in detail (Bandura et al., in press). The experiment proceeded as follows. Adult snake phobics, whose phobias affected their lives adversely, were administered for equivalent periods either participant modeling, modeling alone, or no treatment. In participant modeling, which operates through direct mastery experiences, subjects were assisted, by whatever induction aids were needed, to engage in progressively more threatening interactions with a boa constrictor. After completing all the therapeutic tasks, which included holding the snake,

placing open hands in front of its head as it moved about the room, holding the snake in front of their faces, and allowing it to crawl freely in their laps, the subjects engaged in a brief period of self-directed mastery. In the present experiment, the modeling aid was used only briefly if needed to help initiate performance in order to minimize overlap of this element in the two modes of treatment.

Subjects receiving the modeling treatment merely observed the therapist perform the same activities for an equivalent period. These subjects did not engage in any behavior themselves, and consequently they had no performance sources of information for their efficacy expectations. Enactive and vicarious procedures were selected for study to assess the predictive value of self-efficacy created by quite different modes of treatment.

The level, strength, and generality of the subjects' efficacy expectations were measured at critical junctures in the change process. Subjects privately designated, on a list of 18 performance tasks ranked in order of increasing threat, those tasks they considered themselves capable of executing. They then rated the strength of their expectations for each of these tasks on a 100-point probability scale ranging, in 10-unit intervals, from great uncertainty, through intermediate values of certainty, to complete certainty. They rated their efficacy expectations for coping with snakes of the same variety used in treatment as well as dissimilar snakes to measure the generality of their efficacy expectations. These measures were obtained prior to treatment, following treatment but before the behavioral posttest, and after completing the posttest. Approach behavior was assessed in the posttest by a series of performance tasks requiring increasingly more threatening interactions with a different type of boa constrictor from the one used in treatment and with a corn snake of markedly different appearance but equivalent threat value. Different phobic objects were used to provide a test of the generalized effects of changes in efficacy expectations along a dimension of similarity to the threat used in treatment.

Subjects assigned to the control condition participated in the assessment procedures without receiving any intervening treatment. Following completion of the posttest, the controls and those in the modeling condition who failed to achieve terminal performances received the participant modeling treatment.

Consistent with the social learning analysis of the sources of self-efficacy, experiences based on performance accomplishments produced higher, more generalized, and stronger efficacy expectations than did vicarious experience, which in turn exceeded those in the control condition. Figure 3 summarizes the level of efficacy expectations and performance as a function of treatment conditions at different phases of the experiment. As shown in

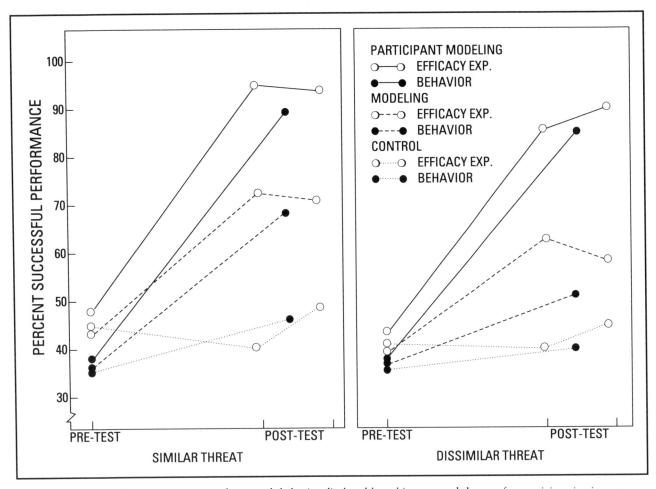

Figure 3. Level of efficacy expectations and approach behavior displayed by subjects toward threats after receiving vicarious or enactive treatments, or no treatment (Bandura et al., in press).

the figure, performance change corresponds closely to the magnitude of expectancy change. The greater the increments in self-perceived efficacy, the greater the changes in behavior. Similar relationships between level of self-efficacy and performance are obtained when the data are considered separately for the two snakes. In accordance with prediction, participant modeling produced the more generalized increases in efficacy expectations and the more generalized behavioral changes.

Although the enactive and vicarious treatments differed in their power to enhance self-efficacy, the efficacy expectations were equally predictive of subsequent performance irrespective of how they were instated. The higher the level of perceived self-efficacy at the completion of treatment the higher was the level of approach behavior for efficacy expectations instated enactively $(r = .83)$ and vicariously $(r = .84)$. It might be noted here that all subjects had at their disposal the component responses for producing the interactive patterns of behavior, and they all had some incentive to overcome their phobic behavior. Under conditions in which people differ

substantially in component capabilities and motivation, skill and incentive factors will also contribute to variance in performance.

Correlation coefficients based on aggregate measures do not fully reveal the degree of correspondence between self-efficacy and performance on the specific behavioral tasks from which the aggregate scores are obtained. A subject can display an equivalent number of efficacy expectations and successful performances, but they might not correspond entirely to the same tasks. The most precise index of the relationship is provided by a microanalysis of the congruence between self-efficacy and performance at the level of individual tasks. This measure was obtained by recording whether or not subjects considered themselves capable of performing each of the various tasks at the end of treatment and by computing the percentage of accurate correspondence between efficacy judgment and actual performance. Self-efficacy was a uniformly accurate predictor of performance on tasks varying in difficulty with different threats regardless of whether the changes in self-efficacy were produced through performance accomplishments (89% congruence) or by vicarious experience alone (86% congruence). The degree of congruence between perceived self-efficacy and subsequent behavior is equally high for enactive (82%) and vicarious (79%) treatments when the microanalysis is conducted only on the subset of tasks that subjects had never performed in the pretest assessment.

In the preceding analysis efficacy expectations were considered without regard to strength. A weak sense of self-efficacy thus received the same weight as one reflecting complete certitude. However, the intensity and persistence of effort, and hence level of performance, should be higher with strong than with weak self-efficacy. The likelihood that a task will be performed as a function of the strength of the corresponding efficacy expectation therefore provides a further refinement in the analysis of the relationship between self-efficacy and performance. The probability of successful performance of any given task as a function of strength of efficacy expectations is plotted in Figure 4. Because the control subjects performed few responses and had correspondingly restricted efficacy expectations, their data were plotted after they had received the participant modeling treatment. In all conditions, the stronger the efficacy expectations, the higher was the likelihood that a particular task would be successfully completed. The positive relationship between strength of self-efficacy and probability of successful performance is virtually identical for the similar and the dissimilar threats.

In brief, the theory systematizes a variety of findings. As the preceding results show, it predicts accurately the magnitude and generality of behavioral change for efficacy expectations induced enactively and vicariously. Moreover, it orders variations in level of behavioral change occurring within the same treatment condition. Subjects who received participant modeling, either as the primary or as the supplementary treatment, successfully performed all of the behaviors in treatment that were later assessed in the posttest toward different threats. Although all had previously achieved maximal performances, not all expressed maximal efficacy expectations. One can therefore compare the error rates of predictions made from maximal efficacy expectations. It would be predicted from the proposed theory that among these successful performers, those who acquire maximal efficacy expectations should attain terminal performances, whereas those holding lower expectations should not. If one predicts that those who performed maximally in treatment will likewise achieve terminal performances when assessed with similar tasks, the error rate is relatively low for the similar threat (28%) but high for the dissimilar threat (52%). If, on the other hand, one predicts that those who express maximal expectations will perform maximally, the error rate is comparably low for

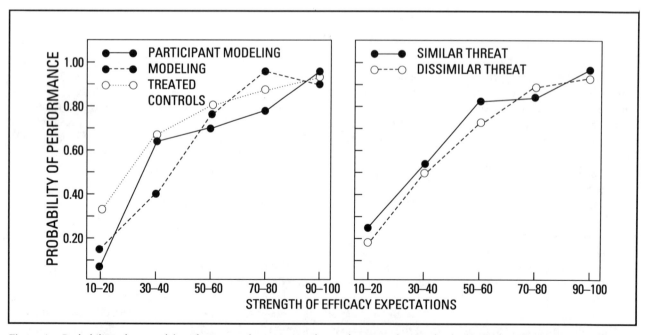

Figure 4. Probability of successful performance of any given task as a function of strength of self-efficacy. The figure on the left shows the relationship for vicarious and enactive treatments; the figure on the right shows the relationship between strength of self-efficacy and successful approach responses toward similar and dissimilar threats combined across treatments (Bandura et al., in press).

both the similar (21%) and the dissimilar (24%) threats. The predictive superiority of efficacy expectations over past performance is significant for total approach behavior and for approach behavior toward the dissimilar threat. These differential findings indicate that experienced mastery altered subjects' sense of personal efficacy rather than merely providing behavioral cues for judgments of self-efficacy.

The theory also accounts for variations in behavioral change produced by modeling alone. To equate for duration of treatment, subjects in the modeling condition were yoked to matched counterparts in participant modeling, who received treatment until they performed all the therapeutic tasks. The subjects in the participant modeling condition varied in the time they required to complete treatment, so some of the subjects in the modeling conditions had only brief exposure to successful performances, whereas others had the benefit of observing feared activities modeled repeatedly without any untoward consequences. The findings are consistent with hypothesized increases in self-efficacy as a function of repeated observation of successful modeling. Brief exposure produced limited increases in the level (9%) and strength (5%) of efficacy expectations and correspondingly little behavior change (10%). In contrast, repeated observation of successful performances increased by a substantial amount the level (44%) and strength (38%) of self-efficacy which, in turn, was accompanied by similarly large increments in performance (35%).

COMPARISON OF SELF-EFFICACY AND DUAL-PROCESS THEORY

As a further test of the generality of the theory under discussion, a microanalysis was conducted of efficacy expectations instated by desensitization procedures, which are aimed at reducing emotional arousal. Social learning theory and the dual-process theory of anxiety, on which the desensitization approach is based, posit different explanatory mechanisms for the changes accompanying this mode of treatment. The alternative views therefore give rise to differential predictions that can be readily tested.

The standard desensitization approach is based on the assumption that anxiety activates defensive behavior (Wolpe, 1974). According to this view, association of neutral events with aversive stimulation creates an anxiety drive that motivates defensive behavior; the defensive behavior, in turn, is reinforced by reducing the anxiety aroused by conditioned aversive stimuli. Hence, to eliminate defensive responding, it is considered necessary to eradicate its underlying anxiety. Treatment strategies are therefore keyed to reduction of emotional arousal. Aver-

sive stimuli are presented at graduated levels in conjunction with relaxation until anxiety reactions to the threats are eliminated.

Although desensitization produces behavioral changes, there is little evidence to support the original rationale that defensive behavior is diminished because anxiety is eliminated either by reciprocal physiological inhibition or by associative recoupling of threatening stimuli to relaxation. Desensitization does not require graduated exposure, and anxiety-reducing activities are at most facilitory, not necessary, conditions for eliminating defensive behavior (Bandura, 1969; Wilson & Davison, 1971).

The principal assumption that defensive behavior is controlled by anxiety arousal is also disputed by several lines of evidence. Autonomic arousal, which constitutes the principal index of anxiety, is not necessary for defensive learning. Because autonomic reactions take much longer to activate than do avoidance responses, the latter cannot be caused by the former. Studies in which autonomic and avoidance responses are measured concurrently indicate that these two modes of activity may be partially correlated in the acquisition phase but are not causally related (Black, 1965). Avoidance behavior, for example, can persist long after autonomic reactions to threats have been extinguished. Surgical removal of autonomic feedback capability in animals has little effect on the acquisition of avoidance responses (Rescorla & Solomon, 1967). Maintenance of avoidance behavior is even less dependent on autonomic feedback. Once defensive behavior has been learned, depriving animals of autonomic feedback does not hasten the rate at which such activities are extinguished.

Research casts doubt on the postulated reinforcement sources, as well as the activated sources, of defensive behavior. In the dual-process theory, the anxiety reduction occasioned by escape from the feared stimulus presumably reinforces the defensive behavior. The evidence, however, reveals that whether or not defensive behavior removes the feared stimulus has variable effects on the maintenance of the behavior (Bolles, 1972a). Moreover, defensive behavior can be acquired and maintained by its success in diminishing the frequency of aversive stimulation, even though there are no feared stimuli to arouse anxiety and to provide the source of decremental reinforcement (Herrnstein, 1969). The substantial negative evidence concerning an anxiety mediational mechanism in avoidance behavior suggests that the effects of desensitization treatment must result from some other mechanism of operation.

Social learning theory regards anxiety and defensive behavior as coeffects rather than as causally linked (Bandura, 1977). Aversive experiences, either of a personal or vicarious sort, create expectations of injurious effects that can activate both fear and defensive behavior. Being coeffects, there is no fixed relationship between autonomic arousal and actions. Until effective coping behaviors are achieved, perceived threats produce high emotional arousal and various defensive maneuvers. But after people become adept at self-protective behaviors, they perform them in potentially threatening situations without having to be frightened (Notterman et al., 1952). Should their habitual coping devices fail, they experience heightened arousal until new defensive learning reduces their vulnerability.

Perceived threats activate defensive behavior because of their predictive value rather than their aversive quality. That is, when formerly neutral stimuli are associated with painful experiences, it is not that the stimuli have become aversive but that individuals have learned to anticipate aversive consequences. It is people's knowledge of their environment, not the stimuli, that are changed by correlated experience. Stimuli having predictive significance signal the likelihood of painful consequences unless protective measures are taken. Defensive behavior, in turn, is maintained by its success in forestalling or reducing the occurrence of aversive events. Once established, self-protective behavior is difficult to eliminate even though the hazards no longer exist. This is because consistent avoidance prevents a person from learning that the real-life conditions have changed. Hence, the nonoccurrence of anticipated hazards reinforces the expectation that the defensive maneuvers forestalled them.

From the perspective of dual-process theory, thorough extinction of anxiety should eliminate avoidance behavior. In the desensitization treatment, however, anxiety reactions are typically extinguished to visualized representations of feared situations. One would expect some transfer loss of extinction effects from symbolic to real-life threats, as is indeed the case (Agras, 1967; Barlow et al., 1969). It is not uncommon for people to fear and avoid real-life situations to which they have been desensitized in imagery. Therefore, according to this view, thorough extinction of anxiety to visualized threats should produce substantial, though less than complete, reductions in defensive behavior. However, dual-process theory provides no basis for predicting either the level of behavior change or the variability in behavior displayed by subjects who have all been equally desensitized.

In the social learning analysis presented earlier, reducing physiological arousal improves performance by raising efficacy expectations rather than by eliminating a drive that instigates the defensive behavior. This information-based view of the mediating mechanism predicts that the higher and stronger the efficacy expectations instated by desensitization procedures, the greater are the reductions in defensive behavior. Because arousal is only one of several sources of efficacy information, and not necessarily the most dependable one, extinguishing anxiety arousal

is rarely a sufficient condition for eliminating defensive behavior.

To test the theory that desensitization changes behavior through its intervening effects on efficacy expectations, severe snake phobics were administered the standard desensitization treatment until their emotional reactions were completely extinguished to imaginal representations of the most aversive scenes (Bandura & Adams, in press). The assessment procedures were identical to those used in the preceding experiment. Subjects' approach behavior was tested on the series of performance tasks before and after the desensitization treatment. The level, strength, and generality of their efficacy expectations were similarly measured before treatment, upon completion of treatment but prior to the posttest, and following the posttest.

The findings show that phobics whose anxiety reactions to visualized threats have been thoroughly extinguished emerge from the desensitization treatment with widely differing efficacy expectations. As depicted graphically in Figure 5, performance corresponds closely to level of self-efficacy. The higher the subjects' level of perceived self-efficacy at the end of treatment, the more approach behavior they subsequently performed in the posttest assessment ($r = .74$).

Results of the microanalysis of congruence between self-efficacy at the end of treatment and performance on each of the tasks administered in the posttest are consistent with the findings obtained from enactive and vicarious treatment. Self-efficacy was an accurate predictor of subsequent performance on 85% for all the tasks, and 83% for the subset of tasks that subjects were unable to perform in the pretest assessment. Subjects successfully executed tasks within the range of their perceived self-efficacy produced by the desensitization treatment, whereas they failed at tasks they perceived to be beyond their capabilities.

MICROANALYSIS OF SELF-EFFICACY AND PERFORMANCE DURING THE PROCESS OF CHANGE

The preceding series of experiments examined the predictive value of self-efficacy at the completion of different modes of treatment. A further study investigated the process of efficacy and behavioral change during the course of treatment itself. Participant modeling was selected for this purpose because the amount of treatment can be well-regulated and it promotes rapid change.

As in the previous studies, adults whose lives were adversely affected by severe snake phobias were tested for their efficacy expectations and approach behavior using

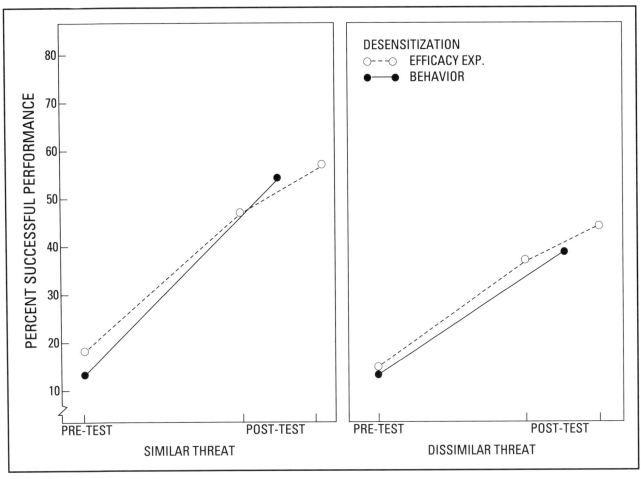

Figure 5. Level of efficacy expectations and approach behavior displayed by subjects toward different threats after their emotional reactions to symbolic representations of feared activities were eliminated through systematic desensitization. (Bandura & Adams, in press.)

the microanalytic methodology described earlier. The various treatment activities were segmented into natural blocks of tasks of increasing difficulty and threat value. Items in the initial block included looking at a snake from progressively closer distances; intermediate blocks required subjects to touch and to hold the snake with gloved and bare hands for increasing intervals; the terminal block required them to tolerate the snake crawling about freely in their laps for an extended period. Subjects received the participant modeling treatment only for the block of items they failed in the hierarchy of assessment tasks. Treatment was continued until they could perform the activities in the failed block, whereupon they were tested for their efficacy expectations and approach responses on the succeeding tasks. Subjects who attained terminal performances received no further treatment. For those who achieved only partial improvement, the sequence of treatment on the failed block followed by assessments of self-efficacy and approach behavior on

succeeding blocks was repeated until they achieved terminal performances.

Findings of the microanalysis lend further support to the postulated cognitive mechanism of change. Subjects who mastered the same intermediate performances during the course of treatment varied considerably in their behavioral attainments when tested on succeeding blocks of tasks. Past performance was therefore of limited value in predicting what subjects would be able to do when confronted with more threatening tasks. However, efficacy judgments proved to be good predictors of degree of behavioral change resulting from partial mastery experiences. Self-efficacy predicted subsequent performance as measured at different points in treatment in 92% of the total assessment tasks. This relationship holds even when the measure of congruence is based only on the subset of activities that subjects could not perform in pretest because they found them too threatening, and did not perform in treatment because the activities extended beyond the failed block. Expectations of personal effectiveness formed through partial mastery experiences during the course of treatment predicted, at a 84% level of accuracy, performance on highly threatening tasks that subjects had never done before.

CONCLUDING REMARKS

The present theoretical formulation orders variations in the level of behavioral changes produced by different modes of treatment; it accounts for behavioral variations displayed by individuals receiving the same type of treatment; and it predicts performance successes at the level of individual tasks during and after treatment. It is possible to generate alternative explanations for particular subsets of data, but the mechanism proposed in the present theory appears to account equally well for the different sets of findings. It might be argued, for example, that self-efficacy proved to be an accurate predictor of performance in the enactive mode of treatment because subjects were simply judging their future performance from their past behavior. However, an interpretation of this type has no explanatory value for the vicarious and emotive treatments, in which perceived self-efficacy was an equally accurate predictor of performance although subjects engaged in no overt behavior. Even in the enactive treatment, perceived self-efficacy proved to be a better predictor of behavior toward unfamiliar threats than did past performance. Moreover, self-efficacy derived from partial enactive mastery during the course of treatment predicted performance on stressful tasks that the individuals had never done before.

As an alternative explanation, one could invoke a superordinate mediator that controls both efficacy expectations and behavior. Although such a possibility is not inconceivable, the mediator would have to be an exceedingly complex one to account adequately for the diverse sets of relationships. To cite but a few examples, it would have to affect differentially efficacy expectations and behavior resulting from maximal enactive mastery; somehow, it would have to produce different levels of self-efficacy from equivalent reductions in emotional arousal; and it would have to generate some variation in efficacy expectations from similar partial mastery experiences. The theory presented here posits a central processor of efficacy information. That is, people process, weigh, and integrate diverse sources of information concerning their capability, and they regulate their choice behavior and effort expenditure accordingly.

Evidence that people develop somewhat different efficacy expectations from similar enactive mastery and fear extinction warrants comment. One possible explanation for the variance is in terms of differential cognitive processing of efficacy information. To the extent that individuals differ in how they cognitively appraise their arousal decrements and behavioral attainments, their percepts of self-efficacy will vary to some degree. A second possibility concerns the multiple determination of self-efficacy. Because people have met with different types and amounts of efficacy-altering experiences, providing one new source of efficacy information would not be expected to affect everyone uniformly. Thus, for example, extinguishing arousal to threats will enhance self-efficacy, but more so in individuals whose past coping attempts have occasionally succeeded than in those who have consistently failed.

The research completed thus far has tested the predictive power of the conceptual scheme for efficacy expectations developed through enactive, vicarious, and emotive-based procedures. Additional tests of the generality of this approach need to be extended to efficacy expectations arising from verbal persuasion and from other types of treatments aimed at reducing emotional arousal.

Cognitive processing of efficacy information, which is an important component function in the proposed theory, is an especially relevant area for research. A number of factors were identified as influencing the cognitive appraisal of efficacy information conveyed by each of the major sources of self-efficacy. Previous research from a number of different perspectives demonstrating that some of these factors affect attitudinal and behavioral changes has suggestive value. But it is investigations that include assessment of the intervening self-efficacy link that can best provide validity for the present theory.

The operative process involved in the relationship between efficacy expectations and action also requires further investigation. It will be recalled that efficacy expectations are presumed to influence level of performance by enhancing intensity and persistence of effort. In the preceding experiments, the behavioral tasks were ordered in level of difficulty and subjects either persisted in their efforts until they completed all of the tasks or they quit at varying points along the way. The number of tasks successfully completed reflects degree of perseverance. As a further step toward elucidating the intervening process, it would be of interest to measure the intensity and duration of effort subjects exert in attempts to master arduous or insoluble tasks as a function of the level and strength of their efficacy expectations. Further research on the processes postulated in the present theoretical formulation should increase our understanding of the relationship between cognitive and behavioral change.

REFERENCES

Agras, W. S. Transfer during systematic desensitization therapy. *Behaviour Research and Therapy.* 1967, *5,* 193–199.

Averill, J. R. Personal control over aversive stimuli and its relationship to stress. *Psychological Bulletin*, 1973, *80*, 286–303.

Bandura, A. *Principles of behavior modification*. New York: Holt, Rinehart & Winston, 1969.

Bandura, A. (Ed.). *Psychological modeling: Conflicting theories*. Chicago: Aldine-Atherton, 1971.

Bandura, A. Effecting change through participant modeling. In J. D. Krumboltz & C. E. Thoresen (Eds.), *Counseling methods*. New York: Holt, Rinehart & Winston, 1976. (a)

Bandura, A. Self-reinforcement: Theoretical and methodological considerations. *Behaviorism*, 1976, *4*, 135–155. (b)

Bandura, A. *Social learning theory*. Englewood Cliffs, N.J.: Prentice-Hall, 1977.

Bandura, A., & Adams, N. E. Analysis of self-efficacy theory of behavioral change. *Cognitive Therapy and Research*, in press.

Bandura, A., Adams, N. E., & Beyer, J. Cognitive processes mediating behavioral changes. *Journal of Personality and Social Psychology*, in press.

Bandura, A., & Barab, P. G. Processes governing disinhibitory effects through symbolic modeling. *Journal of Abnormal Psychology*, 1973, *82*, 1–9.

Bandura, A., Blanchard, E. B., & Ritter, B. The relative efficacy of desensitization and modeling approaches for inducing behavioral, affective, and attitudinal changes. *Journal of Personality and Social Psychology*, 1969, *13*, 173–199.

Bandura, A., Jeffery, R. W., & Gajdos, E. Generalizing change through participant modeling with self-directed mastery. *Behaviour Research and Therapy*, 1975, *13*, 141–152.

Bandura, A., Jeffery, R. W., & Wright, C. L. Efficacy of participant modeling as a function of response induction aids. *Journal of Abnormal Psychology*, 1974, *83*, 56–64.

Bandura, A., & Menlove, F. L. Factors determining vicarious extinction of avoidance behavior through symbolic modeling. *Journal of Personality and Social Psychology*, 1968, *8*, 99–108.

Barlow, D. H., Leitenberg, H., Agras, W. S., & Wincze, J. P. The transfer gap in systematic desensitization: An analogue study. *Behaviour Research and Therapy*, 1969, *7*, 191–196.

Baron, A., Kaufman, A., & Stauber, K. A. Effects of instructions and reinforcement-feedback on human operant behavior maintained by fixed-interval reinforcement. *Journal of the Experimental Analysis of Behavior*, 1969, *12*, 701–712.

Baum, W. M. The correlation-based law of effect. *Journal of the Experimental Analysis of Behavior*, 1973, *20*, 137–153.

Bem, D. J. Self-perception theory. In L. Berkowitz (Ed.), *Advances in experimental social psychology* (Vol. 6). New York: Academic Press, 1972.

Black, A. H. Cardiac conditioning in curarized dogs: The relationship between heart rate and skeletal behaviour. In W. F. Prokasy (Ed.), *Classical conditioning: A symposium*. New York: Appleton-Century-Crofts, 1965.

Blanchard, E. B. The generalization of vicarious extinction effects. *Behaviour Research and Therapy*, 1970, *7*, 323–330. (a)

Blanchard, E. B. Relative contributions of modeling, informational influences, and physical contact in extinction of phobic behavior. *Journal of Abnormal Psychology*, 1970, *76*, 55–61. (b)

Bolles, R. C. The avoidance learning problem. In G. Bower (Ed.), *The psychology of learning and motivation* (Vol. 6). New York: Academic Press, 1972. (a)

Bolles, R. C. Reinforcement, expectancy, and learning. *Psychological Review*, 1972, *79*, 394–409. (b)

Borkovec, T. D. The role of expectancy and physiological feedback in fear research: A review with special reference to subject characteristics. *Behavior Therapy*, 1973, *4*, 491–505.

Bootzin, R. R., Herman, C. P., & Nicassio, P. The power of suggestion: Another examination of misattribution and insomnia. *Journal of Personality and Social Psychology*, 1976, *34*, 673–679.

Calvert-Boyanowsky, J., & Leventhal, H. The role of information in attenuating behavioral responses to stress: A reinterpretation of the misattribution phenomenon. *Journal of Personality and Social Psychology*, 1975, *32*, 214–221.

Davison, G. C., & Wilson, G. T. Processes of fear-reduction in systematic desensitization: Cognitive and social reinforcement factors in humans. *Behavior Therapy*, 1973, *4*, 1–21.

Dawson, M. E., & Furedy, J. J. The role of awareness in human differential autonomomic classical conditioning: The necessary-gate hypothesis. *Psychophysiology*, 1976, *13*, 50–53.

Dulany, D. E. Awareness, rules, and propositional control: A confrontation with S-R behavior theory. In T. R. Dixon & D. L. Horton (Eds.), *Verbal behavior and general behavior theory*. Englewood Cliffs, N. J.: Prentice-Hall, 1968.

Emmelkamp, P. M. G., & Wessels, H. Flooding in imagination vs. flooding *in vivo*: A comparison with agoraphobics. *Behaviour Research and Therapy*, 1975, *13*, 7–15.

Estes, W. K. Reinforcement in human behavior. *American Scientist*, 1972, *60*, 723–729.

Flanders, J. P. A review of research on imitative behavior. *Psychological Bulletin*, 1968, *69*, 316–337.

Gaupp, L. A., Stern, R. M., & Galbraith, G. G. False heart-rate feedback and reciprocal inhibition by aversion relief in the treatment of snake avoidance behavior. *Behavior Therapy*, 1972, *3*, 7–20.

Grings, W. W. The role of consciousness and cognition in autonomic behavior change. In F. J. McGuigan & R. A. Schoonover (Eds.), *The psychophysiology of thinking*. New York: Academic Press, 1973.

Heneman, H. G., III, & Schwab, D. P. Evaluation of research on expectancy theory predictions of employee performance. *Psychological Bulletin*, 1972, *78*, 1–9.

Herrnstein, R. J. Method and theory in the study of avoidance. *Psychological Review*, 1969, *76*, 49–69.

Howlett, S. C., & Nawas, M. M. Exposure to aversive imagery and suggestion in systematic desensitization. In R. D. Rubin, A. A. Lazarus, H. Fensterheim, & C. M. Franks

(Eds.), *Advances in behavior therapy.* New York: Academic Press, 1971.

Hunt, J. McV., Cole, M. W., & Reis, E. E. S. Situational cues distinguishing anger, fear, and sorrow. *American Journal of Psychology,* 1958, *71,* 136–151.

Irwin, F. W. *Intentional behavior and motivation: A cognitive view.* Philadelphia: Lippincott, 1971.

Kaufman, A., Baron, A., & Kopp, E. Some effects of instructions on human operant behavior. Psychonomic Monograph Supplements, 1966, *1,* 243–250.

Kazdin, A. E. Covert modeling and the reduction of avoidance behavior. *Journal of Abnormal Psychology,* 1973, *81,* 87–95.

Kazdin, A. E. Comparative effects of some variations of covert modeling. *Journal of Behavior Therapy and Experimental Psychiatry,* 1974, *5,* 225–232. (a)

Kazdin, A. E. Covert modeling, model similarity, and reduction of avoidance behavior. *Behavior Therapy,* 1974, *5,* 325–340. (b)

Kazdin, A. E. Effects of covert modeling and reinforcement on assertive behavior. *Journal of Abnormal Psychlogy,* 1974, *83,* 240–252. (c)

Kazdin, A. E. Covert modeling, imagery assessment, and assertive behavior. *Journal of Consulting and Clinical Psychology,* 1975, *43,* 716–724.

Kazdin, A. E. Effects of covert modeling, multiple models, and model reinforcement on assertive behavior. *Behavior Therapy,* 1976, *7,* 211–222.

Kellogg, R., & Baron, R. S. Attribution theory, insomnia, and the reverse placebo effect: A reversal of Storms and Nisbett's findings. *Journal of Personality and Social Psychology,* 1975, *32,* 231–236.

Kent, R. N., Wilson, G. T., & Nelson, R. Effects of false heart-rate feedback on avoidance behavior: An investigation of "cognitive desensitization." *Behavior Therapy,* 1972, *3,* 1–6.

Kopel, S., & Arkowitz, H. The role of attribution and self-perception in behavior change: Implications for behavior therapy. *Genetic Psychology Monographs,* 1975, *92,* 175–212.

Lewis, S. A. A comparison of behavior therapy techniques in the reduction of fearful avoidance behavior. *Behavior Therapy,* 1974, *5,* 648–655.

Lick, J., & Bootzin, R. Expectancy factors in the treatment of fear: Methodological and theoretical issues. *Psychological Bulletin,* 1975, *82,* 917–931.

Litvak, S. B. A comparison of two brief group behavior therapy techniques on the reduction of avoidance behavior. *The Psychological Record,* 1969, *19,* 329–334.

LoPiccolo, J. Effective components of systematic desensitization (Doctoral dissertation, Yale University, 1969). *Dissertation Abstracts International,* 1970, *31,* 1543B. (University Microfilms No. 70-16300)

Maier, S. F., & Seligman, M. E. Learned helplessness: Theory and evidence. *Journal of Experimental Psychology,* 1976, *105,* 3–46.

Mandler, G. *Mind and emotion.* New York: Wiley, 1975.

McGlynn, F. D., & Mapp, R. H. Systematic desensitization of snake-avoidance following three types of suggestion. *Behavior Research and Therapy,* 1970, *8,* 197–201.

McGlynn, F. D., Mealiea, W. L., & Nawas, M. M. Systematic desensitization of snake-avoidance under two conditions of suggestion. *Psychological Reports,* 1969, *25,* 220–222.

McGlynn, F. D., Reynolds, E. J., & Linder, L. H. Systematic desensitization with pre-treatment and intra-treatment therapeutic instructions. *Behavior Research and Therapy,* 1971, *9,* 57–63.

Meichenbaum, D. H. Examination of model characteristics in reducing avoidance behavior. *Journal of Personality and Social Psychology,* 1971, *17,* 298–307.

Moore, N. Behaviour therapy in bronchial asthma: A controlled study. *Journal of Psychosomatic Research,* 1965, *9,* 257–276.

Nisbett, R. E., & Schachter, S. Cognitive manipulation of pain. *Journal of Experimental Social Psychology,* 1966, *2,* 227–236.

Notterman, J. M., Schoenfeld, W. N., & Bersh, P. J. A comparison of three extinction procedures following heart rate conditioning. *Journal of Abnormal and Social Psychology,* 1952, *47,* 674–677.

Paul, G. L. *Insight vs. desensitization in psychotherapy.* Stanford, Calif.: Stanford University Press, 1966.

Rabavilas, A. D., Boulougouris, J. C., & Stefanis, C. Duration of flooding sessions in the treatment of obsessive-compulsive patients. *Behavior Research and Therapy,* 1976, *14,* 349–355.

Rescorla, R. A., & Solomon, R. L. Two-process learning theory: Relationships between Pavlovian conditioning and instrumental learning. *Psychological Review,* 1967, *74,* 151–182.

Ritter, B. The use of contact desensitization, demonstration-plus-participation, and demonstration alone in the treatment of acrophobia. *Behaviour Research and Therapy,* 1969, *7,* 157–164.

Röper, G., Rachman, S., & Marks, I. Passive and participant modelling in exposure treatment of obsessive-compulsive neurotics. *Behaviour Research and Therapy,* 1975, *13,* 271–279.

Rosen, G. M., Rosen, E., & Reid, J. B. Cognitive desensitization and avoidance behavior: A reevaluation. *Journal of Abnormal Psychology,* 1972, *80,* 176–182.

Ross, L., Rodin, J., & Zimbardo, P. T. Toward an attribution therapy: The reduction of fear through induced cognitive-emotional misattribution. *Journal of Personality and Social Psychology,* 1969, *12,* 279–288.

Rotter, J. B. Generalized expectancies for internal versus external control of reinforcement. *Psychological Monographs,* 1966, *80*(1, Whole No. 609).

Sarason, I. G. Anxiety and self-preoccupation. In I. G. Sarason & C. D. Spielberger (Eds.), *Stress and anxiety* (Vol. 2). Washington, D.C.: Hemisphere, 1976.

Schachter, S. The interaction of cognitive and physiological determinants of emotional state. In L. Berkowitz (Ed.), *Advances in experimental social psychology.* New York: Academic Press, 1964.

Schachter, S., & Singer, J. E. Cognitive, social, and physiological determinants of emotional state. *Psychological Review,* 1962, *69,* 379–399.

Sherman, A. R., Real-life exposure as a primary therapeutic factor in the desensitization treatment of fear. *Journal of Abnormal Psychology,* 1972, *79,* 19–28.

Singerman, K. J., Borkovec, T. D., & Baron, R. S. Failure of a "misattribution therapy" manipulation with a clinically relevant target behavior. *Behavior Therapy,* 1976, *7,* 306–313.

Stern, R., & Marks, I. Brief and prolonged flooding: A comparison in agoraphobic patients. *Archives of General Psychiatry,* 1973, *28,* 270–276.

Strahley, D. F. Systematic desensitization and counterphobic treatment of an irrational fear of snakes (Doctoral dissertation, University of Tennessee, 1965). *Dissertation Abstracts,* 1966, *27,* 973B. (University Microfilms No. 66-5366)

Sushinsky, L. W., & Bootzin, R. R. Cognitive desensitization as a model of systematic desensitization. *Behavior Research and Therapy,* 1970, *8,* 29–33.

Szpiler, J. A., & Epstein, S. Availability of an avoidance response as related to autonomic arousal. *Journal of Abnormal Psychology,* 1976, *85,* 73–82.

Thase, M. E., & Moss, M. K. The relative efficacy of covert modeling procedures and guided participant modeling in the reduction of avoidance behavior. *Journal of Behavior Therapy and Experimental Psychiatry,* 1976, *7,* 7–12.

Valins, S., & Nisbett, R. E. *Attribution processes in the development and treatment of emotional disorders.* Morristown, N.J.: General Learning Press, 1971.

Valins, S., & Ray, H. Effects of cognitive desensitization on avoidance behavior. *Journal of Personality and Social Psychology,* 1967, *7,* 345–350.

Watson, J. P., Mullett, G. E., & Pillay, H. The effects of prolonged exposure to phobic situations upon agoraphobic patients treated in groups. *Behaviour Research and Therapy,* 1973, *11,* 531–545.

Weiner, B. *Theories of motivation.* Chicago: Markham, 1972.

White, R. W. Motivation reconsidered: The concept of competence. *Psychological Review,* 1959, *66,* 297–333.

Wilson, G. T., & Davison, G. C. Processes of fear reduction in systematic desensitization: Animal studies. *Psychological Bulletin,* 1971, *76,* 1–14.

Wolpe, J. *The practice of behavior therapy.* New York: Pergamon Press, 1974.

Rational Psychotherapy

Albert Ellis
1958

The central theme of this paper is that psychotherapists can help their clients to live the most self-fulfilling, creative, and emotionally satisfying lives by teaching these clients to organize and discipline their thinking. Does this mean that *all* human emotion and creativity can or should be controlled by reason and intellect? Not exactly.

The human being may be said to possess four basic processes—perception, movement, thinking, and emotion—all of which are integrally interrelated. Thus, thinking, aside from consisting of bioelectric changes in the brain cells, and in addition to comprising remembering, learning, problem-solving, and similar psychological processes, also is, and to some extent has to be, sensory, motor, and emotional behavior (1, 4). Instead, then, of saying, "Jones thinks about this puzzle," we should more accurately say, "Jones perceives-moves-feels-THINKS about this puzzle." Because, however, Jones' activity in relation to the puzzle may be *largely* focussed upon solving it, and only *incidentally* on seeing, manipulating, and emoting about it, we may perhaps justifiably emphasize only his thinking.

Emotion, like thinking and the sensori-motor processes, we may define as an exceptionally complex state of human reaction which is integrally related to all the other perception and response processes. It is not *one* thing, but a combination and holistic integration of several seemingly diverse, yet actually closely related, phenomena (1).

Normally, emotion arises from direct stimulation of the cells in the hypothalamus and autonomic nervous system (e.g., by electrical or chemical stimulation) or from indirect excitation via sensori-motor, cognitive, and other conative processes. It may theoretically be controlled, therefore, in four major ways. If one is highly excitable and wishes to calm down, one may (a) take electroshock or drug treatments; (b) use soothing baths or relaxation techniques; (c) seek someone one loves and quiet down for his sake; or (d) reason oneself into a state of calmness by showing oneself how silly it is for one to remain excited.

Although biophysical, sensori-motor, and emotive techniques are all legitimate methods of controlling emotional disturbances, they will not be considered in this paper, and only the rational technique will be emphasized. Rational psychotherapy is based on the assumption that thought and emotion are not two entirely different processes, but that they significantly overlap in many respects and that therefore disordered emotions can often (though not always) be ameliorated by changing one's thinking.

A large part of what we call emotion, in other words, is nothing more or less than a certain kind—a biased, prejudiced, or strongly evaluative kind—of thinking. What we usually label as thinking is a relatively calm and dispassionate appraisal (or organized perception) of a given situation, an objective comparison of many of the elements in this situation, and a coming to some conclusion as a result of this comparing or discriminating process (4). Thus, a thinking person may observe a piece of bread, see that one part of it is mouldy, remember that eating this kind of mould previously made him ill, and therefore cut off the mouldy part and eat the non-mouldy section of the bread.

An emoting individual, on the other hand, will tend to observe the same piece of bread, and remember so vio-

Note. From "Rational Psychotherapy" by A. Ellis, 1958, *The Journal of General Psychology, 58,* 35–49. Copyright 1958 by Heldref Publications. Reprinted by permission of the Helen Dwight Reed Educational Foundation.

lently or prejudicedly his previous experience with the mouldy part, that he will quickly throw away the whole piece of bread and therefore go hungry. Because the thinking person is relatively calm, he uses the maximum information available to him—namely, that mouldy bread is bad but non-mouldy bread is good. Because the emotional person is relatively excited, he may use only part of the available information—namely, that mouldy bread is bad.

It is hypothesized, then, that thinking and emoting are closely interrelated and at times differ mainly in that thinking is a more tranquil, less somatically involved (or, at least, perceived), and less activity-directed mode of discrimination than is emotion. It is also hypothesized that among adult humans raised in a social culture thinking and emoting are so closely interrelated that they usually accompany each other, act in a circular cause-and-effect relationship, and in certain (though hardly all) respects are essentially the *same thing*, so that one's thinking *becomes* one's emotion and emoting *becomes* one's thought. It is finally hypothesized that since man is a uniquely sign-, symbol-, and language-creating animal, both thinking, and emoting tend to take the form of self-talk or internalized sentences; and that, for all practical purposes, the sentences that human beings keep telling themselves *are* or *become* their thoughts and emotions.

This is not to say that emotion can under *no* circumstances exist without thought. It probably can; but it then tends to exist momentarily, and not to be sustained. An individual, for instance, steps on your toe, and you spontaneously, immediately become angry. Or you hear a piece of music and you instantly begin to feel warm and excited. Or you learn that a close friend has died and you quickly begin to feel sad. Under these circumstances, you may feel emotional without doing any concomitant thinking. Perhaps, however, you do, with split-second rapidity, start thinking "This person who stepped on my toe is a blackguard!" or "This music is wonderful!" or "Oh, how awful it is that my friend died!"

In any event, assuming that you don't, at the very beginning, have any conscious or unconscious thought accompanying your emotion, it appears to be difficult to *sustain* an emotional outburst without bolstering it by repeated ideas. For unless you keep telling yourself something on the order of "This person who stepped on my toe is a blackguard!" or "How could he do a horrible thing like that to me!" the pain of having your toe stepped on will soon die, and your immediate reaction will die with the pain. Of course, you can keep getting your toe stepped on, and the continuing pain may sustain your anger. But assuming that your physical sensation stops, your emotional feeling, in order to last, normally has to be bolstered by some kind of thinking.

We say "normally" because it is theoretically possible for your emotional circuits, once they have been made to reverberate by some physical or psychological stimulus, to keep reverberating under their own power. It is also theoretically possible for drugs or electrical impulses to keep acting directly on your hypothalamus and autonomic nervous system and thereby to keep you emotionally aroused. Usually, however, these types of continued direct stimulation of the emotion-producing centers do not seem to be important and are limited largely to pathological conditions.

It would appear, then, that positive human emotions, such as feelings of love or elation, are often associated with or result from thoughts, or internalized sentences, stated in some form or variation of the phrase "This is good!" and that negative human emotions, such as feelings of anger or depression, are frequently associated with or result from thoughts or sentences which are stated in some form or variation of the phrase "This is bad!" Without an adult human being's employing, on some conscious or unconscious level, such thoughts and sentences, much of his emoting would simply not exist.

If the hypothesis that sustained human emotion often results from or is directly associated with human thinking and self-verbalization is true, then important corollaries about the origin and perpetuation of states of emotional disturbance, or neurosis, may be drawn. For neurosis would appear to be disordered, over- or under-intensified, uncontrollable emotion; and this would seem to be the result of (and, in a sense, the very same thing as) illogical, unrealistic, irrational, inflexible, and childish thinking.

That neurotic or emotionally disturbed behavior is illogical and irrational would seem to be almost definitional. For if we define it otherwise, and label as neurotic *all* incompetent and ineffectual behavior, we will be including actions of *truly* stupid and incompetent individuals—for example, those who are mentally deficient or brain injured. The concept of neurosis only becomes meaningful, therefore, when we assume that the disturbed individual is *not* deficient or impaired but that he is theoretically capable of behaving in a more mature, more controlled, more flexible manner than he actually behaves. If, however, a neurotic is essentially an individual who acts significantly below his own potential level of behaving, or who defeats his own ends though he is theoretically capable of achieving them, it would appear that he behaves in an illogical, irrational, unrealistic way. Neurosis, in other words, consists of stupid behavior by a non-stupid person.

Assuming that emotionally disturbed individuals act in irrational, illogical ways, the questions which are therapeutically relevant are: (a) How do they originally get to be illogical? (b) How do they keep perpetuating their irrational thinking? (c) How can they be helped to be less illogical, less neurotic?

Unfortunately, most of the good thinking that has been done in regard to therapy during the past 60 years, especially by Sigmund Freud and his chief followers (5, 6, 7), has concerned itself with the first of these questions rather than the second and the third. The assumption has often been made that if psychotherapists discover and effectively communicate to their clients the main reasons why these clients originally became disturbed, they will thereby also discover how their neuroses are being perpetuated and how they can be helped to overcome them. This is a dubious assumption.

Knowing exactly how an individual originally learned to behave illogically by no means necessarily informs us precisely how he *maintains* his illogical behavior, nor what he should do to change it. This is particularly true because people are often, perhaps usually, afflicted with *secondary* as well as *primary* neuroses, and the two may significantly differ. Thus, an individual may originally become disturbed because he discovers that he has strong death wishes against his father and (quite illogically) thinks he should be blamed and punished for having these wishes. Consequently, he may develop some neurotic symptom, such as a phobia against dogs because, let us say, dogs remind him of his father, who is an ardent hunter.

Later on, this individual may grow to love or be indifferent to his father; or his father may die and be no more of a problem to him. His fear of dogs, however, may remain: not because, as some theorists would insist, they still remind him of his old death wishes against his father, but because he now hates himself so violently for *having* the original neurotic symptom—for behaving, to his mind, so stupidly and illogically in relation to dogs—that every time he thinks of dogs his self-hatred and fear of failure so severely upset him that he cannot reason clearly and cannot combat his illogical fear.

In terms of self-verbalization, this neurotic individual is first saying to himself: "I hate my father—and this is awful!" But he ends up by saying: "I have an irrational fear of dogs—and this is awful!" Even though both sets of self-verbalizations are neuroticizing, and his secondary neurosis may be as bad as or worse than his primary one, the two can hardly be said to be the same. Consequently, exploring and explaining to this individual—or helping him gain insight into—the origins of his primary neurosis will not necessarily help him to understand and overcome his perpetuating or secondary neurotic reactions.

If the hypotheses so far stated have some validity, the psychotherapist's main goals should be those of demonstrating to clients that their self-verbalizations have been and still are the prime source of their emotional disturbances. Clients must be shown that their internalized sentences are illogical and unrealistic at certain critical points and that they now have the ability to control their emotions by telling themselves more rational and less self-defeating sentences.

More precisely: the effective therapist should continually keep unmasking his client's past and, especially, his present illogical thinking or self-defeating verbalizations by (a) bringing them to his attention or consciousness; (b) showing the client how they are causing and maintaining his disturbance and unhappiness; (c) demonstrating exactly what the illogical links in his internalized sentences are; and (d) teaching him how to re-think and re-verbalize these (and other similar) sentences in a more logical, self-helping way. Moreover, before the end of the therapeutic relationship, the therapist should not only deal concretely with the client's specific illogical thinking, but should demonstrate to this client what, in general, are the main irrational ideas that human beings are prone to follow and what more rational philosophies of living may usually be substituted for them. Otherwise, the client who is released from one specific set of illogical notions may well wind up by falling victim to another set.

It is hypothesized, in other words, that human beings are the kind of animals who, when raised in any society similar to our own, tend to fall victim to several major fallacious ideas; to keep reindoctrinating themselves over and over again with these ideas in an unthinking, autosuggestive manner; and consequently to keep actualizing them in overt behavior. Most of these irrational ideas are, as the freudians have very adequately pointed out, instilled by the individual's parents during his childhood, and are tenaciously clung to because of his attachment to these parents and because the ideas were ingrained, or imprinted, or conditioned before later and more rational modes of thinking were given a chance to gain a foothold. Most of them, however, as the freudians have not always been careful to note, are also instilled by the individual's general culture, and particularly by the media of mass communication in this culture.

What are some of the major illogical ideas or philosophies which, when originally held and later perpetuated by men and women in our civilization, inevitably lead to self-defeat and neurosis? Limitations of space preclude our examining all these major ideas, including their more significant corollaries; therefore, only a few of them will be listed. The illogicality of some of these ideas will also, for the present, have to be taken somewhat on faith, since there again is no space to outline the many reasons *why* they are irrational. Anyway, here, where angels fear to tread, goes the psychological theoretician!

1. The idea that it is a dire necessity for an adult to be loved or approved by everyone for everything he does—instead of his concentrating on his own self-respect, on winning approval for necessary purposes (such as job advancement), and on loving rather than being loved.

2. The idea that certain acts are wrong, or wicked, or

villainous, and that people who perform such acts should be severely punished—instead of the idea that certain acts are inappropriate or antisocial, and that people who perform such acts are invariably stupid, ignorant, or emotionally disturbed.

3. The idea that it is terrible, horrible, and catastrophic when things are not the way one would like them to be—instead of the idea that it is too bad when things are not the way one would like them to be, and one should certainly try to change or control conditions so that they become more satisfactory, but that if changing or controlling uncomfortable situations is impossible, one had better become resigned to their existence and stop telling oneself how awful they are.

4. The idea that much human unhappiness is externally caused and is forced on one by outside people and events—instead of the idea that virtually all human unhappiness is caused or sustained by the view one takes of things rather than the things themselves.

5. The idea that if something is or may be dangerous or fearsome one should be terribly concerned about it—instead of the idea that if something is or may be dangerous or fearsome one should frankly face it and try to render it non-dangerous and, when that is impossible, think of other things and stop telling oneself what a terrible situation one is or may be in.

6. The idea that it is easier to avoid than to face life difficulties and self-responsibilities—instead of the idea that the so-called easy way is invariably the much harder way in the long run and that the only way to solve difficult problems is to face them squarely.

7. The idea that one needs something other or stronger or greater than oneself on which to rely—instead of the idea that it is usually far better to stand on one's own feet and gain faith in oneself and one's ability to meet difficult circumstances of living.

8. The idea that one should be thoroughly competent, adequate, intelligent, and achieving in all possible respects—instead of the idea that one should *do* rather than always try to do *well* and that one should accept oneself as a quite imperfect creature, who has general human limitations and specific fallibilities.

9. The idea that because something once strongly affected one's life, it should indefinitely affect it—instead of the idea that one should learn from one's past experiences but not be overly-attached to or prejudiced by them.

10. The idea that it is vitally important to our existence what other people do, and that we should make great efforts to change them in the direction we would like them to be—instead of the idea that other people's deficiencies are largely *their* problems and that putting pressure on them to change is usually least likely to help them do so.

11. The idea that human happiness can be achieved by inertia and inaction—instead of the idea that humans tend to be happiest when they are actively and vitally absorbed in creative pursuits, or when they are devoting themselves to people or projects outside themselves.

12. The idea that one has virtually no control over one's emotions and that one cannot help feeling certain things—instead of the idea that one has enormous control over one's emotions if one chooses to work at controlling them and to practice saying the right kinds of sentences to oneself.

It is the central theme of this paper that it is the foregoing kinds of illogical ideas, and many corollaries which we have no space to delineate, which are the basic causes of most emotional disturbances or neuroses. For once one believes the kind of nonsense included in these notions, one will inevitably tend to become inhibited, hostile, defensive, guilty, anxious, ineffective, inert, uncontrolled, or unhappy. If, on the other hand, one could become thoroughly released from all these fundamental kinds of illogical thinking, it would be exceptionally difficult for one to become too emotionally upset, or at least to sustain one's disturbance for very long.

Does this mean that all the other so-called basic causes of neurosis, such as the Oedipus complex or severe maternal rejection in childhood, are invalid, and that the freudian and other psychodynamic thinkers of the last 60 years have been barking up the wrong tree? Not at all. It only means, if the main hypotheses of this paper are correct, that these psychodynamic thinkers have been emphasizing secondary causes or results of emotional disturbances rather than truly prime causes.

Let us take, for example, an individual who acquires, when he is young, a full-blown Oedipus complex: that is to say, he lusts after his mother, hates his father, is guilty about his sex desires for his mother, and is afraid that his father is going to castrate him. This person, when he is a child, will presumably be disturbed. But, if he is raised so that he acquires none of the basic illogical ideas we have been discussing, it will be virtually impossible for him to remain disturbed.

For, as an adult, this individual will not be too concerned if his parents or others do not approve all his actions, since he will be more interested in his *own* self-respect than in *their* approval. He will not believe that his lust for his mother is wicked or villainous, but will accept it as a normal part of being a limited human whose sex desires may easily be indiscriminate. He will realize that the actual danger of his father castrating him is exceptionally slight. He will not feel that because he was once afraid of his Oedipal feelings he should forever remain so. If he still feels it would be improper for him to have sex relations with his mother, instead of castigating himself for even thinking of having such relations he will merely resolve not to carry his desires into practice and will stick determinedly to his resolve. If, by any chance, he weakens and actually has incestuous relations, he will again refuse to castigate himself mercilessly for being weak but will keep showing himself how self-defeating his behavior is and will actively work and practice at changing it.

Under these circumstances, if this individual has a truly logical and rational approach to life in general, and to the problem of Oedipal feelings, in particular, how can he possibly *remain* disturbed about his Oedipal attachment?

Take, by way of further illustration, the case of an individual who, as a child, is continually criticized by his parents, who consequently feels himself loathesome and inadequate, who refuses to take chances at failing at difficult tasks, who avoids such tasks, and who therefore comes to hate himself more. Such a person will be, of course, seriously neurotic. But how would it be possible for him to *sustain* his neurosis if he began to think in a truly logical manner about himself and his behavior?

For, if this individual does use a consistent rational approach to his own behavior, he will stop caring particularly what others think of him and will start primarily caring what he thinks of himself. Consequently, he will stop avoiding difficult tasks and, instead of punishing himself for being incompetent when he makes a mistake, will say to himself something like: "Now this is not the right way to do things; let me stop and figure out a better way." Or: "There's no doubt that I made a mistake this time; now let me see how I can benefit from making it."

This individual, furthermore, will if he is thinking straight, not blame his defeats on external events, but will realize that he himself is causing them by his illogical or impractical behavior. He will not believe that it is easier to avoid facing difficult things, but will realize that the so-called easy way is always, actually, the harder and more idiotic one. He will not think that he needs something greater or stronger than himself to help him, but will independently buckle down to difficult tasks himself. He will not feel that because he once defeated himself by avoiding doing things the hard way that he must always do so.

How, with this kind of logical thinking, could an originally disturbed person possibly maintain and continually revivify his neurosis? He just couldn't. Similarly, the spoiled brat, the worry-wart, the ego-maniac, the autistic stay-at-home—all of these disturbed individuals would have the devil of a time indefinitely prolonging their neuroses if they did not continue to believe utter nonsense: namely, the kinds of basic irrational postulates previously listed.

Neurosis, then, usually seems to originate in and be perpetuated by some fundamentally unsound, irrational ideas. The individual comes to believe in some unrealistic, impossible, often perfectionistic goals—especially the goals that he should always be approved by everyone, should do everything perfectly well, and should never be frustrated in any of his desires—and then, in spite of considerable contradictory evidence, refuses to give up his original illogical beliefs.

Some of the neurotic's philosophies, such as the idea that he should be loved and approved by everyone, are not entirely inappropriate to his childhood state; but all of them are quite inappropriate to average adulthood. Most of his irrational ideas are specifically taught him by his parents and his culture; and most of them also seem to be held by the great majority of adults in our society—who theoretically should have been but actually never were weaned from them as they chronologically matured. It must consequently be admitted that the neurotic individual we are considering is often statistically normal; or that ours is a generally neuroticizing culture, in which most people are more or less emotionally disturbed because they are raised to believe, and then to internalize and to keep reinfecting themselves with, arrant nonsense which must inevitably lead them to become ineffective, self-defeating, and unhappy. Nonetheless: it is not absolutely *necessary* that human beings believe the irrational notions which, in point of fact, most of them seem to believe today; and the task of psychotherapy is to get them to disbelieve their illogical ideas, to change their self-sabotaging attitudes.

This, precisely, is the task which the rational psychotherapist sets himself. Like other therapists, he frequently resorts to the usual techniques of therapy which the present author has outlined elsewhere (2, 3), including the techniques of relationship, expressive-emotive, supportive, and insight-interpretive therapy. But he views these techniques, as they are commonly employed, as kinds of preliminary strategies whose main functions are to gain rapport with the client, to let him express himself fully, to show him that he is a worthwhile human being who has the ability to change, and to demonstrate how he originally became disturbed.

The rational therapist, in other words, believes that most of the usual therapeutic techniques wittingly or unwittingly show the client *that* he is illogical and how he *originally* became so. They often fail to show him, however, how he is presently *maintaining* his illogical thinking, and precisely what he must do to change it by building general rational philosophies of living and by applying these to practical problems of everyday life. Where most therapists directly or indirectly show the client that he is behaving illogically, the rational therapist goes beyond this point to make a forthright, unequivocal *attack* on the client's general and specific irrational ideas and to try to *induce* him to adopt more rational ones in their place.

Rational psychotherapy makes a concerted attack on the disturbed individual's irrational positions in two main ways: (a) the therapist serves as a frank counter-propagandist who directly contradicts and denies the self-defeating propaganda and superstitions which the client has originally learned and which he is now self-propagandistically perpetuating. (b) The therapist encourages, persuades, cajoles, and at times commands the client to partake of some kind of activity which itself will act as a forceful counter-propagandist agency against the nonsense he believes. Both these main therapeutic activities are consciously performed with one main goal in mind: namely, that of finally getting the client to internalize a rational philosophy of living just as he originally learned and internalized the illogical propaganda and superstitions of his parents and his culture.

The rational therapist, then, assumes that the client somehow imbibed illogical ideas or irrational modes of thinking and that, without so doing, he could hardly be as disturbed as he is. It is the therapist's function not merely to show the client that he has these ideas or thinking processes but to persuade him to change and substitute for them more rational ideas and thought processes. If, because the client is exceptionally disturbed when he first comes to therapy, he must first be approached in a rather cautious, supportive, permissive, and warm manner, and must sometimes be allowed to ventilate his feeling in free association, abreaction, role playing, and other expressive techniques, that may be all to the good. But the therapist does not delude himself that these relationship-building and expressive-emotive techniques in most instances really get to the core of the client's illogical thinking and induce him to think in a more rational manner.

Occasionally, this is true: since the client may come to see, through relationship and emotive-expressive methods, that he *is* acting illogically, and he may therefore resolve to change and actually do so. More often than not, however, his illogical thinking will be so ingrained from constant self-repetitions, and will be so inculcated in motor pathways (or habit patterns) by the time he comes for therapy, that simply showing him, even by direct interpretation, *that* he is illogical will not greatly help. He will often say to the therapist: "All right, now I understand that I have castration fears and that they are illogical. But I *still* feel afraid of my father."

The therapist, therefore, must keep pounding away, time and again, at the illogical ideas which underlie the client's fears. He must show the client that he is afraid, really, not of his father, but of being blamed, of being disapproved, of being unloved, of being imperfect, of being a failure. And such fears are thoroughly irrational because (a) being disapproved is not half so terrible as one *thinks* it is; because (b) no one can be thoroughly blameless or perfect; because (c) people who worry about being blamed or disapproved essentially are putting themselves

at the mercy of the opinion of *others,* over whom they have no real control; because (d) being blamed or disapproved has nothing essentially to do with one's *own* opinion of oneself; etc.

If the therapist, moreover, merely tackles the individual's castration fears, and shows how ridiculous *they* are, what is to prevent this individual's showing up, a year or two later, with some *other* illogical fear—such as the fear that he is sexually impotent? But if the therapist tackles the client's *basic* irrational thinking, which underlies *all* kinds of fear he may have, it is going to be most difficult for this client to turn up with a new neurotic symptom some months or years hence. For once an individual truly surrenders ideas of perfectionism, of the horror of failing at something, of the dire need to be approved by others, of the notion that the world owes him a living, and so on, what else is there for him to be fearful of or disturbed about?

To give some idea of precisely how the rational therapist works, a case summary will now be presented. A client came in one day and said he was depressed but did not know why. A little questioning showed that he had been putting off the inventory keeping he was required to do as part of his job as an apprentice glass-staining artist. The therapist immediately began showing him that his depression was related to his resenting having to keep inventory and that this resentment was illogical for several reasons:

(a). The client very much wanted to learn the art of glass-staining and could only learn it by having the kind of job he had. His sole logical choice, therefore, was between graciously accepting this job, in spite of the inventory-keeping, or giving up trying to be a glass-stainer. By resenting the clerical work and avoiding it, he was choosing neither of these two logical alternatives, and was only getting himself into difficulty.

(b). By blaming the inventory-keeping, and his boss for making him perform it, the client was being irrational since, assuming that the boss was wrong about making him do this clerical work, the boss would have to be wrong out of some combination of stupidity, ignorance, or emotional disturbance; and it is silly and pointless blaming people for being stupid, ignorant, or disturbed. Besides, maybe the boss was quite right, from his own standpoint, about making the client keep the inventory.

(c). Whether the boss was right or wrong, resenting him for his stand was hardly going to make him change it; and the resentment felt by the client was hardly going to do him, the client, any good or make him feel better. The saner attitude for him to take, then, was that it was too bad that inventory-keeping was part of his job, but that's the way it was, and there was no point in resenting the way things were when they could not, for the moment, be changed.

(d). Assuming that the inventory-keeping was irksome, there was no sense in making it still *more* annoying by the client's continually telling himself how awful it was. Nor was there any point in shirking this clerical work, since he eventually would have to do it anyway and he might as well get this unpleasant task out of the way quickly. Even more important: by shirking a task that he knew that, eventually, he just had to do, he would lose respect for himself, and his loss of self-respect would be far worse than the slight, rather childish satisfaction he might receive from trying to sabotage his boss's desires.

While showing this client how illogical was his thinking and consequent behavior, the therapist specifically made him aware that he must be telling himself sentences like these: "My boss makes me do inventory-keeping. I do not like to do this. . . . There is no reason why I have to do it. . . . He is therefore a blackguard for making me do it. . . . So I'll fool him and avoid doing it. . . . And then I'll be happier." But these sentences were so palpably foolish that the client could not really believe them, and began to finish them off with sentences like: "I'm not really fooling my boss, because he sees what I'm doing. . . . So I'm not solving my problem this way. . . . So I really should stop this nonsense and get the inventory-keeping done. . . . But I'll be damned if I'll do it for him! . . . However, if I don't do it, I'll be fired. . . . But I still don't want to do it for him! . . . . I guess I've got to, though. . . . Oh, why must I always be persecuted like this? . . . And why must I keep getting myself into such a mess? . . . I guess I'm just no good. . . . And people are against me. . . . Oh, what's the use?"

Whereupon, employing these illogical kinds of sentences, the client was becoming depressed, avoiding doing the inventory-keeping, and then becoming more resentful and depressed. Instead, the therapist pointed out, he could tell himself quite different sentences, on this order: "Keeping inventory is a bore. . . . But it is presently an essential part of my job. . . . And I also may learn something useful by it. . . . Therefore, I had better go about this task as best I may and thereby get what I want out of this job."

The therapist also emphasized that whenever the client found himself intensely angry, guilty, or depressed, there was little doubt that he was then thinking illogically, and that he should immediately question himself as to what was the irrational element in his thinking, and set about replacing it with a more logical element or chain of sentences.

The therapist then used the client's current dilemma—that of avoiding inventory-keeping—as an illustration of his general neurosis, which in his case largely took the form of severe alcoholic tendencies. He was shown that his alcoholic trends, too, were a resultant of his trying to do things the easy way, and of poor thinking preluding his

avoidance of self-responsibilities. He was impressed with the fact that, as long as he kept thinking illogically about relatively small things, such as the inventory-keeping, he would also tend to think equally illogically about more important aspects, such as the alcoholism.

Several previous incidents of illogical thinking leading to emotional upheaval in the client's life were then reviewed, and some general principles of irrational thought discussed. Thus, the general principle of blamelessness was raised and the client was shown precisely why it is illogical to blame anyone for anything. The general principle of inevitability was brought up and he was shown that when a frustrating or unpleasant event is inevitable, it is only logical to accept it uncomplainingly instead of dwelling on its unpleasant aspects. The general principle of self-respect was discussed, with the therapist demonstrating that liking oneself is far more important than resentfully trying to harm others.

In this matter, by attempting to show or teach the client some of the general rules of logical living, the therapist tried to go beyond his immediate problem and to help provide him with a generalized mode of thinking or problem solving that would enable him to deal effectively with almost any future similar situation that might arise.

The rational therapist, then, is a frank propagandist who believes wholeheartedly in a more rigorous application of the rules of logic, of straight thinking, and of scientific method to everyday life, and who ruthlessly uncovers every vestige of irrational thinking in the client's experience and energetically urges him into more rational channels. In so doing, the rational therapist does not ignore or eradicate the client's emotions; on the contrary, he considers them most seriously, and helps change them, when they are disordered and self-defeating, through the same means by which they commonly arise in the first place—that is, by thinking and acting. Through exerting consistent interpretive and philosophic pressure on the client to change his thinking or his self-verbalizations and to change his experiences or his actions, the rational therapist gives a specific impetus to the client's movement toward mental health without which it is not impossible, but quite unlikely, that he will move very far.

Can therapy be effectively done, then, with *all* clients mainly through logical analysis and reconstruction? Alas, no. For one thing, many clients are not bright enough to follow a rigorously rational analysis. For another thing, some individuals are so emotionally aberrated by the time they come for help that they are, at least temporarily, in no position to comprehend and follow logical procedures. Still other clients are too old and inflexible; too young and impressionable; too biophysically deficient; or too something else to accept, at least at the start of therapy, rational analysis.

In consequence, the therapist who *only* employs logical reconstruction in his therapeutic armamentarium is not likely to get too far with many of those who seek his help. It is vitally important, therefore, that any therapist who has a basically rational approach to the problem of helping his clients overcome their neuroses also be quite eclectic in his use of supplementary, less direct, and somewhat less rational techniques.

Admitting, then, that rational psychotherapy is not effective with all types of clients, and that it is most helpful when used in conjunction with, or subsequent to, other widely employed therapeutic techniques, I would like to conclude with two challenging hypotheses: (a) that psychotherapy which includes a high dosage of rational analysis and reconstruction, as briefly outlined in this paper, will prove to be more effective with more types of clients than any of the non-rational or semi-rational therapies now being widely employed; and (b) that a considerable amount of—or, at least, proportion of—rational psychotherapy will prove to be virtually the only type of treatment that helps to undermine the basic neuroses (as distinguished from the superficial neurotic symptoms)

of many clients, and particularly of many with whom other types of therapy have already been shown to be ineffective.

REFERENCES

1. Cobb, S. *Emotions and clinical medicine.* New York: Norton, 1950.
2. Ellis, A. New approaches to psychotherapy techniques. *J. Clin. Psychol. Monog. Suppl.,* No. 11. Brandon, Vermont: *J. Clin. Psychol.,* 1955.
3. ———. Psychotherapy techniques for use with psychotics. *Amer. J. Psychother.,* 1955, 9, 452–476.
4. ———. An operational reformulation of some of the basic principles of psychoanalysis. *Psychoanal. Rev.,* 1956, 43, 163–180.
5. Fenichel, O. *The psychoanalytic theory of neurosis.* New York: Norton, 1945.
6. Freud, S. *Basic writings.* New York: Modern Library, 1938.
7. ———. *Collected papers.* London: Hogarth Press, 1924–1950.

Excerpts from
A Theory of Human Motivation

Abraham H. Maslow
1943

I. INTRODUCTION

In a previous paper (*13*) various propositions were presented which would have to be included in any theory of human motivation that could lay claim to be definitive. These conclusions may be briefly summarized as follows:

1. The integrated wholeness of the organism must be one of the foundation stones of motivation theory.

2. The hunger drive (or any other physiological drive) was rejected as a centering point or model for a definitive theory of motivation. Any drive that is somatically based and localizable was shown to be atypical rather than typical in human motivation.

3. Such a theory should stress and center itself upon ultimate or basic goals rather than partial or superficial ones, upon ends rather than means to these ends. Such a stress would imply a more central place for unconscious than for conscious motivations.

4. There are usually available various cultural paths to the same goal. Therefore conscious, specific, local-cultural desires are not as funda-

mental in motivation theory as the more basic, unconscious goals.

5. Any motivated behavior, either preparatory or consummatory, must be understood to be a channel through which many basic needs may be simultaneously expressed or satisfied. Typically an act has *more* than one motivation.

6. Practically all organismic states are to be understood as motivated and as motivating.

7. Human needs arrange themselves in hierarchies of prepotency. That is to say, the appearance of one need usually rests on the prior satisfaction of another, more prepotent need. Man is a perpetually wanting animal. Also no need or drive can be treated as if it were isolated or discrete; every drive is related to the state of satisfaction or dissatisfaction of other drives.

8. *Lists* of drives will get us nowhere for various theoretical and practical reasons. Furthermore any classification of motivations must deal with the problem of levels of specificity or generalization of the motives to be classified.

9. Classifications of motivations must be based upon goals rather than upon instigating drives or motivated behavior.

10. Motivation theory should be human-centered rather than animal-centered.

Note. From "A theory of human motivation" by A. H. Maslow, 1943, *Psychological Review, 50,* 370–396. Copyright 1943 by the American Psychological Association. Reprinted by permission.

11. The situation or the field in which the organism reacts must be taken into account but the field alone can rarely serve as an exclusive explanation for behavior. Furthermore the field itself must be interpreted in terms of the organism. Field theory cannot be a substitute for motivation theory.

12. Not only the integration of the organism must be taken into account, but also the possibility of isolated, specific, partial or segmental reactions.

It has since become necessary to add to these another affirmation.

13. Motivation theory is not synonymous with behavior theory. The motivations are only one class of determinants of behavior. While behavior is almost always motivated, it is also almost always biologically, culturally and situationally determined as well.

The present paper is an attempt to formulate a positive theory of motivation which will satisfy these theoretical demands and at the same time conform to the known facts, clinical and observational as well as experimental. It derives most directly, however, from clinical experience. This theory is, I think, in the functionalist tradition of James and Dewey, and is fused with the holism of Wertheimer (*19*), Goldstein (*6*), and Gestalt Psychology, and with the dynamicism of Freud (*4*) and Adler (*1*). This fusion or synthesis may arbitrarily be called a "general-dynamic" theory.

It is far easier to perceive and to criticize the aspects in motivation theory than to remedy them. Mostly this is because of the very serious lack of sound data in this area. I conceive this lack of sound facts to be due primarily to the absence of a valid theory of motivation. The present theory then must be considered to be a suggested program or framework for future research and must stand or fall, not so much on facts available or evidence presented, as upon researches yet to be done, researches suggested perhaps, by the questions raised in this paper.

II. THE BASIC NEEDS

The "Physiological" Needs

The needs that are usually taken as the starting point for motivation theory are the so-called physiological drives. Two recent lines of research make it necessary to revise our customary notions about these needs, first, the development of the concept of homeostasis, and second,

the finding that appetites (preferential choices among foods) are a fairly efficient indication of actual needs or lacks in the body.

Homeostasis refers to the body's automatic efforts to maintain a constant, normal state of the blood stream. Cannon (*2*) has described this process for (1) the water content of the blood, (2) salt content, (3) sugar content, (4) protein content, (5) fat content, (6) calcium content, (7) oxygen content, (8) constant hydrogen-ion level (acid-base balance) and (9) constant temperature of the blood. Obviously this list can be extended to include other minerals, the hormones, vitamins, etc.

Young in a recent article (*21*) has summarized the work on appetite in its relation to body needs. If the body lacks some chemical, the individual will tend to develop a specific appetite or partial hunger for that food element.

Thus it seems impossible as well as useless to make any list of fundamental physiological needs for they can come to almost any number one might wish, depending on the degree of specificity of description. We can not identify all physiological needs as homeostatic. That sexual desire, sleepiness, sheer activity and maternal behavior in animals, are homeostatic, has not yet been demonstrated. Furthermore, this list would not include the various sensory pleasures (tastes, smells, tickling, stroking) which are probably physiological and which may become the goals of motivated behavior.

In a previous paper (*13*) it has been pointed out that these physiological drives or needs are to be considered unusual rather than typical because they are isolable, and because they are localizable somatically. That is to say, they are relatively independent of each other, of other motivations and of the organism as a whole, and secondly, in many cases, it is possible to demonstrate a localized, underlying somatic base for the drive. This is true less generally than has been thought (exceptions are fatigue, sleepiness, maternal responses) but it is still true in the classic instances of hunger, sex, and thirst.

It should be pointed out again that any of the physiological needs and the consummatory behavior involved with them serve as channels for all sorts of other needs as well. That is to say, the person who thinks he is hungry may actually be seeking more for comfort, or dependence, than for vitamins or proteins. Conversely, it is possible to satisfy the hunger need in part by other activities such as drinking water or smoking cigarettes. In other words, relatively isolable as these physiological needs are, they are not completely so.

Undoubtedly these physiological needs are the most prepotent of all needs. What this means specifically is, that in the human being who is missing everything in life in an extreme fashion, it is most likely that the major motivation would be the physiological needs rather than any others. A person who is lacking food, safety, love, and esteem would most probably hunger for food more strongly than for anything else.

If all the needs are unsatisfied, and the organism is then dominated by the physiological needs, all other needs may become simply non-existent or be pushed into the background. It is then fair to characterize the whole organism by saying simply that it is hungry, for consciousness is almost completely preempted by hunger. All capacities are put into the service of hunger-satisfaction, and the organization of these capacities is almost entirely determined by the one purpose of satisfying hunger. The receptors and effectors, the intelligence, memory, habits, all may now be defined simply as hunger-gratifying tools. Capacities that are not useful for this purpose lie dormant, or are pushed into the background. The urge to write poetry, the desire to acquire an automobile, the interest in American history, the desire for a new pair of shoes are, in the extreme case, forgotten or become of secondary importance. For the man who is extremely and dangerously hungry, no other interests exist but food. He dreams food, he remembers food, he thinks about food, he emotes only about food, he perceives only food and he wants only food. The more subtle determinants that ordinarily fuse with the physiological drives in organizing even feeding, drinking or sexual behavior, may now be so completely overwhelmed as to allow us to speak at this time (but *only* at this time) of pure hunger drive and behavior, with the one unqualified aim of relief.

Another peculiar characteristic of the human organism when it is dominated by a certain need is that the whole philosophy of the future tends also to change. For our chronically and extremely hungry man, Utopia can be defined very simply as a place where there is plenty of food. He tends to think that, if only he is guaranteed food for the rest of his life, he will be perfectly happy and will never want anything more. Life itself tends to be defined in terms of eating. Anything else will be defined as unimportant. Freedom, love, community feeling, respect, philosophy, may all be waved aside as fripperies which are useless since they fail to fill the stomach. Such a man may fairly be said to live by bread alone.

It cannot possibly be denied that such things are true but their *generality* can be denied. Emergency conditions are, almost by definition, rare in the normally functioning peaceful society. That this truism can be forgotten is due mainly to two reasons. First, rats have few motivations other than physiological ones, and since so much of the research upon motivation has been made with these animals, it is easy to carry the rat-picture over to the human being. Secondly, it is too often not realized that culture itself is an adaptive tool, one of whose main functions is to make the physiological emergencies come less and less often. In most of the known societies, chronic extreme hunger of the emergency type is rare, rather than

common. In any case, this is still true in the United States. The average American citizen is experiencing appetite rather than hunger when he says "I am hungry." He is apt to experience sheer life-and-death hunger only by accident and then only a few times through his entire life.

Obviously a good way to obscure the "higher" motivations, and to get a lopsided view of human capacities and human nature, is to make the organism extremely and chronically hungry or thirsty. Anyone who attempts to make an emergency picture into a typical one, and who will measure all of man's goals and desires by his behavior during extreme physiological deprivation is certainly being blind to many things. It is quite true that man lives by bread alone—when there is no bread. But what happens to man's desires when there *is* plenty of bread and when his belly is chronically filled?

At once other (and "higher") needs emerge and these, rather than physiological hungers, dominate the organism. And when these in turn are satisfied, again new (and still "higher") needs emerge and so on. This is what we mean by saying that the basic human needs are organized into a hierarchy of relative prepotency.

One main implication of this phrasing is that gratification becomes as important a concept as deprivation in motivation theory, for it releases the organism from the domination of a relatively more physiological need, permitting thereby the emergence of other more social goals. The physiological needs, along with their partial goals, when chronically gratified cease to exist as active determinants or organizers of behavior. They now exist only in a potential fashion in the sense that they may emerge again to dominate the organism if they are thwarted. But a want that is satisfied is no longer a want. The organism is dominated and its behavior organized only by unsatisfied needs. If hunger is satisfied, it becomes unimportant in the current dynamics of the individual.

This statement is somewhat qualified by a hypothesis to be discussed more fully later, namely that it is precisely those individuals in whom a certain need has always been satisfied who are best equipped to tolerate deprivation of that need in the future, and that furthermore, those who have been deprived in the past will react differently to current satisfactions than the one who has never been deprived.

The Safety Needs

If the physiological needs are relatively well gratified, there then emerges a new set of needs, which we may categorize roughly as the safety needs. All that has been said of the physiological needs is equally true, although in lesser degree, of these desires. The organism may equally well be wholly dominated by them. They may serve as the almost exclusive organizers of behavior, recruiting all the capacities of the organism in their service, and we may then fairly describe the whole organism as a safety-seeking mechanism. Again we may say of the receptors, the effectors, of the intellect and the other capacities that they are primarily safety-seeking tools. Again, as in the hungry man, we find that the dominating goal is a strong determinant not only of his current world-outlook and philosophy but also of his philosophy of the future. Practically everything looks less important than safety, (even sometimes the physiological needs which being satisfied, are now underestimated). A man, in this state, if it is extreme enough and chronic enough, may be characterized as living almost for safety alone.

Although in this paper we are interested primarily in the needs of the adult, we can approach an understanding of his safety needs perhaps more efficiently by observation of infants and children, in whom these needs are much more simple and obvious. One reason for the clearer appearance of the threat or danger reaction in infants, is that they do not inhibit this reaction at all, whereas adults in our society have been taught to inhibit it at all costs. Thus even when adults do feel their safety to be threatened we may not be able to see this on the surface. Infants will react in a total fashion and as if they were endangered, if they are disturbed or dropped suddenly, startled by loud noises, flashing light, or other unusual sensory stimulation, by rough handling, by general loss of support in the mother's arms, or by inadequate support.[1] . . .

Confronting the average child with new, unfamiliar, strange, unmanageable stimuli or situations will too frequently elicit the danger or terror reaction, as for example, getting lost or even being separated from the parents for a short time, being confronted with new faces, new situations or new tasks, the sight of strange, unfamiliar or uncontrollable objects, illness or death. Particularly at such times, the child's frantic clinging to his parents is eloquent testimony to their role as protectors (quite apart from their roles as food-givers and love-givers).

From these and similar observations, we may generalize and say that the average child in our society generally prefers a safe, orderly, predictable, organized world, which he can count on, and in which unexpected, unmanageable or other dangerous things do not happen, and in which, in any case, he has all-powerful parents who protect and shield him from harm.

That these reactions may so easily be observed in children is in a way a proof of the fact that children in our society, feel too unsafe (or, in a word, are badly brought up). Children who are reared in an unthreatening, loving family do *not* ordinarily react as we have described above (*17*). In such children the danger reactions are apt to come mostly to objects or situations that adults too would consider dangerous.[2]

The healthy, normal, fortunate adult in our culture is largely satisfied in his safety needs. The peaceful, smoothly running, "good" society ordinarily makes its members feel safe enough from wild animals, extremes of temperature, criminals, assault and murder, tyranny, etc. Therefore, in a very real sense, he no longer has any safety needs as active motivators. Just as a sated man no longer feels hungry, a safe man no longer feels endangered. If we wish to see these needs directly and clearly we must turn to neurotic or near-neurotic individuals, and to the economic and social underdogs. In between these extremes, we can perceive the expressions of safety needs only in such phenomena as, for instance, the common preference for a job with tenure and protection, the desire for a savings account, and for insurance of various kinds (medical, dental, unemployment, disability, old age). . . .

The neurosis in which the search for safety takes its clearest form is in the compulsive-obsessive neurosis. Compulsive-obsessives try frantically to order and stabilize the world so that no unmanageable, unexpected or unfamiliar dangers will ever appear (*14*). They hedge themselves about with all sorts of ceremonials, rules and formulas so that every possible contingency may be provided for and so that no new contingencies may appear. They are much like the brain injured cases, described by Goldstein (*6*), who manage to maintain their equilibrium by avoiding everything unfamiliar and strange and by ordering their restricted world in such a neat, disciplined, orderly fashion that everything in the world can be counted upon. They try to arrange the world so that anything unexpected (dangers) cannot possibly occur. If, through no fault of their own, something unexpected does occur, they go into a panic reaction as if this unexpected occurrence constituted a grave danger. What we can see only as a none-too-strong preference in the healthy person, *e.g.*, preference for the familiar, becomes a life-and-death necessity in abnormal cases.

---

[1] As the child grows up, sheer knowledge and familiarity as well as better motor development make these "dangers" less and less dangerous and more and more manageable. Throughout life it may be said that one of the main conative functions of education is this neutralizing of apparent dangers through knowledge, e.g., I am not afraid of thunder because I know something about it.

[2] A "test battery" for safety might be confronting the child with a small exploding firecracker, or with a bewhiskered face, having the mother leave the room, putting him upon a high ladder, a hypodermic injection, having a mouse crawl up to him, etc. Of course I cannot seriously recommend the deliberate use of such "tests" for they might very well harm the child being tested. But these and similar situations come up by the score in the child's ordinary day-to-day living and may be observed. There is no reason why these stimuli should not be used with, for example, young chimpanzees.

The Love Needs

If both the physiological and the safety needs are fairly well gratified, then there will emerge the love and affection and belongingness needs, and the whole cycle already described will repeat itself with this new center. Now the person will feel keenly, as never before, the absence of friends, or a sweetheart, or a wife, or children. He will hunger for affectionate relations with people in general, namely, for a place in his group, and he will strive with great intensity to achieve this goal. He will want to attain such a place more than anything else in the world and may even forget that once, when he was hungry, he sneered at love.

In our society the thwarting of these needs is the most commonly found core in cases of maladjustment and more severe psychopathology. Love and affection, as well as their possible expression in sexuality, are generally looked upon with ambivalence and are customarily hedged about with many restrictions and inhibitions. Practically all theorists of psychopathology have stressed thwarting of the love needs as basic in the picture of maladjustment. Many clinical studies have therefore been made of this need and we know more about it perhaps than any of the other needs except the physiological ones (*14*).

One thing that must be stressed at this point is that love is not synonymous with sex. Sex may be studied as a purely physiological need. Ordinarily sexual behavior is multi-determined, that is to say, determined not only by sexual but also by other needs, chief among which are the love and affection needs. Also not to be overlooked is the fact that the love needs involve both giving *and* receiving love.[3]

The Esteem Needs

All people in our society (with a few pathological exceptions) have a need or desire for a stable, firmly based, (usually) high evaluation of themselves, for self-respect, or self-esteem, and for the esteem of others. By firmly based self-esteem, we mean that which is soundly based upon real capacity, achievement and respect from others. These needs may be classified into two subsidiary sets. These are, first, the desire for strength, for achievement, for adequacy, for confidence in the face of the world, and for independence and freedom.[4] Secondly, we have what we may call the desire for reputation or prestige (defining it as respect or esteem from other people), recognition, attention, importance or appreciation.[5] These needs have been relatively stressed by Alfred Adler and his followers, and have been relatively neglected by Freud and the psychoanalysts. More and more today however there is appearing widespread appreciation of their central importance.

Satisfaction of the self-esteem need leads to feelings of self-confidence, worth, strength, capability and adequacy of being useful and necessary in the world. But thwarting of these needs produces feelings of inferiority, of weakness and of helplessness. These feelings in turn give rise to either basic discouragement or else compensatory or neurotic trends. An appreciation of the necessity of basic self-confidence and an understanding of how helpless people are without it, can be easily gained from a study of severe traumatic neurosis (*8*).[6]

The Need for Self-Actualization

Even if all these needs are satisfied, we may still often (if not always) expect that a new discontent and restlessness will soon develop, unless the individual is doing what he is fitted for. A musician must make music, an artist must paint, a poet must write, if he is to be ultimately happy. What a man *can* be, he *must* be. This need we may call self-actualization.

This term, first coined by Kurt Goldstein, is being used in this paper in a much more specific and limited fashion. It refers to the desire for self-fulfillment, namely, to the tendency for him to become actualized in what he is potentially. This tendency might be phrased as the desire to become more and more what one is, to become everything that one is capable of becoming.

The specific form that these needs will take will of course vary greatly from person to person. In one individual it may take the form of the desire to be an ideal mother, in another it may be expressed athletically, and in still another it may be expressed in painting pictures or

---

We may assume on the basis of commonly known clinical data that a man who has known true freedom (not paid for by giving up safety and security but rather built on the basis of adequate safety and security) will not willingly or easily allow his freedom to be taken away from him. But we do not know that this is true for the person born into slavery. The events of the next decade should give us our answer. See discussion of this problem in (*5*).

[5] Perhaps the desire for prestige and respect from others is subsidiary to the desire for self-esteem or confidence in oneself. Observation of children seems to indicate that this is so, but clinical data give no clear support for such a conclusion.

[6] For more extensive discussion of normal self-esteem, as well as for reports of various researches, see (*11*).

---

[3] For further details see (*12*) and (*16*, Chap. *5*).

[4] Whether or not this particular desire is universal we do not know. The crucial question, especially important today, is "Will men who are enslaved and dominated, inevitably feel dissatisfied and rebellious?"

in inventions. It is not necessarily a creative urge although in people who have any capacities for creation it will take this form.

The clear emergency of these needs rests upon prior satisfaction of the physiological, safety, love and esteem needs. We shall call people who are satisfied in these needs, basically satisfied people, and it is from these that we may expect the fullest (and healthiest) creativeness.[7] Since, in our society, basically satisfied people are the exception, we do not know much about self-actualization, either experimentally or clinically. It remains a challenging problem for research.

The Preconditions for the Basic Need Satisfactions

There are certain conditions which are immediate prerequisites for the basic need satisfactions. Danger to these is reacted to almost as if it were a direct danger to the basic needs themselves. Such conditions as freedom to speak, freedom to do what one wishes so long as no harm is done to others, freedom to express one's self, freedom to investigate and seek for information, freedom to defend one's self, justice, fairness, honesty, orderliness in the group are examples of such preconditions for basic need satisfactions. Thwarting in these freedoms will be reacted to with a threat or emergency response. These conditions are not ends in themselves but they are *almost* so since they are so closely related to the basic needs, which are apparently the only ends in themselves. These conditions are defended because without them the basic satisfactions are quite impossible, or at least, very severely endangered.

If we remember that the cognitive capacities (perceptual, intellectual, learning) are a set of adjustive tools, which have, among other functions, that of satisfaction of our basic needs, then it is clear that any danger to them, any deprivation or blocking of their free use, must also be indirectly threatening to the basic needs themselves. Such a statement is a partial solution of the general problems of curiosity, the search for knowledge, truth and wisdom, and the ever-persistent urge to solve the cosmic mysteries.

We must therefore introduce another hypothesis and

speak of degrees of closeness to the basic needs, for we have already pointed out that *any* conscious desires (partial goals) are more or less important as they are more or less close to the basic needs. The same statement may be made for various behavior acts. An act is psychologically important if it contributes directly to satisfaction of basic needs. The less directly it so contributes, or the weaker this contribution is, the less important this act must be conceived to be from the point of view of dynamic psychology. A similar statement may be made for the various defense or coping mechanisms. Some are very directly related to the protection or attainment of the basic needs, others are only weakly and distantly related. Indeed if we wished, we could speak of more basic and less basic defense mechanisms, and then affirm that danger to the more basic defenses is more threatening than danger to less basic defenses (always remembering that this is so only because of their relationship to the basic needs).

The Desires to Know and to Understand

So far, we have mentioned the cognitive needs only in passing. Acquiring knowledge and systematizing the universe have been considered as, in part, techniques for the achievement of basic safety in the world, or, for the intelligent man, expressions of self-actualization. Also freedom of inquiry and expression have been discussed as preconditions of satisfactions of the basic needs. True though these formulations may be, they do not constitute definitive answers to the question as to the motivation role of curiosity, learning, philosophizing, experimenting, etc. They are, at best, no more than partial answers.

This question is especially difficult because we know so little about the facts. Curiosity, exploration, desire for the facts, desire to know may certainly be observed easily enough. The fact that they often are pursued even at great cost to the individual's safety is an earnest of the partial character of our previous discussion. In addition, the writer must admit that, though he has sufficient clinical evidence to postulate the desire to know as a very strong drive in intelligent people, no data are available for unintelligent people. It may then be largely a function of relatively high intelligence. Rather tentatively, then, and largely in the hope of stimulating discussion and research, we shall postulate a basic desire to know, to be aware of reality, to get the facts, to satisfy curiosity, or as Wertheimer phrases it, to see rather than to be blind.

This postulation, however, is not enough. Even after we know, we are impelled to know more and more minutely and microscopically on the one hand, and on the other, more and more extensively in the direction of a world philosophy, religion, etc. The facts that we acquire, if they are isolated or atomistic, inevitably get theorized

---

[7] Clearly creative behavior, like painting, is like any other behavior in having multiple determinants. It may be seen in "innately creative" people whether they are satisfied or not, happy or unhappy, hungry or sated. Also it is clear that creative activity may be compensatory, ameliorative or purely economic. It is my impression (as yet unconfirmed) that it is possible to distinguish the artistic and intellectual products of basically satisfied people from those of basically unsatisfied people by inspection alone. In any case, here too we must distinguish, in a dynamic fashion, the overt behavior itself from its various motivations or purposes.

about, and either analyzed or organized or both. This process has been phrased by some as the search for "meaning." We shall then postulate a desire to understand, to systematize, to organize, to analyze, to look for relations and meanings.

Once these desires are accepted for discussion, we see that they too form themselves into a small hierarchy in which the desire to know is prepotent over the desire to understand. All the characteristics of a hierarchy of prepotency that we have described above, seem to hold for this one as well.

We must guard ourselves against the too easy tendency to separate these desires from the basic needs we have discussed above, *i.e.,* to make a sharp dichotomy between "cognitive" and "conative" needs. The desire to know and to understand are themselves conative, *i.e.,* have a striving character, and are as much personality needs as the "basic needs" we have already discussed (*19*).

REFERENCES

1. Adler, A. *Social interest.* London: Faber & Faber, 1938.
2. Cannon, W. B. *Wisdom of the body.* New York: Norton, 1932.
3. Freud, A. *The ego and the mechanisms of defense.* London: Hogarth, 1937.
4. Freud, S. *New introductory lectures on psychoanalysis.* New York: Norton, 1933.
5. Fromm, E. *Escape from freedom.* New York: Farrar and Rinehart, 1941.
6. Goldstein, K. *The organism.* New York: American Book Co., 1939.
7. Horney, K. *The neurotic personality of our time.* New York: Norton, 1937.
8. Kardiner, A. *The traumatic neuroses of war.* New York: Hoeber, 1941.
9. Levy, D. M. Primary affect hunger. *Amer. J. Psychiat.,* 1937, *94,* 643–652.
10. Maslow, A. H. Conflict, frustration, and the theory of threat. *J. abnorm. (soc.) Psychol.,* 1943, *38,* 81–86.
11. _____. Dominance, personality and social behavior in women. *J. soc. Psychol.,* 1939, *10,* 3–39.
12. _____. The dynamics of psychological security-insecurity. *Character & Pers.,* 1942, *10,* 331–344.
13. _____. A preface to motivation theory. *Psychosomatic Med.,* 1943, *5,* 85–92.
14. _____, & Mittelmann, B. *Principles of abnormal psychology.* New York: Harper & Bros., 1941.
15. Murray, H. A., *et al. Explorations in personality.* New York: Oxford University Press, 1938.
16. Plant, J. *Personality and the cultural pattern.* New York: Commonwealth Fund, 1937.
17. Shirley, M. Children's adjustments to a strange situation. *J. abnorm. (soc.) Psychol.,* 1942, *37,* 201–217.
18. Tolman, E. C. *Purposive behavior in animals and men.* New York: Century, 1932.
19. Wertheimer, M. Unpublished lectures at the New School for Social Research.
20. Young, P. T. *Motivation of behavior.* New York: John Wiley & Sons, 1936.
21. _____. The experimental analysis of appetite. *Psychol. Bull.,* 1941, *38,* 129–164.

Excerpts from *Contributions of Existential Psychotherapy*

Rollo May
1958

The fundamental contribution of existential therapy is its understanding of man as *being*. It does not deny the validity of dynamisms and the study of specific behavior patterns in their rightful places. But it holds that drives or dynamisms, by whatever name one calls them, can be understood only in the context of the structure of the existence of the person we are dealing with. The distinctive character of existential analysis is, thus, that it is concerned with *ontology*, the science of being, and with *Dasein*, the existence of this particular being sitting opposite the psychotherapist.

Before struggling with definitions of *being* and related terms, let us begin existentially by reminding ourselves that what we are talking about is an experience every sensitive therapist must have countless times a day. It is the experience of the instantaneous encounter with another person who comes alive to us on a very different level from what we know *about* him. "Instantaneous" refers, of course, not to the actual time involved but to the quality of the experience. We may know a great deal about a patient from his case record, let us say, and may have a fairly good idea of how other interviewers have described him. But when the patient himself steps in, we often have a sudden, sometimes powerful, experience of here-is-a-new-person, an experience that normally carries with it an element of surprise, not in the sense of perplexity or bewilderment, but in its etymological sense of being "taken from above." This is of course in no sense a criticism of one's colleagues' reports; for we have this experience of encounter even with persons we have known or worked with for a long time.[1] The data we learned *about* the patient may have been accurate and well worth learning. But the point rather is that *the grasping of the being of the other person occurs on a quite different level from our knowledge of specific things about him*. Obviously a knowledge of the drives and mechanisms which are in operation in the other person's behavior is useful; a familiarity with his patterns of interpersonal relationships is highly relevant; information about his social conditioning, the meaning of particular gestures and symbolic actions is of course to the point, and so on *ad infinitum*. But all these fall on to a quite different level when we confront the overarching, most real fact of all—namely, the immediate, living person himself. When we find that all our voluminous knowledge about the person suddenly forms itself into a new pattern in this confrontation, the implication is not that the knowledge was wrong; it is rather that it takes its meaning, form, and significance from the reality of the person of whom these specific things are expressions. Nothing we are saying here in the

[1] We may have it with friends and loved ones. It is not a once-and-for-all experience; indeed, in any developing, growing relationship it may—probably should, if the relationship is vital—occur continually.

slightest deprecates the importance of gathering and studying seriously all the specific data one can get about the given person. This is only common sense. But neither can one close his eyes to the experiential fact that this data forms itself into a configuration given in the encounter with the person himself. This also is illustrated by the common experience we all have had in interviewing persons; we may say we do not get a "feeling" of the other person and need to prolong the interview until the data "breaks" into its own form in our minds. We particularly do not get this "feeling" when we ourselves are hostile or resenting the relationship—that is, keeping the other person out—no matter how intellectually bright we may be at the time. This is the classical distinction between *knowing* and *knowing about*. When we seek to know a person, the knowledge *about* him must be subordinated to the overarching fact of his actual existence.

In the ancient Greek and Hebrew languages the verb "to know" is the same word as that which means "to have sexual intercourse." This is illustrated time and again in the King James translation of the Bible—"Abraham knew his wife and she conceived . . ." and so on. Thus the etymological relation between knowing and loving is exceedingly close. Though we cannot go into this complex topic, we can at least say that knowing another human being, like loving him, involves a kind of union, a dialectical participation with the other. This Binswanger calls the "dual mode." One must have at least a readiness to love the other person, broadly speaking, if one is to be able to understand him.

The encounter with the being of another person has the power to shake one profoundly and may potentially be very anxiety-arousing. It may also be joy-creating. In either case, it has the power to grasp and move one deeply. The therapist understandably may be tempted for his own comfort to abstract himself from the encounter by thinking of the other as just a "patient" or by focusing only on certain mechanisms of behavior. But if the technical view is used dominantly in the relating to the other person, obviously one has defended himself from anxiety at the price not only of the isolation of himself from the other but also of radical distortion of reality. For one does not then really *see* the other person. It does not disparage the importance of technique to point out that technique, like data, must be subordinated to the fact of the reality of two persons in the room.

This point has been admirably made in a slightly different way by Sartre. If we "consider man," he writes, "as capable of being analyzed and reduced to original data, to determined drives (or 'desires'), supported by the subject as properties of an object," we may indeed end up with an imposing system of substances which we may then call mechanisms or dynamisms or patterns. But we find ourselves up against a dilemma. Our human being has

become "a sort of indeterminate clay which would have to receive [the desires] passively—or he would be reduced to a simple bundle of these irreducible drives or tendencies. In either case the *man* disappears; we can no longer find 'the one' to whom this or that experience has happened."[2]

I. TO BE AND NOT TO BE

It is difficult enough to give definitions of "being" and *Dasein,* but our task is made doubly difficult by the fact that these terms and their connotations encounter much resistance. Some readers may feel that these words are only a new form of "mysticism" (used in its disparaging and quite inaccurate sense of "misty") and have nothing to do with science. But this attitude obviously dodges the whole issue by disparaging it. It is interesting that the term "mystic" is used in this derogatory sense to mean anything we cannot segmentize and count. The odd belief prevails in our culture that a thing or experience is not real if we cannot make it mathematical, and somehow it must be real if we can reduce it to numbers. But this means making an abstraction out of it—mathematics is the abstraction par excellence, which is indeed its glory and the reason for its great usefulness. Modern Western man thus finds himself in the strange situation, after reducing something to an abstraction, of having then to persuade himself it is real. This has much to do with the sense of isolation and loneliness which is endemic in the modern Western world; for the only experience we let ourselves believe in as real is that which precisely is not. Thus we deny the reality of our own experience. The term "mystic," in this disparaging sense, is generally used in the service of obscurantism; certainly avoiding an issue by derogation is only to obscure it. Is not the scientific attitude rather, to try to see clearly what it is we are talking about and then to find whatever terms or symbols can

---

[2] Jean-Paul Sartre, *Being and Nothingness,* trans. by Hazel Barnes (1956), p. 561. Sartre goes on, ". . . either in looking for the *person* we encounter a useless, contradictory metaphysical substance—or else the being whom we seek vanishes in a dust of phenomena bound together by external connections. But what each of us requires in this very effort to comprehend another is that he should never resort to this idea of substance, which is inhuman because it is well this side of the human" (p. 52). Also, "If we admit that the person is a totality, we can not hope to reconstruct him by an addition or by an organization of the diverse tendencies which we have empirically discovered in him. . . ." Every attitude of the person contains some reflection of this totality, holds Sartre. "A jealousy of a particular date in which a subject posits himself in history in relation to a certain woman, signifies for the one who knows how to interpret it, the total relation to the world by which the subject constitutes himself as a self. In other words this *empirical attitude* is by itself the expression of the 'choice of an intelligible character.' There is no mystery about this" (p. 58).

best, with least distortion, describe this reality? It should not so greatly surprise us to find that "being" belongs to that class of realities, like "love" and "consciousness" (for two other examples), which we cannot segmentize or abstract without losing precisely what we set out to study. This does not, however, relieve us from the task of trying to understand and describe them.

A more serious source of resistance is one that runs through the whole of modern Western society—namely, the psychological need to avoid and, in some ways, repress, the whole concern with "being." In contrast to other cultures which may be very concerned with being—particularly Indian and Oriental—and other historical periods which have been so concerned, the characteristic of our period in the West, as Marcel rightly phrases it, is precisely that the awareness of "the sense of the ontological —the sense of being—is lacking. Generally speaking, modern man is in this condition; if ontological demands worry him at all, it is only dully, as an obscure impulse."[3]

Marcel points out what many students have emphasized, that this loss of the sense of being is related on one hand to our tendency to subordinate existence to function: a man knows himself not as a man or self but as a ticket-seller in the subway, a grocer, a professor, a vice president of A.T.&T., or by whatever his economic function may be. And on the other hand, this loss of the sense of being is related to the mass collectivist trends and widespread conformist tendencies in our culture. Marcel then makes this trenchant challenge: "*Indeed I wonder if a psychoanalytic method, deeper and more discerning than any that has been evolved until now, would not reveal the morbid effects of the repression of this sense and of the ignoring of this need.*"[4]

"As for defining the word 'being,'" Marcel goes on, "let us admit that it is extremely difficult; I would merely suggest this method of approach: being is what withstands—or what would withstand—an exhaustive analysis bearing on the data of experience and aiming to reduce them step by step to elements increasingly devoid of intrinsic or significant value. (An analysis of this kind is attempted in the theoretical works of Freud.)"[5] This last sentence I take to mean that when Freud's analysis is pushed to the ultimate extreme, and we know, let us say, everything about drives, instincts, and mechanisms, we have everything *except* being. Being is that which remains. It is that which constitutes this infinitely complex set of deterministic factors into a person to *whom* the experiences happen and who possess some element, no

matter how minute, of freedom to become aware that these forces are acting upon him. This is the sphere where he has the potential capacity to pause before reacting and thus to cast some weight on whether his reaction will go this way or that. And this, therefore, is the sphere where he, the human being, is never merely a collection of drives and determined forms of behavior.

The term the existential therapists use for the distinctive character of human existence is *Dasein*. Binswanger, Kuhn, and others designate their school as *Daseinsanalyse*. Composed of *sein* (being) plus *da* (there), *Dasein* indicates that man is the being who is *there* and implies also that he *has* a "there" in the sense that he can know he is there and can take a stand with reference to that fact. The "there" is moreover not just any place, but the particular "there" that is mine, the particular point *in time* as well as space of my existence at this given moment. Man is the being who can be conscious of, and therefore responsible for, his existence. It is this capacity to become aware of his own being which distinguishes the human being from other beings. The existential therapists think of man not only as "being-in-itself," as all beings are, but also as "being-for-itself." Binswanger and other authors . . . speak of "*Dasein* choosing" this or that, meaning "the person-who-is-responsible-for-his-existence choosing. . . ."

The full meaning of the term "human being" will be clearer if the reader will keep in mind that "being" is a participle, a verb form implying that someone is in the process of *being something*. It is unfortunate that, when used as a general noun in English, the term "being" connotes a static substance, and when used as a particular noun such as *a* being, it is usually assumed to refer to an entity, say, such as a soldier to be counted as a unit. Rather, "being" should be understood, when used as a general noun, to mean *potentia*, the source of potentiality; "being" is the potentiality by which the acorn becomes the oak or each of us becomes what he truly is. And when used in a particular sense, such as *a* human being, it always has the dynamic connotation of someone in process, the person being something. Perhaps, therefore, *becoming* connotes more accurately the meaning of the term in this country. We can understand another human being only as we see what he is moving toward, what he is becoming; and we can know ourselves only as we "project our *potentia* in action." The significant tense for human beings is thus the *future*—that is to say, the critical question is what I am pointing toward, becoming, what I will be in the immediate future.

Thus, being in the human sense is not given once and for all. It does not unfold automatically as the oak tree does from the acorn. For an intrinsic and inseparable element in being human is self-consciousness. Man (or *Dasein*) is the particular being who has to be aware of

<hr>

[3] Gabriel Marcel. *The Philosophy of Existence* (1949), p. 1.

[4] *Ibid.* Italics mine. For data concerning the "morbid effects of the repression" of the sense of being, cf. Fromm, *Escape from Freedom*, and David Riesman, *The Lonely Crowd*.

[5] *Ibid.*, p. 5.

himself, be responsible for himself, if he is to become himself. He also is that particular being who knows that at some future moment he will not be; he is the being who is always in a dialectical relation with non-being, death. And he not only knows he will sometime not be, but he can, in his own choices, slough off and forfeit his being. "To be and not to be"—the "and" in our subtitle to this section is not a typographical error—is not a choice one makes once and for all at the point of considering suicide; it reflects to some degree a choice made at every instant. The profound dialectic in the human being's awareness of his own being is pictured with incomparable beauty by Pascal:

Man is only a reed, the feeblest reed in nature, but he is a thinking reed. There is no need for the entire universe to arm itself in order to annihilate him: a vapour, a drop of water, suffices to kill him. But were the universe to crush him, man would yet be more noble than that which slays him, because he knows that he dies, and the advantage that the universe has over him; of this universe knows nothing.[6]

---

[6] Pascal's *Penseés,* Gertrude B. Burfurd Rawlings, trans. and ed. (Peter Pauper Press), p. 35. Pascal goes on, "Thus all our dignity lies in thought. By thought we must raise ourselves, not by space and time, which we cannot fill. Let us strive, then, to think well,—therein is the principle of morality." It is perhaps well to remark that of course by "thought" he means not intellectualism nor technical reason but self-consciousness, the reason which also knows the reasons of the heart.

Some Issues Concerning the Control of Human Behavior: A Symposium

Carl R. Rogers
and B. F. Skinner
1956

I   [SKINNER]

Science is steadily increasing our power to influence, change, mold—in a word, control—human behavior. It has extended our "understanding" (whatever that may be) so that we deal more successfully with people in non-scientific ways, but it has also identified conditions or variables which can be used to predict and control behavior in a new, and increasingly rigorous, technology. The broad disciplines of government and economics offer examples of this, but there is special cogency in those contributions of anthropology, sociology, and psychology which deal with individual behavior. Carl Rogers has listed some of the achievements to date in a recent paper (1). Those of his examples which show or imply the control of the single organism are primarily due, as we should expect, to psychology. It is the experimental study of behavior which carries us beyond awkward or inaccessible "principles," "factors," and so on, to variables which can be directly manipulated.

It is also, and for more or less the same reasons, the

conception of human behavior emerging from an experimental analysis which most directly challenges traditional views. Psychologists themselves often do not seem to be aware of how far they have moved in this direction. But the change is not passing unnoticed by others. Until only recently it was customary to deny the possibility of a rigorous science of human behavior by arguing, either that a lawful science was impossible because man was a free agent, or that merely statistical predictions would always leave room for personal freedom. But those who used to take this line have become more vociferous in expressing their alarm at the way these obstacles are being surmounted.

Now, the control of human behavior has always been unpopular. Any undisguised effort to control usually arouses emotional reactions. We hesitate to admit, even to ourselves, that we are engaged in control, and we may refuse to control, even when this would be helpful, for fear of criticism. Those who have explicitly avowed an interest in control have been roughly treated by history. Machiavelli is the great prototype. As Macaulay said of him, "Out of his surname they coined an epithet for a knave and out of his Christian name a synonym for the devil." There were obvious reasons. The control that Machiavelli analyzed and recommended, like most political control, used techniques that were aversive to the con-

Note. From "Some issues concerning the control of human behavior" by C. R. Rogers and B. F. Skinner, 1956, *Science, 124,* 1057–1066. Copyright 1956 by the American Association for the Advancement of Science. Reprinted by permission.

trollee. The threats and punishments of the bully, like those of the government operating on the same plan, are not designed—whatever their success—to endear themselves to those who are controlled. Even when the techniques themselves are not aversive, control is usually exercised for the selfish purposes of the controller and, hence, has indirectly punishing effects upon others.

Man's natural inclination to revolt against selfish control has been exploited to good purpose in what we call the philosophy and literature of democracy. The doctrine of the rights of man has been effective in arousing individuals to concerted action against governmental and religious tyranny. The literature which has had this effect has greatly extended the number of terms in our language which express reactions to the control of men. But the ubiquity and ease of expression of this attitude spells trouble for any science which may give birth to a powerful technology of behavior. Intelligent men and women, dominated by the humanistic philosophy of the past two centuries, cannot view with equanimity what Andrew Hacker has called "the specter of predictable man" (2). Even the statistical or actuarial prediction of human events, such as the number of fatalities to be expected on a holiday weekend, strikes many people as uncanny and evil, while the prediction and control of individual behavior is regarded as little less than the work of the devil. I am not so much concerned here with the political or economic consequences for psychology, although research following certain channels may well suffer harmful effects. We ourselves, as intelligent men and women, and as exponents of Western thought, share these attitudes. They have already interfered with the free exercise of a scientific analysis, and their influence threatens to assume more serious proportions.

Three broad areas of human behavior supply good examples. The first of these—*personal control*—may be taken to include person-to-person relationships in the family, among friends, in social and work groups, and in counseling and psychotherapy. Other fields are *education* and *government*. A few examples from each will show how nonscientific preconceptions are affecting our current thinking about human behavior.

Personal Control

People living together in groups come to control one another with a technique which is not inappropriately called "ethical." When an individual behaves in a fashion acceptable to the group, he receives admiration, approval, affection, and many other reinforcements which increase the likelihood that he will continue to behave in that fashion. When his behavior is not acceptable, he is criticized, censured, blamed, or otherwise punished. In the first case

the group calls him "good"; in the second, "bad." This practice is so thoroughly ingrained in our culture that we often fail to see that it is a technique of control. Yet we are almost always engaged in such control, even though the reinforcements and punishments are often subtle.

The practice of admiration is an important part of a culture, because behavior which is otherwise inclined to be weak can be set up and maintained with its help. The individual is especially likely to be praised, admired, or loved when he acts for the group in the face of great danger, for example, or sacrifices himself or his possessions, or submits to prolonged hardship, or suffers martyrdom. These actions are not admirable in any absolute sense, but they require admiration if they are to be strong. Similarly, we admire people who behave in original or exceptional ways, not because such behavior is itself admirable, but because we do not know how to encourage original or exceptional behavior in any other way. The group acclaims independent, unaided behavior in part because it is easier to reinforce than to help.

As long as this technique of control is misunderstood, we cannot judge correctly an environment in which there is less need for heroism, hardship, or independent action. We are likely to argue that such an environment is itself less admirable or produces less admirable people. In the old days, for example, young scholars often lived in undesirable quarters, ate unappetizing or inadequate food, performed unprofitable tasks for a living or to pay for necessary books and materials or publication. Older scholars and other members of the group offered compensating reinforcement in the form of approval and admiration for these sacrifices. When the modern graduate student receives a generous scholarship, enjoys good living conditions, and has his research and publication subsidized, the grounds for evaluation seem to be pulled from under us. Such a student no longer *needs* admiration to carry him over a series of obstacles (no matter how much he may need it for other reasons), and, in missing certain familiar objects of admiration, we are likely to conclude that such *conditions* are less admirable. Obstacles to scholarly work may serve as a useful measure of motivation—and we may go wrong unless some substitute is found—but we can scarcely defend a deliberate harassment of the student for this purpose. The productivity of any set of conditions can be evaluated only when we have freed ourselves of the attitudes which have been generated in us as members of an ethical group.

A similar difficulty arises from our use of punishment in the form of censure or blame. The concept of responsibility and the related concepts of foreknowledge and choice are used to justify techniques of control using punishment. Was So-and-So aware of the probable consequences of his action, and was the action deliberate? If so, we are justified in punishing him. But what does this mean? It appears to be a question concerning the efficacy of the contingent relations between behavior and punishing consequences. We punish behavior because it is objectionable to us or the group, but in a minor refinement of rather recent origin we have come to withhold punishment when it cannot be expected to have any effect. If the objectionable consequences of an act were accidental and not likely to occur again, there is no point in punishing. We say that the individual was not "aware of the consequences of his action" or that the consequences were not "intentional." If the action could not have been avoided —if the individual "had no choice"—punishment is also withheld, as it is if the individual is incapable of being changed by punishment because he is of "unsound mind." In all these cases—different as they are—the individual is held "not responsible" and goes unpunished.

Just as we say that it is "not fair" to punish a man for something he could not help doing, so we call it "unfair" when one is rewarded beyond his due or for something he could not help doing. In other words, we also object to wasting *reinforcers* where they are not needed or will do no good. We make the same point with the words *just* and *right*. Thus we have no right to punish the irresponsible, and a man has no right to reinforcers he does not earn or deserve. But concepts of choice, responsibility, justice, and so on, provide a most inadequate analysis of efficient reinforcing and punishing contingencies because they carry a heavy semantic cargo of a quite different sort, which obscures any attempt to clarify controlling practices or to improve techniques. In particular, they fail to prepare us for techniques based on other than aversive techniques of control. Most people would object to forcing prisoners to serve as subjects of dangerous medical experiments, but few object when they are induced to serve by the offer of return privileges—even when the reinforcing effect of these privileges has been created by forcible deprivation. In the traditional scheme the right to refuse guarantees the individual against coercion or an unfair bargain. But to what extent *can* a prisoner refuse under such circumstances?

We need not go so far afield to make the point. We can observe our own attitude toward personal freedom in the way we resent any interference with what we want to do. Suppose we want to buy a car of a particular sort. Then we may object, for example, if our wife urges us to buy a less expensive model and to put the difference into a new refrigerator. Or we may resent it if our neighbor questions our need for such a car or our ability to pay for it. We would certainly resent it if it were illegal to buy such a car (remember Prohibition); and if we find we cannot actually afford it, we may resent governmental control of the price through tariffs and taxes. We resent it if we discover that we cannot get the car because the manufacturer is holding the model in deliberately short supply in order to push a model we

do not want. In all this we assert our democratic right to buy the car of our choice. We are well prepared to do so and to resent any restriction on our freedom.

But why do we not ask *why* it is the car of our choice and resent the forces which made it so? Perhaps our favorite toy as a child was a car, of a very different model, but nevertheless bearing the name of the car we now want. Perhaps our favorite TV program is sponsored by the manufacturer of that car. Perhaps we have seen pictures of many beautiful or prestigeful persons driving it—in pleasant or glamorous places. Perhaps the car has been designed with respect to our motivational patterns: the device on the hood is a phallic symbol; or the horsepower has been stepped up to please our competitive spirit in enabling us to pass other cars swiftly (or, as the advertisements say, "safely"). The concept of freedom that has emerged as part of the cultural practice of our group makes little or no provision for recognizing or dealing with these kinds of control. Concepts like "responsibility" and "rights" are scarcely applicable. We are prepared to deal with coercive measures, but we have no traditional recourse with respect to other measures which in the long run (and especially with the help of science) may be much more powerful and dangerous.

Education

The techniques of education were once frankly aversive. The teacher was usually older and stronger than his pupils and was able to "make them learn." This meant that they were not actually taught but were surrounded by a threatening world from which they could escape only by learning. Usually they were left to their own resources in discovering how to do so. Claude Coleman has published a grimly amusing reminder of these older practices (3). He tells of a schoolteacher who published a careful account of his services during 51 years of teaching, during which he administered: ". . . 911,527 blows with a cane; 124,010 with a rod; 20,989 with a ruler; 136,715 with the hand; 10,295 over the mouth; 7,905 boxes on the ear; [and] 1,115,800 slaps on the head. . . ."

Progressive education was a humanitarian effort to substitute positive reinforcement for such aversive measures, but in the search for useful human values in the classroom it has never fully replaced the variables it abandoned. Viewed as a branch of behavioral technology, education remains relatively inefficient. We supplement it, and rationalize it, by admiring the pupil who learns *for himself;* and we often attribute the learning process, or knowledge itself, to something *inside* the individual. We admire behavior which seems to have inner sources. Thus we admire one who *recites* a poem more than one who simply *reads* it. We admire one who *knows* the answer more than one who *knows where to look it up*. We admire the *writer* rather than the *reader*. We admire the arithmetician who can do a problem in his head rather than with a slide rule or calculating machine, or in "original" ways rather than by a strict application of rules. In general we feel that any aid or "crutch"—except those aids to which we are now thoroughly accustomed—reduces the credit due. In Plato's *Phaedrus,* Thamus, the king, attacks the invention of the alphabet on similar grounds! He is afraid "it will produce forgetfulness in the minds of those who learn to use it, because they will not practice their memories. . . ." In other words, he holds it more admirable to remember than to use a memorandum. He also objects that pupils "will read many things without instruction . . . [and] will therefore seem to know many things when they are for the most part ignorant." In the same vein we are today sometimes contemptuous of book learning, but, as educators, we can scarcely afford to adopt this view without reservation.

By admiring the student for knowledge and blaming him for ignorance, we escape some of the responsibility of teaching him. We resist any analysis of the educational process which threatens the notion of inner wisdom or questions the contention that the fault of ignorance lies with the student. More powerful techniques which bring about the same changes in behavior by manipulating *external* variables are decried as brainwashing or thought control. We are quite unprepared to judge effective educational measures. As long as only a few pupils learn much of what is taught, we do not worry about uniformity or regimentation. We do not fear the feeble technique; but we should view with dismay a system under which every student learned everything listed in a syllabus—although such a condition is far from unthinkable. Similarly, we do not fear a system which is so defective that the student must *work* for an education; but we are loath to give credit for anything learned without effort—although this could well be taken as an ideal result—and we flatly refuse to give credit if the student already knows what a school teaches.

A world in which people are wise and good without trying, without "having to be," without "choosing to be," could conceivably be a far better world for everyone. In such a world we should not have to "give anyone credit"— we should not need to admire anyone—for being wise and good. From our present point of view we cannot believe that such a world would be admirable. We do not even permit ourselves to imagine what it would be like.

Government

Government has always been the special field of aversive control. The state is frequently defined in terms of the power to punish, and jurisprudence leans heavily upon the associated notion of personal responsibility. Yet it is becoming increasingly difficult to reconcile current practice and theory with these earlier views. In criminology, for example, there is a strong tendency to drop the notion of responsibility in favor of some such alternative as capacity or controllability. But no matter how strongly the facts, or even practical expedience, support such a change, it is difficult to make the change in a legal system designed on a different plan. When governments resort to other techniques (for example, positive reinforcement), the concept of responsibility is no longer relevant and the theory of government is no longer applicable.

The conflict is illustrated by two decisions of the Supreme Court in the 1930's which dealt with, and disagreed on, the definition of control or coercion (4, p. 233). The Agricultural Adjustment Act proposed that the Secretary of Agriculture make "rental or benefit payments" to those farmers who agreed to reduce production. The government agreed that the Act would be unconstitutional if the farmer had been *compelled* to reduce production but was not, since he was merely *invited* to do so. Justice Roberts (4) expressed the contrary majority view of the court that "The power to confer or withhold unlimited benefits is the power to coerce or destroy." This recognition of positive reinforcement was withdrawn a few years later in another case in which Justice Cardozo (4, p. 244) wrote "To hold that motive or temptation is equivalent to coercion is to plunge the law in endless difficulties." We may agree with him, without implying that the proposition is therefore wrong. Sooner or later the law must be prepared to deal with all possible techniques of governmental control.

The uneasiness with which we view government (in the broadest possible sense) when it does not use punishment is shown by the reception of my utopian novel, *Walden Two* (4a). This was essentially a proposal to apply a behavioral technology to the construction of a workable, effective, and productive pattern of government. It was greeted with wrathful violence. *Life* magazine called it "a travesty on the good life," and "a menace . . . a triumph of mortmain or the dead hand not envisaged since the days of Sparta . . . a slur upon a name, a corruption of an impulse." Joseph Wood Krutch devoted a substantial part of his book, *The Measure of Man* (5), to attacking my views and those of the protagonist, Frazier, in the same vein, and Morris Viteles has recently criticized the book in a similar manner in *Science* (6). Perhaps the reaction is best expressed in a quotation from *The Quest for Utopia* by Negley and Patrick (7):

Halfway through this contemporary utopia, the reader may feel sure, as we did, that this is a beautifully ironic satire on what has been called "behavioral engineering." The longer one stays in this better world of the psychologist, however, the plainer it becomes that the inspiration is not satiric, but messianic. This is indeed the behaviorally engineered society, and while it was to be expected that sooner or later the principle of psychological condition-ing would be made the basis of a serious construction of utopia—Brown anticipated it in *Limanora*—yet not even the effective satire of Huxley is adequate prepara-tion for the shocking horror of the idea when positively presented. Of all the dictatorships espoused by uto-pists, this is the most profound, and incipient dictators might well find in this utopia a guidebook of political practice.

One would scarcely guess that the authors are talking about a world in which there is food, clothing, and shelter for all, where everyone chooses his own work and works on the average only 4 hours a day, where music and the arts flourish, where personal relationships develop under the most favorable circumstances, where education pre-pares every child for the social and intellectual life which lies before him, where—in short—people are truly happy, secure, productive, creative, and forward-looking. What is wrong with it? Only one thing: someone "planned it that way." If these critics had come upon a society in some remote corner of the world which boasted similar advantages, they would undoubtedly have hailed it as providing a pattern we all might well follow—provided that it was clearly the result of a natural process of cultural evolution. Any evidence that intelligence had been used in arriving at this version of the good life would, in their eyes, be a serious flaw. No matter if the planner of *Walden Two* diverts none of the proceeds of the community to his own use, no matter if he has no current control or is, indeed, unknown to most of the other mem-bers of the community (he planned that, too), somewhere back of it all he occupies the position of prime mover. And this, to the child of the democratic tradition, spoils it all.

The dangers inherent in the control of human behavior are very real. The possibility of the misuse of scientific knowledge must always be faced. We cannot escape by denying the power of a science of behavior or arresting its development. It is no help to cling to familiar philoso-phies of human behavior simply because they are more reassuring. As I have pointed out elsewhere (8), the new techniques emerging from a science of behavior must be subject to the explicit countercontrol which has already been applied to earlier and cruder forms. Brute force and deception, for example, are now fairly generally sup-pressed by ethical practices and by explicit governmental and religious agencies. A similar countercontrol of scien-tific knowledge in the interests of the group is a feasible and promising possibility. Although we cannot say how devious the course of its evolution may be, a cultural

pattern of control and countercontrol will presumably emerge which will be most widely supported because it is most widely reinforcing.

If we cannot foresee all the details of this (as we obvi-ously cannot), it is important to remember that this is true of the critics of science as well. The dire consequences of new techniques of control, the hidden menace in original cultural designs—these need some proof. It is only another example of my present point that the need for proof is so often overlooked. Man has got himself into some pretty fixes, and it is easy to believe that he will do so again. But there is a more optimistic possibility. The slow growth of the methods of science, now for the first time being applied to human affairs, *may* mean a new and exciting phase of human life to which historical analogies will not apply and in which earlier political slogans will not be appropriate. If we are to use the knowledge that a science of behavior is now making available with any hope of success, we must look at human nature as it is brought into focus through the methods of science rather than as it has been presented to us in a series of historical accidents.

If the advent of a powerful science of behavior causes trouble, it will not be because science itself is inimical to human welfare but because older conceptions have not yielded easily or gracefully. We expect resistance to new techniques of control from those who have heavy invest-ments in the old, but we have no reason to help them preserve a series of principles that are not ends in them-selves but rather outmoded means to an end. What is needed is a new conception of human behavior which is compatible with the implications of a scientific analysis. All men control and are controlled. The question of gov-ernment in the broadest possible sense is not how free-dom is to be preserved but what kinds of control are to be used and to what ends. Control must be analyzed and considered in its proper proportions. No one, I am sure, wishes to develop new master-slave relationships or bend the will of the people to despotic rulers in new ways. These are patterns of control appropriate to a world with-out science. They may well be the first to go when the experimental analysis of behavior comes into its own in the design of cultural practices.

II [ROGERS]

There are, I believe, a number of matters in connection with this important topic on which the authors of this article, and probably a large majority of psychologists, are in agreement. These matters then are not issues as far as we are concerned, and I should like to mention them briefly in order to put them to one side.

Points of Agreement

I am sure we agree that men—as individuals and as societies—have always endeavored to understand, predict, influence, and control human behavior—their own behavior and that of others.

I believe we agree that the behavioral sciences are making and will continue to make increasingly rapid progress in the understanding of behavior, and that as a consequence the capacity to predict and to control behavior is developing with equal rapidity.

I believe we agree that to deny these advances, or to claim that man's behavior cannot be a field of science, is unrealistic. Even though this is not an issue for us, we should recognize that many intelligent men still hold strongly to the view that the actions of men are free in some sense such that scientific knowledge of man's behavior is impossible. Thus Reinhold Niebuhr, the noted theologian, heaps scorn on the concept of psychology as a science of man's behavior and even says, "In any event, no scientific investigation of past behavior can become the basis of predictions of future behavior" (9). So, while this is not an issue for psychologists, we should at least notice in passing that it is an issue for many people.

I believe we are in agreement that the tremendous potential power of a science which permits the prediction and control of behavior may be misused, and that the possibility of such misuse constitutes a serious threat.

Consequently Skinner and I are in agreement that the whole question of the scientific control of human behavior is a matter with which psychologists and the general public should concern themselves. As Robert Oppenheimer told the American Psychological Association last year (10) the problems that psychologists will pose for society by their growing ability to control behavior will be much more grave than the problems posed by the ability of physicists to control the reactions of matter. I am not sure whether psychologists generally recognize this. My impression is that by and large they hold a laissez-faire attitude. Obviously Skinner and I do not hold this laissez-faire view, or we would not have written this article.

Points at Issue

With these several points of basic and important agreement, are there then any issues that remain on which there are differences? I believe there are. They can be stated very briefly: Who will be controlled? Who will exercise control? What type of control will be exercised?

Most important of all, toward what end or what purpose, or in the pursuit of what value, will control be exercised?

It is on questions of this sort that there exist ambiguities, misunderstandings, and probably deep differences. These differences exist among psychologists, among members of the general public in this country, and among various world cultures. Without any hope of achieving a final resolution of these questions, we can, I believe, put these issues in clearer form.

Some Meanings

To avoid ambiguity and faulty communication, I would like to clarify the meanings of some of the terms we are using.

Behavioral science is a term that might be defined from several angles but in the context of this discussion it refers primarily to knowledge that the existence of certain describable conditions in the human being and/or in his environment is followed by certain describable consequences in his actions.

Prediction means the prior identification of behaviors which then occur. Because it is important in some things I wish to say later, I would point out that one may predict a highly specific behavior, such as an eye blink, or one may predict a class of behaviors. One might correctly predict "avoidant behavior," for example, without being able to specify whether the individual will run away or simply close his eyes.

The word *control* is a very slippery one, which can be used with any one of several meanings. I would like to specify three that seem most important for our present purpose. *Control* may mean: (i) The setting of conditions by B for A, A having no voice in the matter, such that certain predictable behaviors then occur in A. I refer to this as external control. (ii) The setting of conditions by B for A, A giving some degree of consent to these conditions, such that certain predictable behaviors that occur in A. I refer to this as the influence of B on A. (iii) The setting of conditions by A such that certain predictable behaviors then occur in himself. I refer to this as internal control. It will be noted that Skinner lumps together the first two meanings, external control and influence, under the concept of control. I find this confusing.

Usual Concept of Control of Human Behavior

With the underbrush thus cleared away (I hope), let us review very briefly the various elements that are involved in the usual concept of the control of human behavior as mediated by the behavioral sciences. I am drawing here on the previous writings of Skinner, on his present statements, on the writings of others who have considered in either friendly or antagonistic fashion the meanings that would be involved in such control. I have not excluded the science fiction writers, as reported recently by Vandenburg (*11*), since they often show an awareness of the issues involved, even though the methods described are as yet fictional. These then are the elements that seem common to these different concepts of the application of science to human behavior.

1) There must first be some sort of decision about goals. Usually desirable goals are assumed, but sometimes, as in George Orwell's book *1984,* the goal that is selected is an aggrandizement of individual power with which most of us would disagree. In a recent paper Skinner suggests that one possible set of goals to be assigned to the behavioral technology is this: "Let men be happy, informed, skillful, well-behaved and productive" (*12*). In the first draft of his part of this article, which he was kind enough to show me, he did not mention such definite goals as these, but desired "improved" educational practices, "wiser" use of knowledge in government, and the like. In the final version of his article he avoids even these value-laden terms, and his implicit goal is the very general one that scientific control of behavior is desirable, because it would perhaps bring "a far better world for everyone."

Thus the first step in thinking about the control of human behavior is the choice of goals, whether specific or general. It is necessary to come to terms in some way with the issue, "For what purpose?"

2) A second element is that, whether the end selected is highly specific or is a very general one such as wanting "a better world," we proceed by the methods of science to discover the means to these ends. We continue through further experimentation and investigation to discover more effective means. The method of science is self-correcting in thus arriving at increasingly effective ways of achieving the purpose we have in mind.

3) The third aspect of such control is that as the conditions or method are discovered by which to reach the goal, some person or some group establishes these conditions and uses these methods, having in one way or another obtained the power to do so.

4) The fourth element is the exposure of individuals to the prescribed conditions, and this leads, with a high degree of probability, to behavior which is in line with the goals desired. Individuals are now happy, if that has been the goal, or well-behaved, or submissive, or whatever it has been decided to make them.

5) The fifth element is that if the process I have described is put in motion then there is a continuing social organization which will continue to produce the types of behavior that have been valued.

Some Flaws

Are there any flaws in this way of viewing the control of human behavior? I believe there are. In fact the only element in this description with which I find myself in agreement is the second. It seems to me quite incontrovertibly true that the scientific method is an excellent way to discover the means by which to achieve our goals. Beyond that, I feel many sharp differences, which I will try to spell out.

I believe that in Skinner's presentation here and in his previous writings, there is a serious underestimation of the problem of power. To hope that the power which is being made available by the behavioral sciences will be exercised by the scientists, or by a benevolent group, seems to me a hope little supported by either recent or distant history. It seems far more likely that behavior scientists, holding their present attitude, will be in the position of the German rocket scientists specializing in guided missiles. First they worked devotedly for Hitler to destroy the U.S.S.R. and the United States. Now, depending on who captured them, they work devotedly for the U.S.S.R. in the interest of destroying the United States, or devotedly for the United States in the interest of destroying the U.S.S.R. If behavioral scientists are concerned solely with advancing their science, it seems most probable that they will serve the purposes of whatever individual or group has the power.

But the major flaw I see in this review of what is involved in the scientific control of human behavior is the denial, misunderstanding, or gross underestimation of the place of ends, goals or values in their relationship to science. This error (as it seems to me) has so many implications that I would like to devote some space to it.

Ends and Values in Relation to Science

In sharp contradiction to some views that have been advanced, I would like to propose a two-pronged thesis: (i) In any scientific endeavor—whether "pure" or applied science—there is a prior subjective choice of the purpose or value which that scientific work is perceived as serving. (ii) This subjective value choice which brings the scientific endeavor into being must always lie outside of that endeavor and can never become a part of the science involved in that endeavor.

Let me illustrate the first point from Skinner himself. It is clear that in his earlier writing (*12*) it is recognized that a prior value choice is necessary, and it is specified as the goal that men are to become happy, well-behaved, productive, and so on. I am pleased that Skinner has retreated from the goals he then chose, because to me they seem to be stultifying values. I can only feel that he was choosing these goals for others, not for himself. I would hate to see Skinner become "well-behaved," as that term would be defined for him by behavioral scientists. His recent article in the *American Psychologist* (13) shows that he certainly does not want to be "productive" as that value is defined by most psychologists. And the most awful fate I can imagine for him would be to have him constantly "happy." It is the fact that he is very unhappy about many things which makes me prize him.

In the first draft of his part of this article, he also included such prior value choices, saying for example, "We must decide how we are to use the knowledge which a science of human behavior is now making available." Now he has dropped all mention of such choices, and if I understand him correctly, he believes that science can proceed without them. He has suggested this view in another recent paper, stating that "We must continue to experiment in cultural design . . . testing the consequences as we go. Eventually the practices which make for the greatest biological and psychological strength of the group will presumably survive" (8, p. 549).

I would point out, however, that to choose to experiment is a value choice. Even to move in the direction of perfectly random experimentation is a value choice. To test the consequences of an experiment is possible only if we have first made a subjective choice of a criterion value. And implicit in his statement is a valuing of biological and psychological strength. So even when trying to avoid such choice, it seems inescapable that a prior subjective value choice is necessary for any scientific endeavor, or for any application of scientific knowledge.

I wish to make it clear that I am not saying that values cannot be included as a subject of science. It is not true that science deals only with certain classes of "facts" and that these classes do not include values. It is a bit more complex than that, as a simple illustration or two may make clear.

If I value knowledge of the "three R's" as a goal of education, the methods of science can give me increasingly accurate information on how this goal may be achieved. If I value problem-solving ability as a goal of education, the scientific method can give me the same kind of help.

Now, if I wish to determine whether problem-solving ability is "better" than knowledge of the three R's, then scientific method can also study those two values but *only*—and this is very important—in terms of some other value which I have subjectively chosen. I may value college success. Then I can determine whether problem-solving ability or knowledge of the three R's is most closely associated with that value. I may value personal integration or vocational success or responsible citizenship. I can determine whether problem-solving ability or knowledge of the three R's is "better" for achieving any

one of these values. But the value or purpose that gives meaning to a particular scientific endeavor must always lie outside of that endeavor.

Although our concern in this symposium is largely with applied science, what I have been saying seems equally true of so-called "pure" science. In pure science the usual prior subjective value choice is the discovery of truth. But this is a subjective choice, and science can never say whether it is the best choice, save in the light of some other value. Geneticists in the U.S.S.R., for example, had to make a subjective choice of whether it was better to pursue truth or to discover facts which upheld a governmental dogma. Which choice is "better"? We could make a scientific investigation of those alternatives but only in the light of some other subjectively chosen value. If, for example, we value the survival of a culture, then we could begin to investigate with the methods of science the question of whether pursuit of truth or support of governmental dogma is most closely associated with cultural survival.

My point then is that any endeavor in science, pure or applied, is carried on in the pursuit of a purpose or value that is subjectively chosen by persons. It is important that this choice be made explicit, since the particular value which is being sought can never be tested or evaluated, confirmed or denied, by the scientific endeavor to which it gives birth. The initial purpose or value always and necessarily lies outside the scope of the scientific effort which it sets in motion.

Among other things this means that if we choose some particular goal or series of goals for human beings and then set out on a large scale to control human behavior to the end of achieving those goals, we are locked in the rigidity of our initial choice, because such a scientific endeavor can never transcend itself to select new goals. Only subjective human persons can do that. Thus if we chose as our goal the state of happiness for human beings (a goal deservedly ridiculed by Aldous Huxley in *Brave New World*), and if we involved all of society in a successful scientific program by which people became happy, we would be locked in a colossal rigidity in which no one would be free to question this goal, because our scientific operations could not transcend themselves to question their guiding purposes. And without laboring this point, I would remark that colossal rigidity, whether in dinosaurs or dictatorships, has a very poor record of evolutionary survival.

If, however, a part of our scheme is to set free some "planners" who do not have to be happy, who are not controlled, and who are therefore free to choose other values, this has several meanings. It means that the purpose we have chosen as our goal is not a sufficient and a satisfying one for human beings but must be supplemented. It also means that if it is necessary to set up an elite group which is free, then this shows all too clearly that the great majority are only the slaves—no matter by what high-sounding name we call them—of those who select the goals.

Perhaps, however, the thought is that a continuing scientific endeavor will evolve its own goals; that the initial findings will alter the directions, and subsequent findings will alter them still further, and that science somehow develops its own purpose. Although he does not clearly say so, this appears to be the pattern Skinner has in mind. It is surely a reasonable description, but it overlooks one element in this continuing development, which is that subjective personal choice enters in at every point at which the direction changes. The findings of a science, the results of an experiment, do not and never can tell us what next scientific purpose to pursue. Even in the purest of science, the scientist must decide what the findings mean and must subjectively choose what next step will be most profitable in the pursuit of his purpose. And if we are speaking of the application of scientific knowledge, then it is distressingly clear that the increasing scientific knowledge of the structure of the atom carries with it no necessary choice as to the purpose to which this knowledge will be put. This is a subjective personal choice which must be made by many individuals.

Thus I return to the proposition with which I began this section of my remarks—and which I now repeat in different words. Science has its meaning as the objective pursuit of a purpose which has been subjectively chosen by a person or persons. This purpose or value can never be investigated by the particular scientific experiment or investigation to which it has given birth and meaning. Consequently, any discussion of the control of human beings by the behavioral sciences must first and most deeply concern itself with the subjectively chosen purposes which such an application of science is intended to implement.

Is the Situation Hopeless?

The thoughtful reader may recognize that, although my remarks up to this point have introduced some modifications in the conception of the processes by which human behavior will be controlled, these remarks may have made such control seem, if anything, even more inevitable. We might sum it up this way: Behavioral science is clearly moving forward; the increasing power for control which it gives will be held by someone or some group; such an individual or group will surely choose the values or goals to be achieved; and most of us will then be increasingly controlled by means so subtle that we will not even be aware of them as control. Thus, whether a council of wise psychologists (if this is not a contradiction

in terms), or a Stalin, or a Big Brother has the power, and whether the goal is happiness, or productivity, or resolution of the Oedipus complex, or submission, or love of Big Brother, we will inevitably find ourselves moving toward the chosen goal and probably thinking that we ourselves desire it. Thus, if this line of reasoning is correct, it appears that some form of *Walden Two* or of *1984* (and at a deep philosophic level they seem indistinguishable) is coming. The fact that it would surely arrive piecemeal, rather than all at once, does not greatly change the fundamental issues. In any event, as Skinner has indicated in his writings, we would then look back upon the concepts of human freedom, the capacity for choice, the responsibility for choice, and the worth of the human individual as historical curiosities which once existed by cultural accident as values in a prescientific civilization.

I believe that any person observant of trends must regard something like the foregoing sequence as a real possibility. It is not simply a fantasy. Something of that sort may even be the most likely future. But is it an inevitable future? I want to devote the remainder of my remarks to an alternative possibility.

Alternative Set of Values

Suppose we start with a set of ends, values, purposes, quite different from the type of goals we have been considering. Suppose we do this quite openly, setting them forth as a possible value choice to be accepted or rejected. Suppose we select a set of values that focuses on fluid elements of process rather than static attributes. We might then value: man as a process of becoming, as a process of achieving worth and dignity through the development of his potentialities; the individual human being as a self-actualizing process, moving on to more challenging and enriching experiences; the process by which the individual creatively adapts to an ever-new and changing world; the process by which knowledge transcends itself, as, for example, the theory of relativity transcended Newtonian physics, itself to be transcended in some future day by a new perception.

If we select values such as these we turn to our science and technology of behavior with a very different set of questions. We will want to know such things as these: Can science aid in the discovery of new modes of richly rewarding living? more meaningful and satisfying modes of interpersonal relationships? Can science inform us on how the human race can become a more intelligent participant in its own evolution—its physical, psychological and social evolution? Can science inform us on ways of releasing the creative capacity of individuals, which seem so necessary if we are to survive in this fantastically expanding atomic age? Oppenheimer has pointed out

(*14*) that knowledge, which used to double in millennia or centuries, now doubles in a generation or a decade. It appears that we must discover the utmost in release of creativity if we are to be able to adapt effectively. In short, can science discover the methods by which man can most readily become a continually developing and self-transcending process, in his behavior, his thinking, his knowledge? Can science predict and release an essentially "unpredictable" freedom?

It is one of the virtues of science as a method that it is as able to advance and implement goals and purposes of this sort as it is to serve static values, such as states of being well-informed, happy, obedient. Indeed we have some evidence of this.

Small Example

I will perhaps be forgiven if I document some of the possibilities along this line by turning to psychotherapy, the field I know best.

Psychotherapy, as Meerloo (*15*) and others have pointed out, can be one of the most subtle tools for the control of A by B. The therapist can subtly mold individuals in imitation of himself. He can cause an individual to become a submissive and conforming being. When certain therapeutic principles are used in extreme fashion, we call it brainwashing, an instance of the disintegration of the personality and a reformulation of the person along lines desired by the controlling individual. So the principles of therapy can be used as an effective means of external control of human personality and behavior. Can psychotherapy be anything else?

Here I find the developments going on in client-centered psychotherapy (*16*) an exciting hint of what a behavioral science can do in achieving the kinds of values I have stated. Quite aside from being a somewhat new orientation in psychotherapy, this development has important implications regarding the relation of a behavioral science to the control of human behavior. Let me describe our experience as it relates to the issues of this discussion.

In client-centered therapy, we are deeply engaged in the prediction and influencing of behavior, or even the control of behavior. As therapists, we institute certain attitudinal conditions, and the client has relatively little voice in the establishment of these conditions. We predict that if these conditions are instituted, certain behavioral consequences will ensue in the client. Up to this point this is largely external control, no different from what Skinner has described, and no different from what I have discussed in the preceding sections of this article. But here any similarity ceases.

The conditions we have chosen to establish predict such behavioral consequences as these: that the client will become self-directing, less rigid, more open to the evidence of his senses, better organized and integrated, more similar to the ideal which he has chosen for himself. In other words, we have established by external control conditions which we predict will be followed by internal control by the individual, in pursuit of internally chosen goals. We have set the conditions which predict various classes of behaviors—self-directing behaviors, sensitivity to realities within and without, flexible adaptiveness—which are by their very nature unpredictable in their specifics. Our recent research (*17*) indicates that our predictions are to a significant degree corroborated, and our commitment to the scientific method causes us to believe that more effective means of achieving these goals may be realized.

Research exists in other fields—industry, education, group dynamics—which seem to support our own findings. I believe it may be conservatively stated that scientific progress has been made in identifying those conditions in an interpersonal relationship which, if they exist in B, are followed in A by greater maturity in behavior, less dependence on others, an increase in expressiveness as a person, an increase in variability, flexibility and effectiveness of adaptation, an increase in self-responsibility and self-direction. And, quite in contrast to the concern expressed by some, we do not find that the creatively adaptive behavior which results from such self-directed variability of expression is a "happy accident" which occurs in "chaos." Rather, the individual who is open to his experience, and self-directing, is harmonious not chaotic, ingenious rather than random, as he orders his responses imaginatively toward the achievement of his own purposes. His creative actions are no more a "happy accident" than was Einstein's development of the theory of relativity.

Thus we find ourselves in fundamental agreement with John Dewey's statement: "Science has made its way by releasing, not by suppressing, the elements of variation, of invention and innovation, of novel creation in individuals" (*18*). Progress in personal life and in group living is, we believe, made in the same way.

Possible Concept of the Control of Human Behavior

It is quite clear that the point of view I am expressing is in sharp contrast to the usual conception of the relationship of the behavioral sciences to the control of human behavior. In order to make this contrast even more blunt, I will state this possibility in paragraphs parallel to those used before.

1) It is possible for us to choose to value man as a self-actualizing process of becoming; to value creativity, and the process by which knowledge becomes self-transcending.

2) We can proceed, by the methods of science, to discover the conditions which necessarily precede these processes and, through continuing experimentation, to discover better means of achieving these purposes.

3) It is possible for individuals or groups to set these conditions, with a minimum of power or control. According to present knowledge, the only authority necessary is the authority to establish certain qualities of interpersonal relationship.

4) Exposed to these conditions, present knowledge suggests that individuals become more self-responsible, make progress in self-actualization, become more flexible, and become more creatively adaptive.

5) Thus such an initial choice would inaugurate the beginnings of a social system or subsystem in which values, knowledge, adaptive skills, and even the concept of science would be continually changing and self-transcending. The emphasis would be upon man as a process of becoming.

I believe it is clear that such a view as I have been describing does not lead to any definable utopia. It would be impossible to predict its final outcome. It involves a step-by-step development, based on a continuing subjective choice of purposes, which are implemented by the behavioral sciences. It is in the direction of the "open society," as that term has been defined by Popper (*19*), where individuals carry responsibility for personal decisions. It is at the opposite pole from his concept of the closed society, of which *Walden Two* would be an example.

I trust it is also evident that the whole emphasis is on process, not on end-states of being. I am suggesting that it is by choosing to value certain qualitative elements of the process of becoming that we can find a pathway toward the open society.

The Choice

It is my hope that we have helped to clarify the range of choice which will lie before us and our children in regard to the behavioral sciences. We can choose to use our growing knowledge to enslave people in ways never dreamed of before, depersonalizing them, controlling them by means so carefully selected that they will perhaps never be aware of their loss of personhood. We can choose to utilize our scientific knowledge to make men happy, well-behaved, and productive, as Skinner earlier suggested. Or we can insure that each person learns all the syllabus which we select and set before him, as Skinner

now suggests. Or at the other end of the spectrum of choice we can choose to use the behavioral sciences in ways which will free, not control; which will bring about constructive variability, not conformity; which will develop creativity, not contentment; which will facilitate each person in his self-directed process of becoming; which will aid individuals, groups, and even the concept of science to become self-transcending in freshly adaptive ways of meeting life and its problems. The choice is up to us, and, the human race being what it is, we are likely to stumble about, making at times some nearly disastrous value choices and at other times highly constructive ones.

I am aware that to some, this setting forth of a choice is unrealistic, because a choice of values is regarded as not possible. Skinner has stated: "Man's vaunted creative powers . . . his capacity to choose and our right to hold him responsible for his choice—none of these is conspicuous in this new self-portrait (provided by science). Man, we once believed, was free to express himself in art, music, and literature, to inquire into nature, to seek salvation in his own way. He could initiate action and make spontaneous and capricious changes of course. . . . But science insists that action is initiated by forces impinging upon the individual, and that caprice is only another name for behavior for which we have not yet found a cause" (*12*, pp. 52–53).

I can understand this point of view, but I believe that it avoids looking at the great paradox of behavioral science. Behavior, when it is examined scientifically, is surely best understood as determined by prior causation. This is one great fact of science. But responsible personal choice, which is the most essential element in being a person, which is the core experience in psychotherapy, which exists prior to any scientific endeavor, is an equally prominent fact in our lives. To deny the experience of responsible choice is, to me, as restricted a view as to deny the possibility of a behavioral science. That these two important elements of our experience appear to be in contradiction has perhaps the same significance as the contradiction between the wave theory and the corpuscular theory of light, both of which can be shown to be true, even though incompatible. We cannot profitably deny our subjective life, any more than we can deny the objective description of that life.

In conclusion then, it is my contention that science cannot come into being without a personal choice of the values we wish to achieve. And these values we choose to implement will forever lie outside of the science which implements them; the goals we select, the purposes we wish to follow, must always be outside of the science which achieves them. To me this has the encouraging meaning that the human person, with his capacity of subjective choice, can and will always exist, separate from and prior to any of his scientific undertakings. Unless as individuals and groups we choose to relinquish our capacity of subjective choice, we will always remain persons, not simply pawns of a self-created science.

III [SKINNER]

I cannot quite agree that the practice of science *requires* a prior decision about goals or a prior choice of values. The metallurgist can study the properties of steel and the engineer can design a bridge without raising the question of whether a bridge is to be built. But such questions are certainly frequently raised and tentatively answered. Rogers wants to call the answers "subjective choices of values." To me, such an expression suggests that we have had to abandon more rigorous scientific practices in order to talk about our own behavior. In the experimental analysis of other organisms I would use other terms, and I shall try to do so here. Any list of values is a list of reinforcers—conditioned or otherwise. We are so constituted that under certain circumstances food, water, sexual contact, and so on, will make any behavior which produces them more likely to occur again. Other things may acquire this power. We do not need to say that an organism chooses to eat rather than to starve. If you answer that it is a very different thing when a man chooses to starve, I am only too happy to agree. If it were not so, we should have cleared up the question of choice long ago. An organism can be reinforced by—can be made to "choose"—almost any given state of affairs.

Rogers is concerned with choices that involve multiple and usually conflicting consequences. I have dealt with some of these elsewhere (20) in an analysis of self-control. Shall I eat these delicious strawberries today if I will then suffer an annoying rash tomorrow? The decision I am to make used to be assigned to the province of ethics. But we are now studying similar combinations of positive and negative consequences, as well as collateral conditions which affect the result, in the laboratory. Even a pigeon can be taught some measure of self-control! And this work helps us to understand the operation of certain formulas—among them value judgments—which folk-wisdom, religion, and psychotherapy have advanced in the interests of self-discipline. The observable effect of any statement of value is to alter the relative effectiveness of reinforcers. We may no longer enjoy the strawberries for thinking about the rash. If rashes are made sufficiently shameful, illegal, sinful, maladjusted, or unwise, we may glow with satisfaction as we push the strawberries aside in a grandiose avoidance response which would bring a smile to the lips of Murray Sidman.

People behave in ways which, as we say, conform to ethical, governmental, or religious patterns because they are reinforced for doing so. The resulting behavior may

have far-reaching consequences for the survival of the pattern to which it conforms. And whether we like it or not, survival is the ultimate criterion. This is where, it seems to me, science can help—not in choosing a goal, but in enabling us to predict the survival value of cultural practices. Man has too long tried to get the kind of world he wants by glorifying some brand of immediate reinforcement. As science points up more and more of the remoter consequences, he may begin to work to strengthen behavior, not in a slavish devotion to a chosen value, but with respect to the ultimate survival of mankind. Do not ask me why I want mankind to survive. I can tell you why only in the sense in which the physiologist can tell you why I want to breathe. Once the relation between a given step and the survival of my group has been pointed out, I will take that step. And it is the business of science to point out just such relations.

The values I have occasionally recommended (and Rogers has not led me to recant) are transitional. Other things being equal, I am betting on the group whose practices make for healthy, happy, secure, productive, and creative people. And I insist that the values recommended by Rogers are transitional, too, for I can ask him the same kind of question. Man as a process of becoming—*what?* Self-actualization—for what? Inner control is no more a goal than external.

What Rogers seems to me to be proposing, both here and elsewhere (1), is this: Let us use our increasing power of control to create individuals who will not need and perhaps will no longer respond to control. Let us solve the problem of our power by renouncing it. At first blush this seems as implausible as a benevolent despot. Yet power has occasionally been foresworn. A nation has burned its Reichstag, rich men have given away their wealth, beautiful women have become ugly hermits in the desert, and psychotherapists have become nondirective. When this happens, I look to other possible reinforcements for a plausible explanation. A people relinquish democratic power when a tyrant promises them the earth. Rich men give away wealth to escape the accusing finger of their fellowmen. A woman destroys her beauty in the hope of salvation. And a psychotherapist relinquishes control because he can thus help his client more effectively.

The solution that Rogers is suggesting is thus understandable. But is he correctly interpreting the result? What evidence is there that a client ever becomes truly *self*-directing? What evidence is there that he ever makes a truly *inner* choice of ideal or goal? Even though the therapist does not do the choosing, even though he encourages "self-actualization"—he is not out of control as long as he holds himself ready to step in when occasion demands —when, for example, the client chooses the goal of becoming a more accomplished liar or murdering his boss. But supposing the therapist does withdraw completely or is no longer necessary—what about all the other forces acting upon the client? Is the self-chosen goal independent of his early ethical and religious training? of the folk-wisdom of his group? of the opinions and attitudes of others who are important to him? Surely not. The therapeutic situation is only a small part of the world of the client. From the therapist's point of view it may appear to be possible to relinquish control. But the control passes, not to a "self," but to forces in other parts of the client's world. The solution of the therapist's problem of power cannot be *our* solution, for we must consider *all* the forces acting upon the individual.

The child who must be prodded and nagged is something less than a fully developed human being. We want to see him hurrying to his appointment, not because each step is taken in response to verbal reminders from his mother, but because certain temporal contingencies, in which dawdling has been punished and hurrying reinforced, have worked a change in his behavior. Call this a state of better organization, a greater sensitivity to reality; or what you will. The plain fact is that the child passes from a temporary verbal control exercised by his parents to control by certain inexorable features of the environment. I should suppose that something of the same sort happens in successful psychotherapy. Rogers seems to me to be saying this: Let us put an end, as quickly as possible, to any pattern of master-and-slave, to any direct obedience to command, to the submissive following of suggestions. Let the individual be free to adjust himself to more rewarding features of the world about him. In the end, let his teachers and counselors "wither away," like the Marxist state. I not only agree with this as a useful ideal, I have constructed a fanciful world to demonstrate its advantages. It saddens me to hear Rogers say that "at a deep philosophic level" *Walden Two* and George Orwell's *1984* "seem indistinguishable." They could scarcely be more unlike—at any level. The book *1984* is a picture of immediate aversive control for vicious selfish purposes. The founder of *Walden Two*, on the other hand, has built a community in which neither he nor any other person exerts any current control. His achievement lay in his original *plan*, and when he boasts of this ("It is enough to satisfy the thirstiest tyrant") we do not fear him but only pity him for his weakness.

Another critic of *Walden Two*, Andrew Hacker (*21*), has discussed this point in considering the bearing of mass conditioning upon the liberal notion of autonomous man. In drawing certain parallels between the Grand Inquisition passage in Dostoevsky's *Brothers Karamazov*, Huxley's *Brave New World,* and *Walden Two,* he attempts to set up a distinction to be drawn in any society between conditioners and conditioned. He assumes that "the conditioner can be said to be autonomous in the traditional liberal sense." But then he notes: "Of course the condi-

tioner has been conditioned. But he has not been conditioned by the conscious manipulation of another *person*." But how does this affect the resulting behavior? Can we not soon forget the origins of the "artificial" diamond which is identical with the real thing? Whether it is an "accidental" cultural pattern, such as is said to have produced the founder of *Walden Two,* or the engineering environment which is about to produce his successors, we are dealing with sets of conditions generating human behavior which will ultimately be measured by their contribution to the strength of the group. We look to the future, not the past, for the test of "goodness" or acceptability.

If we are worthy of our democratic heritage we shall, of course, be ready to resist any tyrannical use of science for immediate or selfish purposes. But if we value the achievements and goals of democracy we must not refuse to apply science to the design and construction of cultural patterns, even though we may then find ourselves in some sense in the position of controllers. Fear of control, generalized beyond any warrant, has led to a misinterpretation of valid practices and the blind rejection of intelligent planning for a better way of life. In terms which I trust Rogers will approve, in conquering this fear we shall become more mature and better organized and shall, thus, more fully actualize ourselves as human beings.

REFERENCES AND NOTES

1. C. R. Rogers, *Teachers College Record, 57,* 316 (1956).
2. A. Hacker, *Antioch Rev., 14,* 195 (1954).
3. C. Coleman, *Bull. Am. Assoc. Univ. Professors, 39,* 457 (1953).
4. P. A. Freund *et al., Constitutional Law: Cases and Other Problems,* vol. 1 (Little, Brown, Boston, 1954).
4a. B. F. Skinner, *Walden Two* (Macmillan, New York, 1948).
5. J. W. Krutch, *The Measure of Man* (Bobbs-Merrill, Indianapolis, 1953).
6. M. Viteles, *Science, 122,* 1167 (1955).
7. G. Negley and J. M. Patrick, *The Quest for Utopia* (Schuman, New York, 1952).
8. B. F. Skinner, *Trans. N.Y. Acad. Sci., 17,* 547 (1955).
9. R. Niebuhr, *The Self and the Dramas of History* (Scribner, New York, 1955), p. 47.
10. R. Oppenheimer, *Am. Psychol., 11,* 127 (1956).
11. S. G. Vandenberg, *ibid., 11,* 339 (1956).
12. B. F. Skinner, *Am. Scholar, 25,* 47 (1955–56).
13. ———, *Am. Psychol., 11,* 221 (1956).
14. R. Oppenheimer, *Roosevelt University Occasional Papers* 2 (1956).
15. J. A. M. Meerloo, *J. Nervous Mental Disease, 122,* 353 (1955).
16. C. R. Rogers, *Client-Centered Therapy* (Houghton-Mifflin, Boston, 1951).

17. _____ and R. Dymond, Eds., *Psychotherapy and Personality Change* (Univ. of Chicago Press, Chicago, 1954).
18. J. Ratner, Ed., *Intelligence in the Modern World: John Dewey's Philosophy* (Modern Library, New York, 1939), p. 359.
19. K. R. Popper, *The Open Society and Its Enemies* (Routledge and Kegan Paul, London, 1945).
20. B. F. Skinner, *Science and Human Behavior* (Macmillan, New York, 1953).
21. A. Hacker, *J. Politics, 17,* 590 (1955).

Behavior Therapy Versus Psychoanalysis: Therapeutic and Social Implications

Joseph Wolpe
1981

Abstract: *Although the specific efficacy of psychoanalytic therapy in the treatment of the neuroses has never been demonstrated, psychoanalytic theory and practices continue to dominate the field of clinical psychology. That psychoanalytic theory has not been displaced by the behavioral theory of neurosis is remarkable in view of the persuasive evidence that exists for the efficacy of behavior therapy. One reason for this seems to be the persistence of widespread misperceptions of behavior therapy. It has been represented to the public as an "inhuman" treatment that routinely resorts to electric shocks and other unpleasant agents and to the profession as a therapy incognizant of the patient's feelings or thoughts and applicable only to neuroses that are "simple," such as phobias—an image regularly reinforced by "authorities" who are misinformed. This article attempts to correct these misperceptions. It also draws attention to the suffering imposed on many by years of psychoanalysis. The promise of widespread availability of behavior therapy as an alternative will only be fulfilled when more high-quality training is funded.*

The present century has seen the birth (Jones, 1924) and the development (Ayllon & Azrin, 1968; Wolpe,

Note. From "Behavior therapy versus psychoanalysis" by J. Wolpe, 1981, *American Psychologist, 36*(2), 159–164. Copyright 1981 by the American Psychological Association. Reprinted by permission.

1958) of behavior therapy—methods of psychotherapeutic change founded on principles of learning established in the psychological laboratory. Its results in the treatment of human neuroses have been quite impressive. Paul (1966), on the basis of a survey of controlled studies on systematic desensitization, has stated, "For the first time in the history of psychological treatments, a specific therapeutic package reliably produced measurable benefits for clients across a broad range of distressing problems in which anxiety was of fundamental importance" (p. 159). Nevertheless, it is *psychoanalytic* theory that has continued to be the most pervasive influence in psychotherapeutic practice.

THE REIGN OF PSYCHOANALYSIS

According to psychoanalytic theory, mental activity is partly conscious and partly out of reach of consciousness in the "unconscious mind." Neurotic symptoms are regarded as the manifestations of emotional forces that have been "repressed" in the unconscious. Freud (1922/1950) regarded these symptoms as "compromise formations between the repressed sexual instincts and the repressive ego instincts" (p. 107). Psychoanalytic therapy aims to overcome a neurosis by bringing the putative repressed impulses into consciousness, through such means as free association and dream analysis. All the derivatives of psychoanalysis (the theories of Adler, Sullivan, and others) exert their main therapeutic effort toward making the unconscious conscious (Munroe, 1955).

The clinical effectiveness of psychoanalytic therapy has never been established. Eysenck (1966), in a review of 24 studies encompassing over 7,000 cases, concluded that the data failed to show that psychoanalytic therapy facilitates the recovery of neurotic patients. Erwin (1980) has convincingly defended Eysenck's conclusion against challenges by Bergin (1971), Bergin and Suinn (1975), and Brown and Herrnstein (1975). A particularly noteworthy study is that of the Fact-Gathering Committee of the American Psychoanalytic Association (Note 1). Out of 595 patients, 306 were judged to have been "completely analyzed" (in a mean of about 600 sessions); 210 of these were followed up afterwards, and 126 were stated to have been cured or greatly improved. This is 60% of the completely analyzed group but only about 31% of the original total.

It is customary to turn a blind eye to such poor results and to contend that the treatment is nevertheless on the right track because the psychoanalytic theory of neurosis is true. In actuality, not a single one of the theory's main propositions has ever been supported by scientifically acceptable evidence (see, e.g., Bailey, 1964; Salter, 1952; Valentine, 1946). But this too is brushed aside. That this happens is a tribute to the expository brilliance with which Freud presented his theories. His writing weaves a magic web from which few can extricate themselves once enmeshed. To the convinced it is sacrilegious to suggest the need for anything so mundane as empirical testing.

After a phase of outraged opposition to psychoanalysis early in the 20th century, converts to it were legion. In 1939, it was officially approved by the American Medical Association. By then it had become widely accepted by Western intellectuals as a philosophy of life. They saw it, in vibrant contrast to the dry abstractions of academic psychology, as a psychology of reality, dealing with things that mattered and revealing dark and mysterious aspects of the mind.

Not everybody was persuaded. There were many who saw the flaws in the theory and some who vigorously criticized it. One of the most noteworthy critics was Wohlgemuth, whose *Critical Examination of Psychoanalysis* appeared in 1923. But critiques like his had little effect—illustrating Conant's (1947) maxim that theories are not abandoned on the basis of contradictory evidence. On the other hand, Conant attests that they *are* abandoned when better theories arrive on the scene. There was no better theory in 1923. But now, in 1981, a seemingly better theory—the behavioral theory of neuroses—has been with us for a quarter of a century. Yet psychoanalysis sits firmly in the clinical saddle. The first step in attempting to explain why this is so is to examine what evidence

there is that behavioral theory and the therapy that emerged from it are really better.

CONCEPTUAL ORIGINS AND THERAPEUTIC EFFICACY OF BEHAVIOR THERAPY OF NEUROSES

I shall now review the foundations of the behavioral theory of neurosis and the evidence of the clinical efficacy of behavior therapy. At the beginning of this century, Pavlov produced "experimental neuroses" in animals—a long-lasting susceptibility to the triggering of strong anxiety responses by particular stimulus conditions, a susceptibility in many respects similar to the neuroses of human beings (Wolpe, 1967). Many experimenters in the United States subsequently confirmed Pavlov's observations, often using variations of his procedure (for a review, see Wolpe, 1952). Using a method described by Dimmick, Ludlow, and Whiteman (1939), I produced experimental neuroses in cats by administering painful but non-damaging electrical stimuli (high voltage, low amperage) of two seconds' duration to an animal in a small cage (Wolpe, 1925, 1958). This stimulation elicited strong fear reactions: The animal's pupils dilated, its hair stood on end, and it breathed rapidly. Repeating the stimulation at irregular intervals of minutes resulted in the animal's becoming very fearful of the cage and surrounding stimuli in between 5 and 20 repetitions. The autonomous power of these stimuli strongly to arouse fear would have lasted the life of the animal if left untreated (Gantt, 1944). The fear was undiminished by exposures, short or long, to the experimental cage, nor was it alleviated by months of absence from the cage. In every animal, however, the fear could be systematically weakened, eventually to zero, by arranging for small amounts of it (evoked at first by generalized stimuli) to be inhibited by the competition of eating behavior. This suggested that a therapeutic principle resided in response competition. Clinical trials showed that the competition of feeding also overcame children's fears (Jones, 1924) but not those of adults (Wolpe & Wolpe, in press). Fortunately, a considerable number of other responses were found to have the ability to inhibit and consequently to overcome adults' fears. Fear can be inhibited by the calmness generated by deep muscle relaxation, by the expression of legitimate anger in the context of certain inappropriate social fears, and by the use of sexual responses in cases of sexual fear, as well as by a number of more esoteric methods, including flooding (Wolpe, 1973).

The important question, however, is whether these experimentally derived methods actually achieve an unusual percentage of favorable results and are significantly more economical of time and effort. The answer lies in a comparison with the well-documented fact that the practitioners of practically any system of psychotherapy obtain recoveries or marked improvements in 40%–50% of the cases they treat (e.g., Eysenck, 1966). If the followers of different systems—Freudian and Jungian analysts, nondirective therapists, encounter groupers, and primal screamers—all achieve this percentage, there must be a common process working for all of them that has nothing to do with their respective techniques. The distinctive procedures of a therapeutic system cannot be said to be helpful unless a recovery rate significantly above the common baseline can be shown.

The question then becomes, Does behavior therapy improve on the common run of results? The first published statistical analysis of behavior therapy was based on my own uncontrolled clinical observations (Wolpe, 1958). In a mean of 30 sessions, 188 (89%) out of 210 neurotic cases I had treated were either apparently recovered or at least 80% improved on the criteria proposed by Knight (1941): symptomatic improvement, increased productiveness, improved adjustment in pleasure and sex, improvement in interpersonal relationships, and ability to handle ordinary psychological conflicts and reasonable reality stresses. It has since that time been commonplace for skilled behavior therapists to report marked improvement in at least 80% of their neurotic cases. A relatively recent development has been the striking success of flooding and response prevention in the treatment of those obsessive-compulsive neuroses in which the patient is preoccupied with avoiding and washing away "contamination" (Foa & Steketee, 1979; Meyer, 1966; Rachman, Hodgson, & Marzillier, 1970). These cases used to be one of psychiatry's knottiest problems; and now the great majority of patients can expect to recover or improve markedly in a matter of weeks.

Further support for behavior therapy comes from a large number of controlled studies, of which I shall mention two of the more notable. Paul (1966) had psychoanalytically oriented therapists treat severe fears of public speaking with three techniques—their own accustomed short-term in-sight therapy, systematic desensitization, and a control procedure called "attention placebo." The therapists did significantly better with systematic desensitization than with their own techniques or with attention placebo.

The second study is that of Sloane, Staples, Cristol, Yorkston, and Whipple (1975). "Mild" and "moderately severe" neurotic patients were randomly assigned to two treatments—behavior therapy or brief psychoanalytically oriented psychotherapy—or to a waiting-list control group. At the end of the four-month treatment period, on a rating scale of overall improvement, 93% of the behavior therapy patients, in contrast to 77% of the

psychotherapy and waiting-list groups, were considered either improved or recovered, a difference significant at the .05 level. Patients treated by behavior therapy also showed significant improvement in work and social adjustment, while psychotherapy patients showed only marginal improvement in work and none in social adjustment. At one year, only those who had been treated by behavior therapy showed greater improvement in target symptoms than waiting-list subjects.

THE FALSE IMAGE OF BEHAVIOR THERAPY

The use of procedures similar to those successful in extinguishing strong anxiety-response habits in experimental animals has thus increased our power to overcome unadaptive, learned anxiety-response habits in humans. Behavior therapy does what had been predicted on theoretical grounds. This is a unique achievement in the field of psychotherapy that should surely entitle the behavioral approach to center stage. Why has that position been denied it?

It is a matter of its image, which has been distorted in two major ways. To the public, behavior therapy has been represented as being made up of cruel and degrading treatments that emphasize aversive shocks and include sensory deprivation, brainwashing, electroconvulsive therapy, and psychosurgery. This is the accepted newspaper image. Mitford's (1973) book, *Kind and Usual Punishment: The Prison Business*, is particularly derogatory. This kind of vilification began with reports of treatments in prisons that were actually conducted by persons who were not behavior therapists (for a review, see Friedman, 1975). Although the accusations against behavior therapy were rebutted by Goldiamond (1975), the adverse implications have remained in the public mind. A particularly baneful influence in the same direction was the film *Clockwork Orange*, in which a repulsive and entirely fictional treatment was represented as behavior therapy.

Within the fields of psychiatry and clinical psychology, there is a widespread misperception of behavior therapy as a simplistic and perfunctory enterprise applicable only to phobias and some sexual difficulties. Its practitioners are supposed to be insensitive to and uninterested in the subtleties and complexities inherent in most human problems. One factor that has contributed to this image is the predominance of simple phobias, and especially snake phobias, in reports of research. Most damaging have been the negative opinions frequently expressed by prominent but ill-informed psychiatrists and psychologists of various orientations. For example, Marmor (1980) recently declared that behavior therapy's major emphasis is on "removing the presenting symptom or symptoms by behavior modification; and the patient's subjective problems, feelings, or thoughts are considered essentially irrelevant to the psychotherapeutic process" (p. 410). Similarly, Lazarus (1977) asserted that behavior therapy is characterized by the "eschewal of most cognitive processes" and by a view of cognitive processes as "entirely secondary to sub-cortical autonomic conditioning as the *real* basis of emotional and behavioral change" (p. 552). And Marks, a British psychiatrist who is very popular with American psychiatrists, has repeatedly proclaimed that behavior therapy is applicable to "perhaps 10% of adult psychiatric outpatients," those with phobias, obsessions, and some sexual problems (Marks, 1975, p. 254). These examples typify the stream of inaccuracies about behavior therapy that pervade the literature.

That behavior therapy is neither indifferent to patients' thoughts nor narrow in its clinical scope is quite evident from its own literature. It has been applied with success not only to phobias and sexual problems but to the whole range of neurotic problems, including the most complex social neuroses and so-called existential problems. Again and again, in a modest time span, it has secured recovery in neurotics for whom lengthy psychoanalyses have failed (e.g., Wolpe, 1958, 1964).

The accusation that behavior therapists consider their patients' "subjective problems, feelings, or thoughts" irrelevant to the psychotherapeutic process is a transparent absurdity, as I showed in detail in a previous article (Wolpe, 1978, p. 442). It is the subjective problem, the complaint, that drives the neurotic patient to seek treatment, no matter of what kind. To the behavior therapist the patient's story is the primary data. The behavior therapist carefully probes all seemingly relevant experiences because consequent therapeutic actions depend completely on an assessment of what triggers what. The patient's "feelings and thoughts" are the main source of information, augmented by various questionnaires that the patient thoughtfully answers. No therapy is more "personalized" than behavior therapy; no other therapist knows as much detail about the patient as the behavior therapist does before commencing treatment; and nobody else tailors the therapy as explicitly to the individual's problems.

The process of acquiring the necessary information, *behavior analysis,* identifies and defines the stimulus sources of anxiety and establishes the causal connections between anxiety and any consequences it may have, such as sexual difficulties, depression, obsessions and compulsions, or antisocial habits like exhibitionism and kleptomania. The behavior analysis determines which neurotic anxieties are based on autonomic conditioning and which on cognitive errors or misinformation. It is the therapist's skill in conducting this analysis that makes it possible for behavior therapy to succeed in even the most complex neuroses.

However, it is unfortunate that a great many people who use behavior therapy techniques have not learned much about behavior analysis or have not understood the need for it. They fail to identify intricate stimulus-response relations, and they do not distinguish conditioned anxiety from cognitively based anxiety. They have trouble with complex cases. They give package treatments for diagnoses like agoraphobia, a practice that Barlow (1979) aptly deplored. Inevitably, these people have much less success with patients than they would with the help of behavior analysis; and then they write articles stating that the favorable reports of the efficacy of behavior therapy are exaggerated.

SOCIAL IMPLICATIONS

The failures of psychoanalysis and the rationalizations that are given for them have very serious social consequences. One might complain that I am a biased judge, and of course I am. So let me quote from Schmideberg (1970), a distinguished psychoanalyst:

> From time to time patients come to one who have had years of unsuccessful psychotherapy and are in desperate need of help. They have been made to feel that analysis is the only worthwhile therapy, and that there must be something quite specially wrong with them if it cannot help them as it has helped others; so their depression and sense of failure are reinforced. Often it is not only their psychological condition but also their realistic situation that has deteriorated, sometimes beyond repair. (p. 195)

One of Schmideberg's illustrative examples concerns a 54-year-old man who had first sought treatment in his early twenties for various anxieties and inhibitions that were largely the manifestations of the timidity of an inexperienced young man, the son of poor parents. *Thirty years* of analysis with leading American analysts had not helped him. When he came to Schmideberg, he had spent all his money on therapy, could not afford to have an office, and had to practice his accountancy at home. Another of Schmideberg's cases was a woman of 28 who had originally had no definite symptoms, but had entered psychoanalysis in the hope of leading a fuller life and making a happy marriage. During her analysis she developed an agoraphobia, which steadily grew worse. She then continued with two other analysts, steadily deteriorating. Schmideberg first saw her after 12 years of treatment, when she was very much overweight and had lost her looks and any chance of getting married—the only thing she really wanted.

I have seen many such cases. Psychoanalytically oriented therapists rationalize lack of progress by saddling the patient with the responsibility for it. The patient is told that failure to improve is due to his or her "resistance" and not to anything wrong or inappropriate about the therapy. An impartial observer would surely question the competence or the integrity of a therapist whose skill is supposed to be to break down resistances but who fails to do this for a patient in 5 or 10 years and recommends more of the same!

To keep patients interminably in chancery is an immoral practice and a social blot on the psychological profession. We are all tainted by it. Perhaps in years gone by, one could have argued that there was nothing better to offer and that the still-suffering patient at least had the benefit of support. But it is a moral requirement of any health professional to know the state of the art in his or her field and to be able to offer patients alternatives when the methods used have failed.

At a symposium at the meeting of the American Psychiatric Association in May 1980, I asked 500 psychiatrists how many of them had *any* acquaintance with the literature of behavior therapy and about 25% raised their hands. If you had pneumonia, would you entrust yourself to an internist who confessed not seriously to have read the literature on penicillin and who, when confronted with evidence of its efficacy, expressed skepticism of that kind of thing?

What is even worse is that the purveyors of the psychoanalytic philosophy continued to control the teaching of psychotherapy in most of our departments of psychiatry and clinical psychology. The saving grace for them is the 40% or more of neurotic subjects who do well in any psychotherapeutic interview situation as a result of emotional arousal by their therapists.

How can this sorry state of affairs be changed? Perhaps to some extent by exposing, as I have here tried to do, the iniquity of these practices. But people are unlikely to change course unless they have something to gain or to lose. Now a threat looms in the recent statements from the National Institute of Mental Health and the insurance companies of their unwillingness to go on paying for psychotherapy without evidence of its efficacy.

So there is hope for tomorrow. But if tomorrow were to give behavior therapy its rightful place in the clinical world, would the abuses end, and would the public be better off? In theory, the answer is *yes*. In practice, the answer is *not yet*. In the whole of North America there are no more than 200 practitioners with adequate skills in behavior analysis. High-quality training is very hard to find. Only about a dozen programs out of more than a hundred being offered include instruction and supervision by teachers skilled in behavior analysis. This can only be remedied by a rechanneling of the mainstream of financial support for psychotherapy so that the programs needed to train good teachers and good therapists can be established. Only then will the state of the art reach and benefit the suffering public.

REFERENCE NOTE

1. American Psychoanalytic Association. *Summary and final report of the Central-Fact-Gathering Committee.* Unpublished manuscript, 1958. (For a summary, see Brody, M. W. Prognosis and results of psychoanalysis. In J. H. Nodine & J. H. Moyer [Eds.], *Psychosomatic medicine.* Philadelphia: Lea & Febiger, 1962.)

REFERENCES

Ayllon, T., & Azrin, H. N. *The token economy: A motivational system for therapy and rehabilitation.* New York: Appleton-Century-Crofts, 1968.

Bailey, P. Sigmund Freud: Scientific period (1873–1897). In J. Wolpe, A. Salter, & L. J. Reyna (Eds.), *The conditioning therapies.* New York: Holt, Rinehart & Winston, 1964.

Barlow, D. H. President's message. *Behavior Therapist,* 1979, *2,* 8.

Bergin, A. The evaluation of therapeutic outcomes. In A. E. Bergin & S. L. Garfield (Eds.), *Handbook of psychotherapy and behavior change: An empirical analysis.* New York: Wiley, 1971.

Bergin, A., & Suinn, R. M. Individual psychotherapy and behavior therapy. *Annual Review of Psychology,* 1975, *26,* 509–556.

Brown, R., & Herrnstein, R. *Psychology.* Boston: Little, Brown, 1975.

Conant, J. B. *On understanding science.* New Haven, Conn.: Yale University Press, 1947.

Dimmick, F. L., Ludlow, N., & Whiteman, A. A study of "experimental neurosis" in cats. *Journal of Comparative Psychology,* 1939, *28,* 39–43.

Erwin, E. Psychoanalytic therapy: The Eysenck argument. *American Psychologist,* 1980, *35,* 435–443.

Eysenck, H. J. *The effects of psychotherapy.* New York: Interscience, 1966.

Foa, E. B., & Steketee, G. Obsessive-compulsives: Conceptual issues and treatment interventions. In M. Hersen, R. M. Eisler, & P. M. Miller (Eds.), *Progress in behavior modification* (Vol. 8). New York: Academic Press, 1979.

Freud, S. Psychoanalysis. In E. Jones (Ed.), *Collected papers* (Vol. 5). London: Hogarth, 1950. (Originally published, 1922.)

Friedman, P. R. Legal regulation of applied behavior analysis in mental institutions and prisons. *Arizona Law Review,* 1975, *17,* 39–104.

Gantt, W. H. Experimental basis for neurotic behavior. *Psychosomatic Medicine Monograph,* 1944, *3,* Nos. 3 & 4.

Goldiamond, I. Singling out behavior modification for legal regulations: Some effects on patient care psychotherapy and research in general. *Arizona Law Review,* 1975, *17,* 105–126.

Jones, M. C. The elimination of children's fears. *Journal of Experimental Psychology,* 1924, *7,* 382–390.

Knight, R. P. Evaluation of the results of psychoanalytic therapy. *American Journal of Psychiatry,* 1941, *98,* 434.

Lazarus, A. Has behavior therapy outlived its usefulness? *American Psychologist,* 1977, *32,* 550–554.

Marks, I. M. Behavioral treatments of phobic and obsessive-compulsive disorders: A critical appraisal. In M. Hersen, R. M. Eisler, & P. M. Miller (Eds.), *Progress in behavior modification.* New York: Academic Press, 1975.

Marmor, J. Recent trends in psychotherapy. *American Journal of Psychiatry,* 1980, *137,* 409–416.

Meyer, V. Modifications of expectations in cases with obsessional rituals. *Behaviour Research and Therapy,* 1966, *4,* 273–280.

Mitford, J. *Kind and usual punishment: The prison business.* New York: Knopf, 1973.

Munroe, R. *Schools of psychoanalytic thought.* New York: Holt, Rinehart & Winston, 1955.

Paul, G. L. *Insight versus desensitization in psychotherapy.* Stanford, Calif.: Stanford University Press, 1966.

Rachman, S. J., Hodgson, R. J., & Marzillier, J. Treatment of an obsessional-compulsive disorder by modelling. *Behavioural Research and Therapy,* 1970, *8,* 385–390.

Salter, A. *The case against psychoanalysis.* New York: Holt, Rinehart & Winston, 1952.

Schmideberg, M. Psychotherapy with failures of psychoanalysis. *British Journal of Psychiatry,* 1970, *116,* 195–200.

Sloane, R. B., Staples, F. R., Cristol, A. H., Yorkston, N. J. & Whipple, K. *Psychotherapy versus behavior therapy.* Cambridge, Mass.: Harvard University Press, 1975.

Valentine, C. W. *The psychology of early childhood* (3rd ed.). London: Methuen, 1946.

Wohlgemuth, A. *A critical examination of psychoanalysis.* London: Allen & Unwin, 1923.

Wolpe, J. Experimental neurosis as learned behavior. *British Journal of Psychology,* 1952, *43,* 243–268.

Wolpe, J. *Psychotherapy by reciprocal inhibition.* Stanford, Calif.: Stanford University Press, 1958.

Wolpe, J. Behavior therapy in complex neurotic states. *British Journal of Psychiatry,* 1964, *110,* 28–34.

Wolpe, J. Parallels between animal and human neuroses. In J. Zubin & H. F. Hunt (Eds.), *Comparative psychopathology.* New York: Grune & Stratton, 1967.

Wolpe, J. *The practice of behavior therapy* (2nd ed.). New York: Pergamon Press, 1973.

Wolpe, J. Cognition and causation in human behavior and its therapy. *American Psychologist,* 1978, *33,* 437–446.

Wolpe, J., & Wolpe, D. *Our useless fears.* Boston: Houghton Mifflin, in press.

Section III

CHILDHOOD DISORDERS

The initial selection in this section is Leo Kanner's remarkable paper that, in 1943, was the first to document the existence of a serious childhood disorder called autism. Kanner presents eleven clinical cases and then discusses the commonality of symptoms that led him to identify autism as a unique behavioral syndrome separate from childhood schizophrenia.

In the second selection, Lauretta Bender discusses the disorder designated as childhood schizophrenia. Basing her conclusions on her study of 100 schizophrenic children, Bender uses illuminating excerpts from case histories to describe the children's characteristic problems in vascular responses, growth, motor behavior, and reflex responses, among other physiological variables, and comments on their art, language, and thought.

The third article by Bruno Bettelheim is a case history of a schizophrenic child who converted himself into a mechanical boy. The seriousness of his disorder and Bettelheim's success in reaching him provide fascinating reading.

Autistic Disturbances of Affective Contact

Leo Kanner
1943

To understand and measure emotional qualities is very difficult. Psychologists and educators have been struggling with that problem for years but we are still unable to measure emotional and personality traits with the exactness with which we can measure intelligence.

—Rose Zeligs in *Glimpses into Child Life*

Since 1938, there have come to our attention a number of children whose condition differs so markedly and uniquely from anything reported so far, that each case merits—and, I hope, will eventually receive—a detailed consideration of its fascinating peculiarities. In this place, the limitations necessarily imposed by space call for a condensed presentation of the case material. For the same reason, photographs have also been omitted. Since none of the children of this group has as yet attained an age beyond 11 years, this must be considered a preliminary report, to be enlarged upon as the patients grow older and further observation of their development is made.

CASE 1

Donald T. was first seen in October, 1938, at the age of 5 years, 1 month. Before the family's arrival from their home town, the father sent a thirty-three-page typewritten history that, though filled with much obsessive detail,

gave an excellent account of Donald's background. Donald was born at full term on September 8, 1933. He weighed nearly 7 pounds at birth. He was breast fed, with supplementary feeding, until the end of the eighth month; there were frequent changes of formulas. "Eating," the report said, "has always been a problem with him. He has never shown a normal appetite. Seeing children eating candy and ice cream has never been a temptation to him." Dentition proceeded satisfactorily. He walked at 13 months.

At the age of 1 year "he could hum and sing many tunes accurately." Before he was 2 years old, he had "an unusual memory for faces and names, knew the names of a great number of houses" in his home town. "He was encouraged by the family in learning and reciting short poems, and even learned the Twenty-third Psalm and twenty-five questions and answers of the Presbyterian Catechism." The parents observed that "he was not learning to ask questions or to answer questions unless they pertained to rhymes or things of this nature, and often then he would ask no question except in single words." His enunciation was clear. He became interested in pictures "and very soon knew an inordinate number of pictures in a set of *Compton's Encyclopedia.*" He knew the pictures of the presidents "and knew most of the pictures of his ancestors and kinfolks on both sides of the house." He quickly learned the whole alphabet "backward as well as forward" and to count to 100.

It was observed at an early time that he was happiest when left alone, almost never cried to go with his mother, did not seem to notice his father's homecomings, and was indifferent to visiting relatives. The father made a special point of mentioning that Donald even failed to pay the slightest attention to Santa Claus in full regalia.

He seems to be self-satisfied. He has no apparent affection when petted. He does not observe the fact that anyone comes or goes, and never seems glad to see father or mother or any playmate. He seems almost to draw into his shell and live within himself. We once secured a most attractive little boy of the same age from an orphanage and brought him home to spend the summer with Donald, but Donald has never asked him a question nor answered a question and has never romped with him in play. He seldom comes to anyone when called but has to be picked up and carried or led wherever he ought to go.

In his second year, he "developed a mania for spinning blocks and pans and other round objects." At the same time, he had

A dislike for self-propelling vehicles, such as Taylor-tots, tricycles, and swings. He is still fearful of tricycles and seems to have almost a horror of them when he is forced to ride, at which time he will try to hold onto the person assisting him. This summer [1937] we bought him a playground slide and on the first afternoon when other children were sliding on it he would not get about it, and when we put him up to slide down it he seemed horror-struck. The next morning when nobody was present, however, he walked out, climbed the ladder, and slid down, and he has slid on it frequently since, but slides only when no other child is present to join him in sliding. . . . He was always constantly happy and busy entertaining himself, but resented being urged to play with certain things.

When interfered with, he had temper tantrums, during which he was destructive. He was "dreadfully fearful of being spanked or switched" but "could not associate his misconduct with his punishment."

In August, 1937, Donald was placed in a tuberculosis preventorium in order to provide for him "a change of environment." While there, he had a "disinclination to play with children and do things children his age usually take an interest in." He gained weight but developed the habit of shaking his head from side to side. He continued spinning objects and jumped up and down in ecstasy as he watched them spin. He displayed

An abstraction of mind which made him perfectly oblivious to everything about him. He appears to be always thinking and thinking, and to get his attention almost requires one to break down a mental barrier between his inner consciousness and the outside world.

The father, whom Donald resembles physically, is a successful, meticulous, hard-working lawyer who has had two "breakdowns" under strain of work. He always took every ailment seriously, taking to his bed and following doctors' orders punctiliously even for the slightest cold. "When he walks down the street, he is so absorbed in thinking that he sees nothing and nobody and cannot remember anything about the walk." The mother, a college graduate, is a calm, capable woman, to whom her husband feels vastly superior. A second child, a boy, was born to them on May 22, 1938.

Donald, when examined at the Harriet Lane Home in October, 1938, was found to be in good physical condition. During the initial observation and in a two-week study by Drs. Eugenia S. Cameron and George Frankl at the Child Study Home of Maryland, the following picture was obtained:

There was a marked limitation of spontaneous activity. He wandered about smiling, making stereotyped movements with his fingers, crossing them about in the air. He shook his head from side to side, whispering or humming the same three-note tune. He spun with great pleasure anything he could seize upon to spin. He kept throwing things on the floor, seeming to delight in the sounds they made. He arranged beads, sticks, or blocks in groups of different series of colors. Whenever he finished one of these performances, he squealed and jumped up and down. Beyond this he showed no initiative, requiring constant instruction (from his mother) in any form of activity other than the limited ones in which he was absorbed.

Most of his actions were repetitions carried out in exactly the same way in which they had been performed originally. If he spun a block, he must always start with the same face uppermost. When he threaded buttons, he arranged them in a certain sequence that had no pattern to it but happened to be the order used by the father when he first had shown them to Donald.

There were also innumerable verbal rituals recurring all day long. When he desired to get down after his nap, he said, "Boo [his word for his mother], say 'Don, do you want to get down?'"

His mother would comply, and Don would say: "Now say 'All right.'"

The mother did, and Don got down. At mealtime, repeating something that had obviously been said to him often, he said to his mother, "Say 'Eat it or I won't give you tomatoes, but if you don't eat it I will give you tomatoes,'" or "Say 'If you drink to there, I'll laugh and I'll smile.'"

And his mother had to conform or else he squealed, cried, and strained every muscle in his neck in tension. This happened all day long about one thing or another. He seemed to have much pleasure in ejaculating words or phrases, such as "Chrysanthemum"; "Dahlia, dahlia, dahlia"; "Business"; "Trumpet vine"; "The right one is on, the left one is off"; "Through the dark clouds shining." Irrelevant utterances such as these were his ordinary mode of speech. He always seemed to be parroting what he had heard said to him at one time or another. He used the personal pronouns for the persons he was quoting, even imitating the intonation. When he wanted his mother to pull his shoe off, he said: "Pull off your shoe." When he wanted a bath, he said. "Do you want a bath?"

Words to him had a specifically literal, inflexible meaning. He seemed unable to generalize, to transfer an expression to another similar object or situation. If he did so occasionally, it was a substitution, which then "stood" definitely for the original meaning. Thus he christened each of his water color bottles by the name of one of the Dionne quintuplets—Annette for blue, Cécile for red, etc. Then, going through a series of color mixtures, he proceeded in this manner: "Annette and Cécile make purple."

The colloquial request to "put that *down*" meant to him that he was to put the thing on the floor. He had a "milk glass" and a "water glass." When he spit some milk into the "water glass," the milk thereby became "white water."

The word "yes" for a long time meant that he wanted his father to put him up on his shoulder. This had a definite origin. His father, trying to teach him to say "yes" and "no," once asked him, "Do you want me to put you on my shoulder?"

Don expressed his agreement by repeating the question literally, echolalia-like. His father said, "If you want me to, say 'Yes'; if you don't want me to, say 'No.'"

Don said "yes" when asked. But thereafter "yes" came to mean that he desired to be put up on his father's shoulder.

He paid no attention to persons around him. When taken into a room, he completely disregarded the people and instantly went for objects, preferably those that could be spun. Commands or actions that could not possibly be disregarded were resented as unwelcome intrusions. But he was never angry at the interfering *person*. He angrily shoved away the *hand* that was in his way or the *foot* that stepped on one of his blocks, at one time referring to the foot on the block as "umbrella." Once the obstacle was removed, he forgot the whole affair. He gave no heed to the presence of other children but went about his favorite pastimes, walking off from the children if they were so bold as to join him. If a child took a toy from him, he passively permitted it. He scrawled lines on the picture books the other children were coloring, retreating or putting his hands over his ears if they threatened him in anger. His mother was the only person with whom he had any contact at all, and even she spent all of her time developing ways of keeping him at play with her.

After his return home, the mother sent periodic reports about his development. He quickly learned to read flu-

ently and to play simple tunes on the piano. He began, whenever his attention could be obtained, to respond to questions "which require yes or no for an answer." Though he occasionally began to speak of himself as "I" and of the person addressed as "you," he continued for quite some time the pattern of pronominal reversals. When, for instance, in February, 1939, he stumbled and nearly fell, he said of himself, "*You* did not fall down."

He expressed puzzlement about the inconsistencies of spelling: "bite" should be spelled "bight" to correspond to the spelling of "light." He could spend hours writing on the blackboard. His play became more imaginative and varied, though still quite ritualistic.

He was brought back for a check-up in May, 1939. His attention and concentration were improved. He was in better contact with his environment, and there were some direct reactions to people and situations. He showed disappointment when thwarted, demanded bribes promised him, gave evidence of pleasure when praised. It was possible, at the Child Study Home, to obtain with constant insistence some conformity to daily routine and some degree of proper handling of objects. But he still went on writing letters with his fingers in the air, ejaculating words —"Semicolon"; "Capital"; "Twelve, twelve"; "Slain, slain"; "I could put a little comma or semicolon"— chewing on paper, putting food on his hair, throwing books into the toilet, putting a key down the water drain, climbing onto the table and bureau, having temper tantrums, giggling and whispering autistically. He got hold of an encyclopedia and learned about fifteen words in the index and kept repeating them over and over again. His mother was helped in trying to develop his interest and participation in ordinary life situations.

The following are abstracts from letters sent subsequently by Donald's mother:

September, 1939. He continues to eat and to wash and dress himself only at my insistence and with my help. He is becoming resourceful, builds things with his blocks, dramatizes stories, attempts to wash the car, waters the flowers with the hose, plays store with the grocery supply, tries to cut out pictures with the scissors. Numbers still have a great attraction for him. While his play is definitely improving, he has never asked questions about people and shows no interest in our conversation. . . .

October, 1939 [a school principal friend of the mother's had agreed to try Donald in the first grade of her school]. The first day was very trying for them but each succeeding day he has improved very much. Don is much more independent, wants to do many things for himself. He marches in line nicely, answers when called upon, and is more biddable and obedient. He never voluntarily relates any of his experiences at school and never objects to going. . . .

November, 1939. I visited his room this morning and was amazed to see how nicely he cooperated and responded. He was very quiet and calm and listened to what the teacher was saying about half the time. He does not squeal or run around but takes his place like the other children. The teacher began writing on the board. That immediately attracted his attention. She wrote:

BETTY MAY FEED A FISH.

DON MAY FEED A FISH.

JERRY MAY FEED A FISH.

In his turn he walked up and drew a circle around his name. Then he fed a goldfish. Next, each child was given his weekly reader, and he turned to the proper page as the teacher directed and read when called upon. He also answered a question about one of the pictures. Several times, when pleased, he jumped up and down and shook his hand once while answering. . . .

March, 1940. The greatest improvement I notice is his awareness of things about him. He talks very much more and asks a good many questions. Not often does he voluntarily tell me of happenings at school, but if I ask leading questions, he answers them correctly. He really enters into the games with other children. One day he enlisted the family in one game he had just learned, telling each of us just exactly what to do. He feeds himself some better and is better able to do things for himself. . . .

March, 1941. He has improved greatly, but the basic difficulties are still evident. . . .

Donald was brought for another check-up in April, 1941. An invitation to enter the office was disregarded, but he had himself led willingly. Once inside, he did not even glance at the three physicians present (two of whom he well remembered from his previous visits) but immediately made for the desk and handled papers and books. Questions at first were met with the stereotyped reply, "I don't know." He then helped himself to pencil and paper and wrote and drew pages and pages full of letters of the alphabet and a few simple designs. He arranged the letters in two or three lines, reading them in vertical rather than horizontal succession, and was very much pleased with the result. Occasionally he volunteered a statement or question: "I am going to stay for two days at the Child Study Home." Later he said, "Where is my mother?"

"Why do you want her?" he was asked.

"I want to hug her around the neck."

He used pronouns adequately and his sentences were grammatically correct.

The major part of his "conversation" consisted of questions of an obsessive nature. He was inexhaustible in bringing up variations: "How many days in a week, years in a century, hours in a day, hours in half a day, weeks in a century, centuries in half a millennium," etc., etc.; "How many pints in a gallon, how many gallons to fill four gallons?" Sometimes he asked, "How many hours in a minute, how many days in an hour?" etc. He looked thoughtful and always wanted an answer. At times he temporarily compromised by responding quickly to some other question or request but promptly returned to the same type of behavior. Many of his replies were metaphorical or otherwise peculiar. When asked to subtract 4 from 10, he answered: "I'll draw a hexagon."

He was still extremely autistic. His relation to people had developed only in so far as he addressed them when he needed or wanted to know something. He never looked at the person while talking and did not use communicative gestures. Even this type of contact ceased the moment he was told or given what he had asked for.

A letter from the mother stated in October, 1942:

Don is still indifferent to much that is around him. His interests change often, but always he is absorbed in some kind of silly, unrelated subject. His literal-mindedness is still very marked, he wants to spell words as they sound and to pronounce letters consistently. Recently I have been able to have Don do a few chores around the place to earn picture show money. He really enjoys the movies now but not with any idea of a connected story. He remembers them in the order in which he sees them. Another of his recent hobbies is with old issues of *Time* magazine. He found a copy of the first issue of March 3, 1923, and had attempted to make a list of the dates of publication of each issue since that time. So far he has gotten to April, 1934. He has figured the number of issues in a volume and similar nonsense.

CASE 2

Frederick W. was referred on May 27, 1942, at the age of 6 years, with the physician's complaint that his "adaptive behavior in a social setting is characterized by attacking as well as withdrawing behavior." His mother stated:

The child has always been self-sufficient. I could leave him alone and he'd entertain himself very happily, walking around, singing. I have never known him to cry in demanding attention. He was never interested in hide-and-seek, but he'd roll a ball back and forth, watch his father shave, hold the razor box and put the razor back in, put the lid on the soap box. He never was very good with cooperative play. He doesn't care to play with the ordinary things that other children play with, anything with wheels on. He is afraid of mechanical things; he runs from them. He used to be afraid of my egg beater, is perfectly petrified of my vacuum cleaner. Elevators are simply a terrifying experience to him. He is afraid of spinning tops.

Until the last year, he mostly ignored other people. When we had guests, he just wouldn't pay any attention.

He looked curiously at small children, and then would go off all alone. He acted as if people weren't there at all, even with his grandparents. About a year ago, he began showing more interest in observing them, would even go up to them. But usually people are an interference. He'll push people away from him. If people come too close to him, he'll push them away. He doesn't want me to touch him or put my arm around him, but he'll come and touch *me*.

To a certain extent, he likes to stick to the same thing. On one of the bookshelves we had three pieces in a certain arrangement. Whenever this was changed, he always rearranged it in the old pattern. He won't try new things, apparently. After watching for a long time, he does it all of a sudden. He wants to be sure he does it right.

He has said at least two words ["Daddy" and "Dora," the mother's first name] before he was 2 years old. From then on, between 2 and 3 years, he would say words that seemed to come as a surprise to himself. He'd say them once and never repeat them. One of the first words he said was "overalls." [The parents never expected him to answer any of their questions, were *once* surprised when he did give an answer—"Yes"]. At about 2½ years, he began to sing. He sang about twenty or thirty songs, including a little French lullaby. In his fourth year, I tried to make him ask for things before he'd get them. He was stronger-willed than I was and held out longer, and he would not get it but he never gave in about it. Now he can count up into the hundreds and can add numbers, but he is not interested in numbers as they apply to objects. He has great difficulty in learning the proper use of personal pronouns. When receiving a gift, he would say of himself: "You say 'Thank you.'"

He bowls, and when he sees the pins go down, he'll jump up and down in great glee.

Frederick was born May 23, 1936, in breech presentation. The mother had "some kidney trouble" and an elective cesarean section was performed about two weeks before term. He was well after birth; feeding presented no problem. The mother recalled that he was never observed to assume an anticipatory posture when she prepared to pick him up. He sat up at 7 months, walked at about 18 months. He had occasional colds but no other illness. Attempts to have him attend nursery school were unsuccessful: "he would either be retiring and hide in a corner or would push himself into the middle of a group and be very aggressive."

The boy is an only child. The father, aged 44, a university graduate and a plant pathologist, has traveled a great deal in connection with his work. He is a patient, even-tempered man, mildly obsessive; as a child he did not talk "until late" and was delicate, supposedly "from lack of vitamin in diet allowed in Africa." The mother, aged 40, a college graduate, successively a secretary to physicians, a purchasing agent, director of secretarial studies in a girls' school, and at one time a teacher of history, is described as healthy and even-tempered.

The paternal grandfather organized medical missions in Africa, studied tropical medicine in England, became an authority on manganese mining in Brazil, was at the same time dean of a medical school and director of an art museum in an American city, and is listed in *Who's Who* under two different names. He disappeared in 1911, his whereabouts remaining obscure for twenty-five years. It was then learned that he had gone to Europe and married a novelist, without obtaining a divorce from his first wife. The family considers him "a very strong character of the genius type, who wanted to do as much good as he could."

The paternal grandmother is described as "a dyed-in-the-wool missionary if ever there was one, quite dominating and hard to get along with, at present pioneering in the South at a college for mountaineers."

The father is the second of five children. The oldest is a well known newspaperman and author of a best-seller. Next comes a brother who writes for adventure magazines. The youngest, a painter, writer, and radio commentator, "did not talk until he was about 6 years old," and the first words he is reported to have spoken were "When a lion can't talk he can whistle."

The mother said of her own relatives, "Mine are very ordinary people." Her family is settled in a Wisconsin town, where her father is a banker; her mother is "mildly interested" in church work, and her three sisters, all younger than herself, are average middle-class matrons.

Frederick was admitted to the Harriet Lane Home on May 27, 1942. He appeared to be well nourished. The circumference of his head was 21 inches, of his chest 22 inches, of his abdomen 21 inches. His occiput and frontal region were markedly prominent. There was a supernumerary nipple in the left axilla. Reflexes were sluggish but present. All other findings, including laboratory examinations and X ray of his skull, were normal, except for large and ragged tonsils.

He was led into the psychiatrist's office by a nurse, who left the room immediately afterward. His facial expression was tense, somewhat apprehensive, and gave the impression of intelligence. He wandered aimlessly about for a few moments, showing no sign of awareness of the three adults present. He then set down on the couch, ejaculating unintelligible sounds, and then abruptly lay down, wearing throughout a dreamy-like smile. When he responded to questions or commands at all, he did so by repeating them echolalia fashion. The most striking feature in his behavior was the difference in his reactions to objects and to people. Objects absorbed him easily and he showed good attention and perseverance in playing with them. He seemed to regard people as unwelcome intruders to whom he paid as little attention as they would permit. When forced to respond, he did so briefly and returned to his absorption in things. When a hand was held out before him so that he could not possibly ignore it, he played with it briefly as if it were a detached object. He blew out a match with an expression of satisfaction with the achievement, but did not look up to the person who had lit the match. When a fourth person entered the room, he retreated for a minute or two behind the bookcase, saying, "I don't want you," and waving him away, then resumed his play, paying no further attention to him or anyone else.

Test results (Grace Arthur performance scale) were difficult to evaluate because of his lack of cooperation. He did best with the Seguin form board (shortest time, 58 seconds). In the mare and foal completion test he seemed to be guided by form entirely, to the extent that it made no difference whether the pieces were right side up or not. He completed the triangle but not the rectangle. With all the form boards he showed good perseverance and concentration, working at them spontaneously and interestedly. Between tests, he wandered about the room examining various objects or fishing in the wastebasket without regard for the persons present. He made frequent sucking noises and occasionally kissed the dorsal surface of his hand. He became fascinated with the circle from the form board, rolling it on the desk and attempting, with occasional success, to catch it just before it rolled off.

Frederick was enrolled at the Devereux Schools on September 26, 1942.

CASE 3

Richard M. was referred to the Johns Hopkins Hospital on February 5, 1941, at 3 years, 3 months of age, with the complaint of deafness because he did not talk and did not respond to questions. Following his admission, the interne made this observation:

> The child seems quite intelligent, playing with the toys in his bed and being adequately curious about instruments used in the examination. He seems quite self-sufficient in his play. It is difficult to tell definitely whether he hears, but it seems that he does. He will obey commands, such as "Sit up" or "Lie down," even when he does not see the speaker. He does not pay attention to conversation going on around him, and although he does make noises, he says no recognizable words.

His mother brought with her copious notes that indicated obsessive preoccupation with details and a tendency to read all sorts of peculiar interpretations into the child's performances. She watched (and recorded) every gesture and every "look," trying to find their specific significance and finally deciding on a particular, sometimes very farfetched explanation. She thus accumulated an account that, though very elaborate and richly illus-

trated, on the whole revealed more of her own version of what had happened in each instance than it told of what had actually occurred.

Richard's father is a professor of forestry in a southern university. He is very much immersed in his work, almost entirely to the exclusion of social contacts. The mother is a college graduate. The maternal grandfather is a physician, and the rest of the family, in both branches, consists of intelligent professional people. Richard's brother, thirty-one months his junior, is described as a normal, well developed child.

Richard was born on November 17, 1937. Pregnancy and birth were normal. He sat up at 8 months and walked at 1 year. His mother began to "train" him at the age of 3 weeks, giving him a suppository every morning "so his bowels would move by the clock." The mother, in comparing her two children, recalled that while her younger child showed an active anticipatory reaction to being picked up, Richard had not shown any physiognomic or postural sign of preparedness and had failed to adjust his body to being held by her or the nurse. Nutrition and physical growth proceeded satisfactorily. Following smallpox vaccination at 12 months, he had an attack of diarrhea and fever, from which he recovered in something less than a week.

In September, 1940, the mother, in commenting on Richard's failure to talk, remarked in her notes:

> I can't be sure just when he stopped the imitation of word sounds. It seems that he has gone backward mentally gradually for the last two years. We have thought it was because he did not disclose what was in his head, that it was there all right. Now that he is making so many sounds, it is disconcerting because it is now evident that he can't talk. Before, I thought he could if he only would. *He gave the impression of silent wisdom to me. . . .* One puzzling and discouraging thing is the great difficulty one has in getting his attention.

On physical examination, Richard was found to be healthy except for large tonsils and adenoids, which were removed on February 8, 1941. His head circumference was $54\frac{1}{2}$ cm. His electroencephalogram was normal.

He had himself led willingly to the psychiatrist's office and engaged at once in active play with the toys, paying no attention to the persons in the room. Occasionally, he looked up at the walls, smiled and uttered short staccato forceful sounds—"Ee! Ee! Ee!" He complied with a spoken and gestural command of his mother to take off his slippers. When the command was changed to another, this time without gestures, he repeated the original request and again took off his slippers (which had been put on again). He performed well with the unrotated form board but not with the rotated form board.

Richard was again seen at the age of 4 years, 4 months. He had grown considerably and gained weight. When started for the examination room, he screamed and made a great fuss, but once he yielded he went along willingly. He immediately proceeded to turn the lights on and off. He showed no interest in the examiner or any other person but was attracted to a small box that he threw as if it were a ball.

At 4 years, 11 months, his first move in entering the office (or any other room) was to turn the lights on and off. He climbed on a chair, and from the chair to the desk in order to reach the switch of the wall lamp. He did not communicate his wishes but went into a rage until his mother guessed and procured what he wanted. He had no contact with people, whom he definitely regarded as an interference when they talked to him or otherwise tried to gain his attention.

The mother felt that she was no longer capable of handling him, and he was placed in a foster home near Annapolis with a woman who had shown a remarkable talent for dealing with difficult children. Recently, this woman heard him say clearly his first intelligible words. They were, "Good night."

CASE 4

Paul G. was referred in March, 1941, at the age of 5 years, for psychometric assessment of what was thought to be a severe intellectual defect. He had attended a private nursery school, where his incoherent speech, inability to conform, and reaction with temper outbursts to any interference created the impression of feeblemindedness.

Paul, an only child, had come to this country from England with his mother at nearly 2 years of age. The father, a mining engineer, believed to be in Australia now, had left his wife shortly before that time after several years of an unhappy marriage. The mother, supposedly a college graduate, a restless, unstable, excitable woman, gave a vague and blatantly conflicting history of the family background and the child's development. She spent much time emphasizing and illustrating her efforts to make Paul clever by teaching him to memorize poems and songs. At 3 years, he knew the words of not less than thirty-seven songs and various and sundry nursery rhymes.

He was born normally. He vomited a great deal during his first year, and feeding formulas were changed frequently with little success. He ceased vomiting when he was started on solid food. He cut his teeth, held up his head, sat up, walked, and established bowel and bladder control at the usual age. He had measles, chickenpox, and pertussis without complications. His tonsils were removed when he was 3 years old. On physical examination, phimosis was found to be the only deviation from otherwise good health.

The following features emerged from observation on his visits to the clinic, during five weeks' residence in a boarding home, and during a few days' stay in the hospital.

Paul was a slender, well built, attractive child, whose face looked intelligent and animated. He had good manual dexterity. He rarely responded to any form of address, even to the calling of his name. At one time he picked up a block from the floor on request. Once he copied a circle immediately after it had been drawn before him. Sometimes an energetic "Don't!" caused him to interrupt his activity of the moment. But usually, when spoken to, he went on with whatever he was doing as if nothing had been said. Yet one never had the feeling that he was willingly disobedient or contrary. He was obviously so remote that the remarks did not reach him. He was always vivaciously occupied with something and seemed to be highly satisfied, unless someone made a persistent attempt to interfere with his self-chosen actions. Then he first tried impatiently to get out of the way and, when this met with no success, screamed and kicked in a full-fledged tantrum.

There was a marked contrast between his relations to people and to objects. Upon entering the room, he instantly went after objects and used them correctly. He was not destructive and treated the objects with care and even affection. He picked up a pencil and scribbled on paper that he found on the table. He opened a box, took out a toy telephone, singing again and again: "He wants the telephone," and went around the room with the mouthpiece and receiver in proper position. He got hold of a pair of scissors and patiently and skillfully cut a sheet of paper into small bits, singing the phrase "Cutting paper," many times. He helped himself to a toy engine, ran around the room holding it up high and singing over and over again, "The engine is flying." While these utterances, made always with the same inflection, were clearly connected with his actions, he ejaculated others that could not be linked up with immediate situations. These are a few examples: "The people in the hotel"; "Did you hurt your leg?" "Candy is all gone, candy is empty"; "You'll fall off the bicycle and bump your head." However, some of those exclamations could be definitely traced to previous experiences. He was in the habit of saying almost every day, "Don't throw the dog off the balcony." His mother recalled that she had said those words to him about a toy dog while they were still in England. At the sight of a saucepan he would invariably exclaim, "Peten-eater." The mother remembered that this particular association had begun when he was 2 years old and she happened to drop a saucepan while reciting to him the nursery rhyme about "Peter, Peter, pumpkin eater." Reproductions of warnings of bodily injury constituted a major portion of his utterances.

None of these remarks was meant to have communicative value. There was, on his side, no affective tie to people. He behaved as if people as such did not matter or even exist. It made no difference whether one spoke to him in a friendly or a harsh way. He never looked up at people's faces. When he had any dealings with persons at all, he treated them, or rather parts of them, as if they were objects. He would use a hand to lead him. He would, in playing, butt his head against his mother as at other times he did against a pillow. He allowed his boarding mother's hands to dress him, paying not the slightest attention to *her*. When with other children, he ignored them and went after their toys.

His enunciation was clear and he had a good vocabulary. His sentence construction was satisfactory, with one significant exception. He never used the pronoun of the first person, nor did he refer to himself as Paul. All statements pertaining to himself were made in the second person, as literal repetitions of things that had been said to him before. He would express his desire for candy by saying, "*You* want candy." He would pull his hand away from a hot radiator and say "*You* get hurt." Occasionally there were parrot-like repetitions of things said to him.

Formal testing could not be carried out, but he certainly could not be regarded as feebleminded in the ordinary sense. After hearing his boarding mother say grace three times, he repeated it without a flaw and has retained it since then. He could count and name colors. He learned quickly to identify his favorite victrola records from a large stack and knew how to mount and play them.

His boarding mother reported a number of observations that indicated compulsive behavior. He often masturbated with complete abandon. He ran around in circles emitting phrases in an ecstatic-like fashion. He took a small blanket and kept shaking it, delightedly shouting, "Ee! Ee!" He could continue in this manner for a long time and showed great irritation when he was interfered with. All these and many other things were not only repetitions but recurred day after day with almost photographic sameness.

CASE 5

Barbara K. was referred in February, 1942, at 8 years, 3 months of age. Her father's written note stated:

> First child, born normally October 30, 1933. She nursed very poorly and was put on bottle after about a week. She quit taking any kind of nourishment at 3 months. She was tube-fed five times daily up to 1 year of age. She began to eat then, though there was much diffi-
> culty until she was about 18 months old. Since then she has been a good eater, likes to experiment with food, tasting, and now fond of cooking.
>
> Ordinary vocabulary at 2 years, but always slow at putting words into sentences. Phenomenal ability to spell, read, and a good writer, but still has difficulty with verbal expression. Written langauge has helped the verbal. Can't get arithmetic except as a memory feat.
>
> Repetitious as a baby, and obsessive now: holds things in hands, takes things to bed with her, repeats phrases, gets stuck on an idea, game, etc., and rides it hard, then goes to something else. She used to talk using "you" for herself and "I" for her mother or me, as if she were saying things as we would in talking to her.
>
> Very timid, fearful of various and changing things, wind, large animals, etc. Mostly passive, but passively stubborn at times. Inattentive to the point where one wonders if she hears. (She does!) No competitive spirit, no desire to please her teacher. If she knew more than any member in the class about something, she would give no hint of it, just keep quiet, maybe not even listen.
>
> In camp last summer she was well liked, learned to swim, is graceful in water (had always appeared awkward in her motility before), overcame fear of ponies, played best with children of 5 years of age. At camp she slid into avitaminosis and malnutrition but offered almost no verbal complaints.

Barbara's father is a prominent psychiatrist. Her mother is a well educated, kindly woman. A younger brother, born in 1937, is healthy, alert, and well developed.

Barbara "shook hands" upon request (offering the left upon coming, the right upon leaving) by merely raising a limp hand in the approximate direction of the examiner's proffered hand; the motion definitely lacked the implication of greeting. During the entire interview there was no indication of any kind of affective contact. A pin prick resulted in withdrawal of her arm, a fearful glance at the pin (not the examiner), and utterance of the word "Hurt!" not addressed to anyone in particular.

She showed no interest in test performances. The concept of test, of sharing an experience or situation, seemed foreign to her. She protruded her tongue and played with her hand as one would with a toy. Attracted by a pen on the desk stand, she said: "Pen like yours at home." Then, seeing a pencil, she inquired: "May I take this home?"

When told that she might, she made no move to take it. The pencil was given to her, but she shoved it away, saying, "It's not my pencil."

She did the same thing repeatedly in regard to other objects. Several times she said, "Let's see Mother" (who was in the waiting room).

She read excellently, finishing the 10-year Binet fire story in thirty-three seconds and with no errors, but was unable to reproduce from memory anything she had read. In the Binet pictures, she saw (or at least reported) no action or relatedness between the single items, which she had no difficulty enumerating. Her handwriting was legible. Her drawing (man, house, cat sitting on six legs, pumpkin, engine) was unimaginative and stereotyped. She used her right hand for writing, her left for everything else; she was left-footed and right-eyed.

She knew the days of the week. She began to name them: "Saturday, Sunday, Monday," then said, "You go to school" (meaning, "on Monday"), then stopped as if the performance were completed.

Throughout all these procedures, in which—often after several repetitions of the question or command—she complied almost automatically, she scribbled words spontaneously: "oranges"; "lemons"; "bananas"; "grapes"; "cherries"; "apples"; "apricots"; "tangerine"; "grapefruits"; "watermelon juice"; the words sometimes ran into each other and were obviously not meant for others to read.

She frequently interrupted whatever "conversation" there was with references to "motor transports" and "piggy-back," both of which—according to her father— had preoccupied her for quite some time. She said, for instance, "I saw motor transports"; "I saw piggy-back when I went to school."

Her mother remarked, "Appendages fascinate her, like a smoke stack or a pendulum." Her father had previously stated: "Recent interest in sexual matters, hanging about when we take a bath, and obsessive interest in toilets."

Barbara was placed at the Devereux Schools, where she is making some progress in learning to relate herself to people.

CASE 6

Virginia S., born September 13, 1931, has resided at a state training school for the feebleminded since 1936, with the exception of one month in 1938, when she was paroled to a school for the deaf "for educational opportunity." Dr. Esther L. Richards, who saw her several times, clearly recognized that she was neither deaf nor feebleminded and wrote in May, 1941:

> Virginia stands out from other children [at the training school] because she is absolutely different from any of the others. She is neat and tidy, does not play with other children, and does not seem to be deaf from gross tests, but does not talk. The child will amuse herself by the hour putting picture puzzles together, sticking to them until they are done. I have seen her with a box filled with the parts of two puzzles gradually work out the pieces for each. All findings seem to be in the nature of a congenital abnormality which looks as if it were more of a personality abnormality than an organic defect.

Virginia, the younger of two siblings, was the daughter of a psychiatrist, who said of himself (in December, 1941): "I have never liked children, probably a reaction on my part to the restraint from movement (travel), the minor interruptions and commotions."

Of Virginia's mother, her husband said: "She is not by any means the mother type. Her attitude [toward a child] is more like toward a doll or pet than anything else."

Virginia's brother, Philip, five years her senior, when referred to us because of severe stuttering at 15 years of age, burst out in tears when asked how things were at home and he sobbed: "The only time my father has ever had anything to do with me was when he scolded me for doing something wrong."

His mother did not contribute even that much. He felt that all his life he had lived in "a frosty atmosphere" with two inapproachable strangers.

In August, 1938, the psychologist at the training school observed that Virginia could respond to sounds, the calling of her name, and the command, "Look!"

> She pays no attention to what is said to her but quickly comprehends whatever is expected. Her performance reflects discrimination, care, and precision.

With the nonlanguage items of the Binet and Merrill-Palmer tests, she achieved an I.Q. of 94. "Without a doubt," commented the psychologist,

> Her intelligence is superior to this. . . . She is quiet, solemn, composed. Not once have I seen her smile. She retires within herself, segregating herself from others. She seems to be in a world of her own, oblivious to all but the center of interest in the presiding situation. She is mostly self-sufficient and independent. When others encroach upon her integrity, she tolerates them with indifference. There was no manifestation of friendliness or interest in persons. On the other hand, she finds pleasure in dealing with things, about which she shows imagination and initiative. Typically, there is no display of affection. . . .

> *Psychologist's note, October, 1939.* Today Virginia was much more at home in the office. She remembered (after more than a year) where the toys were kept and helped herself. She could not be persuaded to participate in test procedures, would not wait for demonstrations when they were required. Quick, skilled moves. Trial and error plus insight. Very few futile moves. Immediate retesting reduced the time and error by more than half. There are times, more often than not, in which she is completely oblivious to all but her immediate focus of attention. . . .

> *January, 1940.* Mostly she is quiet, as she has always worked and played alone. She has not resisted authority or caused any special trouble. During group activities, she

soon becomes restless, squirms, and wants to leave to satisfy her curiosity about something else. She does make some vocal sounds, crying out if repressed or opposed too much by another child. She hums to herself, and in December I heard her hum the perfect tune of a Christmas hymn while she was pasting paper chains.

June, 1940. The school girls have said that Virginia says some words when at the cottage. They remember that she loves candy so much and says "Chocolate," "Marshmallow," also "Mama" and "Baby."

When seen on October 11, 1942, Virginia was a tall, slender, very neatly dressed 11-year-old girl. She responded when called by getting up and coming nearer, without ever looking up to the person who called her. She just stood listlessly, looking into space. Occasionally, in answer to questions, she muttered, "Mamma, baby." When a group was formed around the piano, one child playing and the others singing, Virginia sat among the children, seemingly not even noticing what went on, and gave the impression of being self-absorbed. She did not seem to notice when the children stopped singing. When the group dispersed she did not change her position and appeared not to be aware of the change of scene. She had an intelligent physiognomy, though her eyes had a blank expression.

CASE 7

Herbert B. was referred on February 5, 1941, at 3 years, 2 months of age. He was thought to be seriously retarded in intellectual development. There were no physical abnormalities except for undescended testicles. His electroencephalogram was normal.

Herbert was born November 16, 1937, two weeks before term by elective cesarean section; his birth weight was 6¼ pounds. He vomited all food from birth through the third month. Then vomiting ceased almost abruptly and, except for occasional regurgitation, feeding proceeded satisfactorily. According to his mother, he was "always slow and quiet." For a time he was believed to be deaf because "he did not register any change of expression when spoken to or when in the presence of other people; also, he made no attempt to speak or to form words." He held up his head at 4 months and sat at 8 months, but did not try to walk until 2 years old, when suddenly "he began to walk without any preliminary crawling or assistance by chairs." He persistently refused to take fluid in any but an all-glass container. Once, while at a hospital, he went three days without fluid because it was offered in tin cups. He was "tremendously frightened by running water, gas burners, and many other things." He became upset by any change of accustomed pattern:

"if he notices change, he is very fussy and cries." But he himself liked to pull blinds up and down, to tear cardboard boxes into small pieces and play with them for hours, and to close and open the wings of doors.

Herbert's parents separated shortly after his birth. The father, a psychiatrist, is described as "a man of unusual intelligence, sensitive, restless, introspective, taking himself very seriously, not interested in people, mostly living within himself, at times alcoholic." The mother, a physician, speaks of herself as "energetic and outgoing, fond of people and children but having little insight into their problems, finding it a great deal easier to accept people rather than try to understand them." Herbert is the youngest of three children. The second is a normal, healthy boy. The oldest, Dorothy, born in June, 1934, after thirty-six hours of hard labor, seemed alert and responsive as an infant and said many words at 18 months, but toward the end of the second year she "did not show much progression in her play relationships or in contacts with other people." She wanted to be left alone, danced about in circles, made queer noises with her mouth, and *ignored persons completely* except for her mother, to whom she clung "in panic and general agitation." (Her father hated her ostensibly.) "Her speech was very meager and expression of ideas completely lacking. She had *difficulties with her pronouns* and would repeat 'you' and 'I' instead of using them for the proper persons." She was first declared to be feebleminded, then schizophrenic, but after the parents separated (the children remaining with their mother), she "blossomed out." She now attends school, where she makes good progress; she talks well, has an I.Q. of 108, and—though sensitive and moderately apprehensive—is interested in people and gets along reasonably well with them.

Herbert, when examined on his first visit, showed a remarkably intelligent physiognomy and good motor coordination. Within certain limits, he displayed astounding purposefulness in the pursuit of self-selected goals. Among a group of blocks, he instantly recognized those that were glued to a board and those that were detachable. He could build a tower of blocks as skillfully and as high as any child of his age or even older. He could not be diverted from his self-chosen occupations. He was annoyed by any interference, shoving intruders away (without ever looking at them), or screaming when the shoving had no effect.

He was again seen at 4 years, 7 months, and again at 5 years, 2 months of age. He still did not speak. Both times he entered the office without paying the slightest attention to the people present. He went after the Seguin form board and instantly busied himself putting the figures into their proper spaces and taking them out again adroitly and quickly. When interfered with he whined impatiently. When one figure was stealthily removed, he immediately noticed its absence, became disturbed, but promptly forgot all about it when it was put back. At times, after he had finally quieted down following the upset caused by the removal of the form board, he jumped up and down on the couch with an ecstatic expression on his face. He did not respond to being called or to any other words addressed to him. He was completely absorbed in whatever he did. He never smiled. He sometimes uttered inarticulate sounds in a monotonous sing-song manner. At one time he gently stroked his mother's leg and touched it with his lips. He very frequently brought blocks and other objects to his lips. There was an almost photographic likeness of his behavior during the two visits, with the main exception that at 4 years he showed apprehension and shrank back when a match was lighted, while at 5 years he reacted by jumping up and down ecstatically.

CASE 8

Alfred L. was brought by his mother in November, 1935, at 3½ years of age with this complaint:

> He has gradually shown a marked tendency toward developing one special interest which will completely dominate his day's activities. He talks of little else while the interest exists, he frets when he is not able to indulge in it (by seeing it, coming in contact with it, drawing pictures of it), and it is difficult to get his attention because of his preoccupation. . . . There has also been the problem of an overattachment to the world of objects and failure to develop the usual amount of social awareness.

Alfred was born in May, 1932, three weeks before term. For the first two months, "the feeding formula caused considerable concern but then he gained rapidly and became an unusually large and vigorous baby." He sat up at 5 months and walked at 14.

> Language developed slowly; he seemed to have no interest in it. He seldom tells experience. He still confuses pronouns. He never asks questions in the form of questions (with the appropriate inflection). Since he talked, there has been a tendency to repeat over and over one word or a statement. He almost never says a sentence without repeating it. Yesterday, when looking at a picture, he said many times, "Some cows standing in the water." We counted fifty repetitions, then he stopped after several more and then began over and over.

He had a good deal of "worrying":

> He frets when the bread is put in the oven to be made into toast, and is afraid it will get burned and be hurt. He is upset when the sun sets. He is upset because the moon

does not always appear in the sky at night. He prefers to play alone; he will get down from a piece of apparatus as soon as another child approaches. He likes to work out some project with large boxes (make a trolley, for instance) and does not want anyone to get on it or interfere.

When infantile thumb sucking was prevented by mechanical devices, he gave it up and instead put various objects into his mouth. On several occasions pebbles were found in his stools. Shortly before his second birthday, he swallowed cotton from an Easter rabbit, aspirating some of the cotton, so that tracheotomy became necessary. A few months later, he swallowed some kerosene "with no ill effects."

Alfred was an only child. His father, 30 years old at the time of his birth, "does not get along well with people, is suspicious, easily hurt, easily roused to anger, has to be dragged out to visit friends, spends his spare time reading, gardening, and fishing." He is a chemist and a law school graduate. The mother, of the same age, is a "clinical psychologist," very obsessive and excitable. The paternal grandparents died early; the father was adopted by a minister. The maternal grandfather, a psychologist, was severely obsessive, had numerous tics, was given to "repeated hand washing, protracted thinking along one line, fear of being alone, cardiac fears." The grandmother, "an excitable, explosive person, has done public speaking, published several books, is an incessant solitaire player, greatly worried over money matters." A maternal uncle frequently ran away from home and school, joined the marines, and later "made a splendid adjustment in commercial life."

The mother left her husband two months after Alfred's birth. The child has lived with his mother and maternal grandparents. "In the home is a nursery school and kindergarten (run by the mother), which creates some confusion for the child." Alfred did not see his father until he was 3 years, 4 months old, when the mother decided that "he should know his father" and "took steps to have the father come to the home to see the child."

Alfred, upon entering the office, paid no attention to the examiner. He immediately spotted a train in the toy cabinet, took it out, and connected and disconnected the cars in a slow, monotonous manner. He kept saying many times, "More train—more train—more train." He repeatedly "counted" the car windows: "One, two windows—one, two windows—one, two windows—four window, eight window, eight windows." He could not in any way be distracted from the trains. A Binet test was attempted in a room in which there were no trains. It was possible with much difficulty to pierce from time to time through his preoccupations. He finally complied in most instances in a manner that clearly indicated that he wanted to get through with the particular intrusion; this was repeated with each individual item of the task. In the end he achieved an *I.Q. of 140.*

The mother did not bring him back after this first visit because of "his continued distress when confronted with a member of the medical profession." In August, 1938, she sent upon request a written report of his development. From this report, the following passages are quoted:

> He is called a lone wolf. He prefers to play alone and avoids groups of children at play. He does not pay much attention to adults except when demanding stories. He avoids competition. He reads simple stories to himself. He is very fearful of being hurt, talks a great deal about the use of the electric chair. He is thrown into a panic when anyone accidentally covers his face.

Alfred was again referred in June, 1941. His parents had decided to live together. Prior to that the boy had been in eleven different schools. He had been kept in bed often because of colds, bronchitis, chickenpox, streptococcus infection, impetigo, and a vaguely described condition which the mother—the assurances of various pediatricians to the contrary notwithstanding—insisted was "rheumatic fever." While in the hospital, he is said to have behaved "like a manic patient." (The mother liked to call herself a psychiatrist and to make "psychiatric" diagnoses of the child.) From the mother's report, which combined obsessive enumeration of detailed instances with "explanations" trying to prove Alfred's "normalcy," the following information was gathered.

He had begun to play with children younger than himself, "using them as puppets—that's all." He had been stuffed with music, dramatics, and recitals, and had an excellent rote memory. He still was "terribly engrossed" in his play, didn't want people around, just couldn't relax:

> He had many fears, almost always connected with mechanical noise (meat grinders, vacuum cleaners, street cars, trains, etc.). Usually he winds up with an obsessed interest in the things he was afraid of. Now he is afraid of the shrillness of a dog's barking.

Alfred was extremely tense during the entire interview, and very serious-minded, to such an extent that had it not been for his juvenile voice, he might have given the impression of a worried and preoccupied little old man. At the same time, he was very restless and showed considerable pressure of talk, which had nothing personal in it but consisted of obsessive questions about windows, shades, dark rooms, especially the X-ray room. He never smiled. No change of topic could get him away from the topic of light and darkness. But in between he answered the examiner's questions, which often had to be repeated several times, and to which he sometimes responded as

the result of a bargain—"You answer my question, and I'll answer yours." He was painstakingly specific in his definitions. A balloon "is made out of lined rubber and has air in it and some have gas and sometimes they go up in the air and sometimes they can hold up and when they got a hole in it they'll bust up; if people squeeze they'll bust. Isn't it right?" A tiger "is a thing, animal, striped, like a cat, can scratch, eats people up, wild, lives in the jungle sometimes and in the forests, mostly in the jungle. Isn't it right?" The question "Isn't it right?" was definitely meant to be answered; there was a serious desire to be assured that the definition was sufficiently complete.

He was often confused about the meaning of words. When shown a picture and asked, "What is this picture about?" he replied, "People are moving *about.*"

He once stopped and asked, very much perplexed, why there was "The Johns Hopkins Hospital" printed on the history sheets: "Why do they have to say it?" This, to him, was a real problem of major importance, calling for a great deal of thought and discussion. Since the histories were taken at the hospital, why should it be necessary to have the name on every sheet, though the person writing on it knew where he was writing? The examiner, whom he remembered very well from his visit six years previously, was to him nothing more nor less than a person who was expected to answer his obsessive questions about darkness and light.

CASE 9

Charles N. was brought by his mother on February 2, 1943, at 4½ years of age, with the chief complaint, "The thing that upsets me most is that I can't reach my baby." She introduced her report by saying: "I am trying hard not to govern my remarks by professional knowledge which has intruded in my own way of thinking by now."

As a baby, the boy was inactive, "slow and phlegmatic." He would lie in the crib, just staring. He would act almost as if hypnotized. He seemed to concentrate on doing one thing at a time. Hypothyroidism was suspected, and he was given thyroid extract, without any change of the general condition.

> His enjoyment and appreciation of music encouraged me to play records. When he was 1½ years old, he could discriminate between eighteen symphonies. He recognized the composer as soon as the first movement started. He would say "Beethoven." At about the same age, he began to spin toys and lids of bottles and jars by the hour. He had a lot of manual dexterity in ability to spin cylinders. He would watch it and get severely excited and jump up and down in ecstasy. Now he is interested in reflecting light from mirrors and catching reflections. When he is interested in a thing, you cannot change it. He would pay

no attention to me and show no recognition of me if I enter the room. . . .

The most impressive thing is his detachment and his inaccessibility. He walks as if he is in a shadow, lives in a world of his own where he cannot be reached. No sense of relationship to persons. He went through a period of quoting another person; never offers anything himself. His entire conversation is a replica of whatever has been said to him. He used to speak of himself in the second person, now he uses the third person at times; he would say, "He wants"—never "I want." . . .

He is destructive; the furniture in his room looks like it has hunks out of it. He will break a purple crayon into two parts and say, "*You* had a beautiful purple crayon and now it's two pieces. Look what *you* did."

He developed an obsession about feces, would hide it anywhere (for instance, in drawers), would tease me if I walked into the room: "You soiled your pants, now you can't have your crayons!"

As a result, he is still not toilet trained. He never soils himself in the nursery school, always does it when he comes home. The same is true of wetting. He is proud of wetting, jumps up and down with ecstasy, says, "Look at the big puddle *he* made."

When he is with other people, he doesn't look up at them. Last July, we had a group of people. When Charles came in, it was just like a foal who'd been let out of an enclosure. He did not pay attention to them but their presence was felt. He will mimic a voice and he sings and some people would not notice any abnormality in the child. At school, he never envelops himself in a group, he is detached from the rest of the children, except when he is in the assembly; if there is music, he will go to the front row and sing.

He has a wonderful memory for words. Vocabulary is good, except for pronouns. He never initiates conversation, and conversation is limited, extensive only as far as objects go.

Charles was born normally, a planned and wanted child. He sat up at 6 months and walked at less than 15 months—"just stood up and walked one day—no preliminary creeping." He has had none of the usual children's diseases.

Charles is the oldest of three children. The father, a high-school graduate and a clothing merchant, is described as a "self-made, gentle, calm, and placid person." The mother has "a successful business record, theatrical booking office in New York, of remarkable equanimity." The other two children were 28 and 14 months old at the time of Charles' visit to the Clinic. The maternal grandmother, "very dynamic, forceful, hyperactive, almost hypomanic," has done some writing and composing. A maternal aunt, "psychoneurotic, very brilliant, given to hysterics," has written poems and songs. Another aunt was referred to as "the amazon of the family." A maternal uncle, a psychiatrist, has considerable

musical talent. The paternal relatives are described as "ordinary simple people."

Charles was a well developed, intelligent-looking boy, who was in good physical health. He wore glasses. When he entered the office, he paid not the slightest attention to the people present (three physicians, his mother, and his uncle). Without looking at anyone, he said, "Give me a pencil!" and took a piece of paper from the desk and wrote something resembling a figure 2 (a large desk calendar prominently displayed a figure 2; the day was February 2). He had brought with him a copy of *Readers Digest* and was fascinated by a picture of a baby. He said, "Look at the funny baby," innumerable times, occasionally adding, "Is he not funny? Is he not sweet?"

When the book was taken away from him, he struggled with the hand that held it, without looking at the *person* who had taken the book. When he was pricked with a pin, he said, "What's this?" and answered his own question: "It is a needle."

He looked timidly at the pin, shrank from further pricks, but at no time did he seem to connect the pricking with the *person* who held the pin. When the *Readers Digest* was taken from him and thrown on the floor and a foot placed over it, he tried to remove the foot as if it were another detached and interfering object, again with no concern for the *person* to whom the foot belonged. He once turned to his mother and excitedly said, "Give it to you!"

When confronted with the Seguin form board, he was mainly interested in the names of the forms, before putting them into their appropriate holes. He often spun the forms around, jumping up and down excitedly while they were in motion. The whole performance was very repetitious. He never used language as a means of communicating with people. He remembered names, such as "octagon," "diamond," "oblong block," but nevertheless kept asking, "What is this?"

He did not respond to being called and did not look at his mother when she spoke to him. When the blocks were removed, he screamed, stamped his feet, and cried, "I'll give it to you!" (meaning "You give it to me"). He was very skillful in his movements.

Charles was placed at the Devereux Schools.

CASE 10

John F. was first seen on February 13, 1940, at 2 years, 4 months of age.

The father said: "The main thing that worries me is the difficulty in feeding. That is the essential thing, and secondly his slowness in development. During the first days of life he did not take the breast satisfactorily. After fifteen days he was changed from breast to bottle but did not take the bottle satisfactorily. There is a long story of trying to get food down. We have tried everything under the sun. He has been immature all along. At 20 months he first started to talk. He sucks his thumb and grinds his teeth quite frequently and rolls from side to side before sleeping. If we don't do what he wants, he will scream and yell."

John was born September 19, 1937; his birth weight was $7\frac{1}{2}$ pounds. There were frequent hospitalizations because of the feeding problem. No physical disorder was ever found, except that the anterior fontanelle did not close until he was $2\frac{1}{2}$ years of age. He suffered from repeated colds and otitis media, which necessitated bilateral myringotomy.

John was an only child until February, 1943. The father, a psychiatrist, is "a very calm, placid, emotionally stable person, who is the soothing element in the family." The mother, a high-school graduate, worked as secretary in a pathology laboratory before marriage—"a hypomanic type of person; sees everything as a pathological specimen rather than well; throughout the pregnancy she was very apprehensive, afraid she would not live through the labor." The paternal grandmother is "obsessive about religion and washes her hands every few minutes." The maternal grandfather was an accountant.

John was brought to the office by both parents. He wandered about the room constantly and aimlessly. Except for spontaneous scribbling, he never brought two objects into relation to each other. He did not respond to the simplest commands, except that his parents with much difficulty elicited bye-bye, pat-a-cake, and peek-a-boo gestures, performed clumsily. His typical attitude toward objects was to throw them on the floor.

Three months later, his vocabulary showed remarkable improvement, though his articulation was defective. Mild obsessive trends were reported, such as pushing aside the first spoonful of every dish. His excursions about the office were slightly more purposeful.

At the end of his fourth year, he was able to form a very limited kind of affective contact, and even that only with a very limited number of people. Once such a relationship had been established, it had to continue in exactly the same channels. He was capable of forming elaborate and grammatically correct sentences, but he used the pronoun of the second person when referring to himself. He used language not as a means of communication but mainly as a repetition of things he had heard, without alteration of the personal pronoun. There was very marked obsessiveness. Daily routine must be adhered to rigidly; any slightest change of the pattern called forth outbursts of panic. There was endless repetition of sentences. He had an excellent rote memory and could recite many prayers, nursery rhymes, and songs "in different languages"; the mother did a great deal of stuffing in this respect

and was very proud of these "achievements": "He can tell victrola records by their color and if one side of the record is identified, he remembers what is on the other side."

At $4\frac{1}{3}$ years, he began gradually to use pronouns adequately. Even though his direct interest was in objects only, he took great pains in attracting the attention of the examiner (Dr. Hilde Bruch) and in gaining her praise. However, he never addressed her directly and spontaneously. He wanted to make sure of the sameness of the environment literally by keeping doors and windows closed. When his mother opened the door "to pierce through his obsession," he became violent in closing it again and finally, when again interfered with, burst helplessly into tears, utterly frustrated.

He was extremely upset upon seeing anything broken or incomplete. He noticed two dolls to which he had paid no attention before. He saw that one of them had no hat and became very much agitated, wandering about the room to look for the hat. When the hat was retrieved from another room, he instantly lost all interest in the dolls.

At $5\frac{1}{2}$ years, he had good mastery of the use of pronouns. He had begun to feed himself satisfactorily. He saw a group photograph in the office and asked his father, "When are they coming out of the picture and coming in here?"

He was very serious about this. His father said something about the pictures they have at home on the wall. This disturbed John somewhat. He corrected his father: "We have them *near* the wall" ("on" apparently meaning to him "above" or "on top").

When he saw a penny, he said, "Penny. That's where you play tenpins." He had been given pennies when he knocked over tenpins while playing with his father at home.

He saw a dictionary and said to his father, "That's where you left the money?"

Once his father had left some money in a dictionary and asked John to tell his mother about it.

His father whistled a tune and John instantly and correctly identified it as "Mendelssohn's violin concerto." Though he could speak of things as big or pretty, he was utterly incapable of making comparisons ("Which is the bigger line? Prettier face?" etc.).

In December, 1942, and January, 1943, he had two series of predominantly right-sided *convulsions,* with conjugate deviation of the eyes to the right and transient paresis of the right arm. Neurologic examination showed no abnormalities. His eyegrounds were normal. An electroencephalogram indicated "focal disturbance in the left occipital region," but "a good part of the record could not be read because of the continuous marked artefacts due to the child's lack of cooperation."

CASE 11

Elaine C. was brought by her parents on April 12, 1939, at the age of 7 years, 2 months, because of "unusual development": "She doesn't adjust. She stops at all abstractions. She doesn't understand other children's games, doesn't retain interest in stories read to her, wanders off and walks by herself, is especially fond of animals of all kinds, occasionally mimics them by walking on all fours and making strange noises."

Elaine was born on February 3, 1932 at term. She appeared healthy, took feedings well, stood up at 7 months and walked at less than a year. She could say four words at the end of her first year but made no progress in linguistic development for the following four years. Deafness was suspected but ruled out. Because of a febrile illness at 13 months, her increasing difficulties were interpreted as possible postencephalitic behavior disorder. Others blamed the mother, who was accused of inadequate handling of the child. Feeblemindedness was another diagnosis. For eighteen months, she was given anterior pituitary and thyroid preparations. "Some doctors," struck by Elaine's intelligent physiognomy, "thought she was a normal child and said that she would outgrow this."

At 2 years, she was sent to a nursery school, where "she independently went her way, not doing what the others did. She, for instance, drank the water and ate the plant when they were being taught to handle flowers." She developed an early interest in pictures of animals. Though generally restless, she could for hours concentrate on looking at such pictures, "especially engravings."

When she began to speak at about 5 years, she started out with complete though simple sentences that were "mechanical phrases" not related to the situation of the moment or related to it in a peculiar metaphorical way. She had an excellent vocabulary, knew especially the names and "classifications" of animals. She did not use pronouns correctly, but used plurals and tenses well. She "could not use negatives but recognized their meaning when others used them."

There were many peculiarities in her relation to situations:

> She can count by rote. She can set the table for numbers of people if the names are given her or enumerated in any way, but she cannot set the table "for three." If sent for a specific object in a certain place, she cannot bring it if it is somewhere else but still visible.

She was "frightened" by noises and anything moving toward her. She was so afraid of the vacuum cleaner that she would not even go near the closet where it was kept, and when it was used, ran out into the garage, covering her ears with her hands.

Elaine was the older of two children. Her father, aged 36, studied law and the liberal arts in three universities (including the Sorbonne), was an advertising copy writer, "one of those chronically thin persons, nervous energy readily expended." He was at one time editor of a magazine. The mother, aged 32, a "self-controlled, placid, logical person," had done editorial work for a magazine before marriage. The maternal grandfather was a newspaper editor, the grandmother was "emotionally unstable."

Elaine had been examined by a Boston psychologist at nearly 7 years of age. The report stated among other things:

> Her attitude toward the examiner remained vague and detached. Even when annoyed by restraint, she might vigorously push aside a table or restraining hand with a scream, but she made no personal appeal for help or sympathy. At favorable moments she was competent in handling her crayons or assembling pieces to form pictures of animals. She could name a wide variety of pictures, including elephants, alligators, and dinosaurs. She used language in simple sentence structure, but rarely answered a direct question. As she plays, she repeats over and over phrases which are irrelevant to the immediate situation.

Physically the child was in good health. Her electroencephalogram was normal.

When examined in April, 1939, she shook hands with the physician upon request, without looking at him, then ran to the window and looked out. She automatically heeded the invitation to sit down. Her reaction to questions—after several repetitions—was an echolalia type reproduction of the whole question or, if it was too lengthy, of the end portion. She had no real contact with the persons in the office. Her expression was blank, though not unintelligent, and there were no communicative gestures. At one time, without changing her physiognomy, she said suddenly: "Fishes don't cry." After a time, she got up and left the room without asking or showing fear.

She was placed at the Child Study Home of Maryland, where she remained for three weeks and was studied by Drs. Eugenia S. Cameron and George Frankl. While there, she soon learned the names of all the children, knew the color of their eyes, the bed in which each slept, and many other details about them, but never entered into any relationship with them. When taken to the playgrounds, she was extremely upset and ran back to her room. She was very restless but when allowed to look at pictures, play alone with blocks, draw, or string beads, she could entertain herself contentedly for hours. Any noise, any interruption disturbed her. Once, when on the toilet seat, she heard a knocking in the pipes; for several days thereafter, even when put on a chamber pot in her own room, she did not move her bowels, anxiously listening for the noise. She frequently ejaculated stereotyped phrases, such as, "Dinosaurs don't cry"; "Crayfish, sharks, fish, and rocks"; "Crayfish and forks live in children's tummies"; "Butterflies live in children's stomachs, and in their panties, too"; "Fish have sharp teeth and bite little children"; "There is war in the sky"; "Rocks and crags, I will kill" (grabbing her blanket and kicking it about the bed); "Gargoyles bite children and drink oil"; "I will crush old angle worm, he bites children" (gritting her teeth and spinning around in a circle, very excited); "Gargoyles have milk bags"; "Needle head. Pink wee-wee. Has a yellow leg. Cutting the dead deer. Poison deer. Poor Elaine. No tadpoles in the house. Men broke deer's leg" (while cutting the picture of a deer from a book); "Tigers and cats"; "Seals and salamanders"; "Bears and foxes."

A few excerpts from the observations follow:

> Her language always has the same quality. Her speech is never accompanied by facial expression or gestures. She does not look into one's face. Her voice is peculiarly unmodulated, somewhat hoarse; she utters her words in an abrupt manner.
>
> Her utterances are impersonal. She never uses the personal pronouns of the first and second persons correctly. She does not seem able to conceive the real meaning of these words.
>
> Her grammar is inflexible. She uses sentences just as she has heard them, without adapting them grammatically to the situation of the moment. When she says, "Want me to draw a spider," she means, "I want you to draw a spider."
>
> She affirms by repeating a question literally, and she negates by not complying. Her speech is rarely communicative. She has no relation to children, has never talked to them, to be friendly with them, or to play with them. She moves among them like a strange being, as one moves between the pieces of furniture of a room.
>
> She insists on the repetition of the same routine always. Interruption of the routine is one of the most frequent occasions for her outbursts. Her own activities are simple and repetitive. She is able to spend hours in some form of daydreaming and seems to be very happy with it. She is inclined to rhythmical movements which always are masturbatory. She masturbates more in periods of excitement than during calm happiness. . . . Her movements are quick and skillful.

Elaine was placed in a private school in Pennsylvania. In a recent letter, the father reported "rather amazing changes":

> She is a tall, husky girl with clear eyes that have long since lost any trace of that animal wildness they periodically showed in the time you knew her. She speaks well

on almost any subject, though with something of an odd intonation. Her conversation is still rambling talk, frequently with an amusing point, and it is only occasional, deliberate, and announced. She reads very well, but she reads fast, jumbling words, not pronouncing clearly, and not making proper emphases. Her range of information is really quite wide, and her memory almost infallible. It is obvious that Elaine is not "normal." Failure in anything leads to a feeling of defeat, of despair, and to a momentary fit of depression.

DISCUSSION

The eleven children (eight boys and three girls) whose histories have been briefly presented offer, as is to be expected, individual differences in the degree of their disturbance, the manifestation of specific features, the family constellation, and the step-by-step development in the course of years. But even a quick review of the material makes the emergence of a number of essential common characteristics appear inevitable. These characteristics form a unique "syndrome," not heretofore reported, which seems to be rare enough, yet is probably more frequent than is indicated by the paucity of observed cases. It is quite possible that some such children have been viewed as feebleminded or schizophrenic. In fact, several children of our group were introduced to us as idiots or imbeciles, one still resides in a state school for the feebleminded, and two had been previously considered as schizophrenic.

The outstanding, "pathognomonic," fundamental disorder is the children's *inability to relate themselves* in the ordinary way to people and situations from the beginning of life. Their parents referred to them as having always been "self-sufficient"; "like in a shell"; "happiest when left alone"; "acting as if people weren't there"; "perfectly oblivious to everything about him"; "giving the impression of silent wisdom"; "failing to develop the usual amount of social awareness"; "acting almost as if hypnotized." This is not, as in schizophrenic children or adults, a departure from an initially present relationship; it is not a "withdrawal" from formerly existing participation. There is from the start an *extreme autistic aloneness* that, whenever possible, disregards, ignores, shuts out anything that comes to the child from the outside. Direct physical contact or such motion or noise as threatens to disrupt the aloneness is either treated "as if it weren't there" or, if this is no longer sufficient, resented painfully as distressing interference.

According to Gesell, the average child at 4 months of age makes an anticipatory motor adjustment by facial tension and shrugging attitude of the shoulders when lifted from a table or placed on a table. Gesell commented:

It is possible that a less definite evidence of such adjustment may be found as low down as the neonatal period. Although a habit must be conditioned by experience, the opportunity for experience is almost universal and the response is sufficiently objective to merit further observation and record.

This universal experience is supplied by the frequency with which an infant is picked up by his mother and other persons. It is therefore highly significant that almost all mothers of our patients recalled their astonishment at the children's *failure to assume at any time an anticipatory posture* preparatory to being picked up. One father recalled that his daughter (Barbara) did not for years change her physiognomy or position in the least when the parents, upon coming home after a few hours' absence, approached her crib talking to her and making ready to pick her up.

The average infant learns during the first few months to adjust his body to the posture of the person who holds him. Our children were not able to do so for two or three years. We had an opportunity to observe 38-month-old Herbert in such a situation. His mother informed him in appropriate terms that she was going to lift him up, extending her arms in his direction. There was no response. She proceeded to take him up, and he allowed her to do so, remaining completely passive as if he were a sack of flour. It was the mother who had to do all the adjusting. Herbert was at that time capable of sitting, standing, and walking.

Eight of the eleven children acquired the *ability to speak* either at the usual age or after some delay. Three (Richard, Herbert, Virginia) have so far remained "mute." In none of the eight "speaking" children has language over a period of years served to convey meaning to others. They were, with the exception of John F., capable of clear articulation and phonation. Naming of objects presented no difficulty; even long and unusual words were learned and retained with remarkable facility. Almost all the parents reported, usually with much pride, that the children had learned at an early age to repeat an inordinate number of nursery rhymes, prayers, lists of animals, the roster of presidents, the alphabet forward and backward, even foreign-language (French) lullabies. Aside from the recital of sentences contained in the ready-made poems or other remembered pieces, it took a long time before they began to put words together. Other than that, "language" consisted mainly of "naming," of nouns identifying objects, adjectives indicating colors, and numbers indicating nothing specific.

Their *excellent rote memory*, coupled with the inability to use language in any other way, often led the parents to stuff them with more and more verses, zoologic and botanic names, titles and composers of victrola record pieces, and the like. Thus, from the start, language —which the children did not use for the purpose of communication—was deflected in a considerable measure to a self-sufficient, semantically and conversationally valueless or grossly distorted memory exercise. To a child 2 or 3 years old, all these words, numbers, and poems ("questions and answers of the Presbyterian Catechism"; "Mendelssohn's violin concerto"; "the Twenty-third Psalm"; a French lullaby; an encyclopedia index page) could hardly have more meaning than sets of nonsense syllables to adults. It is difficult to know for certain whether the stuffing as such has contributed essentially to the course of the psychopathologic condition. But it is also difficult to imagine that it did not cut deeply into the development of language as a tool for receiving and imparting meaningful messages.

As far as the communicative functions of speech are concerned, there is no fundamental difference between the eight speaking and the three mute children. Richard was once overheard by his boarding mother to say distinctly, "Good night." Justified skepticism about this observation was later dispelled when this "mute" child was seen in the office shaping his mouth in silent repetition of words when asked to say certain things. "Mute" Virginia—so her cottage mates insisted—was heard repeatedly to say, "Chocolate"; "Marshmallow"; "Mama"; "Baby."

When sentences are finally formed, they are for a long time mostly parrot-like repetitions of heard word combinations. They are sometimes echoed immediately, but they are just as often "stored" by the child and uttered at a later date. One may, if one wishes, speak of *delayed echolalia*. Affirmation is indicated by literal repetition of a question. "Yes" is a concept that it takes the children many years to acquire. They are incapable of using it as a general symbol of assent. Donald learned to say "Yes" when his father told him that he would put him on his shoulders if he said "Yes." This word then came to "mean" only the desire to be put on his father's shoulders. It took many months before he could detach the word "yes" from this specific situation, and it took much longer before he was able to use it as a general term of affirmation.

The same type of *literalness* exists also with regard to prepositions. Alfred, when asked, "What is this picture about?" replied: "People are moving *about*."

John F. corrected his father's statement about pictures on the wall; the pictures were "*near* the wall." Donald T., requested to put something *down*, promptly put it on the floor. Apparently the meaning of a word becomes inflexible and cannot be used with any but the originally acquired connotation.

There is no difficulty with plurals and tenses. But the absence of spontaneous sentence formation and the echolalia type reproduction has, in every one of the eight speaking children, given rise to a peculiar grammatical phenomenon. *Personal pronouns are repeated just as heard,* with no change to suit the altered situation. The child, once told by his mother, "Now I will give you your milk," expresses the desire for milk in exactly the same words. Consequently, he comes to speak of himself always as "you," and of the person addressed as "I." Not only the words, but even the intonation is retained. If the mother's original remark has been made in form of a question, it is reproduced with the grammatical form and the inflection of a question. The repetition "Are you ready for your dessert?" means that the child is ready for his dessert. There is a set, not-to-be-changed phrase for every specific occasion. The pronominal fixation remains until about the sixth year of life, when the child gradually learns to speak of himself in the first person, and of the individual addressed in the second person. In the transitional period, he sometimes still reverts to the earlier form or at times refers to himself in the third person.

The fact that the children echo things heard does not signify that they "attend" when spoken to. It often takes numerous reiterations of a question or command before there is even so much as an echoed response. Not less than seven of the children were therefore considered as deaf or hard of hearing. There is an all-powerful need for being left undisturbed. Everything that is brought to the child from the outside, everything that changes his external or even internal environment, represents a dreaded intrusion.

Food is the earliest intrusion that is brought to the child from the outside. David Levy observed that affect-hungry children, when placed in foster homes where they are well treated, at first demand excessive quantities of food. Hilde Bruch, in her studies of obese children, found that overeating often resulted when affectionate offerings from the parents were lacking or considered unsatisfactory. Our patients, reversely, anxious to keep the outside world away, indicated this by the refusal of food. Donald, Paul ("vomited a great deal during the first year"), Barbara ("had to be tube-fed until 1 year of age"), Herbert, Alfred, and John presented severe feeding difficulty from the beginning of life. Most of them, after an unsuccessful struggle, constantly interfered with, finally gave up the struggle and of a sudden began eating satisfactorily.

Another intrusion comes from *loud noises and moving objects,* which are therefore reacted to with horror. Tricycles, swings, elevators, vacuum cleaners, running water, gas burners, mechanical toys, egg beaters, even the wind could on occasions bring about a major panic. One of the children was even afraid to go near the closet in which the vacuum cleaner was kept. Injections and examinations with stethoscope or otoscope created a grave emotional crisis. Yet it is not the noise or motion itself that is dreaded. The disturbance comes from the noise or

motion that intrudes itself, or threatens to intrude itself, upon the child's aloneness. The child himself can happily make as great a noise as any that he dreads and move objects about to his heart's desire.

But the child's noises and motions and all of his performances are as *monotonously repetitious* as are his verbal utterances. There is a marked limitation in the variety of his spontaneous activities. The child's behavior is governed by an *anxiously obsessive desire for the maintenance of sameness* that nobody but the child himself may disrupt on rare occasions. Changes of routine, of furniture arrangement, of a pattern, of the order in which everyday acts are carried out, can drive him to despair. When John's parents got ready to move to a new home, the child was frantic when he saw the moving men roll up the rug in his room. He was acutely upset until the moment when, in the new home, he saw his furniture arranged in the same manner as before. He looked pleased, all anxiety was suddenly gone, and he went around affectionately patting each piece. Once blocks, beads, sticks have been put together in a certain way, they are always regrouped in exactly the same way, even though there was no definite design. The children's memory was phenomenal in this respect. After the lapse of several days, a multitude of blocks could be rearranged in precisely the same unorganized pattern, with the same color of each block turned up, with each picture or letter on the upper surface of each block facing in the same direction as before. The absence of a block or the presence of a supernumerary block was noticed immediately, and there was an imperative demand for the restoration of the missing piece. If someone removed a block, the child struggled to get it back, going into a panic tantrum until he regained it, and then promptly and with sudden calm after the storm returned to the design and replaced the block.

This insistence on sameness led several of the children to become greatly disturbed upon the sight of anything broken or incomplete. A great part of the day was spent in demanding not only the sameness of the wording of a request but also the sameness of the sequence of events. Donald would not leave his bed after his nap until he had said, "Boo, say 'Don, do you want to get down?'" and the mother had complied. But this was not all. The act was still not considered completed. Donald would continue, "Now say 'All right.'" Again the mother had to comply, or there was screaming until the performance was completed. All of this ritual was an indispensable part of the act of getting up after a nap. Every other activity had to be completed from beginning to end in the manner in which it had been started originally. It was impossible to return from a walk without having covered the same ground as had been covered before. The sight of a broken crossbar on a garage door on his regular daily tour so upset

Charles that he kept talking and asking about it for weeks on end, even while spending a few days in a distant city. One of the children noticed a crack in the office ceiling and kept asking anxiously and repeatedly who had cracked the ceiling, not calmed by any answer given her. Another child, seeing one doll with a hat and another without a hat, could not be placated until the other hat was found and put on the doll's head. He then immediately lost interest in the two dolls; sameness and completeness had been restored, and all was well again.

The dread of change and incompleteness seems to be a major factor in the explanation of the monotonous repetitiousness and the resulting *limitation in the variety of spontaneous activity.* A situation, a performance, a sentence is not regarded as complete if it is not made up of exactly the same elements that were present at the time the child was first confronted with it. If the slightest ingredient is altered or removed, the total situation is no longer the same and therefore is not accepted as such, or it is resented with impatience or even with a reaction of profound frustration. The inability to experience wholes without full attention to the constituent parts is somewhat reminiscent of the plight of children with specific reading disability who do not respond to the modern system of configurational reading instruction but must be taught to build up words from their alphabetic elements. This is perhaps one of the reasons why those children of our group who were old enough to be instructed in reading immediately became excessively preoccupied with the "spelling" of words, or why Donald, for example, was so disturbed over the fact that "light" and "bite," having the same phonetic quality, should be spelled differently.

Objects that do not change their appearance and position, that retain their sameness and never threaten to interfere with the child's aloneness, are readily accepted by the autistic child. He has a good *relation to objects;* he is interested in them, can play with them happily for hours. He can be very fond of them, or get angry at them if, for instance, he cannot fit them into a certain space. When with them, he has a gratifying sense of undisputed power and control. Donald and Charles began in the second year of life to exercise this power by spinning everything that could be possibly spun and jumping up and down in ecstasy when they watched the objects whirl about. Frederick "jumped up and down in great glee" when he bowled and saw the pins go down. The children sensed and exercised the same power over their own bodies by rolling and other rhythmic movements. These actions and the accompanying ecstatic fervor strongly indicate the presence of *masturbatory orgastic gratification.*

The children's *relation to people* is altogether different. Every one of the children, upon entering the office, immediately went after blocks, toys, or other objects, without paying the least attention to the persons present. It would be wrong to say that they were not aware of the presence of persons. But the people, so long as they left the child alone, figured in about the same manner as did the desk, the bookshelf, or the filing cabinet. When the child was addressed, he was not bothered. He had the choice between not responding at all or, if a question was repeated too insistently, "getting it over with" and continuing with whatever he had been doing. Comings and goings, even of the mother, did not seem to register. Conversation going on in the room elicited no interest. If the adults did not try to enter the child's domain, he would at times, while moving between them, gently touch a hand or a knee as on other occasions he patted the desk or the couch. But he never looked into anyone's face. If an adult forcibly intruded himself by taking a block away or stepping on an object that the child needed, the child struggled and became angry with the hand or the foot, which was dealt with per se and not as a part of a person. He never addressed a word or a look to the owner of the hand or foot. When the object was retrieved, the child's mood changed abruptly to one of placidity. When pricked, he showed fear of the *pin* but not of the person who pricked him.

The relation to the members of the household or to other children did not differ from that to the people at the office. Profound aloneness dominates all behavior. The father or mother or both may have been away for an hour or a month; at their homecoming, there is no indication that the child has been even aware of their absence. After many outbursts of frustration, he gradually and reluctantly learns to compromise when he finds no way out, obeys certain orders, complies in matters of daily routine, but always strictly insists on the observance of his rituals. When there is company, he moves among the people "like a stranger" or, as one mother put it, "like a foal who had been let out of an enclosure." When with other children, he does not play with them. He plays alone while they are around, maintaining no bodily, physiognomic, or verbal contact with them. He does not take part in competitive games. He just is there, and if sometimes he happens to stroll as far as the periphery of a group, he soon removes himself and remains alone. At the same time, he quickly becomes familiar with the names of all the children of the group, may know the color of each child's hair, and other details about each child.

There is a far better relationship with pictures of people than with people themselves. Pictures, after all, cannot interfere. Charles was affectionately interested in the picture of a child in a magazine advertisement. He remarked repeatedly about the child's sweetness and beauty. Elaine was fascinated by pictures of animals but would not go near a live animal. John made no distinction between real and depicted people. When he saw a group photograph, he asked seriously when the people would step out of the picture and come into the room.

Even though most of these children were at one time or another looked upon as feebleminded, they are all unquestionably endowed with good *cognitive potentialities.* They all have strikingly intelligent physiognomies. Their faces at the same time give the impression of *serious-mindedness* and, in the presence of others, an anxious *tenseness,* probably because of the uneasy anticipation of possible interference. When alone with objects, there is often a placid smile and an expression of beatitude, sometimes accompanied by happy though monotonous humming and singing. The astounding vocabulary of the speaking children, the excellent memory for events of several years before, the phenomenal rote memory for poems and names, and the precise recollection of complex patterns and sequences, bespeak good intelligence in the sense in which this word is commonly used. Binet or similar testing could not be carried out because of limited accessibility. But all the children did well with the Seguin form board.

Physically, the children were essentially normal. Five had relatively large heads. Several of the children were somewhat clumsy in gait and gross motor performances, but all were very skillful in terms of finer muscle coordination. Electroencephalograms were normal in the case of all but John, whose anterior fontanelle did not close until he was $2\frac{1}{2}$ years old, and who at $5\frac{1}{4}$ years had two series of predominantly right-sided convulsions. Frederick had a supernumerary nipple in the left axilla; there were no other instances of congenital anomalies.

There is one other very interesting common denominator in the backgrounds of these children. *They all come of highly intelligent families.* Four fathers are psychiatrists, one is a brilliant lawyer, one a chemist and law school graduate employed in the government Patent Office, one a plant pathologist, one a professor of forestry, one an advertising copy writer who has a degree in law and has studied in three universities, one is a mining engineer, and one a successful business man. Nine of the eleven mothers are college graduates. Of the two who have only high-school education, one was a secretary in a pathology laboratory, and the other ran a theatrical booking office in New York City before marriage. Among the others, there was a free-lance writer, a physician, a psychologist, a graduate nurse, and Frederick's mother was successively a purchasing agent, the director of secretarial studies in a girls' school, and a teacher of history. Among the grandparents and collaterals there are many physicians, scientists, writers, journalists, and students of art. All but three of the families are represented in *Who's Who in America* or *American Men of Science,* or in both.

Two of the children are Jewish, the others are all of Anglo-Saxon descent. Three are "only" children, five are the first-born of two children in their respective families, one is the oldest of three children, one is the younger of the two, and one the youngest of three.

COMMENT

The combination of extreme autism, obsessiveness, stereotypy, and echolalia brings the total picture into relationship with some of the basic schizophrenic phenomena. Some of the children have indeed been diagnosed as of this type at one time or another. But in spite of the remarkable similarities, the condition differs in many respects from all other known instances of childhood schizophrenia.

First of all, even in cases with the earliest recorded onset of schizophrenia, including those of De Sanctis' dementia praecocissima and of Heller's dementia infantilis, the first observable manifestations were preceded by at least two years of essentially average development; the histories specifically emphasize a more or less graduate *change* in the patients' behavior. The children of our group have all shown their extreme aloneness from the very beginning of life, not responding to anything that comes to them from the outside world. This is most characteristically expressed in the recurrent report of failure of the child to assume an anticipatory posture upon being picked up, and of failure to adjust the body to that of the person holding him.

Second, our children are able to establish and maintain an excellent, purposeful, and "intelligent" relation to objects that do not threaten to interfere with their aloneness, but are from the start anxiously and tensely impervious to people, with whom for a long time they do not have any kind of direct affective contact. If dealing with another person becomes inevitable, then a temporary relationship is formed with the person's hand or foot as a definitely detached object, but not with the person himself.

All of the children's activities and utterances are governed rigidly and consistently by the powerful desire for aloneness and sameness. Their world must seem to them to be made up of elements that, once they have been experienced in a certain setting or sequence, cannot be tolerated in any other setting or sequence; nor can the setting or sequence be tolerated without all the original ingredients in the identical spatial or chronologic order. Hence the obsessive repetitiousness. Hence the reproduction of sentences without altering the pronouns to suit the occasion. Hence, perhaps, also the development of a truly phenomenal memory that enables the child to recall and reproduce complex "nonsense" patterns, no matter how unorganized they are, in exactly the same form as originally construed.

Five of our children have by now reached ages between 9 and 11 years. Except for Virginia S., who has been dumped in a school for the feebleminded, they show a very interesting course. The basic desire for aloneness and sameness has remained essentially unchanged, but there has been a varying degree of emergence from solitude, an acceptance of at least some people as being within the child's sphere of consideration, and a sufficient increase in the number of experienced patterns to refute the earlier impression of extreme limitation of the child's ideational content. One might perhaps put it this way: While the schizophrenic tries to solve his problem by stepping out of a world of which he has been a part and with which he has been in touch, our children gradually *compromise* by extending cautious feelers into a world in which they have been total strangers from the beginning. Between the ages of 5 and 6 years, they gradually abandon the echolalia and learn spontaneously to use personal pronouns with adequate reference. Language becomes more communicative, at first in the sense of a question-and-answer exercise, and then in the sense of greater spontaneity of sentence formation. Food is accepted without difficulty. Noises and motions are tolerated more than previously. The panic tantrums subside. The repetitiousness assumes the form of obsessive preoccupations. Contact with a limited number of people is established in a two-fold way: people are included in the child's world to the extent to which they satisfy his needs, answer his obsessive questions, teach him how to read and to do things. Second, though people are still regarded as nuisances, their questions are answered and their commands are obeyed reluctantly, with the implication that it would be best to get these interferences over with, the sooner to be able to return to the still much desired aloneness. Between the ages of 6 and 8 years, the children begin to play in a group, still never *with* the other members of the play group, but at least on the periphery *alongside* the group. Reading skill is acquired quickly, but the children read monotonously, and a story or a moving picture is experienced in unrelated portions rather than in its coherent totality. All of this makes the family feel that, in spite of recognized "difference" from other children, there is progress and improvement.

It is not easy to evaluate the fact that all of our patients have come of highly intelligent parents. This much is certain, that there is a great deal of obsessiveness in the family background. The very detailed diaries and reports and the frequent remembrance, after several years, that the children had learned to recite twenty-five questions and answers of the Presbyterian Catechism, to sing thirty-seven nursery songs, or to discriminate between eighteen symphonies, furnish a telling illustration of parental obsessiveness.

One other fact stands out prominently. In the whole group, there are very few really warmhearted fathers and mothers. For the most part, the parents, grandparents, and collaterals are persons strongly preoccupied with abstractions of a scientific, literary, or artistic nature, and limited in genuine interest in people. Even some of the happiest marriages are rather cold and formal affairs. Three of the marriages were dismal failures. The question arises whether or to what extent this fact has contributed to the condition of the children. The children's aloneness from the beginning of life makes it difficult to attribute the whole picture exclusively to the type of the early parental relations with our patients.

We must, then, assume that these children have come into the world with innate inability to form the usual, biologically provided affective contact with people, just as other children come into the world with innate physical or intellectual handicaps. If this assumption is correct, a further study of our children may help to furnish concrete criteria regarding the still diffuse notions about the constitutional components of emotional reactivity. For here we seem to have pure-culture examples of *inborn autistic disturbances of affective contact.**

---

* Since the completion of this paper, 2 more cases of inborn autistic disturbance of affective contact have come under our observation.

Childhood Schizophrenia: Clinical Study of One Hundred Schizophrenic Children

Lauretta Bender
1947

More than one hundred preadolescent children, who have presented the clinical picture of childhood schizophrenia, have been observed on the Children's Ward of the Psychiatric Division of Bellevue Hospital in the past ten years. Our own definition of childhood schizophrenia has been a clinical entity, occurring in childhood before the age of eleven years, which "reveals pathology in behavior at every level and in every area of integration or patterning within the functioning of the central nervous system, be it vegetative, motor, perceptual, intellectual, emotional, or social. Furthermore, this behavior pathology disturbs the pattern of every functioning field in a characteristic way. The pathology cannot therefore be thought of as focal in the architecture of the central nervous system, but rather as striking at the substratum of integrative functioning or biologically patterned behavior" (1). At present the only concept we can have of this pathology is in terms of field forces in which temporal rather than spatial factors are emphasized. Within the concept of field forces, one can accept some idea of a focal order, since no one integrated function is ever completely lost or inhibited, and since there are different degrees of severity of disturbance in the

life history of any child and between two different children. This also differs with the period of onset.

The diagnostic criteria for the 100 schizophrenic children which make up this study have been rigid. In each child it has been possible to demonstrate characteristic disturbances in every patterned functional field of behavior. Every schizophrenic child reacts to the psychosis in a way determined by his own total personality including the infantile experiences and the level of maturation of the personality. This reaction is usually a neurotic one determined by the anxiety stirred up by the disturbing phenomena in the vaso-vegetative, motility, perceptual, and psychological fields. Interferences in normal developmental patterns and regressive phenomena with resulting primitive reactions are related to both the essential psychosis and the reaction of the anxiety-ridden personality.

There are, of course, children in whom the differential diagnosis is very difficult. Those with some form of diffuse encephalopathy or diffuse developmental deviations in which the normally strong urges for normal development push the child into frustration and reactive anxiety may present many schizophrenic features in the motility disturbances, intellectual interferences, and psychological reactions. Some children with a deep anxiety due to disturbances in interpersonal relationships may react with profound biological disturbance and regressive behavior akin to the schizophrenic. The common feature is the anxiety and the fact that the developing child is a biological society entity with only a certain number of ways of reacting to life traumas and always reacts holistically whether the traumas arise internally or externally or at whatever point in the developmental curve. Schizophrenia adds nothing to childhood experiences or behavior which an otherwise normal child might not also be capable of under some other condition.

Schizophrenia in childhood may otherwise be defined as a form of encephalopathy appearing at different points in the developmental curve, interfering with the normal developmental pattern of the biological unit and the social personality in a characteristic way and, because of frustration, causing anxiety to which the individual must react according to his own capacities.

In every schizophrenic child, we can see disturbances in the vaso-vegetative functioning. They may be either excessively labile or unresponsive in their vasomotor behavior; they may flush, perspire, or be colorless with blue cold extremities; they react to minor and major illnesses in an unpredictable way. A simple cold may make them appear to be in a state of shock for a short time, and they may completely recover in an hour or two. They may react with no temperature fluctuation to a severe infection or show an excessive response to a slight illness. Hoskins (2) has emphasized the difficulties that lie in the integration or control or cooperation in the different fields of vasomotor, vegetative, or endocrine functions in the adult. The rapidly growing organism of the child seems to accentuate these problems although little specific work has been done on children. Leonard Gold (3) showed that there was a disturbance in equilibrium of the autonomic nervous system in that the sympathetic was more sluggish than the para-sympathetic. In 9 of our patients the autonomic nervous system maintained its own homeostasis and was sluggish in its recuperative powers once it was thrown out of equilibrium by mecholyl chloride as compared with 19 non-schizophrenic problem children.

The physiological rhythms of daily living lose their normal rhythmic pattern. This is seen in the sleeping, eating, and elimination habits. Mothers complain of it as a part of the early disorder in behavior, and we observe it in trying to adapt the children to the ward routine suitable for the normal child. Growth discrepancies are marked. The children are too big or too little, too fat or too thin. The growth problems become interrelated with the psychological problems because of both the essential schizophrenic process and the reactive anxiety. Stuart, in whom schizophrenia began in the first two years, when anxiety is at its height in relationship to oral activities, was at $8\frac{1}{2}$ years as tall as a 12 year old boy and was obese. Most of his activities and preoccupations centered on oral problems with biting, spitting, excessive verbalization and obscenities, and overeating. He distressed his mother by identifying her as "horse face."

Menstruation has occurred in several girls at age 7 and 10 years without other gross endocrine anomalies, but with the onset of schizophrenia. Delay in the onset of menses in girls with schizophrenia at puberty is well known. Precocious or delayed puberty in boys also occurs. Unevenness in the somatic growth and nonspecific endocrine dyscrasias would seem to explain the dysplastic features of many adult schizophrenics. It remains to be determined whether in such cases the clinical picture of schizophrenia was apparent in the stage of childhood at which the deviation in physical development asserted itself. Such cases have been referred to as a constitutional type of schizophrenia (Bowman 4), and it has been shown that they have a schizoid type of prepsychotic personality in childhood which may well have been a childhood schizophrenia.

Electroencephalograms show a disproportionate number of dysrhythmic records with periodic bursts of slow-high voltage waves, but as yet, one cannot interpret the EEG as a projection of a specific cortical pattern disorder in schizophrenia.

Characteristic disturbances in patterned motor behavior or motility can be demonstrated in every schizophrenic child. Mothers will tell us in retrospect of unevenness in the motor development of the child. They complain of motor awkwardness and poor control of limbs. The child seemed insecure and unhappy in gaining new motor patterns and expressed anxiety to a distressing degree in forming new motor habits independent of the mother, such as walking alone, climbing stairs, stepping over or off of small objects, or using swings, tricycles, or even being left alone in a carriage or high chair. The motor independence may have been established and lost again with the onset of the schizophrenic illness. This is probably one of the most significant early causes for the reactive anxiety and guilt on the part of the mother who cannot understand why she cannot make her child independent in his motor habits when he seems otherwise quite normal in his physical development.

Early or primitive reflex patterned activities may outlive the stage to which they belong and be retained throughout childhood as a mode of play or of expressing anxiety, etc. A good example of this is the choreoathetotic activities of the hands of the infant which is normal in the first few months, and is used as a play pattern in the latter half of the first year as the child discovers its hands and relates them to the visual motor patterns and eating-grasping patterns. In children who develop schizophrenia in the first two years of life, this motor pattern is retained and seems compulsively determined, along with other motor reflex patterns. Later in childhood, it may assume the pattern of mannerisms. Some children will relate them to oral habits, biting and sucking the fingers until they are sore and abscessed.

Others relate them to jumping activities either in play or anger, as in temper tantrums. Seven-year-old Richard, schizophrenic since his second year, says, "It is my nervousness and it makes me happy. If I didn't do it, I wouldn't be nervous, but maybe I wouldn't be happy." It occurred most characteristically in him after an elaborately patterned and symbolic play situation. Whatever the pattern, it is always a pattern and not an isolated neurological sign of known brain pathology such as choreoathetosis.

There are postural reflex responses (5) (6) (7) which are nearly specific for childhood schizophrenia. Postural reflexes are tested by having the child stand with his arms outstretched in front of him and his eyes closed while the head is turned on the neck by the examiner. The primitive response to this test is to turn the body so as to bring it in line again with the head. So long as the examiner continues to turn the head, the child will continue to turn on the longitudinal axis. This is a normal response for the young child from the time he is old enough to stand alone and cooperate with the test procedure without losing his balance (otherwise he will resist the test) until the age of six years in the average normal child. After this, the normal child will accept the turning of the head without rotating the body and, after an initial displacement of the arms, will correct the displacement. This is a highly sensitive test procedure for many types of motor disabilities in children (8). The schizophrenic child responds with a graceful fluid whirling which he quickly accepts as a new pattern of activity, if he has not already discovered it himself, and will carry it on spontaneously. Sometimes the examiner need only put his finger on the top of the head which suggests a pivot. This should not be misunderstood as an acquired trained pattern in a child anxious to please the adult. Normal children do not usually respond in this way. The schizophrenic child finds that the test stimulus conforms with his own impulse tendencies. Rotating and whirling motor play in all planes make up a large part of their activity. It finds expression in their dreams and all other forms of fantasies, and is the nucleus of many of their psychological problems such as fear of or preoccupation with losing their limbs, inability to determine the periphery of their own body or the boundaries of their personality or "ego boundaries," their relationship to the reality of the outer world, to determine their own center of gravity, to relate themselves to time and space, or even be sure of their own identity.

There are two other related phenomena. The schizophrenic child shows a physical or bodily dependence which can be seen by simple physical contact. He seeks instantly to use the body or the motility of the adult and will either lean so completely on the other person as to fall to the ground if that support is withdrawn or will readily sink completely and passively into the lap and arms of the accepting adult as though to melt his body into that of the other and thereby identify himself with the other's more secure center of gravity. With the same impulse, he clings to and holds on to the adult at every opportunity. The second phenomenon is a cohesiveness of the body surface such that there seems to be no limiting membrane between the two proximating skin surfaces. One can obtain complete motor compliance from the child by contact through the palmar surfaces and induce *cerea flexibilitas* or push the child about at will. Sometimes negativism or ambivalence may lead to an initial resistance to such phenomena but it is quickly overcome. The examining adult must lend himself sympathetically to the relationship since he must always be an active and passive participant in every patient-physician relationship. The child's motor compliance (9) suggests a strong need or impulse to be completely dependent upon the body of another person as though seeking a dependable center of gravity which can be used to control his own disorganizing impulses and undetermined ego boundaries.

The schizophrenic child of three to five or six years may become largely preoccupied with motor play which is composed of many interrevolving systems of reflex activity. Effort to get the child to conform to the pattern of life about him by acquired habit patterns may give the impression of awkwardness and dissociated behavior, but when left to his own devices, he carries on endless rhythmic and graceful dancing behavior with changing tempos.

There are also some unconnected impulse activities, best described as darting, which are sudden and usually at a tangent from the other rhythmic activities. It is as though there were two impulses for activity, one that keeps the child at a constant rhythmic play about a changing center or multiple centers which he is trying to fixate, and the other in which he tries to escape from the organized center of gravity and its determined reflex pattern. In articulate children, this desire to escape may be expressed in psychological as well as motor terms. They strive either to escape from the dependence on the mother (due to the disease process with its motor insecurity and frustrated oral cravings) or to escape from whatever environment they are in and feel is confining them, or again, to escape from their own identity and the frustrating disorder of the psychosis. Ten-year-old Francine wrote a letter to her doctor; "For the doctor, I am sure I will escape though and go to the real world. It is better there. He isn't a guardian angel and neither is this a guardian angel hospital meant for all who come here. I, Francine, that is what they call me, was very unhappy there. It was a terrible world. I thought it was a real one but it seems it isn't. I may some day go to the real one."

An uncertain control of the facial musculature leads to grimacing, carefully patterned, and belonging in some way to the total psychological problem. Various oral mannerisms, often with associated oral or vocal noises, are common. If there is some inequality in the physical make-up in the child (common to all organic patterns and all individuals), it tends to be exaggerated in the schizophrenic child while the normal child compensates for inequalities. Thus, inequalities of the head or face may be reflected into the musculature as a mannerism so marked as to confuse the diagnosis. Other so-called "soft neurological signs" which do not make a syndrome are not uncommon in schizophrenia and can be explained in the same way. The voice is wooden-like in quality, mechanically modulated, and seems not to belong to the child. It has something of a ventriloquistic character as though it too could not be sure of the ego boundary or center or identity of the child which is producing it.

The child's inability to locate the periphery of his body seems related to his inability to take care of his body secretions, body extensions, and his clothes. He has no concern about nasal secretions, saliva, tears, urine and feces, and they drip from him without his awareness. Hair is neglected, but that the problem is something more than simple neglect is evidenced by the observation that many schizophrenic children cut their hair with the schoolroom scissors.

It is clear that it is impossible to discuss problems of motor activity, concern or awareness of body functional problems, body image problems, and other perceptual problems separately. The perceptual problems of schizophrenic children are easily seen, as one need only observe their visual motor patterning with the use of pencil and paper. Most schizophrenic children are highly productive with the various projective techniques although they tend to lose this as they deteriorate, and some, in whom schizophrenia has started early and progressed rapidly, may never show any productivity.

In the study of the genesis of visually perceived form (*10*), it was determined that a vortical movement is the basis for the organization of the visual field and is the beginning of all form. The young child starts with a large whole arm circular scribble; action is the initial impulse for form. It is never unpatterend and the pattern always includes action or motor elements and visual or form elements and spatial and temporal elements. At three or four, the child begins to control the vortical movement into discrete circles, also related to each other concentrically and directionally on a horizontal plane. At four, a modified circle is a square; at five, a triangle; at six, a diamond. A point is the center of a circle. The vertical plane is obtained at four or five by rotating the horizontal plane circle-wise (*11*).

With the use of gestalt figures which give sufficient play to these problems, and which may be copied, these genetic features can be determined. One can also deter-

mine the disorders in visual motor pattern in pathological states. The schizophrenic child copying these figures shows many of the same problems which are shown in his motility. There is a tendency to use old primitive responses interlocked with the more mature capacities which are expected from the maturational level of the child. There is therefore an excessive use of the vortical movement even with good diamond forms. A series of figures on a horizontal plane may be pulled around into a vortical figure. The boundaries of circles are uncertain and may be gone over several times. The centers of circles are uncertain; there are no points but many little circles, and for the same reason angular and crossed forms are fragmented. Action cannot be readily controlled and figures are elaborated, enlarged, repeated. The total product makes a pattern itself with a great deal of fluidity to it based upon vortical movement. The perceptual patterns lose their boundaries and therefore their relationship to the background. One may speak here, too, of a motor compliance and cohesiveness between the boundaries of two objects. There is also an effort to explore and fixate depth or third and fourth dimensions. In this well-patterned fluid matrix, are areas in which the pattern is broken; a part of a figure is separated from the whole and made to rotate faster; a group of small circles is separated from the whole mass. It is a new wave movement. One's best understanding is to think in terms of a disturbance in the time factor in patterned behavior characteristic for each field of behavior, such a time factor being of biological origin and related to this disease process alone. Other forms of behavior such as regressive, projective and introjective, elaborative, inhibitive, distractive and concretistic, are efforts on the part of the personality to orient itself to this pathology and, if possible, control it.

The spontaneous art of schizophrenic children is a field so fertile that its study would bring us not only a very advanced understanding of the disease entity, but also of many normal human problems. The characteristic pathology of schizophrenia with the impulse to action, the reactive anxiety with the desire to understand and correct the pathology, and the accelerated creativeness of the six to twelve-year-old child all combine so that often the schizophrenic child shows remarkable art ability which may express itself in various fields—graphic art, dancing, music, and verbalization.

The schizophrenic child usually employs three topics for his spontaneous graphic art, the human figure, natural scenes, and abstractions. The latter two subjects are extremely intriguing, but cannot be discussed here.

When the child draws the human form, it is essentially a projection of his body image and its problems; it is a self-portrait. It is not surprising that the schizophrenic child with his body image problems, motility, and perceptual disturbances, uncertainty as to his identity, and his drive for action, finds ready expression for his problems in drawing the human form. The techniques that are used have a wide range even in one child. The most primitive use of vortical movement with graduated variations may be the sole form used to draw a human figure, but it expresses just that whirling motility, impulse to action, fluid ego boundary and uncertain center of gravity which represents the schizophrenic child and his problems. He is by no means limited to this technical device. Without training and by sheer self experimentation, these children develop the most amazing capacity to express human form in action, always related to some total situation which is immediately evident from the picture itself. Not all develop the gifts, of course; some express the problems crudely, unesthetically, but nevertheless express it. In others, the gift is dramatic and bears no relationship to the child's endowment but seems to be a hypertrophied capacity arising from the disease. It is fleeting and deteriorates with the progress of the illness or diminishes if the child improves, and as he passes into puberty. The problems which are expressed in the drawings of the human form are his identity and relationship to people about him, the accelerated impulse to motion, action, whirling, dancing, and aggression, the functions of different parts of the body, the boundaries and peripheries and extensions of the body; i.e.—multiplicity of heads and limbs, facial expression of anxiety and terror—feeling of external influence, changing states of consciousness, interpersonal relationships, and social problems.

It is a never-ending source of amazement to see a child who is perhaps underdeveloped, infantile in motor play, physically dependent, unconcerned with his body excreta and clothing, unsure of his own identity, inarticulate to the point of mutism, unable to make any school or social adjustment, but who will cover paper with the most expressive human forms in all kinds of motor patterns and in the most intricate interhuman and social relationships, and experimenting—Picasso-like—in techniques and art forms.

The study of the genesis of the thought and language disturbance of the schizophrenic child will help clarify many of the problems of schizophrenic thought and language in general (*12*). When schizophrenia occurs in the first few years or before language is well established, there is usually more or less retardation, inhibition or blocking, often with complete mutism which may appear as an initial symptom but may later be partially overcome with a return of speech that is distorted; or speech may gradually "deteriorate" or "regress" by use of simpler language forms, dropping out of connecting words, loss of more recently acquired language forms, and fragmentary speech. Language may be used as a repetitive expression of anxiety with questions concerning identity and orientation, but never waiting or attending to an answer or ceasing to use it as a means of communication or interpersonal relationship; it is used as a chanting accompaniment of motor play. There are occasional explosive expletives, aggressive or obscene in nature. Language may be only experimentally imitative, echoing, repetitive or perseverative, compulsive and obsessional. Isolated words may be played or experimented with, and new word forms created, at first varying only slightly from recognizable words and having some significant sign value in the child's emotional problems. Using the third person pronoun for himself and confusing or evading all other pronouns may represent an echolalic repetition of language as he hears it, or may represent concretistic use of language forms, regression to infantile levels, or expressing his difficulties with identity of himself and orientation to the world. When language returns after a period of mutism, it may show all types of deviation as though the child were experimenting with all forms of aphasia and language pathology (*12*) (*13*) (*14*) (*15*).

On the other hand, the child who has already mastered language may show an increased activity in the field of language and in thinking processes. In some there is an early precocious language development. In psychometric tests, his language development may be beyond the level anticipated for his endowment. In this field, too, the drive for action expresses itself. There is no better way of describing the thought processes than to say that they are vortical, gyrating, circling about a nuclear point of gravity which cannot be fixated. There seems to be experimentation with many alternate thought forms and ideas, and only some fragments can be projected since the recording apparatus of speech is slower than the field of language action. Thus what we hear sounds fragmented, dissociated, bizarre; occasional tangent, darting expletives may break through.

Symbol formation is a part of normal thought and language development. Just as there are form disturbances in all other fields of language, so there are in symbol formation in the schizophrenic child. The function of symbol formation (*17*) normally is to use the biologically determined perceptual motor patterns as a sign reference for emotional, psychological, and personality problems. Thus the motile circle in visual motor patterns is used to express body image problems projected and integrated by the maturing child into the human form. At times, unacceptable human traits or partial traits, such as oral aggression in response to aggressive parents, are symbolized as animal forms (*18*). For the young child whose problems are those relating to his relationship with his mother, the family and the outer world, the circle becomes a boat upon a motile flowing ocean, the boat is the mother, the sun is the father and the child himself is inside the boat (*19*). This can and is elaborated indefinitely to meet the needs of the individual child. For seven-year-old

Richard, schizophrenic since his second year, the circle is a "rat-cheese-hole" dealing with his problems of introjection, anality, an aggressive father image and his anxiety concerning aggression. If the circle becomes a square, it is still a "rat-cheese-hole" but it is now derived from electric wall plugs and the rat will be electrocuted by the wires if he goes into the hole. One sees in such symbolization tendencies for condensation or the superimposing of many levels of thinking and of many psychological problems, mixing of abstract and concrete thinking, and of regressive and accelerated drives. At the same time, the child becomes fixated on his symbolic forms and cannot leave them because they never solve his problems. For the normal child, his symbol formation is quickly digested by ceasing to be concrete and becoming abstract, contributing to his growth once they are experienced. Symbols become either amnestic or appear as dreams and recognized fables, fairy stories and fantasies. In the schizophrenic child, such symbol formations are the best examples of the patterned form that the schizophrenic thought disorder tends to take to express, by condensation, all the problems which concern the child.

The psychological problems of childhood schizophrenia are different from those of the adolescent or adult. They are appropriate for the period of childhood and also for critical developmental periods within childhood which may be the period of onset of the illness. The significant problems are identity, body image and body function problems, object relationship and interpersonal relationship both in the family and the larger social world, orientation in time and space, meaning of language and, finally, the problem of anxiety. The disturbance in identification processes; that is, difficulties in identifying one's self and thereby relating to the rest of the world, is the essential psychological problem. The resulting anxiety is a reactive problem, and the symptom formation is related to both.

The youngest schizophrenic children, those in the first two or three years of life, show disturbances in the vegetative rhythms and habit patterns, in motility, and in object relationship. Mothers are most distressed by this inability of the child to relate to herself, to siblings, play material, food or clothes. Language has no objective use for sign value, communication, or interpersonal relations. Kanner (*13*) speaks of "autistic disturbances in affective contact." The child may be fixated on one kind of object relationship such as round objects which can be spun like a top. Robert who was seen by me at age four and again at five and a half, could only relate himself to buttons, silver dollars, and "pepper-pot tops." Kanner (*14*) reports a similar case in detail. For the child between three and five, whose language is not inhibited, we may get a revealing expression of the psychological problems which may again be fixated on one or another problem at a time, as

Richard's rat-cheese-holes, or they may show a spread over almost every problem of childhood. Five-and-a-half-year-old Judy says, "I say, hello, doctor, have you any new toys? Let me open your radiator with this screw driver. I say let me open it. I say, so what! Can I copy your animals? I am in a doctor's office. You and I are twins, aren't we? I am coloring this camel brown. I said I am coloring it brown. I said I am coloring it brown. Have you a little scissors? Have you a big scissors? I say, have you a big scissors? Well here's what I will use, what do you think. It is called a knife. How does my voice sound? What? What? Judy what? Is that your name? I'm cutting out this camel. Is it pretty enough to hang on the wall? Can you cut as pretty as this? My sisters say, camel talk. Isn't that funny? Camel talk. My voice sounds like up in the library. Doesn't it? In the hospital my voice sounds like up in the library. Can you say li-bra-ri-an? The library is where you get books."

An eleven-year-old girl (*20*) had been placed in a shelter with her brother and sisters because of a crisis in the family. When the mother called for the children, the child refused to go with her, saying, "I have two sisters and one brother. . . . Their mother came for them but my mother didn't come for me. My mother didn't take me home because she didn't come for me. Another lady came for them. It was their mother. She didn't have the same look. She was darker. She didn't have my mother's hat or clothes. My mother told me she didn't come. My mother is a colored woman with nice brown hair and brown eyes. She is not so dark. The one that came wasn't so nice and I knew it wasn't my mother. The other children thought so. I am different from the other children. I'm dumber. They catch it before I do. I am harder to catch on anything. They don't want me to play with them. They like me a lot. They like me more and more. There ain't no others. I like them lots and lots and lots. I am an oddicle person because I belong catching one before they do. I don't think my sister is my sister. She went home with her mother. She plays my sister." Later, she said, "I want to go home with my mother, I made a mistake. Her eyes seemed bigger, she looked taller, her feet were bigger, she had a long head and she was blacker. She didn't speak with the same voice as my mother. People on the street seemed to be talking about my mother, I imagined it wasn't nice, maybe something like I was being mean to my mother. The girls would lay on the bed and make up things about my mother. They weren't my sisters. They were the ones that went home with the woman who says she was our mother."

The sexual problems of early childhood may be accentuated in schizophrenia with excessive and open masturbation and preoccupation with the functions of elimination. There may be distressing preoccupations with masturbatory impulses and internalized objects in the pelvic region. One young boy, whenever alone, would cry out "Every minute, every minute, I can't get it out, a big one, too, Jesus Christ, every minute, its getting bigger." He would not explain, but compress his thighs and writhe in his chair and point to his buttocks, and only say "There is something in my arms, there is clay—they feel stiff." There is never the complaint that someone outside is responsible for these experiences. Verbal hallucinations akin to the adult's are so uncommon as to be of no diagnostic value. When present, they seem to have the same mechanism as in non-schizophrenic children, are neurotically determined, and clearly represent a voice of conscience usually related to the introjected body and to unsatisfactory ego-ideals. They readily disappear with treatment (21). In childhood we look for introjection instead of projection (22). The introjected object is often the good and/or bad mother, the devil or guardian angel, the whole of hell or the world at war, "a little man with a big old long hat" and Francine's (22) "brain bodies" which her bad mother put in her to make her have a baby.

These are the internalized objects which Melanie Klein (23) has found important in the normal development of the early infantile period. In childhood schizophrenia, they can be demonstrated and usually persist until nearly puberty. They have considerable influence on the child; in adults they are treated as hallucinations or persecutory objects.

It is a general principle that all of the normal mechanisms of early childhood will be used as points of fixation in childhood schizophrenia. They will be exaggerated by repetition, by finding expression in various forms, by condensing with other mechanisms and carried into later periods of development.

In the same way, the problem of aggression is very important to children especially in the parent-child relationship and sibling relationships. A nine-year-old says, "I want a hammer to kill my bed. I'm mad at it, it won't come to me at night and I have to go find it when I want it. I'm mad at my mother too, she takes food to bed and eats it in bed. If my grandmother found out, she'd kill her. I got a gun to shoot somebody's head off and a razor to cut my finger off. My thumb hurts. I hope I get an operation on my throat, it hurts. I want a very terrible operation on my throat to get something out. It might be poison. I ate something I thought it was candy. Is that a lady or a man doll? What a funny face. It must be a skeleton. They kill people, jump on your back and bite you all to pieces. Know why I want to get hurt? Because my family won't leave me alone. My sisters tell lies about me. They beat me. I want to get hurt real bad. I dreamed a fox was after me. I fell on top of a stump and hurt me. A fox came behind me. I jumped off the roof. But the fox couldn't jump. I landed right on my head and got hurt. I liked that. When you get hurt and wake up, it is beautiful. I dreamed

you tried to tip-toe down the stairs and tripped and fell down and half killed yourself. My mother doesn't love me. She shouldn't have had me. I should have stayed in her guts. I am in my own gizzard. I think I will go back to heaven where I came from."

Anxiety is the nucleus of the schizophrenic problem in the earlier stages. It is the reactive mechanism of the threatened personality, threatened by the disrupting effects of the schizophrenic process in all the functioning fields of the personality, the ego, or the biological unit. The way the individual deals with this anxiety determines much of the symptom formation. The presence of a severe anxiety in a child, unaccounted for by a reality situation, is in itself suggestive of schizophrenia. The suffering on the part of the child and those about him is proportionate to this anxiety and the resulting symptom formation.

Our therapeutic approach at present is directed essentially at the anxiety and secondary symptom formation. In the child, we also attempt to help in the integration of the pattern of behavior and the promotion of such identification processes as possible. So long as the anxiety is evident, the child shows considerable affect. The excessive impulse to action drives the child as much toward social contacts as away from it. The great anxiety also leads him to cling physically and psychologically. Failure to get satisfaction from such contact may gradually lead to withdrawal but not until there has been a long period of illness. The gyrating thought processes of such children, and the tendency to experiment in the hope that they can seek a solution to their problems, leads to what may well be called an ambivalence in personal relationships. Their great charm results in a strong reciprocal relationship. The most dearly beloved of the problem children on the ward in the past ten years have usually been schizophrenic children.

In discussing the disturbances in the interpersonal relationships of the schizophrenic child, we cannot omit comments on the reactions of the mothers, and also of others in the child's world. The mother of the schizophrenic child, especially the child in whom the process has developed insidiously over a long period, shows a specific mechanistic patterning due to her efforts to help the child in his distorted identification processes, to understand what is happening and to identify herself with the child. The mother bears an intolerable burden of anxiety and guilt, and is more bewildered than the child himself. She will try every mechanism for denying, evading, displacing, or absolving the child's psychosis. The motor and physical dependence of the child, his intriguing charm, his distressing anxiety, all bind the child to the mother while she cannot identify with his problems or follow his disturbed thought process and development.

The relationship between siblings, when one is schizophrenic, is particularly difficult because the essential problem in sibling relationship is identification. But the negative and positive features in such a relationship are exaggerated and disturbed. In the same way, other children are both attracted to the schizophrenic child and his exaggeration of childhood problems and frightened by his anxiety and inability to solve his problems. Two schizophrenic children have a strong tendency to identify with each other even though the identification has its difficulties. An eight-year-old girl says, "Do you like Melvin? I hate him. Everybody tries to make him be my boy friend."

In the family situation the problem is further complicated by strong hereditary tendencies. In many of the schizophrenic children in this study, there were other schizophrenic individuals in the family which, of course, amplified the problems of identification and anxiety in the family circle even among those who were not psychotic. (To be reported in more detail in a subsequent report.)

By contrast with adults, one can often make an unusually good contact with schizophrenic children. There is generally a searching, penetrating, even aggressive clinging dependence. They are attractive, intriguing, and appear gifted. They attempt to solve their problems by an excessive identification or interpenetrating relationship. Six-year-old Martin for a while would eat only what I fed him. He was given an Indian suit in the hospital and would not permit it to be removed for sleeping or bathing except by me. If permitted he would sit all day in the corner of my office with his thumb in his mouth, and if put out of the room, would be content if only the toe of his shoe could be pushed over the door sill. At such periods the sight of his mother threw him into a screaming panic. Now, at 16, he is still glad to see me (the process is quiescent now) and talks vaguely of his problems.

In the classification of childhood schizophrenia, the most important factor is the age of onset of the illness. The second factor is the progression or severity of the illness, whether it is rapid and profound or slow and slight, accelerating or regressive, and if the progression is steady or subject to remissions or arrests.

As to the age of onset, there are three critical periods. 1) The first two years of life not uncommonly includes the onset of a mental illness in children which subsequently proves to be schizophrenia. The development is reported by the mother to have been uneven and there may be no point at which the child appeared normal and then regressed. If the progress is rapid and profound, it is difficult to differentiate from organic deficiencies (24). However, there are no gross somatic deficiencies such as microcephaly; the motility disorder is typical of the schizophrenic child and does not make any other neurological syndrome; the disorder in object relationship is conspicuous and there is evidence of excessive anxiety;

there may be no language development at all, but if there is, it may be lost again or misused as a play pattern. Some children, in whom the onset is clearly set in the first two years by the mother, may continue to develop to good intellectual levels, be physically precocious and demonstrate profound motility and psychological disorders, and show anxiety continuously.

2) From three to four and a half years is the most common period of onset. This group is more readily recognized because of the normal development up to this period. The regression may be insidious and very slow, or abrupt and very rapid, so that in six months the child may lose all he has gained in three years, especially the socially oriented behavior patterns, leaving him well developed physically with good gait and exaggerated graceful motility, but having lost many of his acquired habit patterns, language, object relationship, with increased anxiety and physical dependence on the mother. Subsequently, the anxiety may also be lost. It is then we speak of deterioration. Having regressed as far as possible, the child may then slowly begin to regain some patterned behavior but now distorted by the schizophrenic patterning. A variety of unevenness in the patterned disorder may occur. The child may show increased activity with anxiety, emotional instability, irritability, excitement, unprovoked aggression (usually oral) and temper tantrums with fears, phobias, disturbed sleep, accelerated language development, and considerable preoccupation with all of the psychological problems of identity, body functions, physical and social orientation. There will be an aggressive dependence on the mother and all adults. There may be a general acceleration of the developmental tendencies in all fields including physical growth, a general regression, or any mixture of the two. Regressive mental illnesses or infantile dementia commonly starting at this age have been recognized for some time as Heller's disease (24), (25).

It is difficult if not impossible to differentiate this group of cases from what appears to be the more rapidly and evenly regressive schizophrenia or from some of the regressive organic dementias. The family history and ultimate course of the disorder may help in diagnosis. In general, those children with onset of schizophrenia before age five, who show severe interference or regression in fundamental habit patterns, language, object relationship, and motility, and show a loss of anxiety, are the most severe cases. In our experience they do not indicate a tendency to remissions nor do they respond much to shock treatment. On the other hand, children in whom the onset may be just as early but who show the accelerated type of response with a great deal of anxiety, may pass through very severe disturbances, respond to shock therapy and psychotherapy, have good remissions and return to their homes and school. They may withstand the pubertal period and be relatively well, though on clinical examination still show residual signs of schizophrenia in motility, thought disturbances, some defect in object relationship, and in the handling of their emotional life. They remain dependent on their family. It appears that the prognosis for schizophrenia for even this infantile type is as good as it is in adults, which means that a third to a half will make a fair to good social recovery or remission but remain vulnerable. However, this prognosis is possible only if the criteria for diagnosis are clearly delineated and those children who have the milder forms of schizophrenia and those subject to remissions are also diagnosed. The prognosis is improved by early recognition and active treatment.

Children of school age are often brought to the psychiatrist's attention with the history of onset apparently at six to eight years. In most of these, however, it is probable that the onset was three to four years and only recognized when the child was brought to school and into community activities.

3) The third common childhood period of onset is the prepubertal period, age 10 to 11½. In these children the clinical picture is quite different. While in the infantile period, we have difficulties in differentiating between schizophrenia and organic brain disorders, at the prepubertal period the differentiation must be made with the neuroses, especially anxiety states and obsessional-compulsive states. With the obsessional-compulsive thinking added to the psychological problems of the schizophrenic child with his disturbance in identification and orientation, he evolves persecutory systems in which he suspects that either he or his parents are changed and that other children are against him because he cannot identify with them. His efforts to control his motility lead to mannerisms which may appear compulsive. Inability to keep track of the periphery of his body leads to a breakdown in personal habits and care. In some cases the behavior is like delinquency; the child truants, wanders away from home and enters strange dwellings in an effort to orient himself.

His problems in identification are now not only to orient himself in his family, but his family in the social group. His concern about body function includes a concern about his mental processes and his own psychological problems, states of consciousness, life and death, social aggression. He may be suicidal and threaten the welfare of siblings or children his own age level. These problems are often graphically expressed in behavior, in language directly or symbolically, and in art media. There is a good deal of concern with language. Many children read a great deal, most of them show accelerated development in language fields in contrast to performance functioning. The budding sexual problems lead to diffuse exaggerated identifications, most clearly seen in girls who

identify with their brothers. In the past few years they have fantasied themselves in war experiences and the love life of their adolescent brothers. This problem leads to a disrupting ambivalence in all their relationships.

Similarly, there is a tendency to identify with negative characters, such as our enemies during the war. One boy cooperated dramatically with shock treatment because he said we were turning him into a good Jap. The problems are the same as those of early childhood, but are dealt with by a ten-year-old experience and abilities. By this time introjected superegos tend to become projected. Hallucinations are not clear and are not concerned with sexual matters, but there is a tendency to be vaguely aware of the various perceptions being projected just beyond the body periphery. The anxiety tends to focus at this point with considerable concern as to whether they themselves or something outside themselves is identified with this distressing feeling that something is going on which they cannot control.

In conclusion, may I say that the problems of the schizophrenic child are the problems of all growing children, but the patterning is modified by mixed tendencies to expansions and contractions, accelerations and regressions which follow configurational tendencies specific for schizophrenia.

BIBLIOGRAPHY

1. Bender, Lauretta. Childhood Schizophrenia. *Nervous Child*, *1*, 1942, p. 138.
2. Hoskins, Roy G. *The Biology of Schizophrenia*. Norton, New York, 1946.
3. Gold, Leonard. Autonomic Balance in Patients Treated with Insulin Shock as Measured by Mecholyl Chloride. *Arch. Neurol. and Psych.*, *50*, 1943, p. 311.
4. Bowman, Karl, and Jacob Kasanin. Constitutional Schizophrenia. *Am. J. Psychiatry*, *8*, 1933, p. 655.
5. Schilder, Paul. *The Relation between the Personality and Motility of Schizophrenia in Brain and Personality*. Part II. Nerv. and Ment. Dis. Monog. Series No. 53.
6. Bender, Lauretta, and Paul Schilder. Mannerisms as Organic Motility Syndrome (Paracortical Disturbances.) *Confinia Neurologica*, *3*, 1941, p. 21.
7. Hoff, Hans, and Paul Schilder, *Die Lagerreflexe des Menschen*. Vienna, 1927.
8. Teicher, Joseph D. Preliminary Survey of Motility in Children. *J. Nerv. and Ment. Dis.*, *94*, 1941, p. 277.
9. Schilder, Paul. Psychology of Schizophrenia. *Psychoanal. Review*, *26*, 1939, p. 380.
10. Bender, Lauretta. *A Visual Motor Gestalt Test and Its Clinical Use*. Am. Orthopsychiatric Assoc. Monograph Series, No. 3, 1938.
11. Fabian, A. A. Vortical Rotation in Visual Motor Performance. *J. Ed. Psychology*, March 1945, p. 129.
12. Despert, J. Louise. Comparative Study in Thinking in

Schizophrenic Children and Children of Pre-school Age. *Am. J. Psychiatry,* 97, 1940, p. 189.

13. Curran, Frank J., and Paul Schilder. Paraphasic Signs in Diffuse Lesions of the Brain. *J. Nerv. and Ment. Dis.,* 82, 1935, p. 613.

14. Kanner, Leo. Autistic Disturbances of Affective Contact. *Nervous Child,* 2, 1942, p. 217.

15. Despert, J. Louise. Prophylactic Aspects of Schizophrenia in Childhood. *Nervous Child,* 1, 1942, p. 189.

16. _____. Thinking and Motility Disorders in a Schizophrenic Child. *Psychiatric Quarterly,* 15, 1941, p. 522.

17. Schilder, Paul. The Child and the Symbol. *Scientia,* July 1938, p. 21.

18. Bender, Lauretta, and Jack Rapoport. Animal Drawings of Children. *Am. J. Orthopsychiatry,* 14, 1944, p. 512.

19. _____, and William Wolfson. The Nautical Theme in the Art and Fantasy of Children. *Ibid.,* 13, 1943, p. 462.

20. Bender, Lauretta. *Behavior Problems in Children of Psychotic Parents.* Genetic Psychology Monograph No. 18, 1937.

21. _____, and Harry H. Lipkowitz, Hallucinations in Children. *Am. J. Orthopsychiatry,* 10, 1940, p. 471.

22. Rapoport, Jack. Phantasy Objects in Children. *Psychoanal. Rev.,* 31, 1944.

23. Klein, Melanie, *The Psychoanalysis of Children.* Hogarth Press, London, 1932.

24. Bender, Lauretta, and Helen Yarnell. An Observation Nursery. *Am. J. Psychiatry,* 97, 1941, p. 1158.

25. Kanner, Leo. *Child Psychiatry.* Charles C. Thomas, Springfield, Ill., 1932.

Joey: A "Mechanical Boy"

Bruno Bettelheim
1959

A case history of a schizophrenic child who converted himself into a "machine" because he did not dare be human. His story sheds light on emotional development in a mechanized society.

Joey, when we began our work with him, was a mechanical boy. He functioned as if by remote control, run by machines of his own powerfully creative fantasy. Not only did he himself believe that he was a machine but, more remarkably, he created this impression in others. Even while he performed actions that are intrinsically human, they never appeared to be other than machine-started and executed. On the other hand, when the machine was not working we had to concentrate on recollecting his presence, for he seemed not to exist. A human body that functions as if it were a machine and a machine that duplicated human functions are equally fascinating and frightening. Perhaps they are so uncanny because they remind us that the human body can operate without a human spirit, that body can exist without soul. And Joey was a child who had been robbed of his humanity.

Not every child who possesses a fantasy world is possessed by it. Normal children may retreat into realms of imaginary glory or magic powers, but they are easily recalled from these excursions. Disturbed children are not always able to make the return trip; they remain withdrawn, prisoners of the inner world of delusion and fantasy. In many ways Joey presented a classic example of this state of infantile autism.

At the Sonia Shankman Orthogenic School of the University of Chicago it is our function to provide a therapeutic environment in which such children may start life over again. I have previously described in this magazine the rehabilitation of another of our patients ["Schizophrenic Art: A Case Study"; *Scientific American*, April, 1952]. This time I shall concentrate upon the illness, rather than the treatment. In any age, when the individual has escaped into a delusional world, he has usually fashioned it from bits and pieces of the world at hand. Joey, in his time and world, chose the machine and froze himself in its image. His story has a general relevance to the understanding of emotional development in a machine age.

Joey's delusion is not uncommon among schizophrenic children today. He wanted to be rid of his unbearable humanity, to become completely automatic. He so nearly succeeded in attaining this goal that he could almost convince others, as well as himself, of his mechanical character. The descriptions of autistic children in the literature take for their point of departure and comparison the normal or abnormal human being. To do justice to Joey I would have to compare him simultaneously to a most inept infant and a highly complex piece of machinery. Often we had to force ourselves by a conscious act of will to realize that Joey was a child. Again and again his acting out of his delusions froze our own ability to respond as human beings.

During Joey's first weeks with us we would watch absorbedly as this at once fragile-looking and imperious nine-year-old went about his mechanical existence. Entering the dining room, for example, he would string an imaginary wire from his "energy source"—an imaginary electric outlet—to the table. There he "insulated" himself with paper napkins and finally plugged himself in. Only

Note. From "Joey: A 'Mechanical Boy'" by B. Bettelheim, 1959, *Scientific American,* 200, 116–127. Copyright 1959 by Scientific American. Reprinted by permission.

then could Joey eat, for he firmly believed that the "current" ran his ingestive apparatus. So skillful was the pantomime that one had to look twice to be sure there was neither wire nor outlet nor plug. Children and members of our staff spontaneously avoided stepping on the "wires" for fear of interrupting what seemed the source of his very life.

For long periods of time, when his "machinery" was idle, he would sit so quietly that he would disappear from the focus of the most conscientious observation. Yet in the next moment he might be "working" and the center of our captivated attention. Many times a day he would turn himself on and shift noisily through a sequence of higher and higher gears until he "exploded," screaming "Crash, crash!" and hurling items from his ever present apparatus—radio tubes, light bulbs, even motors or, lacking these, any handy breakable object. (Joey had an astonishing knack for snatching bulbs and tubes unobserved.) As soon as the object thrown had shattered, he would cease his screaming and wild jumping and retire to mute, motionless nonexistence.

Our maids, inured to difficult children, were exceptionally attentive to Joey; they were apparently moved by his extreme infantile fragility, so strangely coupled with megalomaniacal superiority. Occasionally some of the apparatus he fixed to his bed to "live him" during his sleep would fall down in disarray. This machinery he contrived from masking tape, cardboard, wire and other paraphernalia. Usually the maids would pick up such things and leave them on a table for the children to find or disregard them entirely. But Joey's machine they carefully restored: "Joey must have the carburetor so he can breathe." Similarly they were on the alert to pick up and preserve the motors that ran him during the day and the exhaust pipes through which he exhaled.

How had Joey become a human machine? From intensive interviews with his parents we learned that the process had begun even before birth. Schizophrenia often results from parental rejection, sometimes combined ambivalently with love. Joey, on the other hand, had been completely ignored.

"I never knew I was pregnant," his mother said, meaning that she had already excluded Joey from her consciousness. His birth, she said, "did not make any difference." Joey's father, a rootless draftee in the wartime civilian army, was equally unready for parenthood. So, of course, are many young couples. Fortunately most such parents lose their indifference upon the baby's birth. But not Joey's parents. "I did not want to see or nurse him," his mother declared. "I had no feeling of actual dislike—I simply didn't want to take care of him." For the first three months of his life Joey "cried most of the time." A colicky baby, he was kept on a rigid four-hour feeding schedule, was not touched unless necessary and was never cuddled

or played with. The mother, preoccupied with herself, usually left Joey alone in the crib or playpen during the day. The father discharged his frustrations by punishing Joey when the child cried at night.

Soon the father left for overseas duty and the mother took Joey, now a year and a half old, to live with her at her parents' home. On his arrival the grandparents noticed that ominous changes had occurred in the child. Strong and healthy at birth, he had become frail and irritable; a responsive baby, he had become remote and inaccessible. When he began to master speech, he talked only to himself. At an early date he became preoccupied with machinery, including an old electric fan which he could take apart and put together again with surprising deftness.

Joey's mother impressed us with a fey quality that expressed her insecurity, her detachment from the world and her low physical vitality. We were struck especially by her total indifference as she talked about Joey. This seemed much more remarkable than the actual mistakes she made in handling him. Certainly he was left to cry for hours when hungry, because she fed him on a rigid schedule; he was toilet-trained with great rigidity so that he would give no trouble. These things happen to many children. But Joey's existence never registered with his mother. In her recollections he was fused at one moment with one event or person; at another, with something or somebody else. When she told us about his birth and infancy, it was as if she were talking about some vague acquaintance, and soon her thoughts would wander off to another person or to herself.

When Joey was not yet four, his nursery school suggested that he enter a special school for disturbed children. At the new school his autism was immediately recognized. During his three years there he experienced a slow improvement. Unfortunately a subsequent two years in a parochial school destroyed this progress. He began to develop compulsive defenses, which he called his "preventions." He could not drink, for example, except through elaborate piping systems built of straws. Liquids had to be "pumped" into him, in his fantasy, or he could not suck. Eventually his behavior became so upsetting that he could not be kept in the parochial school. At home things did not improve. Three months before entering the Orthogenic School he made a serious attempt at suicide.

To us Joey's pathological behavior seemed the external expression of an overwhelming effort to remain almost nonexistent as a person. For weeks Joey's only reply when addressed was "Bam." Unless he thus neutralized whatever we said, there would be an explosion, for Joey plainly wished to close off every form of contact not mediated by machinery. Even when he was bathed he rocked back and forth with mute engine-like regularity, flooding the bathroom. If he stopped rocking, he did this like a machine too; suddenly he went completely rigid. Only once, after months of being lifted from his bath and carried to bed, did a small expression of puzzled pleasure appear on his face as he said softly: "They even carry you to your bed here."

For a long time after he began to talk he would never refer to anyone by name, but only as "that person" or "the little person" or "the big person." He was unable to designate by its true name anything to which he attached feelings. Nor could he name his anxieties except through neologisms or word contaminations. For a long time he spoke about "master paintings" and "a master painting room" (i.e., masturbating and masturbating room). One of his machines, the "criticizer," prevented him from "saying words which have unpleasant feelings." Yet he gave personal names to the tubes and motors in his collection of machinery. Moreover, these dead things had feelings; the tubes bled when hurt and sometimes got sick. He consistently maintained this reversal between animate and inanimate objects.

In Joey's machine world everything, on pain of instant destruction, obeyed inhibitory laws much more stringent than those of physics. When we came to know him better, it was plain that in his moments of silent withdrawal, with his machine switched off, Joey was absorbed in pondering the compulsive laws of his private universe. His preoccupation with machinery made it difficult to establish even practical contacts with him. If he wanted to do something with a counselor, such as play with a toy that had caught his vague attention, he could not do so: "I'd like this very much, but first I have to turn off the machine." But by the time he had fulfilled all the requirements of his preventions, he had lost interest. When a toy was offered to him, he could not touch it because his motors and his tubes did not leave him a hand free. Even certain colors were dangerous and had to be strictly avoided in toys and clothing, because "some colors turn off the current, and I can't touch them because I can't live without the current."

Joey was convinced that machines were better than people. Once when he bumped into one of the pipes on our jungle gym he kicked it so violently that his teacher had to restrain him to keep him from injuring himself. When she explained that the pipe was much harder than his foot, Joey replied: "That proves it. Machines are better than the body. They don't break; they're much harder and stronger." If he lost or forgot something, it merely proved that his brain ought to be thrown away and replaced by machinery. If he spilled something, his arm should be broken and twisted off because it did not work properly. When his head or arm failed to work as it should, he tried to punish it by hitting it. Even Joey's feelings were mechanical. Much later in his therapy, when he had

formed a timid attachment to another child and had been rebuffed, Joey cried: "He broke my feelings."

Gradually we began to understand what had seemed to be contradictory in Joey's behavior—why he held on to the motors and tubes, then suddenly destroyed them in a fury, then set out immediately and urgently to equip himself with new and larger tubes. Joey had created these machines to run his body and mind because it was too painful to be human. But again and again he became dissatisfied with their failure to meet his need and rebellious at the way they frustrated his will. In a recurrent frenzy he "exploded" his light bulbs and tubes, and for a moment became a human being—for one crowning instant he came alive. But as soon as he had asserted his dominance through the self-created explosion, he felt his life ebbing away. To keep on existing he had immediately to restore his machines and replenish the electricity that supplied his life energy.

What deep-seated fears and needs underlay Joey's delusional system? We were long in finding out, for Joey's preventions effectively concealed the secret of his autistic behavior. In the meantime we dealt with his peripheral problems one by one.

During his first year with us Joey's most trying problem was toilet behavior. This surprised us, for Joey's personality was not "anal" in the Freudian sense; his original personality damage had antedated the period of his toilet-training. Rigid and early toilet-training, however, had certainly contributed to his anxieties. It was our effort to help Joey with this problem that led to his first recognition of us as human beings.

Going to the toilet, like everything else in Joey's life, was surrounded by elaborate preventions. We had to accompany him; he had to take off all his clothes; he could only squat, not sit, on the toilet seat; he had to touch the wall with one hand, in which he also clutched frantically the vacuum tubes that powered his elimination. He was terrified lest his whole body be sucked down.

To counteract this fear we gave him a metal wastebasket in lieu of a toilet. Eventually, when eliminating into the wastebasket, he no longer needed to take off all his clothes, nor to hold on to the wall. He still needed the tubes and motors which, he believed, moved his bowels for him. But here again the all-important machinery was itself a source of new terrors. In Joey's world the gadgets had to move their bowels, too. He was terribly concerned that they should, but since they were so much more powerful than men, he was also terrified that if his tubes moved their bowels, their feces would fill all of space and leave him no room to live. He was thus always caught in some fearful contradiction.

Our readiness to accept his toilet habits, which obviously entailed some hardship for his counselors, gave Joey the confidence to express his obsessions in drawings. Drawing these fantasies was a first step toward letting us in, however distantly, to what concerned him most deeply. It was the first step in a year-long process of externalizing his anal preoccupations. As a result he began seeing feces everywhere; the whole world became to him a mire of excrement. At the same time he began to eliminate freely wherever he happened to be. But with this release from his infantile imprisonment in compulsive rules, the toilet and the whole process of elimination became less dangerous. Thus far it had been beyond Joey's comprehension that anybody could possibly move his bowels without mechanical aid. Now Joey took a further step forward; defecation became the first physiological process he could perform without the help of vacuum tubes. It must not be thought that he was proud of this ability. Taking pride in an achievement presupposes that one accomplishes it of one's own free will. He still did not feel himself an autonomous person who could do things on his own. To Joey defecation still seemed enslaved to some incomprehensible but utterly binding cosmic law, perhaps the law his parents had imposed on him when he was being toilet-trained.

It was not simply that his parents had subjected him to rigid, early training. Many children are so trained. But in most cases the parents have a deep emotional investment in the child's performance. The child's response in turn makes training an occasion for interaction between them and for the building of genuine relationships. Joey's parents had no emotional investment in him. His obedience gave them no satisfaction and won him no affection or approval. As a toilet-trained child he saved his mother labor, just as household machines saved her labor. As a machine he was not loved for his performance, nor could he love himself.

So it had been with all other aspects of Joey's existence with his parents. Their reactions to his eating or noneating, sleeping or wakening, urinating or defecating, being dressed or undressed, washed or bathed did not flow from any unitary interest in him, deeply embedded in their personalities. By treating him mechanically his parents made him a machine. The various functions of life—even the parts of his body—bore no integrating relationship to one another or to any sense of self that was acknowledged and confirmed by others. Though he had acquired mastery over some functions, such as toilet-training and speech, he had acquired them separately and kept them isolated from each other. Toilet-training had thus not gained him a pleasant feeling of body mastery; speech had not led to communication of thought or feeling. On the contrary, each achievement only steered him away from self-mastery and integration. Toilet-training had

enslaved him. Speech left him talking in neologisms that obstructed his and our ability to relate to each other. In Joey's development the normal process of growth had been made to run backward. Whatever he had learned put him not at the end of his infantile development toward integration but, on the contrary, farther behind than he was at its very beginning. Had we understood this sooner, his first years with us would have been less baffling.

It is unlikely that Joey's calamity could befall a child in any time and culture but our own. He suffered no physical deprivation; he starved for human contact. Just to be taken care of is not enough for relating. It is a necessary but not a sufficient condition. At the extreme where utter scarcity reigns, the forming of relationships is certainly hampered. But our society of mechanized plenty often makes for equal difficulties in a child's learning to relate. Where parents can provide the simple creature-comforts for their children only at the cost of significant effort, it is likely that they will feel pleasure in being able to provide for them; it is this, the parents' pleasure, that gives children a sense of personal worth and sets the process of relating in motion. But if comfort is so readily available that the parents feel no particular pleasure in winning it for their children, then the children cannot develop the feeling of being worthwhile around the satisfaction of their basic needs. Of course parents and children can and do develop relationships around other situations. But matters are then no longer so simple and direct. The child must be on the receiving end of care and concern given with pleasure and without the exaction of return if he is to feel loved and worthy of respect and consideration. This feeling gives him the ability to trust; he can entrust his well-being to persons to whom he is so important. Out of such trust the child learns to form close and stable relationships.

For Joey relationship with his parents was empty of pleasure in comfort-giving as in all other situations. His was an extreme instance of a plight that sends many schizophrenic children to our clinics and hospitals. Many months passed before he could relate to us; his despair that anybody could like him made contact impossible.

When Joey could finally trust us enough to let himself become more infantile, he began to play at being a papoose. There was a corresponding change in his fantasies. He drew endless pictures of himself as an electrical papoose. Totally enclosed, suspended in empty space, he is run by unknown, unseen power, through wireless electricity. . . .

As we eventually came to understand, the heart of Joey's delusional system was the artificial, mechanical womb he had created and into which he had locked himself. In his papoose fantasies lay the wish to be entirely reborn in a womb. His new experiences in the school suggested that life, after all, might be worth living. Now he was searching for a way to be reborn in a better way. Since machines were better than men, what was more natural than to try rebirth through them? This was the deeper meaning of his electrical papoose.

As Joey made progress, his pictures of himself became more dominant in his drawings. Though still machine-operated, he has grown in self-importance. . . . Now he has acquired hands that do something, and he has had the courage to make a picture of the machine that runs him. Later still the papoose became a person, rather than a robot encased in glass.

Eventually Joey began to create an imaginary family at the school: the "Carr" family. Why the Carr family? In the car he was enclosed as he had been in his papoose, but at least the car was not stationary; it could move. More important, in a car one was not only driven but also could drive. The Carr family was Joey's way of exploring the possibility of leaving the school, of living with a good family in a safe, protecting car. . . .

Joey at last broke through his prison. In this brief account it has not been possible to trace the painfully slow process of his first true relations with other human beings. Suffice it to say that he ceased to be a mechanical boy and became a human child. This newborn child was, however, nearly 12 years old. To recover the lost time is a tremendous task. That work has occupied Joey and us ever since. Sometimes he sets to it with a will; at other times the difficulty of real life makes him regret that he ever came out of his shell. But he has never wanted to return to his mechanical life.

One last detail and this fragment of Joey's story has been told. When Joey was 12, he made a float for our Memorial Day parade. It carried the slogan: "Feelings are more important than anything under the sun." Feelings, Joey had learned, are what make for humanity; their absence, for a mechanical existence. With this knowledge Joey entered the human condition.

Section IV

THERAPIES

❦ ❦ ❦

This section includes examples of case studies and interventions associated with each major approach to treating emotional disorders. It begins with psychoanalytic therapy: the case of Miss Lucy R., age 30, a young woman treated by Sigmund Freud in 1892. Miss Lucy's symptoms were quite interesting, particularly her recurrent olfactory hallucinations—specifically, "a smell of burnt pudding." This case occurred early in Freud's career, and he reveals how he experimented with therapeutic procedures throughout the analysis, which resulted in an apparently complete recovery after 9 weeks of treatment.

Three selections pertaining to behavior therapy are included. Joseph Wolpe, the father of "systematic desensitization," is the author of the first article, which describes the success of behavior therapy in treating complex neurotic states. Wolpe was concerned by charges that behavior therapy was useful in treating such relatively simple problems as phobias, but was inappropriate for dealing with complex neuroses. He presents three clinical cases featuring the use of systematic desensitization to illustrate the effectiveness of behavior therapy.

An article by Aubrey Yates also responds to charges that behavior therapy is superficial. In this case the claim is that the behavioral focus on removing troublesome symptoms leaves untreated the patient's underlying anxiety, which can then manifest new symptoms ("symptom substitution"). Yates systematically details reasons against this argument.

Arnold Lazarus's article presents his theory for comprehensive treatment procedures, which he calls multimodal behavior therapy. This work, published in 1973, reflects his progression from a relatively traditional behavioral perspective to an eclectic approach that incorporates techniques and strategies emanating from a variety of perspectives. Lazarus's writing shows his knowledge of the breadth of treatments available, his willingness to swim against the tide of all established approaches, and his clever sense of humor.

The section dealing with cognitive therapy begins with an article by Donald Meichenbaum and Joseph Goodman, published in 1971. This study illustrates the growing transition in school-based interventions from strictly behavioral approaches featuring the manipulation of external contingencies for behavior to cognitive/behavioral procedures characterized by altered self-talk. Meichenbaum's innovative "self-instructional" training was a particularly important application of cognitive strategies because it was directed at impulsive, externalizing children rather than toward depressed or anxious individuals who internalize their problems.

In the next offering Aaron Beck compiles a comprehensive list of the cognitive distortions that depressed individuals exhibit. Beck illustrates many of the characteristic types of depressive thought by citing incidents from his clinical experience. Beck's observation that the affective disturbance associated with depression may be secondary to the thinking disorder is a keystone of cognitive therapy.

The final example of cognitive therapy is a case study by Albert Ellis documenting the use of rational-emotive therapy to treat a psychopath. The term *psychopath* was typically applied to highly egocentric individuals who exploited others without remorse and who seemingly were incapable of establishing any true bonds of love and trust with others. Many of these individuals run afoul of the law, and they are not considered good candidates for psychotherapy. Ellis clearly loves a challenge and shows how appeals to reason may be successful with the most recalcitrant individuals.

Phenomenological therapy is represented by Carl Rogers's presentation of the strategies he would use to help an antisocial young man whose behavior he has viewed on film. Never one to miss a chance to deride behavioral interventions, Rogers begins by negating the possibility of success with that approach and then spells out his own approach. As usual, Rogers writes with clarity and conviction, stressing the importance of the therapist-client relationship and even admitting that he may get carried away by his anticipation of the client's positive responses to his strategies.

Two case studies, one by R. D. Laing and A. Esterson and one by Ludwig Binswanger, represent existential therapy. Laing and Esterson write about Sarah Danzig, a young woman whose hallucinations, delusions, and generally bizarre behavior are characteristic of schizophrenia, a disorder usually classified as having a biochemical etiology. They document the family interactions with Sarah that they regard as key components in her illness.

Binswanger reports the case of Ilse, a thirty-nine year old woman. Ilse also is delusional and sufficiently bizarre to be considered insane. Binswanger discusses Ilse's affliction in terms of her life history and presents a marvelous treatise on society's response, including psychiatric judgment, to behavior that deviates from the norm. Regarding the etiology of the problem, he invites the reader to remember that it is not the brain that thinks but the person and that mind and body are one. The issues Binswanger raises in his discussion of this case are weighty, but they convey the essence of this perspective.

The ecological approach is represented by Fritz Redl's article on the therapeutic milieu. Redl was one of the foremost representatives of ecological principles in the United States, and the clinical techniques he developed remain in use today. This article shows his deep involvement with and understanding of children with emotional problems and conveys the strategies he used to work with them.

Psychoanalytic Therapy

The Case of Miss Lucy R., Age 30

Sigmund Freud
1938

At the end of the year 1892 a colleague of my acquaintance referred a young lady to me who was being treated by him for chronically recurrent suppurative rhinitis. It subsequently turned out that the obstinate persistence of her trouble was due to caries of the ethmoid bone. Latterly she had complained of some new symptoms which the well-informed physician was no longer able to attribute to a local affection. She had entirely lost her sense of smell and was almost continuously pursued by one or two subjective olfactory sensations. She found these most distressing. She was, moreover, in low spirits and fatigued, and she complained of heaviness in the head, diminished appetite and loss of efficiency.

The young lady, who was living as a governess in the house of the managing director of a factory in Outer Vienna, came to visit me from time to time in my consulting hours. She was an Englishwoman. She had a delicate constitution, with a poor pigmentation, but was in good health apart from her nasal affection. Her first statements confirmed what the physician had told me. She was suffering from depression and fatigue and was tormented by subjective sensations of smell. As regards hysterical symptoms, she showed a fairly definite general analgesia, with no loss of tactile sensibility, and a rough examination (with the hand) revealed no restriction of the visual field. The interior of her nose was completely analgesic and without reflexes; she was sensitive to tactile pressure there, but the perception proper to it as a sense-organ was absent, alike for specific stimuli and for others (e.g. ammonia or acetic acid). The purulent nasal catarrh was just then in a phase of improvement.

In our first attempts at making the illness intelligible it was necessary to interpret the subjective olfactory sensations, since they were recurrent hallucinations, as chronic hysterical symptoms. Her depression might perhaps be the affect attaching to the trauma, and it should be possible to find an experience in which these smells, which had now become subjective, had been objective. This experience must have been the trauma which the recurring sensations of smell symbolized in memory. It might be more correct to regard the recurrent olfactory hallucinations, together with the depression which accompanied them, as equivalents of a hysterical *attack*. The nature of recurrent hallucinations makes them unsuitable in point of fact for playing the part of *chronic* symptoms. But this question did not really arise in a case like this which showed only a rudimentary development. It was essential, however, that the subjective sensations of smell should have had a specialized origin of a sort which would admit of their being derived from some quite particular real object.

This expectation was promptly fulfilled. When I asked her what the smell was by which she was most constantly troubled she answered: "A smell of burnt pudding." Thus I only needed to assume that a smell of burnt pudding had actually occurred in the experience which had operated as a trauma. It is very unusual, no doubt, for olfactory sensations to be chosen as mnemic symbols of traumas, but it was not difficult to account for this choice. The patient was suffering from suppurative rhinitis and consequently her attention was especially focused on her nose and nasal sensations. What I knew of the circumstances of the patient's life was limited to the fact that the two children whom she was looking after had no mother; she had died some years earlier of an acute illness.

I therefore decided to make the smell of burnt pudding the starting-point of the analysis. I will describe the course of this analysis as it might have taken place under favourable conditions. In fact, what should have been a single session spread over several. This was because the patient could only visit me in my consulting hours, when I could only devote a short time to her. Moreover, a single discussion of this sort used to extend over more than a week, since her duties would not allow her to make the long journey from the factory to my house very often. We used therefore to break our conversation off short and take up the thread at the same place next time.

Miss Lucy R. did not fall into a state of somnambulism when I tried to hypnotize her. I therefore did without somnambulism and conducted her whole analysis while she was in a state which may in fact have differed very little from a normal one.

I shall have to go into this point of my technical procedure in greater detail. When, in 1889, I visited the Nancy clinics, I heard Dr. Liébeault, the *doyen* of hypnotism, say: "If only we had the means of putting every patient into a state of somnambulism, hypnotic therapy would be the most powerful of all." In Bernheim's clinic it almost seemed as though such an art really existed and as though it might be possible to learn it from Bernheim. But as soon as I tried to practise this art on my own patients, I discovered that *my* powers at least were subject to severe limits, and that if somnambulism were not brought about in a patient at the first three attempts I had no means of inducing it. The percentage of cases amenable to somnambulism was very much lower in my experience than what Bernheim reported.

I was accordingly faced with the choice of either abandoning the cathartic method in most of the cases which might have been suitable for it, or of venturing on the experiment of employing that method without somnambulism and where the hypnotic influence was light or even where its existence was doubtful. It seemed to me a matter of indifference what degree of hypnosis—according to one or other of the scales that have been proposed for measuring it—was reached by this nonsomnambulistic state; for, as we know, each of the various forms taken by suggestibility is in any case independent of the others, and the bringing about of catalepsy, automatic movements, and so on, does not work either for or against what I required for my purposes, namely that the awakening of forgotten memories should be made easier. Moreover, I soon dropped the practice of making tests to show the degree of hypnosis reached, since in quite a number of cases this roused the patients' resistance and shook their confidence in me, which I needed for carrying out the more important psychical work. Furthermore, I soon began to tire of issuing assurances and commands such as "You are going to sleep! . . . sleep!" and of hearing the patient, as so often happened when the degree of hypnosis was light, remonstrate with me: "But, doctor, I'm *not* asleep," and of then having to make highly ticklish distinctions: "I don't mean ordinary sleep; I mean hypnosis. As you see, you are hypnotized, you can't open your eyes" etc., "and in any case, there's no need for you to go to sleep" and so on. I feel sure that many other physicians who practise psychotherapy can get out of such difficulties with more skill than I can. If so, they may adopt some procedure other than mine. It seems to me, however, that if one can reckon with such frequency on finding oneself in an embarrassing situation through the use of a particular word, one will be wise to avoid both the word and the embarrassment. When, therefore, my first attempt did not lead either to somnambulism or to a degree of hypnosis involving marked physical changes, I ostensibly dropped hypnosis, and only asked for "concentration"; and I ordered the patient to lie down and deliberately shut his eyes as a means of achieving this "concentration." It is possible that in this way I obtained with only a slight effort the deepest degree of hypnosis that could be reached in the particular case.

But in doing without somnambulism I might be depriving myself of a precondition without which the cathartic method seemed unusable. For that method clearly rested on the patients in their changed state of consciousness having access to memories and being able to recognize connections which appeared not to be present in their normal state of consciousness. If the somnambulistic extension of memory were absent there could also be no possibility of establishing any determining causes which the patient could present to the physician as something unknown to him (the patient); and, of course, it is precisely the pathogenic memories which, as we have already said in our "Preliminary Communication" . . . are "absent from the patients' memory, when they are in a normal psychical state, or are only present in a highly summary form."

I was saved from this new embarrassment by remembering that I had myself seen Bernheim producing evidence that the memories of events during somnambulism are only *apparently* forgotten in the waking state and can be revived by a mild word of command and a pressure with the hand intended to indicate a different state of consciousness. He had, for instance, given a woman in a state of somnambulism a negative hallucination to the effect that he was no longer present, and had then endeavoured to draw her attention to himself in a great variety of ways, including some of a decidedly aggressive kind. He did not succeed. After she had been woken up he asked her to tell him what he had done to her while she thought he was not there. She replied in surprise that she knew nothing of it. But he did not accept this. He insisted that she could remember everything and laid his hand on her forehead to help her to recall it. And lo and behold! she ended by describing everything that she had ostensibly not perceived during her somnambulism and ostensibly not remembered in her waking state.

This astonishing and instructive experiment served as my model. I decided to start from the assumption that my patients knew everything that was of any pathogenic significance and that it was only a question of obliging them to communicate it. Thus when I reached a point at which, after asking a patient some question such as: "How long have you had this symptom?" or: "What was its origin?", I was met with the answer: "I really don't know," I proceeded as follows. I placed my hand on the patient's forehead or took her head between my hands and said: "You will think of it under the pressure of my hand. At the moment at which I relax my pressure you will see something in front of you or something will come into your head. Catch hold of it. It will be what we are looking for.—Well, what have you seen or what has occurred to you?"

On the first occasions on which I made use of this procedure (it was not with Miss Lucy R.) I myself was surprised to find that it yielded me the precise results that I needed. And I can safely say that it has scarcely ever left me in the lurch since then. It has always pointed the way which the analysis should take and has enabled me to carry through every such analysis to an end without the use of somnambulism. Eventually I grew so confident that, if patients answered, "I see nothing" or "nothing has occurred to me" I could dismiss this as an impossibility and could assure them that they had certainly become aware of what was wanted but had refused to believe that that was so and had rejected it. I told them I was ready to repeat the procedure as often as they liked and they would see the same thing every time. I turned out to be invariably right. The patients had not yet learned to relax their critical faculty. They had rejected the memory that had come up or the idea that had occurred to them, on the ground that it was unserviceable and an irrelevant interruption; and after they had told it to me it always proved to be what was wanted. Occasionally, when, after three or four pressures, I had at last extracted the information, the patient would reply: "As a matter of fact I knew that the first time, but it was just what I didn't want to say," or: "I hoped that would not be it."

This business of enlarging what was supposed to be a restricted consciousness was laborious—far more so, at least, than an investigation during somnambulism. But it nevertheless made me independent of somnambulism, and gave me insight into the motives which often determine the "forgetting" of memories. I can affirm that this forgetting is often intentional and desired; and its success is never more than *apparent*.

I found it even more surprising perhaps that it was possible by the same procedure to bring back numbers and dates which, on the face of it, had long since been forgotten, and so to reveal how unexpectedly accurate memory can be.

The fact that in looking for numbers and dates our choice is so limited enables us to call to our help a proposition familiar to us from the theory of aphasia, namely that recognizing something is a lighter task for memory than thinking of it spontaneously.[1] Thus, if a patient is unable to remember the year or month or day when a particular event occurred, we can repeat to him the dates of the possibly relevant years, the names of the twelve months and the thirty-one numbers of the days of the month, assuring him that when we come to the right number or the right name his eyes will open of their own accord or that he will feel which is the right one. In the great majority of cases the patient will in fact decide on a particular date. Quite often (as in the case of Frau Cäcilie M.) it is possible to prove from documents belonging to the period in question that the date has been recognized correctly; while in other cases and on other occasions the indisputable accuracy of the date thus chosen can be inferred from the context of the facts remembered. For instance, after a patient had had her attention drawn to the date which had been arrived at by this "counting over" method, she said: "Why, that's my father's birthday!" and added: "Of course! It was because it was his birthday that I was expecting the event we were talking about."

Here I can only touch upon the theme in passing. The conclusion I drew from all these observations was that experiences which have played an important pathogenic part, and all their subsidiary concomitants, are accurately retained in the patient's memory even when they seem to be forgotten—when he is unable to call them to mind.[2]

---

[1] [Freud had written his book on aphasia (1891b) not long before.]

[2] As an example of the technique which I have described above of carrying out investigations in non-somnambulistic states—that is, where there is no extension of consciousness—I will describe an instance which I happen to have analysed in the course of the last few days. I was treating a woman of thirty-eight, suffering from anxiety neurosis (agoraphobia, attacks of fear of death, etc.). Like so many such patients, she had a disinclination to admitting that she had acquired these troubles in her married life and would have liked to push them back into her early youth. Thus she told me that she was seventeen when she had had a first attack of dizziness, with anxiety and feelings of faintness, in the street in her small native town, and that these attacks had recurred from time to time, till a few years ago they had given place to her present disorder. I suspected that these first attacks of dizziness, in which the anxiety faded more and more into the background, were hysterical and I made up my mind to embark on an analysis of them. To begin with she only knew that this first attack came over her while she was out shopping in the principal street.

After this long but unavoidable digression I will return to the case of Miss Lucy R. As I have said, then, my attempts at hypnosis with her did not produce somnambulism. She simply lay quietly in a state open to some mild degree of influence, with her eyes closed all the time, her features somewhat rigid, and without moving hand or foot. I asked her if she could remember the occasion on which she first had the smell of burnt pudding. "Oh yes, I know exactly. It was about two months ago, two days before my birthday. I was with the children in the schoolroom and was playing at cooking with them" (they were two little girls). "A letter was brought in that had just been left by the postman. I saw from the postmark and the handwriting that it was from my mother in Glasgow and wanted to open it and read it; but the children rushed at me, tore the letter out of my hands and cried: 'No, you shan't read it now! It must be for your birthday; we'll keep it for you!' While the children were having this game with me there was suddenly a strong smell. They had forgotten the pudding they were cooking and it was getting burnt. Ever since this I have been pursued by the smell. It is there all the time and becomes stronger when I am agitated."

"Do you see this scene clearly before your eyes?"—"As large as life, just as I experienced it."—"What could there be about it that was so agitating?"—"I was moved because the children were so affectionate to me."—"Weren't they always?"—"Yes—but just when I got the letter from my mother."—"I don't understand why there is a contrast between the children's affection and your mother's letter, for that's what you seem to be suggesting."—"I was intending to go back to my mother's, and the thought of leaving the dear children made me feel so sad."—"What's wrong with your mother? Has she been feeling lonely and sent for you? Or was she ill at the time, and were you expecting news of her?"—"No; she isn't very strong, but she's not exactly ill, and she has a companion with her."—"Then why must you leave the children?"—"I couldn't bear it any longer in the house. The housekeeper, the cook and the French governess seem to have thought that I was putting myself above my station. They joined in a little intrigue against me and said all sorts of things against me to the children's grandfather, and I didn't get as much support as I had expected from the two gentlemen when I complained to them. So I gave notice to the Director" (the children's father). "He answered in a very friendly way that I had better think the matter over

---

"What were you going to buy?"—"Different things, I believe; they were for a ball I had been invited to."—"When was this ball to take place?"—"Two days later, I think."—"Something must have happened to agitate you a few days before, something that made an impression on you."—"I can't think of anything. After all, it was twenty-one years ago."—"That makes no difference; you will remember all the same. I shall press on your head, and when I relax the pressure, you will think of something or see something, and you must tell me what that is." I went through this procedure; but she remained silent. "Well, has nothing occurred to you?"—"I have thought of something, but it can't have any connection with this."—"Tell it to me anyway."—"I thought of a friend of mine, a girl, who is dead. But she died when I was eighteen—a year later, that is."—"We shall see. Let's stick to this point. What about this friend of yours?"—"Her death was a great shock to me, as I used to see a lot of her. A few weeks earlier another girl had died, and that had made a great stir in the town. So after all, I must have been seventeen at the time."—"There, you see, I told you we could rely on the things that come into your head under the pressure of my hand. Now, can you remember what you were thinking about when you felt dizzy in the street?"—"I wasn't thinking of anything; I only felt dizzy."—"That's not possible. States like that never happen without being accompanied by some idea. I shall press once more and the thought you had will come back to you. . . . Well, what has occurred to you?"—"The idea that I am the third."—"What does that mean?"—"When I got the attack of dizziness I must have thought: "Now I am dying, like the other two girls."—"That was the idea, then. As you were having the attack you thought of your friend. So her death must have made a great impression on you."—"Yes, it did. I can remember now that when I heard of her death I felt it was dreadful to be going to a ball, while she was dead. But I was looking forward so much to the ball and was so busy with preparations for it; I didn't want to think of what had happened at all." (We may observe here a deliberate repression from consciousness, which rendered the patient's memory of her friend pathogenic.)

The attack was now to some extent explained. But I still required to know of some precipitating factor which had provoked the memory at that particular time. I formed what happened to be a lucky conjecture. "Do you remember the exact street you were walking along just then?"—"Certainly. It was the principal street, with its old houses. I can see them now."—"And where was it that your friend lived?"—"In a house in the same street. I had just passed it, and I had the attack a couple of houses further on."—"So when you went by the house it reminded you of your dead friend, and you were once more overcome by the contrast which you did not want to think of."

I was still not satisfied. There might, I thought, be something else at work as well that had aroused or reinforced the hysterical disposition of a girl who had till then been normal. My suspicions turned to her monthly periods as an appropriate factor, and I asked: "Do you know at what time in the month your period came on?" The question was not a welcome one. "Do you expect me to know that, too? I can only tell you that I had them very seldom then and very irregularly. When I was seventeen I only had one once."—"Very well, then, we will find out when this once was by counting over." I did the counting over, and she decided definitely on one particular month and hesitated between two days immediately preceding the date of a fixed holiday. "Does that fit in somehow with the date of the ball?" She answered

---

sheepishly: "The ball was on the holiday. And now I remember, too, what an impression it made on me that my only period that year should have had to come on just before the ball. It was my first ball."

There is no difficulty now in reconstructing the interconnection between the events, and we can now see into the mechanism of this hysterical attack. It is true that the achievement of this result had been a laborious business. It required complete confidence in my technique on my side, and the occurrence to the patient of a few key ideas, before it was possible to re-awaken, after an interval of twenty-one years, these details of a forgotten experience in a sceptical person who was, in fact, in a waking state. But once all this had been gone through, the whole thing fitted together.

for a couple of weeks before I finally gave him my decision. I was in this state of uncertainty at the time, and thought I should be leaving the house; but I have stayed on."—"Was there something particular, apart from their fondness for you, which attached you to the children?"—"Yes. Their mother was a distant relation of my mother's, and I had promised her on her death-bed that I would devote myself with all my power to the children, that I would not leave them and that I would take their mother's place with them. In giving notice I had broken this promise."

This seemed to complete the analysis of the patient's subjective sensation of smell. It had turned out in fact to have been an objective sensation originally, and one which was intimately associated with an experience—a little scene—in which opposing affects had been in conflict with each other: her regret at leaving the children and the slights which were nevertheless urging her to make up her mind to do so. Her mother's letter had not unnaturally reminded her of her reasons for this decision, since it was her intention to join her mother on leaving here. The conflict between her affects had elevated the moment of the letter's arrival into a trauma, and the sensation of smell that was associated with this trauma persisted as its symbol. It was still necessary to explain why, out of all the sense-perceptions afforded by the scene, she had chosen this smell as a symbol. I was already prepared, however, to use the chronic affection of her nose as a help in explaining the point. In response to a direct question she told me that just at that time she had once more been suffering from such a heavy cold in the nose that she could hardly smell anything. Nevertheless, while she was in her state of agitation she perceived the smell of the burnt pudding, which broke through the organically-determined loss of her sense of smell.

But I was not satisfied with the explanation thus arrived at. It all sounded highly plausible, but there was something that I missed, some adequate reason why these agitations and this conflict of affects should have led to hysteria rather than anything else. Why had not the whole thing remained on the level of normal psychical life? In other words, what was the justification for the conversion which occurred? Why did she not always call to mind the scene itself, instead of the associated sensation which she singled out as a symbol of the recollection? Such questions might be over-curious and superfluous if we were dealing with a hysteric of long standing in whom the mechanism of conversion was habitual. But it was not until this trauma, or at any rate this small tale of trouble, that the girl had acquired hysteria.

Now I already knew from the analysis of similar cases that before hysteria can be acquired for the first time one essential condition must be fulfilled: an idea must be *intentionally repressed from consciousness* and excluded from associative modification. In my view this intentional repression is also the basis for the conversion, whether total or partial, of the sum of excitation. The sum of excitation, being cut off from psychical association, finds its way all the more easily along the wrong path to a somatic innervation. The basis for repression itself can only be a feeling of unpleasure, the incompatibility between the single idea that is to be repressed and the dominant mass of ideas constituting the ego. The repressed idea takes its revenge, however, by becoming pathogenic.

I accordingly inferred from Miss Lucy R.'s having succumbed to hysterical conversion at the moment in question that among the determinants of the trauma there must have been one which she had sought intentionally to leave in obscurity and had made efforts to forget. If her fondness for the children and her sensitiveness on the subject of the other members of the household were taken together, only one conclusion could be reached. I was bold enough to inform my patient of this interpretation. I said to her: "I cannot think that these are all the reasons for your feeling about the children. I believe that really you are in love with your employer, the Director, though perhaps without being aware of it yourself, and that you have a secret hope of taking their mother's place in actual fact. And then we must remember the sensitiveness you now feel toward the servants, after having lived with them peacefully for years. You're afraid of their having some inkling of your hopes and making fun of you."

She answered in her usual laconic fashion: "Yes, I think that's true."—"But if you knew you loved your employer why didn't you tell me?"—"I didn't know—or rather I didn't want to know. I wanted to drive it out of my head and not think of it again; and I believe latterly I have succeeded."[3] "Why was it that you were unwilling to admit this inclination? Were you ashamed of loving a man?"—"Oh no, I'm not unreasonably prudish. We're not responsible for our feelings, anyhow. It was distressing to me only because he is my employer and I am in his service and live in his house. I don't feel the same com-

---

[3] I have never managed to give a better description than this of the strange state of mind in which one knows and does not know a thing at the same time. It is clearly impossible to understand it unless one has been in such a state oneself. I myself have had a very remarkable experience of this sort, which is still clearly before me. If I try to recollect what went on in my mind at the time I can get hold of very little. What happened was that I saw something which did not fit in at all with my expectation; yet I did not allow what I saw to disturb my fixed plan in the least, though the perception should have put a stop to it. I was unconscious of any contradiction in this; nor was I aware of my feelings of repulsion, which must nevertheless undoubtedly have been responsible for the perception producing no psychical effect. I was afflicted by that blindness of the seeing eye which is so astonishing in the attitude of mothers to their daughters, husbands to their wives and rulers to their favourites.

plete independence towards him that I could towards anyone else. And then I am only a poor girl and he is such a rich man of good family. People would laugh at me if they had any idea of it."

She now showed no resistance to throwing light on the origin of this inclination. She told me that for the first few years she had lived happily in the house, carrying out her duties and free from any unfulfillable wishes. One day, however, her employer, a serious, overworked man whose behaviour towards her had always been reserved, began a discussion with her on the lines along which children should be brought up. He unbent more and was more cordial than usual and told her how much he depended on her for looking after his orphaned children; and as he said this he looked at her meaningly. . . . Her love for him had begun at that moment, and she even allowed herself to dwell on the gratifying hopes which she had based on this talk. But when there was no further development, and when she had waited in vain for a second hour's intimate exchange of views, she decided to banish the whole business from her mind. She entirely agreed with me that the look she had caught during their conversation had probably sprung from his thoughts about his wife, and she recognized quite clearly that there was no prospect of her feelings for him meeting with any return.

I expected that this discussion would bring about a fundamental change in her condition. But for the time being this did not occur. She continued to be in low spirits and depressed. She felt somewhat refreshed in the mornings by a course of hydropathic treatment which I prescribed for her at the same time. The smell of burnt pudding did not disappear completely, though it became less frequent and weaker. It only came on, she said, when she was very much agitated. The persistence of this mnemic symbol led me to suspect that, in addition to the main scene, it had taken over the representation of the many minor traumas subsidiary to that scene. We therefore looked about for anything else that might have to do with the scene of the burnt pudding; we went into the subject of the domestic friction, the grandfather's behaviour, and so on, and as we did so the burnt smell faded more and more. During this time, too, the treatment was interrupted for a considerable while, owing to a fresh attack of her nasal disorder, and this now led to the discovery of the caries of the ethmoid. . . .

On her return she reported that at Christmas she had received a great many presents from the two gentlemen of the house and even from the servants, as though they were all anxious to make it up with her and to wipe out her memory of the conflicts of the last few months. But these signs of goodwill had not made any impression on her.

When I enquired once more about the smell of burnt pudding, she informed me that it had quite disappeared but that she was being bothered by another, similar smell, resembling cigar-smoke. It had been there earlier as well, she thought, but had, as it were, been covered by the smell of the pudding. Now it had emerged by itself.

I was not very well satisfied with the result of the treatment. What had happened was precisely what is always brought up against purely symptomatic treatment: I had removed one symptom only for its place to be taken by another. Nevertheless, I did not hesitate to set about the task of getting rid of this new mnemic symbol by analysis.

But this time she did not know where the subjective olfactory sensation came from—on what important occasion it had been an objective one. "People smoke every day in our house," she said, "and I really don't know whether the smell I notice refers to some special occasion." I then insisted that she should try to remember under the pressure of my hand. I have already mentioned . . . that her memories had the quality of plastic vividness, that she was a "visual" type. And in fact, at my insistence, a picture gradually emerged before her, hesitatingly and piecemeal to begin with. It was the dining-room in her house, where she was waiting with the children for the two gentlemen to return to luncheon from the factory. "Now we are all sitting round the table, the gentlemen, the French governess, the housekeeper, the children and myself. But that's like what happens every day."—"Go on looking at the picture; it will develop and become more specialized."—"Yes, there is a guest. It's the chief accountant. He's an old man and he is as fond of the children as though they were his own grandchildren. But he comes to lunch so often that there's nothing special in that either."—"Be patient and just keep looking at the picture; something's sure to happen."—"Nothing's happening. We're getting up from the table; the children say their good-byes, and they go upstairs with us as usual to the second floor."—"And then?"—"It *is* a special occasion, after all. I recognize the scene now. As the children say good-bye, the accountant tries to kiss them. My employer flares up and actually shouts at him: 'Don't kiss the children!' I feel a stab at my heart; and as the gentlemen are already smoking, the cigar-smoke sticks in my memory."

This, then, was a second and deeper-lying scene which, like the first, operated as a trauma and left a mnemic symbol behind it. But to what did this scene owe its effectiveness? "Which of the two scenes was the earlier," I asked, "this one or the one with the burnt pudding?"—"The scene I have just told you about was the earlier, by almost two months."—"Then why did you feel this stab when the children's father stopped the old man? His reprimand wasn't aimed at you."—"It wasn't right for him to shout at an old man who was a valued friend of his and, what's more, a guest. He could have said it quietly."—"So it was only the violent way he put it that hurt you? Did you feel embarrassed on his account? Or perhaps you thought: 'If he can be so violent about such a small thing with an old friend and guest, how much more so might he be with me if I were his wife.' "—"No, that's not it."—"But it had to do with his violence, hadn't it?"—"Yes, about the children being kissed. He has never liked that."

And now, under the pressure of my hand, the memory of a third and still earlier scene emerged, which was the really operative trauma and which had given the scene with the chief accountant its traumatic effectiveness. It had happened a few months earlier still that a lady who was an acquaintance of her employer's came to visit them, and on her departure kissed the two children on the mouth. Their father, who was present, managed to restrain himself from saying anything to the lady, but after she had gone, his fury burst upon the head of the unlucky governess. He said he held her responsible if anyone kissed the children on the mouth, that it was her duty not to permit it and that she was guilty of a dereliction of duty if she allowed it; if it ever happened again he would entrust his children's upbringing to other hands. This had happened at a time when she still thought he loved her, and was expecting a repetition of their first friendly talk. The scene had crushed her hopes. She had said to herself: "If he can fly out at me like this and make such threats over such a trivial matter, and one for which, moreover, I am not in the least responsible, I must have made a mistake. He can never have had any warm feelings for me, or they would have taught him to treat me with more consideration."—It was obviously the recollection of this distressing scene which had come to her when the chief accountant had tried to kiss the children and had been reprimanded by their father.

After this last analysis, when, two days later, Miss Lucy visited me once more, I could not help asking her what had happened to make her so happy. She was as though transfigured. She was smiling and carried her head high. I thought for a moment that after all I had been wrong about the situation, and that the children's governess had become the Director's fiancée. But she dispelled my notion. "Nothing has happened. It's just that you don't know me. You have only seen me ill and depressed. I'm always cheerful as a rule. When I woke yesterday morning the weight was no longer on my mind, and since then I have felt well."—"And what do you think of your prospects in the house?"—"I am quite clear on the subject. I know I have none, and I shan't make myself unhappy over it."—"And will you get on all right with the servants now?"—"I think my own oversensitiveness was responsible for most of that."—"And are you still in love with your employer?"—"Yes, I certainly am, but that makes no difference. After all, I can have thoughts and feelings to myself."

I then examined her nose and found that its sensitivity to pain and reflex excitability had been almost com-

pletely restored. She was also able to distinguish between smells, though with uncertainty and only if they were strong. I must leave it an open question, however, how far her nasal disorder may have played a part in the impairment of her sense of smell.

This treatment lasted in all for nine weeks. Four months later I met the patient by chance in one of our summer resorts. She was in good spirits and assured me that her recovery had been maintained.

DISCUSSION

I am not inclined to under-estimate the importance of the case that I have here described, even though the patient was suffering only from a slight and mild hysteria and though only a few symptoms were involved. On the contrary it seems to me an instructive fact that even an illness such as this, so unproductive when regarded as a neurosis, called for so many psychical determinants. Indeed, when I consider this case history more closely, I am tempted to regard it as a model instance of one particular type of hysteria, namely the form of this illness which can be acquired even by a person of sound heredity, as a result of appropriate experiences. It should be understood that I do not mean by this a hysteria which is independent of *any* pre-existing disposition. It is probable that no such hysteria exists. But we do not recognize a disposition of this sort in a subject until he has actually become a hysteric; for previously there was no evidence of its existence. A neuropathic disposition, as generally understood, is something different. It is already marked out before the onset of the illness by the amount of the subject's hereditary taint or the sum of his individual psychical abnormalities. So far as my information goes, there was no trace in Miss Lucy R. of either of these factors. Her hysteria can therefore be described as an acquired one, and it presupposed nothing more than the possession of what is probably a very widespread proclivity—the proclivity to acquire hysteria. We have as yet scarcely a notion of what the features of this proclivity may be. In cases of this kind, however, the main emphasis falls upon the nature of the trauma, though taken in conjunction, of course, with the subject's reaction to it. It turns out to be a *sine qua non* for the acquisition of hysteria that an incompatibility should develop between the ego and some idea presented to it. I hope to be able to show elsewhere[4] how different neurotic disturbances arise from the different methods adopted by

---

[4] [Freud sketched out the distinction between the mechanisms used in hysteria, obsessions and paranoia in a communication to Fliess of January 1, 1896 (Freud, 1950a, Draft K); in the following May he published these findings in his second paper on "The Neuro-Psychoses of Defence" (1896b).]

the "ego" in order to escape from this incompatibility. The hysterical method of defence—for which, as we have seen, the possession of a particular proclivity is necessary —lies in the conversion of the excitation into a somatic innervation; and the advantage of this is that the incompatible idea is repressed from the ego's consciousness. In exchange, that consciousness now contains the physical reminiscence which has arisen through conversion (in our case, the patient's subjective sensations of smell) and suffers from the affect which is more or less clearly attached to precisely that reminiscence. The situation which has thus been brought about is now not susceptible to further change; for the incompatibility which would have called for a removal of the affect no longer exists, thanks to the repression and conversion. Thus the mechanism which produces hysteria represents on the one hand an act of moral cowardice and on the other a defensive measure which is at the disposal of the ego. Often enough we have to admit that fending off increasing excitations by the generation of hysteria is, in the circumstances, the most expedient thing to do; more frequently, of course, we shall conclude that a greater amount of moral courage would have been of advantage to the person concerned.

The actual traumatic moment, then, is the one at which the incompatibility forces itself upon the ego and at which the latter decides on the repudiation of the incompatible idea. That idea is not annihilated by a repudiation of this kind, but merely repressed into the unconscious. When this process occurs for the first time there comes into being a nucleus and centre of crystallization for the formation of a psychical group divorced from the ego—a group around which everything which would imply an acceptance of the incompatible idea subsequently collects. The splitting of consciousness in these cases of acquired hysteria is accordingly a deliberate and intentional one. At least it is often *introduced* by an act of volition; for the actual outcome is something different from what the subject intended. What he wanted was to do away with an idea, as though it had never appeared, but all he succeeds in doing is to isolate it psychically.

In the history of our present patient the traumatic moment was the moment of her employer's outburst against her about his children being kissed by the lady. For a time, however, that scene had no manifest effect. (It may be that her oversensitiveness and low spirits began from it, but I cannot say.) Her hysterical symptoms did not start until later, at moments which may be described as "auxiliary." [5] The characteristic feature of such an auxiliary moment is, I believe, that the two divided psychical groups temporarily converge in it, as they do in the extended consciousness which occurs in somnambulism. In Miss Lucy R.'s case the first of the auxiliary moments, at which conversion took place, was the scene at table when the chief accountant tried to kiss the children. Here the traumatic memory was playing a part: she did not behave as though she had got rid of everything connected with her devotion to her employer. (In the history of other cases these different moments coincide; conversion occurs as an immediate effect of the trauma.)

The second auxiliary moment repeated the mechanism of the first one fairly exactly. A powerful impression temporarily reunited the patient's consciousness, and conversion once more took the path which had been opened out on the first occasion. It is interesting to notice that the second symptom to develop masked the first, so that the first was not clearly perceived until the second had been cleared out of the way. It also seems to me worth while remarking upon the reversed course which had to be followed by the analysis as well. I have had the same experience in a whole number of cases; the symptoms that had arisen later masked the earlier ones, and the key to the whole situation lay only in the last symptom to be reached by the analysis.

The therapeutic process in this case consisted in compelling the psychical group that had been split off to unite once more with the ego-consciousness. Strangely enough, success did not run *pari passu* with the amount of work done. It was only when the last piece of work had been completed that recovery suddenly took place.

---

[5] [Freud had already discussed such "auxiliary" traumatic moments in Section I of his first paper on "The Neuro-Psychoses of Defence" (1894a).]

Behavioral Therapy

Behaviour Therapy in Complex Neurotic States

Joseph Wolpe
1964

In recent years it has become widely known that behaviour therapy (conditioning therapy) is effective in the treatment of neuroses. However, in many minds, this knowledge has come to be hedged by some erroneous qualifications, of which the commonest are: (*a*) that behaviour therapy leaves the "deep" cause of neurosis untouched, and (*b*) that it is successful with "monosymptomatic" and allegedly simple cases like phobias, but not with more complex neuroses, such as obsessions and "character neuroses."

Obviously, behaviour therapy, or, for that matter, any form of therapy, can influence the alleged "deep" neurotic process only if there really is such a process, as the psychoanalysts claim. But, as pointed out elsewhere (Wolpe, 1963a) because the psychoanalysts have misapprehended the requirements of scientific evidence they have adduced no acceptable support for their theory, beguiling themselves with surmises, analogies and extrapolations. Until now, whenever direct tests have been made of major tenets of the theory (e.g. the Oedipus theory [Valentine, 1946]) or of major implications of it (e.g. the likelihood of relapse in unpsychoanalysed recovery [Wolpe, 1961a]), the facts have been contrary to psychoanalytic expectations. It would be futile to consider whether behaviour therapy has effects on processes whose causal relationship to neurosis we have no reason to credit and whose very existence may be doubted.

The belief that the efficacy of behaviour therapy is limited to phobias can scarcely be maintained by anybody who has followed the relevant literature (e.g. Wolpe, 1958; Eysenck, 1960; Bond and Hutchison, 1960). But it is a belief that has been encouraged by several factors. First, in the case material which behaviour therapists have used to illustrate their techniques phobias are prominent, precisely because they are well-defined. Second, a good deal of press publicity was given a few years ago to the successful treatment of a cat phobia (Freeman and Kendrick, 1960). Third, and perhaps most important, the behaviouristic analysis of a case frequently results in its acquiring a phobia-like appearance. The distinctive feature of a classical phobia is the presence of ostensible stimulus antecedents of anxiety. *A behaviouristic analysis aims at establishing the stimulus antecedents of all reactions in every variety of neurosis.* When subsequently the case is reported and the non-behaviouristic reader finds himself presented with cut-and-dried relationships between stimuli and anxiety-responses, he may be constrained to comment, "*My* cases are not as clear-cut as that!" The behaviour therapist might justly retort, "If *this* had been your case it would not have seemed clear-cut either, for your training does not lead you to analyse stimulus-response relationships."

The basic premise of behaviour therapy of neurosis is that neuroses are persistent unadaptive learned habits of reaction that have been acquired under conditions of emotional disturbance (anxiety) (Wolpe, 1958). Almost universally anxiety is prominent among the reactions learned; and since this learning is at a primitive (hypothalamic) level it can be reversed only through applying the learning process so as to involve this primitive level. That is why neuroses cannot be overcome by appealing solely to reason.

It was in the context of experimental neuroses that it first became clear that neuroses are learned, and can be unlearned by counteracting anxiety by feeding (Wolpe, 1952, 1958). This finding suggested the *reciprocal inhibition principle* of therapy of the neuroses—that *if a response inhibitory of anxiety can be made to occur in the presence of anxiety-evoking stimuli it will weaken the bond between these stimuli and the anxiety*. In human neuroses, not only feeding but also a considerable number of other responses each of which, empirically, appears to inhibit anxiety, have been successfully used to weaken neurotic anxiety-response habits as well as other neurotic habits. Many of the techniques have been described in detail (Wolpe, 1958), and at least one more has since emerged (Lazarus and Abramovitz, 1962). The most widely used techniques employ assertive responses, relaxation responses (systematic desensitization), and sexual responses.

While the reciprocal inhibition mechanism is central in the elimination of neurotic autonomic response habits, the usual extinction mechanism can sometimes be effectively used to remove neurotic motor habits (e.g. Yates, 1958; Walton, 1961).

VARIETY OF COMPLEXITY IN NEUROSIS

Starting from the clinical fact that neuroses generally present themselves as unadaptive, obstinate habits of behavior (with anxiety most often to the forefront), a patient may be regarded as having a *simple* neurosis if he has only one such habit and if it consists of responses to a single and obvious family of stimuli. For example, he may be afraid only of heights, or only of dogs, or only of asserting himself.

There are several kinds of features that can give complexity to a neurosis and they are often found in combination:

1. Multiple families of hierarchies may be conditioned to neurotic reactions.

2. The reactions may involve unadaptiveness in important areas of social behavior ("character neuroses").

3. The neurosis may involve obsessional behaviour.

4. The neurosis may have somatic consequences.

5. There may be continuous anxiety in addition to that which is associated with specific stimuli.

6. Essential stimulus antecedents of the neurotic reactions may be obscured by conditioned inhibition of associations.

1. Multiple Families of Stimuli Conditioned to Neurotic Reactions

While neurotic reactions confined to single families of stimuli are undoubtedly widespread in the general population, many of them, consisting of fears such as of mice, harmless snakes, the sight of much blood, or the appearance of "madness," do not intrude into the individual's life sufficiently to motivate him to seek treatment, especially if the reactions are relatively mild. In people who come for treatment several families of stimuli producing neurotic reactions are usually to be found. Of the 88 cases upon whom I reported in 1958, anxiety was aroused by direct interpersonal interchanges of various kinds in 57, and in 51 of these there were also other families of stimuli that evoked neurotic anxiety. Sometimes there are many such families. For example, one patient had fears of self-assertion, criticism from others, rejection, silences, social occasions, people in authority, his mother, dirt and disorder, being heard in a toilet or seen emerging from one. When neurotic reactions are producible by a great many situations the patient may be said to have a *disseminated neurosis*.

2. Reactions Involving Unadaptiveness in Social Behavior (Character Neuroses)

The unadaptive social behavior that is observed in some patients takes various forms—e.g. inability to get on with people, inefficiency at work, constant changing of jobs, kleptomania, sexual promiscuity, homosexuality and exhibitionism. In the great majority of such cases the deviant behaviour is secondary to anxiety, whose sources need to be carefully ferreted out. If this is not done, therapeutic failure can almost be guaranteed. It is perhaps because psychoanalysts do not concern themselves with anxiety-arousing stimuli that they find such cases especially difficult to treat. An example is afforded by Case 2.

3. Obsessional Neuroses

In certain cases of neurosis, in addition to the usual autonomic discharges, there may be prominent ideational, motor or sensory responses. The term obsessional is applied to such in detail, consisting of well-defined and often elaborate thought-sequences or relatively intricate acts . . ." (Wolpe, 1958, p. 89). As I have pointed out, some obsessional behaviour elevates the level of anxiety; other obsessional behaviour reduces it. In either case the deconditioning of neurotic anxiety is usually the crux of therapy. (Case 3 provides an interesting example.) It is sometimes found that obsessional behaviour continues even when there is no longer any apparent basis for it in terms of anxiety. Such autonomous habits have been effectively treated by aversive conditioning (Wolpe, 1958). (In some cases, e.g. transvestism (e.g. Glynn and Harper, 1961) or fetishism (Raymond, 1956), aversive conditioning has been the sole treatment used, with beneficial effects that appear to have been durable.)

4. Neuroses with Somatic Consequences

Somatic disorders are of course central in classical hysteria; but somatic effects also frequently accompany the much more common anxiety-dominated neuroses. These effects have, as is well known, been "explained" by the psychoanalysts as due to the operation of unconscious agencies that purposely select the malfunctioning of one organ system rather than another.

However in every case a physiological explanation is possible. In different individuals different combinations of reactive elements make up an anxiety reaction; and even in the same individual variously constituted disturbed reactions may be conditioned. It is postulated that, because of peculiarities of physiological development, or because of special features either of earlier conditioning or of the conditioning of the neurosis itself, the anxiety reaction may be characterized by especially strong autonomic discharges in a particular organ system. It is because of this that in one patient emotional disturbance is accompanied by migraine, in another by asthma, in a third by dermatitis, in a fourth by the development of peptic ulceration. In yet other persons anxiety leads to interference with the speech mechanism (stammering). It has been found neurosis can be abolished by eliminating neurotic anxiety and without treating the somatic symptom itself or paying the least attention to the supposed "significance" that "dynamic" theories allege symptoms to have.

5. Reactions That Include Continuous Anxiety

There are some psychiatrists who say that while they can understand how anxiety reactions triggered by specific stimuli may be subject to deconditioning, they do not see how conditioning can be relevant to anxiety that is present all the time and in all situations. They seem to suggest that there is a variety of neurotic anxiety that has no stimulus antecedents.

If the word "stimulus" is employed according to Lundberg's (1937) excellent definition—"that to which response is made"—it is obvious that every response must have stimulus antecedents, for no response can be causeless. It is true that under certain conditions, e.g. beri-beri, there is continuous anxiety that does not depend on any *particular* neural inputs, because, apparently, thresholds in the autonomic nervous system are so greatly lowered that practically all stimulation has anxiety-like consequents. The remedy here is, of course, biochemical.

But if neuroses are due to learning, continuous anxiety that is actually neurotic must also be due to learning. Observations upon patients reveal three conditioned sources of continuous anxiety.

1. The patient may be continuously anxious in all situations except when a specific "security-object" is present. For example, there are cases of agoraphobia in which the patient is free from anxiety only when an intimate person is near him.

2. There may be a conditioned habit of dwelling upon contents of thought that would evoke anxiety in almost everybody. One finds, most often, continual imaginings of scenes of the patient's death or that of loved ones.

3. There may be true "free-floating anxiety," which I have suggested should be re-named *pervasive anxiety*. This anxiety is not attributable to any clear-cut stimulus configuration either in thought or in the outer world, but appears to be conditioned to various more or less pervasive aspects of stimulation in general. The most pervasive aspects of experience are the awareness of space, time, and one's own body (Kant, 1781). Any or all of these may be conditioned to anxiety. Less pervasive concomitants of experience, such as light, verticality, and light-and-shade contrasts may also be conditioned. A wide range of further possibilities for pervasive conditioning may be found in Taylor's important book on perception (1962). When closely questioned, many patients can clearly identify the pervasive stimulus-elements that are connected with their continuous anxiety.* The mechanisms of perva-

---

* In most cases the level of pervasive anxiety can be sharply reduced by 1–4 full capacity inhalations of a mixture of 65 per cent carbon dioxide and 35 per cent oxygen and remains at the lower level until the patient is again exposed to *specific* anxiety-evoking stimuli (see Wolpe, 1958).

sive anxiety and the conditions under which it occurs are matters that urgently call for research.

A fourth kind of continuous anxiety is not due to conditioning but occurs with exposure to an ongoing conflict situation, such as an undesired marriage. Here we have *unconditioned* anxiety, that is automatically generated when the organism has simultaneous impulses to opposing actions (Fonberg, 1956).

6. Reactions in Which Crucial Stimulus Antecedents Are Obscure

Obscurity of central stimulus antecedents may be due to lack of skill or care on the part of the therapist or to concealment on the part of the patient. Such concealment might be deliberate, but occasionally the patient may simply be unaware of certain of his reactions. This may be due to conditioned inhibition of awareness of particular responses. For example, a recent case presented herself as an acute fear of scrutiny of 8 years' duration. Attempts at desensitization failed, because on the face of it no viable dimension of generalization could be found. When (after about 25 sessions) I was about to abandon the case, a clue emerged of unacknowledged rebellion at her domination by her husband. The complete exposure of this set of attitudes within her led to the possibility of expressing these attitudes and to therapeutic change.

This kind of phenomenon, of course, gave rise to the repression theory of neurosis, but it is an infrequent incident without causal significance (Wolpe, 1958, 1961a).

ILLUSTRATIVE CASES

Case 1

Mrs. Y., aged 56, had suffered much anxiety since early childhood. She had been very timid and inadequate in interpersonal situations, but had improved considerably in these during the past ten years. Her general level of anxiety had fluctuated a good deal over the years, being at its worst in association with periods of special stress, when it tended to be displaced by a particularly unpleasant sort of depression. Numerous "phobic" constellations were also present.

There was a good deal in her history to account for her disturbed reactions. She was the only child of a father who was rarely at home, and a harsh, brutal mother who beat her frequently and often confined her alone in an upstairs room. Later experiences compounded the anxious conditioning that these unhappy circumstances began.

She had had a good deal of therapy intermittently. Between 1950 and 1956, she had had a sustained course of psychoanalysis, averaging about three times a week to an estimated total of about 1,000 sessions. She did not feel that the psychoanalytic procedures had produced any beneficial change, but the analyst, who was a down-to-earth person, had instigated a good deal of assertive behaviour, which was instrumental in overcoming to a considerable extent the interpersonal inadequacies. However, her general level of anxiety remained very high, with no improvement at all in the phobias and phobia-like sources of disturbance.

When Mrs. Y. was first seen in May, 1960, she was extremely anxious all day, but gradually improved towards evening, though the measure of this improvement was affected by exposure to a variety of possible situations to which anxiety had been conditioned. Especially important among these situations were rejection and aloneness, which had recently become an increasing problem because her children, growing up, were often away from home.

A great deal of effort was expended upon determining the stimulus antecedents of the patient's reactions. Some of these were quite obvious, but others required a considerable amount of probing.

Treatment consisted partly of extending the assertive training begun during the psychoanalysis, to remove such anxieties as persisted in interpersonal situations. Much the greater part of the sessions was spent on the systematic desensitization of a large number of anxiety hierarchies. The more important of these were: (1) aloneness; (2) rejection; (3) heights; (4) aeroplanes; (5) her mother; (6) waking times; (7) her own early morning depression; (8) prospects of journeys; (9) being lied to; (10) saying goodbye to dear ones; (11) urinating while people waited outside.

In some of these hierarchies sensitivity was extreme so that the amount of work required was very great indeed. For example, in the case of fear of aloneness, Mrs. Y. was initially so sensitive that if she were at home accompanied only by her daughter, anxiety would be evoked if the daughter closed herself up in a room for five minutes in order to make a phone call. Desensitization began with the use of this particular situation, and separation in time and distance was then progressively increased until the patient was able without anxiety, to imagine being quite alone at home for periods of ten days, separated from the nearest person of consequence to her by 300 miles. She could then also endure without anxiety this situation in reality. Her neurotic fear of aeroplanes was also initially very great, so that even the sound of a plane overhead, or the sight of a stationary one in a distant airfield produced very substantial anxiety. For purposes of desensitization it was found necessary to commence with getting her to imagine that she was looking at a toy plane with a six-inch wing span. At subsequent presentations the size of the plane was gradually increased, and a succession of increasingly large model planes were presented standing on a large lawn, and then real planes which she was gradually made to "board," at first silent and, later, with engines running. Eventually an air liner at an exhibition was made a stepping stone to the boarding of commercial air-liners which first made short hops and then ever longer flights. This patient has recently been able to fly wherever she needs to in the United States with equanimity and indeed with pleasure.

Similar systematic deconditioning led to the elimination of all the other reactions. It is not unlikely that if the case and its treatment had first come to the attention of the same analyst after the conditioning therapy, he would have judged it to be different from his usual run of cases!

Case 2

Mrs. Z. was a 36-year-old divorced social worker with a lifelong history of emotional disturbance that had become much worse when she had developed tuberculosis at the age of 23 and her husband, who could not bear illness, had kept away from her. She had subsequently manifested general fecklessness, shiftlessness at work, and considerable sexual promiscuity. In the course of the years she was thrice divorced and attempted suicide very many times. For 9 years she had undergone psychoanalysis with only brief interruptions but without any benefit. She had felt better only when she was running a particularly exciting love affair. Each of her five analysts had regarded her as having a severe character neurosis and had spent countless hours endeavouring to get at its "unconscious roots."

When I first saw Mrs. Z. she was engrossed in a fairly recent love affair with a man she wanted to marry but who was much less enthusiastic about her. She usually entered my consulting room tearful and distrait, and during our first few weeks made several further attempts at suicide.

A behaviouristic analysis of the case revealed interpersonal fear of disapproval that inhibited almost any kind of assertiveness and thus made her largely incapable of withstanding the demands of others or of making known her own. The therapist strongly urged her to express her legitimate demands; and soon grasping the reasonableness of this she made efforts to comply. An early success occurred when her supervisor criticized her on the ground that she was allowing a client's problems to activate her own emotions. Mrs. Z. disagreed.

Mrs. Z.: "That is not so. You have no justification for that statement and it's unfair of you to say it."

Supervisor: "That's your reaction because you have unconscious expectations of unfairness and interpret remarks accordingly."

Mrs. Z.: "Why not? You *are* often unfair."

She proceeded to give instances of his unfairness and had the best of the interchange. There was great satisfaction in this, for in the past this kind of criticism from him "would have left me helpless, and I would have curled up and cried."

Within the general framework of her fear of disapproval were two areas of acute sensitivity that lent themselves to systematic desensitization—fears of rejection and ridicule. Hierarchies were constructed on each of these two themes. (Examples of low intensity items from the rejection hierarchy were: (1) an acquaintance not reciprocating her invitations; (2) a teacher does not see the merit of her viewpoint; and high level examples were: (1) a respected friend behaves condescendingly; (2) her foster mother is angry with her.)

Mrs. Z's treatment was a combination of sustained encouragement of self-expression and desensitization of the hierarchies. After 31 sessions she felt well and "really calm," more so than she could ever remember. She was mastering situations with people and was no longer upset by the neurotic range of "disapprovals." She worked well and handled her lover with new confidence and was shortly able to give him up. At a 9-month follow-up she had married somebody else and her gains had been maintained, both emotionally and socially.

Case 3

Mr. T. was an 18-year-old youth with a very severe washing compulsion. The basis of this was a fear of contamination by urine, and most especially his own urine, mainly because he dreaded to contaminate others with it. When the treatment to be described began, the patient was almost completely impotentiated by his neurosis. After urinating, he would spend up to 45 minutes in an elaborate ritual of cleaning up his genitalia, followed by about two hours of hand-washing. When he woke in the morning, his first need was to shower, which took him about four hours to do. To these "basic requirements" of his neurosis were added many others occasioned by the incidental contaminations inevitable on any day. It is scarcely surprising that Mr. T. had come to conclude that getting up was not worth the effort, and for two months had spent most of his time in bed.

The neurosis evidently originated in an unusual situation at home. Until the age of 15 Mr. T. had been made to share a bed with his sister, two years older, because she had a fear of being alone. Having sexual responses to his sister had made him feel very guilty and ashamed. He had become angry with his parents for imposing this on him and had hostile and at times destructive phantasies about them. He had been horrified at these, and had begun to regard himself as a despicable individual.

Treatment in the first place consisted of the usual form of desensitization, employing imaginary scenes against a background of relaxation. Since he was also disturbed at the idea of anybody else's independent contamination with urine, the first scene he was asked to imagine was the sight of an unknown person dipping his hand into a forty-cubic-foot trough of water into which one drop of urine had been deposited. Even this scene produced some disturbance in Mr. T. at first, but this waned and disappeared in the course of a few presentations. The concentration of urine was then "increased" until the man was imagined to be inserting his hand into pure urine. At each stage a particular scene was repeated until it no longer evoked any anxiety.

In the next series of imaginary situations Mr. T. himself was inserting his hand into increasingly concentrated solutions of urine.

During the course of these procedures, which occupied about five months of sessions taking place about five times a week and lasting, as a rule, about twenty minutes, there was considerable improvement in Mr. T.'s clinical condition. For example, his hand-washing time went down to about 30 minutes, his shower time to just over an hour, and he no longer found it necessary to interpose the *New York Times* between himself and his chair during interviews. However, at about this time it also became evident that there was an increasing lack of transfer between what he could imagine himself doing and what he actually could do. Whereas he could imagine himself immersing his hand in pure urine, to do so in actuality was out of the question.

It was therefore decided to try desensitization *in vivo*. This means that relaxation was opposed to increasingly strong real stimuli evoking anxiety. Accordingly, he was, to begin with, exposed to the word "urine" printed in big block letters. This evoked a little anxiety which he was asked to relax away. The next step was to put him at one end of a long room and a closed bottle of urine at the other end. Again, he had to relax away the anxiety; and then step by step the bottle of urine was moved closer until eventually he was handling it with only minimal anxiety which again he was able to relax away. When the bottle of urine was no longer capable of evoking anxiety, the next series of manoeuvres was started. First of all, a very dilute solution of urine (1 drop to a gallon) was smeared on the back of his hand and he was made to relax until all anxiety disappeared; and then, from session to session the concentration was gradually increased. When he was able to endure pure urine his own urine began to be used; and finally, he was made to "contaminate" all kinds of objects

with his uriniferous hands—magazines, doorknobs, and people's hands.

The numerous acts of desensitization outlined were completed at the end of June, 1961. By then Mr. T. had achieved greatly increased freedom of movement; he was dressing daily, his hand-washing time had gone down to 7 minutes and his shower time to 40 minutes, and his cleaning-up ritual was almost eliminated. In September, 1961, he went back to school and was seen only occasionally until March, 1962. During this time, without active treatment, he made virtually no further progress. In March, 1962, he began weekly sessions and improvement was resumed. When last seen in June, 1962, his hand-washing time was 3 minutes and his shower time 20 minutes. He said that he was coming to think of urine as "sticky and smelly and nothing else." During the later stages measures were also applied to overcome sexual and social anxieties.

RESULTS OF BEHAVIOUR THERAPY IN COMPLEX NEUROSES

In respect of the whole range of neurotic cases presenting for treatment, I have reported (1958) that 89 per cent of 210 patients in 3 series treated by behaviour therapy were either apparently recovered or at least four-fifths improved on Knight's (1941) criteria (symptomatic improvement, increased stress tolerance, and improved function at work, sex and socially). In the last series, comprising 88 patients, the median number of interviews was 23 and the mean 45.6. All neurotic patients were accepted for treatment but no psychotics. (More recently Hussain [1963] has claimed 95 per cent of favourable results on Knight's criteria in 105 patients; and Lazarus [1963] states that of 408 neurotic patients who consulted him, including even those who came only once or twice, 321 [78 per cent] "derived marked benefit on very stringent criteria.")

In reviewing the 88 cases I have found that 65 were *complex* in one or more of the senses defined in this paper, 21 were non-complex, and 2 turned out to be schizophrenic. Fifty-eight of the 65 (89 per cent) were judged either apparently cured or much improved. This percentage is the same as that obtained for the whole group. However, the median number of sessions for the complex group is 29 and the mean 54.8, in contrast to a median for the non-complex remainder of 11.5 and a mean of 14.9 (see Table 1).

Thus, complex cases respond to behaviour therapy as often as simple ones do, but therapy takes longer, presumably because there is more to be done. The principles are the same. There is a constant need to find new methods that utilize these principles as well as to improve our skills in the methods we have.

TABLE 1. *Comparison of Numbers of Sessions in Complex and Single Neuroses. The Total is only 86 because 2 Cases that turned out to be Schizophrenic are Excluded*

	Number	Median Number of Sessions	Mean Number of Sessions
Complex neuroses	65	29	54.8
Simple neuroses	21	11.5	14.9
Whole group	86	23	45.4

Meanwhile it must be stressed that the unravelling of the stimulus-response relations of neurotic reactions is usually no simple matter and quite often very difficult. In general, a high level of knowledge and skill is required for the adequate practice of behaviour therapy. A presumption has arisen that "anyone can do it," and assessments of it have been made (e.g. Cooper, 1963) on the results obtained by untrained and inexperienced therapists—a practice that obscures the realities (Wolpe, 1963b).

SUMMARY

This paper seeks to examine the allegation that behaviour therapy is of value only for "simple" neuroses. One of the major experimental bases of behaviour therapy is described and its main techniques are outlined. Six types of features that give complexity to a neurosis are defined.

A previously published series of 88 cases treated by behaviour therapy is re-examined to see what differences of outcome there were between "simple" cases and those that were complex in one or more of the ways defined. The recovery rate (apparently cured, or much improved) was the same in both groups, but the median number of sessions used for the complex group was two and a half times that for the noncomplex group, and the mean was almost quadruple.

REFERENCES

Bond, I. K., and Hutchison, H. C. (1960). "Application of reciprocal inhibition therapy to exhibitionism." *Canad. Med. Assoc. J., 83,* 23–25.

Cooper, J. E. (1963). "A study of behaviour therapy." *Lancet, i,* 411.

Eysenck, H. J. (1960). *Behaviour Therapy and the Neuroses.* Oxford: Pergamon Press.

Fonberg, E. (1956). "On the manifestation of conditioned defensive reactions in stress." *Bull. Soc. Sci. Letter. 7,* 1–12. Lodz. Class III.

Freeman, H. L., and Kendrick, D. C. (1960). "A case of cat phobia." *Brit. med. J., ii,* 497–502.

Glynn, J. D., and Harper, P. (1961). "Behaviour therapy in transvestism." *Lancet, i,* 619.

Hussain, A. (1963). "Behaviour therapy in 105 cases." In *The Challenge in Psychotherapy.* (Ed.: Wolpe, J., Salter, A., and Reyna, L. J.) New York; Holt, Rinehart & Winston.

Kant, I. (1781). *Critique of Pure Reason.*

Knight, R. P. (1941). "Evaluation of the results of psychotherapy." *Amer. J. Psychiat., 98,* 434–438.

Lazarus, A. A. (1959). "The elimination of children's phobias by deconditioning." *Med. Proc., 5,* 261–264.

_____ (1963). "An evaluation of behaviour therapy." *Behavior Research and Therapy, I,* 69–79.

_____ and Abramovitz, A. (1962). "The use of emotive imagery in the treatment of children's phobias." *J. Ment. Sci., 108,* 191–195.

Lundberg, G. A. (1937). *Foundations of Sociology.* New York: Macmillan.

Raymond, M. J. (1956). "Case of fetishism treated by aversion therapy." *Brit. med. J., ii,* 854–857.

Taylor, J. G. (1962). *The Behavioural Basis of Perception.* New Haven: Yale University Press.

Valentine, C. W. (1946). *The Psychology of Early Childhood.* London: Methuen.

Walton, D. (1961). "Experimental psychology and the treatment of a tiqueur." *J. Child Psychol. Psychiat., 2,* 148–155.

Wolpe, J. (1952). "Experimental neuroses as learned behaviour." *Brit. J. Psychol., 43,* 243–268.

_____ (1958). *Psychotherapy by Reciprocal Inhibition.* Stanford: Stanford University Press.

_____ (1961a). "The prognosis in unpsychoanalysed recovery from neuroses." *Amer. J. Psychiat., 117,* 35–39.

_____ (1961b). "The systmatic desensitization treatment of neuroses." *J. Nerv. Ment. Dis., 132,* 189–203.

Symptoms and Symptom Substitution

Aubrey J. Yates
1958

In recent years there has been a number of attempts to derive rational methods of symptomatic treatment of the behavioral disorders, based mainly on learning theory (1, 2, 3, 4, 5, 6) and information theory (7). Nevertheless symptomatic treatment has not been favorably considered by most clinical psychologists and the failure to appreciate its possibilities is perhaps best shown by the almost total neglect of Dunlap's classic work (8) on habit formation and the remedial treatment of undesirable habits. The object of this paper is to point out some misconceptions on which objections to symptomatic treatment are based, and to show that such treatment can in fact be firmly founded on modern learning theory.

The argument that symptomatic treatment is a waste of time has had as its strongest proponent the psychoanalytic school, which has insisted that symptoms are but the surface indicators of underlying conflicts, anxieties, etc. This argument has been accepted by most "dynamic" psychologists who concluded that removing the symptom without also effectively treating the anxiety or conflict underlying it would lead to symptom substitution. For example, even if tics could be treated directly and extinguished, the patient would quickly develop either new tics or some other form of symptomatic response. Even orthodox psychiatrists who have little patience with Freudian psychodynamics have accepted this point of view. Thus Kanner writes that "symptomatic therapy which does not care what the complaint is a 'symptom' of is rarely successful and leads to unwarranted pessimism"

(9, p. 244). Mowrer has summed up the position neatly and abusively: "the behavioral manifestations which we now call 'symptoms' are not the essence of neurosis and . . . the modes of treatment that are aimed at the direct alleviation are as ill-considered theoretically as they are futile practically" (10, p. 620).

This point of view has become so widely accepted that until recently almost no symptomatic treatment was carried out, except in the educational field of remedial teaching and speech therapy. However, the distinction between a "fundamental" underlying anxiety and a "superficial" surface symptom is open to a number of objections.

(1) The term "symptom" has been employed very loosely in psychology. In general medicine a clear distinction is made "between symptoms, that is disorders described by the patient, and physical signs or the deviations from the normal revealed by examination" (11, p. 1). In other words, a symptom is a subjectively experienced abnormality, a sign is an objective indication of abnormality. In many cases the symptom may, of course, also be a sign.

Mowrer, having accepted, as we have seen, Freud's conclusion with regard to the meaning and functions of symptoms, was considerably embarrassed by his own empirical finding that "symptomatic" treatment of enuresis was not only 100 per cent successful with regard to the symptoms, but was not followed by symptom substitution in a single case! Instead, however, of rejecting Freud's hypothesis Mowrer took the extraordinary step of denying that enuresis was a symptom in any of the cases he treated. He distinguished between habits which were also symptoms, and habits which were not. Thus: " 'symptoms' differ from ordinary 'habits' primarily in that the former are motivated by and are perpetuated because they lessen the drive of anxiety, whereas 'normal' habits are motivated by and are perpetuated because they lessen other drives, such as hunger, thirst, cold, fatigue, sex, fear, etc." (*10*, p. *546*).

Now the above distinction is clearly a meaningful and possibly a valid one. As far as the author is aware, however, Mowrer has not presented any evidence that the distinction can be sustained in the form in which he has put it, and his own experimental results seem strongly to contraindicate the validity of any such distinction. Mowrer's acrobatics in this regard are as good an example as any of an *a priori* clinical bias being allowed to outweigh cogent experimental evidence.[1]

It is clear that, as used by Freud (*12*), Mowrer (*10*), and other "dynamic" psychologists, the symptom is regarded as a response to some hidden, basic conflict or anxiety. It will be suggested that this "vertical," dualistic approach is unnecessary and should be replaced by a "horizontal," monistic approach, as described below.

(2) The "dynamic" approach ignores the distinction between neuroticism and neurosis (*13*). Neuroticism may be conceptualized as an innate predisposition to develop a neurosis under certain specifiable conditions. This conceptualization is at least as plausible as the alternative outlined above. But, if such a predisposition exists, then it follows that a neurosis *is* symptoms and nothing else, i.e., that a particular neurosis consists of a particular set of learned responses; and that treatment on psychological grounds can only be symptomatic, since treatment of the predisposition must ultimately be by genetic or chemical means.

(3) Finally, it should be noted that belief in symptom substitution seems to be based largely on clinical experience. Considering the significant role such a distinction has played in clinical psychology, experimental demonstration of its existence is singularly lacking. We conclude, therefore, that the reasons generally given for rejecting symptomatic treatment in favor of "dynamic" treatment are not soundly based. Nevertheless, the definition of a neurosis as a system of learned responses is not in itself incompatible with the notion of symptom substitution. We must now turn to the question whether there are any theoretical reasons to suppose that symptom substitution would take place, if symptomatic treatment were to be undertaken. It will be maintained that learning theory suggests both that symptomatic treatment is a rational procedure and that symptom substitution would not be expected except under certain specifiable conditions.

This may perhaps be most easily shown by reference to some recent work on the symptomatic treatment of tics (*6*). A model was constructed to account for the genesis of some tics in terms of two-actor learning theory. It was hypothesized that the tic is a conditioned avoidance response to anxiety, the latter being also a learned response (the conditioned form of the original fear response). A method of treatment was derived in terms of the Hullian concepts of I_R and $_sI_R$, making use of massed practice.[2] With regard to this theory, the following points are specifically relevant to this discussion:

(a) Both the anxiety and the tic are learned responses. Now it would be a logical error to suppose that the fact that the tic is a response *to* the anxiety necessarily means that the anxiety must therefore be more fundamental or that it must receive prior treatment. It seems more reasonable to regard the situation simply as one in which two sets of responses (anxiety and the response to anxiety) are learned over time. This may be termed the "horizontal" approach, as opposed to the dualistic "vertical" approach rejected above.

(b) From this point of view it does not much matter which aspect of behavior (anxiety or tic) is treated first. The fact is, however, that in our present state of knowledge it is easier to treat the tic than the anxiety. The former is more readily manipulated and measured, and, since it usually involves motor behavior, is easily dealt with in relation to the concepts of learning theory. It turns out, however, that in treating the symptoms we are also treating the anxiety. For suppose the symptom is destroyed; then the anxiety, instead of being reduced by it, will persist. But since in fact no traumatic event occurs if the anxiety is allowed to persist, the latter, being itself a learned response, will begin to extinguish. This is what in fact seems to happen, though the principle of partial irreversibility of traumatic anxiety (*14*), if valid, suggests that extinction of the anxiety would never be complete.[3]

This formulation is, of course, derived directly from Mowrer's two-actor theory of learning. That removal of the symptom will affect the learned anxiety is hinted at by Mowrer, when he explains why a symptom "is at one and the same time both self-perpetuating and self-defeating. It is self-perpetuating because it is reinforced by the satisfaction provided through the resultant anxiety reduction;

---

[1] Mowrer admits that it is impossible to "know from the incontinence alone that it is a symptom rather than simply a reflection of pedagogical inadequacy" (*10*, p. *414*). Presumably, therefore, decision as to whether the incontinence is a symptom or a habit can be determined only by carrying out "symptomatic" treatment and seeing what happens.

---

[2] In this study (*6*) it was found convenient to use the concepts of I_R and $_sI_R$ in deriving the method of treatment. This aspect could also, however, have been conceptualized in terms of two-factor learning theory, as Mowrer has shown in connection with studies in the field of general motor behavior (*10*, p. *169*, footnote 4).

[3] The nature of traumatic avoidance learning is a very complex problem, which has been greatly oversimplified here. The reader is referred to recent papers by Solomon and Brush (*15*) and by Solomon and Wynne (*14*) for comprehensive discussions of the current position.

and it is self-destructive in that it *prevents the individual from experiencing the full force of his anxiety and being modified by it in such a direction as to eliminate the occasion for the anxiety*" (*10*, p. 535, footnote 3; italics not in original).

Supposing, therefore, both the symptom and the anxiety to be alleviated, we would be left with a basically neurotic person without a current behavior disorder. But, in terms of learning theory, there would be no reason to suppose that this person would develop new anxieties or symptoms unless put into a new traumatic situation. This would, of course, involve knowledge of what situations would be likely to be traumatic for a particular patient.[4]

Such empirical evidence as there is supports the position outlined above. Symptom substitution has not been found in those instances where a single patient has been subjected to intensive investigation and symptomatic treatment (*16, 2, 6*); nor in those few instances where large-scale follow-up has been carried out on groups of subjects. For example, two recent investigations (*17, 18*) of the results of symptomatic (*pace* Mowrer) treatment of enuresis indicate 70–80 per cent success, and a failure to find symptom substitution over periods up to two years. Mowrer himself (*3*), reported 100 per cent success. The critical point seems to be that we are faced in such cases with a vicious circle (as Mowrer has indeed pointed out): the tic, for example, is a response to anxiety, but performance of the tic increases the general level of drive (irritability, annoyance, etc.), which increases the rate of responding, and so on. The important factor seems to be the breaking of this vicious circle; it does not much matter whether this is accomplished by treating the anxiety or the symptom, since both react upon each other. Thus, in the shadowing method described by Cherry and Sayers (*7*) for the treatment of stammering, the mere fact of demonstrating to the patient that he can speak normally (even though under special conditions and before treatment has started) usually has a very striking effect on the patient's general well-being. In many instances it seems that the symptom itself generates a good deal of anxiety, which can be alleviated by a direct attack on the symptom.

The seriousness of the present situation is clearly demonstrated by Eysenck's recent contention (*19*, p. 271) that, in spite of the experimental validation of symptomatic treatment of enuresis, this technique is not used in any child guidance clinic in Great Britain. It is obvious that a re-orientation is highly desirable, in which the "vertical" approach is abandoned, the use of the term "symptom" dropped altogether, and the patient considered as an individual who has developed a series of learned responses to certain situations. Clinical psychologists may then perhaps begin to apply that large body of knowledge and theory to be found in general psychology in which they are specially trained, and apply the principles of behavior to the abnormal field as well as to the normal.

---

[4] In the case of the patient treated by the author, for example, any situation involving anaesthesia (such as dental or medical operations) would be potentially traumatic.

REFERENCES

1. Liversedge, L. A., and Sylvester, J. D. (1955). Conditioning techniques in the treatment of writer's cramp. *Lancet, 2,* 1147–1195.
2. Meyer, V. (1957). The treatment of two phobic patients on the basis of learning principles. *J. Abnorm. (Soc.) Psychol., 55,* 261–266.
3. Mowrer, O. H. (1938). Enuresis: A method for its study and treatment. *Amer. Orthopsychiat., 8,* 436–459.
4. Raymond, M. J. (1956). Case of fetishism treated by aversion therapy. *Brit. Med. J., 2,* 854–857.
5. Wolpe, J. (1952). Experimental neuroses as learned behaviour. *Brit. J. Psychol., 43,* 243–268.
6. Yates, A. J. (1958). The application of learning theory to the treatment of tics. *J. Abnorm. (Soc.) Psychol., 56,* 175–182.
7. Cherry, C., and Sayers, M. McA. (1956). Experiments upon the total inhibition of stammering by external control and some clinical results. *J. Psychosom. Res., 1,* 233–246.
8. Dunlap, K. (1932). *Habits. Their Making and Unmaking.* Liveright, New York.
9. Kanner, L. (1935). *Child Psychiatry.* Charles C. Thomas, Springfield, Ill.
10. Mowrer, O. H. (1950). *Learning Theory and Personality Dynamics.* Ronald Press. New York.
11. Holmes, G. (1946). *Introduction to Clinical Neurology.* Livingstone, Edinburgh.
12. Freud, S. (1936). *The Problem of Anxiety.* Norton, New York.
13. Eysenck, H. J. (1952). *The Scientific Study of Personality.* Routledge & Kegan Paul, London.
14. Solomon, R. L., and Wynne, L. C. (1954). Traumatic avoidance learning: The principles of anxiety conservation and partial irreversibility. *Psychol. Rev., 61,* 353–385.
15. Solomon, R. L., and Brush, E. S. (1956). Experimentally derived conceptions of anxiety and aversion. In *Nebraska Symposium on Motivation.* Ed. by M. R. Jones. Pages 212–305. Univ. Nebraska Press, Lincoln.
16. Jones, H. G. (1956). The application of conditioning and learning techniques to the treatment of a psychiatric patient. *J. Abnorm. (Soc.) Psychol., 52,* 414–419.
17. Baller, W., and Schalock, H. (1956). Conditioned response treatment of enuresis. *Except. Child, 22,* 233–236.
18. Martin, B., and Kubly, D. (1955). Results of treatment of enuresis by a conditioned response method. *J. Consult. Psychol., 19,* 71–73.
19. Eysenck, H. J. (1957). *Dynamics of Anxiety and Hysteria.* Routledge & Kegal Paul, London.

Multimodal Behavior Therapy: Treating the "BASIC ID"

Arnold A. Lazarus
1973

This paper examines the necessary and sufficient conditions for achieving long-lasting therapeutic change. The rationale for recommending direct intervention across seven distinct but inter-related modalities is outlined in some detail. Other systems of psychotherapy are briefly compared to the multimodal behavior therapy procedures advocated herein. A case presentation is provided in order to lend substance to the general notion that durable clinical results are in direct proportion to the number of specific modalities deliberately invoked by any therapeutic system.

Progress in the field of psychotherapy is hindered by a factor that is endemic in our society: an item is considered newsworthy, and accolades are accorded when claims run counter to the dictates of common sense. Thus everything from megavitamins to anal lavages and primal screams gains staunch adherents who, in their frenetic search for a panacea, often breed confusion worse confounded. The present paper emphasizes that patients are usually troubled by a multitude of *specific* problems which should be dealt with by a similar multitude of *specific* treatments. The approach advocated herein is very different from those systems which cluster presenting problems into ill-defined constructs and then direct one or two treatment procedures at these constructs. The basic assumption is

that durable (long-lasting) therapeutic results depend upon the amount of effort expended by patient and therapist across at least six or seven parameters.

Research into the interaction between technique and relationship variables in therapy has shown that an effective therapist "must be more than a 'nice guy' who can exude prescribed interpersonal conditions—he must have an armamentarium of scientifically derived skills and techniques to supplement his effective interpersonal relations" (19, p. 8). Deliberately excluded from the present formulation is the empathic, nonjudgmental warmth, wit and wisdom which characterize those therapists who help rather than harm their clients (2). If this were an article on surgical techniques and procedures, we would presuppose that individuals who apply the prescribed methods are free from pronounced tremors and possess more than a modicum of manual dexterity. Thus, it is hoped that multimodal behavioral procedures will attract nonmechanistic therapists who are flexible, empathic and genuinely concerned about the welfare of their clients.

The main impetus for all forms of treatment probably stems from the general urgency of human problems and the need for practical assistance. This has lent acceptance to technically faulty work that would not pass muster in other fields, and every informed practitioner is all too well aware of the fragmentary and contradictory theories that hold sway in the absence of experimental evidence. Apart from the plethora of different techniques, systems and theories, we have conflicting models and paradigm clashes as exemplified by the difference between radical behaviorists and devout phenomenologists. Attempts to blend divergent models into integrative or eclectic harmony may often result in no more than syncretistic muddles (*17, 19*). And yet without general guiding principles that cut across all systems of therapy, we are left with cabalistic vignettes in place of experimental data or even clinical evidence. Multimodal behavior therapy encompasses: 1) specification of goals and problems; 2) specification of treatment techniques to achieve these goals and remedy these problems; and 3) systematic measurement of the relative success of these techniques.

Since all patients are influenced by processes that lie beyond the therapist's control and comprehension, the field of psychological treatment and intervention is likely to foster superstitious fallacies as readily as well established facts. The tendency to ascribe causative properties to the *last* event in any sequence is all too well known (*e.g.*, her stomach pains must be due to the sausage she just ate for lunch). Thus a patient, after grappling with a problem for years, starts massaging his left kneecap while plucking his right ear lobe and experiences immediate and lasting relief from tenacious symptoms. If a therapist happens to be close at hand, a new technique is likely to be born and placed alongside the parade of other "breakthroughs" with the screamers, confronters, disclosers, relaxers, dreamers, and desensitizers. And if the therapist happens to be sufficiently naive, enthusiastic and charismatic, we will probably never convince him, his students, or his successful patients that the knee-and-ear technique per se is not the significant agent of change. To guard against this penchant, we must insist upon the precise specification of the operations by which systematic assessment of the efficacy of a treatment for a specific problem is made on a regular basis.

The foregoing variables plus the power struggle between psychiatrists and psychologists and the various schools therein tend to hamper progress. The field, over the span of the past 8 years, is described by two leading research clinicians as "chaotic" (*4, 5*). Part of the confusion may also be ascribed to the fact that there is a human (but unscientific) penchant to search for unitary treatments and cures. How nice if insight alone or a soul-searing scream could pave the way to mental health. How simple and convenient for countless addicts if aversion therapy afforded long-lasting results. And what a boon to phobic sufferers if their morbid fears were enduringly assuaged by systematic desensitization and assertive training methods. But while short-lived relief is available to most, we must concur with Lesse that for most syndromes "there is very little proof at this time that any one given technique is superior to another in the long-range therapy of a particular type of psychogenic problem" (*13,* p. 330).

Notwithstanding the biases that lead to theoretical befuddlement, most clinicians would probably agree with the pragmatic assumption that the more a patient learns in therapy, the less likely he is to relapse afterwards. Thus, an alcoholic treated only by aversion therapy would be more likely to relapse than his counterpart who had also received relaxation therapy (*3*). The benefits that accrue from aversion therapy plus relaxation training would be further potentiated by the addition of assertive training, family therapy, and vocational guidance (*12*). This general statement implies that *lasting change* is at the very least a function of combined *techniques, strategies,* and *modalities.* This vitiates the search for a panacea, or a single therapeutic modality. But a point of diminishing returns obviously exists. If two aspirins are good for you, 10 are not 5 times better. When and why should we stop pushing everything from transcendental meditation to hot and cold sitz baths at our clients? Conversely, how, when, where, and why do we infer that in a given instance, meditation plus sensitivity training is preferable to psychodrama and contingency contracting? Above all, how can we wield Occam's razor to dissect the chaos of these diverse psychotherapeutic enterprises into meaningful and congruent components?

SEVEN MODALITIES

An arbitrary division created *sui generis* would simply turn back the clock on the composite theories and facts that psychologists have amassed to date. It is no accident that ever since the publication of Brentano's *Psychologie vom empirischen Standpunkte* in 1874, acts like ideation, together with feeling states and sensory judgments, have comprised the main subject matter of general psychology. In other words, psychology as the scientific study of behavior has long been concerned with sensation, imagery, cognition, emotion, and interpersonal relationships. If we examine psychotherapeutic processes in the light of each of these basic modalities, seemingly disparate systems are brought into clearer focus and the necessary and sufficient conditions for long-lasting therapeutic change might readily be discerned.

Every patient-therapist interaction involves *behavior* (be it lying down on a couch and free associating, or actively role playing a significant encounter), *affect* (be it the silent joy of nonjudgmental acceptance, or the sobbing release of pent-up anger), *sensation* (which covers a wide range of sensory stimuli from the spontaneous awareness of bodily discomfort to the deliberate cultivation of specific sensual delights), *imagery* (be it the fleeting glimpse of a childhood memory, or the contrived perception of a calm-producing scene), and *cognition* (the insights, philosophies, ideas, and judgments that constitute our fundamental values, attitudes and beliefs). All of these take place within the context of an *interpersonal* relationship, or various interpersonal relationships. An added dimension with many patients is their need for medication or *drugs (e.g.,* phenothiazine derivatives and various antidepressants and mood regulators). Taking the first letter of each of the foregoing italicized words, we have the acronym BASIC ID. Obviously, the proposed seven modalities are interdependent and interactive.

If we approach a patient *de novo* and inquire in detail about his salient behaviors, affective responses, sensations, images, cognitions, interpersonal relationships, and his need for drugs or medication, we will probably know more about him than we can hope to obtain from routine history taking and psychological tests. Whether or not these general guidelines can provide all that we need to know in order to be of therapeutic service is an empirical question.[1]

OTHER SYSTEMS

While it is important to determine whether the BASIC ID and the various combinations thereof are sufficiently exhaustive to encompass most vagaries of human conduct, it is perhaps more compelling first to view very briefly a few existing systems of therapy in the light of these modalities. Most systems deal with the majority of modalities *en passant;* very few pay specific and direct attention to each particular zone. Psychoanalysis deals almost exclusively with cognitive-affective interchanges. The neo-Reichian school of bioenergetics (*14*) focuses upon behavior (in the form of "body language"), and the sensory-affective dimension. Encounter groups and Gestalt therapy display a similar suspicion of the "head" and are inclined to neglect cognitive material for the sake of "gut reactions" or affective and sensory responses. Gestalt therapists also employ role playing and imagery techniques. The Masters and Johnson (*15*) sex-training regimen deals explicitly with sexual behavior, affective processes, the "sensate focus," various re-educative features and the correction of misconceptions, all within a dyadic context, preceded by routine medical and laboratory examinations. They do not avail themselves of imagery techniques (*e.g.,* desensitization, self-hypnosis, or fantasy projection), a fact which may limit their overall success rate.

Perhaps it is worth stressing at this point that the major hypothesis, based by the writer's clinical data (*8, 11*), is

that *durable results are in direct proportion to the number of specific modalities deliberately invoked by any therapeutic system.* Psychoanalysis, for instance, is grossly limited because penetrating insights can hardly be expected to restore effective functioning in people with deficient response repertoires—they need explicit training, modeling, and shaping for the acquisition of adaptive social patterns. Conversely, nothing short of coercive manipulation is likely to develop new response patterns that are at variance with people's fundamental belief systems. Indeed, insight, self-understanding, and the correction of irrational beliefs must usually precede behavior change whenever faulty assumptions govern the channels of manifest behavior. In other instances, behavior change must occur before "insight" can develop (*8*). Thus, cognitive restructuring and overt behavior training are often reciprocal. This should not be misconstrued as implying that a judicious blend of psychoanalysis and behavior therapy is being advocated. Psychoanalytic theory is unscientific and needlessly complex; behavioristic theory is often mechanistic and needlessly simplistic. The points being emphasized transcend any given system or school of therapy. However, adherence to social learning theory (*1*) as the most elegant theoretical system to explain our therapeutic sorties places the writer's identification within the province of behavior therapy—hence "multimodal behavior therapy." Perhaps the plainest way of expressing our major thesis is to stress that comprehensive treatment at the very least calls for the correction of irrational beliefs, deviant behaviors, unpleasant feelings, intrusive images, stressful relationships, negative sensations, and possible biochemical imbalance. To the extent that problem identification (diagnosis) systematically explores each of these modalities, whereupon therapeutic intervention remedies whatever deficits and maladaptive patterns emerge, treatment outcomes will be positive and long-lasting. To ignore any of these modalities is to practice a brand of therapy that is incomplete. Of course, not every case requires attention to each modality, but this conclusion can only be reached after each area has been carefully investigated during problem identification (*i.e.,* diagnosis). A similar position stressing comprehensive assessment and therapy has been advocated by Kanfer and Saslow (*7*).

PROBLEM IDENTIFICATION

Faulty problem identification (inadequate assessment) is probably the greatest impediment to successful therapy. The major advantage of a multimodal orientation is that it provides a systematic framework for conceptualizing presenting complaints within a meaningful context. A young man with the seemingly monosymptomatic com-

---

[1] Some may argue that the absence of a "spiritual" dimension is an obvious hiatus, although in the interests of parsimony, it can be shown that cognitive-affective interchanges readily provide the necessary vinculum.

plaint of "claustrophobia" was seen to be troubled by much more than "confined or crowded spaces" as soon as the basic modalities had been scanned. The main impact upon his *behavior* was his inability to attend social gatherings, plus the inconvenience of avoiding elevators, public transportation, and locked doors. The *affective* concomitants of his avoidance behavior were high levels of general anxiety and frequent panic attacks (*e.g.*, when a barber shop became crowded, and at the check-out counter of a supermarket). The *sensory* modality revealed the fact that he was constantly tense and suffered from muscle spasms. His *imagery* seemed to focus on death, burials, and other morbid themes. The *cognitive* area revealed a tendency to catastrophize and to demean himself. At the *interpersonal* level his wife was inclined to mother him and to reinforce his avoidance behavior. This information *obtained after a cursory 10- to 15-minute inquiry,* immediately underscored crucial antecedent and maintaining factors that warranted more detailed exploration as a prelude to meaningful therapeutic intervention.

In contrast with the foregoing case, little more than *sensory unawareness* in a 22-year-old woman seemed to be the basis for complaints of pervasive anxiety, existential panic and generalized depression. She was so preoccupied with lofty thoughts and abstract ideation that she remained impervious to most visual, auditory, tactile and other sensory stimuli. Treatment was simply a matter of instructing her to attend to a wide range of specific sensations. "I want you to relax in a bath of warm water and to examine exact temperature contrasts in various parts of your body and study all the accompanying sensations." "When you walk into a room I want you to pay special attention to every object, and afterwards, write down a description from memory." "Spend the next 10 minutes listening to all the sounds that you can hear and observe their effects upon you." "Pick up that orange. Look at it. Feel its weight, its texture, its temperature. Now start peeling it with that knife. Stop peeling and smell the orange. Run your tongue over the outside of the peel. Now feel the difference between the outside and the inside of the peel. . . ." These simple exercises in sensory awareness were extraordinarily effective in bringing her in touch with her environment and in diminishing her panic, anxiety and depression. She was then amenable to more basic therapy beyond her presenting complaints.

The multimodal approach to therapy is similar to what is called "the problem-oriented record approach." This emphasis upon problem specification is just coming into its own in psychiatry as evidenced in a recent article by Hayes-Roth, Longabaugh, and Ryback (6). In medicine this approach to record keeping and treatment is slightly older, being best illustrated by Weed's work (*18*). Multimodal behavior therapy not only underscores the value of this new approach, but also provides a conceptual framework for its psychiatric implementation. Let us now turn to a case illustration of its use.

CASE ILLUSTRATION

A case presentation should lend substance to the string of assertions outlined on the foregoing pages.

Mary Ann, aged 24, was diagnosed as a chronic undifferentiated schizophrenic. Shortly after her third admission to a mental hospital, her parents referred her to the writer for treatment. According to the hospital reports, her prognosis was poor. She was overweight, apathetic and withdrawn, but against a background of lethargic indifference, one would detect an ephemeral smile, a sparkle of humor, a sudden glow of warmth, a witty remark, an apposite comment, a poignant revelation. She was heavily medicated (Trilafon 8 mg. t.i.d., Vivactil 10 mg. t.i.d., Cogentin 2 mg. b.d.), and throughout the course of therapy she continued seeing a psychiatrist once a month who adjusted her intake of drugs.

A life history questionnaire, followed by an initial interview, revealed that well intentioned but misguided parents had created a breeding ground for guilty attitudes, especially in matters pertaining to sex. Moreover, an older sister, 5 years her senior, had aggravated the situation "by tormenting me from the day I was born." Her vulnerability to peer pressure during puberty had rendered her prone to "everything but heroin." Nevertheless, she had excelled at school, and her first noticeable breakdown occurred at age 18, shortly after graduating from high school. "I was on a religious kick and kept hearing voices." Her second hospital admission followed a suicidal gesture at age 21, and her third admission was heralded by her sister's sudden demise soon after the patient turned 24.

Since she was a mine of sexual misinformation, her uncertainties and conflicts with regard to sex became an obvious area for therapeutic intervention. The book *Sex Without Guilt* by Albert Ellis (1965 Grove Press edition) served as a useful springboard toward the correction of more basic areas of sexual uncertainty and anxiety. Meanwhile, careful questioning revealed the following Modality Profile:

MODALITY PROFILE

Modality	Problem	Proposed Treatment
Behavior	Inappropriate with-drawal responses	Assertive training
	Frequent crying	Nonreinforcement
	Unkempt appearance	Grooming instructions

Continued

MODALITY PROFILE *Continued*

Modality	Problem	Proposed Treatment
	Excessive eating	Low calorie regimen
	Negative self-statements	Positive self-talk assignments
	Poor eye contact	Rehearsal techniques
	Mumbling of words with poor voice projection	Verbal projection exercises
	Avoidance of hetero-sexual situations	Re-education and desensitization
Affect	Unable to express overt anger	Role playing
	Frequent anxiety	Relaxation training and reassurance
	Absence of enthusi-asm and sponta-neous joy	Positive imagery pro-ceedings
	Panic attacks (usually precipitated by crit-icism from authority figures)	Desensitization and assertive training
	Suicidal feelings	Time projection tech-niques
	Emptiness and alone-ness	General relationship building
Sensation	Stomach spasms	Abdominal breathing and relaxing
	Out of touch with most sensual plea-sures	Sensate focus method
	Tension in jaw and neck	Differential relaxation
	Frequent lower back pains	Orthopedic exercises
	Inner tremors	Gendlin's focusing methods (*8*, p. 232)
Imagery	Distressing scenes of sister's funeral	Desensitization
	Mother's angry face shouting "You fool!"	Empty chair technique
	Performing fellatio on God	Blow up technique (implosion)
	Recurring dreams about airplane bombings	Eidetic imagery invok-ing feelings of being safe
Cognition	Irrational self-talk: "I am evil." "I must suffer." "Sex is dirty." "I am inferior."	Deliberate rational disputation and corrective self-talk
	Syllogistic reasoning, overgeneralization	Parsing of irrational sentences

MODALITY PROFILE *Continued*

Modality	Problem	Proposed Treatment
	Sexual misinformation	Sexual education
Interpersonal relationships	Characterized by childlike depen-dence	Specific self-sufficiency assign-ments
	Easily exploited/submissive	Assertive training
	Overly suspicious	Exaggerated role tak-ing
	Secondary gains from parental concern	Explain reinforcement principles to par-ents and try to en-list their help
	Manipulative tenden-cies	Training in direct and confrontational behaviors

The Modality Profile may strike the reader as a frag-mented, or mechanistic barrage of techniques that would call for a disjointed array of therapeutic maneuvers. In actual practice, the procedures follow logically and blend smoothly into meaningful interventions.

During the course of therapy as more data emerged and as a clearer picture of the patient became apparent, the Modality Profile was constantly revised. Therapy was mainly a process of devising ways and means to remedy Mary Ann's shortcomings and problem areas throughout the basic modalities. The concept of "technical eclecti-cism" came into its own (*10*). In other words, a wide array of therapeutic methods drawn from numerous disciplines was applied, but to remain theoretically consistent, the active ingredients of every technique were sought within the province of social learning theory.

In Mary Ann's case, the array of therapeutic methods selected to restructure her life included familiar behavior therapy techniques such as desensitization, assertive train-ing, role playing, and modeling, but many additional pro-cedures were employed such as time projection, cognitive restructuring, eidetic imagery, and exaggerated role tak-ing as described in some of the writer's recent publica-tions (*8, 9*). The empty chair technique (*16*) and other methods borrowed from Gestalt therapy and encounter group procedures were added to the treatment regimen. Mary Ann was also seen with her parents for eight ses-sions, and was in a group for 30 weeks.

During the course of therapy she became engaged and was seen with her fiancé for premarital counseling for several sessions.

The treatment period covered the span of 13 months at the end of which time she was coping admirably without medication and has continued to do so now for more than a year. This case was chosen for illustrative purposes because so often, people diagnosed as "psychotic" receive little more than chemotherapy and emotional support. Yet, in the writer's experience, once the florid symptoms are controlled by medication, many people are amenable to multimodal behavior therapy. It is tragic that large numbers of people who can be reached and helped by multimodal behavior therapy are often left to vegetate.

CONCLUSIONS

Those who favor working with one or two specific modalities may inquire what evidence there is to support the contention that *multimodal* treatment is necessary. At present, the writer's follow-up studies (*e.g., 8, 11*) have shown that relapse all too commonly ensues after the usual behavior therapy programs, despite the fact that behavioral treatments usually cover more modalities than most other forms of therapy. Of course, the run of the mill behavior therapist does not devote as much attention to imagery techniques as we are advocating (even when using covert reinforcement procedures and imaginal desensitization), nor does he delve meticulously enough into cognitive material, being especially neglectful of various philosophical values and their bearing on self-worth.

Another fact worth emphasizing is that in order to offset "future shock" multimodal therapy attempts to anticipate areas of stress that the client is likely to experience in time to come. Thus, one may use imaginal rehearsal to prepare people to cope with the marriage of a child, a possible change in occupation, the purchase of a new home, the process of aging, and so forth. In my experience, these psychological "fire drills" can serve an important preventive function.

As one investigates each modality, a clear understanding of the individual and his interpersonal context emerges. Even with a "simple phobia," new light is shed, and unexpected information is often gleaned when examining the behavioral, affective, sensory, imaginal, cognitive and interpersonal consequences of the avoidance responses. Whenever a plateau is reached in therapy and progress falters, the writer has found it enormously productive to examine each modality in turn in order to determine a possibly neglected area of concern. More often than not, new material emerges and therapy proceeds apace.

REFERENCES

1. Bandura, A. *Principles of Behavior Modification.* Holt, Rinehart and Winston. New York, 1969.
2. Bergin, A. E. The evaluation of therapeutic outcomes. In Bergin, A. E., and Garfield, S. I., Eds. *Handbook of Psychotherapy and Behavior Change,* pp. 217–220. Wiley, New York, 1971.
3. Blake, B. G. The application of behavior therapy to treatment of alcoholism. *Behav. Res. Ther., 3:* 75–85, 1965.
4. Colby, K. M. Psychotherapeutic processes. *Annu. Rev. Psychol., 15:* 347–370, 1964.
5. Frank, J. D. Therapeutic factors in psychotherapy. *Am. J. Psychother., 25:* 350–361, 1971.
6. Hayes-Roth, F., Longabaugh, R., and Ryback, R. The problem-oriented medical record and psychiatry. *Br. J. Psychiatry, 121:* 27–34, 1972.
7. Kanfer, F. H., and Saslow, G. Behavioral diagnosis. In C. M. Franks, Ed. *Behavior Therapy: Appraisal and Status,* pp. 417–444. McGraw-Hill, New York, 1968.
8. Lazarus, A. A. *Behavior Therapy and Beyond.* McGraw-Hill, New York, 1971.
9. Lazarus, A. A., Ed. *Clinical Behavior Therapy.* Brunner, Mazel, New York, 1972.
10. Lazarus, A. A. In support of technical eclecticism. *Psychol. Rep., 21:* 415–416.
11. Lazarus, A. A. Notes on behavior therapy, the problem of relapse and some tentative solutions. *Psychotherapy. 3:* 192–196, 1971.
12. Lazarus, A. A. Towards the understanding and effective treatment of alcoholism. *S. Afr. Med. J., 39:* 736–741, 1965.
13. Lesse, S. Anxiety—Its relationship to the development and amelioration of obsessive-compulsive disorders. *Am. J. Psychother., 26:* 330–337, 1972.
14. Lowen, A. *The Betrayal of the Body.* Macmillan. New York, 1967.
15. Masters, W. H., and Johnson, V. E. *Human Sexual Inadequacy.* Little Brown. Boston, 1970.
16. Perls, F. S. *Gestalt Therapy Verbatim.* Real People Press Lafayette, California, 1969.
17. Reisman, J. M. *Toward the Integration of Psychotherapy.* Wiley, New York, 1971.
18. Weed, L. L. Medical records that guide and teach. *N. Engl. J. Med., 278:* 593–600, 1968.
19. Woody, R. H. *Psychobehavioral Counseling and Therapy.* Appleton-Century-Crofts, New York, 1971.

Cognitive Therapy

❧ ❧ ❧

Training Impulsive Children to Talk to Themselves: A Means of Developing Self-Control

Donald H. Meichenbaum
and Joseph Goodman
1971

The efficacy of a cognitive self-instructional (SI) training procedure in altering the behavior of "impulsive" school children was examined in two studies. Study I employed an individual training procedure which required the impulsive child to talk to himself, initially overtly and then covertly, in an attempt to increase self-control. The results indicated that the SI group ($N = 5$) improved significantly relative to attentional and assessment control groups on the Porteus Maze test, Performance IQ on the WISC, and on a measure of cognitive impulsivity. The improved performance was evident in a 1-mo. follow-up assessment. Study II examined the efficacy of the components of the cognitive treatment procedure in altering the impulsive child's performance on Kagan's measure of cognitive impulsivity. The results indicated that cognitive modeling alone was sufficient to slow down the impulsive child's response time for initial selection, but only with the addition of SI training was there a significant decrease in errors. The treatment and research implications of modifying S's cognitions are discussed.

The development of the functional interaction between self-verbalization and nonverbal behavior has received much attention (Luria, 1961; Piaget, 1947; Reese, 1962; and see specially a review by Kohlberg, Yaeger, & Hjertholm, 1968). Two general research strategies have been employed to assess the influence of self-verbalizations on behavior. The first strategy is characterized by S's performance on a task and E's subsequent inference as to the presence or absence of specific cognitive activities. In general, this approach has used the concept of "deficiency" to explain poor performance. Reese (1962) has suggested a mediation deficiency hypothesis; Flavell and his co-workers (Flavell, Beach, & Chinsky, 1966; Moely, Olson, Halwes, & Flavell, 1967) have offered a production deficiency hypothesis, and most recently Bem (1970) has suggested a comprehension deficiency hypothesis. The developing child is characterized as going through stages during which he (a) does not mediate or regulate his overt behavior verbally; (b) does not spontaneously produce relevant mediators; and (c) does not comprehend the nature of the problem in order to discover what mediators to produce. Thus, problem solving is viewed as a three-stage process of comprehension, production, and mediation, and poor performance can result from a "deficiency" at any one of these stages. The deficiency literature suggests that a training program designed to improve task performance and engender self-control should provide explicit training in the comprehension of the task, the spontaneous production of mediators, and the use of such mediators to control nonverbal behavior. The present cognitive self-guidance treatment program was designed to provide such training for a group of "impulsive" children.

The other strategy, which is designed to assess the functional role of private speech in task performance, directly manipulates the child's verbalizations and examines resulting changes in nonverbal behavior. Vygotsky (1962) has suggested that internalization of verbal commands is the critical step in the child's development of voluntary control of his behavior. Data from a wide range of studies (Bem, 1967; Klein, 1963; Kohlberg et al., 1968; Lovaas, 1964; Luria, 1959, 1961; Meichenbaum & Goodman, 1969a, 1969b) provide support for the age increase in cognitive self-guiding private speech, and the increase in internalization with age. These results suggest a progression from external to internal control. Early in development, the speech of others, usually adults, mainly controls and directs a child's behavior; somewhat later, the child's own overt speech becomes an effective regulator of his behavior; and still later, the child's covert or inner speech can assume a regulatory role. The present studies were designed to examine the efficacy of a cognitive self-guidance treatment program which followed the developmental sequence by which overt verbalizations of an adult or *E,* followed by the child's overt self-verbalizations, followed by covert self-verbalization would result in the child's own verbal control of his nonverbal behavior. By using this fading procedure, we hoped to (a) train impulsive *S*s to provide themselves with internally originated verbal commands or self-instructions and to respond to them appropriately; (b) strengthen the mediational properties of the children's inner speech in order to bring their behavior under their own verbal or discriminative control; (c) overcome any possible "comprehension, production, or mediational deficiencies"; and finally (d) encourage the children to appropriately self-reinforce their behavior. We hoped to have the child's private speech gain a new functional significance, to have the child develop a new cognitive style or "learning set" and thus to engender self-control.

Two studies are reported which apply the cognitive self-guidance treatment regimen to impulsive school children. The first study, using second-grade children who had been assigned to an "opportunity remedial class," provided four ½-hr. individual training sessions over a 2-wk. period. The effects of training on performance measures and classroom behavior is reported. The second study examines the modification value of a particular component of the treatment regimen, namely modeling, which is designed to alter the child's impulsive cognitive style in one treatment session as assessed on Kagan's

(1966) Matching Familiar Figures (MFF) Test. The impulsive *S*s in the second study have been selected from kindergarten and first-grade classes as assessed by their failure to follow an instruction to "go slower" on a pre-assessment of the MFF test. Both studies indicate the general treatment regimen designed to train impulsive children to talk to themselves, a possible means of developing self-control.

STUDY I

Method

Subjects

The *S*s were 15 second-grade children (8 females, 7 males) whose ages ranged from 7 to 9 yr. with a mean of 8 yr., 2 mo. and who had been placed in an "opportunity remedial class" in a public elementary school. The children were placed into the opportunity class because of behavioral problems such as hyperactivity and poor self-control, and/or they had low IQs on one of a variety of school-administered intelligence tests. The cutoff point on the IQ measures was 85, but for several *S*s the last assessment was several years prior to the present research project. The children's behavior both in class and on performance measures was measured before and after treatment as well as in a 1-mo. follow-up assessment described below. Following the pretreatment assessment, *S*s were assigned to one of three groups. One group comprised the cognitive self-guidance treatment group ($N = 5$). The remaining two groups included in the study were control groups. One control group met with *E* with the same regularity as did the cognitively trained *S*s. This attention control group ($N = 5$) afforded an index of behavioral change due to factors of attention, exposure to training materials, and any demand characteristics inherent in our measures of improvement. In addition, an assessment control group of *S*s who received no treatment was included. The assessment control group ($N = 5$) provided an index of the contribution of intercurrent life experiences to any behavioral change (*e.g.,* being a member of the opportunity remedial class). Assignment to these three groups was done randomly, subject to the two constraints of (*a*) equating the groups on sex composition and (*b*) matching the groups on their prorated WISC IQ performance scores taken prior to treatment.

Treatments

Cognitive training group. The *S*s in this group were seen individually for four ½-hr. treatment sessions over a 2-wk. period. The cognitive training technique proceeded as follows: First, *E* performed a task talking aloud while *S*

observed (E acted as a model); then S performed the same task while E instructed S aloud; then S was asked to perform the task again while instructing himself aloud; then S performed the task while whispering to himself (lip movements); and finally S performed the task covertly (without lip movements). The verbalizations which E modeled and S subsequently used included: (a) questions about the nature and demands of the task so as to compensate for a possible comprehension deficiency; (b) answers to these questions in the form of cognitive rehearsal and planning in order to overcome any possible production deficiency; (c) self-instructions in the form of self-guidance while performing the task in order to overcome any possible mediation deficiency; and (d) self-reinforcement. The following is an example of E's modeled verbalizations which S subsequently used (initially overtly, then covertly):

> Okay, what is it I have to do? You want me to copy the picture with the different lines. I have to go slow and be careful. Okay, draw the line down, down, good; then to the right, that's it; now down some more and to the left. Good, I'm doing fine so far. Remember go slow. Now back up again. No, I was supposed to go down. That's okay. Just erase the line carefully. . . . Good. Even if I make an error I can go on slowly and carefully. Okay, I have to go down now. Finished. I did it.

Note in this example an error in performance was included and E appropriately accommodated. In prior research with impulsive children, Meichenbaum and Goodman (1969b) observed a marked deterioration in their performance following errors. The E's verbalizations varied with the demands of each task, but the general treatment format remained the same throughout. The treatment sequence was also individually adapted to the capabilities of the S and the difficulties of the task.

A variety of tasks was employed to train the child to use self-instructions to control his nonverbal behavior. The tasks varied along a dimension from simple sensorimotor abilities to more complex problem-solving abilities. The sensorimotor tasks, such as copying line patterns and coloring figures within certain boundaries, provided S with an opportunity to produce a narrative description of his behavior, both preceding and accompanying his performance. Over the course of a training session, the child's overt self-statements on a particular task were faded to the covert level, what Luria (1961) has called "interiorization of language." The difficulty level of the training tasks was increased over the four training sessions requiring more cognitively demanding activities. Such tasks as reproducing designs and following sequential instructions taken from the Stanford-Binet intelligence test, completing pictorial series as on the Primary

Mental Abilities test, and solving conceptual tasks as on the Ravens Matrices test, required S to verbalize the demands of the task and problem-solving strategies. The E modeled appropriate self-verbalizations for each of these tasks and then had the child follow the fading procedure. Although the present tasks assess many of the same cognitive abilities required by our dependent measures, there are significant differences between the training tasks and the performance and behavioral indexes used to assess improvement. It should be noted that the attentional control group received the same opportunities to perform on each of the training tasks, but without cognitive self-guidance training.

One can imagine a similar training sequence in the learning of a new motor skill such as driving a car. Initially the driver actively goes through a mental checklist, sometimes aloud, which includes verbal rehearsal, self-guidance, and sometimes appropriate self-reinforcement, especially when driving a stick-shift car. Only with repetition does the sequence become automatic and the cognitions become short-circuited. This sequence is also seen in the way children learn to tie shoelaces and in the development of many other skills. If this observation has any merit, then a training procedure which makes these steps explicit should facilitate the development of self-control.

In summary, the goals of the training procedure were to develop for the impulsive child a cognitive style or learning set in which the child could "size up" the demands of a task, cognitively rehearse, and then guide his performance by means of self-instructions, and when appropriate reinforce himself.

Attention control group. The children in this untutored group had the same number of sessions with E as did the cognitive training Ss. During this time, the child was exposed to identical materials and engaged in the same general activities, but did not receive any self-instructional training. For example, these attentional control Ss received the same number of trials on a task as did the cognitively trained Ss, but they did not receive self-instructional training. An attempt was made to provide both the experimental and attention control groups with equal amounts of social reinforcement for behavioral performance on the tasks.

Assessment control group. This untreated control group received only the same pretreatment, posttreatment, and follow-up assessments as the cognitive treatment and attention control groups.

Instruments

Two general classes of dependent measures were used to assess the efficacy of the cognitive self-guidance treatment regimen to improve performance and engender self-control. The first class of measures involved performance on a variety of psychometric instruments which have been previously used to differentiate impulsive from nonimpulsive children. The second class of measures assessed the generalizability of the treatment effects to the classroom situation. The female E who performed the pretreatment, posttreatment, and follow-up assessments on the performance measures and the two female Es who made classroom observations during pretreatment and posttreatment periods were completely unaware of which children received which treatment.

Performance measures. Three different psychometric tests were used to assess changes in behavioral and cognitive impulsivity during the pretreatment, posttreatment, and follow-up periods. Several investigators (Anthony, 1959; Eysenck, 1955; Foulds, 1951; Porteus, 1942) have demonstrated that the Porteus Maze test, especially the qualitative score which is based upon errors in style and quality of execution, distinguishes between individuals differing in impulsiveness. Most recently, Palkes, Stewart, and Kahana (1968) have reported that hyperactive boys significantly improved on Porteus Maze performance following training in self-directed verbal commands. Thus, the Porteus Maze performance provided one indicant of behavioral change. Because of the length of the assessment (some 45 min.), only years 8–11 of the Porteus Maze test were used. On the posttest the Vineland Revision form of the Porteus Maze test was used.

A second measure which has been used to assess cognitive impulsivity is Kagan's (1966) MFF test. The S's task on the MFF test is to select from an array of variants one picture which is identical to a standard picture. The tendency toward fast or slow decision times and the number of errors are used to identify the degree of conceptual impulsivity. Further support for the use of the MFF test in the present study comes from research by Meichenbaum and Goodman (1969a), who have reported a positive relationship between a child's relative inability to verbally control his motor behavior by means of covert self-instructions and an impulsive conceptual tempo on the MFF test. Parallel forms of the MFF test were developed by using six alternate items in the pretreatment and posttreatment assessments, with the pretreatment MFF test being readministered on the follow-up assessment.

The final set of performance measures was derived from three performance subtests of the WISC. The three subtests selected were Picture Arrangement, Block Design, and Coding. Respectively, these subtests are designed to assess (a) the ability to comprehend and size up a total situation requiring anticipation and planning; (b) the ability to analyze and form abstract designs as illustrated by S's performance and approach to the problems; and (c) the child's motor speed and activity level (Kitzinger & Blumberg, 1957; Lutey, 1966; Wechsler, 1949). The results from the WISC subtests are reported in scaled scores and as a prorated IQ performance estimate.

In summary, the performance measures were designed to assess the range of abilities from sensorimotor, as indicated by qualitative scores on Porteus Maze and Coding tasks on the WISC, to more cognitively demanding tasks such as the MFF test, Block Design, and Picture Arrangement subtests.

Classroom measures. Two measures were used to ascertain whether any of the expected changes would extend into the classroom. The first measure behaviorally assessed the 15 children on their appropriateness and attentiveness within the classroom setting. We used a time-sampling observational technique (10 sec. observe, 10 sec. record) which was developed by Meichenbaum, Bowers, and Ross (1968, 1969) to rate inappropriate classroom behavior. Inappropriate classroom behavior was defined as any behavior which was not consistent with the task set forth by the teacher, that is, behavior which was not task specific. The children were observed for 2 school days 1 wk. before and immediately after treatment. The second measure involved a teacher's questionnaire which was designed to assess each child's behavioral self-control, activity level, cooperativeness, likeability, etc. The questionnaire consisted of 10 incomplete statements, each of which was followed by three forced choice alternative completions. The teacher filled out the scale immediately prior to treatment and 3 wk. later at the conclusion of the posttreatment assessment.

Results

The relative efficacy of the cognitive self-guidance treatment program was assessed by means of a Lindquist (1953) Type I analysis of variance which yields a treatment effect, trials effect (pretreatment and posttreatment assessments), and a Treatment × Trials interaction. The results from the 1-mo. follow-up measures were analyzed separately. Multiple *t*-test comparisons (one-tailed) were performed on the change scores for each of the dependent measures. Figure 1 presents the performance measures.

The analyses of the three WISC subtests revealed only a significant Group × Trials interaction on the Picture Arrangement subtest ($F = 4.56$, $df = 2/12$, $p = .033$) and a strong trend toward significance on the Coding subtest (Group × Trials $F = 2.87$, $df = 2/12$, $p = .10$). The performances on the Block Design subtest did not yield any significant groups, trials, or Group × Trials interactions. When the performances on the three WISC subtests were combined to yield a prorated IQ score, the relative efficacy of the cognitive training procedure is further revealed in a significant Group × Trials interaction ($F = 3.97$, $df = 2/12$, $p = .05$). The cognitive training group

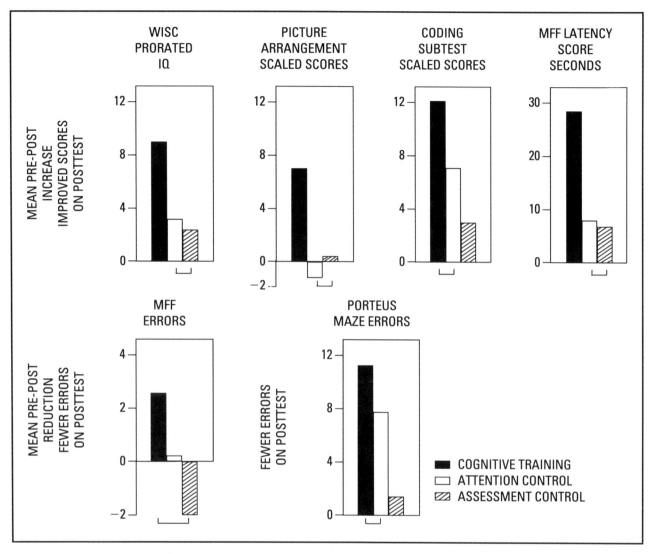

Figure 1. Mean change scores from pretreatment to posttreatment on performance measures. (Groups not connected by solid line are significantly different at .05 level.)

improved 8.3 IQ points (SD = 3.8), from an IQ of 88.4 to an IQ of 96.7. In comparison, the attention control group and the assessment control group improved, respectively, 3.4 (SD = 4.1) and 2.2 (SD = 3.0) IQ points. Multiple t comparisons indicated that the cognitive training group was significantly different (p < .05) from the attentional and assessment control groups on the Picture Arrangement and Coding subtests, and on the prorated IQ scores, whereas the two control groups did not significantly differ from each other on the WISC measures.

Further evidence for the efficacy of the cognitive training is derived from the measure of cognitive impulsivity, namely, the MFF test. A significant Group × Trials interaction (F = 9.49, df = 2/12, p = .004) was found on the initial decision time or latency score on the MFF test. The cognitive training group increased its mean total decision

time for the six MFF items from pretest to posttest by 27.4 sec. (SD = 10.3), in comparison to the attention and assessment control groups who, respectively, increased their total posttest decision times by 7.4 sec. (SD = 3.8) and 6.8 sec. (SD = 9.9). The differential increase in response time indicates that the impulsive Ss in the cognitively trained group took significantly longer before responding on the posttest. The analyses of the error scores on the MFF test did not yield any significant differences, although the trend of the results did suggest differential effectiveness for the cognitively trained Ss. The cognitively trained Ss had a group total decrease on the posttest of 8 errors in comparison to the attentional control Ss, who had a group total decrease of only 2 errors on the posttest, and the assessment control Ss, who had a group total increase of 10 errors on the posttest. The absence of statistical significance on the error scores may be due to the relative ease of the MFF test for this age level and the use of a shortened version of the test in order to develop parallel forms (i.e., 6 items were used instead of the usual 12-item test). The potential usefulness of the cognitive training procedure in altering cognitive impulsivity was examined in the second study which is described below.

An analysis of the performance on the Porteus Maze test indicated a significant Group × Trials interaction ($F = 5.52$, $df = 1/12$, $p = .02$), with the cognitive training and the attentional control groups making significantly ($p < .05$) less errors on the posttest than the assessment control group. The mean change scores indicated that (*a*) Ss who received cognitive training improved most with 10.8 ($SD = 4.3$) less errors on the posttest; (*b*) Ss in the attentional control group made 7.8 ($SD = 6.8$) less errors on the posttest; and (*c*) the assessment control group made 1.2 ($SD = 4.7$) more errors on the posttest. Both the cognitive training group and the attentional control group decreased errors on the posttest by cutting fewer corners, crossing over fewer lines, lifting their pencils less frequently, and producing fewer irregular lines. Palkes et al. (1968) have reported a significant improvement on the Porteus Maze test for a self-directed verbal command group relative to an assessment or no-treatment control group, but they did not include an attentional control group. The present results indicated that an attentional control group which received only practice on a variety of sensorimotor and cognitive tasks also significantly improved their performance on the Porteus Maze test. The inclusion of such an attentional control group is thus necessary in order to exclude alternative hypotheses.

The analyses of the Ss' classroom behavior by means of time-sampling observations and by teachers' ratings did not yield any significant differences. The absence of a significant treatment effect in the classroom may be due to a lack of generalization because of the limited number of training sessions and/or the lack of sensitivity of the assessment measures. The analyses of the 4-wk. follow-up assessment revealed that the cognitive training group maintained their improved performance on the test battery, relative to the attentional and assessment control groups. The analyses of the follow-up test performances relative to the pretreatment performance indicated that on the Picture Arrangement subtest, the WISC prorated IQ score, and the decision time on the MFF, the cognitive training group was significantly different ($p < .05$) from the two control groups. The analysis of the qualitative performance on the Porteus Maze test indicated that both the cognitive training group and the attentional control group maintained their improved performance relative to the assessment control group.

The results of the first study proved most encouraging and suggested that a cognitive self-guidance training program can significantly alter behavior of impulsive children. The purpose of the second study was to examine the differential contribution of the various components of the treatment program in modifying impulsive behavior. The cognitive training procedure involved both modeling by *E* and subsequent self-instructional training by *S*. In this study a comparison is made between the relative efficacy of modeling alone versus modeling plus self-instructional training in modifying cognitive impulsivity as measured by the MFF test. Kagan (1965) has defined cognitive impulsivity as a conceptual tempo or decision-time variable representing the time *S* takes to consider alternate solutions before committing himself to one of them in a situation with high response uncertainty. Kagan and his associates (Kagan, 1965, 1966; Kagan, Rosman, Day, Albert, & Phillips, 1964) have shown that performance on the MFF test has high stability and intertest generality and is related to performance on visual discrimination tasks, inductive reasoning, serial recall, and reading skills. Most recently, investigators have been interested in the modification of cognitive impulsivity. Kagan, Pearson, and Welsh (1966) have attempted to train, in three individual sessions, inhibition of impulsive responding by requiring the child to defer his answer for a fixed period of 10 to 15 sec. During this period the child was encouraged to study the stimuli in the task and to think about his answer, but he did *not* receive training in more efficient procedures to emit during this interval. Significant changes in latency or decision time occurred, but no corresponding significant change in errors was evident. Debus (1970) examined the usefulness of filmed modeling of reflective behavior and found a decrease only in decision time, and, like Kagan, Pearson and Welch (1966), no corresponding change in errors. The studies by Kagan et al. (1966) and Debus (1970) have concentrated on increasing latency times without paying sufficient attention to inducing improved cognitive and/or scanning strategies in the impulsive child. Siegelman (1969) and Drake (1970) have demonstrated that different attentional and cognitive strategies seem to underlie the performance of impulsive and reflective Ss. The data from Siegelman and Drake indicate that the impulsive child on the MFF test (*a*) displays a greater biasing of attention both in extent of scanning and in number of alternatives ignored; (*b*) is simply in search of some variant that globally resembles the standard and is not very discriminating or analytic in his viewing. In comparison, the reflective child seems to follow a strategy to find explicit differences among alternatives and then to check the standard for verification. The impulsive child's approach or strategy on the MFF task results in many errors and quick decision times. The purpose of the present study was to examine the usefulness of the cognitive self-guidance training procedure in altering the attentional strategy of the impulsive child on the MFF test. The efficacy of the self-instructional training procedure in modifying cognitive impulsivity is compared with a modeling-alone procedure. An attentional control group which received exposure to the practice materials but no explicit training was included for comparative purposes.

STUDY II

Method

Subjects

The 15 impulsive children who received training were selected from a larger group of kindergarten ($N = 30$) and first-grade ($N = 30$) public school children on the basis of two behavioral criteria. All of the children were individually tested on parallel forms of six items each of the MFF test. Interspersed between the two MFF forms the instruction "You don't have to hurry. You should go slowly and carefully" was given to all Ss. The 15 impulsive Ss (4 male and 4 female kindergartners and 4 male and 3 female first graders) were selected on the basis of the S's initial performance on Form I of the MFF test and the absence of any appreciable improvement in performance on Form II of the MFF test. Thus, the selected impulsive children were initially cognitively impulsive, and they did not significantly alter their style of responding even though they were instructed to do so. The use of an instructional manipulation to select Ss is consistent with Vygotsky's (1962) suggestion that a child's capabilities are best reflected by his response to instructions.

Following Session 1, the 15 selected impulsive Ss were randomly assigned to one of the treatment groups (viz., modeling alone or modeling plus self-instructional training) or to the attentional control group, subject to the constraint of comparable age and sex representation in each group. One week later in a second session, each of the impulsive Ss was individually seen by a different E (female), who conducted the treatment, after which Ss were tested on a third form of the six-item MFF test by the first E (male) who had conducted the testing in Session 1. The E who administered the three forms of the MFF test was thus unaware into which group S had been placed. The training materials consisted of the Picture Matching subtest from the Primary Mental Abilities (PMA) test and items from the Ravens' Matrices test. These materials elicit similar task abilities to the MFF test and provide a useful format for modeling reflective behaviors. The training procedure which lasted some 20 min. consisted of E performing or modeling behavior on one item of the

practice material and then S doing an item. There were in all eight practice trials.

Treatments

Cognitive modeling group. The Ss in this group ($N = 5$) initially observed the E who modeled a set of verbalizations and behaviors which characterizes the reflective child's proposed strategy on the MFF test. The following is an example of E's modeled verbalizations on the PMA Picture Matching test:

> I have to remember to go slowly to get it right. Look carefully at this one (the standard), now look at these carefully (the variants). Is this one different? Yes, it has an extra leaf. Good, I can eliminate this one. Now, let's look at this one (another variant). I think it's this one, but let me first check the others. Good, I'm going slow and carefully. Okay, I think it's this one.

The impulsive child was exposed to a model which demonstrated the strategy to search for differences that would allow him successively to eliminate as incorrect all variants but one. The E modeled verbal statements or a strategy to make detailed comparisons across figures, looking at all variants before offering an answer. As in the first study, E also modeled errors and then how to cope with errors and improve upon them. For example, following an error E would model the following verbalizations:

> It's okay, just be careful. I should have looked more carefully. Follow the plan to check each one. Good, I'm going slowly.

After E modeled on an item, S was given an opportunity to perform on a similar practice item. The S was encouraged and socially reinforced for using the strategy E had just modeled, but did not receive explicit practice in self-instructing. This modeling-alone group was designed to indicate the degree of behavioral change from exposure to an adult model.

Cognitive modeling plus self-instructional training group. The Ss in this group were exposed to the same modeling behavior by E as were Ss in the modeling-alone group, but in addition they were explicitly trained to produce the self-instructions E emitted while performing the task. After E modeled on an item, S was instructed to perform the task while talking aloud to himself as E had done. Over the course of the eight practice trials, the child's self-verbalizations were faded from initially an overt level to a covert level, as in Study I.

Attentional control groups. The Ss in this group observed the E perform the task and were given an opportunity to perform on each of the practice items. The E's verbalizations consisted only of general statements to "go slow, be careful, look carefully," but did not include the explicit modeling of verbalizations dealing with scanning strategies as did the two treatment groups. The Ss were encouraged and socially reinforced to go slow and be careful, but were not trained to self-instruct. In many ways this group approximates the methods teachers and parents use to demonstrate a task in which they make general prohibitions, but do not explicate the strategies or details involved in solving the task. This group can be considered a minimal modeling condition or an attentional control group for exposure to E and practice on task materials.

An attempt was made to provide all three groups with equal amounts of social reinforcement for their performance. At the completion of the modeling session, all Ss were told, "Can you remember to do just like I did whenever you play games like this? Remember to go slowly and carefully." The E who conducted the training departed, and the first E then administered Form III of the MFF test.

Results

Selection of Ss

Table 1 presents the performance of reflective and impulsive Ss on the initial MFF test (Form I) and on the MFF test (Form II) which was administered immediately after the instructions to "go slower." Of the original 60 Ss tested, 45 were classified into either the reflective or impulsive groups, based on the S's response time and errors relative to the performance of the same age and sex peer group. The instructions to go slower resulted in a significant ($p < .05$) increase in the mean total response time on initial decisions for reflective Ss (i.e., from 99.8 to 123.8 sec.), but no comparable change in errors. The latter finding may be due to a "ceiling effect" and/or a

TABLE 1. *Impulsive and Reflective Ss' Performance on Initial MFF Test (Form I) and on the MFF Test (Form II) Administered after Instructions to "Go Slower"*

Ss	MFF performance			
	Form I		Form II	
	X̄	SD	X̄	SD
Reflectives (N = 20)				
Total errors	6.3	3.5	7.7	4.0
Total decision time	99.8	6.5	123.8	10.5
Impulsives (N = 25)				
Total errors	16.4	3.8	11.4	7.0
Total decision time	42.9	5.5	58.1	7.6

TABLE 2. *A Breakdown of Impulsive Ss' Performance on Forms I and II of the MFF Test*

Ss	MFF performance			
	Form I		Form II	
	X̄	SD	X̄	SD
Impulsive Ss selected for treatment (N = 15)				
Total errors	15.2	3.5	12.2	4.6
Total decision time	42.8	5.3	51.2	5.9
Impulsive Ss *not* selected for treatment (N = 10)				
Total errors	17.6	4.2	10.5	5.4
Total decision time	43.0	6.0	65.0	8.3

slight decrement in performance resulting from anxiety. Several reflective Ss indicated that they interpreted E's instruction to go slower as an indicant that they were not performing adequately. Ward (1968) has reported that anxiety over failure played a greater role in the performance of impulsive children. The impulsive Ss demonstrated a marked variability in how their performance changed as a result of the instructional manipulation. This variability permitted selection of the 15 most impulsive Ss whose performance changed minimally. In a second session, these impulsive Ss were provided with treatment. Table 2 presents the performance scores for the impulsive Ss who were selected for treatment and those impulsive Ss who significantly improved their performance from the minimal instructional manipulation.

In summary, from a group of 60 kindergarten and first-grade children, 15 Ss were selected who were most cognitively impulsive on initial testing and who minimally altered their response style when explicitly given the instruction to do so.

Analysis of treatment efficacy

Figure 2 presents the performance of the modeling group, modeling plus self-instructional group, and the attentional control group for the three six-item forms of the MFF test. The analyses of the decision times and error scores on Forms I and II of the MFF test yielded no significant group, trials, or Group × Trials interaction, indicating that prior to treatment the three groups performed comparably on initial performance and in response to instructions to go slower. The differential efficacy of the treatment procedures is indicated in the analysis of Form III of the MFF test which was administered immediately after treatment. On the decision time measure, the two treatment groups significantly ($p < .05$) slowed down their decision time on Form III relative to their own prior

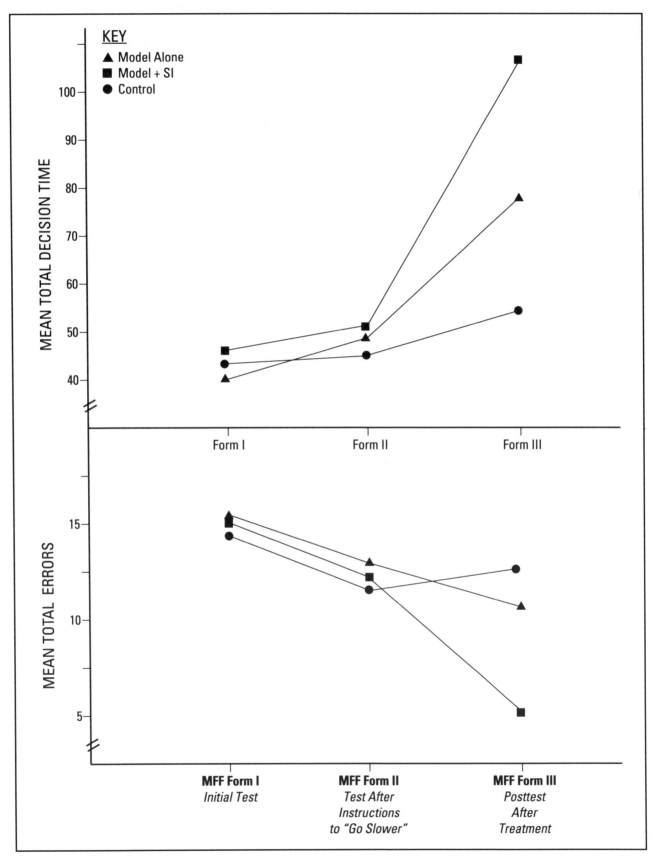

Figure 2. MFF performances of impulsive Ss who were in a modeling-alone group, a modeling plus self-instructional training group, and an additional control group.

performances on Forms I and II and relative to the control group's performance on Form III. The modeling plus self-instructional training group which slowed down the most was significantly different ($t = 8.10$, $df = 8$, $p < .001$) from the modeling-alone group on Form III. The analyses of the error scores indicated that *only* Ss who received modeling plus self-instructional training significantly ($p < .05$) improved their performance relative to the other two groups and relative to their own prior performances.

In summary, the results indicated that the cognitive modeling plus self-instructional group was most effective in altering decision time and in reducing errors. The modeling-alone group significantly decreased decision time, but did not significantly reduce errors. The efficacy of the self-instructional component of the training procedure in fostering behavioral change is underscored by the fact that three of the five Ss in the self-instruction group spontaneously self-verbalized on Form III of the MFF test, whereas none did so in the other two groups. Similarly in Study I, several Ss in the self-instructional training group spontaneously self-verbalized in the post-test and follow-up sessions. It does appear that self-instructional training can bring an impulsive child's overt behavior under his own verbal discriminative control. At a macroscopic level, the impulsive children, after self-instructional training, do seem to be approaching psychometric tasks differently, taking their time, talking to themselves, and improving their performance. Research is now underway to explore the generality, persistence, and behavioral changes that result from self-instructional training.

DISCUSSION

The results of the two studies indicate that a cognitive self-guidance program which trains impulsive children to talk to themselves is effective in modifying their behavior on a variety of psychometric tests which assess cognitive impulsivity, Performance IQ, and motor ability. The results of Study II indicate that the addition of explicit self-instructional training to modeling procedures significantly alters the attentional strategies of the impulsive children and facilitates behavioral change. The impulsive children were taught to use their private speech for orienting, organizing, regulating, and self-rewarding functions with the consequence of greater self-control. The present self-instructional procedure seems applicable to the culturally deprived child, who has been described by Bereiter and Engelmann (1966) and Blank and Solomon (1968, 1969) as having a "central language deficit," namely, the inability to relate what he says to what he does. The deprived child does not spontaneously use language to direct his problem-solving behavior, especially when spe-

cific demands to do so are removed, nor does he exhibit normal capacities for self-control. An examination of the usefulness of the present self-instructional training procedures over a prolonged period of time with such deprived children is now underway.

The present studies indicate that the therapist can now attempt to modify not only the patient's overt behavioral response, but also the antecedent and/or accompanying cognitions. For example, cognitive self-guidance training procedures may be used to influence the attentional and cognitive strategies patients emit in a variety of situations. The possibilities of using self-instructional training procedures to alter (*a*) the "attentional deficit" in schizophrenics (Lang & Buss, 1965); (*b*) psychophysiological reactions of psychiatric patients (Grings, 1965; Schachter, 1966); and (*c*) cognitive styles in general (Ellis, 1963) are most promising. The application of the self-instructional procedure to operant conditioning programs with human Ss, especially children, also seems worthwhile. We suggest that having S self-verbalize, initially aloud and subsequently covertly, the contingencies of reinforcement will result in greater change and more generalization. Reinforcement can be made contingent upon not only the emission of the desired behavior, but also S's self-verbalization of what he must do to secure reinforcement. The literature on awareness (see review by Bandura, 1969) provides further support for the possible efficacy of having S learn to self-verbalize the correct reinforcement rules which influence his subsequent responding.

With the cognitive training procedure, the response chain to be modified is broadened and may thus be subjected to such modification techniques as modeling, reinforcement, and aversive consequences. We have explored in a series of studies the use of behavior modification techniques to alter the self-verbalizations of such patients as phobics, schizophrenics, smokers, speech- and test-anxious Ss, as well as impulsive children (Meichenbaum, 1970, 1971; Meichenbaum, Gilmore, & Fedoravicius, 1971, in press; Steffy, Meichenbaum, & Best, 1970). In each case, therapeutically attending to the patient's self-verbalizations, as well as his overt maladaptive behavior, has led to greater behavioral change, greater generalization, and greater persistence of treatment effects. In each of these therapy studies the goal has been to bring S's overt behavior under his own discriminative control, a means of developing the self-regulatory function of private speech.

In conclusion, a *heuristic* assumption underlying the present line of investigation has been that symbolic activities obey the same psychological laws as do overt behaviors and that private speech is teachable. Thus, behavior modification techniques which have been used to modify overt behaviors may be applied to cognitive processes. Only future research will indicate the validity of this assumption, but the by-products, in terms of the development of new treatment techniques, will be sizable.

REFERENCES

Anthony, A. Normal and neurotic qualitative Porteus Maze performance under stress and non-stress. Unpublished PhD thesis, Columbia University, 1959.

Bandura, A. *Principles of behavior modification.* New York: Holt, Rinehart and Winston, 1969.

Bem, S. Verbal self-control: The establishment of effective self-instruction. *Journal of Experimental Psychology,* 1967, *74,* 485–491.

Bem, S. The role of comprehension in children's problem-solving. *Developmental Psychology,* 1970, *2,* 351–358.

Bereiter, C., & Engelmann, S. *Teaching disadvantaged children in the preschool.* Englewood-Cliffs, N.J.: Prentice-Hall, 1966.

Blank, M., & Solomon, F. A tutorial language program to develop abstract thinking in socially disadvantaged preschool children. *Child Development,* 1968, *39,* 379–389.

Blank, M., & Solomon, F. How should the disadvantaged child be taught? *Child Development,* 1969, *40,* 47–61.

Debus, R. L. Effects of brief observation of model behavior on conceptual tempo of impulsive children. *Developmental Psychology,* 1970, *2,* 22–32.

Drake, D. M. Perceptual correlates of impulsive and reflective behavior. *Developmental Psychology,* 1970, *2,* 202–214.

Ellis, A. *Reason and emotion in psychotherapy.* New York: Holt, Rinehart and Winston, 1962.

Eysenck, A. J. A dynamic theory of anxiety and hysteria. *Journal of Mental Science,* 1955, *101,* 128–151.

Flavell, J. H., Beach, D. R., & Chinsky, J. M. Spontaneous verbal rehearsal in a memory task as a function of age. *Child Development,* 1966, *37,* 283–299.

Foulds, G. A. Temperamental differences in maze performance. *British Journal of Psychology,* 1951, *42,* 209–217.

Grings, W. W. Verbal-perceptual factors in the conditioning of autonomic responses. In W. F. Prokasy (Ed.), *Classical conditioning: A symposium.* New York: Appleton-Century-Crofts, 1965.

Kagan, J. Impulsive and reflective children: Significance of conceptual tempo. In J. D. Krumboltz (Ed.), *Learning and the educational process.* Chicago: Rand McNally, 1965.

Kagan, J. Reflection-impulsivity: The generality and dynamics of conceptual tempo. *Journal of Abnormal Psychology,* 1966, *71,* 17–24.

Kagan, J., Pearson, L., Welch, L. The modifiability of an impulsive tempo. *Journal of Educational Psychology,* 1966, *57,* 359–365.

Kagan, J., Rosman, B. L., Day, D., Albert, J., & Phillips, W. Information processing in the child: Significance of analytic and reflective attitudes. *Psychological Monographs,* 1964, *78,* (1, Whole No. 578).

Kitzinger, H., & Blumberg, E. Supplementary guide for admin-istering and scoring the Wechsler-Bellevue. Intelligence Scale (Form I). *Psychological Monographs,* 1951, *65,* (10, Whole No. 319).

Klein, W. L. An investigation of the spontaneous speech of children during problem solving. Unpublished doctoral dissertation, University of Rochester, 1963.

Kohlberg, L., Yaeger, J., & Hjertholm, E. Private speech: Four studies and a review of theories. *Child Development,* 1968, *39,* 691–736.

Lang, P. J., & Buss, A. H. Psychological deficit in schizophrenia: Interference activation. *Journal of Abnormal Psychology,* 1965, *70,* 77–106.

Lindquist, E. F. *Design and analysis of experiments in psychology and education.* Boston: Houghton Mifflin, 1953.

Lovaas, O. I. Cue properties of words: The control of operant responding by rate and content of verbal operants. *Child Development,* 1964, *35,* 245–256.

Luria, A. R. The directive function of speech in development. *Word,* 1959, *15,* 341–352.

Luria, A. R. *The role of speech in the regulation of normal and abnormal behavior.* New York: Liveright, 1961.

Lutey, C. *Individual intelligence testing: A manual.* Greeley, Colo.: Executary, 1966.

Meichenbaum, D. Cognitive factors in behavior modification: Modifying what people say to themselves. Unpublished manuscript, University of Waterloo, 1970.

Meichenbaum, D. Examination of model characteristics in reducing avoidance behavior. *Journal of Personality and Social Psychology,* 1971, *17,* 298–307.

Meichenbaum, D., Bowers, K., & Ross, R. Modification of classroom behavior of institutionalized female adolescent offenders. *Behaviour Research and Therapy,* 1968, *6,* 343–353.

Meichenbaum, D., Bowers, K., & Ross, R. A behavioral analysis of teacher expectancy effect. *Journal of Personality and Social Psychology,* 1969, *13,* 306–316.

Meichenbaum, D., Gilmore, J. B., & Fedoravicius, A. Group insight versus group desensitization in treating speech anxiety. *Journal of Consulting and Clinical Psychology,* 1971, in press.

Meichenbaum, D., & Goodman, J. The developmental control of operant motor responding by verbal operants. *Journal of Experimental Child Psychology,* 1969, *7,* 553–565. (a)

Meichenbaum, D., & Goodman, J. Reflection-impulsivity and verbal control of motor behavior. *Child Development,* 1969, *40,* 785–797. (b)

Moely, B., Olson, F., Halwes, T., & Flavell, J. Production deficiency in young children's recall. *Developmental Psychology,* 1969, *1,* 26–34.

Palkes, H., Stewart, W., & Kahana, B. Porteus Maze performance of hyperactive boys after training in self-directed verbal commands. *Child Development,* 1968, *39,* 817–826.

Piaget, J. *The psychology of intelligence.* London: Routledge & Kegan Paul, 1947.

Porteus, S. E. *Qualitative performance in the maze test.* Vineland, N.J.: Smith, 1942.

Reese, H. W. Verbal mediation as a function of age level. *Psychological Bulletin*, 1962, *59*, 502–509.

Schachter, S. The interaction of cognitive and physiological determinants of emotional state. In C. D. Speilberger (Ed.), *Anxiety and behavior*. New York: Academic Press, 1966.

Siegelman, E. Reflective and impulsive observing behavior. *Child Development*, 1969, *40*, 1213–1222.

Steffy, R., Meichenbaum, D., & Best, A. Aversive and cognitive factors in the modification of smoking behavior. *Behavior Research and Therapy*, 1970, *8*, 115–125.

Vygotsky, L. S. *Thought and language*. New York: Wiley, 1962.

Ward, W. C. Reflection-impulsivity in kindergarten children. *Child Development*, 1968, *39*, 867–874.

Wechsler, D. *Manual: Wechsler Intelligence Scale for Children*. New York: Psychological Corporation, 1949.

Thinking and Depression: Idiosyncratic Content and Cognitive Distortions

Aaron T. Beck
1963

The clinical and theoretical papers dealing with the psychological correlates of depression have predominantly utilized a motivational-affective model for categorizing and interpreting the verbal behavior of the patients. The cognitive processes as such have received little attention except insofar as they were related to variables such as hostility, orality, or guilt.[1]

The relative lack of emphasis on the thought processes in depression may be a reflection of—or possibly a contributing factor to—the widely held view that depression is an affective disorder, pure and simple, and that any impairment of thinking is the result of the affective disturbance.[2] The opinion has been buttressed by the failure to demonstrate any consistent evidence of abnormalities in the formal thought processes in the responses to the standard battery of psychological tests.[3] Furthermore, the few experimental studies of thinking in depression have revealed no consistent deviations other than a retardation in the responses to "speed tests"[4] and a lowered responsiveness to a Gestalt Completion Test.[5]

In his book on depression, Kraines[6] on the basis of clinical observations indicated several characteristics of a thought disorder in depression. The objective of the present study has been to determine the prevalence of a thought disorder among depressed patients in psychotherapy and to delineate its characteristics. An important

corollary of this objective has been the specification of the differences from and the similarities to the thinking of nondepressed psychiatric patients. This paper will focus particularly on the following areas: (1) the idiosyncratic thought content indicative of distorted or unrealistic conceptualizations; (2) the processes involved in the deviations from logical or realistic thinking; (3) the formal characteristics of the ideation showing such deviations; (4) the relation between the cognitive distortions and the affects characteristic of depression.

CLINICAL MATERIAL

The data for this study were accumulated from interviews with 50 psychiatric patients seen by the author in psychotherapy or formal psychoanalysis. Of the patients, four were hospitalized for varying periods of time during the treatment. The rest of the patients were seen on an ambulatory basis throughout their treatment.

The frequency of interviews varied from one to six a week with the median number of interviews three a week. The total length of time in psychotherapy ranged from six months to six years; the median was two years. In no case did a single episode of depression last longer than a year. A large proportion of the patients continued in psychotherapy for a substantial period of time after the remission of their initial depressive episode. Thirteen patients either had recurrent depressions while in psychotherapy or returned to psychotherapy because of a recurrence. In this recurrent depression group, six had completely asymptomatic intervals between the recurrences and seven

Note. From "Thinking and depression: Idiosyncratic content and cognitive distortions" by A. Beck, 1963, *Archives of General Psychiatry, 9,* 324–333. Copyright 1963 by the American Medical Association. Reprinted by permission.

had some degree of hypomanic elevation. It was, therefore, possible to obtain data from these patients during each phase of the cycle.

Of the 50 patients in the sample, 16 were men and 34 were women. The age range was from 18 to 48 with a median of 34. An estimate of their intelligence suggested that they were all of at least bright average intelligence. The socioeconomic status of the patients was judged to be middle or upper class. Twelve of the patients were diagnosed as psychotic depressive or manic-depressive reactions and 38 as neurotic depressive reactions. (A study based on six of the patients in this group has already been published.[7])

In establishing the diagnosis of depression the following diagnostic indicators were employed: (*a*) objective signs of depression in the faces, speech, posture, and motor activity; (*b*) a major complaint of feeling depressed or sad and at least 11 of the following 14 signs and symptoms: loss of appetite, weight loss, sleep disturbance, loss of libido, fatiguability, crying, pessimism, suicidal wishes, indecisiveness, loss of sense of humor, sense of boredom or apathy, overconcern about health, excessive self-criticisms, and loss of initiative.

Patients showing evidence of organic brain damage or of a schizophrenic process and cases in which anxiety or some other psychopathological state was more prominent than depression were excluded from this group.

In addition to the group of depressed patients, a group of 31 nondepressed patients were also seen in psychotherapy. The composition of this group was similar to the depressed group in respect to age, sex, and social position. These patients constituted a "control group" for this study.

PROCEDURE

Face-to-face interviews were conducted during the periods of time when the depressions were regarded as moderate to severe in intensity. The author was active and supportive during these periods. Formal analysis was employed for the long-term patients except when they appeared to be seriously depressed; the couch was utilized, free association was encouraged, and the psychiatrist followed the policy of minimal activity. The recorded data used as the basis for this paper were handwritten notes made by the author during the psychotherapeutic interviews. These data included retrospective reports by the patients of feelings and thoughts prior to the sessions as well as spontaneous reports of their feelings and thoughts during the sessions. In addition, several patients regularly kept notes of their feelings and thoughts between psychotherapeutic sessions and reported these to the psychiatrist.

During the period in which these data were collected

handwritten records of the verbalizations of the nondepressed patients were made. These notes were used for purposes of comparison with the verbal reports of the depressed group.

FINDINGS

It was found that each of the depressed patients differed from the patients in the nondepressed groups in the preponderance of certain themes, which will be outlined below. Moreover, each of the other nosological groups showed an idiosyncratic ideational content which distinguished them from each other as well as from the depressed group. The typical ideational content of the depressed patients was characterized by themes of low self-esteem, self-blame, overwhelming responsibilities, and desires to escape; of the anxiety states by themes of personal danger; of the hypomanic states by themes of self-enhancement; and of the hostile paranoid states by themes of accusations against others.

Although each nosological group showed particular types of thought content specific for that group, the formal characteristics and processes of distortion involved in the idiosyncratic ideation were similar for each of these nosological categories. The processes of distortion and the formal characteristics will be described in later sections of the paper.

Thematic Content of Cognitions

The types of cognitions* outlined below were reported by the depressed patients to occur under two general conditions. First, the typical depressive cognitions were observed in response to particular kinds of external "stimulus situations." These were situations which contained an ingredient, or combination of ingredients, whose content had some relevance to the content of the idiosyncratic response. This stereotyped response was frequently completely irrelevant and inappropriate to the situation as a whole. For instance, any experience which touched in any way on the subject of the patient's personal attributes might immediately make him think he was inadequate.

A young man would respond with self-derogatory thoughts to any interpersonal situation in which another person appeared indifferent to him. If a passerby on the street did not smile at him, he was prone to think he was inferior. Similarly, a woman consistently had the thought

---

* The term cognition is used in the present treatment to refer to a specific thought, such as an interpretation, a self-command, or a self-criticism. The term is also applied to wishes (such as suicidal desires) which have a verbal content.

she was a bad mother whenever she saw another woman with a child.

Secondly, the typical depressive thoughts were observed in the patients' ruminations or "free associations," ie, when they were not reacting to an immediate external stimulus and were not attempting to direct their thoughts. The severely depressed patients often experienced long, uninterrupted sequences of depressive associations, completely independent of the external situation.

Low self-regard

The low self-evaluations formed a very prominent part of the depressed patients' ideation. This generally consisted of an unrealistic downgrading of themselves in areas that were of particular importance to them. A brilliant academician questioned his basic intelligence, an attractive society woman insisted she had become repulsive-looking, and a successful businessman began to believe he had no real business acumen and was headed for bankruptcy.

The low self-appraisal was applied to personal attributes, such as ability, virtue, attractiveness, and health; acquisitions of tangibles or intangibles (such as love or friendship); or past performance in one's career or role as a spouse or parent. In making these self-appraisals the depressed patient was prone to magnify any failures or defects and to minimize or ignore any favorable characteristics.

A very common feature of the self-evaluations was the comparison with other people, particularly those in his own social or occupational group. Almost uniformly, in making his comparisons, the depressed patient tended to rate himself as inferior. He regarded himself as less intelligent, less productive, less attractive, less financially secure, or less successful as a spouse or parent than those in his comparison group. These types of self-ratings comprise the "feeling of inferiority," which have been noted in the literature on depressives.

Ideas of deprivation

Allied to the low self-appraisals are the ideas of destitution that were seen in certain depressed patients. These ideas were noted in the patient's verbalized thoughts that he was alone, unwanted, and unlovable, often in the face of overt demonstrations of friendship and affection from other people. The sense of deprivation was also applied to material possessions, despite obvious evidence to the contrary.

Self-criticisms and self-blame

Another prominent theme in the reported thoughts of the depressed patients was concerned with self-criticisms and self-condemnations. These themes should be differ-

entiated from the low self-evaluations described in the previous section. While the low self-evaluation refers simply to the appraisal of themselves relative to their comparison group or their own standards, the self-criticisms represent the reproaches they leveled against themselves for their perceived shortcomings. It should be pointed out, however, that not all patients with low self-evaluations showed self-criticisms.

It was noteworthy that the self-criticisms, just as the low self-evaluations, were applied to those specific attributes or behaviors which were highly valued by the individual. A depressed woman, for example, condemned herself for not having breakfast ready for her husband. On another occasion, however, she reported a sexual affair with one of his colleagues without any evidence of regret, self-criticism, or guilt: Competence as a housewife was one of her expectations of herself whereas marital fidelity was not.

The patients' tendency to blame themselves for their mistakes or shortcomings generally had no logical basis. This was demonstrated by a housewife who took her children on a picnic. When a thunderstorm suddenly appeared she blamed herself for not having picked a better day.

Overwhelming problems and duties

The patients consistently magnified the magnitude of problems or responsibilities that they would consider minor or insignificant when not depressed.

A depressed housewife, when confronted with the necessity of sewing "name tags" on her children's clothes in preparation for camp, perceived this as a gigantic undertaking which would takes weeks to complete. When she finally did get to work at it, she was able to finish the task in less than a day.

Self-commands and injunctions

Self-coercive cognitions, while not prominently mentioned in the literature on depression, appeared to form a substantial portion of the verbalized thoughts of the patients in the sample. These cognitions consisted of constant "nagging" or prodding to do particular things. The prodding would persist even though it was impractical, undesirable, or impossible for the person to implement these self-instructions.

In a number of cases, the "shoulds" and "musts" were applied to an enormous range of activities, many of which were mutually exclusive. A housewife reported that in a period of a few minutes, she had compelling thoughts to clean the house, lose some weight, visit a sick friend, be a "Den Mother," get a full-time job, plan the week's menu, return to college for a degree, spend more time with her children, take a memory course, to be more active in women's organizations, and start putting away her family's winter clothes.

Escape and suicidal wishes

Thoughts about escaping from the problems of life were frequent among all the patients. Some had daydreams of being a hobo or going to a tropical paradise. It was unusual, however, that evading the tasks brought any relief. Even when a temporary respite was taken on the advice of the psychiatrist, the patients were prone to blame themselves for "shirking responsibilities."

The desire to escape seemed to be related to the patients' viewing themselves at an impasse. On the one hand, they saw themselves as incapable, incompetent, and helpless. On the other hand they saw their tasks as ponderous and formidable. Their response was a wish to withdraw from the "unsolvable" problems. Several patients spent considerable time in bed; some hid under the covers.

The suicidal preoccupations similarly seemed related to the patient's conceptualization of his situation as untenable or hopeless. He believed he could not tolerate a continuation of his suffering and he could see no solution to the problem: The psychiatrist could not help him, his symptoms could not be alleviated, and his various problems could not be solved. The suicidal patients generally stated that they regarded suicide as the only possible solution for their "desperate" or "hopeless" situation.

Typology of Cognitive Distortions

The preceding section attempted to delineate the typical thematic content of the verbalizations of the depressed patients. A crucial characteristic of the cognitions with this content was that they represented varying degrees of distortion of reality. While some degree of inaccuracy and inconsistency would be expected in the cognitions of any individual, the distinguishing characteristic of the depressed patients was that they showed a *systematic error;* viz, a bias against themselves. Systematic errors were also noted in the idiosyncratic ideation of the other nosological groups.

The typical depressive cognitions can be categorized according to the ways in which they deviate from logical or realistic thinking. The processes may be classified as paralogical (arbitrary inference, selective abstraction, and over-generalization), stylistic (exaggeration), or semantic (inexact labeling). These cognitive distortions were observed at all levels of depression, from the mild neurotic depression to the severe psychotic. While the thinking disorder was obvious in the psychotic depressions, it was observable in more subtle ways among all the neurotic depressed.

Arbitrary interpretation is defined as the process of forming an interpretation of a situation, event, or experience when there is no factual evidence to support the conclusion or when the conclusion is contrary to the evidence.

A patient riding on the elevator had the thought, "He (the elevator operator) thinks I'm a nobody." The patient then felt sad. On being questioned by the psychiatrist, he realized there was no factual basis for his thought.

Such misconstructions are particularly prone to occur when the cues are ambiguous. An intern, for example, became quite discouraged when he received an announcement that all patients "worked-up" by the interns should be examined subsequently by the resident physicians. His thought on reading the announcement was, "The chief doesn't have faith in my work." In this instance, he personalized the event although there was no ostensible reason to suspect that his particular performance had anything to do with the policy decision.

Intrinsic to this type of thinking is the lack of consideration of the alternative explanations that are more plausible and more probable. The intern, when questioned about other possible explanations for the policy decision, then recalled a previous statement by his "chief" to the effect that he wanted the residents to have more contact with the patients, as part of their training. The idea that this explicitly stated objective was the basis for the new policy had not previously occurred to him.

Selective abstraction refers to the process of focusing on a detail taken out of context, ignoring other more salient features of the situation, and conceptualizing the whole experience on the basis of this element.

A patient, in reviewing her secretarial work with her employer, was praised about a number of aspects of her work. The employer at one point asked her to discontinue making extra carbon copies of his letters. Her immediate thought was, "He is dissatisfied with my work." This idea became paramount despite all the positive statements he had made.

Overgeneralization was manifested by the patients' pattern of drawing a general conclusion about their ability, performance, or worth on the basis of a single incident.

A patient reported the following sequence of events which occurred within a period of half an hour before he left the house: His wife was upset because the children were slow in getting dressed. He thought, "I'm a poor father because the children are not better disciplined." He then noticed a faucet was leaky and thought this showed he was also a poor husband. While driving to work, he thought, "I must be a poor driver or other cars would not be passing me." As he arrived at work he noticed some other personnel had already arrived. He thought, "I can't be very dedicated or I would have come earlier." When he noticed folders and papers piled up on his desk, he concluded, "I'm a poor organizer because I have so much work to do."

Magnification and minimization refer to errors in evaluation which are so gross as to constitute distortions. As described in the section on thematic content, these processes were manifested by underestimation of the individual's performance, achievement or ability, and inflation of the magnitude of his problems and tasks. Other examples were the exaggeration of the intensity or significance of a traumatic event. It was frequently observed that the patients' initial reaction to an unpleasant event was to regard it as a catastrophe. It was generally found on further inquiry that the perceived disaster was often a relatively minor problem.

A man reported that he had been upset because of damage to his house as the result of a storm. When he first discovered the damage, his sequence of thoughts were, "The side of the house is wrecked. . . . It will cost a fortune to fix it." His immediate reaction was that his repair bill would be several thousand dollars. After the initial shock had dissipated, he realized that the damage was minor and that the repairs would cost around $50.

Often *inexact labeling* seems to contribute to this kind of distortion. The affective reaction is proportional to the descriptive labeling of the event rather than to the actual intensity of a traumatic situation.

A man reported during his therapy hour that he was very upset because he had been "clobbered" by his superior. On further reflection, he realized that he had magnified the incident and that a more adequate description was that his supervisor "corrected an error" he had made. After re-evaluating the event, he felt better. He also realized that whenever he was corrected or criticized by a person in authority he was prone to describe this as being "clobbered."

Formal Characteristics of Depressive Cognitions

The previous sections have attempted to categorize the typical thematic contents of the verbalized thoughts of depressed patients and to present observations regarding the processes involved in the conceptual errors and distortions.

The inaccurate conceptualizations with depressive content have been labeled "depressive cognitions." This section will present a summary of the specific formal characteristics of the depressive cognitions as reported by the patients.

One of the striking features of the typical depressive cognitions is that they generally were experienced by the patients as arising as though they were *automatic*

responses, ie, without any apparent antecedent reflection or reasoning.

A patient, for example, observed that when he was in a situation in which somebody else was receiving praise, he would "automatically" have the thought, "I'm nobody . . . I'm not good enough." Later, when he reflected on his response, he would then regard it as inappropriate. Nonetheless, his immediate responses to such situations continued to be a self-devaluation.

The depressive thoughts not only appeared to be "automatic," in the sense just described, but they seemed, also, to have an *involuntary* quality. The patients frequently reported that these thoughts would occur even when they had resolved "not to have them" or were actively trying to avoid them. This involuntary characteristic was clearly exemplified by repetitive thoughts of suicidal content but was found in a less dramatic way in other types of depressive cognitions. A number of the patients were able to anticipate the kind of depressive thoughts that would occur in certain specific situations and would prepare themselves in advance to make a more realistic judgment of the situation. Nevertheless, despite the intention to ward off or control these thoughts, they would continue to pre-empt a more rational response.**

Another characteristic of the depressive thoughts is their *plausibility* to the patient. At the beginning of therapy the patients tended to accept the validity of the cognitions uncritically. It often required considerable experience in observing these thoughts and attempting to judge them rationally for the patients to recognize them as distortions. It was noted that the more plausible the cognitions seemed (or the more uncritically the patient regarded them), the stronger the affective reaction. It was also observed that when the patient was able to question the validity of the thoughts, the affective reaction was generally reduced. The converse of this also appeared to be true: When the affective reaction to a thought was particularly strong, its plausibility became enhanced and the patient found it more difficult to appraise its validity. Furthermore, once a strong affect was aroused in response to a distorted cognition, any subsequent distortions seemed to have an increased plausibility. This characteristic appeared to be present irrespective of whether the affect was sadness, anger, anxiety, or euphoria. Once the affective response was dissipated, however, the patient

---

** The foregoing features may suggest that the depressive thoughts are essentially a type of obsessional thinking. The depressive thoughts, however, differ from classical obsessional thinking in that their specific content varies according to the particular stimulus situation and also in that they are associated with an affective response. Obsessional thoughts, on the other hand, tend to retain essentially the same "wording" with each repetition, are generally regarded by the patient as a "strange" or "alien" idea, and are not associated with any feeling.

could then appraise these cognitions critically and recognize the distortions.

A final characteristic of the depressive cognitions was their *perseveration*. Despite the multiplicity and complexity of life situations, the depressed patient was prone to interpret a wide range of his experiences in terms of a few stereotyped ideas. The same type of cognition would be elicited by highly heterogeneous experiences. In addition, these idiosyncratic cognitions tended to occur repetitively in the patients' ruminations and stream of associations.

Relation of Depressive Thoughts to Affects

As part of the psychotherapy, the author encouraged the patients to attempt to specify as precisely as possible their feelings and the thoughts they had in relation to these feelings.

A number of problems were presented in the attempt to obtain precise description and labeling of the feelings. The patients had no difficulty in designating their feelings as pleasant or unpleasant. In the unpleasant group of affects they were readily able to specify whether they felt depressed (or sad), anxious, angry, and embarrassed. When they were asked to discriminate further among the depressed feelings, there was considerable variability in the group. Most of the patients were able to differentiate with a reasonable degree of certainty among the following feelings: sad, discouraged, hurt, humiliated, guilty, empty, and lonely.

In attempting to determine the relation of specific feelings to a specific thought, the patients developed the routine of trying to focus their attention on their thoughts whenever they had an unpleasant feeling or when the feeling became intensified. This often meant "thinking back" after they were aware of the unpleasant feeling to recall the content of the preceding thought. They frequently observed that an unpleasant thought preceded the unpleasant affect.

The most noteworthy finding was that when the thoughts associated with the depressive affects were identified they were generally found to contain the type of conceptual distortions or errors already described as well as the typical depressive thematic content. Similarly, when the affect was anxiety, anger, or elation, the associated cognitions had a content congruent with these feelings.

An attempt was made to classify the cognitions to determine whether there were any specific features that could distinguish among the types of cognitions associated respectively with depression, anger, or elation. It was found, as might be expected, that the typical thoughts associated with the depressive affect centered around the ideas that the individual was deficient in some sort of way. Furthermore, the specific types of depressive affect were generally consistent with the specific thought content. Thus, thoughts of being deserted, inferior, or derelict in some way, were associated respectively with feelings of loneliness, humiliation, or guilt.

In the nondepressed group, the thoughts associated with the affect of anxiety had the theme of anticipation of some unpleasant event. Thoughts associated with anger had an element of blame directed against some other person or agency. Finally, feelings of euphoria were associated with thoughts that were self-inflating in some way.

COMMENT

It has been noted that "the schizophrenic excels in his tendency to misconstrue the world that is presented. . . ."[8] While the validity of this statement has been supported by numerous clinical and experimental studies, it has not generally been acknowledged that misconstructions of reality may also be a characteristic feature of other psychiatric disorders. The present study indicates that, even in mild phases of depression, systematic deviations from realistic and logical thinking occur. A crucial feature of these cognitive distortions is that they consistently appeared only in the ideational material that had a typically depressive content; for example, themes of being deficient in some way. The other ideational material reported by the depressed patients did not show any systematic errors.

The thinking-disorder typology outlined in this paper is similar to that described in studies of schizophrenia. While some of the most flagrant schizophrenic signs (such as word-salad, metaphorical speech, neologisms, and condensations) were not observed, the kinds of paralogical processes in the depressed patients resembled those described in schizophrenics.[8] Moreover, the same kind of paralogical thinking was observed in the nondepressed patients in the control group.

While each nosological category showed a distinctive thought *content*, the differences in terms of the *processes* involved in the deviant thinking appeared to be quantitative rather than qualitative. These findings suggest that a thinking disorder may be common to all types of psychopathology. By applying this concept to psychiatric classification, it would be possible to characterize the specific nosological categories in terms of the degree of cognitive impairment and the particular content of the idiosyncratic cognitions.

The failure of various psychological tests to reflect a thinking disorder in depression[3,4,5] warrants consideration. It may be suggested that the particular tests employed may not have been adequately designed for the purpose of detecting the thinking deviations in depression. Since clinical observation indicates that the typical cognitive distortions in depression are limited to specific content areas (such as self-devaluations), the various object-sorting, proverb-interpreting, and projective tests may have missed the essential pathology. It may be noted that even in studies of schizophrenia, the demonstration of a thinking disorder is dependent on the type of test administered and the characteristics of the experimental group. Cohen et al,[5] for example, found that the only instrument eliciting abnormal responses in acute schizophrenics was the Rorschach test whereas chronic schizophrenics showed abnormalities on a Gestalt Completion test as well as on the Rorschach.

The clinical finding of a thinking disorder at all levels of depression should focus attention on the problem of defining the precise relationship of the cognitive distortions to the characteristic affective state in depression. The diagnostic manual of the American Psychiatric Association (APA)[2] defines the psychotic affective reactions in terms of "a primary, severe disorder of mood with resultant disturbance of thought and behavior, in consonance with the affect." Although this is a widely accepted concept, the converse would appear to be at least as plausible; viz, that there is primary disorder of thought with resultant disturbance of affect and behavior in consonance with the cognitive distortions. This latter thesis is consistent with the conception that the way an individual structures an experience determines his affective response to it. If, for example, he perceives a situation as dangerous, he may be expected to respond with a consonant affect, such as anxiety.

It is proposed, therefore, that the typical depressive affects are evoked by the erroneous conceptualizations: If the patient incorrectly perceives himself as inadequate, deserted or sinful, he will experience corresponding affects such as sadness, loneliness, or guilt. On the other hand, the possibility that the evoked affect may, in turn, influence the thinking should be considered. It is conceivable that once a depressive affect has been aroused, it will facilitate the emergence of further depressive-type cognitions. A continuous interaction between cognition and affect may, consequently, be produced and, thus, lead to the typical downward spiral observed in depression. Since it seems likely that this interaction would be highly complex, appropriately designed experiments would be warranted to clarify the relationships.

A thorough exposition of the theoretical significance of the clinical findings is beyond the scope of this paper. It may be tentatively suggested that in depression there is a significant rearrangement of the cognitive organization. This modified organization channels a large proportion of the thinking in the direction of negative self-evaluations, nihilistic predictions, and plans for escape or suicide. It is postulated that this particular shift in the thought content results specifically from the activation and dominance of certain idiosyncratic cognitive patterns (schemas), which have a content corresponding to the typical depressive themes in the verbal material. To the extent that these idiosyncratic schemas supersede more appropriate schemas in the ordering, differentiation, and analysis of experience, the resulting conceptualizations of reality will be distorted. A more complete formulation of the cognitive organization in depression has been presented in another paper.[9]

Before this discussion is concluded, a few methodological problems should be mentioned. A question could be raised, for example, regarding the generalizability of the observations. Since the sample consisted largely of psychotherapy patients of a relatively narrow range of intelligence and social index, there may be some uncertainty as to whether the findings are applicable to the general population of depressed patients. A previous study by the author and his coinvestigators is pertinent to this question. An inventory was derived from the verbalized self-appraisals of the depressed patients included in the present study. A systematic study of the responses to this instrument by a much larger and more heterogeneous clinic and hospitalized sample demonstrated that the self-reports of the psychotherapy group were representative of the much broader group.[10]

In view of the obvious methodological problems associated with using data from handwritten notes of psychotherapy sessions, it is apparent that the findings of the present study will have to be subjected to verification by more refined and systematic studies. One promising approach has been developed by Gottschalk et al.[11] who utilized verbatim recordings of five-minute periods of free association by depressed patients and subjected this material to blind scoring by trained judges. Such a procedure circumvents the hazards of therapist bias and suggestion associated with verbal material recorded in psychotherapy interviews.

SUMMARY AND CONCLUSIONS

A group of 50 depressed patients in psychotherapy and a control group of 31 nondepressed patients were studied to determine the prevalence and types of cognitive abnormalities. Evidence of deviation from logical and realistic thinking was found at every level of depression from mild neurotic to severe psychotic.

The ideation of the depressed patients differed from that of the nondepressed in the prominence of certain typical themes; viz, low self-evaluation, ideas of deprivation, exaggeration of problems and difficulties, self-criticisms and self-commands, and wishes to escape and die. Similarly, each of the nondepressed nosological groups could be differentiated on the basis of their idiosyncratic thought content.

Abnormalities were detected consistently only in those verbalized thoughts that had the typical thematic content of the depressed groups. The other kinds of ideation did not show any consistent distortion. Among the deviations in thinking, the following processes were identified: arbitrary inference, selective abstraction, over-generalization, and magnification and minimization.

Since paralogical processes were also observed in the idiosyncratic ideation of nondepressed patients, it was suggested that a thought disorder may be common to all types of psychopathology. The thesis was advanced that the various nosological groups could be classified on the basis of the degree of cognitive distortion and the characteristic content of their verbalized thoughts.

In view of the observation that the distorted ideas of the depressed patients appeared immediately before the arousal or intensification of the typical depressive affects, it was suggested that the affective disturbance may be secondary to the thinking disorder. The possibility of a reciprocal interaction between cognition and affect was also raised.

The thesis was advanced that the cognitive distortions in depression result from the progressive dominance of the thought processes by idiosyncratic schemas. By superseding more appropriate schemas, the idiosyncratic schemas force the conceptualization of experience into certain rigid patterns with the consequent sacrifice of realistic and logical qualities.

REFERENCES

1. Mendelson, M.: *Psychoanalytic Concepts of Depression.* Springfield, Ill.; Charles C Thomas, Publisher, 1960.
2. American Psychiatric Association: *Diagnostic and Statistical Manual of Mental Disorders.* 1952.
3. Schafer, R.: *The Clinical Application of Psychological Tests.* New York: International Universities Press, 1948.
4. Payne, R. W., and Hewlett, J. H.; "Thought Disorder in Psychotic Patients," in H. H. Eysenck, editor: *Experiments in Personality.* London; Routledge & Kegan Paul, Ltd, 1961.
5. Cohen, B.; Senf, R.; and Huston, P.: Perceptual Accuracy in Schizophrenia, Depression, and Neurosis and Effects of Amytal, *J Abnorm Soc Psychol* 52:363, 1956.
6. Kraines, S. H.: *Mental Depressions and Their Treatment.* New York: The Macmillan Company, 1957.
7. Beck, A. T., and Hurvich, M.; Psychological Correlates of Depression, *Psychosom Med* 21:50, 1959.
8. Kasanin, J. S.: *Language and Thought in Schizophrenia.* Berkeley and Los Angeles: University of California Press, 1944.
9. Beck, A. T.: *Thinking and Depression: 2. A Theoretical Exploration.* Mimeographed Paper, 1963.
10. Beck, A. T.; Ward, C. H.; Mendelson, M.; Mock, J.; and Erbaugh, J.: An Inventory for Measuring Depression, *Arch Gen Psychiat* 4:561, 1961.
11. Gottschalk, L.; Glesser, G.; and Springer, K.: Three Hostility Scales Applicable to Verbal Samples, to be published, 1963.

The Treatment of a Psychopath with Rational-Emotive Psychotherapy

Albert Ellis
1963

So-called psychopaths, or individuals suffering severe character disorder whose behavior is distinctly antisocial, are exceptionally difficult to treat with any form of psychotherapy. They only rarely come for treatment on a voluntary basis; and when they are involuntarily forced into treatment they tend to be resistant, surly, and in search of a "cure" that will involve no real effort on their part. Even when they come for private treatment, they are usually looking for magical, effortless "cures," and they tend to stay in treatment only for a short period of time and to make relatively little improvement.

Psychoanalytic techniques of approaching psychopaths are particularly ineffective for several reasons. These individuals are frequently nonintrospective and nonverbal; they tend to be not overly bright or well educated; they are impatient of long-winded procedures; and they are highly skeptical or afraid of involved psychological analysis or interpretation. It is therefore only the exceptional psychopath who can be helped with analytic methods such as those employed by Lindner in his *Rebel Without a Cause* (1944). Considerably modified techniques of interpretation, such as advocated by Cleckley (1950) and Schmideberg (1959), are usually recommended, instead of the classical psychoanalytic methods.

Before attempting to treat any young delinquents or older criminals in my present private practice of psycho-

therapy, I had considerable experience in examining and treating them when I was Chief Psychologist at the New Jersey State Diagnostic Center and later Chief Psychologist of the New Jersey Department of Institutions and Agencies. At that time I became impressed with the fact that whether the offender was a thief, a sex deviate, a dope addict, or a murderer, about the very worst way to try to help him rehabilitate himself was to give him a moral lecture, appeal to his conscience or superego, or in any way blame him for his misdeeds.

I began to see that, in their own peculiar ways, virtually all these offenders really were anxious and guilty underneath their facade of psychopathic bravado; and that, in fact, their criminal acts were frequently committed as a defensive attempt to protect them against their own feelings of low self-esteem. I saw that many of them were already being compulsively driven to psychopathic behavior by underlying guilt and anxiety; and that to endeavor to make them more guilty and anxious, as is often at first attempted in some forms of counseling and psychotherapy, would hardly help them lose their need for their compulsive defenses.

Instead, I found that if I temporarily showed the offender that I was *not* critical of his behavior, and if I at first allied myself with him (if necessary) against the authorities of the institution in which he was incarcerated (and whom he almost invariably saw as being persecutory), a notable degree of rapport could be established between us. Then, once the prisoner felt that I was really on his side, it was often possible to show him that his pattern of criminal behavior was not merely immoral and antisocial (which he of course knew without my telling him so) but that, more importantly, it was *self-defeating*. If I could convince him, which I often could, that however much society might be (from his standpoint, justifiably and revengefully) harmed by his crimes, he *himself* was inevitably even more self-sabotaged by these acts and their usual consequences, then I had a fairly good chance of getting him to change his behavior in the future.

My many investigatory and therapeutic relationships with criminals taught me, then, that so-called hardened psychopaths, like other disturbed human beings, act in an irrational and self-defeating manner because they believe, quite falsely, that they are helping themselves thereby. And when they are calmly, unblamefully, and yet vigorously disabused of this belief, they are often capable of radically changing their philosophic orientation and their antisocial behavior which springs from that orientation. Because many or most of the classic psychopaths are, as Cleckley points out, basically psychotic, they are often most difficult to treat; and one must usually be content with reasonably limited gains in therapy with them. Nonetheless, remarkable improvements in their general living patterns, and particularly in the reduction of their antisocial behavior, may result from proper treatment.

Partly as a result of my experiences in treating youthful and older offenders, as well as considerable experience in working with run-of-the-mill neurotics and psychotics, I have in recent years developed the technique of rational-emotive psychotherapy expounded in this volume. A case involving the rational therapeutic treatment of a psychopath will now be described.

The patient was a 25 year old son of a well-to-do family and had been engaging in antisocial behavior, including lying, stealing, sexual irresponsibility, and physical assaults on others since the age of 14. He had been in trouble with the law on five different occasions, but had only been convicted once and spent one year in the reformatory. He displayed no guilt about his offenses and seemed not at all concerned about the fact that he had once helped cripple an old man whose candy store he and his youthful comrades had held up. He had had two illegitimate children by different girls, but made no effort to see them or contribute to their financial support. He came for psychotherapy only at the insistence of his lawyer, who told him that his one chance of being put on probation, instead of being sent to prison, for his latest offense (rifling several vending machines) was to plead emotional disturbance and convince the court that he was really trying to do something to help himself get better. He was first seen by a psychiatrist, who diagnosed him as a hopeless psychopath and thought that treatment would be futile. But I agreed to see him because I thought he presented a challenging problem for psychotherapy.

For the first few sessions the patient was only moderately cooperative, kept postponing appointments without good cause, and came 10 or 15 minutes late to almost every interview. He would listen fairly attentively and take an active part in the session; but as soon as he left the therapist's office he would, in his own words, "forget almost everything we said," and come in for the next session without giving any thought to his problems or their possible alleviation. It was not that he was resentfully resisting therapy; but he quite frankly was doing little or nothing to "get with it."

During the first several sessions, I made little attempt to get the full details of the patient's history. I merely determined that he was the only son of a doting mother, who had always given him his way, and of a merchant father who had ostensibly been friendly and permissive, but who actually had held up to him almost impossibly high standards of achievement and who was severely disappointed whenever he fell below these standards. The patient—whom we shall call Jim—had behaved as a spoiled brat with other children, over whom he was always trying to lord it; had never lived up to his potentialities in school; had started to gain attention from his peers and his teachers at an early age by nasty, show-off behavior; and had been able to get along only reasonably well with girls, one or more of whom he usually managed to have serve him while he sadistically exploited her masochistic tendencies.

Although the patient was quite intelligent and could easily understand psychodynamic explanations of his behavior—such as the possible connection between his failing to satisfy his father's high standards of excellence and his trying to prove to others, by quite opposite antisocial actions, how "great" he was—no attempt to interpret or clarify such connections was made. For one thing, he stoutly opposed such "psychoanalytic crap" whenever the psychodynamics of his situation were even hinted at; for another thing, the rational-emotive therapist frequently makes relatively little use of this kind of historical clarification, since he deems it highly interesting but not necessarily conducive to basic personality change.

Instead, the patient's current circumstances were first focused upon, and he was quickly and intensively shown that he kept defeating himself in the present—as well as in the past. Thus, he kept discussing with me the possibility of his violating the terms of his bail and "skipping out of town." Without being in the least moralistic about his idea or taking any offense at the implied notion that therapy was not going to help him and therefore he might as well go on living the kind of life he had always lived, I calmly and ruthlessly showed Jim that (*a*) he had very little likelihood of being able to skip town without being caught in short order; (*b*) he would only lead a life of desperate evasion during the time he would remain free; and (*c*) he would most certainly know no mercy from the court if and when he was recaptured. Although, at first, he was most loath to accept these grim facts, I patiently persisted in forcing him to do so.

At the same time, I kept showing Jim the silly and totally unrealistic philosophies behind his self-defeating notions of trying to skip bail. He was shown that he was grandiosely and idiotically telling himself that he *should* be able to do what he wanted just because he wanted to do so; that it was totally unfair and unethical for others, including the law, to stand in his way; and that it was utterly catastrophic when he was frustrated in his one-sided demands. And these assumptions, I kept insisting, were thoroughly groundless and irrational.

"But why," asked Jim at one point in the fourth session, "shouldn't I want things to go my way? Why *shouldn't* I try to get what I want?"

Therapist: No reason at all. To want what you want when you want it is perfectly legitimate. But you, unfortunately, are doing one additional thing—and that's perfectly illegitimate.

Patient: What's that? What's the illegitimate thing?

T: You're not only *wanting* what you want, but *demanding* it. You're taking a perfectly sane desire—to be able to avoid standing trial for your crimes, in this instance—and asininely turning it into an absolute *necessity*.

P: Why is that so crazy?

T: For the simple reason that, first of all, *any* demand or necessity is crazy. Wanting a thing, wanting any damn thing you happen to crave, is fine—as long as you admit the possibility of your not being able to get it. But as soon as you demand something, turn it into a necessity, you simply won't be able to *stand* your not getting it. In that event, either you'll do something desperate to get it—as you usually have done in your long history of antisocial behavior—or else you'll keep making yourself angry, exceptionally frustrated, or anxious about not getting it. Either way, *you* lose.

P: But suppose I *can* get what I want?

T: Fine—as long as you don't subsequently defeat your own ends by getting it. As in this case. Even assuming that you could skip bail successfully—which is very doubtful, except for a short while—would you *eventually* gain by having to live in terror of arrest for the remainder of your life or by having to give up everything and everyone you love here to run, let us say, to South America?

P: Perhaps not.

T: Perhaps? Besides, let's assume, for a moment, that you really could get away with it—that you really could skip bail and wouldn't get caught and wouldn't live in perpetual fear. Even then, would you be doing yourself such a great favor?

P: It seems to me I would! What more could I ask?

T: A lot more. And it is just your *not* asking for a lot

more that proves, to me at least, that you are a pretty sick guy.

P: In what way? What kind of crap are you giving me? Bullshit!

T: Well, I could get highly "ethical" and say that if you get away with things like that, with rifling vending machines, jumping bail, and such things, that you are then helping to create the kind of a world that you yourself would not want to live in, or certainly wouldn't want your friends or relatives to live in. For if you can get away with such acts, of course, others can, too; and in such a pilfering, bail-jumping world, who would want to live?

P: But suppose I said that I didn't mind living in that kind of world—kind of liked it, in fact?

T: Right. You might very well say that. And even mean it—though I wonder whether, if you really gave the matter careful thought, you would. But let us suppose you would. So I won't use that "ethical" argument with a presumably "unethical" and guiltless person like you. But there is still another and better argument, and one that you and people like you generally overlook.

P: And that is?

T: That is—your own skin.

P: My own skin?

T: Yes, your own thick and impenetrable skin. Your guiltless, ever so guiltless skin.

P: I don't get it. What the hell are you talking about?

T: Simply this. Suppose, as we have been saying, you are truly guiltless. Suppose you, like Lucky Luciano and a few other guys who really seem to have got away scot-free with a life of crime, really do have a thick skin, and don't give a good goddam what happens to others who may suffer from your deeds, don't care what kind of a world you are helping to create. How, may I ask, can you—you personally, that is—manufacture and maintain that lovely, rugged, impenetrable skin?

P: What difference does it make how I got it, as long as it's there?

T: Ah, but it does!—it does make a difference.

P: How the hell does it?

T: Simply like this. The only practical way that you can be guiltless, can maintain an impenetrable skin under conditions such as we are describing, where you keep getting away with doing in others and reaping criminal rewards, is by hostility—by resenting, hating, loathing the world against which you are criminally behaving.

P: Can't I get away with these things without hating others? Why can't I?

T: Not very likely. For why would a person do in others without hating them in some manner? And how could he not be at least *somewhat* concerned about the kind of dog-eat-dog social order he was creating unless he downed his potential concern with defensive resentment against others.

P: I don't know—. Why couldn't he?

T: Have *you?*

P: Have I, you mean, managed not to—?

T: Exactly! With your long history of lying to others, leading them on to do all kinds of things they didn't want to do, really, by your misleading them as to your feelings about them. The girls you got pregnant and deserted, for instance. The partners in crime you double-crossed. The parents whose help you've always run back for after breaking promise after promise to them. Would you call that *love* you felt for these people? Affection? Kindliness?

P: Well—uh—no, not exactly.

T: And the hostility, the resentment, the bitterness you felt for these people—and must keep perpetually feeling, mind you, as you keep "getting away" with crime after crime—did these emotions make you feel good, feel happy?

P: Well—at times, I must admit, they did.

T: Yes, at times. But really, deep down, in your inmost heart, *does* it make you feel good, happy, buoyant, joyous to do people in, to hate them, to think that they are no damn good, to plot and scheme against them?

P: No, I guess not. Not always.

T: Even most of the time?

P: No—uh—no. Very rarely, I must admit.

T: Well, there's your answer.

P: You mean to the thick skin business? You mean that I thicken my skin by hating others—and only really hurt myself in the process.

T: Isn't that the way it is? Really is? Isn't your thick skin—like the lamps made of human skin by the Nazis, incidentally—built of, nourished on little but your own corrosive hatred for others? And doesn't that hatred mainly, in the long run, corrode you?

P: Hm. I—. You've given me something to think about there.

T: By all means, think about it. Give it some real, hard thought.

In a similar manner, in session after session with this intelligent psychopath, I kept directly bringing up, ruthlessly examining, and forthrightly attacking some of his basic philosophies of living, and showing him that these philosophies underlay his antisocial thoughts and behavior. I made no negative criticism or attack on the patient *himself:* but merely on his ideas, his thoughts, his assumptions which (consciously and unconsciously) served as the foundation stones for his disordered feelings and actions.

It was quite a battle, the therapeutic process with Jim. Intelligent he was, and he had little difficulty in ostensibly seeing the things I pointed out, and even quickly agreeing with them. But his behavior, which mirrored his *real* beliefs, changed little at first, and he only (as do so many patients) gave lip-service to the new ideas that we were

discussing. Finally, after a year of rational-emotive therapy, Jim was able to admit that for a long time he had vaguely sensed the self-defeatism and wrongness of his criminal behavior, but that he had been unable to make any concerted attack on it largely because he was afraid that he *couldn't* change. That is, he believed that (a) he had no ability to control his antisocial tendencies; and that (b) he would not be able to get along satisfactorily in life if he attempted to live more honestly.

I then started to make a frontal assault on the philosophies behind Jim's defeatist feelings. I showed him that an individual's inability to control his behavior mainly stems from the *idea* that he cannot do so, the *notion* that long-standing feelings are innate and unmanageable, and that he simply *has* to be ruled by them. Instead, I insisted, human feelings *are* invariably controllable—if one seeks out the self-propagandizing sentences (e.g., "I must do this," "I have no power to stop myself from doing that," etc.) which one unconsciously uses to create and maintain these "feelings."

Jim's severe feelings of inadequacy—his original feelings that he never could gain the attention of others unless he was a problem child and his later feelings that he could not compete in a civilized economy unless he resorted to lying or thieving behavior—were also traced to the self-propagated beliefs behind them—that is, to the sentences: "I am utterly worthless unless I am always the center of attention, even though I gain this attention by unsocial behavior." "If I competed with others in an honest manner, I would fall on my face, and that would be utterly disgraceful and unforgivable." Et cetera.

These self-sabotaging beliefs, and the internalized sentences continually maintaining them, were then not merely traced to their source (in Jim's early relations with his parents, teachers, and peers) but were logically analyzed, questioned, challenged, and counterattacked by the therapist, until Jim learned to do a similar kind of self-analyzing, questioning, and challenging for himself. Finally, after considerable progress, retrogression, and then resumption of progress, Jim (who by that time had been placed on probation) voluntarily gave up the fairly easy, well-paid and unchallenging job which his family, because of their financial standing, had been able to secure for him, and decided to return to college to study to be an accountant.

"All my life," he said during one of the closing sessions of therapy, "I have tried to avoid doing things the hard way—for fear, of course, of failing and thereby 'proving' to myself and others that I was no damn good. No more of that crap any more! I'm going to make a darned good try at the hard way, from now on; and if I fail, I fail. Better I fail that way than 'succeed' the stupid way I was 'succeeding' before. Not that I think I *will* fail now. But in case I do—so what?"

A two-year follow-up report on this patient showed that he was finishing college and doing quite well at his school work. There is every reason to believe that he will continue to work and succeed at his chosen field of endeavor. If so, a self-defeating psychopath has finally turned into a forward-looking citizen.

In this case, the patient's high intelligence and good family background unquestionably contributed to making him a more suitable prospect for psychotherapy than the average psychopath would usually be. The same technique of rational-emotive psychotherapy, however, has also been recently used with several other individuals with severe character disorders and symptoms of acute antisocial behavior, and it appears to work far better than the classical psychoanalytic and psychoanalytically-oriented methods which I formerly employed with these same kinds of patients.

This is not to say or imply that RT works wonders with all psychopaths. It (or any other known type of psychotherapy) doesn't. Even mildly neurotic patients can be and usually are difficult to reorient in their thinking: since, as pointed out in the early part of this book, almost all human beings find it *easy* to behave idiotically about themselves and others. Psychopaths and psychotics (who, to my way of thinking, seriously overlap) find it still more difficult to change their own self-defeating ways. Even when they are not organically predisposed to be aberrant

(which they probably usually are), their disordered and delusive thinking is so deeply ingrained that only with the greatest effort on their and their therapists' part can effective inroads against their slippery thinking be made.

Not only, therefore, must the therapist who treats psychopaths himself be unusually sane and nonblaming, but he must be able to vigorously maintain a challenging, circuit-breaking attitude: so that by his very persistence in tackling the slipshod cognitions of his antisocial patients, he at first makes up for their tendency to goof in this very respect. Left to their own devices, psychopathic individuals brilliantly avoid facing basic issues and evade accepting a long-range view of life. If the therapist utterly refuses to let them get away with this kind of cognitive shoddiness, but at the same time refrains from scorning them for presently having it, he has some chance—not, to be honest, a very good but still a fair chance—to interrupt and help break up the rigidly set rationalizing patterns which the psychopath keeps inventing and sustaining.

Directness, forcefulness, and freedom from moralizing are among the most effective methods in the armamentarium of the therapist who would assail the citadels of psychopathy. These therapeutic attributes are all heavily emphasized in rational-emotive psychotherapy; and it is therefore hypothesized that this technique is one of the most effective means of treating individuals with severe character disorders.

Phenomenological Therapy

Client-Centered Theory

Carl R. Rogers
1956

The film presents us with Paul Moody, already quite deeply involved in anti-social behavior, who is now physically available for some sort of help, and who perhaps is at least to some degree psychologically available for help as well. Our problem is this. Do our theories—of personality, of learning, of psychotherapy—provide any basis for a method of altering Paul's anti-social tendencies?

UNDERSTANDING PAUL

We might find it profitable to ask ourselves first, what information is it necessary to obtain in order to apply our particular theory? If our theory demands that we gain information as to the causal sequence of events leading up to the present behavior, before we can suggest the basis of new learning, then we are defeated before we start. The film suggests very faintly the complexity of the many factors which may have conditioned Paul. To feel at all secure in our knowledge of this causal sequence we would need to have thousands of observations about each day of this boy's whole life, and even then would be dubious about the inferences we were making. As a consequence behavior theorists who emphasize the genesis of behavior as a chain of cause and effect responses usually have to lay aside their theories in facing a practical situation, and simply deal with it on a "common sense" basis. Otherwise they are caught in an infinite regression of fact-

Note. From "Client-centered theory" by C. R. Rogers, 1956, *Journal of Counseling Psychology, 3,* 115–120. Copyright 1956 by the American Psychological Association. Reprinted by permission.

seeking. To some degree both Mowrer and Kimble seem to me to be caught in this difficulty.

As a second possibility, if in order to apply our theory we need to gain information about the stimuli to which Paul is responding, our problem is still almost impossibly complex. To know the objective reality of the conflicted and conflicting attitudes of his parents; to know the parents' behaviors; to know the attitudes and behaviors of Paul's peers (friendly and hostile); to know the changing stimuli presented by the social worker, the cop, the neighborhood; to measure or even estimate the character of all these stimuli, in order to gauge Paul's response, would be an impossible task.

But from the point of view of a third approach we are in a more fortunate position. We can form a relationship with Paul in which we can fairly readily come to know his phenomenological field, his field of perceived meanings, as these occur in consciousness. We can learn how he sees himself, his behavior, his father, his mother, his teachers, his friends. We can learn how he perceives the attitudes of each of these toward him. We can learn the meaning that each of these perceptions has for him. We can even predict that if the relationship has certain qualities, the area of his awareness will broaden and come to include experiences which have occurred in his organism, but of which he has not previously been aware. Consequently we can broaden his perceptual field and come to know these additional meanings.

Now this knowledge, which we can realistically obtain, seems like the merest *fragment* of the total reality. We are only talking about the immediately experienced, conscious, phenomenal field. Obviously there also exists the unbelievably long and complex chain of the genetic sequence of his behavior. There also exists all the complex immediate external reality to which it seems that Paul is reacting. There is also the large number of elements in Paul's own experience of which he is unaware. Is this tiny fragment of obtainable information as to Paul's own immediate perceptions of any real use? Or is it too insignificant a fraction to be of value? This is an empirical question.

Now the exciting answer which is suggested by therapeutic experience, and by research in psychotherapy as far as it has gone, is that this small knowable fragment, the immediate internal frame of reference of the individual, is perhaps a very significant basis for the understanding of behavior, and that it provides perhaps the greatest potentiality for alteration in personality and behavior. Contact with this minute knowable fraction of the total reality, gives us, according to our present clinical and research experience, leverage on some very important elements indeed.

HELPING PAUL

So much for the problem of what we can know. Now what can we offer? We can offer rewards for more social behavior—affection, praise, money, friends, a happier situation at home. We can offer punishments for anti-social tendencies—deprivations, unpleasant consequences, loss of affection and friends. But it is already evident that such a gross use of rewards and punishment is totally ineffective in Paul's case. So we can turn to the possibility of changing the stimuli, the environment. If we have enough power in the situation we might put Paul in a new school, and a different settlement house, in contact with a new group of peers. We might even move him to a new home, a foster home. But those with long experience in such efforts are the first to point out how frequently disappointing are the results of trying to change the behavioral response through changing the external stimuli, especially after the first few years of life.

What is left? We can offer him a relationship, but this seems rather insignificant compared to all of the more drastic changes in environment which we have pointed out as being relatively futile. Offering him a relationship is the one personal, human thing entirely within our control, needing no legal sanction, no power to put it into effect. What likelihood is there that such a simple step could have an influence? This, too, is an empirical question, and again the answer, so far as we now know it, is exciting. It seems that if the relationship has certain qualities, the influence may be decidedly marked.

Thus, in regard to the central problem of this panel, our present empirical knowledge permits us to make this hypothesis. If a certain definable type of interpersonal relationship is offered to Paul, in which communicative

contact is made with his internal frame of reference, then he will come to experience changes in his conscious perceptual field, and his attitudes, personality, and behavior will be altered in accordance with these changes.

Let me try to spell this out in relation to Paul's situation at the close of the movie. Our theory would propose first that someone—a counselor, the social worker, anyone with the appropriate attitudes—offer a personal relationship to Paul. Since the parents have asked for help for the boy, it might be suggested that Paul be *required* to have at least five sessions with the counselor, in order to make sure that he had an opportunity to experience this relationship. After that he could make his own choice as to whether or not to continue.

The likelihood of change in Paul's perceptions and behavior would depend on certain qualities of this relationship. To the degree that the counselor is genuine, internally consistent, operating without facade, and with awareness of his own feelings; to the extent that he is acceptant of every aspect of Paul in the relationship; to the degree that he experiences a sensitively emphatic understanding of Paul's inner world of perceptual meanings; and to the degree that Paul senses the counselor's acceptance and understanding—then we could hypothesize that change would take place.

The process by which change would take place is one we have come partially to understand, and the film suggests some of the first steps. Pressed by his own concern and fright about his behavior, Paul would, in this relationship, which is experienced as free from external threat, begin to explore his perceptions of his problems and of himself. He would express the feeling that he is a bad boy, a worthless boy in the eyes of his father, a disappointment to both his father and mother. He would in some fashion probably express the feeling that all of his own impulses—whether to complete the boat building, to do a good job with the scenery, to leave his home so that his parents would not be further disappointed in him—all simply wind up as further proof that he is a bad, wrong, wicked, obnoxious, disappointing person. This is not only the way he thinks he is seen. It is the way he seems himself. He can never do anything quite well enough to be accepted, no matter how good his intentions. It always turns out that he is bad. He has, in theoretical terms, introjected the negative value which he perceives his parents as having placed upon him.

As all of these perceptions are fully accepted by the counselor as meaningful aspects of Paul, worthy of respect, Paul would not need to defend them and could go on to other experiences and meanings which were sharply contradictory. I shall try to suggest some of these in a schematic way. I do not of course mean that each of these would necessarily appear in the relationship, but that expressions of these types would occur.

For example, Paul would experience such contradictory attitudes as these, attitudes which would be threatening because the new element in each of these contradictions is inconsistent with the concept of himself, and hence has not previously been fully permitted in awareness.

> "Of course it was really bad to mess up the dining room the day the guests came, but I got a big kick out of finishing the boat."

> "My father is really a very good man, but to me he sometimes seems very unfair. I even resent him then."

> "I admire my father very much, and want to be like him in my carpentry, and in making the other kids live up to my high standards, but at times I *hate* him."

As the relationship continued, Paul would continue to use it increasingly to explore his own feelings, particularly in relation to himself. The outstanding characteristic of this exploration would be its tendency toward increasing differentiation. Experiences would be valued in a differentiated, not a global way. "I experience finishing the boat as good, my father experiences it as good and then bad, my mother experiences it as a nuisance."

Gradually, over a period of time, these freshly differentiated experiences become assimilated into the self. The reorganization of the self-concept involves the admission into self of many more specific, more differentiated perceptions of experience, much closer to the immediate organismic reaction. Schematically we might say that they would be of this order.

> "I experience pain at disappointing my parents, and I experience satisfaction in some of the very things which to them are disappointing."

> "I resent my father, and at times hate him; and I admire him very much, and at times love him."

> "I love my mother at times, and at times I am disappointed in what seems to me to be her weakness."

> "I experience the positive regard of my therapist for each of my feelings and perceptions, and to some degree have come to feel this same positive regard for myself in these experiences."

> "I am the integrator and the integration of my experience, which I perceive more and more accurately."

> "I find it challenging and worthwhile to be what I am, and to develop."

> "But to be what I am means to experience more vividly pain and disappointment and anger and failure as real parts of myself, as well as satisfaction, and happiness, and achievement and love as equally real elements of myself."

PREDICTING PAUL'S BEHAVIOR

I have probably been somewhat carried away by my schematic design, and I would have to confess that only to some degree would Paul experience the later themes of the schema, and the degree to which he experienced them would depend on the extent to which the relationship offered by the therapist met the conditions mentioned previously.

In any event, we could predict, on the basis of our research knowledge, that Paul would become more open to his experience, would exhibit less defensiveness, would shut fewer experiences out of awareness. We know that he would tend to be more "realistic" in his perceptions of himself, that he would value himself and his reactions more highly. We know that he would tend to become more confident of himself, more self-directing and autonomous. In his behavior he would become more mature, as clinicians define maturity. He would be less frustrated by stress, and would recover from stress more quickly. In personality characteristics and structure he would tend to become more similar to the person he wants to be. Our findings, particularly as contained in our recent volume of research,[1] indicate that there is a reasonable probability of occurrence for all of these outcomes for Paul.

But, some of you may be thinking, what about his delinquency? You are talking about inner change, but we are concerned about social behavior. How do you know that he will not become a more mature delinquent, a more effective housebreaker, a more integrated truant? Here, too, our experience, as well as our research, suggests the answer. It is that when the individual is free to be his experience, to actualize himself in terms of that experience, then he actualizes himself in the direction of a more harmonious relationship with others. Why? The most basic and most satisfying answer is that man is that kind of an animal. It seems that as a species he prefers, *if he is fully aware of all his reactions, and the consequences of all his behavior,* to live in a realistically harmonious relationship to others. He is not, as orthodox Freudian theory might lead us to believe, inwardly a beast who would be utterly destructive if he followed his inner urges.

So we do not need to be concerned as to the *direction* in

[1] *Psychotherapy and Personality Change,* edited by Carl R. Rogers and Rosalind F. Dymond. Chicago: University of Chicago Press, 1954.

which Paul will move, if we can provide a relationship where he can knowingly and freely choose. If he can make progress in becoming himself, he will, because he belongs to the human species, become a more socialized self.

This does not mean that he will be a conformist but that he will be more real, and his reactions real and appropriate reactions to the immediate situation. He will not be so likely to feel bad and doomed, or to behave in ways appropriate to someone who is doomed to be bad. He will be affectionate when he feels affectionate, toward the real object of his affections. Thus he will be quite likely to express resentment to his father, as well as affection; to let his mother know if he feels she is letting him down, as well as to express his response to her affection. He will enter into more real, immediate, and satisfying communication with others, and this leads to positive social relationships.

I have applied our theory of therapy and personality in such a way as to stress the things we know. There are many elements we do not as yet know, and our hypotheses may be faulty in unknown ways. Also I have hypothesized an optimal therapist, and actually all of us fall short of possessing in optimal degree the previously described characteristics of the therapist. So that in many ways the actual conditions we are able to provide may fall short of the theoretically optimal conditions, and to that degree the change in Paul's personality and behavior will fall short of what I have hypothesized. But I would emphasize, in closing, that psychology is at the point where it does have theories which apply to such behavioral situations as Paul's, and that these theories are to some degree confirmed by empirical findings.

THE RESPONSIBILITY FOR PAUL

This concludes my formal remarks, but since I still have a little time left, I should like to differ somewhat with Kimble who says that we can either attempt to alter the motivation or change the habits of this boy. I wish to point out that for myself I have no desire to alter Paul's motives, and I have no interest in any direct effort to change his habits.

Let's take a look at each of these. Kimble describes Paul's motives as being needs for affection, for companionship with his father, for achievement, for recognition. Why would one wish to change these motives? I would agree with this description and add that Paul is trying to become himself, to satisfy these needs and to actualize and enhance himself in the only ways he perceives as leading to these goals. Certainly I have no desire to alter these motives, which seem to me to be the basic motives of all of us.

I would point out further that direct attempts to alter habits are time-consuming and fruitless. On the other hand, if the perceived channel of satisfying needs is altered, habits dissolve almost as if by magic. Take the adolescent boy. For years he has perceived the only avenue to manly behavior to be that of being rough and tough. Hence he resists strongly such "sissy" traits as combing his hair or washing behind his ears. When his sexuality begins to mature, and he pays attention to what girls think, he perceives that a neat and attractive appearance is another way of being manly. As soon as he acquires this new perception, the habit of resisting cleanliness and neatness—a habit which has persisted for years—drops away almost overnight.

So I would simply say that I in no way wish to change Paul's motivation, and I would regard direct efforts to change his habits as a waste of time. My aim would be to set in motion a process which would permit more accurate differentiation of perception. He would then perceive new ways, more satisfying ways of meeting his needs, fulfilling his motives, and actualizing himself. His habits will then change almost automatically. The best way of setting in motion this alteration of the perceptual field is through a personal relationship of acceptance, safety, and freedom, where he can dare to explore his perceived world.

Existential Therapy

The Danzigs

R. D. Laing
and A. Esterson
1964

CLINICAL PERSPECTIVE

From the clinical psychiatric viewpoint, Sarah Danzig began to develop an illness of insidious onset at the age of seventeen. She began to lie in bed all day, getting up only at night and staying up thinking or brooding or reading the Bible. Gradually she lost interest in everyday affairs and became increasingly preoccupied with religious issues. Her attendance at commercial college became intermittent, and she failed to complete her studies. During the next four years Sarah failed to make the grade at whatever job or course of study she undertook.

When she was twenty-one her illness took a sudden turn for the worse. She began to express bizarre ideas, for instance that she heard voices over the telephone and saw people on television talking about her. Soon afterwards she started to rage against members of her family. After one outburst against her mother she fled the house and stayed out all night. On her return she was taken to an observation ward, where she remained for two weeks. Thereafter, she was listless, apathetic, quiet, withdrawn, and lacking in concentration. Although from time to time she made bizarre statements, for example that she had been raped, on the whole she was able to live quietly at home, and even returned to work, this time in her father's office. She continued like this for fifteen months, and then relapsed. Once more she persistently expressed bizarre ideas. She complained that people at the office were talk-

ing about her, were in a plot against her, and did not wish her to work with them. She insisted they intercepted and tore up her letters. She also insisted that her letters were being intercepted at home. She complained to her father that his staff were incompetent, and quarrelled with him and his secretary over keeping the books. Eventually she refused to go to work, and took to lying in her bed all day, getting up only at night to brood or to sit reading the Bible. She spoke hardly at all except to make occasional statements about religion or to accuse her family of discussing her, or to complain that the telephone operators were listening in to her calls. She became irritable and aggressive, particularly towards her father, and it was following an outburst against him that she was again brought into hospital.

STRUCTURE OF INVESTIGATION

The family consisted of mother (aged fifty), father (fifty-six), Sarah (aged twenty-three), John (twenty-one), Ruth (fifteen). At her parents' request, Ruth was not included in the investigation.

Interviews	Occasions
Daughter	13
Father	1
Mother	1
Mother and father	4
Mother and daughter	1
Father and daughter	1

204 ❧ R. D. LAING and A. ESTERSON

Son	3
Son and daughter	3
Mother, father and daughter	8
Mother, father, daughter and son	4
	39

This represents thirty-two hours of interviewing time, of which eighteen hours were tape-recorded.

THE FAMILY SITUATION

In this case the necessity for a variety of "sightings" of the family in action is revealed particularly clearly.

We shall first describe certain aspects of the family interviews, with particular reference to what makes intelligible various delusions and psychotic manifestations relating to Sarah's behaviour in hospital. She said that:

1. The Ward Sister was withholding letters from her and failing to pass on telephone messages from her mother. She knew the letters from her mother were being withheld because her mother was writing to her every other day. She knew that her mother was writing to her every other day because she was her mother's child and her mother loved her.

2. The hospital was maliciously detaining her, while her parents wanted her home at once.

3. She was afraid of being abandoned in hospital and never getting home again. She did not say who would abandon her, but the heart of her fear was that she would be cut off from her mother.

4. She said that her mother had only agreed to her coming into hospital because she had not wanted her to leave home. Her mother did not want to lose her children. She said that she did not blame her mother, and emphasized that she and her mother loved each other.

5. She was angry with her father and was afraid of him. She saw him as the prime agent in her detention in hospital. She said that he was a liar, and would tell lies about her.

Throughout these interviews Sarah, for the most part, passively complied with her parents and her brother.

In the first family session the issue of her fear of being abandoned was raised. Her parents and brother reassured her that they had telephoned every day, and had left mes-

sages for her. This was not in fact so. They told her that she was ill, that they only wanted her to stay in hospital for her own good, not because they wanted to abandon her. They loved her and wanted her back home. Sarah made no attempt to argue.

John was soon to remark that she was unusually amiable and acquiescent, whereas "normally she was highly resistant to suggestion." The significance of this remark emerged more fully when he warned us in private against being fooled by her. She was just pretending to agree with them. It was an act to get out of hospital. With her, however, he was sympathetic and loving, giving *her* no hint that he thought she was trying to fool him.

It seemed therefore that a mistrustful perception of the hospital was necessary for her if she was to maintain her trust in her family, since greater perceptual and cognitive dissonance would have been experienced by Sarah had she distrusted her family rather than the hospital.

When her family was asked in what way they felt she was ill, they replied that she was lazy, stubborn, sluttish, terribly impudent to her father, rebellious, obscene, etc. They seemed to be describing wickedness, not sickness. At least this is how Sarah felt it. She remarked timidly that she had changed her mind about going home.

One of the main features of her illness in the view of her parents was an unreasoned, senseless, persistent hostility to her father, but when she was seen alone, her mother, without any apparent awareness of being inconsistent, also described Sarah's hostility as a meaningful response to various things her father did. Indeed, she said he acted in the same way towards her (mother) and John, making them angry too. In fact it emerged that they were constantly quarrelling. It thus became clear that Sarah's anger against her father, which her family now could not tolerate, was hardly more intense than the enmity her mother and John had directed against him for years. But they objected to Sarah acting similarly. Sarah was finally singled out by her mother, father, and brother as the one person who was *really* expected to comply with her father's wishes. This was not put to her in so many words, but each of the others privately realized that she was put in a special position although without their being fully aware of its consequences for her. They argued that if Sarah could not get on with her father she must be ill.

But it was not her father who was the promoter of the idea that Sarah "had to go." Although he and Sarah fought and screamed at each other more than her mother and John could tolerate, they also got on together in a much more affectionate and intimate way than her mother or John liked to admit.

When interviewed alone, her mother said plainly that if Sarah did not give up her hostility to her father she should remain permanently in hospital. When she was with Sarah, however, she conveyed to her again without any sense of inconsistency that it was not she, but her husband and John, who wanted her put away. She told Sarah plainly that John was fed up with her, that he could not stand her at home, and that he was not going to be bothered with her. This was true, but it contrasted with John's frequent reassurances to Sarah to the contrary. John admitted that Sarah was only saying to his father what he had said to her about him. But, like his mother, he thought that Sarah must be ill if she said such things, since it was not her place.

When he was alone with the interviewer, Mr. Danzig said that his wife had wanted to get rid of Sarah for some time, had wanted to "sacrifice" her, but he had refused to agree. He regarded himself as Sarah's ally, but the support he accorded her was more imaginary than real since he did not support her either when his wife and son were attacking her or when he was alone with her

He did, however, remonstrate with them in Sarah's absence, even to threatening to leave home himself if they did not leave her alone.[1] It is ironical that Mrs. Danzig insisted that it was for her husband's sake that Sarah had to be "treated" in hospital for her "illness."

Thus, Sarah's construction that her father and the hospital, not her mother and John, wished to keep her locked up was as reasonable as it was unreasonable—in fact, with the evidence available to her it was possibly the most likely construction.

Sarah was continually mystified in this respect. For instance, when the interviewer introduced the issue of whether Sarah got on everyone's nerves, and not only her father's, Mrs. Danzig took this as a criticism of Sarah and told her how "ungrateful" she was for upsetting her father. Sarah tried feebly to defend herself, and then pleaded that she was tired. Her mother sympathized, and then went on to describe Sarah in her usual terms as selfish, ungrateful, inconsiderate, and so on. It was always difficult to get past such attributions to specific items of behaviour. When Sarah listlessly fell in with her, her mother took it as evidence that she was right. She then advised Sarah to follow our advice and to stay in hospital, in the interests of her health. We had not given any such advice.

Another mystifying feature of this family is the marked conspiratorial tone and manner they adopt with each other and with us in Sarah's absence. They have then a solidarity otherwise lacking. It is impressive how their conflicts are then forgotten.

On one occasion, when Sarah left the room, her mother, father, and brother began a furtive whispered exchange about her. As Sarah re-entered she said uncer-

tainly that she had the impression that they were talking about her. They denied this and looked at us significantly, as though to say: "See how suspicious she is."

After these glimpses of this family in action in the present and recent past, we shall now try to reconstruct some crucial historical facts.

Sarah left school at sixteen to go to secretarial college for fifteen months, then to art school for two years. Recently she had been working in her father's office. She had had a previous "breakdown" eighteen months ago.

According to her mother and father, until the age of twelve she had been a most lovable child. She had always tended to lack self-confidence, however, and to be concerned about how she appeared to others, continually relying on her parents and her brother to tell her how people saw her. Nevertheless according to them, she had been very popular, and had had a number of friends. She had had a sharp wit, a good sense of humour and she was artistic. She liked paintings, good music, good books, and had an exceptional talent for writing and drawing, showing promise in these respects at school. She had insight into other people's characters and did not like cheap talk. They did not, however, wish her to be an artist.

After fifteen months at secretarial college she stopped attending. She lay in bed until late in the morning, and stayed awake all night thinking or reading. She began to lose her friends one by one. At this time she began to read the Bible and tried to interpret for herself what she read.

Father, mother, John and Sarah all agree on the following features of Sarah's behaviour *before* admission to hospital.

1. She had been saying for some months that telephone operators (or someone) had been listening in to her calls.

2. She believed that people in her father's office had been talking about her and did not want her to work there.

3. She believed that someone at the office intercepted and destroyed her letters, and that some of the staff were incompetent.

4. She believed that her parents and brother were talking about her.

5. She believed that they were keeping letters from her.

6. She was irritable and aggressive towards members of her family, especially her father, towards whom she did not have the right attitude for a daughter. In particular she called him a liar,

---

[1] His motives for leaving home were more mixed than this and he had never been clear about them. . . .

and said she no longer believed in him or trusted him.

7. She was very shy and self-conscious.

8. She did not mix with other people, but was quiet, withdrawn, miserable, and discontented.

9. She lay in bed all day and sat up into the small hours of the morning.

10. She lacked concentration and had been thinking too much.

11. She had been reading the Bible a great deal.

Twelve months earlier Sarah had gone to work in her father's office. She soon began to feel that she was being discussed disparagingly. In her turn she complained to her father that certain employees were incompetent. Finally, she refused to go any more. About this time (it is not clear when it began), she discovered that her salary had been over-stated in the books and told her father. He tried to explain it to her, but she failed to understand either his explanation or that of his son and secretary. "She wore us all out" (mother). She insisted that the clerk responsible was incompetent, and when they did not agree accused them of being against her, and began to act provocatively at home, e.g. by smoking in front of her father on the Sabbath, putting lemonade into his tea, and so on. These acts were regarded with a mixture of anger, guilt, shame, and concern by her parents and brother, who eventually resolved their dilemma by treating them as signs of illness.

Her family regarded Sarah's madness as a calamity visited on the family.

MOTHER: Well I did sort of think all this business of going, you know, thinking unusual things, saying people are not—to me these sort of things—they always happen to other people, they never happen to us. You know the sort of thing, you think it always happens to other people—you know people flooded out, you know, I feel sorry, but you do sort of think "Oh I'll never be flooded out where I'm living now"—you see? I'm only giving you an example. It's never occurred to me that I'll ever get flooded out where I live now—that's how I look at it.

And:

FATHER: We didn't realize what was happening.

MOTHER: We didn't, as I told you, we thought these things only happened to other people's children. You read in the paper a little girl is murdered, or kidnapped, you feel very sorry for the people, but you don't associate it with your own child. As I say, everything terrible happens to other people.

FATHER: When it happens to you—

MOTHER: And then it happens with you unfortunately, then other people say "Oh how terrible," then it becomes a tragedy. It *never* occurred to me that she'd ever go sort of mentally like this, to turn out in this sort of way.

What was the calamity comparable to these floods, murder, and kidnap, that had befallen this family? The more we probed, the more elusive it became, but what was obvious was her parents' shame and fear of scandal. In particular, they were worried about Sarah's social naïvety and lack of discretion. They regarded her as a "breaker of the family front." When she first went to work in her father's office he had urged her to keep quiet about her breakdown. Unfortunately it leaked out and his staff began to gossip behind her back, although to her face they were kind and forbearing. She was also resented for being the boss's daughter. Sarah felt their hostility without being able to get her feeling confirmed by anyone.

She also discovered certain actual mistakes that had been made and told her father. She was resented more than ever now, but she could not be attacked directly. Instead, she was exposed to more innuendoes that no one would confirm explicitly. She became more and more isolated and unhappy. At this time some of her correspondence was mislaid "accidentally" by another employee. She perceived the "unconscious" motive of the other, and tried to challenge her. The other girl insinuated something about her sanity, and in an agitated state she went to her father to complain. Her father, anxious to avoid any open recognition among his employees that his daughter had been a mental case, pooh-poohed her complaints, casting doubt on the validity of her suspicions—"You are unwell. No one dislikes you. No one is talking about you. It's imagination," and so on. Without confirmation from her father she became more agitated, and started calling him a liar, accusing him of being in collusion with the others. She refused to return to the office.

In addition, while working with him, she had discovered that her father, while generally a meticulously honest man, engaged in certain petty dishonesties. We of course have no difficulty in reconciling this paradox, since it is quite characteristic of the compulsive-obsessive person, but Sarah could not understand this and became very confused, especially as her father now had to defend himself desperately, not against his own dissociated impulses, but against her. This involved him, unwittingly, in order to preserve her trust in him, in destroying her trust in herself, and as far as he could he enlisted his secretary, wife, and son to this end.

They said in effect: "You are imagining that there is a flaw in your father" *and,* "You are mad or bad if you imagine such a thing," *and,* "You are mad or bad if you do not believe us when we tell you that you are mad or bad to trust your own perceptions and memory."

Much of what they called her illness consisted in attempts to discuss forbidden issues, comments on their attempts to keep her in the dark, or to muddle her, and angry responses to such mystifications and mystification over mystifications. She had been put in the position of having to try to sort out secrecy and muddle, in the face of being muddled up over the validity of trying to do so. With some justification, therefore, Sarah began to feel that they were in collusion against her.

We have to explain why this girl is so naïve in the first place. It may be argued that with such a naïve girl the family would want to keep her in ignorance of their secrets, that their mystification of her was a consequence of her naïvety. This was partly so. But our evidence shows that her naïvety had itself been preceded by a prior mystification. The family was thus caught in a vicious spiral. The more they mystified her the more she remained naïve and the more she remained naïve the more they felt they had to protect themselves by mystifying her.

Mr. Danzig lived a scrupulously correct family life, and needed to be seen as a man of stern and perfect rectitude, and as the head of the family. His wife complied with him in this, but at the same time encouraged John to "see through" him, but not in public. John helped to maintain his father's public image, but his cooperation at home was intermittent, and he was often supported in these lapses by his mother. Mr. Danzig knew of the mother-son alliance, and mother and son knew he knew, and he knew they knew he knew. There was thus complete understanding among the three of them in this respect.

With Sarah, however, it was different. Mother and son often criticized Mr. Danzig in front of her, but she was not supposed to do so. They thus presented her with a very difficult task. Mr. Danzig's view of his marriage (and, incidentally, something of his style of thinking in general) can be seen in the following passage.

> It may well be that my wife in her moments of forgetfulness speaks to me sharply in the presence of the children. In other words she doesn't show for me the respect that a wife should in the presence of children. And I've told her more than often, "If you've anything to say to me, say it not in front of the children."
>
> We differ a lot on that (keeping the house clean—e.g. the children's bedrooms). One of the excuses is, "I haven't got the time, patience," or, "Have no help."—All right, I try to alleviate her worries. I chime in sometimes. I help her. Then she comes back—I have no right to interfere. I get erratic. I say, "No, I like—I'm only interfering when I see something which I don't like."
>
> I want a certain clean way and it can arise from an attitude—perhaps she may think—indifference on my

wife's part. She feels—er—she can't go out very well. I can accept this. She feels she doesn't go out very well. I object to her—I want her to dress very nicely, very neatly and cleanly and smartly. I want to go out watching her. She doesn't care. She's indifferent to this. I don't like that. I say, "Whatever position arises between me and you privately or otherwise, publicly, come out clean. Go out occasionally. It's not nice for the children. It gives an example to the children if you go out occasionally."

> It may well be perhaps, shall I say—I may even go a bit further than this. It may well be and I've often thought about it, it may well be that I may not have been her ideal in marriage—I'm going to admit to you that *she* may not be *my* ideal in marriage . . .
>
> She was an only child. She was quite an intelligent person, well-read, musical. I thought, "We might blend. Possible, possible. I may be a possible to her." You get near enough the possibilities, near the next best. Maybe she felt the same thing. I did have ideas in my mind but—my wife wasn't bad looking. And so I came to the point. We met and it seemed possible. We didn't dislike one another, not to say—I'm not going to say I was ravingly in love with my wife, and I don't think my wife was with me; but maybe I wasn't experienced enough to understand certain things. Oh I wasn't a bargain—I wasn't a bargain—I was a young man. I hadn't the remotest idea of running around with other people—with other women—picking them up at dance-halls or a ball, when I was single, and I thought, "Well this is a nice set-up—I might be able to work this round"—so we both felt the same thing. We were both of the same mind.

It was not surprising that Sarah maintained an idealized picture of her father, dissociated from her dissonant perceptions, until she was over twenty-one. She had had squabbles with her father before, about unannounced intrusions into her bedroom when she was undressed, unsolicited insistence on tidying up her bedroom, listening in on her telephone calls, intercepting her letters, and so on, but in none of these was she sure that her father was in the wrong. All such behaviour was either denied by him or rationalized as out of love for her. If she found this love annoying, she felt that she was at fault.

As her idealization of her father broke down, she clung all the more desperately to her idealization of her mother, which her mother helped her to maintain. Her mother's behaviour over the issue of Sarah's lying late in bed illustrates this. Both her parents continually reproached her for not getting up early. They shouted at her to mend her ways, saying that now she was grown up, and should not behave like a baby. Their actions, however, were markedly at variance with this, for her father insisted, for instance, on his right to enter her bedroom whenever he wanted, which her mother did not oppose, and she, while complaining bitterly of the inconvenience, continued to cook her meals whenever she chose to get up. When we asked why she did not lay down fixed times for her daughter's meals, and refuse to let her routine be disorganized, she replied that if she did that she would feel guilty and a bad mother. Sarah's father replied indignantly that if that happened he would carry food up to his daughter himself, and Sarah felt that her mother would be mean if she did not give her her meals whenever she felt like eating.

The more her parents did things for her, the more they wanted her gratitude and the more ungrateful she became. Searching for gratitude they did even more for her. Thus, while expecting her to grow up they treated her as a child, and she, while wanting to be considered as an adult, behaved more and more as a baby. Her parents then reproached her for being spoiled by them, and she reproached them for not treating her as an adult.

When Sarah said she was afraid of her father her parents not only could not understand this, they refused to believe it. After all he had never abused her or shouted at her or hit her. Apart from insisting that she obey certain religious rules such as not smoking on the Sabbath, he had made no demands on her. In their opinion the trouble was that he had not been firm enough and had overindulged her. Nor could Sarah gain any support from John. His position was very equivocal. He was, as noted above, privately supported by his mother against his father, and he obtained her open support when he defied him to his face. He was also encouraged by both parents to see Sarah as the favoured and indulged child. For a short time in his teens he had supported his sister, but had broken with her. He then engaged in an alliance with his mother. We have evidence that she was jealous of the closeness between him and his sister. To what extent was she responsible for stimulating John's jealousy of his father's "indulgence" of Sarah as an aid to bringing him to her side? To what extent did she stimulate his defiance of his father, and win him by supporting him in it? What is the evidence that Sarah was indulged more than he?

According to them all Mr. Danzig was "firmer" with John than with Sarah and Ruth, because John was a boy. But John reproached his father for not being firm enough with him. He said that his father should have hit him to make him work better at school. He was not afraid of his father as a child, and he thought he should have been. All children should be afraid of their fathers. He thought his father had bad children, although there have been worse boys than himself. He tried to comply, but did not always succeed. He did not think his father's demands unreasonable, but . . .

Mr. Danzig felt he had over-indulged his son. He should have "bullied" him more. He had spoiled both John and Sarah.

I was patient with him and very happy to say that although I spoilt him—I spoilt Sarah, I spoilt John . . .

We may say that John *believes* Sarah was indulged more than himself. His reasons for so believing, as they emerge, are obscure.

This family therefore functioned largely through a series of alliances—mother and father; mother and son; mother, father, and son. Sarah was left out. She received, as she said, no "backing" from anyone in the family and this seems to have been the case. These alliances offered protection against impossible ideals. Sarah, with no ally, was expected to conform with no let-up to the rules that the others all managed to break. For instance, John was not supposed to have a sexual life, but he had one, with his mother's collusion. Mrs. Danzig broke Sabbath rules, with John's connivance, unbeknown to her husband, and so on. Mr. Danzig was secretly sexually dissatisfied and had often thought of leaving his wife in recent years. Even though regarded as ill, indulged, and spoiled, Sarah alone was expected to govern her thoughts and actions according to Mr. Danzig's obsessive-compulsive interpretation of a rigorous orthodoxy. Her social naïvety has thus to be set within the context of her parents' demand for *total* compliance from her alone.

Nor could she compare her parents' praxis with that of other people, since her contacts with the extra-familial world were effectively cut off. Although her parents were concerned because she had no friends, they were even more worried in case she was seduced if she did mix socially.

FATHER: Well one of the reasons why I personally was interested in her social life is not because I was prying into her private affairs; I was mainly interested in watching that she shouldn't be impressed by funny stories, by all sorts of—all and sundry—I realized she was a very sensitive young lady, very highly impressionable, and that she should not be so impressed, to get wrong impressions. Because there are so many young men around with glib tongues and fancy themselves and able to get hold of a girl like Sarah and tell her all sorts of funny stories, and can lead to a lot of complications—that was the main reason why I was interested in her social standing and social life. But I wasn't interested to pry into her private affairs.

They did not forbid her to go out with boys, in fact they told her she should, but they watched her every move so closely that she felt she had no privacy at all, and when she objected, if they did not deny what they were doing, they reproached her for being ungrateful for their concern. She thus became muddled over whether or not it was right to want to go out with boys, or even to have any private life in the first place. Her father tried to investigate her boy-friends without her knowledge in various ways. As John explained.

JOHN: But I don't want you to get the impression that Dad hangs over like an eagle and tries to control Sarah's social life. Before she was ill he was always very careful about his intrusions into her private life, because he knew that if he did make an obviously nosey approach she would *flare* up, so therefore we tried to—very very carefully about her social life—the questions, if there were any, were always put by Mum, put in a sleeky way, sometimes or—(protest from Father about the word "sneaky")—I didn't say "sneaky" I said "sleeky"—a silky sort of a way (Mother tries to calm Father, explaining John's statement to him). By sheer—by continuous nagging on Mummy's part—"give a name" whether it was the right name or not, she gave a name—that satisfied her.

And while denying that he minded her going out to places where she would meet boys:

FATHER: But I understand, I fully understand a young lady and a young man enjoying themselves—they enjoy flirting or necking what they call it, and young men, I understand that—I'm human—I was once young myself—I'm still young but—

her father implicitly forbade her to enter these places by uttering vague, ominous warnings about their dangers.

FATHER: I didn't say coffee bars generally—there can be certain coffee bars which are very dangerous to visit as well. I'm not particularizing *any* coffee bar, *any* restaurant, *any* dance-hall, or *any* place of amusement—I'm making a general statement how much I am concerned about *both* of you.

Although John could to a large extent see what was going on he failed to back Sarah in this matter, as in others. As we have seen, *he* defied his father's prohibitions and demands with his mother's help, but when similar demands were made of Sarah he sided with his father against her.

> From my point of view when it comes to *Sarah* it's not intrusion—when it comes to me it *is* intrusion.

In the face of this alliance Sarah gave up attempting to meet anyone outside her family.

Sarah at one point had become virtually catatonic, that is, she would not speak or respond to their approaches, or only compliantly. While she was in hospital this quietness and compliance were very noticeable. As we have noted, her family took this as a trick to deceive the doctor and get him to agree to her leaving. Her dilemma at this point appeared to be that if she talked about what she thought, she would have to remain in hospital, and if she remained silent her family would see this as deception, and would demand of the doctor that she be detained and "treated"

until she had the "right" ideas. If she tried to impose the "right" ideas on herself, then in a sense she would be killing herself. But even this would not save her from mental hospital, and from being cut off from her family, because then she would be "dead," "a shadow of herself," "personalityless," to use her brother's description, and so would still need "treatment."

Sarah, they said, was obsessed with religion. For the past few years she had been continually reading the Bible, quoting from it, and trying to understand it. They did not believe she understood anything about it, however. According to them, it did not really mean much to her. She merely repeated it parrot-fashion. They suggested her interest in it was possibly due to guilt. It was "a form of atonement by forced hardship," according to John.

There was deep confusion in this family about the nature of religion.

Mrs. Danzig's parents came from Eastern Europe. They were Orthodox Jews, her father because he believed in Orthodoxy, her mother because she wanted to please him. Mrs. Danzig was an only child. She respected her father, and never did anything in front of him that she thought would upset him. Her parents had been strict with her, but not as strict as her husband's parents had been with him. Her father had been a diplomatic man and knew when to turn a blind eye towards minor infringements of Orthodox regulations.

For example, on the Sabbath it was forbidden to carry money, but in the summer, on the Sabbath, she used to go to town. Her father, as she left the house, tactfully refrained from asking where she was going, or how she was going to get there without carrying money for fares and meals and so forth. She in her turn acted tactfully towards him, and at home she abode strictly by the ritual regulations. Her father never left the house on the Sabbath except to go to Synagogue, while her mother stayed home.

According to Mrs. Danzig, her husband was very Orthodox. His father had been a Hebrew scholar. She did not object to his Orthodoxy. She knew about it when she married, and was happy to keep a kosher house "because that's the way it should be." It was the way her mother had done it.

> I do agree to a certain extent that if you're Jewish you keep to the Jewish religion. You *go* to Synagogue on Saturday, there's no harm in going to the Synagogue on Saturday, that's all right. I mean you can't run away from the fact that you're what you are.

It is true that she disagreed with many of the Orthodox regulations, because they were inconvenient, but she complied with them to please her husband, as her mother had complied to please her father. For example, she now never went out on the Sabbath, and she never struck a light in front of her husband. Although, unlike her mother, she would do certain things such as striking a light if her husband was not present to see it, she would not upset him by doing it in front of him. It was her duty as a wife to comply in these matters, and show respect for her husband. If he wanted her to appear as an Orthodox Jewess, then she was prepared to appear in this way to him. And besides it was not worth having a row about. There were, however, certain areas that had nothing to do with a man: for example, the kitchen, where she tolerated no interference.

Mr. and Mrs. Danzig, although strictly religious, were, in their opinion, also fairly "modern," for instance, in the matter of sex. Particularly was this so with Mrs. Danzig. She liked her daughter to go out with boys. It was the right thing to do. She did not even object to her daughter going out with a boy on the Sabbath, though Sarah herself regularly remained at home on that day trying to comply with her father and with ritual law.

> If she wants to go out with a fellow on a Saturday, I don't think it's such a terrible thing. She's not doing anything immoral. She's not doing anything very bad by going out with a girl or a fellow asks her to go out on a Saturday.

In fact, Mrs. Danzig used to urge Sarah to go out and meet boys. It was good for her. It would help her to get over her self-consciousness.

> I often used to tell her, I said, "I think you ought to go out and meet boys and meet girls. You should go out more and get dates and get to know people and go somewhere else. You meet them if you already know somebody. If you've seen them before you can approach them. You feel you've seen them once before, you know them and it doesn't make you so shy."

Of course the relationship must be of the right kind. In other words, it was not only all right to go out with the opposite sex, it was a social obligation for all normal girls; but naturally nothing sexual must enter into the relationship.

> Well I would have liked her to go out with boys. I think it's very normal for young girls to go out with the opposite sex, and I think it's the right thing that she should go out with the opposite sex, in the right way of course, to go out socially, yes.

Her parents, however, secretly investigated the boys she went out with, and regarded it as their right to listen in on her telephone calls—without, of course, admitting to her that they did so.

Sarah had got into the habit of reading at night and sleeping in the morning. This was repeatedly referred to as "laziness" by all members of the family. In fact, she slept rather less than they did, and they were trying to get her to take sleeping tablets to sleep more, and tranquillizers to "think" less. For it was not only the fact that Sarah lay in bed that upset them, it was also the fact that she was thinking so much. As Mrs. Danzig said,

> Sitting up all night thinking and not telling anyone what she thought. Not that we particularly want to know what Sarah's thinking or doing, although it's only natural that a mother should be curious.

Sarah's "thinking" worried them all a great deal. Mrs. Danzig knew that "thinking," especially a lot of "thinking," was liable to make you have peculiar thoughts, because it "turns the brain."

> . . . sitting up all night in a blue nightdress in the kitchen—just the lights on, nobody making a sound. She's thinking and thinking—goodness knows what the heck she's thinking about. It's enough to twist anybody's mind.

According to mother, father, and John, Sarah's breakdown was due to lying in bed "thinking" instead of getting up and occupying herself and meeting people. No matter how her mother shouted at her she would not stop "thinking," and to their greater alarm she thought inwardly, not out loud. She even pretended to put some beauty preparation on her legs as a pretext for staying up in her room and thinking. Mrs. Danzig reproached herself. She should have called in a psychiatrist sooner. They know how to handle such people.

> They could have knocked some sense into her. I should have called in a doctor, at that time, and said, "Look— she's upstairs, you talk to her." If she refused to listen to him—he's a medical man, he might give me another suggestion. It didn't *dawn* on me at the time that it was a psychiatric case, or whatever you call her.

Her father tells us that he came into a room and he saw Sarah just standing looking out of the window. He asked her what she was thinking, and she said, "I don't need to tell you."

Sarah and her brother argued in front of us about "thinking." Sarah claimed that John "thinks" also.

JOHN: Yes, but not like you do.

SARAH: Well, just yesterday I came into your bedroom and you were lying on your bed—thinking.

JOHN: No I wasn't.

SARAH: Yes you were.

JOHN: I was listening to the radio.

Reading the Bible was also a very doubtful activity, especially for a girl. Religion was one thing, but reading the Bible was another. The Bible was possibly all right to glance through, and perhaps, even, a religious person *should* do that; but to want to sit down and read it and make a fuss if it was missing from its usual place . . .

MOTHER: Well she couldn't find the Bible, raised havoc out of the bookcases—"Where is it?—That one's got it—this one's got it"—I said, "Who wants to read your Bible?" I said, "Is it normal for a girl to sit up all night and read the Bible all night?" I also think it's nice to read. I read. I might read a magazine or a book, but I've never read the Bible. I've never heard of it. If I saw another girl read the Bible, I would come home and say, "That girl's got a kink somewhere"— Yes, know about it, look at it for five minutes— just a glance through; but you never make a study of the Bible. I could never sit down and read the Bible for two to three solid hours. I don't think she reads it. I think she just glances at the pages.

INTERVIEWER: I'm a little surprised at this, I had the impression that this is what your husband would like.

MOTHER: What, to read the Bible all night?—Oh no, oh no, oh no. He likes to get down to things. He thinks every girl should know, you know have natural accomplishments. I used to teach her music. She didn't want to practise—all right, we'll drop that. And now with television, they don't want to. And she used to play—all right, don't learn. He likes her to go out with boys. He likes her to mix, to go to socials, you know, like debates. She used to like to go to debates, they used to have special film shows, you know, interest—show it to a group of people—Oh he likes her to have an interest in all these sort of *normal* things. We used to go very often, the four of us, not Ruth, she was too young—go out at night to the cinema or to a theatre—the four of us, and we'd go out and have dinner. Oh he's not—I tell you—he's been brought up—his father was very religious, he was an officer of the Synagogue and a great Hebrew Talmudist . . .

Sarah's thinking and reading of the Bible evoked a mixture of alarm, concern, dismay, and disparagement. Her brother scorned her, her mother told her she was lazy, her father rebuked her. Yet they all felt that they were judged in some way by her. But it was not difficult for them not to take seriously the stumbling efforts of a girl to come to terms with her experience.

The fact that she read the Bible in an effort to throw light on her present experience was completely incomprehensible to this family. Accustomed to meet with ridicule and admonitions not to be lazy, selfish, or ungrateful, and so on, she either kept silent or gave out a short statement from time to time that only caused her family to lament the more the calamity that had befallen them.

Sarah had taken seriously what she had been taught, so that when she discovered the double standards of her family she was bewildered. She could not bring herself to accept her brother's openly avowed double standards, which were her father's also, but unavowed by him. Indeed, she *was not allowed to do so*. Her mother and father both felt that this was necessary for John, but they insisted that she adopt their point of view without reservation. But it was impossible to do this without adopting their particular stratagems, and this they forbade her to do.

We have presented above only a small fragment of our data on this family. In this rest of our data the mystifications around this girl are in no way attenuated. Once more, we have given, we hope, *enough* to establish the social intelligibility of the events in this family that have prompted the diagnosis of schizophrenia "in" one of its members.

Insanity As Life-Historical Phenomenon and As Mental Disease: The Case of Ilse

Ludwig Binswanger
1958

I. INSANITY AS LIFE-HISTORICAL PHENOMENON

Life-History

Our patient is a thirty-nine-year-old intelligent woman. She was happily married, but not fully satisfied in her marriage, Protestant, religious, mother of three children, daughter of an extremely egotistical, hard and tyrannical father and an "angelic," self-effacing, touchingly kind mother who allowed herself to be treated by her husband like a slave and only lived for him.

From the time she was a child Ilse suffered greatly under these conditions, feeling powerless to change them. For three years she had shown symptoms of overstrain and "nervousness." Following a performance of *Hamlet*, an idea came to her mind to persuade her father through some decisive act to treat her mother more considerately. During her boarding school period she believed she had great influence upon him. Ilse's resolution to carry out her plan was reinforced through that scene in which Hamlet plans to murder the king at his prayer but shrinks back

from doing it. If at a particular time Hamlet had not missed his chance, he could have been saved, Ilse felt. She confessed to her husband that she planned something unusual and was only waiting for the right moment. Four months after the *Hamlet* performance, when asked for help against her father by her mother, she told her husband that she wanted to "demonstrate to her father what love can do." If he forbade her to do it, he would make her unhappy for the rest of her life; she had to "get rid of that."

One day, when her father had once again reproached her, she told him she knew of a way of saving him, and in front of her father she put her right hand up to her forearm into the burning stove, then held out her hands toward him with these words: "Look, this is to show you how much I love you!"

During the act she was oblivious to pain, although she suffered severe burns of the third degree with subsequent suppuration. During the four-week treatment she displayed tremendous energy and perseverance. Immediately after the act she appeared to be in an elated, heroic mood and directed the people around her, who had gotten panicky. Her father did change his behavior toward her mother for some weeks, but, to Ilse's great distress, soon new conflicts occurred. And yet, her husband found her, in the following months, more vigorous, agile, energetic, and busy than ever. Now, she announced, she had no other duties and could devote herself wholly to her husband and children. When her fourth child died in the

213

same year, she bravely overcame her grief but firmly believed that the loss was the atonement for her love for the doctor who had treated the child.

Eight months after the act she was busier and moodier than before and took too much upon herself, intellectually and physically; she read Freud, participated in a Dalcroze gymnastic class, became secretary of a Society for the Improvement of Women's Dress, but felt that her strength was decreasing, particularly before and after periods. One day, thirteen or fourteen months after the burning, she asked the family doctor whether in his opinion she could develop a mental disease. After another three months she decided to take a vacation. She felt like "staking everything on one card." She reported that she was tortured by thoughts which, she felt, were almost thoughts of insanity. . . .

After the patient was placed in our institute, the delusions of reference spread further, along with delusions of love. These latter manifested themselves not only in Ilse's belief that she was loved and tested by the doctors but also in her compulsion to love the doctors. "I cannot eat and drink anymore until the hunger and thirst of my soul are quenched. Please let me have the nourishment I need, you know it as well as I do." Ilse imagined that the doctors increased all the drives in her so as to make her purge herself of them[1]—the drive toward love and the drive toward the truth. That, to her, represented her "treatment," one which she felt was very strenuous. Soon she considered it merely a torture.

> It is not my fault that I got this way. You think it is delusions—religious delusions—that I think, speak, write like this. But this is not true; it is my nature, my innermost nature, which clamors for an outlet in order to relax again, or rather which you have dragged out of me with your torturous tools which torment me deeply. There is nothing other in me than what I have shown you, there is no breath of falsehood and no sensationalism in it, that I know of.
>
> I cannot know what is in you. What is in me, I know, and am telling you everything without reservations. But I *cannot* tell you what is in you; because from the way you have behaved toward me I could draw different conclusions, and I cannot know which is the right one. [*From a letter to her physician.*]

The fact that a picture of a winter scene was on the wall of her room was interpreted by her as an intention to make her "as cold as ice." Another time she had a feeling as though her fingers, hands, and forearms were of wet

clay—as though they were swollen and did not belong to her body at all.

When asked about the burning, she explained: "I wanted to demonstrate to my father that love is something that overcomes itself, not by words but by deeds. This should have had an effect on him like a lightning bolt, like a revelation, and should have made him stop living as an egotist. When the idea first came to me, it was for my mother's sake, but then I thought if I were to do it for his own sake it would be the right thing. I pitied him, and since then had felt even more love and understanding for him. I guess I must love all men so much because I loved my father so much."

Ilse passed through severe states of excitation with suicidal tendencies, mistaking of persons, and numerous ideas of reference, but without ever suffering from actual hallucinations. After thirteen months of institutional care Ilse could return to her home completely cured of her acute psychosis.

The *theme* around which this biography revolves is *father*. At the same time, it shows an attempt at mastering its theme. A sharp dissonance is noticeable, the contradiction between ecstatic love (an almost idolizing veneration of the father) and energetic rebellion against his tyranny, primarily his tyrannizing of the mother. The dissonance in this theme signifies an open, never-healing life sore; it could only be resolved by a change in the mind and behavior of the father, by a divorce of the parents, or by eliminating the father. All these roads were blocked by insurmountable external and internal obstacles. Thus, living turns into suffering from the dissonance of its main theme, into grievous floating in the pains of hopelessness. What from the angle of the world appears as hopelessness is, in terms of the "ego," irresolution, indetermination, shrinking away from decisions. This is the situation Hamlet is in. In his fate Ilse sees her own as in a mirror. The decision which she cannot make for herself she can, at last, make for Hamlet. She believes he should have killed the praying king without consideration of the situation and thus would have saved himself. Only such resolution to act would have saved him "from insanity!" Now the stone starts rolling. In her own situation, the possibility of eliminating the tyrant is excluded. The idea of parricide cannot develop, and if it did, her love for the father would interfere with the act. Both parents are dead set against divorce. What is left to her is an attempt to persuade the father to a change in attitude and behavior toward the mother. The theme that now offers itself is named *sacrifice*. For a sacrifice will offer Ilse the opportunity to prove her love to her father as well as to make the desired "impression." The "sacrifice of love" is designed to overcome the father's brutal tyranny. Through the sacrifice of love Ilse takes the brutality upon herself. It is she who submits to suffering from some brutal pain so that mother

---

[1] When she watched the cleaning of windows, she felt the urge to join in the wiping so that everything would become clean and pure. What Ilse called the "treatment" was, of course, her delusion. No psychoanalytical experiments whatsoever were conducted.

does not have to suffer any more. The father himself is "spared" throughout.

The intended effect of the sacrifice fails in the long run, the sacrifice proves in vain. The life-sore opens again, deeper and more painful than ever. The sacrifice was still a self-chosen decision, still a decision of the "self" to bring about a reconciliation of the discordant forces; but now the self is relieved of any decision. The self succumbs under the heavy task of pursuing further the leitmotif of its history. But the life task posed by the theme as such remains nonetheless and presses for a "solution." This self-effacing solution, according to her own insight, runs as follows: You *must* love all men so much because you love your father so much (*viz.*, delusions of love). This may be complemented by: You *must* attract the attention and interest of *all* people to yourself, because you have attracted the attention and the interest of your father to yourself; you *must* know what impression you are making upon *all* people because you wanted to make an impression upon your father; you must react to everything the others do because you wanted to know how your father reacted to *you*; in short, you must be "in the center of attention" of *all* people (*viz.*, delusions of reference). The lack of insight into the *must* of this loving and attracting-of-attention we call insanity. The cure for such insanity consists in the shaking off of the *must* and in the restoration of the rule of the self.

In our case, the restoration was a lasting one. Ilse stayed perfectly healthy up to her death at the age of seventy-three.

She was able to direct the theme "salvation" and "purification" into healthy channels, that is, to confirm it through social work. Advised and counseled by experts over a period of time, she successfully practiced as a psychological counselor and at times was also the leader of a psychological workshop group.

The Sacrifice

Much as war is described as a continuation of politics by different means, so in our case we could interpret Ilse's delusions as a continuation of her sacrifice, but by different means. Even the sacrifice itself could be explained as a continuation of the earlier life history, but with the help of a different instrument. Already the sacrifice was the outcome and expression of a very complex life-historical network of motives. The rational motive was an intention to make a deep impression upon the father so as to change his attitude and behavior toward the mother. This intention was to be carried out by way of the fire ordeal, of suffering extreme physical pain as proof of what love—her love for her father—could do. If one wants to emphasize convincingly a belief or an intention in the German language, one would say, "For that I would put my hand in the fire." Ilse actually did it. That she tried to confirm how serious she was in her belief and intention not to "let it go on," that is, not to tolerate her mother's treatment at the hands of her father any longer.

But by the same token, Ilse wanted to save the father himself by a sacrifice of love. This act also represents the realization of a salvation phantasy as we know it from psychoanalysis in connection with "incest phantasies." As such the sacrifice expresses a purification wish, the wish to be purged of the incest wish. The salvation of the father is, at the same time, the salvation of her own exaggerated love for her father. The fire offers itself as a proper medium since, like the water, it is in the service of purification and, in our case, of purification by self-inflicted torture, mutilation, repentance, and asceticism. Hence the sacrifice itself is an act of atonement. It serves the expression and confirmation of Ilse's love for her father as well as her atonement for this love. The ambivalent nature of neurotic and psychotic forms of expression has been, since Freud and Bleuler, generally recognized. Ilse appears as a twofold heroine offering a love sacrifice for the father (and only indirectly for the mother) as well as offering her self-sacrifice, the sacrifice of her love for the father. Furthermore the meaning and countermeaning of the sacrifice are expressed in the idea that out of the (partial) death through sacrifice new life was expected to grow: on one hand, the father was to be awakened to a new life, and on the other, her love for her father was to score a new living triumph. (The equation *fire = life* is known from antiquity—*e.g.*, from Heraclitus, and more recently from Paracelsus.)

. . .

We have seen that a verbal testimony of love to the father—perhaps expressed in the words: "I would risk my right hand to prove that my love does not shrink from any sacrifice, if only *you* make the sacrifice of your egotism and your tyranny toward mother"—that such *verbal* testimony was replaced by Ilse's *manual* testimony, her palpable affirmation, the sacrifice of her hand. As any sacrifice this, too, is an act of self-denial, of self-effacement and self-surrender. Hence it would be wrong to dispute the ethical meaning and content of this sacrifice. But that it was not a pure, let alone an "absolute," sacrifice was realized by Ilse herself. The motive of worry about the mother receded more and more behind the motive of the testimony of love to the father and of the test by fire of her influence upon him. The sacrifice is not pure but clouded by passion. The self-surrender is also a surrender of her inner heat to the ice-cold father, it expresses the "insane idea" of touching the father's cold heart by "something decisive," a "decisive event." For that something, Ilse, by no means accidentally, uses again a metaphor from the realm of fire; she wants to touch her father's heart with a "lightning bolt," not in order to sear it, but in order to melt it in the "fire" of her love. Following this, we may rightly say—if not with Ilse's own words—the sacrifice was to be a purifying storm in the close and oppressive atmosphere of her parents' home. Ilse's faith in the power of love was accompanied by a will to power in general, an arrogant drive to trespass storm-like, "like a lightning bolt," the boundaries of man. But Ilse trespasses these boundaries by no means only for the sake of her father, but just as much for the sake of herself. In her attempt to purify her passionate love for her father she tried to accomplish by a sudden violent act against herself, by an act of forced asceticism, what man is permitted to accomplish only in a steady process of slow maturation.

But the sacrifice was in every respect in vain. The lightning did not hit the father as deeply and as decisively as Ilse had hoped, nor did she herself emerge from the cataclysm genuinely purified. We shall understand this the better the more we can clarify for ourselves the meaning of a sacrifice. Such meaning does not exhaust itself in active testimony and substituting symbol; the deepest meaning of any sacrifice lies in *founding,* the founding of a union. The testimony of love must become a union of love to make the sacrifice "meaningful." By my testimony, by my confession of love, I am testifying to my love for you, I am confessing my love for you; but only in the union are you answering me, and only this answer is the foundation of the We. In Ilse's case, however, this answer is missing. The "lightning" does *not* strike, the storm did *not* purify the air, the union was *not* found. Hence the sacrifice of self-purification loses its meaning too. The founding of a new union with the father, purified, made sacred, and conditioned by the sacrifice, would have made the self-sacrifice, the extinction of passion, meaningful; through the failure of the union, of unity with the father on the level of a pure We, the self-purification becomes meaningless. The entire existence is now not only thrown back to the *status quo ante,* but faces a completely new situation: What now?

Insanity

Ilse's "innermost nature" was not made to resign. The inner fire continued burning until one day it threatened to kindle the whole existence. Her failure to establish the union, her shaken confidence, became distrust of all and of herself. The pride of self-conceit turned into the feeling of being threatened in her honor. Since her father cared little for her sacrifice, even spurned it, she came to feel not only misunderstood but actually wounded in her honor. To her love for father was added her extreme disappointment, her distrust in him as well as in her own mission and

strength. These feelings were joined by doubts which can be formulated as follows: Didn't he notice how serious I was about it? Did he believe that I was out for sensationalism, that I wanted to become the center of his interest only to "make an impression" on him and to test the power of my influence upon him? Didn't he notice how much I love him, doesn't he know how greatly he has hurt and offended me?

No discussion of all this came about, and none could come about. What could have been accomplished by words since not even the "deed" had been convincing (that is, not able to create the union). Now Ilse is forced into a defensive position. Everything now seems to depend upon her giving evidence of her good intention and sincerity, upon her defense of her honor and her definite purification of her passion. But here, again, she believes that she meets with resistance; the others refuse to believe her, deride her, scoff at her, just as her father had "scoffed" at her.

. . .

During her insanity, she repeats time and again protestations in defense of her honor, in defense against the reproach of sensationalism, of dishonesty, and of "delusions." They all sound like belated justifications of her sacrifice: *not* out of sensationalism, *not* to place herself in the center of (her mother's) interest, *not* out of self-conceit did she put her hand in the stove! Rather, it was her genuine aim to help her mother to an existence worthy of a human being. Nonetheless, the self-reproaches that her sacrifice was not made in full sincerity could not be silenced. Therefore, to her the treatment had to be a purification of her "drive for love and truth." Here again we face the ambivalence of psychotic manifestations: on one hand, Ilse must love *all* men so much because she loves father so much, and she must feel she is in the center of interest for *all* because she wanted to be in the center of interest for the father. On the other hand, she must make (purifying) amends *for* that love and *for* that wish to be in the center. As far and as long as she believes in the doctors' purifying intention and believes that she can interpret their intention in this sense, the doctors remain her friends and helpers; insofar and as long as she is certain that this is not the case they change into tormentors and enemies. But halfway between the two interpretive possibilities lurks the doubt about "what is in you," the lacking ability really to penetrate the inside of the others. Again, in her certainty about the others being ill-inclined toward her, watching her, we recognize her bad conscience and feelings of guilt (because of her "burning" love for her father). In this way the others become just as tyrannical, inflexible, and inaccessible to her love as is her father! Thus the entire dialectics of her relation to her father continue in the dialectics of her relations to her fellow men in general.

Hence, the actual meaning of her insanity rests in the

pluralization[2] of the father—in the transformation of the singular *thou* and of the dual *we* into the plurality of *you* (plural) and *we*. In this sense the insanity is an expression of the lifting of the "incest taboo." The "inner flames," heretofore constrained by this taboo, now break all dams and seize *all* men who come on the scene. Hence the *thou*, though desecrated and evaluated, is brought closer to its "natural destiny." But still, for Ilse, the married woman, the *thou* remains taboo, a cause of fear and reproach, the reproach that she was "man-crazy." In the dress-loving Figura Leu she sees as though in a mirror her own coquetry and craving for men, just as, in Hamlet, she saw a reflection of her own indecision. With Figura Leu she can identify in yet another respect; this girl is the most enchanting figure among the former lady-loves of the Landvogt; she is described as "standing bathed in light—a heavenly angel who celebrates a mystery." And it was she who refused to marry the Landvogt "because she never knew when she would be called away to that unknown land where the spirits travel."

The real sense of Ilse's insanity (or, as seen from the angle of the healthy, the non-sense of it) we have located in the leveling down and pluralization of the *thou*. We now see that this process is not confined to the positive love motion of attraction but that it extends to its "counter-meaning," to a negative motion of repulsion. Ilse's disappointment in the father develops—always by way of the pluralization of the *thou*—into the delusions of reference. The pluralization of the *thou* is the order principle by which the alleged disorder ("insanity") can be understood; it is the principle which permits us to see not just chaos but method in this insanity.

Thus, the scientific problem which presents itself to the psychiatrist in the form of Ilse's insanity has obtained its methodical foundation.

Review

Ilse's life-history impressed us as appropriate to our topic because it contains only one key theme and because its various phases can with increasing clarity be recognized and presented as specific variations of this theme. This key theme serves us as the *constant* which provides the key to our understanding of Ilse's life as a *history*. History is always thematic. The kind of themes which a person (or a people) is assigned by destiny or which he

selects for "elaboration," and the manner in which he varies them, are not only decisive for his history but *are* his history. In Ilse's case the constant is, as we saw, the father theme. The historic theme, like all others, is not "absolute," not separated from the entire life situation, but it is a very real life problem and as such dominates the life history. It is this father, this adored cold tyrant, who enslaves the beloved mother and poisons the life of Ilse and her family with a close and oppressive atmosphere from which Ilse the child, and Ilse the woman and mother, never manages to emerge and in which she drags her life on in complete helplessness and hopelessness. This marks the first phase of her life-history.

In her fourth life-decade the pressure of this atmosphere condenses so as to produce an intolerable torture. More and more Ilse realizes that only a storm, a lightning bolt, can purify the atmosphere. Her key problem sharpens into a crisis. Her entire existence is in a turmoil and she stakes everything on one chance. It is true, Ilse has independently reached a decisive resolution, but now the self is ruled by this resolution to the point of being driven; thus, it desires nothing more than to free itself from being driven by means of the act. Already, the self is not any more in control of itself; the key problem is overpowering it. This is the second phase of this life history. It comes to its close in the pathetically violent solution of the crisis through action, through the fire sacrifice.

The third phase is initiated by self-mastery regained through the act; but this control is soon upset by another compulsion to be driven, another seemingly aimless restlessness which makes her fall for all sorts of side aims, and is, about fifteen months after the act, replaced by a new variation of the never-ceasing key theme—to be sure, by very different means. First, the passive helplessness, then the active, self-chosen but no longer self-empowered act, and then the extreme "self-disempowering," the yielding to the "theme" that now assumes unlimited power. The theme, of course, is not just a theme but an argument between "I and the world," sharpened by a definite existential situation. This theme now no longer worries about limitations but sweeps the whole existence along with it, perceiving only itself and living only for itself. It forces the person whom it rules to meet the "father" all over in the world of fellow men (*Mitwelt*) and to struggle with it in love and hatred, fight and surrender, and again and again in conflict. The father, to Ilse, was not merely a *thou* but was at the same time an object of *sorge* (combination of "care" and "worry"), something to be "taken at something"[3] (potentially and actually), something to be impressed and influenced. And Ilse, similarly, was accepted

---

[2] [By "pluralization," a term which is used frequently on this and the following pages Binswanger means the spreading, extending of Ilse's relationship to her father to cover a relationship with all men. Pluralization is a dispersing, a "leveling down," as Binswanger puts it on the following page, and thus changes the central and real value of the relationship.—Translator.]

---

[3] See footnote 1.

and rejected by him, disappointed, her honor wounded and tyrannized. Accordingly, things now develop between her and the world-around (*Umwelt*). Instead of father, the latter is now the power with which no union can be formed, no peaceful agreement or accord can be reached. But where thou and object, love and worry, are in constant conflict, the power becomes an insoluble riddle, a riddlesome power. Just as the father's harshness and coldness, inaccessibility to love and sacrifice, turned into a torturous riddle for Ilse, so the entire environment now becomes an enigmatic power; at one time it is a loving You, one to which she would like to surrender not just her hand but herself altogether; at another time it is a harsh, loveless, inaccessible world which scoffs at her love, derides and humiliates her, wounds her honor. Her entire existence is now limited to the motions and unrest of being attracted and being rejected. But with the pluralization of You, with the theme extended all over her existence without limit, and with the loss of the original thematic goal, the father, no solution of the problem is possible any more. The theme spends itself on an inappropriate object, it rotates in eternal repetition around itself. The only remaining question is . . . whether existence will find a way out of this form of self-discussion, return to itself and so clear the road for new possibilities for a solution or whether it will be blunted in the process by endlessly repeating and stereotyping the discussion as such through acts, behavior, or phrases. But as long as the theme remains the theme (even the stereotypization is . . . still thematic variation) there is life-history. . . .

Finally, we have observed a fourth phase in her life-history reaching the end of life, a phase in which the self regained command and led the life-historical problem toward a new but this time definite solution. The pressure of helplessness and indecision, the pathos of lightning swift action driven back and forth by it, are eventually all replaced by what could be termed a "sound" solution: the switching of the problems of love, cleansing, and resistance onto the track of goal-directed and methodical, painstaking, and patient psychological work—in short, into the world of practice. The thou and the world-around (*Umwelt*) were finally reconciled in readiness to help and work for the fellow man. The gap between the thou and the resistance of the apathetic world was bridged, and that resistance showed itself no longer in the "other fellow's" harshness, coldness, contempt, and scorn but in his suffering, which is accessible to work and can be overcome by work.

We understand that in the invention of a musical theme and in the formulation of its variations the total musical existence of the composer plays a decisive part. Similarly, in the acceptance of a life-historical theme and in the formulation of its variations the total existence of the person prevails. The father theme, therefore, is by no means the ultimate; we must not absolutize the "father-complex" into an independent "being." Much less should we, in the manner of psychoanalysis, see in this history merely a history of the libido, of its fixation onto father, its forced withdrawal from father, and its eventual transference to the world-around. For in that way we would misinterpret essential possibilities of human existence into genetic developmental processes, reduce history to natural history. But only human existence is genuinely historical. Although its history is determined by the themes it has been assigned and on which it works and even though its history consists in having and working out these themes, still its historicity rests upon its attitude toward its "ground." Although existence does not lay its own ground itself but takes it over as its being and heritage, it still is left with freedom in relation to the ground. Having a father and a mother is part of man's being, just as is having an organism and a history. (Therefore, where parents are "missing" existence can be exposed to the most serious crises.) But that Ilse got just that father and that mother was her destiny, received as a heritage and as a task; how to bear up under this destiny was the problem of her existence. Hence, in her "father complex" were destiny *and* freedom at work. Both are to be held "responsible" for the choice of the life-historical theme and the formulation of its variations.

Finally, we have to confess that in our case we do not even know the theme in its original form, the form it had in Ilse's childhood. This is not only a flaw in our life-historical discussion, but a real gap. If we knew the infantile arch-form of the father theme, we would probably recognize in it the seeds of all possibilities which we found developed and utilized in the later variations.

Insanity, Existential Analysis, and "Empathy"

Speaking of the life-historical phenomena of helplessness, readiness to sacrifice, insanity, and eventually of work, we also feel obliged to investigate and describe these phenomena in respect to their phenomenal structure. This would be the task of existential analysis or of anthropological phenomenology. All these phenomena are phenomena of being-in-the-world-beyond-the-world; they are specific forms of it and produce, in turn, specific forms of being-oneself and not-being-oneself, being-together and not-being together, of spatialization and temporalization, etc. In this way, the life-historical analysis presses beyond itself toward a phenomenological existential analysis. Since we deal with these questions elsewhere, we may stop at this point. But it should be emphasized that the kind and mode of the given being-in-the-world-beyond-the-world also determines the way in which we fellow men communicate with the person in the various phases of his or her life-history, which is to say, the way we sympathize and come to an understanding with him. The degree of potential and real agreement between my world and his world determines the degree of possible communication or "understanding."

We are now approaching the problem which is usually characterized by the very vague term "empathy." But this label does not help us to get farther; wherever feeling and feelings are introduced, we have to grope as in a fog. We can only proceed into clearer air when we submit to the necessary effort to examine and describe that feeling or feelings in regard to their phenomenal mode of being and their phenomenological content. In the case of "empathy," e.g., we would have to examine to what degree it is phenomenon of *warmth,* a phenomenon of the possibility or impossibility of fusing the *chaleur intime* (as in our instance); or a vocal or *sound* phenomenon, as when the poet Hoelderlin writes to his mother that there could not be a sound alive in her soul with which his soul would not chime in; or phenomenon of *touch,* as when we say, "your sorrow, your joy touches me; or a phenomenon of *sharing* as expressed by Diotima in Hoelderlin's *Hyperion*—"He who understand you must share your greatness and your desperation"; or a phenomenon of *participation,* as in the saying, "I partake in your grief"; or, lastly, a phenomenon of *"identification,"* as when we say, "I would have done the same in your place" (in contrast to, "I don't understand how you could act that way.") All these modes of expression refer to certain phenomenal, intentional, and preintentional modes of being-together (*Mitseinandersein*) and co-being (*Mitsein*) which would have first to be analyzed before the total phenomenon of empathy could be made comprehensive and clarifiable. For this reason alone, the differentiation of psychic life with which we can empathize from psychic life with which we cannot empathize (schizophrenics) loses a great deal of its scientific value, apart from the fact that the limits of empathic possibilities are purely objective and vary according to the empathic ability and "imagination" of the investigator.

Fortunately, today we are in a position to overcome the dichotomy between empathizable and nonempathizable psychic life, because we now have at our disposal a method that enables us to analyze phenomenologically the given being-in-the-world independently from that dichotomy. This method is the anthropological or existential-analytical one which owes its existence to Husserl's phenomenology and which received its decisive stimulation from Heidegger's existential "*Daseins analysis.*" Without yet entering this area we have had to carry the problem of communication to this point in order to find the actual starting point for our approach to the problem, *insanity as a mental disease.*

II. INSANITY AS A MENTAL DISEASE

Wherever in a scientific of prescientific context mental illness is discussed, one speaks of psychic disease symptoms in a certain person. But *what* makes its appearance in these symptoms is, just as in the case of physical illness, by no means "the disease." Indeed, the latter does not at all show in the symptoms; the symptoms rather refer to something which is hidden "behind" them. The disease itself has yet to be brought to light or to be revealed, with the symptoms serving as guides. What are these symptoms like?

At this point, let us look at our case and specifically at Ilse's sacrifice, and let us see how a layman would react to such an act. He would probably ask himself: Would I have done this, or could I have done this in Ilse's place? And his answer would be: No, no normal person would do a thing like this in our day and time. And in view of the pluralization of the "Thou," he would have felt even more emphatically: "Now this woman has gone completely crazy?" So we see that the judgment on the sickness or health is subject to the norm of the social attitude. If an act, behavior, or verbalization deviates from that norm, it is judged even by the layman as morbid, as a symptom of an illness. However, there may be people who see in the sacrifice the expression of a genuinely religious or ethical self-effacement, of a genuinely ethical readiness for sacrifice and love for one's fellow man; such persons would strongly reject the idea that the sacrifice be considered a symptom of disease. We realize that the norm of behavior is by no means fixed once for all, but that it varies according to an individual's education and culture or to a cultural area. What appears abnormal—or a deviation from the norm—to one person may look to another quite normal, or even like the supreme expression of a norm; the judgment "sick" or "sound" is accordingly formed within a cultural frame of reference. Naturally, the same is true for insanity. What we of the twentieth century consider a symptom of disease was seen by the Greeks as a blow from Apollo or as the work of the Furies and by the people of the Christian Middle Ages as possession by the Devil. What at the peak of Pietism could pass for an expression of supreme piety would today be considered a phenomenon of morbid self-reflection and morbid guilt feelings, and so forth. But all this cannot alter the fact that a person is judged "sick" wherever his social behavior deviates from the respective norm of social behavior and thus appears conspicuous or strange.

But we must not be content with this. Although we register by our judgment the deviation from the norm of social behavior, this judgment rests on facts that are pre- and irrational, namely, facts from the area of *communica-*

tio (social intercourse) and of *communio* (love). For example, someone who considers Ilse's sacrifice morbid discloses thereby that such an act or, more correctly, that Ilse in carrying through such an act strikes him as "strange," which is to say that something has got between him and her which is experienced by him as a barrier to *communicatio* and, even more so, to *communio*, the obstacle, turns into an object[4] (of conspicuousness, avoidance, pity, judgment, etc.). Thereby I separate or remove myself from my fellow men, and the closeness of sympathy and intercourse changes into the distance of objective regard, observation, and judgment. Since the manifestation of love and the possibility of communication also greatly depend upon the membership in a cultural community, the cultural relatedness of the judgment "sick" must still be upheld. But we did wish to demonstrate that the symptoms of disease with which psychiatry deals refer to facts in the fellow-human area of sympathy and intercourse or, more precisely, that they are facts of sympathy and intercourse, in short, of understanding in the widest sense of the word.

Even the psychiatrist proceeds at first not unlike the layman. He, too, *judges* Ilse's sacrifice, and he often does so still in a moralizing fashion. He would, for instance, characterize the strangeness of this action as an act of "exaggerated" or "eccentric" love, or as bizarre or deranged, just as he describes the behavior of a hebephrenic or manic as insolent, reckless, frivolous. It appears obvious that he cannot be satisfied with such "subjective" criteria which vary from person to person and from culture to culture, but that he will have to search for comparatively definite criteria. This calls not only for a conscientious review and sifting of the total empirical material of abnormal social behavior but also for a new frame of reference out of which and by which the psychiatric judgment is formed. Such a frame of reference he can find not in the culture, as we know, but in nature. Therefore he can only reach his scientific goal if he succeeds in understanding culturally related behavior as naturally conditioned.

To get to this point the psychiatrist had first to collect and classify observational material like a botanist or zoologist, from a natural-scientific viewpoint, in order to survey and organize it within a natural-scientific system. He sees the complex and dramatic life-historical *phenomenon* of the sacrifice as an individual *event* "in time" and "in" a human being, he places it in the category of bizarre, absurd, or "eccentric" acts, traces them perhaps to the class of "schizoid" or schizophrenic behavior, and lists the latter as a symptom of schizophrenia. It is true that in so doing he has completely neglected the life-historical

structure and significance of the sacrifice; instead, he has used the natural-scientific method of subsumption and now knows in which disease category to include the action.[5] With this, he has reached his first goal, the formation of a diagnostic judgment.

But now we have to ask ourselves: what has happened here? We have, to be sure, far surpassed the concept of abnormality. Where we speak of disease symptoms and make a diagnostic judgment, quite a different frame of reference appears to be in force. It is neither a cultural nor a purely natural-scientific-biological one, but a medical one; it is the reference system of medical pathology. If we judge abnormal social behavior—a cultural fact—psychiatrically as a pathological phenomenon, we have left the area of purely biological judgment and entered the area of judgment of biological *purpose*, just as if we had to deal with physical abnormal behavior. Health and illness are value concepts, objects of judgments based on biological purpose, regardless of whether we measure them with Virchow by the purpose of safety of the organism (illness as threat or danger), with Krehl by the purpose of efficiency and vitality (illness as their limitation), or with Freud by the purpose of enjoyment of life (illness as suffering). The psychiatrist who judges the life-historical phenomenon of insanity or of the sacrifice as symptoms of schizophrenia or generally of a mental disease expresses much more than the fact that he considers them abnormal behavior—namely, that he sees in them a threat, a limitation, a suffering. But he does not stop there, he does not rest until he has, at least, tried to retrace this threat, this limitation, this suffering, to events in a natural object—the one which alone permits us to regard man wholly as a natural object (or to reduce him to it) even if with the greatest loss in observable reality (*anschaulicher Wirklichkeit*). This natural object is the *organism* in the sense of the total context of living and functioning of a human individual.[6] Hence, that which in

---

[4] *Viz.*, René Le Senne, *Obstacle et valeur* (Paris: Editions Montaigne).

[5] We have omitted the question of whether the sacrifice already constitutes the beginning of a schizophrenic episode, a suspicion which is supported among other things by the patient's state of schizophrenia.

[6] But it has to be mentioned that the *complete* reduction of man to his organism is only possible "in abstracto," and that the seeming riddle of the psycho-physical connection stems only from that abstraction. In "reality" there is no organism and no brain that could not be claimed by someone as "my" organism or "my" brain. The possessive relation, however, is fundamentally removed from the categories of natural science. It does not partake in determining what is to be considered an object of nature. This problem had already been touched by Kant when he emphasizes the "trap" in the question of the location of the soul in the bodily world, stressing that the body whose changes are *my* changes is *my* body, and that its location is *my* location. This points already to the fact that "my body" must always at the same time, mean "myself." Later, Hoenigswald (Psychology of Thinking) placed the problem of the *praesenzielle Possessivbestimmung* in the

this context is indicated or registered by the disease symptom, that hidden something to which the symptom refers, is threats to or restrictions of the organism—in short, disturbances in the efficiency or functions of the organism. Of course, what is meant here is only the reference system in general within which the psychiatric-medical judgment occurs.

In the act of passing the psychiatric judgment the psychiatrist does not have to be conscious of this (teleological) system of reference. Indeed, between this system of reference and the given facts to be judged extends the entire empirical knowledge of psychiatry and knowledge of the aforementioned "system" of psychiatric-medical *pathology* developed in accordance with purely natural-scientific principles. It is that knowledge alone on which the psychiatric judgment rests. "Diagnosis" (*diagnosko*) means to discern precisely, to examine accurately, and to *decide* on the basis of such examination and discernment. Only through exact investigation and differentiation of the signs and symptoms of illness—which calls for familiarization and experience with psychiatric pathology—is the physician able to diagnose the hidden disorder to which these signs and symptoms refer and through which it registers. Thereby, however, the hidden is only named— *i.e.*, determined as here and now existent in the organism —but by no means is it revealed in its being (*Sein*) or essence. What psychiatry wants to do and is in a position to do is not at all a revelation of that essence but an increasingly precise and ever deeper penetration into the existing medical fact—as, for example, the fact of schizophrenia—into the causes of its existence and the possibilities of fighting and removing those causes and their effects. Actually revelation of being (essence) is here as everywhere only possible by philosophical ("ontological") revelation.

The reduction of human life-history to events in the organism occurs not simply under the pressure of the natural-scientific-medical method and its successes; it can be and has been philosophically argued that on all occasions where illness is discussed, one has eventually to resort to the organism. . . . But there still remains the great psychiatric problem of what in a behavior diagnosed as pathological can be reduced from a disturbance

of communication to a disturbance in the organism, particularly in the brain. This will always be determined by the currents of contemporary scientific fashion, as so alarmingly demonstrated by positivism. But at this point philosophical demand and empirical research join hands. Whereas the former warns us not to give up a method prematurely and to avoid *Metabasis eis allo genos*, our very case shows how necessary it is to pursue the life-history all the way into insanity. We can demonstrate thereby that it is not permissible to isolate from that insanity single links, such as Ilse's delusions of love or her ideas of reference or the muddy feeling in her hands and their apartness from the body, and to project them separated from the organism or the brain. All we can say is that the total form in which the life-historical theme is treated, the form of solution to the task which is posed by the theme, can be pathological and thus dependent on disturbances in the central organ. Anything beyond this is in the area of brain-pathological speculation; for it is not the "brain" that thinks and treats a life-historical theme, but the "man" (*der Mensch*).

Of course, the question could be raised, what would have become of Ilse if the father had accepted her sacrifice, if he had formed a new union with her and if thereby her love to him had been "purified"? It is very possible, if not sure, that the illness would have come to a standstill or would have assumed a different form. This possibility in itself—and even more so the possibility of "active" psychotherapy in psychoneuroses—suffices to prove that man does not "consist of psyche and soma" but that the "organism" as such is much more than and something different from a mere organism and that the psyche is altogether something different from a mere psyche.[7] Man is and remains a unit. He is not "divided into" body and psyche; rather, the body is also psyche and the psyche is also body. Although not "identical" in empirical observation, the two are borderline concepts mutually calling for each other; considered in separation, however, they are purely theoretical constructs. Only from such a viewpoint are we able to understand that a life-historical turn may bring about a change in physiological events, that a change in the latter can cause a turn in the manner in which a life-historical theme is formulated.

center of the discussion on the coordination of the psyche with the physis, pointing out why the coordination of the psyche to the brain has to be dropped, and that only *my* brain, as the condition for the objectivity of thinking, has an original (*urspruengliche*) relation to the world of norms.

[7] The assumption that these possibilities prove "to what degree psychic and physical events interact" could only be made if one wishes to ingratiate oneself with the psycho-physical theory.

Ecological Therapy

The Concept of a "Therapeutic Milieu"

Fritz Redl
1959

Speculations about the therapeutic value of the "milieu" in which our patients live are neither as new nor as revolutionary as the enthusiasts, as well as the detractors of "milieu therapy" occasionally want them to appear. If I may risk shocking you so early in the game, the most extreme degree of "holy respect" for the tremendous impact that even the "little things" in an environment can have is represented in the original description of the conditions for a Freudian psychoanalytic hour. The ritual of interaction between patient and therapist is certainly sharply circumscribed. Even items such as horizontality of body posture and geographical placement of the analyst's chair are considered important conditions. Of course, the "basic rule" must be strictly adhered to, there should be no noises from the analyst's children coming through from the next room, one would worry whether patients might meet each other on the way out or in. The idea that months of solid work even by the greatest genius of transference manipulation might be endangered if doctor and patient should happen to meet at the Austrian equivalent of a cocktail party, instead of in their usual office terrain, is certainly impressive evidence for the great impact classical psychoanalysis has ascribed to factors such as time, space, and other "external givens."

If you now want to argue with me by reminding me that all this is true only for the duration of the 50-minute hour, and that other "milieu" factors in the patient's wider circle of life have not been deemed as relevant, then I might concede that point. But even so, I would like to remind you that we have always had a holy respect for two sets of "milieu" factors, at least in child analysis: we have always lived under the terror that the parents or teachers of our child patients might do things to them which would be so traumatic that we could, of course, not analyze them while all this was going on; and we would insist we couldn't touch a case unless we could get the child out of the terrain of parental sex life and into a bed of his own, or unless the parents stopped some of the more extreme forms of punitive suppressiveness at once. These are only a few of the illustrations we could think of. You will find a much more impressive list of "milieu variables," which certainly need to be influenced by the therapist, in Anna Freud's classic, *Introduction to the Technique of Child Analysis*, though not under that heading, of course.

The other case in point of my argument that even classical psychoanalysis has not neglected concern with "milieu" influences as much as it is supposed to have, relates to our evaluation of failure and success. At least in our informal appraisals I have time and again observed how easily we ascribe the breakdown of a child analysis to the "negative factors in the youngster's environment," and I have found in myself an inclination to do the same with the other fellow's successes. If my colleague seems to have presented an unusual piece of therapeutic "breakthrough," I find the temptation strong to look for the good luck he had with all the supportive factors that were present in his case and which, to my narcissism, seem to explain his success much better than the technical argument he put forth.

Now, seriously, if we secretly allow "milieu particles" to weigh so strongly that they can make and break even the most skillfully developed emotional therapy bridges between patient and doctor, hadn't we better look into this some more?

The fortunate fact that the answer to this question has, historically, been an enthusiastic "yes," however, has started us off in another problem-direction. Since more and more of us got impressed by more and more "factors" which in some way or other could be subsumed under the "milieu" term, the word has assumed such a variety of connotations that scientific communication has been overstimulated, but at the same time blocked in its development toward precision.

Since avoiding the traps of early concept confusion is an important prelude to a more rigid examination of meanings and to their appropriate scope, we might allow ourselves the luxury of at least a short list of "dangers we ought to watch out for from now on," provided we keep it telegram-style, so as not to take too much attention from the major theme. Since time and space for argument is dear, I shall be presumptuous enough to confront you simply with my personal conclusions, and offer them as warning posts, without further apology.

TRAPS FOR THE MILIEU CONCEPT

1. The cry for *the* therapeutic milieu as a general slogan is futile and in this wide formulation the term doesn't mean a thing. No milieu is "good" or "bad" in itself—it all depends. And it depends on more factors than I want to list, though some of them will turn up as we go along.

2. It won't do to use our own philosophical, ethical, political convictions, or our taste buds, in order to find out what really has or has not "therapeutic effect." Even the most respectable clinical discussions around this theme drift all too easily into A's trying to convince B that his setup is too "autocratic," or that what he called "democratic" group management isn't really good for those youngsters. Whether a ward should have rules, how many and which, must not lead to an argument between those who like rules and those who don't; I have seen many a scientific discussion end up in the same personal taste-bud battle that one otherwise finds acceptable only when people talk about religions or brands of cars.

3. Even a concept of "total milieu therapy" does not imply that all aspects of a given milieu are equally relevant in all moments in clinical life. All games, for instance, have some kind of "social structure" and as part of that, some kind of "pecking order" which determines the power position of the players for the duration of the game. Whether the specific pecking order of the game I let them play today had anything to do with the fact that it blew up in my face after five minutes is a question that can be answered only in empirical terms. I know of cases where the pecking order was clearly it; I have to look no further. I know of others where it was of no *clinical* relevance at the time. The boys blew up because they got too scared

playing hide-and-seek with flashlights in the dark. In short, the scientific establishment of a given milieu aspect as a theoretically valid and important one does not substitute for the need for a diagnosis on the spot. It alone can differentiate between potential milieu impacts and actual ones in each case.

4. The idea of the "modern" and therefore social-science-conscious psychiatrist that he has to sell out to the sociologist if he wants to have his "ward milieu" studied properly is the bunk. Of course, any thoughtful appraisal of a hospital milieu will contain many variables which the mother discipline of a given psychiatrist may never have dreamed about. On the other hand, the thing that counts is not only the description of a variable, but the assessment of the potential impact on the treatment process of a given group of patients. That is basically a *clinical* matter, and it remains the clinician's task. The discipline that merges social science with clinical criteria in a balanced way still has to be invented. There is no short cut to it either by psychiatry's stealing particles of social science concepts or by selling out to the social scientist's domain.

5. The frequently voiced expectation that the discovery of what "milieu" one needs would automatically make it easy to produce that style of milieu in a given place is downright naïve. An instrumentology for the creation of "ward atmosphere," of "clinically correct policies of behavioral intervention," etc., has yet to be created, and it will cost blood and sweat to get it. The idea that all it takes to have a "good treatment milieu" is for a milieu-convinced ward boss to make his nurses feel comfortable with him, and to hold a few gripe sessions between patients and staff, is a daydream, the simplicity of which we can no longer afford.

"THERAPEUTIC"—IN WHICH RESPECT?

The worst trap that explorers of the milieu idea sometimes seem to be goaded into is the ubiquitous use of the term "therapeutic," if it is coupled as an adjective, with "milieu" as a noun. I have described the seven most common meanings squeezed into this word in scientific writings and scientific discussions elsewhere,[1] but I must at least point at this possible confusion before we go on. Whenever people demand that a really good "therapeutic milieu" have this or that quality to it, they may refer to any one—or a combination of—the following issues:

---

[1] "The Meaning of 'Therapeutic Milieu,'" in *Symposium on Preventive and Social Psychiatry*, 15–17 April 1957, Walter Reed Army Institute of Research (Washington, D.C.: U.S. Government Printing Office, 1958).

1. Therapeutic—meaning: *don't put poison in their soup.*

   Example—Demand for absence of crude forms of punishment in a place that calls itself a "residential treatment center."

2. Therapeutic—meaning: *you still have to feed them,* even though that has little to do directly with a specific operation you are planning to perform.

   Example—Youngsters need an activity program, so if you keep them for a while you'd better see that they get it, even if your specific theory of psychiatry thinks nothing of the direct implication of play life and activity diet in terms of therapy as such.

3. Therapeutic—meaning: *developmental phase appropriateness and cultural background awareness.*

   Example—It would not be therapeutic to keep adolescents in an infantilizing "little boy and girl" atmosphere; or: a fine lady fussing over a little boy's hair grooming might convey "warmth" to a neglected middle-class child, but would simply be viewed as a hostile pest by a young toughie from the other side of the tracks.

4. Therapeutic—meaning: *clinically elastic.*

   Example—The fact that rules and regulations were too rigid to fit particular disturbance patterns or needs of patients, I have heard referred to as "untherapeutic," and with all due respect to numbers and group psychology, there is a point where the inability to make exceptions becomes "untherapeutic" too.

5. Therapeutic—meaning: *encompassing fringe-area treatment goals.*

   Example—Johnny is here for treatment of his kleptomania. His therapist works hard on that in individual therapy. Johnny also has a severe deficiency in school learning, and is clumsy in his play life with contemporaries. Even while the therapist is not yet in a position to pull any of these factors in, some other aspect of the milieu to which Johnny is exposed must give him experiences in this direction. Or else, the place is not "therapeutic enough" for him.

6. Therapeutic—in terms of *"the milieu and I."*

   Example—Some types of cases with deficient superego formation can be lured into identification with value issues only through the detour of an identification with the group code within which they live. For those cases the "therapist" is only one of the therapeutic agents. The "institutional atmosphere" that makes the child want to identify with what it stands for is another, *on equal rights.* In this case, this part of the "milieu" is expected to become a direct partner in treatment of the specific disturbance for which the child was brought in.

7. Therapeutic—in terms of *re-education for life.*

   Example—Especially for larger institutions the demand is often made that the institutions should not only provide people who treat the patient, but that they should also have features in them which come as close to "real life outside" as is possible, or else they wouldn't be "therapeutic enough." Thus, all those features that would seem to be needed for a very sick person are considered as rather countertherapeutic and bad, though unfortunately still necessary, while all semblance to open community life is considered a therapeutic ingredient in its own right. How far one and the same institution can cater to illness and at the same time lure into normality is then often a case for debate.

Enough of this dissection of an adjective. I hope I am understood correctly: Any one of these meanings of the term "therapeutic" is a justified issue in its own right. Any one of them may, in a given case, assume priority importance or may fade out in relevance to the zero point. All I am trying to convey is the importance of remembering who is talking about what—and about which patients—when we use the term in a scientific free-for-all. So far I haven't been too impressed with our ability to do so.

By the way, even in all those seven cases the term "therapeutic" may still be used in a double frame of reference: (a) Was it therapeutic for a given patient—if so, how do you know? (b) Is this expected to be potentially "therapeutic"—meaning beneficial for the treatment goal—from what I know about the basic nature of the issue under debate? These two frames of reference need to be kept asunder too.

A "MILIEU"—WHAT'S IN IT?

Obviously I am not going to use the term in the nearly global meaning which its theft from the French language originally insinuated. For practical reasons, I am going to talk here only of one sort of milieu concept: of a "milieu" artificially created for the purpose of the treatment of a group of youngsters. Within this confine you can make it somewhat wider if you want, and think of the "Children's Psychiatric Unit" on the fourth, eighth, or ninth floor of a large hospital, or you may hold before your eyes, while I am speaking, a small residential treatment home for children that is not part of a large unit. Of course, I know that the similarity of what I am talking about to other types of setups may be quite great, but I can't cover them all. Hence, anything else you hold before your eyes while I talk, you do strictly at your own risk.

So, here we are on the doorstep of that treatment home or at the keyhole of that hospital ward. And now you ask me: If you could plan things the way you wanted to, which are the most important "items" in your milieu that will sooner or later become terribly relevant for better or for worse? The choice is hard, and only such a tough proposition gets me over the guilt feeling for oversimplifying and listing items out of context.

1. *The social structure.* This is some term, and I have yet to see the psychiatrist that isn't stunned for a moment at its momentum—many would run and hire a sociologist on the spot. Being short on time, I have no choice, but let me hurry and add: this term in itself is as extendible and collapsible as a balloon. It doesn't mean much without specifications. So, let me just list a few of the things I have in mind.

a) A hospital ward is more like a *harem society than a family,* no matter how motherly or fatherly the particular nurses and doctors may feel toward their youngsters. The place I run at the moment is purposely shaped as much as possible after the model of an American camp, which is the only pattern I could find which children would be familiar with, where a lot of adults walk through children's lives in older brother and parentlike roles without pretending it to be an equivalent to family life.

b) *The role distribution* of the adult figures can be of terrific importance for the amount of clarity with which children perceive what it is all about. Outspokenly or not, sooner or later they must become clear about just who can or cannot be expected to decide what; otherwise, how would one know when one is getting the run-around?

c) The *pecking order* of any outfit does not long remain a secret to an open door neighborhood-

wise toughie, no matter how dumb he may be otherwise. He also smells the outspoken "pecking order" among the adults who take care of him, no matter how carefully disguised it may be under professional role titles or Civil Service Classification codes.

d) The *communication network* of any given institution is an integral part of its "social structure." Just who can be approached about listening to what, is quite a task to learn; and to figure out the real communication lines that are open and those which are secretly clogged in the adult communication network is usually an unsoluble task except for the suspicious outside researcher.

I mentioned only four illustrations of all the things I want included under "social structure." There are many more, and I have no quarrel with the rich inventory many social scientists have invented for this. The quarrel I have goes all against oversimplification, and if you tell me social structure is only what goes into a power line drawing or a sociogram, or that social structure is the only important variable in "milieu" that psychiatrists have neglected in the past, then you have me in a mood to fight. By the way—if I list "social structure" as one of the important milieu variables, I'd better add in a hurry: a mere listing or description of the social structure extant on a given ward is of no interest to me at all if it doesn't go further than that. From a clinical angle, the excitement begins *after* the sociologist tells me what social structure I have before me. Then I really want to know: What does it do to my therapeutic goals? What does it imply for my choice in techniques? In which phase of the therapy of my children is it an asset, and in which other phase does it turn into a serious block? To use just one example for the clinical question to be added to the social scientist's answer: The kind of ward I run—harem society style—makes individual attachments of child to worker difficult to achieve; on the other hand, it pleasantly dilutes too excited libidinous attachment-needs into more harmless distribution over a larger number of live props. Question: Is that good or bad, and for whom during what phase of their treatment?

2. *The value system that oozes out of our pores.* Some people subsume that under social structure. I think I have reasons to want a separate place for it here, but let's not waste time on the question why. The fact is, the youngsters not only respond to what we say or put in mimeographed writing; they smell our value-feelings even when we don't notice our own body odor any more. I am not sure how, and I can't wait until I find out. But I do need to find out which value items are there to smell. Does the arrangement of my furniture call me a liar while

I make a speech about how much at home I want them to feel, or does that gleam in a counselor's eye tell the child: "You are still wanted," even though he means it if he says he won't let you cut up the tablecloth? By the way, in some value studies I have missed one angle many times: the *clinical convictions* of what is professionally correct handling, which sometimes even questionnaire-clumsy workers on a low salary level may develop, and which become a motivating source for their behavior in its own right, besides their own personal moral convictions or their power drives.

3. *Routines, rituals, and behavioral regulations.* The sequence of events and the conditions under which people undergo certain repetitive maneuvers in their life space can have a strong impact on whether they can keep themselves under control, or whether their impulse-control balance breaks down. Since Bruno Bettelheim's classic description of the events inside a child while he seems engaged in the process of getting up or getting himself to sleep, no more words should have to be said about this. And yet, many "therapeutic milieu" discussions still waste their time on arguments between those who like regularity and those who think the existence of a rule makes life an unimaginative drudge. All groups also have a certain "ritual" by which a member gets back into the graces of the group if he has sinned, and others which the group has to go through when an individual has deviated. Which of these ceremonial rites are going on among my boys, thinly disguised behind squabbles and fights, and which of them do adult staff people indulge in, under the even thinner disguise of a discussion on punishment and on the setting of limits? Again—the mere discovery of phenomena fitting into this category is not what I am after. We are still far from having good research data on the *clinical relevance* of whatever specific practice may be in vogue in a specific place.

4. *The impact of the group process.* We had better pause after pronouncing this weighty phrase—it is about as heavy and full of dodges as the phrase "social structure," as previously pointed out. And since this one milieu aspect might well keep us here for a week, let me sink as low as simple wordlisting at this point. Items that I think should go somewhere under this name: over-all group atmosphere, processes like scapegoating, mascot-cultivation, subclique formation, group psychological role suction,[2] experiences of exposure to group psychological intoxication, dependency on contagion clusters, leadership tensions, etc. Whatever you have learned from social psychology, group psychology and group dynamics had

better be written in right here. The point of all this: These phenomena are *not* just interesting things that happen among patients or staff, to be viewed with a clinical grin, a sociological hurrah, or with the curiosity stare of an anthropological slumming party. These processes are forces to which my child patient is exposed, as real as the oedipus complex of his therapist, the food he eats and the toys he plays with. The forces producing such impacts may be hard to see, or even to make visible through x-ray tricks. They are there and as much of his "surroundings" as the unbreakable room in which he screams off his tantrum.

5. *The trait clusters that other people whirl around within a five-yard stretch.* I first wanted to call this item "the other people as persons," but I know this would only call forth a long harangue about feelings, attitudes—Isn't it people anyway, who make up a group?—etc. From bitter discussion experience, I am trying to duck these questions by this somewhat off-the-beat phrase. What I have in mind is this: My youngsters live as part of a group, true enough. But they are also individuals. And Bobby who shares a room with John is within striking distance of whatever personal peculiarities John may happen to throw at others. In short, we expect some children to show "shock" at certain colors on a Rorschach card. We expect children to be lured into excited creativity at the mere vision of some fascinating project outline or plane model seductively placed before their eyes. Well, the boy with whom Bobby shares his room is worse than a Rorschach or a plane model. Not only does his presence and the visualization of his personality do something to Bobby, for John not only *has* character traits and neurotic syndromes; he swings them around his body like a wet bathing towel, and it is going to hit whoever gets in its path, innocent or not. In short, personality traits remain psychological entities for the psychologist who watches them in the youngsters. They are *real things that hit and scratch* if you get in their way, for the roommate and all the other people on the ward.

We have learned to respect the impact of certain extremes in pathologies upon each other, but we are still far from inspecting our milieus carefully enough for what they contain in "trait clusters" that children swing around their heads within a five-yard range. Let me add: not all traits and syndromes are "swung"; some stay put and can only be seen or smelled, so they become visible or a nuisance only to the one who shares the same room. Also: we are far from knowing what this all amounts to clinically. For the question of just what "milieu ingredients" my ward contains, in terms of existent trait clusters of the people who live in it, is still far removed from the question of just which *should* coexist with each other, and which others should be carefully kept asunder.

6. *The staff, their attitudes and feelings—but please*

---

[2] Some more detailed description of this appears in *Group Processes: Transactions of the Fourth (1957) Conference*, Bertram Schaffner, Ed. (New York: Josiah Macy, Jr. Foundation, 1959).

let's not call it all "transference." This one I can be short about, for clinicians all know about it; sociologists will grant it to you, though they may question how heavily it counts. In fact, the attitudes and feelings of staff have been drummed up for so long now as "the" most important aspect of a milieu, often even as the only important one, that I am not afraid this item will be forgotten. No argument needed, it is self-evident. Only two issues I would like to battle around: One, while attitudes and feelings are very important indeed, they are not always all that counts, and sometimes other milieu items may gang up on them so much they may obliterate their impact. My other battle cry: Attitudes and feelings of staff are manifold, and spring from many different sources. Let's limit the term "transference" to those for which it was originally invented. If Nurse's Aide A gets too hostile to Bob because he bit him too hard, let's not throw all of that into the same terminological pot. By the way, if I grant "attitudes and feelings of staff" a place on my list of "powerful milieu ingredients," I mean the attitudes and feelings that really fill the place, that are lived—not those that are only mentioned in research interviews and on questionnaires.

7. Behavior received. I tried many other terms, but it won't work. There just isn't one that fits. In a sentence I would say: what people really *do* to each other counts as much as how they feel. This forces me into a two-hour argument in which I have to justify why it isn't un-psychiatric to say such a thing. For, isn't it the underlying feelings that "really" count? That depends on which side of the fence your "really" is. The very fact that you use such a term already means you know there is another side to it, only you don't want to take it as seriously as yours. In short, there are situations where the "underlying feeling" with which the adult punishes a child counts so much that the rather silly form of punishment that was chosen is negligible. But I could quote you hundreds of other examples where this is not the case. No matter what wonderful motive—if you expose child A to an isolation with more panic in it than he can stand, the effect will be obvious. Your excuse that you "meant well and love the boy" may be as futile as that of the mother who would give the child an overdose of arsenic, not knowing its effect.

This item of *behaviors received in a day's time* by each child should make a really interesting line to assess. We would have to look about at "behaviors received" from other boys as well as from staff, and see what the implications of those behaviors received are, even after deducting from them the mitigating influences of "attitudes that really were aiming at the opposite." The same, by the way, should also be taken into consideration for staff to be hired. I have run into people who really love "crazy youngsters" and are quite willing to sacrifice a lot. Only they simply cannot stand more than half a

pound of spittle in their face a day, professional attitude or no.

In order to make such an assessment, the clinician would of course be interested especially in the *forms* that are being used by staff for intervention—limit-setting—expression of acceptance and love, etc. The totality of prevalence of certain forms of "behavior received" is not a negligible characteristic of the milieu in which a child patient has to live.

8. Activity structure and nature of constituent performances. Part of the impact a hospital or treatment home has on a child lies in the things he is allowed or requested *to do.* Any given activity that is halfway shapeful enough to be described has a certain amount of structure to it—some games, for instance, have a body of rules; demand the splitting up into two opposing sides or staying in a circle; and have certain assessments of roles for the players, at least for the duration. At the same time, they make youngsters "do certain things" while the game lasts. Paul Gump introduced the term "constituent performances" into our Detroit Game Study, and referred by this term to the performances required within the course of a game as basic. Thus, running and tagging are constituent performances of a tag game, guessing word meanings is a constituent performance in many a charade, etc. We have plenty of evidence by now that—other things being equal—the very exposure of children to a given game, with its structure and demand for certain constituent performances, may have terrific clinical impact on the events at least of that day. Wherever we miscalculate the overwhelming effect which the seductive aspect of certain games may have (flashlight hide-and-seek in the dark just before bedtime) we may ask for trouble, while many a seemingly risky game can safely be played if enough ego supportive controls are built right into it (the safety zone to which you can withdraw without having to admit you get tired or scared, etc.). In short, while I would hardly relegate the total treatment job of severely disturbed children in a mental hospital ward to that factor alone, I certainly would want to figure on it as seriously as I would calculate the mental hygiene aspects of other factors more traditionally envisioned as being of clinical concern. What I say here about games goes for many other activities patients engage in—arts and crafts, woodwork, outings, overnight trips, cookouts, discussion groups, musical evening, etc. Which of these things takes place, where, with which feeling tone, and with what structural and activity ingredients is as characteristic of a given "milieu" as the staff that is hired.

9. Space, equipment, time and props. What an assortment of names, but I know as yet of no collective noun that would cover them all equally well. Since I have made such a fuss about this for years, I may try to be shorter about it than seems reasonable. Remember what a bunch of boys do when running through a viaduct with an echo effect? Remember what may happen to a small group who are supposed to discuss plans for their next Scout meeting, who have to hold this discussion unexpectedly, in a huge gym with lots of stuff around, instead of in their usual clubroom? Remember what will happen to a baseball that is put on the table prematurely while they are still supposed to sit quietly and listen, and remember what happens to many a well-intended moral lecture to a group of sloppy campers, if you timed it so badly that the swimming bell started ringing before you had finished? Do I still have to prove why I think that what an outfit does with arrangements of time expectations and time distribution, what prop-exposure the youngsters are expected to stand or avoid, what space arrangements are like, and what equipment does to the goals you have set for yourself, should be listed along with the important "properties" of a place where clinical work with children takes place? So far I have found that in hospitals this item tends to be left out of milieu discussions by psychiatrists and sociologists alike; only the nurses and attendants have learned by bitter experience that it may pay to lend an ear to it.

10. *The seepage from the world outside.* One of the hardest "milieu aspects" to assess in a short visit to any institution is the amount of "impact from the larger universe and the surrounding world" that actually seeps through its walls and finds its way into the lives of the patients. No outfit is airtight, no matter how many keys and taboos are in use. In our own little children's ward-world, for instance, there are the following "seepage ingredients from the world outside" that are as much a part of our "milieu," as it hits the boys, as anything else: Adult visitors and the "past case history" flavor they leave behind. Child visitors and the "sociological body odor" of the old neighborhood, or the new one which they exude. Excursions which we arrange, old haunts from prehospital days, which we happen to drive through unintentionally on our way to our destination. Plenty of purposely pulled-in outside world through movies, television, pictures, and stories we may tell them. And, of course, school is a full-view window hopefully opened wide for many vistas to be seen through it—if we only could get our children to look.

There is the "hospital impact" of the large building that hits them whenever they leave the ward floor in transit, the physically sick patients they meet on the elevator who stir the question up again in their own mind: "Why am I here?" There are the stories other boys tell, the staff tells, the imputed secrets we may be hiding from them whenever we seem eager to divert attention to something else. As soon as the children move into the open cottage, the word "seepage" isn't quite as correct any more. Suffice it to say: the type and amount of "outside world"

particles that are allowed in or even eagerly pulled in constitute a most important part of the lives of the captive population of an institutional setting, and want to be given attention to in an appraisal of just what a given "milieu" holds.

11. *The system of umpiring services and traffic regulations between environment and child.* Those among you who have a sharp nose for methodological speculations may want to object and insist that I am jumping category dimensions in tagging on this item and the next one on my list. I don't want to quarrel about this now. For even though you may be right, it is too late today to start a new chapter, so please let me get away with tagging these two items on here. In some ways they still belong, for whether there are any umpiring services built into an institution, and what they are like, is certainly an important "milieu property" in my estimation.

What I have in mind here has been described in more detail in a previous paper.[3] In short, it runs somewhat like this: Some "milieu impacts" hit the children directly; nobody needs to interpret or translate. Others hit the child all right, but to have their proper impact someone has to do some explaining. It makes a great difference whether a child who is running away unhappy, after a cruel razzing received from a thoughtless group, is left to deal with this all by himself; or whether the institution provides interpretational or first-aid services for the muddled feelings at the time. Some of our children, for instance, might translate such an experience, which was not intended by the institution, into additional resentment against the world. With sympathy in the predicament offered by a friendly adult who tags along and comforts, this same experience may well be decontaminated or even turned into the opposite.

A similar item is the one I had in mind in using the phrase "traffic regulations." Much give-and-take can follow naturally among the inhabitants of a given place. Depending on the amount of their disturbance, though, some social interactions which normal life leaves to the children's own resources require traffic supervision by an adult. I would like to know whether a given milieu has foreseen this and can guarantee the provision of some help in the bartering custom among the youngsters, or whether that new youngster will be mercilessly exposed to the wildest blackmail with no help from anyone, the moment he enters the doors to my ward. In short, it is like asking what medical first-aid facilities are in a town before one moves into it. Whether this belongs to the concept of what makes up a "town," or whether it should be listed under a separate heading I leave for a later

---

[3] *Strategy and Techniques of the Life Space Interview,* Am. J. Orthopsychiatry, 29: 1–19, 1959.

chance to thrash out. All I want to point at now is that the nature of and existence or nonexistence of umpiring services and social traffic regulations is as "real" a property of a setup as its walls, kitchen equipment and clinical beliefs.

12. *The thermostat for the regulation of clinical resilience.* If it is cold in an old cabin somewhere in the midst of "primitive nature," the trouble is obvious: either there isn't any fire going, or something is wrong with the stove and the whole heating system, so it doesn't give off enough heat. If I freeze in a building artificially equipped with all the modern conveniences, such a conclusion might be off the beam. The trouble may simply be that the thermostat isn't working right. This, like the previous item, is a property of a given milieu rather than a "milieu ingredient" in the stricter sense of the word. However, it is of such utmost clinical relevance that it has to go in here somewhere. In fact, I have hardly ever participated in a discussion on the milieu concept without having this item come up somehow or other.

The term under which it is more often referred to is actually that of "flexibility," which most milieu therapy enthusiasts praise as "good" while the bad men in the picture are the ones that think "rigidity" is a virtue. I have more reasons to be tired of these either/or issues than I can list in the remaining time. It seems to me that the "resilience" concept fits better what most of us have so long tried to shoot at with the flexibility label. A milieu certainly needs to be sensitive to the changing needs of the patients during different phases of the treatment process. It needs to "tighten up"—lower the behavioral ceiling when impulse-panic looms on the horizon; and it may have to lift it when self-imposed internal pressures mount. Also, it needs to limit spontaneity and autonomy of the individual patient in early phases of intensive disorder and rampant pathology; it needs to throw in a challenge toward autonomy and even the risking of mistakes, when the patient goes through the later phases of recovery. Especially when severely disturbed children are in the process of going through an intensive phase of "improvement," the resilience of a milieu to make way for its implications is as important as its ability to "shrink back" during a regressive phase.

JUST HOW DOES THE MILIEU DO IT?

Listing these 12 variables of important milieu aspects which can be differentiated as explorable issues in their own right is only part of the story. I hold no brief for this list, and I am well aware of its methodological complications and deficiencies. The major value of listing them at all lies in the insistence that *there are so many of them* and that they *can be separately studied and explored.* This

should at least help us to secure ourselves against falling in love with any one of them to the exclusion of the others, and of forcing any discipline that wants to tackle the job, whether it be psychiatry, sociology or what not, to look beyond its traditional scope and directly into the face of uncompromisingly multifaceted facts.

Since the major sense in all this milieu noise is primarily the impact of these variables on the treatment process of the children we are trying to cure, the question of the clinical assessment of the relevance of each of these items is next on the docket of urgent jobs. This one we shall have to skip for today, but time may allow us to point at the other question leading into the most important core of the problem: If we assume that any one of these milieu ingredients, or whatever you want to call them, may have positive or negative impacts on our therapeutic work—how do they do it? Just what goes on when we claim that any one of those milieu givens "did something to our youngsters"? This gets us into one of the most noteworthy gaps in all our theory of personality, and frankly, I don't think even our most up-to-date models are quite up to it. True enough, we have learned a few things about just how pathology is influenced in the process of a specific form of psychiatric interview, and we know a little about influence of human over human, here or there. We are not so well off when we come to the impact of more abstract sounding entities, such as "group structure." We have even more trouble to figure out just how space, time and props are supposed to do their job, whenever we claim that they have the power to throw an otherwise well-planned therapeutic experience out of gear.

One phase of this problem sounds familiar—when psychiatry first began to take the impact of "culture" seriously, we were confronted with a similar puzzler: just where, within the individual, is what going on at the moment when we say a "cultural" factor had some influence on a given behavior of a person?

This problem is far from solved. I think it might help, though, to introduce a thought that might lead to greater specificity in observation and ultimately to more "usable" forms of data collection. Frankly, I have never seen the "milieu" at work. My children are never hit by "the milieu" as such. It always hits them in a specific form and at a given time and place. I think the researchers who play with the concept of a "setting" have a technical advantage over us in this field. Of course, the setting alone doesn't interest me either. For what it all hinges on is just what *experience* a given setting produces or makes possible within my child patient and what this child patient does with it.

Rather than study the "milieu" per se, and then the "reactions of the children," how about making it a four-step plan? Let's keep the "milieu" as the over-all concept on the fringe; its basic ingredients come close to my youngsters only insofar as they are contained in a given setting. For example, my children on the ward can be found engaged in getting up, eating a meal or snacks; they can be found roaming around the playroom, or in a station wagon, with all their overnight gear, on the way to their camping site. They can be found in their arts and crafts room, or schoolroom, engaged in very specific activities. Enough of illustrations—the point is, in all those settings the whole assortment of milieu aspects hits them in very *specific forms:* There is an outspoken behavioral expectation floating through that arts and crafts room at any time. There are spatial characteristics, tools, and props. There is the potential reaction of the other child or adult, the feeling tone of the group toward the whole situation as such; there is the impact of people's goal values and attitudes as well as that of the behavior of the child's neighbor who clobbers him right now with his newly made viking sword. In short: *I may be able to isolate observations of milieu ingredients as they "hit" the child in a specific setting during a specific activity.* On such a narrowed-down level of observation, I may also be able to trace the actual *experience* which such a concrete situation in a given setting produced in the child; and if I know what the child *did with the experience,* it may make sense, since I have both ends of the line before me. The youngster's reactions to his experience—the nature of the ingredients of the "setting" on both ends of the line, plus plenty of good hunches on the child's experience while exposed to its impact.

It seems to me that much more work needs to be done with the concept of "setting" so as to make it clinically more meaningful, and that sharper observational techniques, capable of catching "implied milieu impact" as well as "child's coping with" the experience produced by the setting, need to be developed. This, however, leads into a theme to be discussed in other sessions of our Annual Meeting.

One more word before closing. It is time that we take Erik Erikson's warning more seriously than we have done so far—and I mention him as symbolizing a point of view that many of us have been increasingly impressed by. If I may try to say what I think he would warn us about after all this discussion of "milieu impacts" on therapy of children, it would run somewhat like this: Why are you still talking most of the time as though "milieu" or "environment" were some sort of rigid structure, and the individuals were good for nothing but to "react" to it?

How does some of that "environment" you talk about come into being, after all? Couldn't we reverse the story just as well, and ask: "What do your child patients do to their milieu?"—not only: "What does the milieu do to them?" Mine, by the way, are doing plenty to it, and I have little doubt but that many of the items which we describe as though they were fixtures on the environmental scene are actually products of the attitudes and actions of the very people who, after they have produced them, are also exposed to their impact in turn.

I, for one, would want to exclaim loudly what I didn't dare whisper too much at the start of my paper, or I would have scared you off too soon. I would like to find out not only what milieu is and how it operates, but also how we can describe it, how we influence it, and by what actions of all involved it is, in turn, created or molded. At the moment I am convinced of only one thing for sure—we all have quite a way to go to achieve either of those tasks.

Section V

ALTERNATIVE APPROACHES

❦ ❦ ❦

This section presents work depicting approaches to therapy that vary from the traditional verbal interaction between a therapist and a single client. It includes selections pertaining to group therapy, play therapy, art therapy, music therapy, dance therapy, and drama therapy.

The first three articles deal with group therapy, beginning with one by Fritz Perls, the father of Gestalt psychology and an innovator in the use of group strategies. Perls believed that emotionally disturbed individuals had to go through a painful maturation process that was expedited by the group; apparently no one was better than he in facilitating growth in group sessions.

In the second paper George Bach discusses his invention of the marathon group. Bach believed that typical group sessions of an hour or so are not long enough for game playing to end and honest exchanges to begin. He also thought that group pressure was responsible for a great deal of progress in therapy sessions. His thorough yet concise discussion provides an excellent introduction to his thought.

In the third paper the ubiquitous Albert Ellis reports on rational group therapy. He provides examples of interactions in typical group sessions that clarify the group process.

The play therapy selections begin with several brief excerpts from a classic book by Melanie Klein, an innovator in the application of psychoanalytic techniques to children. The passages reproduced were selected to illustrate the pervasive influence of the psychoanalytic movement in the 1940s and the interesting intellectual dispute regarding the analysis of children between Klein and Sigmund Freud's daughter Anna, who tailored his psychoanalytical theories for application to children. The second selection in this section, written by Anna Freud, depicts her disagreement with Klein on several issues. One issue involves the extent to which the therapist should interpret children's behavior; the other pertains to the degree to which children's transference (their projection of significant feelings toward others onto the therapist) is like adult transference.

Hiam Ginott's theoretical framework for group play therapy also reflects a psychoanalytic frame of reference, although his work is more current than Anna Freud's article. Unlike Freud, he does not deal with theoretical issues but presents his justification for group therapy, using practical examples to illustrate each of his points.

The last selection in the play therapy section departs from psychoanalytic tenets. Virginia

Axline, a student of Carl Rogers, demonstrates the manner in which nondirective principles are applied in play therapy. In describing a case where she was able to accept the behavior of her client John when he held a knife to her wrist, she provides the most dramatic example of therapy included in this text.

Art therapy is represented by the work of the two greatest women in the field, Margaret Naumburg and Edith Kramer. Naumburg's contribution is an excerpt from her book *An Introduction to Art Therapy; Studies of the "Free" Art Expression of Behavior Problem Children and Adolescents as a Means of Diagnosis and Therapy.* The case included vividly illustrates Naumburg's psychoanalytic orientation to art therapy.

Kramer's work is represented by quotations from an article she wrote comparing art therapy and art education. This piece shows her concern with art as a creative process and as a vehicle for enhancing children's self-esteem. It contrasts nicely with Naumburg's highly clinical perspective.

Music therapy is represented by excerpts from Juliette Alvin's classic book, *Music for the Handicapped Child.* She depicts the use of music with a child afflicted with muscular dystrophy and with an emotionally disturbed child.

An article by Marion Chace, a forerunner in the use of dance with mentally ill persons in hospital settings, demonstrates her intuitive understanding of patients' feelings and capabilities. She viewed dance as a means of communicating with individuals who often are unresponsive to verbal communication.

The last selection in this section consists of excerpts from *Psychodrama*, by Jacob Moreno. Moreno's introduction is particularly fascinating as he documents his early attempts to develop an approach to therapy that moved beyond psychoanalysis and credits himself for initiating the ideas of group therapy and action therapy. He also disputes the "myth" that the American sociologist G. H. Mead was a major conceptualizer of role theory, attributing that concept to psychodrama. Although Moreno clearly was not a modest man, it appears that his innovations had a significant impact on a variety of approaches to treating emotionally disturbed or disordered individuals.

Group Therapy

Group vs. Individual Therapy

F. S. Perls
1967

Marshall McLuhan has written a book in which he expands the notion: the medium is the message.

What is the message we receive from the medium of group therapy? Group therapy tells us, "I am more economical than individual therapy." Individual therapy counters, "Yes, but you are less efficient." "But," asks group therapy, "who says *you* are efficient?"

You will notice that on my private stage these two therapies immediately begin to fight, to get into a conflict.

For a while, I tried to solve this conflict in Gestalt therapy by asking my patients to have both individual and group therapy. Lately, however, I have eliminated individual sessions altogether, except for emergency cases. As a matter of fact, I have come to consider that all individual therapy is obsolete and should be replaced by workshops in Gestalt therapy. In my workshops, I now integrate individual and group work. This is effective with a group, however, only if the therapist's encounter with an *individual patient within the group* is effective.

To understand the effectiveness of Gestalt therapy in workshops, we have, first, to consider another conflict: the dichotomy in present-day psychology between the *experiential* and the *behavioral* approaches. Then we can understand how Gestalt therapy integrates both branches of psychology.

The behaviorist is usually thought of primarily as a conditioner. If he were willing to disassociate himself from the activity of conditioning—from a compulsion to change behavior, essentially by the external means of drill and repetition—he could become an observer, a describer of ongoing processes. He would then learn that learning is discovering, that it is a matter of new experience. On the other hand, he has one advantage over the majority of clinical psychologists: he works in the here and now. He is reality-oriented, though in a rather mechanical way; and he is more observation-oriented than the clinician, who, for the most part, is guided by abstractions and computations. But the clinician has what the behaviorist omits—full concern with the phenomenon of awareness. Whether he calls it consciousness, sensitivity, or awareness does not matter at all.

Freud assumed that the mere transposition of unconscious *memories* into conscious ones would be sufficient for a cure. Existential psychiatry has a similar, though somewhat broader, outlook: to assimilate and to make available *all* those parts of the personality that have been alienated.

What can hinder the experientialist is this: though his focus is on experience, he turns easily away from the here and now of the behaviorist. Either he becomes concerned, like Freud, with the past and with causality, or he becomes concerned, like Adler, with intentions. The actual behavior of *both* the therapist and the patient is usually explained away as "transference" and "counter-transference."

Interest in observable behavior developed early in psychotherapy. The hypnotist wanted not only to relieve the patient of his symptoms, but also to change objectionable habits into desirable ones. The Freudian school saw behavior patterns parallel with the three recognized erog-

Note. From "Group vs. individual therapy" by F. S. Perls, 1967, *ETC: A Review of General Semantics, 24*(3), 306–312. Copyright 1967 by the Society for General Semantics. Reprinted by permission.

enous zones: oral, anal, and genital. Reich's interest in character formation was largely centered on a person's *motoric* behavior. He tried to take a short cut, and so, like most therapists, he neglected to observe the details of *voice* and verbal *behavior*.

The Gestalt school has investigated much of our sensoric behavior. Since our contact with the world is based upon sensory awareness, especially seeing, hearing, and touching, these means of external-object-awareness play as great a part in Gestalt therapy as does the internal proprioceptive system of self-awareness. Since all sensing takes place in the here and now, Gestalt therapy is "present time" oriented, as is the behaviorist.

The sum of the types of overt motoric and verbal behavior—that which is easily observable and verifiable—we call character. We call the place where this behavior originates the mind. Even our secret verbal behavior is called thinking or intellect. But it is actually phantasy, or, as Freud has seen it, to play in life—the rehearsal stage on which we prepare for the roles we want.

The intellect—the whole of intelligence—we might liken to a computer. It is, however a pallid substitute for the vivid immediacy of sensing and experiencing. The psychoanalyst and the so-called rational therapist, by playing interpretation and explanation games, only reinforce this deceptive dominance of the intellect and interfere with the emotional responses which are at the center of our personality. In the emotional desert of neurotic patients, we seldom find any feelings other than boredom, self-pity, and depression.

In short, the clinical psychotherapist lacks full involvement with actuality, with the here and now, whereas the behaviorist denies the importance of awareness. In Gestalt therapy, we integrate the two sides of the coin by doing microscopic psychiatry, by investigating the awareness and avoidance of awareness of every detail of the patient's and the so-called therapist's behavior. This is the true integration of the two psychologies—not just eclectic, not a compromise. But it is most difficult to achieve this synthesis in the combination of group and individual therapy.

A neurotic may be defined as a person who is unable to assume the full identity and responsibility of mature behavior. He will do anything to keep himself in the state of immaturity, even to playing the role of an adult—that is, his infantile concept of what an adult is like. The neurotic cannot conceive of himself as a self-supportive person, able to mobilize his potential in order to cope with the world. He looks for environmental support through direction, help, explanations, and answers. He mobilizes not his own resources, but his *means of manipulating* the environment—helplessness, flattery, stupidity, and

other more or less subtle controls—in order to get support.

The psychoanalyst can play right into the hands of the neurotic who resorts to such behavior by disregarding the essence of human relationships and by turning any relationship into an infantile one, such as father-figure, incest, super-ego dominance. The patient is not made responsible, but the unconscious, the Oedipus complex or what-you-will, receives the catharsis of cause and responsibility.

The basic behavior of a student of mine was wailing. His father was a professional wailer: a cantor. The student *was* aware that he was like his father in many respects and fought this attitude; but the insight was of no help to him, because it never clarified what the essence of his wailing was. The louder he wailed, the greater his disappointment that there was no result. He failed to realize that he *and* his father were barking up the wrong tree. There could be no answer, because nobody, no God, no magician, was there to help him. (The father imitation is not the problem. The irrational behavior of both father and son is.)

Freudianism barks up the wrong tree of cause and interpretations; psychology in general does it by mixing up mind and phantasy. Every patient barks up the wrong tree by expecting that he can achieve maturation through external sources—through being psychoanalysed, reconditioned, hypnotized, or marathonized, or by taking psychedelic drugs. Maturation cannot be achieved *for* him; he has to go through the painful process of growing up by himself. A therapist can do nothing but provide him with the opportunity—by being available both as a catalyst and as a screen upon which he can project his neurosis.

The basic theory of Gestalt therapy is that maturation is a continuous growth process in which environmental support is transformed into self-support. In healthy development, the infant mobilizes and learns to use his own resources. A viable balance of support and frustration enables him to become independent, free to utilize his innate potential.

In contrast, a neurosis develops in an environment that does not facilitate this maturation process adequately. Development is, instead, perverted into a character formation, into a set of behavior patterns that are meant to control the environment by manipulation. The child learns, often by copying some adult, to secure environmental support by playing helpless or stupid, by bullying, by flattering, by trying to be seductive, and so on and on. Thus any helpful and too supportive therapist or member of the group who is sucked in by a patient's manipulations will only spoil that person more—by depriving him of the opportunity to discover his own strength, potential, and resources. The therapist's real tool here is skillful frustration.

At the core of each neurosis lies what the Russians call the *sick point*. Realizing that they can do nothing to cure it, they are satisfied to reorganize it and to sublimate their energies around this sick point. In Gestalt therapy, we call this sick point the *impasse;* and I have as yet seen no method other than Gestalt therapy capable of getting through it. Furthermore, I doubt if it is possible to get through the impasse in individual therapy, and I know that the integration of individual and group therapy holds the possibility to do so.

When approaching the existential impasse (and this does not mean minor hang-ups), the patient gets into a whirl. He becomes panic-stricken, deaf and dumb— unwilling to leave the merry-go-round of compulsive repetition. He truly feels the despair which Kierkegaard recognized as "sickness unto death." The existential impasse is a situation in which no environmental support is forthcoming, and the patient is, or believes himself to be, incapable of coping with life on his own. So he will do anything to hold on to the status quo—rather than grow up and use his own powers. He will change marriage partners, but not his expectations; he will change therapists, but not his neurosis; he will change the content of his inner conflicts, but he will not give up his self-torture games; he will increase the subtlety of his manipulations and his control-madness to secure the environmental support without which he imagines he cannot survive.

Now, in the group situation something happens that is not possible in the private interview. To the whole group *it is obvious* that a person in distress *does not see* the obvious, does not see the way out of the impasse, does not see (for instance) that most of his misery is a purely imagined one. In the face of this collective conviction of the group, he cannot use his usual phobic way of disowning the therapist when he cannot manipulate him. Somehow, trust in the group seems to be greater than trust in the therapist—in spite of all so-called transference confidence.

Behind the impasse there lurks the threatening monster that keeps the patient nailed to the cross of his neurosis. This monster is the catastrophic expectation that, so he imagines, spells his doom and prevents him from taking reasonable risks and enduring the growing pains of maturation.

It is at this point that rational thinking has its place: in the assessment of the degree to which catastrophic expectation is mere imagination or exaggeration of real danger. In the safe emergency of the therapeutic situation, the neurotic discovers that the world does not fall to pieces if he gets angry, sexy, joyous, mournful. Nor is the group's support for his self-esteem and appreciation of his achievements toward authenticity and greater liveliness to be underestimated.

In my Gestalt workshop anyone who feels the urge can work with me. I am available, but never pushing. A dyad is temporarily developed between myself and the patient; but the rest of the group is fully involved, though seldom as active participants. Mostly they act as an audience which is stimulated by the encounter to do quite a bit of silent self-therapy.

There are other advantages in working with a group. A great deal of individual development can be facilitated through doing collective experiments—talking jibberish together, or doing withdrawal experiments, or learning to understand the importance of atmosphere, or showing the person on the spot how he collectively bores, hypnotizes, or amuses the environment. In grief or similar emotionally charged situations, chain reactions often occur. The group soon learns to understand the contrast between helpfulness, however well meaning, and true support. And at the same time, the group's observation of the manipulative games which the neurotic plays, the roles he acts out, in order to keep himself in the infantile state facilitates their own self-recognition.

In other words, in contrast to the usual type of group meetings, *I* carry the load of the session, by either doing individual therapy or conducting mass experiments. I often interfere if the group plays opinion and interpretation games or has similar purely verbal encounters without any experiential substance, but I keep out of it as soon as anything genuine happens.

It is always a deeply moving experience for the group and for me, the therapist, to see previously robotized corpses begin to return to life, gain substance, begin the dance of abandonment and self-fulfillment. *The paper people are turning into real people.*

The Marathon Group: Intensive Practice of Intimate Interaction

George R. Bach
1966

Summary.—Briefly are described the schedule, contents, the psychosocial processes, and the therapeutic effects of Marathon Therapy which is a living-in, intensive interaction experience in which so-called "patients" and so-called "psychotherapists" involve each other as persons in reciprocal influence-pressures to improve their styles of life.

I

Like all effective group psychotherapeutic programs, the *Marathon* is a group practicum in intimate, authentic human interaction. One of the unique aspects of the Marathon technique is an intensification and acceleration of transparency and genuine encounter by a deliberate instigation of group pressure focused on behavioral change.

In the course of conducting over 12,000 therapeutic group hours with a great variety of patients, it is clinically observable that for many patients the 50-minute individual hour or the 1- to 2-hour group sessions are not long enough for either patient or therapist to take off their social masks, i.e., to stop playing games and start interacting truthfully, authentically, and transparently. It takes a longer session for people in our culture to switch from the marketing stance of role-playing and image-making,

which they must practice in the work-a-day world, to feel free to "come out" straight and strong, not hidden behind oblique "sick" roles or other so-called "resistance."

Clinical experience has shown that *group-pressure*, rather than the therapist's individual interventions and interpretations given privately, is a major vehicle which can move people effectively and quickly from impression making and manipulative behavior toward honest, responsible, spontaneous *levelling* with one another. But it takes time for the therapeutic group to generate influence-pressure in intensity and work-oriented kind, sufficient to produce behavioral change. It takes time, also, for group members to display their individual ways of acting within the group which stimulates their ways of being and acting in the world. It takes time for therapists and peers to discern the potential for therapeutic change in each person and then to focus on this potential and to suggest change. Finally, it also takes time to experience the change, experiment with it and practice it here and now while participating in shaping the learning culture of the therapeutic group. All of this, becoming transparent, levelling, exposing to influence-pressure, attempting changes and practicing new behavior, we believe, is a *natural Gestalt*, i.e., *a unit* of learning experience which should not be broken up into bits and pieces but should occur as a whole, mediating a significant turning-point, a big step toward becoming what one can be!

Customary schedules of group therapy tend to break up this experiential learning unit. One-, two-, or even three-hour office meetings are not enough therapeutically, although staff time and fee economics make them universally accepted schedules. We have tried long hour groups and also week-end retreats and closely spaced groups (every other evening). With each of these schedules we noticed that there are always a few patients who "slip by" the experience, always waiting and ready to level truthfully with their peers, but never quite coming out openly transparent in time for the group to get hold of them fully for feedback, confrontation, and pressure to change. These brief interrupted groups rarely generate the right amount and kind of *influence-pressure* to make a crucial impact on the resistant learner. The brief group is an ideal play-ground for time-wasting, psychiatric games, such as diagnosing (labelling) safaris into phantasias, psychological archeology, playing psychoanalysis with "transference" interpretation, collusive acceptance of people's irrational self-propaganda as to "who is the best therapist," "best patient," etc., etc.

Searching for a practical solution, we were delighted to discover last year (in 1963) that a group of younger colleagues (Roger Wickland and Frederick Stoller) had independently developed in a psychiatric hospital setting all-day-long types of group therapeutic sessions which were effective in producing therapeutic changes in "difficult" patients. Adopting this approach to our private practice patients, we re-activated our old week-end retreat program but with a new twist: no interruptions, continuous meetings for 2 days, no sub-grouping, no socializing, minimal breaks, clear-cut ground rules, and admission of people seriously interested in changing themselves rather than the universe. The revision is a success thanks to our consultant, Dr. Frederick Stoller, who working as my co-therapist in the very first Marathon ever done with private patients, has helped me significantly to improve our old weekend live-in program.

Currently, our *Marathon* group therapy retreats take place in a secluded private setting where a selected group of 10 to 14 participants can stay together for 2, 3, or 4 days.[1]

The actual schedule of a particular Marathon varies, depending on setting and the members' goals and values. In the standard procedures members meet non-stop throughout the first night, i.e., without sleeping for 24 hr. or longer. The Marathon terminates in non-verbal, silent communication exercises, conducted in pairs. This is followed by a "closure-party" in which sub-grouping is resumed. Thus, a gradual re-entry into the conventional social atmosphere is reluctantly made. The entire session may be recorded and a feedback follow-up is scheduled 4 to 8 weeks later, which is designed to reinforce those decisions for change which have been emerging during the Marathon itself. In our Institute practice the Marathon retreats for private patients are systematically integrated with the regular group therapy program. Most patients are first seen individually (briefly) and then assigned to a regular 2- to 4-hour weekly therapy group. Marathon retreat experiences are interspersed at intervals of 3 to 6 months. Some Marathons are "specialized" for marital couples, executives of business organizations, or an advanced training session for group psychotherapists or social science researchers.

We conceptualize the Marathon therapeutic process as a practicum in authentic communication, based on freedom from social fears conventionally associated with transparency.

The unique opportunity of participating in honest encounter on a day-and-night basis produces psychological intimacy among the participants. This gives them a taste for what can be achieved with significant others everywhere.

As subjective truths are shared, irrational and ineffectual behavior appears incongruent, to be dropped in favor of new, more intimate, and competent behavioral patterns. The latter emerge and are practiced in the course of the Marathon. Orientation is ahistorical, emphasizing "what" and "how now" rather than "why" and "where from."

The genuine productivity of every group member is the therapist's mission which he procures by whatever means at his disposal. One of the other missions of the therapist is to maximize group feedback and enhance the opportunity for genuine encountering of and exposure to group pressure. For these reasons the Marathon is not unlike a "pressure cooker" in which phony steam boils away and genuine emotions (including negative ones) emerge. The group atmosphere is kept focused every moment on the objectives at hand: to produce *change in orientation* and new ways of dealing with old crucial problems (creativity).

Every member is a co-therapist and co-responsible for the relative success or failure of any given Marathon meeting. Thus, the two or more professional co-therapists will, if and when they genuinely feel it, take their turns to participate "patient-wise," that is, as whole persons rather than just in a technical role-wise form. Decisions for change and serious commitment to follow through in life action are frankly elicited. Follow-up sessions will inquire into their validity.

Concerning *selection*, prospective Marathon participants are not sorted out in the traditional psychiatric-diagnostic sense, but rather on the basis of (1) attitudes toward self-change and (2) group constellation. Before admittance "Marathonians" must convince one and preferably both professional co-therapists that they are anxious to make significant *changes* in their customary

---

[1] The enrollment fee, which includes room and board, ranges from $90.00 to $300.00 per participant depending on duration, setting, and staff. The minimum fee per actual group therapy hour is $3.00.

ways of acting and being in this world. This presumes some degree of basic self-understanding of what one *now* is and what one can potentially become. The purpose of the Marathon is to awaken and strengthen further feelings for new directions and *movement* toward self-actualization in mutual *intimate concert* with others who are growing also. Marathons create a social climate for inter-peer growth stimulation, a sort of *psychological fertility!*

The Marathon group-therapeutic experience is most fully effective with those who wish to exchange their own ways of acting and being in this world and who are ready to quit blaming others and environment for their present unsatisfactory lot. New patients who initially tend to play the psychiatric game: "I am sick—*YOU* cure me" may be admitted to *initiation types of Marathons* whose specific mission is to knock out blamesmanship and other false, irrational, socially destructive operations (Bach, 1954) by which people preserve, cuddle, and justify their sick-roles. A patient who has given up his game of "I am sick—You, Doctor, and you-all (group) do something and take care of me" is a person ready to behave like a problem-solving adult. Such an individual can quickly learn to accept rational group-pressure as a useful means of strengthening his still weak and new "character." Therapeutic group pressure need not be mis-used irrationally (Bach, 1956) and immaturely as a substitute for individuality or as some social womb into which one may regressively crawl and hide there in fearful alienation from the big, bad competitive world of adult "fighters!" The regressive tendency to depend on the group is counteracted by the demand *for everyone to act as therapist to everyone.*

The work-burden of trying to be an effective co-therapist and agent of change to others *fatigues* all Marathonians over the long work hours. It takes devotion mixed with CONSTRUCTIVE AGGRESSION to get people to take off image-masks and put on honest faces. It takes patience and energy to break down resistances against change which all well-entrenched behavioral patterns—however irrational—will put up as part of a person's phony "self-esteem." The exhaustion and *fatigue* produced by the Marathon procedure leads to refusal to spend any energy on "acting up" or "acting out." Tired people tend to be truthful! They do not have the energy to play games.

Therapeutic Effects of Marathon Therapy

It also takes disciplined, concerted group-cooperation to create properly *focused* selective group pressure. Behavioral change is not created by uni-lateral influence, or chaotic, disorganized "free-for-all," cathartic "group-

emotions" *per se*. Marathons are *not* tension-relieving, cathartic acting-out groups. They generate rather high levels of emotional tensions which stimulate cognitive re-orientation for their relief! Generally two new modes of acting, feeling, and being emerge during a Marathon: (1) *transparency of the real self*, which (being accepted and reinforced by the peer group) leads to (2) *psychological intimacy* within the peer-group. This sequence from transparency to intimacy is a natural development because what alienates people from one another are the masks they put on, the roles they take, the images they try to create, and many of the games they play. Parenthetically, there are a few intimacy-producing games played by explicit mutual awareness and consent. These inter-personal stances alienate because they make it harder to know a person and to know where one stands with him. Inter-personal uncertainty is experienced as psychologically dangerous and anxiety-evoking until authenticity and transparency are reciprocally practiced. One or both parties may have hidden ulterior motives which usually turn out to be exploitive or destructive. Unless a person displays himself transparently, one never knows when to come on with him and when to get off or when to give, when to get or when to give up! One must remain alienated, on guard against the possibility of *psychological ambush*, i.e., to be seduced in to spilling one's guts, to expose one's vulnerability, to get one's expectations up, only to be let down, even "destroyed." The con-artist's use of the double bind, i.e., you are damned if you do and damned if you don't, is psychologically lethal, for friends have no effective defenses against the double bind.

In the course of the long work hours of Marathon therapy, a transition from this self-defensive alienation and exploitive game-playing to psychological intimacy is revealed for everyone present to see.

II[2]

Entering a Marathon group implies submitting to a set of *ground rules*. The importance of these rules is such that they have been termed *Ten Marathon Commandments*. How explicit these rules are made depends upon the sophistication of the particular group; many participants grasp them without their having to be concretely outlined. However, there are groups which require that the rules be clearly laid out, and individual participants may behave in such a manner as to force the rules to be spelled

---

[2] Part II was drafted by Dr. Bach and edited by Dr. F. Stoller after both had worked together and also independently with Marathon groups for 2 years. The 10 Marathon Commandments, their purpose and evolution will be discussed in detail in a forthcoming book, *The 300 year weekend*, by G. R. Bach, J. Gibb, G. Hoover, and F. Stoller.

out. In any case, these rules must be crystal clear in the minds of the group leaders and will act as a guide for their direction of the sessions. The following, then, are the basic group rules of the Marathon.

The Ten Marathon Commandments

(1) To stay together in the same place and not leave until the group breaks or ends at its prearranged time. Everyone communicates with the *whole* group. Everyone attends to and reacts to how each individual acts in the group situation. This means that there must be *no sub-grouping,* such as is common at ordinary social gatherings and parties. Only during official group breaks and at the end of the session do people break up into sub-groups.

(2) Creature comforts are to be taken care of on a self-regulatory basis. Eating will be done within the rules of the group, usually on a buffet *basis without disrupting the continuity of the group proceedings!* Participants can move about to different chairs, lie down on the floor, indulge in exercises within the sights and sounds of the group arena. Brief breaks for exercising, sleeping or changing clothes will be decided on by each group as a whole. There will be no alcohol or drugs taken during the Marathon proper. At the conclusion, most groups treat themselves to a "closure-party" and some groups schedule a follow-up meeting.

(3) The group leader is bound by the same rules as everyone else, except that in order to keep his services alert he has the privilege, during every twenty-four hours of work, to rest up to four hours away from the group. During his absence, the group continues the meeting on a self-regulatory basis with every group member responsible for the uninterrupted continuation of the group proceedings and the enforcement of the ground rules. (A group leader in top physical condition may become so involved in the proceedings that he may choose not to exercise his resting privilege.)

(4) All forms of physical assault or threats of physical violence are outlawed. Attacks must be confined to verbal critiques. However, there are no limits as to the straight-forward use of Anglo-Saxon words or slang.

(5) Legitimate, professionally correct group procedures such as Psycho-Drama, Awareness-expansion Exercises, "Sensitivity Training," Transactional Games Analyses, etc., may be used temporarily during a Marathon, but only under *very* special circumstances. We have found that the use of a "technique" may retard rather than facilitate the slow, natural emergence of trust, transparency, and intimacy. Any routine use of any group-process "technique," however valuable it may be in other settings, is definitely contra-indicated in the marathon group situation.

(6) The encountering experience is a four-phase process. Individual expressions are (a) reacted to, and (b) these reactions are shared in a "feedback." (c) The "feedback" in turn generates counter-reactions (d) from the original expressors as well as from the rest of the group. Members are expected to facilitate each of these phases by active participation in the following manner.

(6i) Members share true feelings as clearly and transparently as possible. The expressor is himself responsible for drawing and keeping the full attention of the group onto himself. No one should wait to be "brought out." Every participant is expected to put himself voluntarily into the focus of the group's attention, to seek out the group and to turn attention to himself, preferably a number of times. This applies to *everybody* including the official group leaders. There are *no observers,* only active participants.

By being an attentive audience, the group rewards the expressor. The expressor will remain in focal-position (or "hot-seat") until his feeling-productivity wanes and/or until the expressor himself has had "enough" of the "hot-seat," or until group-interest and group-pressure are dissipated.

(6ii) In the "feedback" reactions to the expressor, no holds are barred! Candid "*levelling*" is expected from everyone, which means participants explicitly share and do *not* hide or mask their here-and-now, on the spot reactions to one another! Tact is "out" and brutal frankness is "in." Any phony, defensive or evasive behavior (such as playing psychiatric games or reciting old "lines") is fair game for the group's critique and verbal attack. "Ought's-manship" (advising others how to solve their problems) can deteriorate into a time-consuming, dulling routine which suppresses spontaneous encounter. Excessive advice-giving is, therefore, undesirable.

(6iii) Trying to make people "feel better" is NOT *the purpose of the Marathon.* Self-appointed, tactful diplomats, amateur "protectors," and "Red Cross nurses" distract and dilute the levelling experience. Any kind of protective "cushioning" or cuddling spoils (for the central "hot-seat" person) the experience of standing up alone to the group, as he must to the world. Cushioning interventions should be held in abeyance until a participant has had the opportunity to express the full range of his Being in the group and to feel the group's reaction to him.

(7) "SHOW ME NOW . . . DO NOT TELL ME WHEN" is *the* Marathon Leitmotif. Owning up to feelings *here* and *now* and sharing them is *the* mode of participation. Telling the group about how one behaves outside the group and how "he" then and there reacted in bygone times and other places, back home or back at the office— is only warm-up material. The thing to do is for each

member to let himself feel his presence in the group and let the *currently active impact* of the others get to him!

The modes of participation recommended in the four paragraphs above (6i, 6ii, 6iii, and 7) provide each group member with the opportunity to become better aware of how he *IS* in the group and in what directions he may want to *change,* and to try out new ways of being in the group.

(8) "AS YOU ARE IN THE GROUP, SO YOU ARE IN THE WORLD." As the members learn to exchange feelings in the group, a pattern of participation automatically emerges which the group will mirror back to the individual member. In the long hours of a Marathon one cannot help being seen for what he really is and to see what he may become. The Marathon group simulates the world of emotionally significant others; and the ways in which the member relates to this world reflect the core pattern of his Being. The group members' reactions give cues as to the effect his behavior patterns have on the world. He has the option to try out new, improved ways of Being.

(9) Group members' changes and improvements in participation will be attended to by the group. Giving affectionate recognition to growth and new learning is as much in order as cuddling, defensive behavior is out of order (cf. Rule 6iii). Reinforcement of new learning is the loving side of critical levelling (cf. Rule 7 for the "attack" part).

(10) While nothing is sacred within the group, the information gained during a Marathon week-end is confidential in the nature of professionally privileged communication. Nothing is revealed to anyone outside. Objective research reporting in anonymous format is the only exception to this "rule of discretion."

The "Ten Commandments," the ground rules for Marathon participants given above, are not arbitrary "rules" or "conventions." Rather, they emerged gradually and painfully in years of clinical experience with interaction groups generally and with Marathon groups in particular. Respecting these blank ground rules does not necessarily guarantee success for a given Marathon. But, we do know that respecting the work-spirit of the situation facilitates the exciting metamorphosis of an assembly of role-playing strangers into a creatively intimate, authentically sharing communion. Since the Marathon leader likes to facilitate and partake of this metamorphosis, he has a vested, professional and personal interest in keeping anybody from distracting him and the group from this beautiful and valuable experience.

REFERENCES

Bach, G. R. *Intensive group psychotherapy.* New York: Ronald, 1954.

Bach, G. R. Pathological aspects of therapeutic groups. *Group Psychotherapy,* 1956, 9, 133–148.

Bach, G. R., & Alexander, S. *Intimate enemies: principles of therapeutic aggression.* New York: Doubleday, in press.

Rational Group Therapy

Albert Ellis
1963

Although I employed group psychotherapy a decade ago and found it to be an effective means of treating institutionalized young delinquents, and although I have been a member of the American Group Psychotherapy Association for a good many years, I resisted doing group therapy with adults in my private practice until fairly recently. One of the main reasons for my resistance was an awareness, through my patients and my professional contacts, of what often was transpiring in the type of psychoanalytically-oriented group therapy which is most prevalent in New York City.

The more rational I became as a therapist, the more irrational most psychoanalytic group therapy seemed to be; and I wanted no part in adding to the New York scene some additional "therapeutic" groups in which patients were encouraged to view each other as members of the same family, to ventilate without ever really eradicating their hostility, to regress to so-called pregenital stages of development, and generally to become sicker (though perhaps more *gratifyingly* sicker) than they had been before entering therapy.

As the theory and practice of rational-emotive psychotherapy developed, however, I began to see how it could be logically applied to group therapy, and I sometimes used it in small groups consisting of members of the same family. Thus, I would fairly frequently see husbands and wives during the same session; and sometimes I saw their children or parents or other relatives along with them. I also occasionally saw a patient and his or her friend simultaneously.

One thing that I particularly noted in the course of seeing these small groups was that considerable therapeutic time was often saved, in that whatever I had to teach one patient was sometimes just as effective with the spouse or other attending patient. Moreover, if I saw, say, a husband and wife together, and convinced even one of them that he was acting irrationally, and that if he looked at his own internalized sentences and challenged and changed them he could behave much more rationally and less neurotically, then this one convinced patient frequently was able to do a better job with the other, less convinced patient than I was able to do myself. The convinced patient became a kind of auxiliary therapist; and his playing this kind of a role frequently was of enormous help, both to the other patient and to himself (Bach, 1954; Hunt, 1962).

Noting this kind of effect from very small therapeutic groups, I decided to experiment with larger groups, and formed my first regular rational therapy group, consisting of seven members, in 1958. From the start, the group was a great success. The members not only enjoyed the sessions but seemed to be appreciably benefited by them. And some members, who had had several years of prior individual therapy and made relatively minor gains, were able to make much greater progress after they had been steady members of a group for awhile. Soon the original group began to expand in size, as more members wanted to join; and at present, I have five fairly sizable groups going on a once-a-week basis.

Rational group therapy is significantly different from many other kinds of group therapy in several respects. In the first place, the groups tend to be larger than are psychoanalytic or other types of groups. Although I naively thought, when I began my first group, that seven or eight members were quite enough to crowd into a single group,

I soon began to see that larger groups were not only quite practical but actually had distinct advantages. With the larger groups, for example, sessions tend to be more lively; more new material, and less stewing around in the same old neurotic juices, tends to arise; more challenging points of view are presented to any individual who brings up his problem during a given session; and, from the standpoint of educational economy, when productive sessions are held more "pupils" are present to learn and benefit from the professional resources (the trained therapist) present.

In consequence of its being able to deal adequately with fairly large groups of patients, rational-emotive group therapy is also financially economical, since each patient may be charged a quite reasonable fee for the hour-and-a-half session in which he participates once a week.

As a result of practical experience, therefore, I soon found it feasible to expand my groups to 10, 12, and sometimes even as many as 14 regular members. At first, I permitted the group members to socialize with each other fairly easily outside the group sessions; but when such socialization soon resulted in lying and evasion on the part of some of the group members who were becoming too friendly with other members, the rules were stiffened, and socialization was confined to the members going, as a group, for coffee after the session (without the presence of the therapist).

Other than this, alternate group sessions, when the therapist is not present, were not allowed, since my observations have led me to believe that group patients who have alternate sessions and who socialize with each other outside the group frequently adopt therapy as a way of life, isolate themselves from other outside contacts, and lead a kind of sheltered, and often very sick, existence which enables them to *avoid* facing and working out some of their main relationship problems and life difficulties.

From the start, rational group therapy has taken a highly didactic and well-integrated course, in that the session normally begins with someone's presenting a troubling problem (or continuing a problem presented at the previous session). Then the other members of the group, acting as auxiliary therapists of a sort, question, challenge, and analytically parse the thinking of the presenting patient, pretty much along the same lines as a rational therapist would handle his patient in an individual interview. If the presenter, for example, says that his boss yelled at him that day and he got very upset, they want to know exactly what he told himself to make himself upset, why he believes this nonsense that he told himself, how he is going to contradict it, what he is going to do the next time the boss yells at him, what the general philosophic principle of his upsetting himself is, etc., etc.

After one patient has been therapeutically interviewed by the other members of the group in this rational-emotive manner, a second or third patient is usually also handled in a similar manner during a given session; though on some occasions the entire session may be devoted to the problems of a single patient, especially one who has not previously presented any of his disturbances in the group. Meanwhile, considerable interaction and rational analysis of this interaction also takes place.

Thus, if one group member is too insistent that another member has a certain problem or should do this or that about his problem, he may be interrupted and challenged by any member of the group as to why he is upsetting himself so much about the first person's problem, or why he is projecting or distorting so much in relation to this problem; and soon the second person rather than the first one may be the center of the group's therapeutic attention. Similarly, if individuals in the group remain too silent, talk too much, keep talking about but never working on their problems, or otherwise acting inappropriately, they may be spontaneously challenged by other group members (or by the therapist) and objectively questioned about their group behavior.

No holds are barred in the group; and no subject of any kind is tabu. If individuals are reluctant to discuss certain aspects of their lives, they may be permitted to remain silent for awhile. But ultimately they will almost certainly be questioned; and their stubborn silences or evasions will be rationally analyzed, until they are convinced that there *is* nothing for them to be ashamed of, that there *is* no horror in revealing themselves to other group members.

Actually, with a few exceptions, the content and the language of the members' statements is unusually free at most times; and sex deviants, thieves, participants in incest, impotent and frigid individuals, paranoid patients, and other committers of socially disapproved acts are continually talking up and discussing their deeds quite openly. So honest is the general tenor of discussion in most instances that the dishonest or avoidant individual soon begins to feel uncomfortable and often feels compelled to bring up whatever fantasies or overt acts he has been hiding.

At the same time, there is no deliberate emphasis on the "true confession" type of session, or on abreaction or catharsis for their own sake. Individuals in the group are often encouraged, by the therapist or by other group members, to speak out and to discuss problems that are bothering them, but that they feel ashamed of discussing. However, they are encouraged to do so not for the cathartic release that they will get thereby, but to show them, on a philosophical level, that there really *is* nothing frightful about their revealing themselves to others, and that the world will *not* come to an end if they do so.

Thus, when anyone is afraid to speak up (as is common, especially among new members of the group), he is not forced to do so against his will. Rather, he is normally asked: "*Why* don't you want to tell us your problem? What are you afraid will happen if you do speak up? Do you think that we won't like you if you tell us the 'terrible' things you have done? Suppose we *don't* like you—what horrible event will *then* occur?" With this kind of questioning, which actually consists of an attack on the philosophic assumptions of the shy or hesitant group member, he is not only induced to ventilate his thoughts and feelings, but to challenge his own premises and to see that there is no good *reason* for his remaining silent.

Similarly, when a group member obviously dislikes what some other member is doing or saying, but will not admit his feelings of dislike or anger, he is frequently encouraged by other group members to express his feelings more openly and honestly. But, again, the purpose of his being urged to express himself is not to help him ventilate or gain emotional release. Rather, it is to show him that (a) there is no good reason why he should not behave as he feels, and (b) there is often even less good reason for his feeling the way he does and for cherishing this self-defeating feeling.

Thus, a member of one of my groups said nothing for the first several sessions he attended, but sat frowning and pouting at many things that the other group members were saying. He was finally challenged: "Well, let's have it, Joe. What's eating you?" At first he insisted that he wasn't upset in any way about what was going on in the group, but had merely been thinking of things outside the group when he frowned and pouted. But then several group members pointed out that when Jack had said this, or Marion had said that, Joe always stewed or sulked or otherwise showed evident negative feeling. How come?

"All right," Joe finally said, "I guess I have been angry. Damn angry, in fact! And why shouldn't I be? Jack keeps talking about himself all the time as if he were the only person in the room, and all the rest of us are just here to hear him and to help him with his problems; and he obviously doesn't give a damn about helping anyone else but himself. And Marion, well, she goes over the same thing, time and again, and asks us to tell her what to do, but she's really not interested in doing anything for herself and makes absolutely no effort to change. I think that she just wants our attention and has no intention of changing at all. So why should I waste my time telling her anything, when she's not even really listening?"

A couple of the group members immediately began to defend Jack and Marion, and to say that they weren't exactly doing what Joe was accusing them of; and that Joe was grossly exaggerating their poor group behavior. But one girl interrupted these two defenders and said:

"Look, this is not the point. Let's suppose that Marion and Jack are acting just as you, Joe, say they are, and that in a sense they're wasting the time of the rest of the group. So? What do you expect disturbed people to do—behave like little angels in a situation like this? Sure they're doing the wrong thing. That's what they're here for! If they were acting the way you seem to want them to act, they wouldn't need therapy at all. Now the real question is: Why the hell can't you *take* their kind of behavior, and try to help them—and help yourself through trying to help them—change it? Sitting in the corner and pouting like you have been doing for the last several sessions isn't going to help you, them, or anyone!"

"Yes," another member of the group chimed in: "Let's assume that Jack and especially Marion—whom I think you're quite right about, incidentally, because I find her, very often, an awful pain in the ass myself, and heartily agree with you that she's not trying very hard to use the group, except to *avoid* doing anything about her problem—let's suppose that they're both just wasting our time acting the way they do, and not really trying to solve their problems. So what? What do you expect neurotics like any of us to do, anyway—act like perfectly sane and healthy people? But, as Grace said, that's not the point. The real point is that *you* are upsetting yourself because Jack and Marion are behaving in their typical upset way. Now what are *you* telling yourself in order to make yourself angry at them?"

Several of the other group members also chimed in, not to induce the angry member to admit he was angry or to get him to give "healthy" vent to his anger; but, rather, to get him to look behind his anger, and discover what *he* was doing to create it. At first, he was startled with this approach, for he felt that he had a perfect *right* to be angry at Jack and Marion. But a short while later, he began to see that other issues were involved, and said:

"Yeah, I'm beginning to get it now. You're not just trying to get me to say what I feel, though that's important, too, I guess, as long as I actually feel it, and I'm not doing myself any good pouting like this and hiding my feelings. But you're really trying to get me to look behind my feelings, and to ask myself what I am doing to create them. I never thought about it that way before, but just as I'm sitting here, I can see you're right. For I was telling myself, while Marion was talking, that she has no intention whatever of changing her ways, and that she's therefore imposing on the rest of us, and especially on myself, whom I think, yes, I think I do want to change, although maybe I'm just rationalizing pretty much the same way she does. Anyway, I kept telling myself that she shouldn't be acting in this anti-group and, yes, I guess anti-me way. And I see now that I'm wrong: there's no reason why she shouldn't be acting this way, though it would be much better for her if she weren't."

"And besides," said one of the other group members,

"you're not helping her in any way by getting angry at her, as you have been doing, isn't that so?"

"Yes, you're absolutely right. If I really want to help Marion, then I shouldn't be angry at her, but should tell her that I don't think that she's really trying to get better, and should try to help her see why she's not trying, and then I might be, uh, really helpful instead of, uh—"

"Stewing in your own juices!"

"Yes, stewing in my own juices. I'm beginning to see that it's my problem for not expressing myself helpfully to her, but for becoming angry and, well, you know, I just thought of something this very minute! It could be, yes, it could well be that I was becoming angry at her because I wanted to help her, and didn't know how to, and thought it was terrible that I didn't know how to, and was afraid to take a chance and speak up, and perhaps put my foot in it before her and before the rest of the group. And I—I, yes, I guess I've been sitting here and stewing because I really hated myself for not knowing how to help her, or at least trying to speak up to try to help her, and then I was blaming her for putting me in this position, when I, of course, really put myself in it, by being afraid to speak up, and I was seeing her as the cause of my keeping my mouth shut when she wasn't, really, at all."

"In other words," said the therapist, "you blamed yourself for not being able to help Marion. Then you blamed her for putting you on this self-blaming spot, as it were. Then you said to yourself—blaming again, mind you!—She just is unhelpable and really doesn't want any of us to help her, so why doesn't she stop this stuff she is talking about when she is pretending she is trying to get help from us and—'"

"—Yes, and then I kind of almost saw what I was doing, even before the group started pointing it out to me, and I blamed myself, once again, for doing it, and for not talking up myself about it, for not bringing out *my* problem, and letting someone like Marion, instead, go on blathering about her problems when she really doesn't intend to do—. See! I can see it right now. I'm already beginning to blame her again and I can feel the blood and the temper rising in me."

"Pretty firmly and strongly set, this blaming habit, isn't it?" asked the therapist. "But don't get discouraged, now, and start blaming yourself for having the blaming habit. That would be the final ironical straw! As long as you can objectively see what you're doing, how you're blaming, as I think you are now beginning to see, the vicious circle, or set of concentric interlocking circles, of blame can be broken. In time! And with effort!"

"Yes, hell knows it's taking *me* a long enough time," interjected one of the other group members. "But it's slowly coming along. And I really do think that I blame myself just a little bit less every other day. Now if I can only apply it to others, and stop blaming people like Marion—who still, I am also forced to confess, gives me a pain in the ass, too, with her talky-talky circumlocutions—"

"You mean," interrupted another group member, "whom *you* give *yourself* a pain in the ass about."

"Yes. Thank you. Whom I give *myself* a pain in the ass about. Well, when I stop *that* kind of blaming, maybe I'll get somewhere myself and be able to live more comfortably in this unholy world."

"You can say that again!" said the group member who had first been pounced upon for his silent pouting.

Although, then, in rational group therapy there is considerable emotional ventilation and expression of cross-feelings by and among the group members, the philosophic purpose of this ventilation is continually brought to light and examined. The final aim, as in all rational-emotive therapy, is to *change* the negative thoughts and feelings of the participants, rather than merely to offer them "healthy" and gratifying expression.

Some of the main advantages of group forms of RT are as follows:

1. Since RT is mainly a mode of attitudinal de-indoctrination, the individual who has an entire group of individuals, including many who are at least as disturbed as he is, attacking and challenging his irrational self-indoctrinations may be more effectively encouraged and persuaded to challenge his own nonsense than may the individual who merely has a single therapist showing him how self-defeating he is. No matter how sane, intelligent, or effective a therapist may be, he is still only one person; and all his work with a patient may often fairly easily be edited out, by the patient's telling himself that the therapist is wrong, stupid, crazy, misguided, etc. It is often harder for a resistant patient to ignore the therapeutic influence of 10 or 12 people than it is for him to by-pass a single therapist.

2. In rational-emotive group therapy, each member of the group who actively participates serves as a kind of therapist in his own right, and tries his best to talk the other members of the group out of their self-sabotaging. In so doing, he usually cannot help seeing that he has just as silly and groundless prejudices himself as have the other people he is trying to help; and that just as they must give up their nonsense, so must he give up a great deal of his. The more stubbornly the other group members hold on to their irrational premises, the more he may be able to note his own stubbornness in holding on to his own. Moreover, the better arguments he may devise, sometimes on the spur of a moment, to assail another group member's illogical views, the better he is sometimes able to use similar arguments to defeat his own defeatism. In group RT, the patients all tend at various times to take the role of a therapist; and this kind of role-playing, as Corsini, Shaw, and Blake (1961) and Moreno

and Borgatta (1951) have shown, is an effective method of self-teaching.

3. In rational-emotive group therapy, as in most forms of group treatment, the mere fact that a patient hears the problems of the other group members is sometimes quite therapeutic. Believing, when he first enters therapy, that he is uniquely disturbed or worthless, he soon finds that his problems are no different from other people's; and that he has plenty of company in the world of emotional disturbance. He may therefore see that he is *not* necessarily hopeless, and that he (like the others) can get over his troubles. Particularly, when a disturbed group member sees equally neurotic individuals slowly but surely improve in the course of group therapy, he is likely to tell himself that at least it is *possible* for him to improve, too—whereas, previously, he may have thought this to be virtually impossible.

4. Disturbed individuals who think about their upsets seriously often come up with individual answers which can be effectively applied by others. Sometimes the specific terminology that they employ to attack their difficulties may be taken over and usefully applied by other group members. Sometimes their philosophic content is helpful. Sometimes the practical homework activity assignments that they give themselves may be successfully applied by others. Thus, one of my patients set herself the task of making an actual written account of what she was telling herself just prior to her becoming upset about something. Then, when she became upset about something similar again, she would pull out her previously made list and go over it, to see what she probably was telling herself *this* time. And she would find it easier to work with and challenge her own negative thinking in this manner. Two other members of her group, on hearing her technique of tackling her own internal verbalizations, used the method themselves and found it quite helpful.

5. Frequently a group member, especially one who has been defensively preventing himself from observing his own behavior clearly (because, with his self-blaming philosophy of life, he would then be compelled to give himself a difficult time), is able to observe, in the course of group treatment, the neurotic behavior of others; and after seeing *their* behavior, is able to recognize this same kind of activity or inactivity in himself. Thus, a good many patients who have little to talk about in individual therapy, because they are glossing over some of their major difficulties, at first listen to the disclosures of others in their group, and *then* they find that they have much to talk about—both in the group itself and in their individual therapy sessions. These people need a sort of spark from without to enable them to see what they are doing; and the group work provides them with this kind of spark in many instances.

Moreover, the mere fact that Jim, who is himself quite hostile, is safely removed from Joe's behavior, frequently enables him to see how hostile Joe is without at first recognizing his own hostility. But after he has seen Joe's (and perhaps Jack's, and Judy's, and Jill's) hostility, he is able to edge up, as it were, on his own anger, and admit that it exists.

6. Group homework assignments are often more effective than those given by an individual therapist. If the individual therapist tells a shy patient that he simply has to go out and meet other people, in order to overcome his fear of them, the patient may resist following the therapist's suggestion for quite a period of time. But if an entire group says to him, "Look fellow, let's have no nonsense about this. We want you to speak to the people in your class at school even though you think it's going to kill you to do so," then the patient may more easily give in to group pressure, may begin to push himself into social activity, and may quickly see that it really *doesn't* blight his entire existence if he fails to be accepted by everyone to whom he talks.

The mere fact that other group members are doing healthier things, after coming to therapy, than they ever did before, may persuade one member to try these same kinds of things; and the fact that he is going to have difficulty explaining to the group that he has *not* carried out its homework assignment may give him the extra drive needed to get him to carry it out. When a group member does healthy acts because of group pressure, he may be doing the right thing for the wrong reasons— that is, getting "better" out of his dire need for group approval. So this kind of "progress" is by no means always genuine movement, but it may at times be of considerable temporary help.

7. Whereas, in individual therapy, the patient can often give a seemingly honest but yet very false account of his interactions with other people, in a group situation his own account is not even needed in many instances, since he *does* socially interact right within the group itself. Therefore, the therapist may literally see how he is interacting, without relying on his reports. In one instance, for example, one of my patients kept coming to me for weeks, telling me how he was refusing to become hostile any more, no matter how his wife or boss provoked him. But after he had been in a group for only a few sessions, it was obvious that he *still* was much more hostile to others than he realized that he was; and this fact could be forcefully brought to his attention and worked at.

8. A group offers a disturbed individual more hypotheses about the causes of some of his behavior than almost any individual therapist might be able to offer him. In one case, one of my patients had been upset about his relations with his girlfriend for many weeks, and both the therapist and his group, in individual and group sessions, had given him many hypotheses as to why he was upset,

such as: he was afraid he couldn't get another girlfriend if she left him; he thought it unfair that she was difficult to cope with; he identified her with his dominating mother; etc. The patient carefully considered all these hypotheses, but felt that none of them really rang a bell in his head.

Finally, however, one of the quietest members of his group, who rarely had anything constructive to offer, at this point, wondered whether, just as in his own case, the patient was worried about his failure to make any significant progress in his relationship with this girl, and was blaming himself for failing to effectively apply his therapy-learned insights to the relationship with her. This hypothesis rang a real bell; and the patient saw more clearly what he was telling himself and began to work on one of his basic problems—fear of failing at the therapy process itself.

9. In some instances, group therapy offers patients, especially those who may be slow to warm up to considering their own problems at any given time, a chance to get more intensively at the bottom of some of their disturbances than does the usual form of individual therapy. Thus, a group therapy session generally lasts for an hour and a half (against an individual session of 45 minutes). If, during this time, a given patient is discussing his problems with the group; and if he then, immediately after, continues to discuss himself for an hour or two more, over coffee with some members of the group, he may finally begin to see things about himself that it would have been much more difficult or even impossible for him to see if he merely had the usual 45 minute single session.

By the same token, his two-, three-, or four-hour total therapeutic participation on a given day, even if he himself is relatively silent during this time, may make such a total impact on the patient that he may continue to think constructively and objectively about himself for hours or days afterward; while, after a single session of individual therapy, he may time and again tend to turn to his usual evasions of thinking concertedly about himself.

In many respects, therefore, rational group therapy (like many other forms of group therapy) has concrete advantages over individual psychotherapy. But it has disadvantages, too. An individual in a group naturally cannot receive as much specialized attention from the therapist as he can when he has individualized sessions. When he sees the therapist alone, he is much more likely to get a degree of concentration on his problem, of consistent focusing on his main tasks, and of steady persuasion, challenging, and encouragement that will almost certainly be significantly diluted when he is but one individual in a group of 10 or 12.

Moreover, group therapy is not suited to all patients. Some are too afraid of group contacts even to try it; some are too sick to stick with it when they do try it; some are so suggestible that they take all therapeutic suggestions, both good and bad, with equal seriousness, and therefore may be more harmed than helped by group treatment. Most general psychotherapy patients, I have found, are sufficiently ready for group therapy even when they have first started therapy, and can appreciably benefit from it. Many of them have a hard time in the group for the first several weeks; but if they stick at it, they find it easier and easier, and benefit enormously.

Just as group therapy is unsuitable for some patients, so is it practically mandatory for others. I have seen quite a few patients who have severe socializing problems, and who seem to be almost impossible to help when they are only in individual therapy, for the simple reason that they can be significantly improved only if and when they have more contact with others, and through this contact (and the therapeutic supervision that continues while they are having it) work through their relationship problems. But they refuse, these patients, to do anything at all about making the required social contacts; and they can go on for years of regular therapy, indefinitely refusing. Finally, they quit therapy in disgust, feeling that they have not been greatly benefited—which, in their cases, is true.

These same individuals, if they can somehow be forced or cajoled into joining a therapeutic group, usually still prove to be difficult patients, in that they say very little, do not interact with other group members, and continue to lead their lonely lives in the midst of the group process. Quite commonly, however, they can be pressured by the therapist and the group to participate more and more in the group activity; and after a time, and sometimes not too long a time, they are socializing much better and are beginning to work through their relationship difficulties.

I have no hesitation, after considerable experience with this kind of patient, in forcing some of them into group therapy by merely telling them that I will not see them any longer on a purely individual basis. Most of the time, this kind of force is not necessary; since individual patients can be persuaded by normal means to join a group. But in the several cases in which I have forced someone to join one of my groups, the worst that has happened is that they have left the group after a few sessions; and in more than half the cases they have stayed with the group and begun to benefit significantly from their association with it.

My experience with rational-emotive group psychotherapy during the past several years has shown that group work, when effectively done, is not merely an adjunct to individual therapy but actually an important part of it. For individual sessions tend to be more interesting and helpful as the member participates in a group. Behavior which the patient exhibited in the course of group sessions may be discussed in detail during the individual sessions; and, similarly, material gone over during individual therapy may be helpfully employed in the course of group sessions.

Ideally, I find that if I see my patients for regular individual sessions (usually about once a week) at the start of therapy, and after a few introductory sessions get them into a once-a-week group session, maximum benefit results. After from one to three months of this individual and group therapy combination, most patients can thereafter be seen once a week in group and once every other week (or even less often) in individual therapy. After a year or two (and sometimes less) has gone by on this kind of basis, most patients can be seen regularly mainly in the group, with individual sessions being infrequent or entirely absent.

All told, the total length of therapeutic contact in most completed cases is from two to four years. But during this period the patient has perhaps been seen for about 75 to 100 times for individual sessions and about 150 times for group sessions. In terms of time and money expended by the patient, this is a considerable saving over classical psychoanalysis or most kinds of psychoanalytically-oriented psychotherapy. And the results, from almost the beginning weeks of therapy until the end, are far better in most instances than the results that seem to be obtained by other therapeutic methods.

Rational group psychotherapy, then, is an integral part of rational-emotive analysis. Group participation is almost ideally adaptable to the rational approach; and many of the severe limitations and the anti-therapeutic results of psychoanalytic group therapy are eliminated or significantly decreased by the use of this kind of group method.

Play Therapy

❦ ❦ ❦

Excerpts from
The Psycho-Analysis of Children

Melanie Klein
1948

INTRODUCTION

The beginnings of Child Analysis go back more than two decades, to the time when Freud himself carried out his analysis of "Little Hans."[1] The first analysis of a child was of great theoretic importance in two respects. Its success in the case of a child of under five showed that psycho-analytic methods could be applied to small children; and, perhaps more important still, it was able fully to demonstrate, by direct contact with the child, the hitherto much-questioned existence of those infantile instinctual tendencies which Freud had discovered in the adult. In addition, the results obtained from it held out the hope that further analyses of small children would give us a deeper and more accurate knowledge of their psychology than analysis of adults had done, and would thus be able to make important and fundamental additions to the theory of Psycho-Analysis. But this hope remained unrealized for a long time. For many years Child Analysis continued to be a relatively unexplored region in the domain of Psycho-Analysis, both as a science and a therapy. Although several analysts, Dr. H. Hug-Hellmuth[2] in especial, have since undertaken analyses of children, no fixed rules as regards its technique or application have

been evolved. This is doubtless the reason why the great practical and theoretical possibilities of Child Analysis have not yet been generally appreciated, and why those fundamental principles and aspects of Psycho-Analysis which have long since been adopted in the case of adults have still to be laid down and proved where children are concerned.

It is only within the last twelve or thirteen years that more considerable work has been done in the field of Child Analysis. This has, in the main, followed two lines of development—one represented by Anna Freud and the other by myself.

Anna Freud has been led by her findings in regard to the ego of the child to modify the classical technique, and has worked out her method of analysing children in the latency period quite independently of my procedure. The theoretic conclusions she has come to are at variance with mine in certain fundamental respects. In her opinion, children do not develop a transference-neurosis,[3] so that a fundamental condition for analytical treatment is absent.

[1] "Analysis of a Phobia in a Five-Year-Old Boy" (1909).
[2] "Zur Technik der Kinderanalyse" (1921).

[3] "Unlike the adult, the child is not prepared to produce a new edition, as it were, of its love-relationships; the reason being that, to continue the metaphor, the original edition is not yet out of print. Its first objects, its parents, are still its love-objects in real life and not merely in imagination, as is the case with grown-up neurotics." And again: "The child has no need to exchange him" (the analyst) "with its parents without more ado; for the analyst does not offer it all those advantages in comparison with its original objects which the adult patient gains who exchanges phantasy-objects for a real person" (*Einfuhrung in die Technik der Kinderanalyse*, 1927, S. 56 and 58).

Moreover, she thinks that a method similar to the one employed for adults should not be applied to children, because their infantile ego-ideal is still too weak.[4]

These views differ from mine. My observations have taught me that children can quite well produce a transference-neurosis, and that a transference-situation arises just as in the case of grown-up persons, so long as we employ a method which is the equivalent of Adult Analysis, *i.e.* which avoids all educational measures and which fully analyses the negative impulses directed towards the analyst. They have also taught me that in children of every age it is very hard even for deep analysis to mitigate the severity of the super-ego. Moreover, in so far as it does so without having recourse to any educational influence, analysis not only does not weaken the child's ego, but actually strengthens it.

It would be an interesting task, no doubt, to compare these two lines of procedure in detail and with reference to the experimental data and to evaluate them from a theoretical point of view. But I must content myself in these pages with giving an account of my technique and of the theoretical conclusions which it has enabled me to come to. Relatively so little is known at present about the analysis of children that our first task must be to throw light on the problems of Child Analysis from various angles and to gather together the results so far obtained.

PREFACE TO THE FIRST EDITION

This book is based on the observations I have been able to make in the course of my psycho-analytic work with children. My original plan was to devote the first part of it to a description of the technique I have elaborated and the second to a statement of the theoretical conclusions to which my practical work has gradually brought me, and which now seem in their turn well fitted to assist the technique I employ. But in the course of writing this book—a task which has extended over several years—the second part has outgrown its limits. In addition to my experience of Child Analysis, the observations I have made in analysing adults have led me to apply my views concerning the earliest developmental stages of the child to the psychology of the adult as well, and I have come to

certain conclusions which I shall bring forward in these pages as a contribution to the general psycho-analytic theory of the earliest stages of the development of the individual.

The contribution is in every respect based on the body of knowledge transmitted to us by Freud. It was by applying his findings that I gained access to the minds of small children and could analyse and cure them. In doing this, moreover, I was able to make those direct observations of early developmental processes which have led me to my present theoretic conclusions. Those conclusions contain a full confirmation of the knowledge Freud has gained from the analysis of adults, and are an endeavour to extend that knowledge in one or two directions.

If this endeavour should in any way be successful, and if this book should really add a few more stones to the growing edifice of psycho-analytic knowledge, my first thanks would be due to Freud himself, who has not only raised that edifice and placed it on foundations that will allow of its further elaboration, but who has always directed our attention to those points where the new work should properly be added.

I should next like to mention the part which my two teachers, Dr. Sándor Ferenczi and Dr. Karl Abraham, have played in furthering my psycho-analytic work. Ferenczi was the first to make me acquainted with Psycho-Analysis. He also made me understand its real essence and meaning. His strong and direct feeling for the unconscious and for symbolism, and the remarkable *rapport* he had with the minds of children, have had a lasting influence on me in my understanding of the psychology of the small child. He also pointed out to me my aptitude for Child Analysis, in whose advancement he took a great personal interest, and encouraged me to devote myself to this field of psychoanalytic therapy, then still very little explored. He furthermore did all he could to help me along this path, and gave me much support in my first efforts. It is to him that I owe the beginnings of my work as an analyst.

In Dr. Karl Abraham I had the great good fortune to find a second teacher with the faculty of inspiring his pupils to put out their best energies in the service of Psycho-Analysis. In Abraham's opinion the progress of Psycho-Analysis depended upon each individual analyst —upon the value of his work, the quality of his character and the level of his scientific attainments. These high standards have been before my mind, when, in this book on Psycho-Analysis, I have tried to repay some part of the great debt I owe to that science. Abraham fully grasped the great practical and theoretic possibilities of Child Analysis. At the First Conference of German Psycho-Analysts at Würzburg in 1924, in summing up a report I had read upon an obsessional neurosis in a child, he declared in words that I shall never forget: "The future of

---

[4] The reasons she adduces are: "the weakness of the child's ego-ideal, the dependence of its requirements, and hence of its neurosis, upon the external world, its inability to control the instincts that have been liberated within it and the consequent necessity the analyst is under of keeping it under his educational guidance" (S. 82). Again: "In children, the negative tendencies they direct towards the analyst, illuminating as they so often are in many ways, are essentially inconvenient, and we must reduce them and weaken them as speedily as possible. It is in their positive relation to the analyst that truly valuable work will always be done" (S. 51).

Psycho-Analysis lies in Play Analysis." My study of the mind of the small child brought certain facts before me which seemed strange at first sight. But the confidence in my work which Abraham expressed encouraged me to go forward on my way. My theoretic conclusions are a natural development of his own discoveries, as I hope this book will show.

In the last few years my work has received the most whole-hearted support from Dr. Ernest Jones. At a time when Child Analysis was still in its first stages, he foresaw the part it would play in the future. It was at his invitation that I gave my first course of lectures in London in 1925 as a guest of the British Psycho-Analytical Society; and these lectures have given rise to the first part of my present book. (A second course of lectures, entitled "Adult Psychology viewed in the light of Child Analysis," given in London in 1927, forms the basis of the second part.) The deep conviction with which Dr. Jones has made himself an advocate of Child Analysis has opened the way for this field of work in England. He himself has made important contributions to the problem of early anxiety-situations, the significance of the aggressive tendencies for the sense of guilt, and the earliest stages of the sexual development of woman. The results of his studies are in close touch with my own in all essential points.

I should like in this place to thank my other English fellow-workers for the sympathetic understanding and cordial support they have given to my work. My friend Miss M. N. Searl, whose views agree with mine and who works along the same lines as myself, has done lasting service towards the advancement of Child Analysis in England, both from a practical and a theoretical point of view, and towards the training of child analysts. My thanks are also due to Mrs. James Strachey for her very able translation of the book, and to her and Mr. Strachey for the great assistance which their stimulating hints and suggestions have given me in its composition. My thanks are next due to Dr. Edward Glover for the warm and unfailing interest he has shown in my work, and for the way in which he has assisted me by his sympathetic criticism. He has been of special service in pointing out the respects in which my conclusions agree with the already existing and accepted theories of Psycho-Analysis. I also owe a deep debt of gratitude to my friend Mrs. Joan Riviere, who has given such active support to my work and has always been ready to help me in every way.

Last but not least, let me very heartily thank my daughter, Dr. Melitta Schmideberg, for the devoted and valuable help which she has given me in the preparation of this book.

The Role of Transference in the Analysis of Children

Anna Freud
1946

Ladies and Gentlemen. I will go briefly over the ground covered at our last meeting.

We directed our attention to the methods of the analysis of children; we remarked that we have to put the case-history together from information furnished by the family, instead of relying exclusively upon that given by the patient; we became familiar with the child as a good dream-interpreter, and evaluated the significance of day dreams and imaginative drawings as technical auxiliaries. On the other hand I had to report that children are not inclined to enter into free association, and by this refusal oblige us to look for some substitute for this most essential of aids in the analysis of adults. We concluded with a description of one of these substitute methods, postponing its theoretical evaluation until to-day.

The play technique worked out by Mrs. Melanie Klein is certainly valuable for observing the child. Instead of taking the time and trouble to pursue it into its domestic environment we establish at one stroke the whole of its known world in the analyst's room, and let it move about in it under the analyst's eye but at first without his interference. In this way we have the opportunity of getting to know the child's various reactions, the strength of its aggressive impulses or of its sympathies, as well as its attitude to the various things and persons represented by the toys. There is this advantage over the observation of real conditions, that the toy environment is manageable

and amenable to the child's will so that it can carry out in it all the actions which in the real world, so much bigger and stronger than itself, remain confined to a phantasy-existence. All these merits make the use of the Klein play-method almost indispensable for familiarisation with small children, who are not yet capable of verbal self-expression.

Mrs. Klein however takes an important further step in the employment of this technique. She assumes the same status for these play-actions of the child as for the free associations of the adult patient, and translates as she goes along the actions undertaken by the child in this way into corresponding thoughts; that is to say, she tries to find beneath everything done in play its underlying symbolic function. If the child overturns a lamp-post or a toy figure she interprets it as something of an aggressive impulse against the father; a deliberate collision between two cars as evidence of an observation of sexual union between the parents. Her procedure consists in accompanying the child's activities with translations and interpretations, which themselves—like the interpretation of the adult's free associations—exert a further influence upon the patient.

Let us examine the justification for equating the child's play activity with the adult's free association. The adult's ideas are "free," that is to say the patient has divested his thoughts of all direction and influence, but his attitude is nevertheless influenced by a certain consideration—that he who is associating has set himself to be analysed. The child lacks this attitude. I think it is possible, as I have explained before, to give the children some idea of the purpose of analysis. But the children for whom Mrs.

Note. From *The psychoanalytical treatment of children* (pp. 28–37) by N. Procter-Gregg (Trans.), 1946, London: Imag Publishing Co. Copyright 1946 by International University Press. Reprinted by permission.

Klein has worked out her play-technique, in the first infantile period, are too young to be influenced in this way. Mrs. Klein considers it as one of the important advantages of her method that by it she is saved the necessity of such a preparation of the child. But if the child's play is not dominated by the same purposive attitude as the adult's free association, there is no justification for treating it as having the same significance. Instead of being invested with symbolic meaning it may sometimes admit of a harmless explanation. The child who upsets a toy lamp-post may on its walk the day before have come across some incident in connection with such an object; the car collision may be reproducing some happening in the street; and the child who runs towards a lady visitor and opens her handbag is not necessarily, as Mrs. Klein maintains, thereby symbolically expressing its curiosity as to whether its mother's womb conceals another little brother or sister, but may be connecting some experience of the previous day when someone brought it a little present in a similar receptacle. Indeed with an adult we do not consider ourselves justified in ascribing a symbolic significance to every one of his acts or ideas, but only to those which arise under the influence of the analytical situation which he has accepted.

In reply to this objection to the Klein technique it may be said that a child's play is certainly open to the harmless interpretation just suggested, but why does it reproduce just those particular scenes with the lamp-post or the cars? Is it not just the symbolic significance behind these observations which cause them to be preferred and reproduced before any others in the analytical hour? Is it true, the argument may proceed, that the child lacks in its actions the purposive attitude of the analytical situation, which guides the adult. But perhaps it does not need it at all. The adult must renounce the guidance of his thoughts by a conscious effort of will and leave their direction entirely to his unconscious impulses. But the child may require no such deliberate modification of its situation. Perhaps it is at all times and in every piece of play entirely surrendered to the domination of its unconscious.

It is not easy to determine by an exchange of theoretical arguments the question of whether the equation of children's play with adults' free association is justifiable or not. This is obviously a matter for review in the light of practical experience.

Let us try criticism on another point. We know that Mrs. Klein utilises for interpretation, besides the things which the child does with the toys provided, all its procedure towards the objects found in her room or towards her own person. Here again she follows strictly the example of adult analysis. We certainly feel justified in drawing into the analysis all the patient's behaviour towards us during the visit, and all the little voluntary and involuntary actions which we observe him to perform. In this we

are relying upon the state of transference in which he finds himself, which can invest even otherwise trivial behaviour with symbolical significance.

Here the question arises as to whether a child finds itself in the same transference situation as the adult; in what manner and in what forms its transference-impulses come to expression; and in what they lend themselves to interpretation. We have come to the important consideration, of *the role of transference as a technical expedient in the analysis of children*. The decision on this question will at the same time furnish fresh material to controvert or support Mrs. Klein's contention.

I explained in the first lecture how I took great pains to establish in the child a strong attachment to myself, and to bring it into a relationship of real dependence on me. I would not have tried so hard to do this, if I had thought the analysis of children could be carried out without a transference of this kind. But the affectionate attachment, the positive transference as it is called in analytical terminology, is the prerequisite for all later work. The child in fact will only believe the loved person, and it will only accomplish something to please that person.

The analysis of children requires much more from this attachment than in the case of adults. There is an educational as well as an analytical purpose with which we shall later be concerned in more detail: Successful upbringing always—not only in children's analysis—stands or falls with the pupil's attachment to the person in charge of it. And we cannot say in regard to the analysis of children that the establishment of a transference is in itself enough for our purpose, regardless of whether it is friendly or hostile. We know that with an adult we can get through long periods with a negative transference, which we turn to our account through consistent interpretation and reference to its origins. But with a child negative impulses towards the analyst—however revealing they may be in many respects—are essentially inconvenient, and should be dealt with as soon as possible. The really fruitful work always takes place with a positive attachment.

I have described the establishment of this affectionate tie during our discussion of the introductory phase to the analysis of children. Its expression in fantasies and small or larger actions is hardly distinguishable from the equivalent processes in adult patients. We are made to feel the negative reactions at every point where we attempt to assist a fragment of repressed material towards liberation from the unconscious, thereby drawing upon ourselves the resistance of the ego. At such a time we appear to the child as the dangerous and to-be-feared tempter, and we bring on ourselves all the expressions of hatred and repulsion with which at other times it treats its own forbidden instinctual impulses.

I will give an account of a positive transference-fantasy

from the six-year-old obsessional patient. The external occasion for it was furnished by myself, for I had visited her in her own home and stayed for her evening bath. She opened her visit on the next day with the words, "you visited me in my bath and next time I'll come and visit you in yours." Some while later she retailed for me the day-dream which she had composed in bed before going to sleep, after I had gone away. I add her own explanatory asides in brackets.

"All the rich people did not like you. And your father who was very rich did not like you at all. (That means I am angry with your father, don't you think?) And you liked no one and gave lessons to no one. And my father and mother hated me and so did John and Billy and Mary and all the people in the world hated us, even the people we did not know, even the dead people. So you liked only me and I liked only you and we always stayed together. All the others were very rich but we two were quite poor. We had nothing, not even clothes for they took away every-thing we had. There was only the sofa left in the room and we slept on that together. But we were quite happy together. And then we thought we ought to have a baby. So we mixed a-a and cissies to make a baby. But then we thought that was not a nice thing to make a baby out of. So we began to mix flower-petals and things that gave me a baby. For the baby was in me. It stayed in me quite a long while (my mother told me that, that babies stay quite a long while in their mothers) and then the doctor took it out. But I was not a bit sick (mothers usually are, my mother said). The baby was very sweet and cunning and so we thought we'd like to be just as cunning and changed ourselves to be very small. I was 'so' high and you were 'so' high. (That is, I think because in our lesson last week we found out that I wanted to be like Billy and Mary.) And as we had nothing at all we started to make ourselves a house out of rose-leaves, and beds out of rose-leaves and pillows and mattresses all out of rose-leaves sewn together. Where the little holes were left we put some-thing white in. Instead of wall-paper we had the thinnest glass and the walls were carved in different patterns. The chairs were made of glass too but we were so light that we were not too heavy for them. (I think I left my mother out because I was angry with her for not coming to see me.)" Then there followed a detailed description of the furni-ture and all the things that were made for the house. The daydream was obviously spun out in this direction until she went to sleep, laying special emphasis on the point that our initial poverty was finally quite made up for and that in the end we had much nicer things than all the first mentioned rich people.

The same little patient at other times related how she was warned against me from within. The inner voice said, "Don't believe Anna Freud. She tells lies. She will not help you and will only make you worse. She will change your face too, so that you look uglier. Everything she says is not true. Just be tired, stay quietly in bed and don't go to her to-day." But she always told this voice to be silent and said to it that it should be told of first of all in the next appointment.

Another small patient envisaged me, at the time when we were discussing her masturbation, in all sorts of degrading roles—as a beggar, as a poor old woman, and once as just myself but standing in the middle of my room with devils dancing round me.

You will notice that we become the object towards which the patient's friendly or hostile impulses are directed, just as we do in the case of adults. It might seem from these examples that a child makes a good trans-ference. Unfortunately that is not really true. The child indeed enters into the liveliest relations with the analyst, and evinces a multitude of reactions which it has acquired in the relationship with its parents; it gives us most impor-tant hints on the formation of its character in the fluctua-tion, intensity, and expression of its feelings; but it forms no transference neurosis.

The analysts amongst you will know what I mean by this. The adult neurotic gradually transforms, in the course of analytic treatment, the symptom on account of which he sought this remedy. He gives up the old objects on which his fantasies were hitherto fixed, and centres his neurosis anew upon the person of the analyst. As we put it, he substitutes transference-symptom for his previous symptoms, transposes his existing neurosis, of whatever kind, into a transference-neurosis, and displays all his abnormal reactions in relation to the new transference person, the analyst. On this new ground, where the analyst feels at home, he can follow up with the patient the origin and growth of the individual symptoms; and on this cleared field of operations there then takes place the final struggle, for gradual insight into the malady and the discovery to the patient of the unconscious processes within him.

There are two possible reasons why this cannot be brought about in the case of a small child. One lies within the psychological structure of the child itself, the other in the child's analyst.

The child is not, like the adult, ready to produce a new edition of its love-relationships, because, as one might say, the old edition is not yet exhausted. Its original objects, the parents, are still real and present as love-objects—not only in fantasy as with the adult neurotic; between them and the child exist all the relations of everyday life, and all its gratifications and disappointments still in reality depend on them. The analyst enters this situation as a new person, and will probably share with the parents the child's love or hate. But there is no necessity for the child to exchange the parents for him, since compared to them he has not the advantages which the adult finds when he can exchange his fantasy-objects for a real person. Let us in this connection reconsider Mrs. Klein's method. She maintains that when a child evinces hostility towards her in the first visit, repulsing or even beginning to strike her, one may see in that a proof of the child's ambivalent attitude towards its mother. The hostile components of this ambivalence are merely displaced onto the analyst. But I believe the truth of the matter is different. The more tenderly a little child is attached to its own mother, the fewer friendly impulses it has towards strangers. We see this most clearly with the baby, who shows only anxious rejection towards everyone other than its mother or nurse. Indeed the converse obtains. It is especially with children who are accustomed to little loving treatment at home, and are not used to showing or receiving any strong affection, that a positive relationship is often most quickly established. They obtain from the analyst what they have up till now expected in vain from the original love objects.

On the other hand, the behaviour of the children's analyst, as we have described him, is not such as to produce a transference that can be well interpreted. We know how we bear ourselves in the analysis of adults for this purpose. We remain impersonal and shadowy, a blank page on which the patient can inscribe his transference-fantasies, somewhat after the way in which at the cinema a picture is thrown upon an empty screen. We avoid either issuing prohibitions, or allowing gratifications. If in spite of this we seem to the patient forbidding or encouraging, it is easy to make it clear to him that he has brought the material for this impression from his own past.

But the children's analyst must be anything but a shadow. We have already remarked that he is a person of interest to the child, endowed with all sorts of interesting and attractive qualities. The educational implications which, as you will hear, are involved in the analysis, result in the child knowing very well just what seems to the analyst desirable or undesirable and what he sanctions or disapproves of. And such a well-defined and in many respects novel personality is unfortunately a bad transference-object, of little use when it comes to interpreting the transference. The difficulty here is, as though, to use our former illustration, the screen on which a film was to be projected already bore another picture. The more elaborate and brightly-coloured it is, the more will it tend to efface the outlines of what is superimposed.

For these reasons the child forms no transference neurosis. In spite of all its positive and negative impulses towards the analyst it continues to display its abnormal reactions where they were displayed before—in the home circle. Because of this the children's analyst is obliged to take into account not only what happens under his own eye but also what occurs in the real scene of the neurotic reactions, i.e. the child's home. Here we come to an infin-

ity of practical technical difficulties in the analysis of children, which I only lay broadly before you without going into actual detail. Working from this standpoint we are dependent upon a permanent news-service about the child; we must know the people in its environment and be sure to some extent of what their reactions to the child are. In the ideal case, we share our work with the persons who are actually bringing up the child; just as we share with them the child's affection or hostility.

Where the external conditions, or the personalities of the parents, do not allow of such co-operative treatment, certain material for the analysis eludes us. On this account I had to conduct some analyses of children almost exclusively by means of dreams and daydreams. There was nothing interpretable in the transference and much of the day-to-day symptomatic neurotic material never became available to me.

But there are ways and means to bring about an equation of the child's situation to that of the adult (so much better suited for the carrying through of analysis); and so to force the child into a transference neurosis. This may become necessary where it is a case of severe neurotic illness in an environment hostile either to analysis or the child. In such a case the child would have to be removed from its family and placed in some suitable institution. As there is no such institution in existence at present we are at full liberty to imagine one, say a home supervised by the children's analyst himself, or—less far-fetched—a school where psycho-analytical principles predominate and the work is attuned to co-operation with the analyst. In both cases a symptom-free period would first occur, in which the child accustoms itself to the new and favourable surroundings. The better it feels at this time, the more unapt and unwilling for analysis shall we find it. We shall probably do best to leave it quite undisturbed. Only when it has "acclimatised itself," that is to say when under the influence of the realities of everyday life it has formed an attachment to the new environment, beside which the original objects gradually pale; when it allows its symptoms to revive again in this new existence, and groups its abnormal reactions around new personages; when it has thus formed its transference-neurosis—will it become analysable once more.

In an institution of the first sort, managed by the children's analyst (and at present we cannot even judge whether such an arrangement is to be desired) it would then be a matter of an actual transference-neurosis in the sense of the adult's, with the analyst as focal object. In the other sort we should simply have artificially bettered the home environment, creating a substitute home which so to say allows us to see into it, as seems necessary for the analytical work, and the reactions of which towards the child we can control and regulate.

Thus the removal of the child from its home might

appear to be the most practical solution. But when we come to consider the termination of a child's analysis, we shall see how many objections there are to it. By this expedient we forestall the natural development at a crucial stage, forcing the child's premature detachment from the parental objects at a time when it neither is capable of any independence in its emotional life, nor has at its disposal, owing to external circumstances, any freedom in the choice of new love-objects. Even if we insist on a very long duration for the analysis of children there still remains in most cases a hiatus between its termination and the development of puberty, during which the child needs education, protection, and guidance in every sense of the words. But what gives us any assurance that after we have secured a successful resolution of the transference the child will find of itself the way to the right objects? It returns home at a time when it has become a stranger there, and its further guidance is now perhaps entrusted to the very persons from whom we have forcibly detached it. On inner grounds it is not capable of self-reliance. We are thus placing it in a position of renewed difficulty, in which it will find again most of the original elements of its conflict. It can now take either once more the path to neurosis or, if this is closed to it by the successful outcome of the analytical treatment, the opposite line of open rebellion. From the purely therapeutical point of view this may seem an advantage; but from that of social adjustment which in the child's case matters most in the end, it is certainly none.

A Theoretical Framework
for Group Play-Therapy

Hiam G. Ginott
1961

The tendency to regard group therapy as "superficial" has abated considerably during the last decade. On both a national and an international scale, group therapy has been gaining acceptance by individual clinicians and treatment agencies. Two factors account for the change in attitude toward group therapy: (1) group therapy has evolved a systematic theory with principles and processes that can be tested scientifically; (2) necessity, the mother of invention, has compelled many therapists to try group therapy in an effort to meet more realistically the growing demands for service. In the course of trial and error, many have found group therapy to be not just a watered-down individual therapy extended simultaneously to several participants but a qualitatively different experience with rich potentialities of its own. Hobbs expressed the thoughts of many group therapists when he wrote: "It is one thing to be understood and accepted by a therapist, it is considerably a more potent experience to be understood and accepted by several people who are also honestly sharing their feelings in a joint search for a more satisfying way of life." . . .

The aim of all therapy, including group therapy, is to effect basic changes in the intrapsychic equilibrium of each patient. Through relationship, catharsis, insight,

reality testing, and sublimation, therapy brings about a new balance in the structure of the personality, with a strengthened ego, modified superego, and improved self-image. The inner experience responsible for curative effects is the same in all therapies, just as the repair value of certain medications is the same, whether administered orally, intramuscularly, or intravenously. Every therapeutic system must explain and justify its effectiveness in terms of its impact on the identifiable variables of therapy. In evaluating a particular therapy approach, the following questions must be answered:

1. Does the method facilitate or hinder the establishment of a therapeutic relationship?

2. Does it accelerate or retard evocation of catharsis?

3. Does it aid or obstruct attainment of insight?

4. Does it augment or diminish opportunities for reality testing?

5. Does it open or block channels for sublimation?

The variations in the intensity and richness of these five elements account largely for differences in treatment results attained in different therapies. The above five criteria will be used in evaluating group play-therapy.

DOES GROUP PLAY-THERAPY FACILITATE OR HINDER THE ESTABLISHMENT OF A THERAPEUTIC RELATIONSHIP?

The presence of several children seems to facilitate the establishment of a desired relationship between the therapist and each child. A group setting proves especially helpful during the initial meeting. The first encounter with the therapist is frequently frightening to the small child. He is reluctant to separate from his mother and to follow a strange person to an unfamiliar room. It is less threatening for him to enter the new situation in the company of two or three children of his own age. In individual therapy, it is not unusual for a child, at his first session, to feel ill at ease, withdraw completely, and spend the whole session without daring to utter a word or touch a toy. In group play-therapy the presence of other children seems to diminish tension and stimulate activity and participation. The group induces spontaneity in the children; they begin to relate to the therapist and to trust him more readily than they do in individual therapy. This is illustrated by the following play-therapy sequence:

Seven-year-old Edna refused to enter the playroom for her first session. She sat in the waiting room, her face buried in mother's lap and her arms around mother's waist. In an emphatic voice she proclaimed, "I ain't going in without my mother." In spite of her loud protests, the therapist led Edna to the playroom. She looked like a lamb going to the slaughter. She stood in the corner of the room crying bitterly, "I want my Mom." The two other girls observed Edna with curiosity. "Why is she crying?" asked Betty. Ruth, who only ten sessions ago had a similar experience, answered, "She's afraid of the doctor. That's why she's crying." Ruth turned to Edna and said sympathetically, "You're scared, aren't you?" Edna did not reply, but she stopped crying. "I know you're scared," Ruth went on. "I felt the same when I first came here." "You did?" said Edna, turning her face away from the wall. She took one step forward and said to Ruth, "You was afraid, too? I'm scared of doctors 'cause they hurt you." "Not this one," assured Ruth. A few minutes later, Edna and her newly acquired friends were busily digging in the sandbox.

Identification is the crucial process whereby the group experience can become therapeutic. The group provides opportunities for multilateral relationships unavailable in individual play-therapy. In addition to an accepting and respecting parent surrogate, the group also offers the patients other identification models. Children identify themselves not only with the therapist but with the other members of the group. An effeminate boy, for example, may derive ego strength from associating with an accepting masculine playmate, and an over-protected child may become more independent by identifying himself with more autonomous group members. The tendency to withdraw into fantasy, so characteristic of the schizoid, is likely to be dispelled by the reminders of reality provided by others in the group. On the other hand, hyperkinetic children may become less active and more introspective under the neutralizing influence of calmer group mates. The result is that both the withdrawn and the over-active achieve a healthier balance between the inner world of fantasy and the outer world of reality.

The focus of treatment in group play-therapy is always the individual child. No group goals are set and no group cohesion is looked for. Each child may engage in activities unrelated to other members. Subgroups form and disband spontaneously according to the ever-changing interests of the participants. Yet, interpatient relations are an important element in group treatment. The therapeutic process is enhanced by the fact that every group member can be a giver and not only a receiver of help. Hobbs summarizes it: "In group therapy a person may achieve mature balance between giving and receiving, between dependence of self and realistic self-sustaining dependence on others." . . . This point is illustrated in the following group therapy excerpt:

Barbara, aged eight, had not seen her father in two years. She missed him keenly. During one of the therapy sessions, while handling a gun, she hurt her finger. It was a minor injury, but she reacted with much emotion. She cried bitterly and pleaded with the therapist.

BARBARA: Please let me go. My finger hurts, and I need my mother.

THERAPIST: It's not only your finger that hurts. Something hurts inside.

Barbara: Yes.

THERAPIST: You miss your Daddy.

BARBARA: My Daddy went away and I don't have a Daddy. He never comes home, and I need my Daddy.

Barbara stood close to the therapist and cried.
Shirley, aged 9, came over, put her arm around Barbara and said: "I don't have a Daddy either. My parents are divorced, and my father is far away in California."
The two girls stood close to each other, sharing their common sorrow.

There are also risks in group play-therapy. For example, a child who is ostracized by the group may relive original trauma too vividly and with damaging results. However, such dangers are not inherent in group therapy; they are a result of faulty grouping. Just as in adult therapy, patients in play-therapy should be grouped for the therapeutic impact they have on each other. . . .

DOES GROUP PLAY-THERAPY ACCELERATE OR RETARD EVOCATION OF CATHARSIS?

Children differ greatly in their use of cathartic media and in their preferences for "playing out" or "saying out" their problems. The therapeutic medium best suited for young children is play. In therapy, the term "play" does not connote its usual recreational meaning, but it is equivalent to freedom to act and react, suppress and express, suspect and respect.

Group play-therapy provides two media for catharsis, play and verbalization, so that each child can utilize the symbolic means of expression which best meet his need. In individual therapy, catharsis is mostly free associative. It consists of the child's free movement from activity to activity and from play to play. Seemingly unrelated activities, like verbal free association, can lead to the emergence of themes related to the patient's core problems. Group play-therapy has an advantage over individual treatment in regard to catharsis. Besides "free associative" catharsis, it provides also "vicarious"[1] and "induced"[1] catharsis. Many children, especially the more fearful ones, participate covertly as spectators in activities that they crave but fear. The group accelerates the child's awareness of the permissiveness of the setting. When one child comes forth with a "daring" activity, others in the group frequently find it easier to do the same. Children who are afraid to initiate any activity on their own gain the courage to do so in the company of others. It is as though the children help each other to realize that the playroom is a safety zone amid life's heavy traffic, where they can rest or roam without fear of authority figures and careless drivers.

It is dramatic to observe a child who stands in the corner of the room, not daring to take a step and yet following with eager eyes the activities in which he would like to indulge. He is frightened and fascinated when another boy spanks the baby doll or shoots the mother doll. It is rewarding to see children moving from passive observation to occasional involvement, to initiation of activities, and finally to cooperation with others.

Ten-year-old Jim held a rubber snake in his hand and said with great venom, "I like this snake better than my brother. I hate my brother. He's not just a nuisance; he's a pest." Nine-year-old Todd, who was standing in the corner of the room, withdrawn and quiet, came over to Jim and said, "My brother's a pest, too." The eyes of the two boys lit up with a strange glitter as they helped each other to express their hatred of siblings.

JIM: I can't stand my brother.

TODD: My brother is no good.

JIM: Mine is more no good.

TODD: Mine's the worst.

JIM: I wish I didn't have a brother.

TODD: I wish my brother would disappear.

JIM: I wish my brother was never born.

TODD: I wish my brother was never thought to be born.

This was Todd's third session. The first two sessions he spent in complete silence.

It must be stressed that catharsis is always grounded in relationship. It occurs only when there is trust between the child and the therapist. Only in a secure atmosphere do children feel free to regress and to relive early emotions in a constructive milieu.

DOES GROUP PLAY-THERAPY AID OR OBSTRUCT ATTAINMENT OF INSIGHT?

There is no direct relationship between insight and adjustment. There are many psychotics who have an uncanny grasp of the dynamics of their personality, whereas the bulk of so-called "normal" people have relatively little insight into the motivation of their behavior. This remark is not made to devalue insight but to point out its limitations as a catalyzer in therapy. Frequently, insight is a result rather than a cause of therapy, attained by persons who have grown emotionally ready to get acquainted with their unconscious. This pertains to both adults and children. Through growth in inner security, children acquire a keener awareness of themselves and of their relations to the significant persons in their lives. This insight is frequently derivative and non-verbal and attained without the aid of interpretations and explanations. As Slavson points out: "In activity groups in which no interpretation is given, children become aware of the change

---

[1] This term was coined by S. R. Slavson.

within themselves and of their former motives and reactions." . . . In play-therapy, insight is both direct and derivative, both verbal and non-verbal.

Some leading therapists feel that with adults individual therapy provides a better setting for achievement of insight than group therapy. They believe that only the deep transference relationship of individual treatment can give patients the security and the courage to face their unconscious. This may possibly be true in adult therapy. However, experience with groups of young children has indicated that mutual stimulation of ideas and feelings brings to the surface profound insights. Self-knowledge is developed through experience with many different relationships. In group play-therapy children are forced to re-evaluate their behavior in the light of peer reactions. The following example from a group session will serve as an illustration.

Horty, aged nine, is extremely domineering and critical. During the therapy hour, there is hardly a moment in which she does not boss, criticize, or belittle the other children. In this session her victim was Linda. When Linda wanted to paint, Horty said, "That's not how you paint. Let me show you how to do it." Without waiting for Linda's consent, Horty poured paint all over Linda's paper. When Linda wanted to use brown paint, Horty commanded, "Don't use brown; use purple." She grabbed the brown paint out of Linda's hand and gave her a jar of purple. When Linda wanted to put starch on her painting, Horty said, "Don't use starch; use water." Over Linda's protests, Horty poured water on the painting. Linda sighed.

The therapist said, "You wish she did not boss you so much."

LINDA: You boss too much.

HORTY: No, I don't.

LINDA: Yes, you do. Listen how you talk. You talk like a teacher. Do this! Do that! You better stop being so bossy!

Horty had no answer. She retreated to a corner of the table, and painted in silence for a long time. Suddenly she turned to Linda and said, "Am I really so bossy?"

It seems that the group crystallized the situation for Horty. It made her aware of her problem, so that she could face it and reflect upon it in the very situation that ordinarily provoked the difficulty. In individual therapy it would have taken much longer for the child to be confronted with the problem.

DOES GROUP PLAY-THERAPY AUGMENT OR DIMINISH OPPORTUNITIES FOR REALITY TESTING?

Unlike individual treatments, group play-therapy provides a tangible social setting for discovering and experimenting with new and more satisfying modes of relating to peers. The group constitutes a milieu where new social techniques can be tested in terms of reality mastery and inter-individual relationships. The inhibited child learns that he can attain objectives by voicing his desires, and the driven child learns that they are also served who only stand and wait.

The presence of several children in the playroom serves to tie the therapy experience to the world of reality. Infantile feelings of omnipotence and magic that interfere with good adjustment are unmasked and modified by the group. The children help each other to become aware of their responsibilities in interpersonal relations. The following excerpt from a case record illustrates the group's ability to put pressure on an unsocialized member, much beyond what could be expected in individual therapy.

The minute Pat, aged nine, gets into the playroom, she starts annoying the other children, and in spite of their protests, she keeps up her attacks. Thus today she shot the airgun into the ears of the other girls, and threatened to put paint on their clothes. In defense, the girls teamed up against Pat with a verbal barrage:

JANET: I bet even your mother doesn't love you.

PAT: Yes, she does.

JANET: Nobody could love anybody like you.

PAT: My mother loves me.

JANET: I bet your mother would like to get rid of you.

PAT: I have the best mother in the world.

MARGIE: You're crazy. You're ready for the nut house.

PAT: I am not crazy.

MARGIE: Are you a tomboy?

PAT: NO!

JANET: Then why do you act like a tomboy?

Pat was surprised by the intensity of the attack, and began to cry. She wanted to leave the playroom.

THERAPIST: You are very unhappy. It hurts you that they don't like you.

PAT: I am not coming back. They hate me.

THERAPIST: You want them to like you.

PAT: Yes.

JANET: How can we like you when you act like that? You don't accept any rules.

MARGIE: Don't fight so much and we'll like you better.

However, the usual circumstance is that the group allows children to experience external reality as satisfying and helpful. To many children, reality has become charged with massive negative expectations. They perceive the world as hostile and depriving, and they expect from it nothing but doom. These children find the conditioned reality of therapy an emotionally moving experience. They have had previous group experiences, but in those they had to be most unlike themselves and constantly on guard. In ordinary groups, they have had to conceal more than reveal, and the barrier between them and other persons was at its highest. The following excerpt from a group play-therapy session will serve as an illustration.

> Garrulous Gracie, aged ten, was in therapy with two very quiet and withdrawn girls. For many sessions Gracie dominated the scene with her ceaseless jabber, and she could really talk a blue streak about everything and about nothing.
> One day Linda, aged eleven, turned to Gracie and said in a very soft and sympathetic voice, "Why do you always talk so fast, Gracie?" The question caught Gracie by surprise. She mumbled unintelligibly for a moment and then blurted out, "Because nobody listens to me, that's why! The minute I open my mouth, my mother says, 'Here she goes again,' and my father yells, 'Shut up!' "
> "Oh," said Linda, "that's too bad. But we're not family. We'll listen to you."

In therapy groups, children are exposed to a new quality of intimate relationships. They learn that they can shed defenses and yet remain protected, that they can get close to contemporaries and an adult and not get hurt. In the security of the therapeutic atmosphere, the children can face each other squarely and honestly and experience emotional closeness to other people. The group as a miniature society offers motivation and support for change, as well as a safe arena for testing new modes of behavior. The children learn that the sharing of materials and ideas is acclaimed by society and that their own contributions are expected and welcomed.

DOES GROUP PLAY-THERAPY OPEN OR BLOCK CHANNELS FOR SUBLIMATION?

One of the aims of child psychotherapy is to help children to develop sublimations consistent with society's standards and expectations. The capacity to accept some, repress a few, and sublimate many primitive urges is the mark of maturity.

Group play-therapy provides children with a richer repertory of sublimatory activities than does individual play-therapy. In individual therapy, a young child may engage in the same activity session after session. For example, he may paint with water colors and never use finger paints, or he may sift sand and never make mud. This self-imposed play restriction may be due to lack of inventiveness or to lack of security on the part of the child. Group play-therapy reduces the child's propensity to repetition; in a group, children teach each other to employ a variety of materials and to engage in a variety of activities, thus increasing each child's stock of sublimatory outlets.

The presence of group mates enables children to engage in competitive games. In group games, children can vent hostility symbolically against substitute siblings. In the initial stage of therapy, children tend to displace hostility upon group mates and the therapist. They attack group members, grab their toys, and interfere with others' activities. As therapy progresses, sublimations replace displacements. Instead of squirting water at one another, children feed dolls; instead of splashing paint, they color pictures; instead of throwing blocks, they build houses; instead of attacking each other, they engage in target shooting and in other competitive games. Such competitive activities, experienced in the accepting atmosphere of the playroom, eventually result in reduced sibling rivalry at home.

SUMMARY

The basic assumptions of this chapter are that the inner experiences responsible for the healing process are the same in all therapies and that every therapy system must explain its effectiveness in terms of its contributions to the identifiable variables common to all therapy. The unique contributions of group play-therapy to the establishment of a therapeutic relationship, to the evocation of catharsis, to the derivation of insight, to the testing of reality, and to the development of sublimations are pointed out and evaluated.

Play Therapy Procedures and Results

Virginia M. Axline
1955

A seven-year-old boy, in the middle of a play therapy session, cried out spontaneously, "Oh, every child just once in his life should have a chance to spill out all over without a 'Don't you dare! Don't you dare! Don't you dare!' " That was his way of defining his play therapy experience at that moment.

An eight-year-old girl suddenly stopped her play and exclaimed, "In here I turn myself inside out and give myself a shake, shake, shake, and finally I get glad all over that I am me."

A twelve-year-old boy who had a long record of delinquency stopped his play, sat down, and looked at the play therapist. He had had many stormy play sessions in this room.

"Strangest thing that happened to me," he commented slowly. "Dragged through one court lecture after another. End up coming here because I'm a no-good kid. What happens? Nothin.' Nothin,' but time for me to spend as I want to spend it. Any way seems all right in here. So I'm used to squandering time, see? The faster it's over, the better I like it, see? Now all of a sudden I'm confused. I turn into a miser about my time. I want this to last, see? I can't understand it at all. I ask myself who is crazy here— you or me? How come, all of a sudden, no lectures? Has everybody finished all the yellin' and cussin' they had for me? Don't you know *who* you got in here? Don't you *know* I'm a no-good kid that'll probably end up killing somebody? Or what cooks?"

"It is baffling and difficult for you to understand how you do feel about all this," said the therapist.

Note. From "Play therapy procedures and results" by V. Axline, 1955, *American Journal of Orthopsychiatry, 25,* 618–626. Copyright 1955 by the American Orthopsychiatric Association. Reprinted by permission.

"It don't really seem to matter what it is that's happening. You stay the same. I ain't suspicious of you any more. I think maybe you're crazy, see. Maybe you don't know about what people are really like—*mean*—and I hate their guts. Maybe I'm crazy! Maybe in here we're *both* of us crazy, see?" He quickly went over to the table and with a sweep of his arm flung all the toys off the table onto the floor. He turned and looked defiantly at the therapist.

"Well?" he demanded. "So what?"

"You say what," the therapist replied quietly.

The boy dug his hands through his hair, uttered a sound like a groan.

"I'm a tough kid, see?" he said with a trace of desperation in his voice. "I can't suddenly get soft spots deep inside of me. I can't get so—so slowed down I—I feel *all* my feelings!"

What is this experience which is known as psychotherapy? There are many different psychological rationales and methods. The over-all objective is probably basic to all procedures: namely, to provide a relationship with the client that will enable him to utilize the capacities that are within him for a more constructive and happier life as an individual and as a member of society. The degree to which we achieve this varies greatly with individual cases. The method by which we seek to achieve the cooperative effort between the therapist and the client varies. This paper will deal with the writer's tentative conclusions that have grown out of the detailed study and analysis of many electrically recorded play therapy sessions, evaluations of the results at termination by parents, teachers, physicians, and follow-up studies.

It seems evident that individuals are learning something all of the time. It is a cumulative, integrative process. A baby is born into a completely new and different world of experience. With his first breath, he begins his long span of accumulating experiences. The first breath leads to the second breath—and while it is similar in process it is not identical. The third breath is different from the preceding ones because of the changes in lung capacity, the experience of breathing, the process of adjusting to the outer world. And this begins the individual's experience in a world of people and things. Life forces interact and the process of learning is under way.

Psychotherapy is a learning experience—a very complex, cumulative, integrative, personal involvement.

The individual's perceptions of himself and his relationships to his world are as uniquely the individual's as are his own heartbeats. Efforts may be made to increase our understanding of how experiences are perceived by the individual and it may be possible to obtain a fairly close approximation of the individual's perceptions. However, the individual alone experiences the total impact of any personal involvement because he feels not single, isolated feelings of the moment but feelings that are created and colored by the affective accompaniment of his total experiences.

Certain descriptive words frequently used in discussions of behavior have become almost stereotyped concepts, lacking accuracy in functional use. For example, is it possible to feel hate without accompanying fear, inadequacy, threat? Does a feeling of guilt come naked and alone? Or does guilt emerge with attendant feelings of insecurity, inadequacy, fear? How does one determine which of the feelings is of greater significance to the individual? Or is this even necessary in order to provide a therapeutic experience for the individual—as "therapeutic experience" is defined in this paper?

In psychotherapy, we are dealing with emotionalized attitudes that have developed out of the individual's past experiencing of himself in relation to others. These emotionalized attitudes influence his perception of himself as either adequate or inadequate, secure or insecure, worthy of respect or not worthy of respect, having personal worth or deficient in this basic feeling. His perception then, in turn, determines his behavior. The individual's behavior at the moment seems to be his best efforts to maintain and defend his selfhood and so maintain a psychological identity and a resistance to threats against his personality. Consequently, the child who is emotionally deprived and who has had experiences that seem to form and reinforce feelings of inadequacy and lack of personal worth learns the kind of behavior that protects his self-esteem and lessens the impact of threats against his personality. He may withdraw from relationships with others in his effort to avoid further emotional abuse. He may refuse to behave in certain ways that are expected or demanded by others in order to maintain a self with integrity. He may be dominated and overwhelmed by his relationships with others that strive to take from him his claim to individu-

ality without giving him the love and feelings of security and worth-whileness that he needs. He may seem to comply to the external pressures and to conform to demands made upon him. However, this type of behavior seems to be symptomatic of his underlying feelings of insecurity and inadequacy and does not have the integrated, purposeful self-involvement that leads to increasing psychological independence and maturity. He may react by hostile, aggressive rebellion. He may strike out at people and things in his world because of his reaction to a weakening concept of self-adequacy. The child who is extremely deprived emotionally shows this deficiency by his apathetic, overwhelming fear of his relationships that seems almost to paralyze him in his efforts to bring something of himself into a relationship with others.

In the past few years, there has been increasing awareness of a kind of behavior that is sometimes termed "pseudo mental retardation." The child's behavior resembles closely the kind of behavior that has been evaluated as indicating mental retardation. There is often lack of responsiveness, lack of progress along developmental lines, deficient social and emotional behavior. The studies that have been made in an attempt to check the validity of the diagnosis of many of these children through psychotherapeutic interviews have raised a significant question in the field of child psychology. These studies and exploratory work have indicated that often this type of behavior is a mask that a child who is emotionally deprived and who feels rejected and unloved and unwanted wears to protect himself. He does not know that this behavior only aggravates the attitudes toward him that create the behavior. It is not premeditated, rational behavior. It is defensive behavior. It is reinforced by the increasing pressures placed upon him where he finds himself more and more frequently in a situation where he is being "tested," put on trial, forced to face an almost endless probing in attempts to understand him, to help him, or to change him.

How can we explain the changes in the child's behavior in those cases where the child has received some form of psychotherapy—and in those cases where the parents have not been willing to participate in any kind of counseling or psychotherapy for themselves?

One ready explanation is that the child would have changed anyhow—that the passage of time alone brought this about. The answer to that explanation can be approached through research projects that have control groups. There is very little research of this kind at the present time.

Another explanation grows out of recorded, objectively observed analysis of therapeutic sessions of growing numbers of children with this behavior pattern. These observations, when followed by evaluation and assessment of the children's behavior after psychotherapy and at later follow-up periods, indicate a theoretical position that should be subjected to the rigors of research procedures to either support or deny the theory.

When such a child comes into a play therapy room and is confronted with a roomful of toys—or a modified selection of toys—and the therapist tries to create the kind of experience that will enable to child to learn how *he* can function on his own, he is involved in a very complex, highly personal, emotional learning experience.

Procedures in the playroom vary greatly. There are, however, basic requirements for all therapists. They should have a genuine respect and interest in the child as a total person. They should have patience and understanding of the complexities of a child's inner world. They should know themselves well enough to be willing and able to serve the child's needs without emotional involvement. They should have sufficient objectivity and sufficient intellectual freedom to set up tentative hypotheses to check—with adequate flexibility to adjust their thinking and responses to further enhance the child's self-discovery. They should have sensitivity, empathy, a sense of humor, and a light touch because a child's world is variable, delicate, full of movement, lights, shadows, rhythm, poetry and grace. The child is quick to respond to the attitudes of respect and love that are offered to him—not thrust upon him.

The child is far more accepting of others—is far more understanding and tolerant than are his elders. He is without prejudice until he catches this attitude from those about him whose insecurity breeds fear and bias.

The therapist and the child meet in the playroom. It is a learning experience for both of them. It is a cooperative effort by which each one learns something that becomes an integral part of both of them.

This is a safety zone that communicates security to the child gradually because of the consistency of the therapist, the stability of the limitations, the friendly understanding, the gentle but firm emphasis on the child's frame of reference, and the patience that keeps out society's pressures to hurry. The child has the time to experience deeply and fully his ability to be a person in his own right through an increasing understanding of his feelings and attitudes and capacities to act and interact with honesty and forthrightness.

If we accept the statement that individuals are learning something all of the time, we are forced to ask ourselves what it is they are learning. It is here that a great discrepancy becomes apparent. If we think of a learning experience as something that is taught, honesty bids us examine closely the relationship between what is taught and what is learned. It seems a probable assumption that people are learning something all of the time—only seldom, if ever, what "the teacher" thinks he is teaching.

Learning is a complex process. There are many psychological concepts and experiments that attempt to explain the process. We read about stimulus, response, reinforcement, extinction, conditioning, retention, forgetting, transference, generalization, discrimination, and other concepts.

In psychotherapy, the learning process is in evidence. It seems to be a cumulative, compound, integrative, affective experience that can be used to illustrate many learning theories. At the same time, it raises many questions as to the adequacy of any existing theory to explain conclusively the learning experience that occurs during psychotherapy.

In play therapy experiences, the child is given an opportunity to learn about himself in relation to the therapist. The therapist will behave in ways that he intends will convey to the child the security and opportunity to explore not only the room and the toys but himself in this experience and relationship.

If play therapy is an experience in self-exploration, self-in-relation-to-others, self-expansion, and self-expression, how can this be achieved and develop a generalization on the part of the child to accept not only himself but others as well, and to learn to use freedom with a sense of responsibility for that privilege? How is the child helped to learn self-understanding that grows into an attempt to understand others? How does the child learn to expand beyond self-centeredness to a recognition and appreciation of others?

If psychotherapy is to be an experience of social and emotional learning for the child, what procedures might facilitate this objective?

There are many glib, overly simplified terms applied to the process of psychotherapy. The usc of the term "permissiveness" has sometimes seemed to put a stamp of approval on completely uncontrolled behavior. It seems more appropriate to define "permissiveness" functionally as the opportunity to utilize the capacities within the individual for the expression of emotionalized attitudes and thoughts and feelings when channelized into symbolic, legitimate activities by the sensible use of limitations in the hope that the child learns responsible freedom of expression.

Limitations or boundaries that prevent the child from either attacking another person or destroying property seem to develop within the child a feeling of security and stability in the therapeutic relationship. If his emotionalized attitudes find outlet in an acceptable manner of externalizing them, it seems probable that he would learn to know his feelings objectively without adding guilt or fear or anxiety that might be precipitated by this lack of symbolic expression.

There needs to be sensitive communication between therapist and child. Here again the attitudes of the therapist show through. The communication seems to be more often on a nonverbal level than on a verbal one. If the therapist considers it important to emphasize the child's frame of reference, there will be an attempt to keep to a minimum any statements or comments that might try to interject the therapist's frame of reference. If the therapist hopes to help the child develop an honest awareness of his emotions, then the therapist will attempt to respond with sensitivity to the child's emotional expressions by a reflection of his expressed feelings, by simple acceptance of what the child says or does, by the manner in which he listens to the child, by the extent to which he is able to get right into the child's frame of reference.

When working with children in play therapy, the therapist must be able to accept the hypothesis that the child has reasons for what he does and that many things may be important to the child that he is not able to communicate to the therapist. It seems quite likely that the play therapy sessions offer the child the opportunity of experiencing affectively this relationship and, because of this present emotional experience, the child can gain much from it even though the therapist does not always know what is going on in the child's inner world—and is unable to find out. Too much insistence on finding out everything may result in a breakdown of communication and rapport.

The child needs a freedom for his expression that can be implemented by a willingness on the part of the therapist to provide a fluidity of use of materials and fantasy and conversation. The child may not always seem rational in his communication from an adult's point of view and yet, from the child's frame of reference, he is communicating something of real down-to-earth feeling. A therapist who is too literal-minded and who cannot tolerate a child's flight into fantasy without ordering it into adult meaningfulness might well be lost at times. Few adults have the flexibility and creative spontaneity of a child. And the use of the term "creative spontaneity" does not always mean expansive activity. In some instances, it can be seen from an adult's point of view as only an idle bit of dawdling—and yet the child's imagination and experience at the moment may bring to the child genuine affective meaning that helps him achieve a meaningful self-realization.

For example, during one series of play sessions, a little Negro boy came into the playroom each week, sat down at the table, tilted back the chair, put his feet up on the table, folded his arms across his chest, sat there with an impassive expression on his face—week after week after week. The therapist was puzzled by this behavior. When the play periods would end, the therapist would announce that time was up. The child would quickly get up and leave. Naturally, many unasked questions crossed the therapist's mind, but up to a point the therapist had not probed, interpreted, encouraged, or prompted the child to either explain himself or do something else. The

therapist finally was about to speak to the child about this situation, to explain that he could play if he wanted to. However, just before the therapist broke into this situation, the boy looked at the therapist and said, "Know what I've been playing?" With eager responsiveness, the therapist replied that she did not know. With a smile and a squaring of his shoulders, the Negro boy replied, "I've been playing White Man!" Who can tell what this experience meant to that child? How can we evaluate the effectiveness of such a play experience?

If we want to provide fluidity of expression, we must keep the experience as free for associations and identifications and changing concepts as is possible. If the child picks up a toy and asks, "What is this?" our answers can determine the use the child can make of it. If we name it, we might tie it so firmly to a world of reality that the free use of it as a medium of expression is restricted. If we say (because we really mean it), "In here it can be anything you'd like it to be—" perhaps we can facilitate his play. For example, sometimes we can see a tin plate change identity many times. Perhaps it starts out as a raft, becomes a flying saucer, a monster, a mother plate, a father plate, a little boy plate. Protected by the flexible self-involvement, the child can bring his feelings out into the open in such a way that he can handle them without fear and self-threat. He can always change the identity of his symbolic figures into something safe and bearable if it seems to become too big to handle.

The limitations of time and space seem important. If the child experiences consistent, predictable boundaries of time and place, he gains a sense of stability and security.

In our experiences with children who have some marked disability, either blindness, deafness, cerebral palsy, or lack or speech, we can observe children using the play sessions in ways that they adapt to their individual needs. It is with these children that we become more aware of the child's abilities to strike at the heart of his difficulties. We note that words, facial expressions, physical activities assume differing values in the relationship. We observe the common element that seems to bring about the changes in behavior that we sometimes term "therapeutic gains." This common element is the opportunity for the child to experience affectively and in exploratory fashion himself in an unrushed, protected relationship with the therapist who appreciates his integrity and personal worth, who offers an opportunity to pour out the feelings and experiences that bother him, who tries to help him achieve responsible freedom of expression so that his capacities can be utilized more constructively for himself as an individual and as a member of a group.

In closing, a brief excerpt from the play interview of a twelve-year-old boy with a record of delinquency is cited.

In the preceding sessions, he had asked the therapist to

get him a penknife so that he could carve some balsa wood. The therapist got a three-bladed penknife. When John came into the playroom, he immediately looked on the table, found the knife, picked it up, snapped open the blade.

"Oh, you fool, you," he cried. "I asked you to get me a knife to carve with, and you walked into the trap. Now you've given me a knife, and I'll cut your wrists." He suddenly reached out, grabbed the therapist's hand and placed the open blade against the vein. "Now what are you going to do?" he demanded.

"It seems to me that is my question," the therapist replied. "You're the one with the knife. What are you going to do?"

"You wonder what?" John asked.

"I certainly do," the therapist said.

"What are you going to do?" John demanded.

"What would you suggest?" the therapist inquired.

"You know what will happen if I get mad enough right now?" John asked threateningly.

"What will?" asked the therapist.

"I'd cut your damn wrists. Then how would you like that? I'd cut that vein right there. What would you do? Tell me that. What would you do?"

"I'd probably bleed," the therapist answered, after some quick thinking.

"And *then* what would happen?" John demanded.

"I don't know," the therapist said. "That would be your problem."

"*My* problem? You'd be the one bleeding to death!" John yelled.

"You'd be the one who did it, though," the therapist said.

"Why don't you try to pull loose?" John demanded.

"Why don't you let go and put away the knife?"

"You were a fool to get me this knife for in here, you know," John said. "You realize what a fool you were? You brought this all on yourself."

"You asked for the knife to carve balsa wood," the therapist replied.

"And *you* turn out to be the balsa wood," shrieked John, laughing hilariously. "So you'll bleed to death. Then what will you do? Tell me. What'll you do then?"

"I don't know," the therapist said, "I've never bled to death before."

John suddenly released the therapist's wrist, closed up the knife, tossed it on the table.

"Some people are too damn dumb to be turned loose," he said. "You're so stupid you could get your very throat cut and wouldn't know what happened. Why did you get this knife? Why did you give it to me?"

"You said you wanted to carve wood. I believe what you say."

Suddenly he sat down with his back to the therapist.

"Some people shouldn't be let out alone," he said. "Some people are too damn dumb. How can I fight you if you won't fight back? How can I cut your wrists if you won't even struggle? All the time here it's like this. It's not me against all the people in the world that I hate and despise. You make it turn out again and again that it's me against myself. All of a sudden I feel all my feelings—and sudden like I just wish I'm not the way I am. I wish I had a feeling of being strong deep inside of me without threats and being afraid really. I feel like I'm too little for too big a world. I don't want to always make war with myself."

John, in his way, indicated what therapists hope to induce in every child with whom they work—an increased awareness of his feelings, a sense of measuring himself against himself, a seeking for an understanding of himself that will bring with it inner peace, and a feeling of being at one with the world.

Art Therapy

❧ ❧ ❧

Excerpts from
An Introduction to Art Therapy

Margaret Naumburg
1950

THE PSYCHODYNAMICS OF THE ART EXPRESSION OF A BOY PATIENT WITH TIC SYNDROME

Introduction

This paper will consider the art expression produced by an 11-year-old Jewish boy, while under treatment at the New York State Psychiatric Institution. His condition was diagnosed as maladie des tics, and his case has been described and discussed by Dr. Margaret Mahler and Dr. Leo Rangell in a paper published under the title of "A Psychosomatic Study of the Maladie des Tics (Gilles de la Tourette's Disease")."

This particular study of the art work of a single patient is one of a series now being reported as aspects of a special research project at the New York State Psychiatric Institute and Hospital in order to investigate the possible use of creative art as an aid in diagnosis and therapy. None of the patients in this study were chosen on the basis of special creative ability and several of them even expressed a dislike for art based on their formal training in the subject at school.

Report on the Patient's Expression

Freddie had been hospitalized for seven months before he commenced art work with the writer. The patient continued these art sessions for six months: five months while hospitalized and one month more while under treatment in the outpatient clinic. After the summer holidays, when the patient returned to school, an attempt was made to continue the art periods. But he was unable to give sufficient time or attention to this effort for besides carrying a full time school program, he was now undertaking psychoanalytic treatment.

While the art sessions were in progress, written records were kept not only to include the manner in which the art work developed, but also to report on whatever significant conversations and other activities occurred during the art periods. In the case of this tiqueur the variations in the patient's involuntary movements were also noted.

Freddie had already been under psychotherapeutic treatment for over two years when the art work was begun. He had, by that time, reached that phase in the development of his disease described by Mahler and Rangell as the third stage when "the tics seemed fewer in number, but also seemed more isolated from awareness and demarcated from the rest of the personality."

In the first few months of art work Freddie was unable to maintain his interest for more than half-hour periods, but as he developed ability to express his experiences in original art forms he would ask for more time in order to complete his pictures. When this patient walked into the art room on the first day, he announced, "I know what I want to make." He chose the plastecine and modelled an airplane with experienced skill. But when the wide-winged plane was completed, the wings dropped off. Without making any effort to repair the damage, the patient sat staring at his broken plane, uttering his complaint that "the wings always fall off."

An attempt was made to show him how he could overcome this difficulty by inserting small wooden sticks as structural supports to brace the wings against the body of the plane. The success of this new technique encouraged and delighted the patient.

When this plane was satisfactorily completed Freddie was asked whether he wished to try painting. But he evaded the use of anything but plastecine by saying: "No, I do that pretty well. I'm not perfect." Only after several more periods of art was Freddie finally willing to try drawing for the first time. It then became evident that he had been disguising his inability to draw or paint by a pretense of expertness.

To do things "perfectly" was evidently a matter of deep concern to this patient; so also was his desire to please and be approved by both adults and children. His behavior on the ward and in school, as well as in the playroom with the psychiatrist, was motivated by this persistent desire to be approved. The ward nurse described his behavior as "too good" and the class teacher was critical of the patient's neglect in completing his school work while striving, nevertheless, to obtain gold star rewards. Similar behavior was evident at first in the patient's response to art work. How this inordinate need of approval was modified as he found himself in creative expression will be discussed as the various phases of the patient's art are described.

On all subjects that related to his own life and relationships he maintained a defensive and noncommittal attitude during the art sessions. Asked by the writer as to which school subjects he liked best, he replied, "Everything; I like arithmetic, reading, geography, everything." When he was questioned as to which he preferred of two movies, he answered "both."

On the first day, however, he went so far as to admit that he did like making "lots and lots of planes and sometimes boats and guns" at home. This corresponded to the aggressive war play described by the psychiatrist in the play therapy sessions.

In the final month of hospitalization, the patient voiced one criticism of his family during the six months of art work. As he was departing for a week-end visit, he was asked by the writer to describe the first thing he would probably do when he reached home. "Talk, I guess," he replied. Pressed further to tell what he liked to talk about with his sister, he explained, somewhat scornfully, "Oh,

she talks a lot about her dolls and school." And then, evidently recalling a recent disagreement with her, he added, *She contradicts me. And I'm afraid I'll be wrong."* In his own words Freddie had expressed, for the first time one of the motivations of his consistently noncommittal attitude on all subjects that related to his life. Having unintentionally revealed resentment against his sister, he immediately tried to disguise it by offering a brotherly expression of approval with the comment: "But my sister's all right."

It seemed possible that the patient was afraid of being wrong in a verbal quarrel with his sister because such an admission came too close to one of his central conflicts; namely, that something was wrong with himself. It was later reported that this boy did show a constant fear of being a damaged person in the course of his psychoanalytic treatment.

This single episode suggests how persistently Freddie had succeeded in repressing vocalization of all hostile feelings against his family. It had been recognized that, as the youngest of three children, he was under the constant strain of competing with two older siblings. A dread of being wrong or of becoming a failure played a dominant part in his feeling of not being a complete person.

Freddie's original doubt of his own power to create in either crayons or water colors was also motivated by a sense of insecurity similar to his vocalized fear of being wrong with the sister. In the first art session, he had attempted to disguise his dread of experimenting with such untried media as chalks and water colors by pretending that he used them so well that he would prefer to model in plastecine. In both situations—at home with his sister, and in the art room with the writer—the patient was making efforts to disguise his exceptional lack of independence to deal with new and unfamiliar situations and media. As in the case of many behavior problem boys, whose ego has remained undeveloped, Freddie strove to conceal his insecurity from others as well as himself; in order to avoid facing new situations he invented devious and varied mechanisms of defense.

The patient began his art sessions by choosing to model bombing planes and other instruments of war. When he gained the confidence to draw his own pet cat in colored chalks, he was less afraid of further experiments. He then attempted to recapture some dreams in crayons and in plastecine. With water colors he was soon able to create landscapes of Riverside Drive. For his aggressive impulses he soon discovered a new release in making scenes of war in a series of crayon drawings. These were promptly followed by a more peaceful Easter Phantasy. In the concluding phases of his art work, Freddie invented a series of episodes to illustrate life in the Armed Services; and he also created many lively sketches showing the activities in modern Sports and Games. A certain male assertiveness was evident in the choice of subject in these final drawings, but they no longer expressed the extreme aggression of his earlier plastecine modelling of implements of war and destruction.

In relation to the modifications observed in Freddie's artistic expression it is interesting to quote a description of this patient's behavior from the Mahler, Luke, Daltroff study.

"F. K. displayed, at the beginning of treatment, quite an active desire to join the children on the block in their group play—gradually the mother's and the big brother's ambivalent anxieties for his well-being were taken over by him, and he gave up the struggle for his freedom, but not before two little accidents, which quite obviously were induced by his inner conflict, 'convinced' him that the rough play 'is not good for me.' "

This description of Freddie's withdrawal from active play throws interesting light on his many pictures of sports and games made in the last phase of his art expression. Such over-determined action drawings will then be understood to serve as a phantasy release from his motor neurosis.

The way in which the patient's aggressive impulses and involuntary movements related themselves to certain changing aspects of his creative expression will become evident as the art products are described.

Since this patient, whose art work is to be described, was under treatment for $2\frac{1}{2}$ years, first at Mt. Sinai Hospital and then at The Psychiatric Institute, a condensation of the clinical history as reported by Mahler and Rangell is reproduced.

Clinical History

Freddie, an 11-year-old Jewish boy, began at the age of 7 to display a series of increasing involuntary tic-like movements of various parts of the body. These were followed later by the uncontrollable emission of inarticulate animal-like noises. Echolalia and echopraxia then appeared but only on occasions of great excitement, as at the movies.

The patient is the youngest of three children, the son of Russian-born immigrants, there being an older brother of 19 and a sister of 13. The mother is a highly emotional, neurotic woman, definitely the dominant member of the family, and the father a passive sort, who is a poor provider, irritable and insecure. The home life is a hectic one, with constant quarrels, shouting, and emotional scenes, superimposed upon ever-present financial distress. There is no history of nervous or mental disease.

Freddie was an unplanned, unwanted child, whose mother, during her pregnancy with him, did everything within her power to induce an abortion. After the birth of the child, the mother felt "he must surely be a cripple,"

and immediately set about compensating for her conscious as well as unconscious guilt feelings toward him by a markedly overprotective attitude and constant anxieties about his health. The patient was a normal infant, and developed normally in all respects. He was overindulged with food and was always overweight. In the last few years, he has shown a voracious appetite and an unusual degree of insatiability, which have resulted in a marked obesity. An important event, which occurred when the patient was 3 months old, and which was probably not unconnected with the emotional and psychological environs of the patient's early life, was the fact that at that time the father, who until then had worked steadily as a taxi driver, suffered an automobile accident which resulted in a serious injury to his spine. This caused a permanent work incapacity which has been responsible for the dire financial straits of the family since that time.

The patient had whooping cough, measles, and chickenpox during childhood, with uneventful courses. Most careful and repeated questioning of mother and father did not reveal illness to support suspicion of encephalitis in the patient's anamnesis. He had a tonsillectomy at four and otitis media at five years. His habits were normal; he was an average student in school, and mixed well with other children. He shared his parents' bedroom, sleeping part of the time with his mother, until the age of 2. From then until 8 years of age, he slept in a bed with his older brother. The mother states: "They could not get along. Freddie used to throw himself around in bed. That's how it all started."

The patient began at the age of 7 to blink his right eye. This seemed at first to be in imitation of a friend of the patient's brother, with whom the latter worked and played. The involuntary winking soon involved the left eye as well, and subsequently movements began to occur in other parts. There developed in succession "twitching movements of the head to the left," "shaking of the right hand and right arm," "puckering up of the lips, and protrusion of the tongue." When trying to fall asleep, "his whole body would shake" and he often would have to be taken out for a walk by the mother at 2 a.m. to relieve his restlessness. The patient then began to make involuntary noises imitating a cat or a dog, sounds which were distressing and resulted in much difficulty at school. During periods of great excitement, it was noted that the patient would imitate the words and actions of others in an uncontrollable manner, as for example when at the movies. The symptoms have progressed, although there have been variable periods of relative quiescence.

After a two week hospitalization on the neurological service of the Mt. Sinai Hospital, diagnosis, psychogenic tic, the patient was referred to the Mental Hygiene Clinic of that hospital in August, 1940, at which time regular observation and psychotherapeutic visits were instituted. After an initial therapeutic success, aggravation of the symptoms occurred in November, 1940, following an accident in which the patient cut one of his fingers and the mother, in her haste to secure aid, fell down a flight of stairs, necessitating treatment for both of them. The patient was admitted to the Children's Service of the New York State Psychiatric Institute on June 2, 1941.

Physical examination showed the patient to be an obese white boy with the general appearance of the Fröhlich habitus.

In the neurological examination only the description of the involuntary movements of the patient will be quoted. These movements were more active and varied in the two years of treatment prior to those final months of hospitalization when the writer began the semi-weekly art sessions with this patient.

There were many involuntary movements, occurring almost in spurts or paroxysms, varying considerably in their frequency and severity, and alternating with periods of relative quiescence. These movements included rapid, lightning-like successive turning movements of the head to the left, followed by forceful turning of the head back to the midline. There occurred lifting of the eyebrows, wrinkling of the forehead, and an occasional winking of the left eye. Often the lips were involuntarily puckered, with the lower lip thrust far forward. The tongue was sometimes forcefully protruded. More rarely, there was a forward thrusting movement of the right shoulder and arm and still less often of the left arm.

The electro-encephalogram was within normal limits, though there were many movement artefacts.

The revised Stanford Binet showed the patient to have an IQ of 118.

The patient was discharged from the Psychiatric Institute in June, 1942. Since that time, he has continued to be followed in the outpatient department of that institution and at the present is under psychoanalytic treatment.

The Rorschach test, which was performed and interpreted by Dr. Z. Piotrowski, confirmed the patient's response during the art sessions. Only that paragraph which describes the patient's psychological responses as they relate to his phantasy life and inhibitions will be quoted. As Dr. Piotrowski states:

"The boy is of superior general intelligence but his intellectual efficiency, especially his conscious control over the thought processes, is inferior. The boy seems to be capable of a great variety of psychological experiences. There is an intensive phantasy life; some tendency to, and even habit of some self-analysis. While there is an intense psychological life, the outward activities of the boy do not seem to be commensurate with his inner experiences because of marked inhibition. The boy is cautious in his dealings with others. If he shows a genuine feeling from time to time, an impulsive emotion now and then, he does this in part because of his poor conscious control over his thoughts and at times also over his actions. He would like to keep himself under strict control but cannot always

succeed in this desire. The prolonged voluntary attention is too poor."

The "marked inhibitions" mentioned by Dr. Piotrowski are overcome with difficulty by the patient in the art sessions and the "intensive phantasy life" for which "his outward activities do not seem commensurate" eventually finds new forms of expression as the art sessions proceed.

How New Themes Developed in the Patient's Art Work

During the first two art sessions Freddie preferred to model such familiar types of war planes and submarines as he had made at home. In the second period he remarked, "I suppose I ought to make a head of George Washington." When this idea was not too enthusiastically received, he proceeded to suggest the substitution of a head of Lincoln or Harrison.

An attempt was made to interest the patient in modelling something with which he was familiar in his own life experience, instead of a head of an American president. Freddie's response was to suggest making a head of his mother.

The Patient Draws His Pet Cat

Since the chance of success with this difficult untried subject seemed doubtful, the conversation was shifted to pets. Freddie was eager to tell all about his cat Queenie. "We thought," he explained, "Queenie was a she when we named it. But the man who gave it to us told my father that Queenie was a he. But we kept the name just the same."

It was not difficult at this point to encourage the patient to try modelling his pet. "But I don't know how," he added. He was asked to decide, first, in what position he wished to model the cat. He replied, "Lying down."

Although Freddie had intended to make Queenie in plastecine, he became so interested in capturing his pet in crayon and chalk drawings that he never modelled his cat. The patient, persisting in his interest during two art sessions, made six drawings of his pet.

He was most critical of his first attempt. "That nose," he remarked, "looks more like a chicken's than a cat's." Freddie was asked, before making another picture of Queenie, to close his eyes and try to recall just how his pet would look. As a result of this imaginative projection, the second profile drawing had more resemblance to the form and quality of a cat. . . .

Since the patient was inclined to tense his entire body as well as his arm and hand whenever he attempted to draw, it was necessary to spend some time in showing him relaxing exercises. Release from misplaced body tension is needed, not only for the large swinging arm movements in good drawing, but it is also essential in directing the control of free brush strokes in painting.

Freddie, like most beginners, tried to set down too many remembered details in small constricted pencil lines. It was therefore necessary to make him aware of the larger rhythmic movements needed in drawing his cat upon the sheet of paper. He was asked to attempt to draw the entire curve of the cat's back in a single easy swing of the pencil across the paper. Then, instead of worrying about the details of the cat's features, he was shown how to sketch in the general position and balance of the head in relation to the rhythm of the body. When the rounded haunch on which the cat rested had also been drawn with a free, swinging stroke, the addition of the features presented less difficulty to the patient; whiskers, paws, and tail were then added in order to complete the design.

So absorbed did the patient become in capturing a likeness of Queenie that he made four outline drawings in the first day. The last one pleased him so well that he decided to fill it in with brown crayon. . . . Pink ears and large white spots were added. "It looks just like Queenie," he commented, as he laid down his crayon at the end of the hour. He then suggested drawing more pictures of his pet in the next art period.

In the following sessions, Freddie began by outlining his cat in purple chalk with a dish of milk beside him. This was the fifth drawing that the patient had made of Queenie. Thus far he had tried for a realistic presentation of his cat. In the sixth picture . . . a great change took place. Interest in a new box of colored chalks led, appar-

ently, to a complete modification of his approach. He was attracted to a brilliant magenta chalk and decided to outline his cat in that color; he then proceeded to fill in the creature's form with a solid mass of this same shade. But instead of completing the rounded haunch of the cat in the same color, he covered it with emerald green. The background of this picture was then filled with deep blue and the floor on which the cat rested was done in purple. . . .

The patient, by overcoming some of his inhibitions had begun to express his affection for his pet cat in original crayon and chalk drawings. This made possible the initial release of that repressed phantasy life which Dr. Piotrowski had described in his interpretation of the Rorschach test. In the final picture of the magenta cat he was able to conceive a creature in unrealistic colors that satisfied his own taste.

The transformation of the patient's repetitive creation of model planes and boats into this varied series of cat pictures now made him able to carry out his own ideas more easily in the following art sessions.

The way in which these cat forms came into existence may serve to suggest how the process of liberation into "free" expression in art cannot take place by merely urging a patient to make whatever he wishes. For, in order to prepare a patient to pour his own experience and imagination into forms of creative expression, he must first gain confidence and discover his ability to do so.

In such an approach, technique is not ignored but is introduced in an incidental manner *after* the patient has begun to express himself. In this, it differs from the traditional method of teaching art; for the formalist tends to introduce rules of technique before the patient has attempted to give shape to his own conceptions.

Selected Quotations from
Art Therapy and Art Education: Overlapping Functions

Edith Kramer
1980

Much of the following material is lengthy quotations from Edith Kramer's article *"Art Therapy and Art Education: Overlapping Functions."* Kramer's theoretical and practical contributions to art therapy are particularly influential because she understood the importance of art education as a therapeutic process and avoided the typical generalizations designed to differentiate between art therapy and art education. She writes: "When distinctions between the work of art therapists and art educators are discussed, it is often stated that art education is product-oriented while art therapy is process-oriented. I find that this over simplification confuses more than it enlightens.

Concerning art education's orientation, we evidently cannot conceive of any genuine art product that is not the culmination of a creative process. Products that are manufactured by plotting and scheming to achieve preconceived results do not partake of art at all. They lack the dignity of even the most abortive artistic attempt and belong at best to the realm of commercially applied art. To designate art education as product-oriented in the latter sense is demeaning to the profession."

Note. From "Art therapy and art education: Overlapping functions" by E. Kramer, 1980, *Art Education, 33,* 16–17. Copyright 1980 by the National Art Education Association. Reprinted by permission.

Kramer's vast experience with the art produced by all types of children enabled her to appreciate that a major difference between the art teacher and art therapist was in their expectations about what the children would produce. Another difference pertained to the difficulties in teaching the processes involved in art to seriously disturbed children. She states,

The art therapist who works with extremely handicapped children must vastly more often than the art teacher be contented with fostering processes that do not culminate in any lasting product. At times all thought of achieving finished paintings or sculptures may have to be abandoned while children endlessly experiment with art materials, vent their anger on them, or desert their work before it is finished. Furthermore, disturbed children's preoccupations with their inner conflicts frequently make them inaccessible to conventional educative methods. Established ways of stimulating the focusing perception and of teaching techniques or of making children aware of the formal elements of art must be subordinated to therapeutic goals, must at times be modified or, perhaps, entirely set aside. In spite of everything, however, any discipline which involves art at all remains committed to processes that ideally culminate in a product that partakes, within the limitations of the child's age and capacities of the quality of art. To lose sight of this commitment is to deprive the disturbed child a priori of the possibility of experiencing the full creative process.

Kramer also was adept at recognizing the differences between conventional verbal therapy and art therapy. She says,

> We cannot simply equate the art produced in art therapy with the words used in adult psychotherapy, or with the play and talk that replace purely verbal interchange in child therapy. Communication in psychotherapy is typically fluid and unformed, and attention is focused in the main on content. While art therapists encourage unconventional form as well as content in art they are nevertheless intent on fostering artistic eloquence. For the depth and verity of the experience in art therapy are in many ways bound up with its formal qualities. Above all, the individual's eloquent productions eloquently speak back to him in the course of work and when he later contemplates the finished product. This dialogue between creator and creation has no exact parallel in verbal psychotherapy. It can be likened only to what happens when the other arts—dance, music, drama, or poetry—are used in therapy. The order and structure with which artistic expression endows experience is of the utmost importance in all these therapies—a powerful aid in recognizing, sorting out, and mastering experience.

Finally, she offered advice to those who undertake the difficult job of working with the seriously disturbed. She says,

> We must try to play down any competition for our attention and services as it arises. To stimulate productive work, we must begin at the beginning: We must celebrate any steps in ego functioning the child may make, much as a mother celebrates any signs of goal-directed behavior in her baby. Such an attitude may seem to infantilize the children, but actually we are addressing ourselves to the infantile, emotional level on which they are indeed functioning, cutting through the defiant or manipulative front which helps such children survive in the world. But we must rejoice only in real achievement, however minute they may be—insincerity inevitably defeats our purpose.

Music and Dance Therapy

Excerpts from
Music for the Handicapped Child

Juliette Alvin
1976

THE STORY OF JOHN

John was one of the many children at the hospital. He had muscular dystrophy, a killing disease for which there is no cure and which leads to a general paralysis. But the illness does not necessarily impair the mind, and John continued to be a normal child with a desire to learn. He had to go into hospital, but there was a school at the hospital and he received schooling as well as medical treatment. Being a naturally easy, sociable, and courageous child, he accepted his condition and integrated quite well with the life in the ward.

Everyone knew that John, who had already lost the use of his legs, would be a permanent wheel-chair case, and get worse and worse. His hands were already showing signs of stiffness. Since treatment could only delay the effects of the disease it was important that the boy's schooling should give him all possible means of mental and emotional development and enable him to enjoy life as much as possible until the end.

Music was one of the most flourishing subjects taught at the hospital; there was music in every ward, singing, playing instruments, listening to music, musical theory and appreciation. Fortunately John was musically sensitive. The music teacher helped him to make his own bamboo pipe, a very exciting experience, and John kept it with

his own small properties. He was taught to play well and seriously, learnt musical notation, and became an enthusiastic and knowledgeable listener to music as well as a proficient player and singer. In time John's musical equipment became the foundation of his life through which he expressed himself and had access to the wide and rich world of music. His pipe playing became so good that he was invited to join the music group of the staff. He helped to entertain visitors and took part in most of the hospital shows. He became a valuable member of the school ensemble even when his fingers became weaker and less flexible. He was helped by the fact that the bamboo pipe requires very little muscular strength and need not be held by the fingers. It can be leant on a table which supports the weight of the instrument. John could also sing quite well, and little by little he acquired a splendid repertoire of short tunes and songs. He could read music notation and was even able to follow on the score recorded performances of chamber or symphonic music. This increased his intelligent and sensitive appreciation of music.

Little by little, as he became older and more aware of his condition, John started to lose hope of recovery, and his love of and need for music increased. He had more difficulty in playing his pipe and in singing, but he passed much time listening actively to music with other children or by himself. Music also helped him to spiritualize his experiences and answered his need for beauty and harmony. Sometimes he also enjoyed the relaxing atmosphere brought by the presence of peaceful background music, on which time flows without conflict and is a help against a feeling of solitude.

John is not expected to live much longer, but his beloved music will follow him to the end. It is difficult to imagine what his short life would have been without music.

THE STORY OF GEORGE

George, a little boy of ten, was not happy, although nothing seemed to worry him particularly. He did not remember his father, who died when he was an infant, and he got on quite well with a half-brother born from his mother's second marriage.

George was intelligent, above the average, very nervous and unstable, unkempt and disorderly. Although he had done music and movement as a young child he was physically incredibly awkward.

He was having great trouble at school, always at the bottom of his form, and got increasingly bad reports which were a source of conflicts with his family. The boy was careless, inattentive, and seemed unable to pull himself together. He was going a bad way and seemed not to care.

At that time music came into his life. He had heard at home a recording of *Swan Lake* and was reached in an extraordinary way by the 'cello part in the score. He identified himself at once with the tune and asked if he could learn the 'cello. When I met him for the first time and asked him why he wished to learn the 'cello, he answered with eagerness that he wanted to be able to play "that tune." I knew nothing then about the child except that he had the right kind of motivation, that he looked very nervous and that he was probably in need of a means of self-expression.

I learnt so much from him about his life, even from the first lesson, that I tried to hide from him the fact that he was quite unfit to play a musical instrument. He had positively no ear, no rhythm, no motor control, and he always moved the wrong way. But he truly loved music and was set on "playing that tune," although I had made it quite clear to him that he could not achieve it before a long time and without hard work.

I gathered very soon that he suffered from loneliness. From the first day he kept his instrument in his room and told me: "My 'cello, that is my best pal. I put it in my room somewhere I can see it when I wake up." We plodded along with meager results, and I sometimes wondered about the wisdom of continuing when the musical results were so unsatisfactory, but he never lost his initial motivation. The child was looking for some kind of satis-factory relationship through which he could express himself. He felt he could find it in his 'cello. After a few weeks he told me that he had had a dream in his sleep: he was in an orchestra and played "that tune." The same dream occurred several times, and each time he was in a different orchestra.

There was then nothing else to do than to go on with much patience and understanding and to call on all the experience needed in such a laborious teaching task. Little by little he told me about the difficulties of his life. He had given up the idea that he could ever be good at school: there was a family crisis every time the school report arrived, and he was becoming quite callous about it. But he thought he would be good at playing the 'cello.

I made his 'cello become a means of rehabilitation. Each of the reports I sent at the end of term contained some of his good features such as eagerness, goodwill, punctuality, and so on, which gave a true and better picture of the boy. This helped to ease the family relationship and the boy was quite aware of it. But the main rehabilitation to be done was in the boy himself. The lessons were an occasion to make him evaluate himself and face his shortcomings. He was careless, unable to criticize himself or to accept criticism, and had no standard in anything. His musical motivation was so strong that I could demand from him all he could give without making him feel that his best was mediocre. In fact, the demands made on him by a teacher he respected and admired made him feel that she respected him and had confidence in his ability to do better.

This relationship helped him to become stronger, more stable, to lose his indifference, and to regain his self-respect. At the same time the 'cello became to him a great source of emotional satisfaction and his love of music increased.

His nervousness and sense of inferiority had made contacts very difficult for him. The change from primary to secondary school might have proved to him a very difficult time. But he integrated at once with his new school because of his 'cello, through which he became a member of the orchestra. He felt he had something valuable to offer to his new school, and he started to form happy relationships through his music first, with the pupils and masters.

From that day he never looked back, and his personality developed normally. He had found himself through his love for a tune that had moved him and led him, with proper guidance, to know, to evaluate, and to express himself. He is now grown-up, but his 'cello is part of his life, and perhaps still "his best pal."

Dance As an Adjunctive Therapy with Hospitalized Mental Patients

Marian Chace
1953

It is widely held that in man's cultural development, the era of language was preceded by nonverbal communication. In contemporary word-centered societies, however, part of acculturation consists of repressing movement as a form of communication. Nevertheless, motor activity does operate unconsciously to express emotion. We unconsciously pay attention to broad, general patterns of muscular action. We expect a fearful, timid person to move with small, ineffectual movements, and a self-confident, aggressive person to use broad, directed, expansive movements.

While verbal utterance of emotion may be withheld or disguised, its nonverbal expression cannot be entirely controlled. An action as simple as walking may reflect the prevailing mood. Likewise, as a group engaged in intellectual discussion becomes emotionally involved, characteristic postural changes and movements occur, and reveal much concerning relationships within the group. When the emotion becomes powerful enough, its physical reflection cannot be ignored, whether it is expressed simply and directly, or rechannelled through the muscular rigidity of "self-control."

In the psychotic, language loses much of its effectiveness as a means of relating to others, serving as a defensive barrier rather than a means of direct communication. The seriously ill mental patient relies to a large extent on nonverbal devices for the communication of his emotions.

Since muscular activity expressing emotion is the substratum of dance, and since dance is a means of structuring and organizing such activity, it might be supposed that the dance could be a potent means of communication with and reintegration of the seriously ill mental patient. We believe we have found this to be the case.

Inasmuch as such patients also suffer from severe isolation, dance therapy serves to reintegrate the individual with the group. Although occasional sessions are held with individual patients, the ultimate aim is their participation in a group.

SETTING

In dance therapy as conducted at St. Elizabeths Hospital in Washington, D.C. and Chestnut Lodge Sanitarium in Rockville, Maryland, no restrictions are laid down as to the type of patient attending sessions, either in terms of diagnosis or in the nature or severity of symptoms. Specific patients are often referred by staff members when they believe this form of treatment is especially indicated. Otherwise, patients are incorporated into the group at their own request, through the suggestion of other patients, or by contact in ward sessions. It is our impression that an initial contact through dancing is most meaningful to the patients whose verbal communication is extremely constricted, ineffectual, threatening, or absent.

The majority of groups meet in a room set apart for dance therapy. Even suicidal and severely disturbed patients can be conducted to the dance room without mishap. Dance sessions are held on the wards primarily to establish contact with newly admitted patients.

STRUCTURING OF THE SESSIONS

As they are assembling, there is a free choice of recorded music by the patients and it usually reflects their mood. To this music, the patients are free to move spontaneously either alone, with the dance therapist, or in small groups. It is the purpose of this warm-up period not only to establish the initial contacts (see under Techniques), but to drain off excitement which might interfere with an effective structuring of the session.

With a group composed largely of depressed patients, the preliminary period is relatively short, while with disturbed patients this period of exciting music, with individualistic movement, may last for half an hour.

After all or nearly all of the group have become involved in this activity, the therapist initiates, to waltz music, a circle. This particular combination of music and pattern has been found to be the only satisfactory means of involving the entire group. Following the lead of the therapist, the circle of patients goes through simple warm-up movements such as arm and leg swings, gradually moving into body stretches and body swings. By this time, some member has fallen into a peculiarly personal movement pattern, and the therapist relinquishes the leadership to this patient, encouraging the group to move with him. A succession of patients will pick up the role of leader in movement and thereafter the therapist largely plays the role of a catalyst.

The movements used in the various dance forms by the patients become broader and more spontaneous. There is also a noticeable increase in the desire and also in the ability of the group to work together in many unison patterns. Simultaneously with this movement in unison, verbal production becomes more spontaneous, body postures more relaxed, and appropriate laughter is often evoked. Miss A. verbalized this feeling by saying, "Dancing makes me aware of me and that is the only time I can be with other people." Patients who are feeling particularly secure within the group structure will give special attention to some of the group who are still withdrawn, and attempt to bring them into the circle of dance movement.

The session moves to its close with a breakdown into individual or small group movement patterns and a final period of listening to music and conversing. It is during this portion of the session that original dances are improvised. This does not mean a return to the bizarre production at the beginning of the session, when the individuals seemed isolated in their own fantasies. Instead, these dances have form and continuity and are organized in response to music rhythms being played. It is possible for the soloist to accept an audience reaction of hand clapping or a dance by the group which is similar to her own, but modified, and still return to the group when his dance is completed.

Music selections throughout the session are consonant with the prevailing emotional tone of the group. A group in which depression predominates will start with slow waltzes and progress through lively waltzes to polkas or square dance music and return to a lively waltz. With a group of excited patients, the session starts by moving to loud, lively music and ends with listening to contemplative music such as a Bach suite or a Debussy prelude.

TECHNIQUES OF DANCE THERAPY

To illustrate some specific, detailed techniques of dance therapy, I shall describe the methods used with a group of acutely disturbed patients. The basic purpose of the therapy with these patients is to establish as direct contact with them as they are able to tolerate.

Initial Contacts

The movement used in establishing initial contact with a patient may be qualitatively similar to those of the patient (not an exact mimicking since this is often construed by the patient as mocking) or they may be expressive of an entirely different emotion with which the therapist has responded to the patient's gestures. Intense alertness is essential in judging which approach should be used so that the dance therapist may immediately establish herself as a "safe" person.

The following is an example of how the patient's muscular tensions are picked up by the therapist and carried into dance action. One patient stands hunched forward, contracted through the abdomen, his whole posture that of a person in terror. The therapist feels the tension within her own abdomen, and using this as a center of action, she develops a tension relaxation dance sequence. The original contraction she feels may be carried into an expansive movement or into some relaxed action, neither of which can be construed as threatening. In either case, it must develop from or be closely related to the patient's own contracted movement. In his response to the therapist, the patient can carry his own contraction into a similar movement, and thus help himself to break away from his fixed emotional-muscular pattern. When action with the therapist has been established, this patient may be able to move away from his fixed spot in the room. Later he may be able to dance by himself, with another patient, or, perhaps even during the same session, join the dance circle for short periods of time.

An assaultive patient, when moving forward with threatening gestures, will evoke fright in the therapist, no matter how transient. This fright usually provokes aggressive, retaliative action. If, however, the fright is put into a dance movement, such as a shrinking to the floor, and then quickly developed into a very broad, friendly, welcoming gesture, the expected retaliation is forestalled. It is vitally important that friendliness be broadly expressed in the face. If the patient continues to come toward the therapist with a threatening movement, the next response is usually one of steadfastness, carried out by wide, firmly planted feet and erectness of the torso, but again with no threat of retaliation This in turn can be developed into a friendly movement, perhaps a broad reaching out of one arm or a wide, sweeping, pushing away movement of both arms simultaneously with a friendly smile.

Following this, I often suggest putting hands on each other's shoulders and pushing back and forth, setting up a swinging motion across the dance floor. This action is in essence a substitution or sublimation of the assaultive action, which for some reason had seemed necessary to the patient.

This entire sequence occurs very rapidly and is usually carried through into a strongly rhythmic dance with much foot and leg action, such as stamping or leaping, always maintaining "reaching-out" movements toward the patient. The usual response of the patient at this time is to join in with movements of a similar quality, although of his own adaptation, and his most common verbalization at this time is to the effect, "Who are you? Where did you come from?"

Another essential element of the therapist's activity in her initial approach is the anticipation of fright in the patient as a result of the inevitable threat consequent to any contact with others. The therapist, therefore, retreats from the contact before the patient does, making it unnecessary for the patient to withdraw, which would reinforce his usual mode of reacting by withdrawal. However, the therapist's retreat is never complete. I leave the patient by moving about the room in continuing dance movement, returning with a warm, friendly, inviting action.

Often, with a passive schizophrenic, who is fearful of aggressive activity on his own part, and remains rooted to one place in the room for many hours, the therapist offers both hands palms upward and moves forward and backward. Most typically, the patient's response is a fixed uplift of the hands in the same position. The therapist very gently claps against the patient's hands a few times and indicates that the movement cannot be

done without help, saying that she might hurt him (a sort of role-reversal). At this, the patient responds with a mild clapping, and as he feels release, gradually accelerates and augments the movement until it is quite actively aggressive. This pattern is interrupted when it becomes violent, through retardation of the therapist's movement and some spontaneous exclamation by her. The patient responds by continuing the clapping more gently and in conventional "patty-cake" movements and seems to feel a reduction, temporarily, of his fear of contact with others.

Although contacts are being made throughout the room on a one-to-one basis between the dance therapist and an individual patient, a number of such contacts may be taking place almost simultaneously. Dance action is so rapid and so flexible that as the therapist leaves one patient momentarily to meet another, the emotion felt and expressed by her may be changed as she turns.

During this period, the therapist has the feeling of building multiple individual lines of communication, none of which may be neglected even momentarily, and all of which will gradually be developed into a group activity, away from herself except as a catalyst.

At the moment when the patient indicates that he is conscious of dancing with another person, rather than merely accepting another dancer moving in a similar fashion, his eyes will suddenly focus on the therapist and he will touch her hands, usually grasping them hard. I always respond with a simple "Hello." Patients who have danced in this fashion often say to me, "You have known me from the beginning."

Since it is inevitable at this stage that some physical contact such as joining hands will occur, this may be a good point at which to comment on touch in dance therapy. Although the therapist always indicates her willingness, availability, or readiness to enter into physical contact by brushing her hands past the patient's uplifted hand, reaching toward a seated patient as if to raise him up, or offering to clap hands with the patient, the act of making actual physical contact is left to the patient, whose freedom to withdraw is never restricted in any way.

It is important that there should be no attempt to alter the way in which a patient wishes to dance. At one session, Miss M. was dancing a free, elated dance to a lively polka. Her patterns were at no time orthodox polka steps, but, nevertheless, her dance conformed to the rhythm and color of the music. A new assistant, not understanding the importance to Miss M. of dancing her own polka in her own way, attempted to coax Miss M. to dance conventional polka steps with her. After a few steps, Miss M. dashed across the room, ripped the phonograph record from the machine, looked at it, and deliberately smashed it. Then she sank on a bench in a posture of despair. It was only by meeting this mood with movement and encouraging her without words to dance again in her own way, conforming to her style of dancing, that she was able to come back into the dance session.

During this period of free dance, aggressive hostility is expressed symbolically. On days when the patients have been especially disturbed, this period will be full of action expressive of destruction, either of self or others, while chants from various people will almost drown out the music. Miss E. was permitted to come to the dance room, but the therapist was warned, "Are you sure you want her? She is so unexpectedly assaultive!" Miss E. danced with intensely emotional movements during this period. Her dances ranged from those which carried her rapidly through the room with movements symbolic of destruction, to utterly despairing ones on the floor, eventually moving into actions which left her whole body twisted into knots. After one such dance she smiled at me and pointing to her diaphragm, said, "Dancing comes from in here, but it leaves you feeling clean." She has never shown hostility toward any member of the dance group and is able to use the group dancing for increasingly longer periods.

Group Development

The dance therapist must use her own judgment as to the moment when the first attempt to use a dance pattern initiated by herself should be attempted. It is when the room is almost totally in action, but before pandemonium arises.

This section of the dance session starts gradually when small circles composed of varying individuals are forming, separating, and reforming. Leadership passes back and forth from members of the groups to the dance therapist and her assistants. Movements begin to lose their bizarre quality returning to it as the circle again dissolves into individuals using movements of their own.

This portion of the session also seems to be a testing period, when patients are discovering whether or not they are still free to act as they wish within the group. As the people involved separate less frequently, verbal communication begins to develop and gradually replaces the relating by movement alone. The dance action becomes more rhythmic, and a patient can stamp his feet on the ground with awareness of the contact, beginning to relax and smile as he hears the sound of the rhythm of many feet. As a patient accepts the rhythms and begins to perform simple basic folk steps, in unison with oth-

ers, his movements can be led gradually into more torso-initiated action.

At that time one frequently hears around the circle, remarks of self awareness: "This is me." "I can live." "These are my hands and those are yours." Quite as many verbalizations take the form of contrast: "I never had a friend." "This I should have known when I was a child." And again, said by too many patients to be coincidental, "My mother never taught me love. How could I learn to be with others?" When these statements are made, they are spontaneous, in rhythm to the music and dance movements, and call forth no answers, unless one accepts broader, more vigorous action of the participants in the circle as an answer.

All over-active patients have very brief attention spans and short periods of tolerance of close contact with others. Consequently, although the feeling of the growth of a group activity remains throughout the session, the shift from a large group doing unison movement to small groups and individualistic solo dancing is rapid and constantly changing.

The session ends with listening to contemplative music for fifteen or twenty minutes, with the Bach Brandenburg Concerto the favorite. During this time, the patients sit or lie in reasonably close groups, but without body contact, and there is no noise from voices. Occasionally, a single patient may use the music to dance some feeling of tragedy or exaltation, but this never seems to disturb the relaxed quiet of the rest of the group.

SUMMARY

Dance therapy, in making use of the basic form of communication, offers the individual a means of relating himself to the environment or to other people when he is cut off in the majority of areas by the patterns of his illness.

His meaningful, though bizarre movements become understandable and acceptable to others as people relate themselves to him on the basis of the emotions expressed through dance action. As his feeling of isolation and his fear of lack of understanding are reduced, he is able to put aside autistic expression to an increasing degree, and this in turn seems to enable him to enter a group and function within it in a manner that is satisfying both to the patient and to others in the group.

Dance therapy is first a method for initial contact and then support. It is a warming-up medium in which a patient becomes more aware of himself as an entity functioning with other entities in comparative safety.

Drama Therapy

Excerpts from
Psychodrama

Jacob Moreno
1985

HISTORIC BACKGROUND

There were in 1914 in Vienna two antitheses to psychoanalysis; the one was the rebellion of the suppressed
group versus the individual; it was the first step beyond
psychoanalysis, "group psychotherapy." I introduced
this particular name to underscore that it concerned itself
first of all with a "therapy" of the group and not merely
with sociological or psychological analysis. The other
was the second step beyond psychoanalysis, the "psychodrama." In the beginning was existence. In the beginning
was the act.

Principle—The merely analytic and verbal method of
group psychotherapy very soon led to difficulties. As long
as group psychotherapy was practiced only *in situ*, that is,
within the family, the factory, etc., where life is lived, in all
dimensions of the present, in action, in thought and
speech, as monologue, dialogue, or drama, the psycho-
motor element of the organism and the creative meaning
of the encounter remained unconscious and uninvesti-
gated. When, however, the moment came to move from a
natural to a synthetic place—for instance, from the family to the clinic—it was necessary to restructure life in all
its dimensions in order to carry out therapy in the actual
meaning of the word. All relationships which occur in
everyday life had, therefore, to be constructed anew; we

Note. From *Psychodrama* (4th ed., pp. 219–222) by J. Moreno, 1985, Ambler,
PA: Beacon House. Copyright 1985 by Beacon House, Inc. Reprinted by
permission.

had to have a space in which the life of the family could be
lived in the same fashion as it occurred in reality as well as
symbolically. The bedroom, the kitchen, the garden, the
dramatis personae of the family—father, mother, child—
the discussions, conflicts, and tensions between them just
as they occur in everyday life, all that which is taken for
granted and remains unconscious had to be reconstructed
but reduced to the truly symbolic elements. What before
appeared as problematic and unfortunate became an asset.
Group psychotherapy was forced to enter into all dimensions of existence in a depth and breadth which were
unknown to the verbally oriented psychotherapist. Group
psychotherapy turned into action psychotherapy and
psychodrama.

ROLE THEORY

The Role Concept

A new body of theory developed in the last thirty years
which aimed to establish a bridge between psychiatry and
the social sciences; it tried to transcend the limitations of
psychoanalysis, behaviorism and sociology. One of the
most significant concepts in this new theoretical framework is the psychiatric role concept.

It is a "myth" that the American sociologist, G. H.
Mead, has had a major influence upon the psychiatric
"role concept" and its psychopathology. The formulation
and development of the psychiatric role concept and of

role playing techniques is the exclusive domain of the psychodramatists. This includes all forms of psychodrama from the extreme non-analytic to the extreme analytic versions, in the U.S.A., France, Germany, Switzerland, Spain, Japan and India. It is the psychodramatists who have not only formulated the concept but have initiated and carried out extensive empirical and clinical research for over forty years. It is my German book *Das Stegreiftheater,* 1923 (translated *The Theatre of Spontaneity*) which set the pace for experimental psychodrama and the techniques in the "here and now."

G. H. Mead's posthumous book, *Mind, Self and Society,* appeared in December 1934, about a year later than my *Who Shall Survive?* which was released in January 1934. At no time does Mead use the term role player, role playing, or role playing techniques, or deal with the psychopathological implications of the role concept. He was an excellent theoretician but never left the plane of theory. Were it left up to him, the vast body of role experimentation and role research would not exist. What we psychodramatists did is (a) to observe the role process within the life context itself; (b) to study it under experimental conditions; (c) to use it as a method of psychotherapy (situation and behavior therapy); and (d) to examine and train behavior in the "here and now" (role trailing, spontaneity and behavior training).

EMERGENCE OF THE SELF

"Role playing is prior to the emergence of the self. Roles do not emerge from the self, but the self emerges from roles." This is, of course, an hypothesis only, which appeals to the sociometrist and the behavioral scientists but may be rejected by the Aristotelians, theologians and metapsychologists. The sociometrist will point out that the playing of roles is not an exclusively human trait, but that roles are also played by animals; they can be observed in the taking of sexual roles, roles of the nest-builder and leader roles, for instance.* In contrast, the Aristotelians will claim that there must be a latent self postulated as pre-existing all role manifestations. Were it not for such a self structure, the role phenomena would be without meaning and direction. They must be grounded in something which unites them.

It is possible to reconcile the opinions of the behavioral scientist with those of the philosophers. The infant lives before and immediately after birth in an undifferentiated universe which I have called "matrix of identity." This matrix is existential but not experienced. It may be considered as the locus from which in gradual stages the self and its branches, the roles, emerge. The roles are the embryos, forerunners of the self; the roles strive toward clustering and unification. I have distinguished physiological or psychosomatic roles, like the role of the eater, the sleeper, and the sexual role; psychological or psychodramatic roles, as ghosts, fairies and hallucinated roles; and then, social roles, as parent, policeman, doctor, etc. The first roles to emerge are the physiological or psychosomatic roles. We know that "operational links" develop between the sexual role, the role of the sleeper, the role of the dreamer, and the role of the eater, which tie them together and integrate them into a unit. At a certain point we might consider it as a sort of physiological self, a "partial" self, a clustering of the physiological roles. Similarly, in the course of development, the psychodramatic roles begin to cluster and produce a sort of psychodramatic self and finally, the social roles begin to cluster and form a sort of social self. The physiological, psychodramatic and social selves are only "part" selves; the really integrated, entire self, of later years is still far from being born. Operational and contact links must gradually develop between the social, the psychological, the physiological role clusters in order that we can identify and experience after their unification, that which we call the "me" or the "I." In this manner, the hypothesis of a latent, metapsychological self can be reconciled with the hypothesis of an emergent, operational self. Role theory is, however, useful in making a mysterious concept of the self tangible and operational. It has been observed that there are frequent imbalances in the clustering of roles within the area of psychosomatic roles or social roles and imbalances between these areas. These imbalances produce delay in the emergence of an actual, experienced self or sharpen disturbances of the self.

As the matrix of identity is at the moment of birth the entire universe of the infant, there is no differentiation between internal and external, between objects and persons, psyche and environment, it is one total existence. It may be useful to think of the psychosomatic roles in the course of their transactions helping the infant to experience what we call the "body"; the psychodramatic roles and their transactions to help the infant to experience what we call the "psyche"; and the social roles to produce what we call "society." Body, psyche and society are then the intermediary parts of the entire self.

If we would start with the opposite postulate, that the self is prior to the roles and the roles emerged from it, we would have to assume that the roles are already embedded in the self and that they emerge by necessity. Pre-established as they are, they would have to assume forms which are predetermined in advance. Such a theory would be difficult to accept in a dynamic, changing, self-creative world. We would be in the same position as the theo-

---

* "Sociometry of Subhuman Groups," Sociometry Monograph No. 38.

logians of the past who assumed that we are born with a "soul," and that from that original, given soul everything a man does or sees or feels emerges or comes forth. Also for the modern theologian it should be of advantage to think of the soul as an entity which evolves and creates itself from millions of small beginnings. The soul is then not in the beginning, but in the end of evolution.

THE TERM ROLE

Role, originally an old French word which penetrated into medieval French and English, is derived from the Latin "rotula." In Greece and also in ancient Rome, the parts in the theater were written on "rolls" and read by the prompters to the actors who tried to memorize their part by heart; this fixation of the word role appears to have been lost in the more illiterate periods of the early and middle centuries of the Dark Ages. It was not until the 16th or 17th centuries, with the emergence of the modern stage, that the parts of the theatrical characters were read from "roles" or paper fascicles. In this manner each scenic "part" becomes a role.

Role is thus not by origin a sociological or psychiatric concept; it came into the scientific vocabulary via the drama. It is often overlooked that modern role theory had its logical origin and its perspectives in the drama. It has a long history and tradition in the European theater from which I gradually developed the therapeutic and social direction of our time. I brought it to the U.S.A. in the middle twenties. From the roles and counter-roles, the role situations and role conserves developed naturally their modern extensions: role player, role playing, role expectation, acting out, and finally, psychodrama and sociodrama. Many American sociologists have monopolized the theory of action and of role, especially T. Parsons, as if they were sociological property. But most terms and meanings which Parsons and associates present in their writings can be found in my prior publications.

DEFINITION AND CONSTRUCTS OF THE ROLE

Role is the functioning form the individual assumes in the specific moment he reacts to a specific situation in which other persons or objects are involved.

The role concept cuts across the sciences of man, physiology, psychology, sociology, anthropology and binds them together on a new plane. The theory of roles is not limited to a single dimension, the social. The psychodramatic role theory, operating with a psychiatric orientation, is more inclusive. It carries the concept of role through all dimensions of life; it begins at birth and continues throughout the lifetime of the individual and the socius. It has constructed models in which the role begins to transact from birth on. We cannot start with the role process at the moment of language development but in order to be consistent we must carry it through the non-verbal phases of living. Therefore, role theory cannot be limited to social roles, it must include the three dimensions—social roles, expressing the social dimension; psychosomatic roles, expressing the physiological dimension; and psychodramatic roles, expressing the psychological dimension of the self.

Illustrations of psychosomatic roles are the role of the eater and the sexual role. Characteristic patterns of interaction between mother and infant in the process of eating produce role constellations of the eater which can be followed up throughout the different life periods. The bodily attachment of infant to mother is a forerunner of the later behavior in the sexual role. Psychodramatic forms of role playing as role reversal, role identification, double and mirror playing, contribute to the mental growth of the individual. The social roles develop at a later stage and lean upon psychosomatic and psychodramatic roles as earlier forms of experience.

Function of the Role

"The function of the role is to enter the unconscious from the social world and bring shape and order into it." The relationship of roles to the situations in which the individual operates (status) and the relation of role as significantly related to ego has been emphasized by myself.

Everybody is expected to live up to his official role in life, a teacher is to act as a teacher, a pupil as a pupil, and so forth. But the individual craves to embody far more roles than those he is allowed to act out in life, and even within the same role one or more varieties of it. Every individual is filled with different roles in which he wants to become active and that are present in him in different stages of development. It is from the active pressure which these multiple individual units exert upon the manifest official role that a feeling of anxiety is often produced.

Every individual—just as he has at all times a set of friends and a set of enemies—has a range of roles in which he sees himself and faces a range of counter-roles in which he sees others around him. They are in various stages of development. The tangible aspects of what is known as "ego" are the roles in which he operates, with the pattern of role-relations around an individual as their focus. We consider roles and relationships between roles as the most significant development within any specific culture.

Role is the unit of culture; ego and role are in continuous interaction.

Role Playing, Role Perception and Role Enactment

Role perception is cognitive and anticipates forthcoming responses. Role enactment is a skill of performance. A high degree of role perception can be accompanied by a low skill for role enactment and vice versa. Role playing is a function of both role perception and role enactment. Role training in contrast to role playing is an effort through the rehearsal of roles, to perform adequately in future situations.

ROLE PATHOLOGY

Regressive behavior is not a true physiological regression but a form of unconscious role playing, a "psychodramatic" regression. The adult catatonic is still an adult, physiologically and psychologically. By acting like a helpless infant, he resorts to the lowest possible denominator of behavior.

"Histrionic neurosis" of actors is due to the intervention of role fragments "alien" to the personality of the actor.

MEASUREMENT OF ROLES

As a general rule, a role can be: 1. rudimentarily developed, normally developed or over-developed; 2. almost or totally absent in a person (indifference); 3. perverted into a hostile function. A role in any of the above categories can also be classified from the point of view of its development in time: 1. it was never present; 2. it is present towards one person but not present towards another; 3. it was once present towards a person but is now extinguished.

Another significant method of measurement is the analysis of role diagrams and sociograms of individuals and groups from the point of role interaction, role clustering, and prediction of future behavior.

CO-UNCONSCIOUS STATES AND THE "INTER-PSYCHE"

By means of "role reversing" one actor tries to identify with another, but reversal of roles can not take place in a vacuum. Individuals who are intimately acquainted reverse roles more easily than individuals who are separated by a wide psychological or ethnic distance. The cause for these great variations are the developments of co-conscious and co-unconscious states. Neither the concept of the individual unconscious (Freud) nor that of the collective unconscious (Jung) can be easily applied to these problems without stretching the meaning of the terms. The free associations of A may be a path to the unconscious states of A; the free associations of B may be a path to the unconscious states of B; but can the unconscious material of A link naturally and directly with the unconscious material of B unless they share in unconscious states? The concept of individual unconscious states becomes unsatisfactory for explaining both movements, from the present situation of A, and in reverse to the present situation of B. We must look for a concept which is so constructed that the objective indication for the existence of this two-way process does not come from a single psyche but a still deeper reality in which the unconscious states of two or several individuals are interlocked with a system of co-unconscious states. They play a great role in the life of people who live in intimate ensembles like father and son, husband and wife, mother and daughter, siblings and twins, but also in other intimate ensembles as in work teams, combat teams in war and revolution, in concentration camps or charysmatic religious groups. Marriage and family therapy for instance, has to be so conducted that the "interpsyche" of the entire group is re-enacted so that all their tele-relations, their co-conscious and co-unconscious states are brought to life. Co-conscious and co-unconscious states are by definition, such states which the partners have experienced and produced jointly and which can, therefore be only jointly reproduced or re-enacted. A co-conscious or a co-unconscious state can not be the property of one individual only. It is always a *common* property and cannot be reproduced but by a combined effort. If a re-enactment of such co-conscious or co-unconscious states is desired or necessary, that re-enactment has to take place with the help of all partners involved in the episode. The logical method of such re-enactment a deux is psychodrama. However great a genius of perception one partner of the ensemble might have, he can not produce that episode alone because they have in common their co-conscious and co-unconscious states which are the matrix from which they drew their inspiration and knowledge.

FUNDAMENTAL RULES

Psychodrama was introduced in the United States in 1925, and since then a number of clinical methods have developed—the therapeutic psychodrama, the sociodrama, the axiodrama, role playing, the analytic psychodrama and various modifications of them.

The chief participants in a therapeutic psychodrama are the protagonist, or subject; the director, or chief therapist; the auxiliary egos; and the group. The protagonist presents either a private or a group problem; the auxiliary egos help him to bring his personal and collective drama to life and to correct it. Meaningful psychological experiences of the protagonist are given shape more thoroughly and more completely than life would permit under normal circumstances. A psychodrama can be produced anywhere, wherever patients find themselves, in a private home, a hospital, a schoolroom, or a military barracks. It sets up its "laboratory" everywhere. Most advantageous is a specially adapted therapeutic space containing a stage. Psychodrama is either protagonist-centered (the private problem of the protagonist) or group-centered (the problem of the group). In general, it is important that the theme, whether it is private or collective, be a truly experienced problem of the participants (real or symbolic). The participants should represent their experiences spontaneously, although the repetition of a theme can frequently be of therapeutic advantage. Next to the protagonist, the auxiliary egos and the chief therapist play an important part. It is their responsibility to bring the therapeutic productivity of the group to as high a level as possible.

The Protagonist—The protagonist, in order to get into the production, must be motivated consciously or unconsciously. The motive may be, among other things, self-realization, relief from mental anguish, ability to function in a social group. He is frustrated, let us say, in the role of the father or any other role in life itself, and he enjoys the feeling of mastery and realization by means of psychodrama which gives him symbolic satisfaction.

RESISTANCE

The term resistance is used here in an operational sense. It means merely that the protagonist does not want to participate in the production. How to overcome his initial resistance is a challenge for the therapist's skill. He may send an auxiliary ego to play the "double" of the protagonist. The double usually places himself back of the patient and begins to soliloquize. He gets the protagonist to participate in the soliloquy and perhaps to admit the hidden reasons he has for refusal. This technique is a "soliloquy-double technique."

The chief therapist himself may use another technique —the "soliloquy technique of the therapist." He may sit on the side of the stage and begin to soliloquize about as follows: "I know that Jack (the patient) doesn't like me. I don't see what other reason he would have for not cooperating." The patient might fall in with this and say, "It isn't *you* I don't like. It is this woman in the front row. She reminds me of my aunt."

Another method is to let the patient (A) step back into the group and start with another patient (B) and then call patient A back to be an auxiliary ego in any episode to B, for instance acting as his father, a policeman or a doctor. This is the "patient's auxiliary ego technique." A, who did not want to present his own problems, may be willing to help another member of the group present his.

A further method of breaking resistance is the "symbolic technique," starting on a symbolic production so that fear of private involvement is eliminated as a cause of resistance. The director addresses the group thus: "There is a conflict between husband and wife because of certain irregularities in the behavior of the husband. He may be a gambler, a drunk, or whatever. They have an only child, a son, who is uncertain on whose side he should be." At this point the director turns towards the group and asks, "Who wants to take the part of the husband, of the wife, or of the son?" These roles being noncommittal for the private lives of the members of the group, the director may more easily provoke some of them to participate.

Another "resistance remover" is the use of significant relations existing between members of the group. The director, for instance, knows that there is a rivalry between two individuals, A and B. He may invite them to fight it out on stage: "Let the group evaluate who is fair and who is unfair."

Another method is to utilize "leader tensions" or "ethnic hostilities," for instance, of refugees versus Americans, Puerto Ricans versus the Negroes in the group.

An effective technique to break resistance is to use comical themes or caricatures in order to arouse the sense of humor of the members.

Last but not least, particular attention should be given to resistance which is directed against the "private" personalities of the chief therapist or of the auxiliary egos. In such cases, the therapist or auxiliary egos may have to be replaced, and it may even be necessary to restructure the group itself so as to meet the needs of the patient.

It is up to the resourcefulness of the director to find clues to get the production started and, once it is started, to see that it grows further along constructive lines. The causes for patient's resistance may thus be summarized as being *private, social, or symbolic*.

THERAPEUTIC, CONTROLLED ACTING OUT

The psychodramatist argues as follows: "Why not let him act out these hidden thoughts and strivings as an alternate to an 'analysis' of his resistance?" The patient on the couch, for instance, may be a woman who suddenly has an urge to get up and dance, or talk to her husband whom she suspects of being disloyal to her, or, ridden by a feeling of guilt, she may want to kneel down and say a prayer. If these activities are forbidden to the patient, certain elements which are upsetting him do not come to the fore and cannot be explained and treated. But if the patient knows that the acting of his hidden thoughts and strivings is tolerated by the therapist, he will display them. The therapist, in turn, will be able to utilize the forthcoming material to the advantage of the patient. If, for instance, the patient plans a suicidal attempt the next day, and if he is permitted to portray this attempt within the framework of a therapeutic session, the therapist may prevent the acting out in life itself. But if he makes nonacting out a rule, the patient may kill himself the next day, and so he may not return to the next psychoanalytic hour, except in the form of an obituary note from the relatives. If acting out does take place during the session and if the episode is not properly carried out by the therapist, this, of course, also can be harmful to the patient. So the crux of the matter is that acting out be tolerated and allowed to take place within a setting which is safe for execution and under the guidance of therapists who are able to utilize the experience.

The whole problem of noninvolvement goes back to the original attitude of many of the early psychoanalysts —fear of direct love or direct hostility, their fear of acting out of the patients toward them and their own acting out toward the patients. The confusion here is particularly increased by the different meanings of the term "acting out." When I introduced this term (1928), it meant acting *that* out which is within the patient, in contrast to acting a role which is assigned to a patient by an outsider. It did not mean that they *should not* be acted out because they camouflage a form of resistance of the patient (psychoanalytic view). I meant just the opposite—that they should be acted out because they may represent important inner experiences of the patient which otherwise remain camouflaged and difficult if not impossible to interpret. In psychodramatic thinking, acting from within, or acting out, is a necessary phase in the progress of therapy; it gives the therapist an opportunity to evaluate the behavior of the patient and gives the patient a chance to evaluate it for himself (action insight). But if natural behavior is persistently prohibited, the psychodramatic effort is in danger of deteriorating to a game of words, a parlor game without feeling and with reduced therapeutic value. In order to overcome the semantic confusion I suggested that we differentiate two types of acting out, *irrational, incalculable acting out* in life itself, harmful to the patient or others, and *therapeutic, controlled acting out* taking place within the treatment setting. An illustration of therapeutic, controlled acting out is the following *Magic Shop Technique*. The director sets up on the stage a "Magic

Shop." Either he himself, or a member of the group selected by him, takes the part of the Shopkeeper. The shop is filled with imaginary items, values of a nonphysical nature. These are not for sale, but they can be obtained in barter, in exchange for other values to be surrendered by the members of the group, either individually or as a group. One after another, the members of the group volunteer to come upon the stage, entering the shop in quest of an idea, a dream, a hope, an ambition. They are expected to come only if they feel a strong desire to obtain a value which they cherish highly or without which their life seems worthless. An illustration follows: A depressive patient, who was admitted in the course of 1948 after a suicidal attempt, came to the Magic Shop requesting "Peace of Mind." The shopkeeper, Justus Randolph, a sensitive young therapist, asked her "What do you want to give in return? You know we cannot give you anything without your willingness to sacrifice something else." "What do you want?," the patient asked. "There is something for which many people who come to this shop long," he replied, "fertility, the ability and willingness to bear children. Do you want to give this up?" "No, that is too high a price to pay, then I do not want peace of mind." With this she walked off the stage and returned to her seat. The shopkeeper had hit a sensitive spot. Maria, the protagonist, was engaged but she refused to get married because of deep-seated fear of sex and childbirth. Her fantasy preoccupations involved images of violent suffering, torture, death, etc., in the act of childbirth.

THE CONCEPT OF THE ENCOUNTER; TELE AND TRANSFERENCE TOWARD THE THERAPIST AND AUXILIARY EGOS

Transference is the development of fantasies (unconscious) which the patient projects upon the therapist, surrounding him with a certain glamour. But there is another process which takes place in the patient, in that part of his ego which is not carried away by autosuggestion. It sizes up the therapist and estimates intuitively what kind of a man he is. These feelings into the immediate behavior of the therapist—physical, mental, or otherwise—are tele relations. *Tele* (from the Greek: far, influence into distance) is feeling of individuals into one another, the cement which holds groups together. It is *Zweifuhlung*, in contrast to *Einfuhlung*. Like a telephone, it has two ends and facilitates two-way communication. Tele is a primary, transference a secondary structure. After transference vanishes, certain tele conditions continue to operate. Tele stimulates stable partnerships and permanent relations. It is assumed that in the genetic development of the infant tele emerges *prior* to transference.

The telic relationships between protagonist, therapist, auxiliary egos, and the significant dramatis personae of the world which they portray are crucial for the therapeutic progress.

ABREACTION AND SPONTANEITY

The difference between abreaction and the psychodramatic process is one of quality and not of quantity. Various abreactions come forth from the patient and the auxiliary egos as well as from the audience, and these are integrated into the psychodramatic production. Psychodramatic production consists of structured scenes, each scene of structured roles, and each role of structured interactions. The various abreactions are obviously interwoven into a symphony of gestures, emotions, strivings, and interactions. Several individuals—the protagonist, the auxiliary egos, the director, and the group—take part in their development. A great deal of emotion, thinking, scientific and artistic skill goes into their making. Although created without rehearsal and without aesthetic pretensions, as human documents they can be well compared with plays such as *Hamlet* or *King Lear*. It would be utter nonsense to call Shakespeare's *Hamlet* just a high form of abreaction. It would be a misuse of words.

OPERATIONAL DEFINITION OF SPONTANEITY

My operational definition of spontaneity is often quoted as follows: The protagonist is challenged to respond with some degree of adequacy to a new situation or with some degree of novelty to an old situation. When the stage actor finds himself without a role conserve, the religious actor without a ritual conserve, they have to "ad lib," to turn to experiences which are not performed and readymade, but are still buried within them in an unformed stage. In order to mobilize and shape them, they need a transformer and catalyst, a kind of intelligence which operates here and now, *hic et nunc*, "spontaneity." Mental healing processes require spontaneity in order to be effective. The technique of free association, for instance, involves spontaneous acting of the individual, although it is restricted to speaking out whatever goes through his mind. What is working here is not only the association of words but the spontaneity which propels them to associate. The larger the volume of word association is, the more significant and more spontaneous is its production. Other conditions being equal, this is true of all other methods de-

signed to assist in mental cures. In psychodrama particularly, spontaneity operates not only in the dimension of words but in all other dimensions of expression, such as acting, interacting, speaking, dancing, singing, and drawing. *It was an important advance to link spontaneity to creativity, the highest form of intelligence we know of, and to recognize them as the primary forces in human behavior.* The dynamic role which spontaneity plays in psychodrama as well as in every form of psychotherapy should not imply however, that the development and presence of spontaneity in itself is the "cure." There are forms of pathological spontaneity which distort perceptions, dissociate the enactment of roles, and interfere with their integration on the various levels of living.

FREE ASSOCIATION, SPEAKING AND ACTING A ROLE

It is not quite accurate to say that psychoanalysis is a dialogue between two. It could be said with more justification that it is a monologue, held in the presence of an interpreter. There are so many varieties called psychoanalytic technique today that it is hard to draw the line. A dialogue, not only in its Socratic but in its common sense, is an encounter of two, each with equal opportunity for combat and repartee. This is definitely *not* the case in psychoanalysis. It is equally inaccurate to call psychodrama a dialogue taking place between several individuals. Just as psychoanalysis is less than a dialogue, psychodrama is more than a dialogue, in the sense that living is more than a dialogue. The contrast between words and actions is difficult to define, speaking being a form of behavior. But the emphasis of psychoanalysis has been the concentration upon word symbols and their interpretation. When a patient free associates, his actions are artificially limited and restrained. He is not permitted to act and interact freely. Because of the natural interweaving of actions and words and their frequent linkage in adult behavior, we should not weaken the profound distinction between action and words which is most pronounced in early childhood and in certain definite mental states. When we say words, we mean words spoken in a specific language, for instance English or German. But English or German, or any other syntaxed language, is not born with us. During a very important part of our life, the earliest part of it, in our infancy, we have no such means of "normalized" social communication, but the impress of this period of our life upon our future development is ever present. In this period, acts are acts and not words, and the action matrices which we develop in infancy are prior to the word matrices which we integrate into them later.

CATHARSIS

Catharsis, as a concept, was introduced by Aristotle. He used this term to express the peculiar effect of the Greek drama upon its spectators. In his *Poetics* he maintains that drama tends to purify the *spectators* by artistically exciting certain emotions which act as a kind of relief from their own selfish passions.

This concept of catharsis has undergone a revolutionary change since systematic psychodramatic work began in Vienna in 1919. This change has been exemplified by the movement away from the written (conserved) drama and toward the spontaneous (psycho) drama, with the emphasis shifted from the spectators to the actors.

In my treatise, *The Spontaneity Theatre (Das Stegreiftheater)*, published in 1923, the new definition of catharsis was: "It (the psychodrama) produces a healing effect—not in the spectator (secondary catharsis) but in the producer-actors who produce the drama and, at the same time liberate themselves from it."

There have been two avenues which led to the psychodramatic view of mental catharsis. The one avenue led from the Greek drama to the conventional drama of today and with it went the universal acceptance of the Aristotelian concept of catharsis. The other avenue led from the religions of the East and the Near East. These religions held that a saint, in order to become a savior, had to make an effort; he had, first, to actualize and save himself. In other words, in the Greek situation the process of mental catharsis was conceived as being localized in the spectator—a passive catharsis. In the religious situation the process of catharsis was localized in the actor, his actual life becoming the stage. This was an active catharsis. In the Greek concept the process of realization of a role took place in an object, in a symbolic person on the stage. In the religious concept the process of realization took place in the subject—the living person who was seeking the catharsis. One might say that passive catharsis is here face to face with active catharsis; aesthetic catharsis with ethical catharsis. These two developments which heretofore have moved along independent paths have been brought to a synthesis by the psychodramatic concept of catharsis. From the ancient Greeks we have retained the drama and the stage, from the Hebrews we have accepted the catharsis of the actor. The spectator has become an actor himself.

Mental catharsis cannot be always attained on the reality level, to meet all the situations and relationships in which there may exist some causes for disequilibrium. But it has to be applied concretely and specifically in order to be effective. The problem has been, therefore, to find a medium which can take care of the disequilibrating phenomena in the most realistic fashion, but still *outside* of reality; a medium which includes a realization as well as a catharsis for the body; a medium which makes catharsis possible on the level of speech; a medium which prepares the way for catharsis not only within an individual but also between two, three, or as many individuals as are interlocked in a life-situation; a medium which opens up for catharsis the world of phantasies and unreal roles and relationships. To all these and many other problems an answer has been found in one of the oldest inventions of man's creative mind—the drama.

THE DIRECTOR

Relation to Production—From the point of view of production, the significant relation between psychodrama and the dream has been often emphasized. Lewis Mumford said on one occasion, "Psychodrama is the essence of the dream." It is correct that in both cases we deal often with fantastic productions in which the protagonist is profoundly involved. Just as in a dream, so a psychodrama appears to be an exposition of unconscious dynamics. But it may be appropriate to point out some fundamental differences. The characters in a dream are hallucinated phantoms. They exist only in the dreamer's mind, and they vanish as soon as the dream is over. But the characters in a psychodrama are real people. The dreamer can go on dreaming the most fantastic things without any resistance from his dream characters, his dream characters and the whole plot being his own production. In a psychodrama, however, the auxiliary egos playing roles frequently resist the reveries of the protagonist, they talk back and fight back and modify the course of the plot, if necessary. There is counter-resistance, one may say, propelled toward the protagonist from all sides. They may for exploratory and therapeutic reasons "interpolate" resistance of all sorts, contrary to the protagonist's design. The protagonist in a psychodrama is never as alone as the nocturnal dreamer. Without the counter-forces which the auxiliary egos and the members of the group inject, the opportunities for the protagonist to learn would be very much reduced.

Relation to Patient—The general rule of directing is to depend chiefly upon the protagonists to provide the *clues* as to how to carry on the production. The first clue of a hallucinating patient may be: "I hear my father screaming."

Th: Where does the voice come from?"

P: "It comes from behind the wall."

Th: "Is your father alone?"

P: "No, he is with my mother, they are fighting."

A clue may or may not be found, but if it is, then the episode is acted out.

The director instructs two auxiliary egos to experiment with the portrayal of father and mother and the conflict between them.

The father sits down.

"No," the protagonist protests, "He is not sitting, he is walking up and down."

P: "No, he doesn't hold his head up. He coughs and spits like this." He tries to show the auxiliary ego how.

The protagonist may ask over and over for new modifications; if he protests too much he may be asked to take the part of the father himself. Now he gives "his own interpretation" of the hallucinated father as he perceives him. Here we notice that "straight" role playing can be insufficient, and we see why psychodramatic techniques need to be introduced. It is (1) to get the protagonist into deeper action by involving him more in his own experience, and (2) to make his hallucinations become more tangible either through his own enactment of them or by an auxiliary ego's enactment. *Our hypothesis is that if such experiments are made at the time when hallucinations are active, controls are interpolated in the patient's mind, conditioning barriers, which become particularly important as a reservoir of preventive measure in case of later relapses.* If he should have a relapse, the previous episodes of similar hallucinations will return to him associated to "controls," not as much in his memory as in his behavior, and these preventives will return with them and reduce the violence of the new attack.

The patient may, of course, use even psychodrama itself as a means of resistance. But the psychodrama director has the opportunity to intervene with various techniques so as to hinder the protagonist from "not playing the game" and using the psychodramatic situation itself as a screen for noncooperation.

Relation to Auxiliary Ego—The directing therapist has a significant relation to the patient; the patient must be aware that the therapist has overall responsibility for the treatment. But the therapist is not left alone in his task. He has a number of therapeutic aides, the auxiliary egos, to help him. An auxiliary ego, may, at times, refuse to play the roles the protagonist wants him to play. The reason for not participating may be that the patient always wants to act in sadistic roles, roles of omnipotence, and, in such episodes to humiliate the partner. For instance, he may always want to sit in the car and let the auxiliary ego be the taxi driver, or he may want to be a big shot in a night club and have the auxiliary ego as a waiter, or to be a big general who orders people around according to his whims. It may very well be that the auxiliary ego comes to the realization that one or two such episodes may have a cathartic value for the patient, but that the repetition may become harmful. He might then step in and suggest that the situation be reversed—that the auxiliary ego be Napoleon and the patient be the little man. If the patient does not accept, the auxiliary ego may further

explain that he has had enough suffering and refuses to act. This kind of resistance may be classified as "resistance for therapeutic reasons." Then there may be a kind of resistance which is private in nature. The auxiliary ego may feel that, by playing the role of an intimate friend in that particular episode, he is getting personally involved and hurt. For instance, I treated a young woman on the stage who was arguing against her husband because of his imagined disloyalties toward her. At this moment the auxiliary ego was ordered to take the part of a woman friend of the patient and was instructed to protect the husband and emphasize his innocence. But when she stepped upon the stage, she did the exact opposite of what she was expected to do. Instead, she supported the wife in her delusions and said that she should throw her man out of the house; that he was not worthy of her love. When the auxiliary ego was stopped afterward and reminded of her complete reversal of behavior on the stage, she broke out in tears and said, "I couldn't help it because I am in the same position as the patient in my own private life." We distinguished, therefore, two kinds of resistance; the one for therapeutic reasons and the other for personal reasons.

AUXILIARY EGOS

As Actors—The auxiliary egos are actors who represent absentee persons as they appear in the private world of the patient. The best auxiliary egos are former patients, who have made at least a temporary recovery and professional therapeutic egos who come from a sociocultural environment similar to the patient's. If there is a choice, "native" auxiliary egos are preferable to professional egos, however well trained the latter may be. Many investigators who tried to apply psychodrama to different cultural settings, have found that the proper choice of auxiliary egos is of primary importance. A middle-aged Puerto Rican woman suffering from weird hallucinations, who did not respond to any form of psychotherapy, responded to psychodrama as soon as native auxiliary egos were used. Many of her religion-tainted hallucinations appeared as quasi-normal to her own people.

As the task of the auxiliary egos is to represent the patient's perceptions of the internal roles or figures dominating his world, the more adequately they are able to present them, the greater will be the effect on the patient. Instead of "talking" to the patient about his inner experiences, the auxiliary egos portray them and make it possible for the patient to encounter his own internal figures externally. Such encounters go beyond verbal communication and help the patient to strengthen his vague internal perceptions to which he can relate himself without external aid. These symbolic figures of his inner life are not mere phantoms but therapeutic actors with real lives of their own.

Relation to Patient—The general rule in classic psychodrama is that the patient can choose or reject the egos portraying the significant roles in his life, and, vice versa, that the egos are free to choose or reject in their willingness to cooperate with the patient. However, there are exceptions where the patient is exposed to a certain ego in a special role, created without his consent, and, at times, the therapist is instructed to assume a role which he does not particularly like to portray. Indications or contraindications are the mental benefits which are expected to be derived by the patient from such traumatic procedures.

On portraying the role it is expected that the ego will identify himself privately with the role to the best of his ability, not only to act and pretend but to "be" it. The hypothesis here is that what certain patients need, more than anything else, is to enter into contact with people who apparently have a profound and warm feeling for him. For instance, if it happens that he, as a child, never had a real father, in a therapeutic situation the one who takes the part of the father should create in the patient the impression that here is a man who acts as he would like to have had his father act; that here is a woman, especially if he never had a mother when he was young, who acts and is like what he wishes his mother to have been, etc. The warmer, more intimate, and genuine the contact is, the greater are the advantages which the patient can derive from the psychodramatic episode. The all-out involvement of the auxiliary ego is indicated for the patient who has been frustrated by the absence of such maternal, paternal, or other constructive and socializing figures in his lifetime. If indicated, the auxiliary ego is permitted to be as active as the patient needs. "Bodily contact" is a basic form of communication. It is not, however, always indicated. In some cases the intimacy and warmth of contact, especially bodily contact, may be contraindicated. There are, for instance, some schizophrenic patients who resent being touched, embraced, or kissed. They would prefer their auxiliary egos to portray symbolic and omnipotent roles. One often sees that they are not quite ready for the realistic approach. They have to go through many symbolic acts before a direct and immediate encounter is acceptable.

TELE AND COUNTERTRANSFERENCE

A minimum of tele structure and resulting cohesiveness of interaction among the therapists and the patients is an indispensable prerequisite for the ongoing therapeutic psychodrama to succeed. If the auxiliary egos are troubled among themselves because of (1) unresolved problems of their own, (2) protest against the psychodramatic director, (3) poor portrayal of the roles assigned to them, (4) lack of faith and negative attitude toward the method used, or (5) interpersonal conflicts among themselves, they create an atmosphere which reflects upon the therapeutic situation. It is obvious, therefore, that if transference and countertransference phenomena dominate the relationship among the auxiliary therapists and toward the patients the therapeutic process will be greatly handicapped. The decisive factor for therapeutic progress is the *tele*.

WARMING UP TO A ROLE

Psychodramatists trained in psychoanalysis often follow the rule of psychoanalysis which has been formulated by Fenichel as "not playing the game" of the patient. Their opinion is that also in psychodrama, the classic psychoanalytic attitude of noninvolvement is desirable. The auxiliary ego is instructed, when he enters a situation in any role, only to go through the motions of the role, but to remain as cold as possible inside, refusing altogether to get warmed up to the role he is supposed to present, playing with indifference, following the principle of neutrality. This kind of resistance of the therapist for methodical reasons is the dogma for one of the French schools of psychodrama (Lebovici and Diatkine). The difficulty with such behavior of the psychodramatist is that if the patient needs a mother or a father, a wife or a child, and the auxiliary ego who is there to portray this role does not convey to the patient the genuine characteristics of it, the patient may be harmed rather than helped. He will feel like a guinea pig rather than a human being. This method might be indicated in certain cases where the patient is autistic to such an extent that he is little aware of what is going on around him, entire self-involved.

THE AUDIENCE GROUP

Group Psychotherapy Versus Group Psychoanalysis

One can look at the formation of synthetic groups from the point of view of the psychoanalytic frame of reference. I assembled the new members of the group (1921) in a room which was fitted out with a number of couches. Every individual was placed on a couch. The fundamental rule of free association was applied to them. The experiment failed; the free association of one began to mingle with the free associations of the other. This confused them and produced a chaotic situation. The reasons for the failure seemed to be twofold. Free association works significantly only along individual tracks; free associations which have significance along the track of individual A have no significance on the track of B or of C and, vice versa. They have no common unconscious; in psychoanalytic theory each individual has its own unconscious. When free association was rigorously applied, a number of individuals were being separately psychoanalyzed. It did not develop into group psychoanalysis but into psychoanalysis of several individuals within a group setting. But my objectives were group therapy and group analysis, not individual analysis. As the psychoanalytic method of free association proved unproductive, I developed a new method which was based on the study of the formation of groups in *statu nascendi*.

Individuals who never met before and who from the first meeting on have to be participants in the same group represent a new problem to the therapist; we see them when they enter spontaneously into interrelations which lead them to form a group *sub species momenti;* we can study their spontaneous reaction in the initial stage of group formation and the activities developed in the course of such organization . . . we can develop the treatment forward instead of backward; we can begin with the initial attitude one person has for the other and follow up to what fate these interrelations lead, what kind of organizations they develop.

In support of the existence of such an initial common matrix, sociometric research has shown that "immediate response between strangers differs significantly from chance. . . ." Barker, in his classic experiment took twelve university students who were complete strangers to each other and were selected from a larger class for its first meeting. Six of these students were men, six were women. Of thirty-six choices of seat mates upon the first occasion, twenty or twenty-five percent were repeated upon the second occasion. Of one-hundred-thirty-two responses to other choices upon the first occasion, eighty-one or sixty-three percent were repeated upon the second occasion. These percents are both considerably higher than would have been obtained if the subjects had chosen entirely at random.

In other words, *there is tele already operating between the members of a group from the first meeting.* This weak, "primary" cohesiveness can be utilized by the therapist toward the developing and sharing of common therapeutic aims. All the interactions between men, abreactions, soliloquies, dialogues, tele, and transference relations to therapist, auxiliary egos, and each other in the course of therapy will be influenced by this original structure and will in turn, modify it. This is the new operational frame of reference from which one can look at the successive stages of a synthetic group.

IMMEDIATE BEHAVIOR OF THE GROUP AND THE "BEDSIDE MANNER" OF THE THERAPIST

Sociograms—The chief concern of the psychodramatic therapist is the immediate behavior of the group. When the therapist faces his group for the first session, he perceives immediately, with his skilled sense for interpersonal relations, some of the interaction between the members, such as the distribution of love, hate, and indifference. It is not just a collection of individuals. He notices one or two sitting all by themselves, physically isolated from the rest; two or three clustered together, smiling and gossiping; one or two engaged in an argument or sitting side by side by giving each other the cold shoulder. In other words, the first contours of a sociogram begin to simmer in his mind. He does not have to give a formal test in order to obtain this knowledge. He takes notices of this "embryonic matrix." It is coming to him through his immediate observation. It becomes his empathic guide for the therapeutic process in becoming. The group has, from the first session on, whatever its size, a specific structure of interpersonal relations which, however, does not reveal itself at once on the surface, an underlying sociometric or group matrix. It is useful to differentiate intuitive recognition of structure (intuitive sociogram; sociogram is a diagram which portrays the forces of attraction, repulsion, and indifference operating in groups), observer's recognition of structure (observer's sociogram), objective recognition of structure (objective sociogram), and perceptual recognition of structure (perceptual sociogram). The therapist may hesitate to impose upon the group a sociometric test to start with, but he will let the sociogram, in its intuitive form, grow in his mind as he looks around, in the "bedside manner" of the group psychotherapist. After one or two sessions he may make (afterward) notations as to the impression he has of the existing structure, and he may ask one of his cotherapists to do the same thing independently and then compare data. Such an observer's sociogram has a greater degree of objectivity and supplements the original intuitions. If after several sessions the group is well established and the contact with the therapist is favorable, the strategic moment may come for a formal sociometric test from which an "objective" sociogram will result. A further step in the clinical exploration of group structure is gained by letting every member of the group make his own sociogram, that is by letting him indicate who among the members of the group, he thinks, chooses or rejects him. He reveals the perceptions he has of what people around him think of him, a perceptual sociogram. He may think of himself as being liked by everyone but in the objective sociogram he may be shown to be a rejected individual. Such a discrepancy between his perceptions and the objective facts may provide important clues to his interpersonal status and a further refinement of his position in the sociogram.

CONCLUSIONS

Behavioristic schools have been limited to observing and experimenting with "external" behavior of individuals, leaving out major portions of the subjective. Many psychological methods, such as psychoanalysis, Rorschach, and TAT, went to the other extreme, focusing on the subjective but limiting the study of direct behavior to a minimum and resorting to the use of elaborate systems of symbolic interpretation. The psychodramatic method brings these two extremes to a new synthesis. It is so designed that it can explore and treat immediate behavior in all its dimensions.

Because we cannot reach into the mind and see what the individual perceives and feels, psychodrama tries, with the cooperation of the patient, to transfer the mind "outside" of the individual and objectify it within a tangible, controllable universe. It may go the whole way in the process of structuring the world of the patient up to the threshold of tolerance, penetrating and surpassing reality ("surplus" reality), and may insist upon the most minute details of episodes in physical, mental, and social space to be explored. Its aim is to make total behavior directly visible, observable, and measurable. The protagonist is being prepared for an encounter with himself. After this phase of objectification is completed, the second phase begins; it is to resubjectify, reorganize, and reintegrate that which has been objectified. (In practice, however, both phases go hand in hand.)

The psychodramatic method rests upon the hypothesis that, in order to provide patients, singly or in groups, with a new opportunity for a psychodynamic and sociocultural reintegration, "therapeutic cultures in miniature" are required, in lieu or in extension of unsatisfactory natural habitats. Vehicles for carrying out this project are (1) existential psychodrama within the framework of community life itself, *in situ,* and (2) the neutral, objective, and flexible therapeutic theater. The latter represents the laboratory method in contrast to the method of nature and is structured to meet the sociocultural needs of the protagonist. . . .

PSYCHODRAMATIC APPROACH TO CHILDREN'S PROBLEMS

I remember the case of a boy whom I treated several years ago using a psychodramatic technique. John used to beat his mother before going to bed and in the presence of guests. Several devices of treatment failed to help the boy to overcome his fits. The first role he portrayed was that of a prince. A member of my staff to whom he showed affinity was dressed as a queen. She acted opposite him as his mother. Otherwise every detail was portrayed as in the actual situations, a mother putting her child to bed, or a mother giving a party and her boy entering the living room to meet the guests. The questions in my mind were these: whether the boy as a prince would beat the mother if she were a queen—whether his fits toward her would be weaker, modified or absent—whether he would not have any fit because he was thinking "it is just a play."

The Therapeutic Process

In the first session I *removed* every possible resistance which might come from the role, the persons acting with him and the scenes—it was a careful elimination of interpersonal resistances on the symbolic level. In later sessions we began to interpolate resistance; the queen mother was ordered to be more aggressive. When prepared for the role the child was influenced to restrain his words or his actions. The boy reacted favorably to the treatment after a few weeks. The symbolic level of princes and queens, royal families and heroes, was apparently the psychological level on which he was spontaneous, and therefore, we hit him on the spot where he was open to influence. Gradually we interpolated new resistances; we moved him from the most extreme autocratic level closer to the realities in which he lived. The next time his mother was merely a college professor; later she was the mayor's wife, a nurse, etc., until the moment arrived when we made the final move; his own mother began to act with him in these roles until a complete duplication of the home scenes were enacted by them. The fits disappeared.

PSYCHODRAMATIC APPROACH TO A CASE OF DEMENTIA PRAECOX

The Auxiliary World

We come now to consider the type of patient with whom communication of any sort is reduced to a minimum. The more sketchy and incomplete the ego, the more articulate and thorough has to be the aid supplied from outside by an auxiliary ego. The more disturbed the mental organization of the patient seems to be, the larger are the number of aids the auxiliary ego has to contribute and the greater is the need for his initiative. Numerous auxiliary egos may become necessary and, in the case of the severe and established psychosis, the task confronting the auxiliary ego is beyond possibility of effective treatment. The milder patient, however many aids he may need for bringing himself to a more satisfactory realization, still lives within the same world with us. In the case of the more severe patient, the reality, as it is usually experienced, is replaced by delusional and hallucinated elements. The patient needs more than an auxiliary ego, he needs an *auxiliary world*.

An illustration is a patient, William, who had been classified as *dementia praecox*. Many of the reality functions were perverted. He did not seem to feel the presence of other people in the house and he was not able to do anything with them. He repeatedly showed the desire to throw visitors, including his father, mother and brothers out of the house. He masturbated frequently and played with his excretions. He ate inconsistently and destroyed certain sorts of foods. He showed one significant trend which dominated the picture. He wrote a proclamation to the world which he wanted to save. He called himself Christ. We took this as a "lead" for the treatment.

We are considering here a type of patient who cannot be reached, either by the psychiatrist for treatment, or by anyone else, to participate in any useful occupation. He does not show signs of emotional interest in any person of his environment. He is shut in and persistently non-cooperative. The most that psychiatry and psychoanalysis have tried to accomplish is to understand these patients, to find some clues for explaining their mental experiences in the psychopathology of dreams, and the unconscious mind. But from the point of view of treatment, we had to go one step further. We translated carefully the patient's utterances, gestures, delusions and hallucinations into a poetic language as a basis to construct a poetic reality, an auxiliary world. In other words, we assumed the attitude of the poet, perhaps, still more, of the dramatist. The auxiliary egos, once acquainted with this poetic language and with the structure of his auxiliary world, would be able to act in this world, to assume roles which would fit the patient's needs, and to talk and live with him in his language and in his own universe. We regarded him so to speak as a poet who is prepossessed at the time by the creations of his own fantasy, the creation of a mad man, a King Lear or Othello, and as we wanted to enter into the drama of his mental confusion we had to learn the grammar of his logic and assume a role which fitted exactly into his universe. The function of the auxiliary ego is to transform himself into a state of mind which enables him to produce at will a role, *if necessary similarly confused* in appearance to that which the patient experiences by compulsion.

We molded an auxiliary psychodrama around the patient. It replaced and shaped every phase of the natural environment. The only person who had his natural role and who lived his own life in the drama was the patient. We people around him assumed roles which fitted him. After more than six months with him he showed no signs of transference, either to the psychiatrist or to the attendants, but he did show numerous and well developed tele-relationships. He was indifferent to certain colors such as red and yellow. His tele was positive for blue and white. This determined the clothes we wore and the color scheme of the house. His tele for certain foods as eggs and meat was negative. It was positive for most fruits and green vegetables. The menu was carefully built around his affinities, however odd they were and however often their pattern changed. He had a tele for some persons but often only in a specific role and for aesthetic reasons, and often even for the role in a specific scene and position. For instance he liked a young attendant to kneel in a corner of a room with his head bowed. He did not like him to kneel in any other room or in any other corner. Outside of this part and position he did not show any sign of interest in the young attendant.

It was the tele complex of the patient which was from moment to moment the guide in the development of his psychodrama. He had been diagnosed as a shut-in personality, but it appears that the "shut-in" is more a clinical than a scientific category of conduct of this sort. It implies that the patient is withdrawn from reality. But as soon as we changed the reality for him and filled it with *his* psychodrama, we saw that sensations and events within it were extremely significant for him. The chart of his psychological network can be drawn. What we call his delusions and hallucinations are probably reactions to the signals which he receives from these private networks.

The Therapeutic Process

The level at which a patient is spontaneous is the working level of the treatment. This level can be so far removed from reality that it may not include the persons and physical objects around the patient. To get William started we had to create a world for him which corresponds to the level in which he lives. The world which we construct for him is a poetical, an auxiliary world. It is filled with roles and masks, with fictitious objects. As the patient improves, the roles and masks can turn more to real persons and the fictitious things more and more into actual things.

Readings in
EMOTIONAL
DISTURBANCE

Edited by
Phyllis L. Newcomer

pro·ed
8700 Shoal Creek Boulevard
Austin, Texas 78757

pro·ed

© 1994 by PRO-ED, Inc.
8700 Shoal Creek Boulevard
Austin, Texas 78757-6897

Library of Congress Cataloging-in-Publication Data

Readings in emotional disturbance / edited by Phyllis L. Newcomer.
        p.   cm.
    Includes index.
    ISBN 0-89079-588-6
    1. Psychotherapy.   2. Mental illness.   3. Child psychopathology.
I. Newcomer, Phyllis L.
RC480.R39   1993
616.89′14—dc20   93-5040
                                                            CIP

This book is designed in Sabon with Univers Condensed.

Production Manager: Alan Grimes
Production Coordinator: Adrienne Booth
Art Director: Lori Kopp
Reprints Buyer: Alicia Woods
Editor: Bruce Bethell
Editorial Assistant: Claudette Landry

Printed in the United States of America

1 2 3 4 5 6 7 8 9 10   98 97 96 95 94